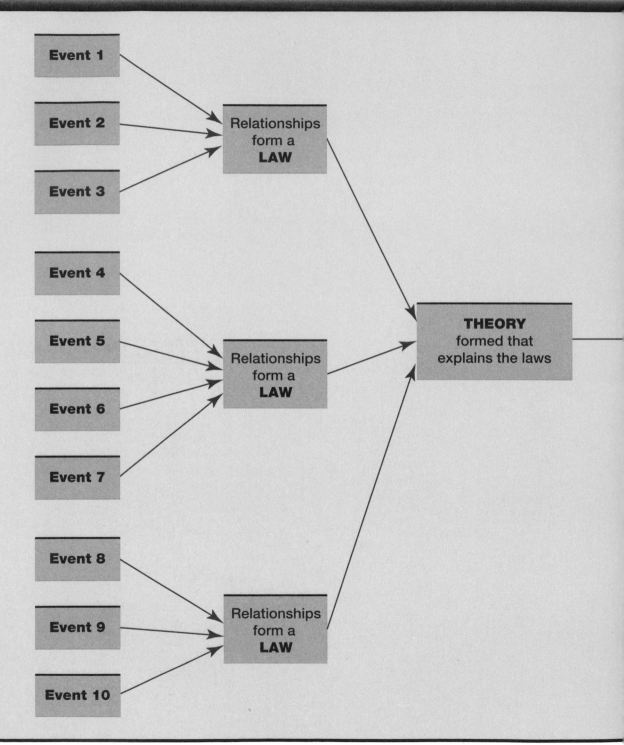

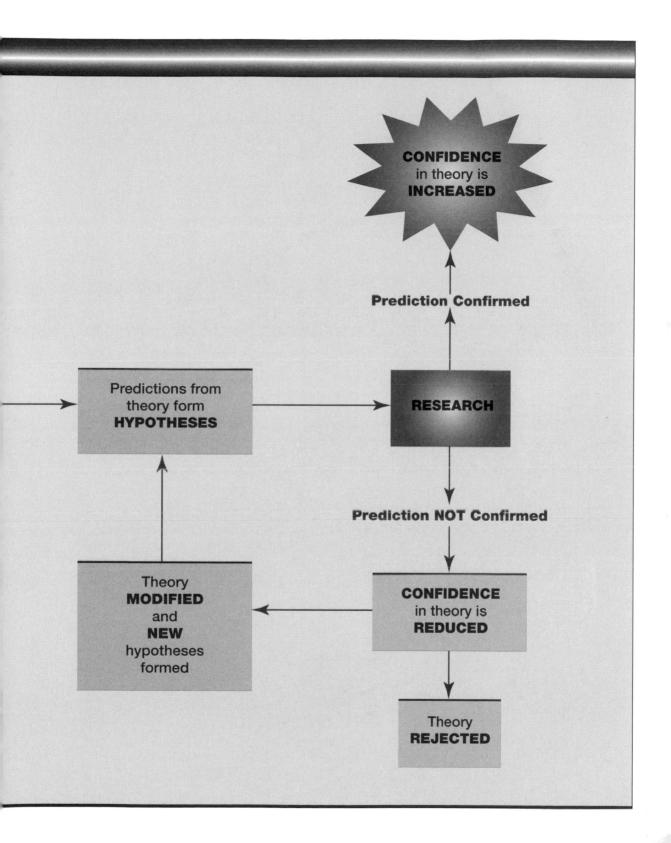

NINTH EDITION

Research Methods

Theresa L. White

*Professor, Le Moyne College and
Adjunct Associate Professor State University of New York,
Upstate Medical University*

Donald H. McBurney

Professor Emeritus, University of Pittsburgh

WADSWORTH
CENGAGE Learning·

Australia • Brazil • Japan • Korea • Mexico • Singapore • Spain • United Kingdom • United States

WADSWORTH
CENGAGE Learning

Research Methods, Ninth Edition
Theresa L. White and Donald H. McBurney

Editor-in-Chief: Linda Ganster-Schreiber

Executive Editor: Jon-David Hague

Acquisitions Editor: Timothy Matray

Assistant Editor: Lauren K. Moody

Editorial Assistant: Nicole Richards

Media Editor: Mary Noel

Senior Art Director: Pamela Galbreath

Marketing Manager: Jessica Egbert

Marketing Program Manager: Janay Pryor

Senior Marketing Communications
Manager: Heather Baxley

Manufacturing Planner: Karen Hunt

Rights Acquisitions Specialist:
Dean Dauphinais

Design Direction, Production Management,
and Composition: PreMediaGlobal

Cover Designer: William Stanton,
Stanton Design

Cover Image: © Dennis Degan/Corbis

For product information and technology assistance, contact us at
Cengage Learning Customer & Sales Support, 1-800-354-9706.

For permission to use material from this text or product,
submit all requests online at **www.cengage.com/permissions**.
Further permissions questions can be e-mailed to
permissionrequest@cengage.com.

Library of Congress Control Number: 2012935969

ISBN-13: 978-1-111-84062-4

ISBN-10: 1-111-84062-8

Wadsworth
20 Davis Drive
Belmont, CA 94002-3098
USA

Cengage Learning is a leading provider of customized learning solutions with office locations around the globe, including Singapore, the United Kingdom, Australia, Mexico, Brazil, and Japan. Locate your local office at: **www.cengage.com/global**.

Cengage Learning products are represented in Canada by Nelson Education, Ltd.

To learn more about Wadsworth, visit **www.cengage.com/wadsworth**.

Purchase any of our products at your local college store or at our preferred online store **www.cengagebrain.com**.

Printed in the United States of America
1 2 3 4 5 6 7 16 15 14 13 12

BRIEF CONTENTS

CONTENTS

8 Nonexperimental Research, Part I: Observational, Archival, and Case-Study Research   191

15   Data Exploration, Part 2: Inferential Statistics   385

It is of the essence of teaching that it seeks to render itself superfluous.

Dietrich Bonhoeffer
The Cost of Discipleship

PREFACE

This book is intended to serve as a text for courses in research methods in psychology at the undergraduate level. We are gratified for the acceptance it has received over the previous eight editions. We particularly appreciate the many comments from students who find the book interesting and clearly written because those characteristics have been high on our list of goals for the book.

The features that have made the book distinctive have been retained in this edition. Our primary intention in writing this text was to put psychological research into a larger scientific context. In teaching the course and looking at possible texts to use, we felt that other books on the topic provided too little emphasis on how psychology fits into the scientific approach to understanding the world. Given the debate that exists among the behavioral, dynamic, biological, humanistic, postmodern, and other types of psychologies as well as the confusion about the nature of science evidenced by the many popular and fringe psychologies, it is not surprising that undergraduate students have questions about how scientific psychology should be done. The first section of the book therefore deals with psychology as a science.

A second goal is to separate the discussion of research methods from its traditional dependence on statistical procedures. Many experimental psychology books are organized around particular statistical methods, especially the analysis of variance. In contrast, we have organized this book around the general problems of validity and how to control for the various threats to validity. With this goal in mind, it made sense to have early chapters that discuss the types of variables encountered in psychological research. The later chapters on true experiments, quasi experiments, and single-subject designs give examples of solutions to the problems of validity, rather than a catalog of statistical applications. Although the last two chapters discuss the graphical and statistical evaluation of data, they are not prescriptive in analysis and instead focus on the process of describing and examining results.

A third goal, closely related to the second, is to convey the idea that designing and conducting research is an exercise in problem solving that can be exciting and creative. We have avoided giving the impression that psychological research involves following a set of cut-and-dried rules or selecting one of a fixed number of available designs. Our belief is that the best research derives from solving particular threats to the validity of a contemplated piece of research and only then asking what kind of design has resulted. Throughout the book we have emphasized the considerations that are involved in designing and conducting research.

Fourth, we have chosen from the psychological literature a wide variety of problems in research and their solutions. Generally, we have avoided non-psychological examples and artificial data. We have instead attempted to include examples from studies examining psychological issues that students may have already encountered, either through everyday life or through their Introductory Psychology course.

Finally, we have tried to convey a feeling for all of the stages of research, from choosing the problem to publishing the results. We have discussed the literature search, the nuts and bolts of research protocols, research ethics, evaluation of data, and the publication process. The only major step that is treated minimally is statistical analysis, which is left to a prerequisite or corequisite course, or to supplementary material, according to the instructor's choice.

Changes in the Ninth Edition

This edition reflects numerous changes and many new examples have been used throughout. The "Suggestions for Further Reading" sections have been updated, as well as web addresses. The Instructor's Manual now has many more multiple choice and essay questions. An updated Power Point presentation is available for all chapters that includes many of the figures seen in the text.

In Chapter 1, we added a set of psychologically interesting questions as the initial paragraph, as well as Box 1.1 with the answers and associated references. These questions should not only whet a student's appetite for the interesting questions in psychology, but should also underscore the importance of becoming a savvy research consumer. The Neil Armstrong example in the section on "authority as a way of knowing" was replaced with one on Barack Obama's birth. A further discussion of the cause and effect relationship was added using John Stuart Mills' classic three criteria for establishing causality: temporal precedence, co-variation of cause and effect, and elimination of alternative explanations. The Simcock and Hayne (2002) example has been replaced with one by DeWall et al. (2010) that shows the ability of acetaminophen to relieve hurt feelings.

In Chapter 2, the section on government and other organizational web sites that provide access to information on psychological topics was updated. All of the references to generally available search engines were updated, and information about GoogleScholar.com was added. For clarity, the information on proprietary databases was restricted to PsycINFO and Web of Science. The PsycINFO search was updated, and three figures were added to show an extended search. Information on searching for databases on the library's homepage was also updated. A "Suggestions for Further Reading" section, with two entries, was also added.

Chapter 3 has been updated to reflect changes made to the APA Ethics Code, including those regarding animal usage, in the 2010 revision. A section on the problems with scientific fraud has been added to Chapter 3 that discusses the recent retraction by *The Lancet* of an article that seemed to show a link between autism and vaccines. The fraud case involving Karen Ruggerio has been replaced by a more recent case involving another psychologist, Marc Hauser. The "Case of the Silver Springs Monkeys" has been replaced by the "Georgie Project," which illustrates animal research at its best. In this example, the research is working well to benefit both animals and people.

Chapter 4 has been substantially revised so as to comply with the Sixth Edition of the *Publication Manual of the American Psychological Association*. All examples have been updated and a discussion on author notes has been added.

Existing concepts have been clarified throughout Chapter 5. Exercises have been altered to more fully cover the information in the chapter, and Exercises 5.3 and 5.5 have been completely replaced.

Chapter 6 was Chapter 7 in previous editions. This chapter has been substantially clarified. The anxiety test used as a manipulation check has been changed from the Taylor Manifest Anxiety Scale to the Beck Anxiety Inventory, as it is more currently used in the assessment of anxiety. Statistical Validity is now called statistical conclusion validity, both to be in keeping with the terminology of Shadish, Cook, & Campbell (2002) and to place an emphasis on the idea that the validity concerns the conclusions. The problem of inaccurate effect size is now discussed in threats to statistical conclusion validity. Another section has been added to the discussion of threats to internal validity, that of Ambiguous Temporal Precedence, which continues the discussion of causality from Chapter 1. The "Nuts and Bolts" section now focuses on the experiment as a social situation, and includes the information on the good subject tendency and evaluation apprehension that was previously in the text. Exercise 6.4 has been changed to reflect a situation in which a correlational study is treated as one that implies causality.

Chapter 7 was Chapter 8 in the last edition of the book. Clarifications, largely in the form of headings or re-ordering of graphs and tables, have been made throughout the chapter. A paragraph further elucidating the difference between general and specific control strategies has been added. The "Reading Between the Lines" discussion problem 7.2 (Cognitive and Arousal Factors in Emotion) has been replaced with a problem concerning the Mozart Effect.

Chapter 8 was Chapter 9 in previous editions. Several new examples have been added to this chapter. A study on attitudes about the Gulf oil spill was added as an example of a case study. In the archival section, the Phillips (1977) example on motor vehicles accidents that are actually suicides has been replaced by a more recent example—a 2004 study showing that people with more traditionally African facial features are given harsher prison sentences. A brief acknowledgement of the process of using mathematical techniques to manage threats to validity in observational studies is included. Details of these methods exceed the scope of this text, but students are made aware that they exist. Motion-sensitive camera is added as a potential recording technique for observational data. A new example of content analysis is included that involves searching messages on Twitter for evidence of mood changes throughout the day. Exercise 8.3 (on the Physical Trace) has been altered to reflect a situation involving Facebook's tracking of their user's activities online.

Chapter 9 was Chapter 10 in previous editions. In this chapter, references to the Mental Measurement Yearbook have been clarified. A new example for branching questions has been included, and the example using Ross Perot's deficit survey question has been replaced with one using Gallup Poll's method of asking questions on the death penalty. The section on computerized administration of surveys has been updated, and more information about the advantages and pitfalls of this method has been included. The example on multi-stage sampling has been updated. The section on randomized response method has been clarified, and a figure has been added.

Chapter 10 was Chapter 11 in previous editions. Initial discussion of true experiments has been expanded to include a short discussion on causality. The example on emotionality in rats has been changed to one involving socialization in tiger cubs. The section on reverse counterbalancing has been clarified, and an example involving rTMS has been added. The Marshall and Teitelbaum (1974) example has been replaced with one involving fMRI of illusory motion.

Chapter 11 was Chapter 12 in previous editions. The section on Interactions and Main Effects has been substantially revised and reorganized. The example of true love and distance has been clarified. Some of the figures and tables that accompanied it have been removed. A summary table now makes the point more succinctly, and the figure surrounding this example has been clarified. The section on Types of Interactions has been revised. Each type of interaction is described more clearly. Previously separate figures have been combined, to make it easier for the student to examine two graphs at once. The section on "Within-Subjects, Between-Subjects, and Mixed Designs" has been clarified. The experimental examples, which previously appeared at the end of the chapter, have been moved nearer to the description of the design that they illustrate. The information about control with a within-subject variable has been moved nearer to the section on within-subjects designs. The example for the mixed factorial design has been changed from one on mood induction to one involving cell phone use while driving. The section previously called "Advantages of Within-Subject Designs" has been moved to the end of the chapter and re-titled "Considering Number of Subjects when Selecting Factorial Designs."

Chapter 12 was Chapter 13 in the previous edition. The example for the ABAB design has been changed. Although the example still deals with self-injurious behavior, the example involving exercise is easier to understand than the previous one. Further clarification of the multiple-baseline design has been included. An additional example has also been added to this section. Two new exercises, one concerning alternate treatment design and one concerning power, have been added.

Chapter 13 was Chapter 14 in previous editions. Clarification has been made to the introduction section. The quasi-experiment's high level of external validity has been highlighted, and an emphasis placed on its ability to examine the "natural experiment." The example for the interrupted-time series design has been changed to one that examines the effect of media policies on suicide rates. The Smith and Glass (1977) efficacy of psychotherapy example for the section on meta-analysis has been updated to include a study by Barak, Hen, Boniel-Nissim, and Shapira (2008) on the effectiveness of internet-based therapy. The fourth point of the summary has been changed to reflect the increased external validity at the cost of internal validity found with true experiments. Exercise 13.1 (Classify a study) has been changed to a problem dealing with sexual abuse and obesity.

Chapter 14 contains some of the information that was found in Chapter 6 of the previous edition, along with some that was previously found in Appendix A. The title of the chapter now reflects its new role in the process of evaluating data. This chapter has been substantially re-ordered, and much new material has been added. The chapter now begins with the assumption that data have been collected, and includes a discussion of data reduction followed by a discussion of descriptive statistics. Finally, the examination of those descriptive statistics in tables and graphs is discussed. Two new exercises were added that require students to create their own graphs.

Chapter 15 contains some of the information that was found in Appendix A of previous editions. A new introduction has been added that invites students to proceed with their inferential analysis following the descriptive evaluations that were begun in Chapter 14. References to descriptive statistics previously found in Appendix A have been removed, as this chapter focuses only on inferential statistics. A "Summary" section has been added, as has a "Suggested Readings" section, and a "Reading Between the Lines" section. A new exercise on pre-school attendance and mathematics performance concerning Chi Square has been added.

In the Epilogue, we updated the figures concerning the amount that the government spends on research, as well as the percentage of articles citing US government support in a reputable journal. An example of data suppression by industry concerning anti-depressants has been added as well as a section encouraging critical thinking when evaluating scientific information reported in the media.

Acknowledgements _____

Many colleagues have contributed to the success of this project over the several editions, now too many to list here. We thank the following reviewers of the eighth edition for their constructive suggestions and comments: Wendy Beller, Quincy University; Benjamin Storm, University of Illinois, Chicago; Elizabeth Krumrei, Pepperdine University; Aurora Sherman, Oregon State University; Christine Browning, Victory University. We would also like to thank the reviewers for the ninth edition. Each new reviewer adds a fresh contribution to the book. Thanks also to Tim Matray, Lauren Moody, and all the other people at Cengage Learning. They have been a true pleasure to work with and have been very supportive of this project.

ABOUT THE AUTHORS

Theresa White

Theresa L. White is a Professor of Psychology at Le Moyne College and an Adjunct Associate Professor of Neuroscience and Physiology at SUNY Upstate Medical University. She received both of her higher degrees in experimental psychology from English universities; her Master of Science degree is from Oxford University and her PhD is from University of Warwick. Dr. White's research is concerned with the way people think about and remember smells and flavors. She currently teaches research methods, sensation and perception, and brain and behavior. Dr. White lives in Syracuse, New York, where the winters sometimes bring more than 180 inches of snow. Whenever the lakes are not frozen, Dr. White enjoys racing her Hobie 16 sailboat. Once the ice is on the lake, she fills her spare time with travel and singing in a gospel choir.

Donald McBurney

Donald H. McBurney is Professor Emeritus of Psychology at the University of Pittsburgh. Previously he taught at the University of Tennessee. He received his PhD in experimental psychology at Brown University. He has numerous publications in his areas of interest, which include the psychophysics of taste, evolutionary psychology, a skeptical approach to the paranormal, and critical thinking. Besides research methods, he taught sensation and perception, evolutionary psychology, and history of psychology. His professional and personal interests intersect in studying the taste of chili peppers. His hobbies include gardening, sailing, and travel.

CHAPTER ONE

Psychology and Science

PREVIEW

Chapter 1 introduces psychology as a science. We see that science is one way of knowing among several. Science has a number of characteristics, such as reliance on objective, empirical facts. Taken together, these characteristics distinguish science from other ways of knowing. Science makes a number of working assumptions, such as that the world is real.

Most people decide to study psychology because they have an interest in understanding their own behavior and the behavior of other people. Trying to gain that understanding can lead people to ask a variety of questions, many of which can be difficult to answer. Consider the following questions for a moment, and try to answer them for yourself: *(1) Are some memories spared in people with Alzheimer's disease? (2) Why are some children able to resiliently overcome abuse situations, while others suffer from serious life difficulties? (3) Are women with bipolar disorder more susceptible to postpartum depression? (4) How does relationship stress affect college students? (5) Do more females suffer from depression than males?* Although some answers to these questions can be found in Box 1.1, finding out the answers on your own would require you to develop skills in research methods. Many students underestimate the importance of research methods, because they do not want to work in a lab in the future. But almost everyone working as a psychologist

---

BOX **1.1**

Answers to Initial Questions and References for Further Reading

1. *Are some memories spared in people with Alzheimer's disease?* Implicit memory, such as that observed in priming or motor learning, seems to be preserved in Alzheimer's patients (Karlsson, Börjesson, Adolfsson, & Nilsson, 2002).

2. *Why are some children able to resiliently overcome abuse situations, while others suffer from serious life difficulties?* Children who show resilience tend to live in lower crime neighborhoods. They also tend to have parents with fewer personality disorders and a lower level of substance abuse (Jaffee, Caspi, Moffitt, Polo-Tomás, & Taylor, 2007).

3. *Are women with bipolar disorder more susceptible to postpartum depression?* Postpartum depression is much more common in women who have been diagnosed with bipolar disorder (Hunt & Silverstone, 1995).

4. *How does relationship stress affect college students?* A higher level of relationship stress is associated with a lower level of academic achievement (Murray-Harvey, 2010).

5. *Do more females suffer from depression than males?* It depends on how old they are as to whether males and females differ in their rates of depression. Prior to adolescence, both genders suffer from depression at relatively equal rates. After puberty, women suffer from depression at a much higher rate than men (Nolen-Hoeksema & Girgus, 1994).

© Cengage Learning

---

encounters questions surrounding their work. While everyone may not want to run their own experiments to answer those questions, it is vital that every psychologist be able to understand and critically evaluate research evidence. In other words, all psychologists should become savvy consumers of experimental psychological research.

Experimental psychology is a science essentially like any other. There may be considerable differences in subject matter between psychology and biology, chemistry, or anthropology, but the essentials are common to all. On the one hand, the differences are fairly obvious. Because animals are more complex than trees, psychological theories may be more complicated than botanical theories; because the behavior of animals varies more than that of rocks, psychology uses statistics more than does physics. On the other hand, the similarities may not be as easy to grasp. For this reason, we devote this chapter to discussing psychology as a science. The goals of science make it different from other human activities. These goals include the description and discovery of regularities, but the main goal is developing a theory to explain facts and laws. Science may be considered a problem-solving activity. First, let us put psychology in context by talking about ways of learning about behavior.

Ways of Knowing About Behavior _____

empirical: based on experience

There is more than one way to learn about human and animal behavior. Every day, all of us use several methods to learn about behavior. We can divide these methods into two broad categories: empirical methods and nonempirical methods. The term empirical simply means based on experience.

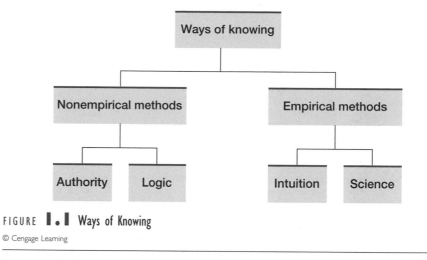

FIGURE **1.1** Ways of Knowing

© Cengage Learning

Nonempirical Methods

First, we will consider two nonempirical methods of learning about behavior: authority and logic. Then, we will consider the empirical methods. Figure 1.1 shows the relationship among them.

Authority

We may believe something because some respected person told us it is true. Religious authorities proclaim the will of God to us about various matters, the government tells us that we should not drive faster than 65 miles per hour, and our parents tell us that we will catch cold if we get our feet wet. Because these authorities often disagree among themselves, we are inclined to reject authority as a way of knowing. How do you know that President Barack Obama was born in Honolulu, Hawaii on August 4, 1961? Or that anyone has been born in Hawaii since then? It is unlikely that you have visited Obama's birthplace, and you certainly were not there when he was born. Perhaps, though, you have heard him talk about it on television, or have seen a copy of his birth certificate online. Yet there are people who believe that Mr. Obama was not born in Hawaii, and that the attempt to portray him as someone born in the United States is a gigantic propaganda hoax perpetrated by the US government. These people point out that seeing a birth certificate is not evidence that the event occurred, since many realistic-looking "birth certificates" can be forged. If you believe that President Obama was born in Hawaii, you do so because of your faith in the credibility of the government, the news media, and the books you have read. These sources all serve as authorities for you if you believe what they say. Although **authority** is often a useful source of information, it also has major limitations as a way of knowing. Authorities often are wrong, even when they assert their beliefs most forcefully. For example, Galileo suffered grievously for daring to hold that the earth goes around the sun. The struggle for intellectual freedom from the dogmas of authority is a continuing theme in the history of science, from Galileo in the 16th century to the recent Soviet dissidents. Still, if you did not have any faith in authority, you would not be reading this book or taking a research methods course from a college professor.

authority: based on someone else's knowledge

Logic

Logic is an important way of helping us know about behavior. Take the following set of statements:

> The behavior of all animals is subject to the laws of natural science.
> Humans are animals.
> Therefore, human behavior is subject to the laws of natural science.

These statements are logical. That is, if the first two are true, then the third follows logically. Use of logic is often crucial in drawing correct conclusions about the world.

Yet, as important as reasoning logically is, logic has limitations as a way of knowing. Logic can tell you that a statement is false because it draws an improper conclusion. But a statement can be logically valid and still not be true because it assumes something to be the case that is not. For example, suppose I say, "If it rains, then there will be no baseball game." If I look out the window and see it is raining, it is valid for me to say, "It is raining; therefore, there will be no baseball game." But the truth of the statement depends on the fact that it is raining. If it is, in fact, not raining, then the statement is false.

Logic is extremely important to science, but it cannot substitute for making the observation that it is raining, or proving that the behavior of all animals is subject to the laws of natural science. In other words, there is no substitute for empirical evidence. As any reader of science fiction can attest, there are many logically possible worlds. Logic alone cannot tell you which world actually exists.

Empirical Methods

Just as we divided ways of knowing into empirical and nonempirical on the basis of whether they depended on experience, we can divide the empirical methods into two categories: intuitive and scientific.

Intuition

We size up strangers within the first few seconds of meeting them. We do this by intuition: a way of knowing based on spontaneous, *instinctive* processes rather than on logic or reasoning. Intuition has a powerful effect on our beliefs about other people. We may distrust a person who seems too sincere to be true. This sizing up has sometimes been called *women's intuition*; today, we are more likely to say that someone gives off *bad vibes*. We use intuition continuously in making the myriad of decisions necessary during the course of a day. Think for a moment how you decide whether to step off the curb in front of an oncoming car at a traffic light. You make a life-or-death decision in a split second. How do you do it? Your decision is probably based on a number of factors, including whether the traffic light has changed to red, whether you are in a hurry, whether the driver looks you in the eye, or whether the car is decelerating. *Somehow* you take all these factors into account. That *somehow* is what we call intuition.

Common sense is a kind of intuition because of its dependence on informal methods. It has the additional characteristic of emphasizing the agreement of a person's judgment with the shared attitudes and experiences of a larger group of people. We are familiar with the example of a recent college graduate who starts working with people who lack formal education. The graduate wants to apply his or her scientific knowledge to the job. The old hands may resist the ideas that don't agree with common sense. After all, their methods worked well before the newcomer arrived.

Common sense as a way of knowing has two basic limitations. First, standards of common sense differ from time to time and from place to place according to the attitudes and experiences of the culture. Years ago, a common-sense method of trying suspects for crimes was having them attempt to chew dry grain. It was believed that if they were innocent, they would be able to eat the grain without difficulty; if they were guilty, their mouths would be too dry to permit swallowing. In reality, this practice does have some scientific basis: A guilty person is likely to be scared spitless. We now know, however, that innocent people can be just as nervous as guilty ones, so today we are usually more scientific in our trial practices. Again, common sense may tell us not to trust a person who will not look us in the eye. In another culture, though, the same behavior may be a sign of respect.

The second limitation of common sense as a way of knowing lies in the fact that the only criterion common sense recognizes for judging the truth of a belief or practice is whether it works. The old hand will tell the college graduate to forget his or her scientific ways because the old ways work well enough. According to the common-sense method, no systematic attempt is made to see why a practice works, or to test its theoretical explanation to see if it is true. As long as a certain practice works, that practice is maintained and the theory behind it is considered true. This principle can be useful at times. Child rearing practices for thousands of years were based on common-sense notions. Perhaps most children turned out reasonably well on this basis. Only in recent years have scientists advocated child-rearing methods that were an improvement over folk practices. Yet following a practice simply because it works does not permit any basis for predicting when the practice will work and when it will not. Common-sense notions of child rearing do not help in dealing with children with autism, for example.

More importantly, because common sense has only practical success as its criterion of truthfulness, it cannot predict new knowledge. Later we will discuss in some detail the idea that science aims at a theoretical explanation of phenomena. Here we will point out only that the absence of theory is one of the major limitations of this method of knowing.

Given that common sense has these two basic limitations—that it changes with time and circumstance and that it is pragmatic rather than theoretical— it is not surprising that scientific knowledge often contradicts common-sense knowledge. We may speak of a scientific result as being counterintuitive; that is, it goes against our notions of common sense. In fact, we consider a scientific theory to be fruitful if it predicts something that we did not expect.

For example, a theory of obesity in humans says that overweight people are controlled more by external cues (sight of food or a clock that indicates dinnertime) and less by internal signals (hunger pangs) than are other people. This theory makes the counterintuitive prediction that there should be

counterintuitive: something that goes against common sense

situations in which overweight people eat less than average-weight people. True to prediction, overweight people do eat less if they have to make a special effort to obtain the food. If there is plenty of food in front of them, however, they will eat more than average-weight people. In one experiment by Richard Nisbett (1968), sandwiches were placed in front of participants who were told to eat all they wanted, and to help themselves to more from the refrigerator if they desired. Half of the participants had only one sandwich in front of them, and the other half had three. Participants of average weight tended to eat about the same in either condition. That is, they would get more from the refrigerator in the one-sandwich condition but leave food on the plate in the three-sandwich condition. Overweight people, however, tended to eat whatever was there, either the small amount or the large amount, and not go to the refrigerator.

Another example of a counterintuitive scientific finding concerns prosocial behavior, or helping people. You might think that the more people who witnessed an emergency situation, the more likely a person would be to receive help. However, research has demonstrated that as the number of bystanders increase, the *fewer* offers of help are made. Darley and Latané (1968) conducted an experiment that included a staged emergency epileptic seizure that occurred during a telephone conference. The researchers varied the number of people who took part in the telephone conference, and found that when people believed that they were the only ones aware of the seizure, 85% of them tried to offer help. When participants in the study thought that there were four other people involved in the conference, only 25% of the participants offered to help. Apparently, the more people who are there, the less people feel responsible for helping in the emergency.

Even though science frequently contradicts common sense, we must not go to the extreme of concluding that we throw away common sense when we start doing science. In fact, science ultimately rests on common sense. Several different theories may be able to explain a given phenomenon. One of them may be rejected by scientists because it strains their common sense. Scientists often say that such-and-such a theory seems plausible, meaning that it agrees with their notion of common sense. Scientists choose among theories on a number of bases, but the theory that is finally accepted must satisfy the common sense of the scientific community. The crucial point here is that the scientist's common sense is different from that of the layperson. Scientists' background in similar problems trains them to think in terms of a particular scientific theory. Laypersons have different backgrounds that may make the theory of the scientists seem ridiculous. Their ideas of common sense differ precisely because they do not have common backgrounds.

Science

In addition to authority, logic, and intuition, the fourth major way of knowing about behavior is science. In the sections that follow, we will consider what science is, how it differs from other ways of knowing, and how psychology fits into the scientific approach to knowing.

What Is Science?

science: a way of obtaining knowledge by means of objective observations

To attempt to define science for a book of this type may seem either totally unnecessary, highly presumptuous, or both. Every reader of this book will have had exposure to science at the high school level, if not in college, which included some study of the scientific method. At this point, there are three reasons why we must discuss the nature of science. First, there is not a scientific method; rather, there are scientific methods. Somewhere you probably learned that the scientific method consisted of executing the following steps: (1) defining the problem, (2) forming a hypothesis, (3) collecting data, (4) drawing conclusions, and (5) communicating the findings. This recipe is usable, if you understand that it is greatly simplified. Research is sometimes done according to these steps, but more often it involves modification of this procedure. As our discussion progresses, the need for modification will become apparent.

The second reason for discussing the nature of science in this book is that even people who have developed a basic idea of how to do science that involves biology, chemistry, or physics often have difficulty seeing how to go about the science of psychology. Yet psychology is highly related to many other scientific disciplines. A study by Boyack, Klavans, and Börner (2005) showed that psychology is a *hub discipline*, along with mathematics, physics, chemistry, earth sciences, medicine, and the social sciences. These hubs are scientific disciplines with ideas and sub-groups that cross scientific boundaries. So, while psychology is distinct from biology, many sub-disciplines, such as animal behavior or neurology, share ideas common to both sciences. To many people it seems that psychology should follow different rules from other sciences because psychology appears by definition to deal with mental events. If you have trouble seeing how psychology can be like the other sciences, don't be discouraged. The experts on psychology took a long time to come to a tentative consensus about how psychology should be done, and the debate is not settled by any means.

A third reason for defining science in an introductory discussion of experimental psychology is that beginning psychology students sometimes feel that they have become amateur psychologists by virtue of observing human and animal behavior for a lifetime. When you took chemistry, you probably had not spent much time thinking about how atoms combine to form molecules. Yet you may have had a lifetime interest in why people are friendly or unfriendly, moody or not moody, and so forth. Sometimes, too, you know exactly why you do things: "I wore a certain style of clothes so I would be accepted by my fellow students." So your very experience with people may make it more difficult for you to think about human behavior scientifically. Studying human behavior might seem easier if you were the mythical Martian sent to spy on the behavior of earthlings. We often are more aware of the customs of a slightly different culture than we are of our own.

Characteristics of Science

To tell the truth, it is impossible to define science neatly because it is too complex an enterprise. It is not like defining a bachelor as an unmarried male. We can characterize science, however, somewhat the way we might characterize happy families by listing their typical attributes: parental interest in children's progress, many shared activities, stable lifestyle, and the like. These are useful in describing a typical happy family even though any one we might mention could be true of some unhappy family, and any one might be missing from some happy family. So we will state several of the important characteristics of science that tend to distinguish it from all other ways of knowing.

Science Is Empirical

You probably have heard the expression "I got it from the horse's mouth." Years ago, some philosophers are said to have argued at great length about how many teeth a horse had. After many logical arguments were presented on various sides of the question, someone suggested looking into a horse's mouth to find out. Although that suggestion seems obvious to us in today's scientific age, it was not clear to the scholastic mind of the Middle Ages that observation could be as good as logic in reaching a conclusion. For example, suppose that the horse was not typical in some respect: It had not yet grown all its teeth, or some had fallen out. The scientific attitude is to rely on experience more than on authority, common sense, or even logic.

Although empiricism is an essential characteristic of science, it is important to note that not all empirical ways of knowing are scientific. The intuitive method is empirical but not scientific.

Science Is Objective

The most important characteristic of science is that it is a way of obtaining knowledge based on objective observations. The key word in this brief definition is *objective*. Objective observations are those made in such a way that any person having normal perception and being in the same place at the same time would arrive at the same observation. Objectivity in science is a concept that is often misunderstood. It does not mean that scientists are coldly detached from their subject matter. It does not mean that they treat people as objects rather than as persons. Nor does it mean that what they observe is necessarily what actually happened. Objectivity simply means that other people would have seen the same things had they been looking over the shoulder of the scientist who made the observation.

In addition, when observations are objectively made and carefully reported, they serve as a sort of recipe for others to follow. Other scientists can repeat the procedures to see if they observe the same things. For this reason, careful records and clear, accurate reports are a crucial part of science. Such documentation permits others to bridge the gaps of space and time, and peer over the shoulder of the scientist, making his or her observations objective. The opposite of objective observations are subjective observations. These are the observations that a person makes that another person is not required to accept as true. Ann may say, "I taste salt." This statement by Ann is subjective because no one else can confirm that she actually experienced a salty taste. She might have tasted nothing because the salt was too weak, and just said "salt" out of perverseness. Then again, the statement "Ann reported tasting salt" is objective because anyone else present in the room could verify the fact that Ann made such a statement. So the experimenter can report objectively about Ann's subjective report. It is the experimenter's report that becomes the object of scientific discussion.

The need for objective observations explains the importance that scientists place on proper research methods. Great care is taken to specify the exact conditions under which observations are made so that other scientists can repeat the observations, if they desire, and try to obtain the same results.

Objectivity is the single most important characteristic in setting science apart from what is not science. Science deals with phenomena that are available to anyone. It cannot deal with phenomena that only one person or a few people can observe. This fact distinguishes science from all systems of knowledge based on authority: religion, politics, nationalism, and so on. Objectivity is what makes science the universal means of achieving understanding, because it eliminates from consideration at the outset any phenomenon that cannot command the agreement of every person. This is not to say that there are no scientific controversies or nationalistic scientists; far from it. But science as a whole is remarkably free from parochialism precisely because it deals only with those phenomena that are available to any person.

Science Is Self-Correcting

Because science is an empirical enterprise, it follows that new evidence is constantly being discovered that contradicts previous knowledge. Science is characterized by a willingness to let new evidence correct previous beliefs. This makes science different from perhaps every other human enterprise. Courts appeal to the Constitution, religions appeal to the writings of prophets, and institutions appeal to their traditions. Science, however, is characterized by a commitment to change based on empirical evidence. A notable example is provided by the French Academy of Sciences, which had a debate in the 18th century about whether stones fell from the sky. When the Academy concluded, on the basis of the best evidence at the time, that stones did not fall from the sky, museums discarded priceless collections of what we now know to be meteorites. Today, as a direct result of more empirical evidence, the existence of meteorites is common knowledge.

A psychological example concerns the relative influence of heredity and environment on behavior. Most psychologists in the middle years of the 20th century emphasized the role of environment in behavior, including personality. Some evidence (e.g., Bouchard, 1999) suggests, however, that heredity has a considerable degree of influence on personality and other behavioral characteristics. This has led to the rewriting of psychology textbooks to a remarkable degree. The willingness of scientists to change their opinions is a hallmark of science.

Science Is Progressive

Because science is empirical and self-correcting, it follows that it is also progressive. Science moves forward toward truth, adding more and more information to what was previously known. Other areas of human activity may change, but it is difficult to argue that they progress. Consider fashions in clothes. What is in fashion today may have been the latest thing 50 years ago and completely out of fashion last year. Literature, music, and painting are different today from what they were a hundred years ago, to be sure, but whether they are better is a matter of taste, not a matter that could be settled by any empirical test. Comparison of science textbooks over the years, however, shows remarkable progress in the amount and quality of knowledge they contain.

Science Is Tentative

What we have just said makes it obvious that science must be tentative. Because science is tentative, the opportunity to be self-correcting is also available. In other words, science never claims to have the whole truth on any question because new information may make current knowledge obsolete at any time. Because of the progressive nature of science, however, we can be reasonably confident that we are increasingly approaching the truth, rather than simply changing our ideas according to fashion or whim.

Science Is Parsimonious

parsimony: using the simplest possible explanation

According to the dictionary, *parsimony* means stinginess. This may seem a peculiar trait to claim as a desirable characteristic of science. In the case of science, the principle of parsimony holds that we should use the simplest explanation possible to account for a given phenomenon. If we want to explain why a mother cat licks and cleans her kittens of the fluids and membranes that cover them when they are born, we could say that she knows that she must clean them up or they will become cold and will not survive. Alternatively, we could suggest that she does so because that stuff tastes good to her. The first explanation may be more appealing to us, and attribute more dignity to the cat, especially if we are cat lovers, but the second explanation is closer to the truth as well as simpler. A good scientist will always prefer a simpler explanation to a more complex one, other things being equal. In our example, the explanation in terms of taste preferences is simpler than attributing sophisticated mental processes to the cat.

This principle of parsimony was advocated by William of Ockham (also spelled Occam), a philosopher who was active in the 14th century. He became so associated with this concept that it is often called "Occam's razor."

Science Is Concerned with Theory

As we will see later in this chapter, one of the major concerns of science is the development of a theory of how something works. The importance of theory to science can be illustrated by contrasting science and technology. These are similar enterprises, and historically the two have developed together. People were concerned with how to grow corn, for example. Techniques of growing better corn tended to lead to an understanding of what made the corn grow. This, in turn, led to better technology. Even today we often hear science and technology mentioned together, and they sometimes appear together in the names of magazines, colleges, and other institutions. But technology has the goal of making something work, whereas science has the task of understanding why it works. So technology would suggest taking an aspirin to alleviate a headache, while science would be concerned with the reason that aspirin reduces headaches and what the parameters are for its effectiveness. A psychological example of technology would be when a therapist applies a flooding technique to a person with a phobia in which they are exposed to the object of their fear. The science behind flooding tries to understand theoretical underpinnings (rooted in behavioral theory in this case) that make the technique effective.

Often the technology is far ahead of the science. A good example is the development of automatic controls. During the early days of the Industrial Revolution, the invention of the steam engine made work much easier. But it was necessary for someone to watch the earliest steam engines constantly, decreasing the supply of steam to the engine when it went too fast, and increasing it when it went too slowly. This was no doubt a boring task, albeit better than turning the wheels by hand. Eventually, in 1788, James Watt invented the automatic governor to control the supply of steam to the engine. He arranged for a pair of balls attached to levers to be spun by a shaft. When the shaft spun too fast, the balls flew outward and the levers shut off the flow of steam. When the shaft spun too slowly, the balls fell back, opening the steam valve. Thus the speed of the engine controlled the supply of steam, permitting the engine to run at a nearly constant rate. Years later, scientists understood that the principle of feedback by which the automatic governor maintains the constant speed of the steam engine is the same principle by which an animal's internal environment is kept constant, also called *homeostasis*. Technology gave us the automatic governor long before scientists understood that it represented a general theoretical principle.

The Relation Between Science and Nonscience

We have noted that science is not uniquely different from other ways of knowing. In fact, we stated that logic and common sense have important roles to play in science. At the same time, science and technology share a number of common characteristics, including empiricism and progress. We should point out that by emphasizing science we are not saying that we must reject other ways of knowing. Scientists are, after all, human, and therefore subject to all the frailties of humankind. They begin their inquiry on the basis of the actual beliefs that they hold at the time, as influenced by authority, logic, and common sense. What makes scientists different is their willingness to change those beliefs based on objectively obtained empirical evidence derived from their method of inquiry.

Authority has a reduced role in science. In virtually every human enterprise, there are people who serve as guardians of orthodoxy. Even in the most democratic organization, a majority vote can render certain opinions heretical. Although a power structure is by no means absent from science, authority plays a different role from the one it plays in other human activities. A clear example can be seen in almost any meeting of a large scientific organization. Anyone who meets minimal requirements—an undergraduate, graduate student, or new PhD—can present a paper that challenges the theories of even the most illustrious scientist. Although the challenger may suffer trepidation, and the senior scientist's arguments may receive more careful attention, the focus of the discussion will be on the soundness of the research methods and the logic of the challenger's position. If the challenger has presented a sound argument based on acceptable methods of observation, other scientists will be motivated to try to repeat the observations. If these repeated observations are successful, the illustrious scientist's ideas are replaced by those of the challenger.

Working Assumptions of Science

To most of us who have come through our Western educational system, science seems an obvious way to learn about the world. The rise of the counterculture in the 1960s, though, and the interest in non-Western modes of thought in recent years have reminded us that behind the scientific approach lie certain assumptions about the world. Many scientists rarely think about these assumptions and take them for granted as part of our Western, scientific outlook. Let us discuss them briefly.

The Reality of the World

realism: the philosophy that objects perceived have an existence outside the mind

Most scientists agree that one of science's fundamental assumptions is the reality of the world. Philosophers call this assumption the doctrine of realism: the notion that the objects of scientific study in the world exist apart from their being perceived by us. The scientist assumes, for example, that a rat does not stop being reinforced in a Skinner box simply because the experimenter fell asleep or went out for coffee or the recorder ran out of paper. This point may seem obvious to you, but a number of philosophers and some scientists would argue fiercely on this point. They are concerned with the valid and difficult question of how we really know the nature of the world. For example, how can we know our senses are not deceiving us when we observe that a piece of coal is black?

In general, scientists have little interest in philosophical debates about the reality of the world. They assume that the world is there, and they go about studying it as best they can. We must note, however, that they do avoid one variety of realism, which is known as common-sense realism, or naive realism. Common-sense realism is the philosophy of the person on the street who never wondered why coal looks black because anybody knows that coal is black. Common-sense realism says that things are just the way they seem: Coal looks black because it is black. The failure of common-sense realism has actually contributed to the development of science in many situations, particularly in psychology. For example, under some conditions, coal can look light gray rather than black. Students of perception devoted a good deal of energy to solving the problem of why a piece of coal can look black at one time and gray at another.

Although the scientist and the layperson both believe in the existence of a real world, the world that the scientist believes in is different from the one the layperson believes in. The layperson's world may contain people who are lazy or hardworking, good or evil. The scientist's world, by contrast, is more likely to consist of people who are influenced by stimuli, cognitions, and emotions.

The scientist and the layperson both assume there is only one reality, but they differ as to what that reality is.

Rationality

rationality: a view that reasoning is the basis for solving problems

Another crucial assumption of science is **rationality**—that the world is understandable by way of logical thinking. If the world were irrational—if it could not be understood by using principles of logic—then there would be no point in trying to understand it by any means whatsoever. We would simply throw up our hands and try to get along as best we could without trying to understand the world around us.

Regularity

regularity: a belief that phenomena exist in recurring patterns that conform with universal laws

The reality and rationality of the world would not be much use to science without the assumption of regularity. **Regularity** means that we assume that the world follows the same laws at all times and in all places. We pick up a book and are confident that it will not have become explosive since we last used it. We go to sleep at night without worrying that we will wake up in the morning as a giant cockroach. The reason regularity is so important for science is that it says that the laws of science are the same today as they were yesterday or a thousand years ago, and they will be the same tomorrow and a thousand years from now. If a new clothing style were to sweep the country tomorrow, a scientist would try to explain it by using the same principles that would have explained the fad for the flapper style of the 1920s, or the punk style of the 1980s. A scientist believes that "there is nothing new under the sun." It is true that the causes of these events may be complex and that we may never have all the facts necessary to explain a particular event in detail, but science assumes that nothing about human behavior falls outside the laws of nature, wherever or whenever the behavior occurs.

Discoverability

discoverability: the belief that it is possible to learn solutions to questions posed

Not only do scientists assume that the world is real, rational, and regular, but they also believe that it is possible to find out how it works. There is a difference between this assumption and the others. It is possible that the world is entirely rational, but that we can never find the key to the puzzle unless it is revealed to us. The scientist assumes that we can discover the way the world works without having a higher being or book reveal it to us. This belief in **discoverability** is the difference between a puzzle and a mystery. A puzzle can be solved by a person using ordinary means. A mystery, using the word in the strict sense, cannot be understood by human means but must have its solution revealed by someone who knows the mystery. Science treats the world as a gigantic puzzle that is mysterious in the loose sense of leading to wonder, but is not mysterious in the strict sense of not being solvable by human means.

This belief in the discoverability of the world by scientific methods must be tempered by an appreciation of the difficulty of the task. Many scientific puzzles have intrigued people throughout recorded history. Nature gives up its secrets reluctantly. Many books on experimental methods in psychology give the false impression that by a straightforward application of simple methods, the pieces of the psychological puzzle will slowly and steadily fall into place—far from it. Many fascinating examples show how solutions to scientific problems require great ingenuity and effort. In a fascinating autobiographical article, B. F. Skinner (1956) describes the processes that led him to become the founder of operant psychology. The basic belief in discoverability is one of the working assumptions of science that motivates people to make the effort necessary to carry on experimental work for large parts of their lifetimes.

Causality

To do science, it is necessary to assume that events do not just happen by themselves or for no reason. Thus, the idea that every event has a cause is a basic tenet of science. In fact, some have defined science as a search for causes of events.

determinism: the doctrine that all events happen because of preceding causes

A belief that all events are caused is called determinism. A strict determinist holds that if it were possible to know all laws of behavior and the exact condition of persons, together with everything that was influencing them at a particular time, it would be possible to predict exactly what they would do next. Others say that because the laws of behavior cannot be stated with certainty, the possibility of free will cannot be ruled out.

The problem of determinism and free will is a thorny one that we can leave to the philosophers. We do not have to decide whether people's behavior is strictly determined, whether we have free will, or whether both positions can be true at the same time. We are only stating that scientists use the concept of causality as a working assumption. People who believe in free will send their children to school because they expect the school to change the children's behavior in a predictable way. Therefore, they believe in determinism to some extent. Similarly, scientists seek causes for behavior without necessarily making the assumption that they will ever completely learn the causes of behavior, or that the idea of free will is an illusion.

temporal precedence: something that occurs prior to another thing

co-variation of cause and effect: when the cause is introduced, the effect occurs

probabilistic co-variation: statistical association of a cause with an effect

While we are discussing causality, we should note that all relationships between events are not of a cause-and-effect nature; some things just happen at the same time. Suppose, for example, you ate chocolate ice cream at a new restaurant and became sick. In order to establish a cause-and-effect relationship between events (such as eating ice cream and becoming sick), at least three criteria must be met (Mill, 2006). First, the cause has to come before the event, which is called temporal precedence. So, whether you ate the ice cream and then became sick, or became sick, then ate some ice cream, becomes important in establishing causality because causes must occur first. The next criterion is co-variation of cause and effect, or basically, that when the cause is present, the effect happens. If you went back to the same restaurant, and again ate chocolate ice cream and felt ill, there would be a high co-variation of cause and effect. It is worth mentioning that the co-variation need not be perfect; some events may be considered causes of other events, even if the relationship between them is less than constant and shows probabilistic co-variation. The classic example is the conclusion that smoking is a cause of lung cancer even though not every person who smokes contracts lung cancer. Similarly, poverty is a probabilistic cause of crime. Even though not every poor person becomes a criminal and not all criminals are poor,

**elimination of alterna-
tive explanations:** no
explanation for an effect
other than the purported
cause is possible

there is a statistical association between poverty and crime. The last criterion for establishing a cause-and-effect relationship is the elimination of alternative explanations. In other words, there is no other possible explanation for the effect except the cause. So, in our example with the ice cream potentially causing illness, you might want to think about whether or not the chocolate ice cream was eaten immediately following a trip to a buffet line where you seriously overate. If so, then maybe the ice cream was not the cause of the illness.

We must not leave the topic of the assumptions of science without pointing out that these need only be methodological, or working, assumptions, rather than assertions of ultimate truth. All scientists operate under such assumptions in the laboratory and in their writing about science. Outside the laboratory, however, some of them make different assumptions. At home they may doubt the existence of the real world. They may believe that human behavior is irrational, that miracles sometimes happen, or that the world really is mysterious in the strict sense. The point is that people are scientists when they are doing science, and to do science, they must make the assumptions we have discussed.

The Goals of Science

Until now, we have discussed the characteristics of science and what its working assumptions are. Now we begin to discuss the goals of science. Although science has a primary goal of understanding the world, this is achieved through two main goals: discovering regularities and developing theories.

The Discovery of Regularities

The goal of discovering regularities can be considered in three ways: the description of behavior, the discovery of lawful relationships among aspects of behavior, and the search for causes. For convenience, we consider them separately, even though they are three aspects of the same goal.

Description

The first step in any science is to describe the phenomena considered to be important for the science to deal with. We must define events and entities such as stimuli and responses, cognitions and beliefs, or neuroses and psychoses. This step seems so modest that often we are tempted to skip it and go on to the next one: the discovery of laws. We must have some agreement, though, on just what it is that we are going to study. Before we can find out what causes a person to become a sociopath, we must carefully describe the behavior of the sociopathic person and find out what sociopaths have in common. Only when we have a fairly clear description of the sociopathic personality can we look for factors in a person's background or physiology that caused him or her to become sociopathic.

The importance of description illustrates the close relationship between psychology and the biological sciences. For many years, a chief occupation of biologists was the description and classification of living forms. This process is still important today, but only in the past few decades have biologists been able to get beyond the descriptive level to study the mechanisms of life processes. Because psychology is a young science, much descriptive work still remains to be done. Perhaps nowhere is this more evident than in the area of personality, where there is fundamental disagreement about the way to go about describing personality.

Several quite different approaches to personality description currently exist. Type theories of personality attempt to classify people by putting them into particular categories or types, much as a botanist would classify a plant. Trait theories, by contrast, see people as differing in amount, rather than kind, on various traits that all people share to a greater or lesser extent. Social learning theories play down the personal causes of behavior in favor of situational causes. There are other theories of personality as well. Without judging the relative merits of these various theories, we may observe that the large number of conflicting approaches to describing personality reflects a relatively primitive state of science.

Lest anyone think we are emphasizing one area of psychology over another, let us consider an example from perception. Complete lack of agreement exists about the classification of odor qualities. Many odor classification schemes have been proposed over the centuries, but so far none has demonstrated its superiority over the others. It is fair to say that the absence of a satisfactory odor classification has severely hampered the development of satisfactory theories of smell and lawful relationships among variables.

Description of phenomena is crucially important to a science because it defines the subject matter for which laws are sought and theories are developed. If the descriptive phase of a science is skipped or done carelessly, it may become necessary to return to square one and start over again. All too often, experiments yielding to the temptation to skip the difficult descriptive phase jump into the next phase of developing laws. You might say, "I have noticed that my cat seems aggressive at certain times, fighting often with other cats and killing lots of mice. I will study the conditions under which this behavior occurs and look for its causes." What you have overlooked is that fighting with other cats and killing mice are two different kinds of behaviors. The cat that is fighting hisses, arches its back, and raises its fur. The cat that is hunting and killing a mouse has sleek fur, slinks quietly, and shows a different behavior pattern. A careful description of the behaviors in these two situations will reveal that they are not the same class of behaviors at all. This kind of mistake is made frequently in psychology. Unfortunately, there is no simple way to avoid it. You must be alert to the danger and diligent in describing behavior thoughtfully.

Not only does description of behavior define the subject matter of a science, but it can also be thought of as creating the subject matter. An example is the use of functional magnetic resonance imaging (fMRI) to examine the auditory hallucinations that people experience in schizophrenia. *Hearing voices* is a common complaint in schizophrenia. Mental health professionals traditionally showed little interest in the auditory hallucinations, dismissing them as only a symptom of the underlying disease. Recently, however, scientists have used the MRI to examine the brains of patients when they are experiencing hallucinations. The resulting brain scans showed that when the patients were hallucinating, brain areas involved in auditory perception, memory, speech, and emotion show increased blood flow (Shergill et al., 2003). This discovery led to further research on hallucinations that has been both exciting and informative. The availability of a behavioral marker of the hallucinations in the MRI data has led to the development of a promising treatment: the delivery of magnetic pulses to the brain areas affected by the hallucinations seems to temporarily quiet the experience of hearing voices in many of the schizophrenic patients (Hoffman et al., 2005).

Discovering Laws

law: a statement that certain events are regularly associated with each other in an orderly way

As the describing of behavior progresses, various regularities appear among behavioral events. These regularities form laws of behavior. A **law** is simply a statement that certain events are regularly associated with each other. The frustration-aggression law states that frustration causes aggression. In other words, the occurrence of frustration is regularly associated with aggression. Psychology has many examples of laws, because any time a regular association between two variables exists, you have a law.

It is not necessary to have a perfect relation between the two variables to have a law. As we noted earlier in the discussion of causality, some laws are probabilistic; that is, there is regularity between two variables, but the regularity is not such that every time one variable is present, the other is too. Because of the complexity of behavior, laws of behavior are often stated in statistical form.

Laws do not have to state cause-effect relationships between events; any regular relationship is a law. When we described the behavior of a fighting cat, we noted that the cat hisses, arches its back, and raises its fur. The arched back doesn't cause the cat to fight; it is simply correlated with fighting. These events are regularly associated together when a cat fights, and so can be considered a law. Thus, description and discovery of laws are actually part of a single activity; we have separated them in our discussion only for the purpose of exposition. In our earlier example, description of the sociopathic personality produces a statement of a lawful relationship among the various characteristics of people we call sociopaths.

Important as laws are, discovery of a law becomes not the capstone of scientific activity, but one of the early steps. The meaning of the term *law* will become clearer later as we contrast law and theory.

The Search for Causes

We have said that the goal of science is to understand the world. Another way of saying this is that scientists search for the causes of the events that we observe. If we know the causes of child abuse, for example, then we believe that we understand child abuse. The search for causes is so important that all the other goals of science that we will talk about can be considered as subgoals of it.

Discovering the cause of some event is not always as easy as explaining why the ice cream has turned to soup inside the freezer: "No wonder—the freezer's plug is lying on the floor!" Finding the cause of something like

Legionnaires' disease or depression is a complicated and exciting detective story. Consider the discovery of the part of the brain responsible for speech.

The extent to which the brain acts as a single unit rather than as an aggregate of specialized parts that perform particular functions was a major topic of controversy in the 19th century. Paul Broca was a French physician of the time. Several of his patients experienced strokes that left them unable to speak, a condition now known as expressive aphasia. A stroke is lay terminology for damage to brain tissue caused by interruption of blood flow to parts of the brain, either by clots that block blood vessels, or by a leak in a blood vessel. In an attempt to determine the part of the brain that might be responsible for speech, Broca performed autopsies on these patients after they died. It happens that strokes are highly variable in their extent and location in the brain. Some are very large, and others are quite small; they can affect any part of the brain.

Following are questions that Broca may have asked himself that also may be applicable in the search for causes of other psychological events:

1. *What do the cases have in common?* All of Broca's aphasic patients were able to speak normally; they then showed impaired speech patterns after the stroke (*temporal precedence*). All of the patients had strokes that affected the left hemisphere of the brain, but the affected areas varied in location and extent. By carefully comparing the brains of all his aphasic patients, he found that one particular area of the frontal cortex was involved in all patients whose strokes left them unable to speak (*co-variation of cause and effect*). This small part of the frontal area that was damaged in all the aphasic patients is now known as Broca's area.

2. *How do the cases differ from some similar cases?* Broca presumably saw many stroke patients who did not have aphasia. Those patients differed from the aphasics in that their strokes occurred in areas other than the frontal area. So Broca could rule out the idea that any stroke whatsoever causes aphasia (*elimination of alternative explanations*).

3. *Does the magnitude of the effect vary with the magnitude of some other event?* This question is similar to the first one, but asks whether the size of an effect varies with the size of something that might be its cause. Suppose that the size of the lesion in Broca's area is correlated with the degree of loss of speech. The more completely Broca's area is destroyed, the more complete is the loss of speech. Suppose that some people have tiny lesions in Broca's area and have barely noticeable speech problems, while those who have extensive damage of the area have extensive loss of speech. We would then have further evidence that lesions of Broca's area caused the aphasia.

Some Things to Keep in Mind

Although the questions above may help you find the cause of some psychological effect, they are not foolproof. In fact, there are often some pretty big obstacles to finding causes.

We often overlook the real cause. Our general knowledge of an area can help us guess the cause of some effect. Broca's background as a physician gave him an understanding of the problem that led him in the right direction. He thought to do autopsies on the patients, to look specifically at their brains, and to notice that one particular small part of the frontal lobe was affected. Others who were not physicians no doubt observed stroke patients with aphasia, but they did not do the autopsies.

Some events are just coincidences. Suppose for a moment that all of Broca's aphasic patients suffered their strokes while fighting with their spouses. The factor of fighting with one's spouse would be common to all cases and therefore a candidate to be the cause of aphasia. Before we concluded that fighting with a spouse is a cause of aphasia, however, we would want to know why that should cause aphasia instead of some other type of stroke. In the absence of some theoretical connection between aphasia and fighting with one's spouse, we would tend to ignore this cause as a candidate.

Sometimes the real cause is another event that is correlated with the suspected cause. Jonathan is a fourth-grader whose father keeps up on the latest scientific methods of improving his children's school performance. After reading that boys who wear longer pants tend to have larger vocabularies, he suggests to his wife that they start buying longer pants for Jonathan. In this case, Jonathan's father overlooked something that was a cause of both long pants and larger vocabularies: age. At the same time he committed the fallacy of ignoring a possible cause: What he thought was a cause was itself caused by a third event that he had overlooked.

Causes cannot happen after their effects. As we have seen, determining the cause of some event can be complicated, yet temporal precedence remains of critical importance. Because time's arrow flies only forward, the cause of an event cannot happen after the event. Germs cause disease, heat causes blisters, and rain makes grass grow, not the other way around. You may think that this point is too obvious to mention, but it is denied by anyone who believes in one particular form of ESP: precognition, which is also called fortune telling or foretelling the future. Anyone who thinks that people can tell the future is claiming that an event that has not yet happened causes people to have a premonition, or knowledge in advance of the event. But precognition is a claim that an event can precede its cause, which is not possible.

The Development of Theories

The ultimate goal of science is the development of a theory to explain the lawful relationships that exist in a particular field. We will define the concept of theory shortly. For now, we can briefly say that a theory is a set of statements that organize a large body of facts (laws) into a single explanatory system. Figure 1.2 demonstrates the relationships among facts, laws, and theories, and these ideas are also described in Table 1.1. In a nutshell, a theory is an explanation for a set of facts.

What Is a Theory?

We can define the concept of theory either broadly or narrowly. Broadly speaking, a theory is a statement or set of statements about the relationships among variables. If the statements concern only a single relationship between variables, we are speaking of a law. However, sometimes a number of laws

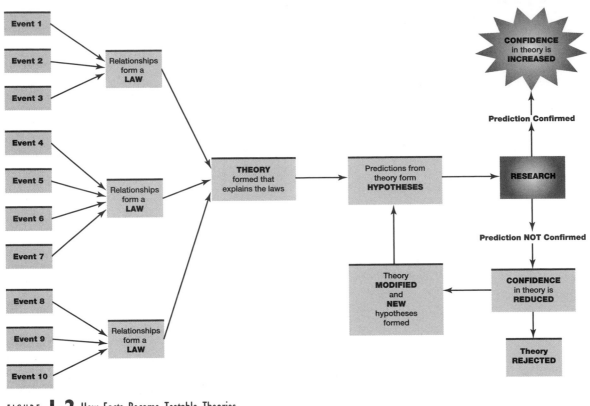

are tied together into a more general set of statements, which is called a theory. A classic example is Skinner's theory of operant conditioning. Skinner (1950) avoided concepts that could not be directly observed. Nevertheless, his system is a theory in the broader sense of a set of interrelated laws.

More often, the term **theory** is used in a second and stricter sense. According to this view, a theory is a statement or a set of statements about relationships among variables that includes at least one concept that is not directly observed but that is necessary to explain these relationships. Refer to Table 1.1. The statement at the bottom, about Elaine's ability to remember a series of numbers, concerns a specific set of observations on one person at one time under particular conditions. This statement has no generality.

The middle statement is about the behavior of people, in general, under similar conditions. This is a general statement that is true whenever certain conditions obtain; therefore, we are justified in calling it a law. At the top is a statement that is different from the middle or the bottom one. Depicted here is a brief outline of the Atkinson-Shiffrin theory of memory. This theory introduces concepts, such as working memory, that are not present at the level of law. These new concepts are theoretical concepts because they are invoked to explain the relationship among the variables in the middle statement. Specifically, the theory introduces the concept of working memory, which is said to be

theory: a statement or set of statements explaining one or more laws, usually including one indirect concept needed to explain the relationship

TABLE **1.1**
Relationship of Data, Law, and Theory
© Cengage Learning

Theory	Information $\longrightarrow$	Working memory	Processing $\longrightarrow$	Long-term memory
Law	People can recall seven bits of information that have been briefly presented.			
Data	On the average, Elaine could remember for 10 seconds a series of seven numbers when they were shown to her for one second on April 12, 2004.			

a stage in the processing of information into permanent form. All information to be remembered is held for a while in working memory before being transferred into long-term memory. Working memory is a theoretical concept because it is not seen or measured directly, but must be inferred from behavior. This stage of processing can be inferred from several bases. Among the more important is the fact that only about seven items can be held briefly in memory after they have been presented together once, as when we remember a telephone number that we have just looked up. If more than about seven numbers are presented together, some of them are lost. In our long-term memory, however, no such limitation exists on the number of things we can recall. Thus, working memory is clearly different from long-term memory in its limited capacity to hold information. Psychology makes use of a number of unobservable concepts, such as working memory, in developing theories of behavior.

Note that working memory is never observed directly. No single way of measuring its effects defines the concept completely. Theoretical concepts are not observed directly; they can be defined only indirectly by reference to events that are directly observed. A theoretical concept is an invention of the scientist to account for laws of behavior. To take an example from physics, no one has ever seen an electron. It is a theoretical concept invented to account for particular laws of physics.

Theories Must Be Falsifiable

The comic strip character, Lucy, once said that she had a perfect theory: it could not be proven right or wrong. This may seem like a good idea to Lucy, but to a scientist, such a theory is worse than useless. A good theory must be capable of being tested in an unambiguous way. It must make a definite prediction that can be proven right or wrong. The reason for this is the empirical nature of science. If science is based on empirical evidence, its theories must be capable of being empirically tested. A theory of how people would behave in space colonies would not be a scientific theory because we cannot test it. Someday we may have space colonies, and such a theory would then be scientific because it could then be tested.

A theory must not only be testable, it must also be capable of being proven wrong. This property of being capable of disproof is called **falsifiability**. When most people attempt to test a theory, they try to prove that it is true. In fact, the more fruitful test of a theory is to set up a condition in which it can fail. You

falsifiability: the property of a good theory that it is capable of disproof

may have heard the joke about the person who kept snapping his fingers to keep the elephants away. When his friend objected that there were no elephants around, he said, "See, it works." Snapping his fingers as a test of this theory was nearly useless. There are many reasons, other than finger snapping, why there may be no elephants in a particular area: climate, food supply, and so forth. A far more useful test would be not snapping his fingers. That test would permit his theory to be proven wrong.

This notion is based on the work of the philosopher, Sir Karl Popper, who said that a scientific theory can never be proven true because there are many false theories that can predict any given outcome. Popper would say that no matter how many times the predicted result occurs, there might still be another theory that actually is the true one. What would be informative would be a disconfirmation, or a result that contradicted the theory. According to Popper, we make up theories and try to knock them down. The ones that survive the testing process can tentatively be accepted as true by a process of elimination. We can never prove the theory to be true for certain, but we gain more confidence in the theory the more tests it survives.

The Role of Theories

We have emphasized the development of theories as a major goal of science. But why are theories so important? Theories play three crucial roles in the development of a science: (1) organizing knowledge and explaining laws, (2) predicting new laws, and (3) guiding research.

Organizing Knowledge and Explaining Laws

First, theories organize knowledge and explain laws. In the absence of a theory, we simply have a collection of descriptions and some laws. The theory pulls these together into a unified framework. According to philosophers of science, relating individual events to laws and laws to theories constitutes scientific explanation. The individual fact is explained by being shown to be an instance of a general law. In turn, the law is explained by its relation to the theory. We explain Elaine's inability to remember more than seven numbers as an instance of the law of the limited nature of working memory. We can go up one level and explain the limited nature of working memory in terms of the way information is processed from a working store into a permanent form according to memory theory. Explanation is a process of relating more particular concepts to more general concepts. The theory explains the laws that have been found.

The better the theory, the more events and laws it can explain. We would have little interest in a theory that explained the behavior of only a few individuals under a limited set of circumstances. In addition, the more specific and precise the explanation, the better the theory is. For this reason, theories that are stated mathematically are considered better than theories that state relationships only in general terms. Of course, these two considerations are often in conflict. A broad general theory can explain more laws and instances, but with less precision than a less ambitious theory can. During the first half of the 20th century, psychology was characterized by many broad theories, such as those of Sigmund Freud, Clark H. Hull, and others, that were designed to encompass much of behavior. More recently, psychologists have devoted themselves to theories that are less ambitious in scope, but have greater explanatory precision, such as theories of speech perception, or problem solving.

Predicting New Laws

The second role of theories is to predict new laws. A fruitful theory not only explains many different laws that were previously unrelated, but also suggests places to look for new laws. For example, a prominent theory of pain perception holds that social pain may be interpreted by the brain similarly to physical pain. C. Nathan DeWall and his colleagues (2010) hypothesized that if this theory were true, then people who had their feelings hurt (social pain) should have their pain reduced through the administration of a product shown to reduce physical pain, such as acetaminophen (the pain reliever found in Tylenol®). DeWall and his colleagues ran an experiment in which undergraduates were randomly chosen to receive either two doses of acetaminophen every day for three weeks or a similarly administered placebo (sugar pill). At the end of each day, participants reported their level of social pain or hurt feelings for the day, as well as positive emotions. By the end of the 21 days, people in the acetaminophen group showed fewer hurt feelings than those who had been in the placebo group, though the level of positive emotions was not different between the groups. This showed that the acetaminophen acted solely to reduce the pain, not simply to elevate emotions. The results of this experiment demonstrate how a theory can lead to new laws, or to new phenomena. In this case, the theory led to the prediction and then confirmation that central pain relievers reduce psychological as well as physiological pain.

Guiding Research

Theories also serve to guide research. Most researchers say that they work within a certain theoretical framework, such as the memory theory just described. A good theory suggests new experiments and helps researchers choose alternative ways of performing them. This role of theory in guiding research goes hand in hand with its role in predicting new laws. When scientists use a theory to predict a new law, they also use the theory to suggest new studies that can be performed to establish that new law. DeWall and his colleagues, guided by the overlapping pain centers theory, derived a prediction from that theory. This prediction led them to study whether acetaminophen reduced psychological pain.

Other Goals

We have stressed theoretical explanation as the ultimate goal of science. However, many books say that the goals of psychology are description, prediction, and control. We have already discussed description as a goal. Prediction and control actually emerge from the description process. If we have done our job of description well, we have established laws of behavior. Knowledge of these laws allows us to predict the occurrence of behavior. If we can predict behavior, we are also able to control it if we have control over the events that cause it. So description, prediction, and control are three aspects of the goal of discovering regularities of behavior.

Hypotheses in Science

If developing laws and theories is the goal of science, how do we go about that process? Let us return for a moment to the theory that psychological pain is processed similarly to physical pain. DeWall and his colleagues reasoned that if the same brain areas are responsible for psychological pain as physical pain, then common pain relievers should also affect hurt feelings. What DeWall and his colleagues did was to propose a hypothesis.

hypothesis: a statement assumed to be true for the purpose of testing its validity

A **hypothesis** is a statement that is assumed to be true for the purpose of testing its validity. A hypothesis can be put in the form of an if-then statement: If A is true, then B should follow. The statement must be one that is either true or false: If people take pain relievers when their feelings are hurt, they will feel better or they won't; it cannot feel both better and worse.

A scientific hypothesis reads like this: If we make certain observations under particular conditions, and a given theory is correct, then we should find the following results. A scientific hypothesis must be capable of empirical testing and, as a result, empirical confirmation or disconfirmation.

DeWall and his colleagues' hypothesis consisted of a law that was predicted from the theory. In other cases, the theory may be the focus of the hypothesis. Take an example from law enforcement. Police may hypothesize that the butler did it. This is a hypothesis that states a theory to be tested: the theory that the butler did it. In actuality, however, we must not suppose that a particular hypothesis can concern only a theory or only a law, to the exclusion of the other. A hypothesis about a law involves certain assumptions about the theory underlying the law. Conversely, it is impossible to test a theory without also testing some lawful prediction of the theory.

DeWall might well have said, *if the overlapping pain centers theory of psychological pain is correct, and if we give people a pain reliever like acetaminophen, then their hurt feelings should be relieved.* This statement contains one hypothesis about the theory and another about the law. If the prediction is not confirmed when it is tested empirically, either the law or the theory—or both—may be false.

Most scientific research, then, is designed to test at least one hypothesis. Much of the rest of this book can be considered a discussion of how one makes and tests scientific hypotheses in the field of psychology.

Defining Theoretical Concepts

We said earlier that science seeks to develop theoretical explanations of phenomena that occur in the world. Developing theoretical explanations is such a complex activity that breaking down the processes into definite steps is difficult. Sometimes we start with a theory and look for phenomena that should occur if the theory is true. At other times we begin with a phenomenon for which we have no explanation and try to develop a satisfactory theory. We now take up the question of how we build theories.

The first and most important question is: how do we go about inferring the existence of the theoretical entities, such as working memory that we develop to account for the facts of behavior? On what basis, that is, are we permitted to construct theoretical concepts such as working memory, learning, and hunger? How do these supposedly scientific concepts differ from nonscientific concepts? To answer these questions, we must recall that science deals with empirical objective knowledge: those events that are available to every person. Operationism, which is associated with physicist Percy Bridgman, states that scientific concepts must be public in the same way that scientific data are public. According to Bridgman, a theoretical concept must be tied to observable operations that any person can observe or perform.

operationism: a view that scientific concepts must be defined in terms of observable operations

If a concept cannot be tied to particular operations, then it is not a scientific concept. Take the concept of the will of God. If we say that everything that happens is the will of God, then the concept is without operational meaning. If it should rain tomorrow, we might say the rain was God's will. Then again, if it should not rain tomorrow, we likewise conclude that not raining was God's will. We have no way to define which future events would be according to God's will and which would not. Few people would say that God's will is a scientific concept.

Let us consider another example. Some people believe that psychic ability (e.g., extrasensory perception) is a scientific concept. Here, the problem is defining psychic ability; the only way to do so is for certain types of unlikely data to occur. No conditions are known that are favorable or unfavorable to the demonstration of psychic ability; that is, no operations exist that increase or decrease the probability of an event that would be defined as reflecting psychic ability. Psychic perceptions take place according to no lawful operations. Most psychologists conclude that the concept of psychic ability has no operational definition and, therefore, is not a scientific concept.

Operationism, then, strictly limits the kinds of concepts with which science can deal. If there is no way of defining the concept according to observable operations, the concept is barred from science.

Operationism has a further, more specific, meaning; namely, that scientific concepts are defined according to the operations by which they are measured. If you were to read the report of an experiment that contrasted the learning rates for young and old people, you probably would want to know what the author meant by learning, as well as what ages they considered *old* or *young*. In the methods section of a paper reporting this experiment, you might read that two groups of people, one 15–25 and one 70–80 years old, had to continue to study a list of 30 words until they could report them accurately 15 minutes later. You would say to yourself, "Ah, when the author says that she looked at learning, she means the rate at which people were able to acquire a verbal task." The statement of what the experimenter did to define learning is called an **operational definition** of learning. The statement of what the experimenter did to define groups as young or old is called an **operational definition** of age. Of first and crucial importance in an operational definition is to state a procedure, or operation, that specifies the meaning of the concept. For the purposes of the experiment, the particular way of

operational definition: a statement of the precise meaning of a procedure or concept within an experiment

inducing learning defines the concept of learning, and a particular range of ages defines young, while another range of ages defines old.

As important as an operational definition of a concept is, it has been misunderstood and misused in psychology. The principal misuse is taking a trivial definition of a concept and attempting to build a theory on it. You may believe that twiddling a button on one's clothing is a sign of anxiety. However, this would probably not be as good a measure of anxiety as the galvanic skin response or the Taylor Manifest Anxiety Scale. Experiments that relied on the button-twiddling measure probably would not be as good tests of an anxiety theory as those that used one of the other measures.

Another misuse of the concept of operational definition is considering every measure of a concept as independent of every other measure. According to this view, learning a list of words until they can be repeated accurately 15 minutes later is a different type of learning from giving people a pair of words to study and having them respond correctly to one member of the pair 15 minutes later. It is true that these two operational definitions of learning may produce somewhat different results in particular situations because of peculiarities inherent in the methods of the learning task.

converging operations: using different operational definitions to arrive at the meaning of a concept

Yet by using different methods of producing learning, we hope that a common core of knowledge about learning will result. Using different ways of honing in on a concept via different operational definitions is called converging operations. Each new way of producing the concept of learning will rule out one possible objection to the explanation, until a high degree of confidence can be reached. The method of converging operations is much like the method a surveyor uses to locate a point on the ground. The point is marked from two or more independent locations in order to get a good fix on it by triangulation. The larger the number of independent locations from which the surveyor knows the distance and direction, the more precisely the new point is located.

Today, operationism is no longer adhered to in the strict sense that Bridgman advocated. Scientists now agree that some of the meaning of a theoretical concept may be defined by its relationship to a larger theory of which it is a part. Learning, for example, may not be defined completely by any of the ways of measuring it, or even by all of them together. From operationism, however, we must remember to define carefully the terms we use so that their meaning is clear with respect to events in the world that can be observed objectively and with respect to the theories we develop to explain those events.

The Nature of Scientific Progress _____

Paradigms

paradigm: a set of laws, theories, methods, and applications that form a scientific research tradition; for example, Pavlovian conditioning

Laypersons commonly believe that science progresses in a straightforward manner by accumulating knowledge, much as a building is built brick by brick. That this stereotype is mistaken has been shown convincingly by Thomas Kuhn (1996). Basic to Kuhn's thought is the concept of a **paradigm:** a pervasive way of thinking about a branch of science that includes all the assumptions and theories that are accepted as true by a group of scientists. During a period of what he calls normal science, nearly all scientists accept the same paradigm and work under its influence. Eventually, problems develop that cannot be explained without difficulty by the paradigm. These anomalies cause a crisis, during which other paradigms are created that compete with the original paradigm. A new paradigm will be accepted when it accounts more successfully for empirical data than did the old paradigm. According to Kuhn, the course of science is not steady progress toward a goal. Rather, it consists of phases of normal science, each dominated by a single paradigm, alternating with revolutions that install new paradigms that last as long as each paradigm is reasonably successful in accounting for empirical data.

Kuhn's concept of paradigm shifts has gained widespread acceptance among scientists because it captures the reality of conflict among competing theories and the often acrimonious debates that take place among scientific camps. His viewpoint also accounts for some proverbs about science, such as the idea that a theory is not rejected because it is disproved, but because a better theory displaces it.

Kuhn holds that it is not possible to choose between different paradigms on the basis of data alone. The reason is that what counts as data depends on the methods, theories, and assumptions of the particular paradigm. These factors are sufficiently complex that the switch from one paradigm to another involves social and personal forces to such an extent that it is sometimes likened to a political revolution.

Larry Laudan (1977, 1996) represents what is perhaps the mainstream opinion about what Kuhn's ideas mean for science. Laudan does not accept the radical relativism of some, and holds that scientists pursue research traditions because they solve theoretical and empirical problems. In this way, science is rational because scientists can choose the paradigm that is currently solving the most problems.

Although most scientists acknowledge the usefulness of Kuhn's ideas, people take considerably different messages from the ideas. Some social scientists and philosophers have used Kuhn to support a radical relativism in science. These relativists hold that various scientific theories are all equally good and no better than other *stories* about reality. They may give the creation myth of a Native American tribe equal validity concerning the tribe's origin as DNA evidence. We discuss this idea of *social constructivism* in the next section.

A Note on Psychology and Science

The view of science that we have presented here is the one that has guided many researchers and much of the history of modern psychology. The reader should be aware that some would say that it is an ideal that is seldom realized in practice. The epilogue to this book discusses some ways that science sometimes fails to achieve the ideal.

Further, another view of science has begun to gain a following in psychology. This view, sometimes called *social construction*, has become highly influential in the humanities. Applied to science, social constructivism claims that science does not deal as much with reality as with the beliefs of scientists. Because scientists are people like everyone else, their views are not necessarily more objective than those of anyone else (e.g., Gergen, 1994, 2001). Janis Bohan (1993) succinctly states the social constructivist position as follows:

> The foundational assertion of social constructivism is that we have no way of knowing with certainty the nature of reality. From this perspective, so-called knowledge does not reflect the free-standing reality, existing apart from the knower and revealed by careful application of procedures. Rather, what we purport to know ... is a construction ... based upon ... the contexts within which it is created.... Thus, knowledge is a product of social exchange; what we call knowledge is simply what we agree to call truth. (pp. 12–13)

Psychologists are divided on the value of social constructivism. (See Haig, 2002, and surrounding articles in the same issue.) M. Brewster Smith (1994) criticizes social construction as follows:

> Psychologists ... can welcome social construction—the recognition that people actively construct their worlds of experience.... They can accept the contextualist criticism that many of the claims of Euro-American psychology are probably history and culture bound.... What I see as most unfortunate, however, is the tendency ... to give up on the conception of science ... as an enterprise that has successfully sought progressively more adequate and comprehensive understanding of the phenomena in its domain. (p. 408)

Smith points out what seems to be the key question dividing social constructivists from other scientists: Does a reality exist independently of the scientist that can be approached, even if only glimpsed dimly, or is reality a story created by the scientist that is no better than other stories? The answer to this question might well be different in the case of whether the sun revolves around the earth or vice versa, than in the case of whether gender is a social construction or a natural category.

Both sides agree that the road to discovering the nature of reality is strewn with obstacles. Readers who prefer not to wait until the end of the book to get more perspective on this question should turn to the epilogue now.

Summary

1. Psychology is a science, essentially like any other science.
2. There are four ways of knowing about behavior: authority, logic, intuition, and science.
3. Authority plays a diminished role in science compared with other social institutions.
4. Logic plays an important role in science, but is secondary in importance to observation.
5. Common sense is limited in its usefulness to science because it changes from time to time and place to place, and cannot predict new knowledge.

6. Scientific knowledge often contradicts common sense, but ultimately it rests on a certain kind of common sense.

7. Science is a way of obtaining knowledge based on objective observations.

8. There is not one scientific method, but many scientific methods.

9. Science has the following characteristics: It is empirical, objective, self-correcting, progressive, tentative, parsimonious, and concerned with theory.

10. Science has five major working assumptions: the reality, rationality, and regularity of the world; the discoverability of how the world works; and the operation of causality.

11. Scientists assume that the world is real, but they do not assume that it is just the way it appears to be.

12. The assumption of rationality means that the world is believed to be understandable via logical thinking.

13. The assumption of regularity means that the world is believed to follow the same laws in all times and places.

14. The assumption of discoverability means that scientists believe that it is possible to find out how the world works.

15. The assumption of causality means that all events are believed to have causes.

16. The criteria of temporal precedence, co-variation of cause and effect, and elimination of alternative explanations are critical to establishing a cause-and-effect relationship between two events.

17. The goals of science include the discovery of regularities and the development of theories.

18. Discovering regularities includes describing behavior, discovering lawful relationships among aspects of behavior, and searching for causes.

19. Description of behavior is crucially important because it defines the subject matter for which laws are to be sought and theories developed.

20. Description can be thought of as creating the subject matter of science.

21. A law is a statement that certain events are regularly associated with one another.

22. The ultimate goal of science is the development of a theory to explain lawful relationships that exist in a particular field.

23. Broadly speaking, a theory is a set of statements about the relationships among variables.

24. More narrowly, a theory is a set of statements about relationships among variables that includes at least one concept that is not directly observed.

25. Theories and hypotheses must be capable of being tested empirically.

26. Theories guide research and, in turn, are modified by research in a continuous cycle.

27. Theories have three main functions in science: (1) organizing knowledge and explaining laws, (2) predicting new laws, and (3) guiding research.

28. A hypothesis is a statement that is assumed to be true for the purpose of testing its validity.

29. Operationism is the doctrine that scientific concepts must be tied to observable operations.
30. Although it is important to define theoretical concepts operationally, scientists agree that an operational definition does not completely define a concept.
31. Progress in science often involves a major shift in theories and assumptions, known as a paradigm shift, rather than a steady accumulation of knowledge.

Suggestions for Further Reading

CAMPBELL, N. (1953). *What is science?* New York: Dover. This book, originally published in 1921, is a classic introduction to the nature of science. It is brief and particularly clear in its discussion of the nature of scientific laws and theories.

CONANT, J. B. (1961). *Science and common sense.* New Haven, CT: Yale University Press. This book shows, by examples from the natural sciences, how science grew out of a concern with practical problems and how science differs from technology in its emphasis on speculative knowledge to satisfy curiosity about the world.

COOPER, H. M. (1989). *Integrating research: A guide for literature reviews.* Newbury Park, CA: Sage. This treatment of literature reviewing emphasizes psychological applications.

COUVALIS, G. (1997). *The philosophy of science: Science and objectivity.* London: Sage. This contemporary introduction to philosophy of science has a good discussion of the objectivity of science.

HACKING, I. (1981). *Scientific revolutions.* London: Oxford University Press. The introduction to this volume gives a concise statement of the basic propositions held by most philosophers of science before Kuhn. The article by Laudan contains a list of beliefs now generally held. The annotated bibliography is a valuable guide to the literature in the area.

HEMPEL, C. G. (1966). *Philosophy of natural science.* Englewood Cliffs, NJ: Prentice-Hall. This excellent brief introduction to the philosophy of science has a particularly good discussion of law, theory, and the nature of scientific explanation.

LADYMAN, J. (2001). *Understanding philosophy of science.* London: Routledge. This is an accessible introduction to modern philosophy of science, with

an emphasis on the debate between realists and antirealists.

LIGHT, R. J., & PILLEMER, D. B. (2005). *Summing up: The science of reviewing research.* Cambridge, MA: Harvard University Press. This book has less technical discussion of the process of literature review than most treatments of meta-analysis.

MARX, M. H., & GOODSON, F. E. (Eds.) (1976). *Theories in contemporary psychology.* New York: Macmillan. This edited volume contains many of the classic papers on the philosophy of science as it relates specifically to psychological theories. The discussion is on a high level, but is essential for serious students.

MCBURNEY, D. H. (2002). *How to think like a psychologist: Critical thinking in psychology* (2nd ed.). Englewood Cliffs, NJ: Prentice-Hall. This book answers common questions that students have about psychology as a science.

RADNER, D., & RADNER, M. (1982). *Science and unreason.* Belmont, CA: Wadsworth. This is an illuminating and entertaining account of some infamous pseudosciences and how they differ from science.

REED, J. G., & BAXTER, P. M. (2003). *Library use: A handbook for psychology* (3rd ed.). Washington, DC: American Psychological Association. This very useful book is designed for undergraduates who are doing library work in psychology for the first time.

SHADISH, W., COOK, T., & CAMPBELL, D. (2002). *Experimental and quasi-experimental designs for generalized causal interference.* Boston: Houghton Mifflin.

STANOVICH, K. E. (2009). *How to think straight about psychology* (9th ed.). Boston, MA: Allyn & Bacon. Stanovich discusses common misconceptions about the nature of psychology as a science.

A CASE IN POINT

Each chapter in this book has a case study that illustrates at least one issue raised in the text. These cases are generally more complex than an exercise and usually have no single best solution. You will need to use your judgment to complete the case, and different people will often come to different justifiable conclusions.

Mike's Research Project

Mike was a sophomore psychology major at State University. One weekend when he was home, he and his family got into a discussion of his experimental psychology project, which concerned the reasons why teenagers use drugs. Mike said that he suspected that teenagers who use drugs are seeking a substitute for the satisfactions others get through close personal relationships. He was describing what he had found so far in his library search when his father suggested that he read an interesting article in last week's Sunday supplement from the local paper. "It quoted several people who worked with drug users, each of whom explained drugs on the basis of their own personal experiences, some as past drug abusers, and all with teenagers. The article said that it was obvious why kids used drugs: too much money and free time, television, and the breakdown of the family."

Mike's mother had a different idea. "It's all caused by grunge rock. There was much less drug use before; now there's a lot. It's a simple matter of logic."

Mike's little sister, Jennifer, had been listening to the conversation. "All the people I know who use drugs are just weird, and there's no point in trying to figure them out; they're just different from everyone else. If you want to know why they use drugs, you'll have to become a pothead and try it for yourself."

This suggestion got his mother's attention in a hurry. "I'm worried enough about your being down there at the university as it is without your getting involved with drugs. There are some things we can never know because we aren't supposed to. You should just pick another topic, or better yet, another major."

Mike's father said, "I think Jennifer has a point. Psychology may be a science, but because it deals with the mind, it can't be done the way chemistry is. You can't put the mind in a test tube. You need to use different methods. You should ask drug users why they do it."

Later, as he drove back to school, Mike realized that he had not been able to answer their arguments. He reread the first chapter in his textbook and wrote a letter to his parents.

Required

Compose Mike's letter for him, identifying the assumptions each person made that violate the assumptions of science. Answer the objections.

Evolutionary Psychology of the Family

This case is based on an article in the *New York Times* by Natalie Angier, "New View of Family: Unstable but Wealth Helps" (August 29, 1995, pp. B5, B7).

Darwin's theory of evolution has long been accepted by scientists as the explanation of the origins of animals, including humans. Relatively recently, psychologists and other scientists have begun to apply evolutionary theory to human behavior. This effort is controversial, not because of creationism, which is held by few scientists, but because many scientists believe that the predictions of evolutionary theory imply that various behaviors are acceptable because they are *natural*. Partly because of its controversial status, this new area of psychology provides an excellent case in point for many of the ideas of this chapter.

Stephen Emlen is an evolutionary biologist at Cornell University who studies family interactions in animals, mainly birds. He is part of a group of evolutionary psychologists who say it is their turn to take a crack at the family. They argue that the application of the basic principles of Darwinian science can illuminate family dynamics in ways not revealed through the social sciences, which generally emphasize the cultural, psychological, and economic roots of behavior, rather than the biological ones (Angier, 1995, p. B7).

Although many scientists might define a family as one or two parents with dependent offspring, Emlen considered an animal to be familial when it

(continued)

sticks around its birthplace as an adult and continues to have contact with its parents and other relatives throughout life. Often the homebound animal may postpone having a family of its own even when it is reproductively capable of doing so. "Some might argue that any case where a parent cares for dependent offspring is a family," Dr. Emlen said. "But I thought that explaining more prolonged interactions, after the offspring have become potential competitors, would be a more useful way to look for parallels to the human situation." (Angier, 1995, p. B7)

For example, the tendency of wealthy human families to form dynasties that remain intact for generations is well known. And biologists have also known about the acorn woodpecker, a species that drills holes in trees to store acorns to tide them over when food is scarce. Emlen sees a similarity between the two situations: He predicts that families will be more stable if they control high-quality resources, such as rich human property owners, or acorn woodpeckers with lots of acorn-producing trees in their territories. The young will tend to stick around in hopes of taking over the resources when the older generation dies off. Offspring of poor families will disperse to seek their fortunes.

> But family stability breaks down if the members are not related by blood: If the biological mother dies, and the father finds a new mate, his grown son will try courting the new female at every opportunity, undermining his father's position. If it is the father who dies, and the male is the dominant sex of that species, the son will eject the mother from the territory and assume lordship. (Angier, 1995, p. B7)

A key idea in the evolutionary approach to families is that the degree of relatedness of the individuals in the family predicts how much they should cooperate. Because close relatives share many genes, behavior that benefits relatives will help perpetuate an individual's genes. This is called *inclusive fitness*. Conversely, individuals who are unrelated have less incentive to be cooperative. Evolutionary theory, therefore, predicts

that individuals may actually be quite hostile to unrelated family members.

Emlen predicts, on the basis of inclusive fitness, that families with stepparents will be less stable and have more incidents of child abuse. When he went to collect data on this question, however,

> he was astonished to learn that information was often not broken down in this manner. "Most social science studies look at two-parent families compared to single-parent families," he said. "The intact families are pooled whether they're biological or stepfamilies."
>
> A Darwinian perspective, he added, "would say you should expect huge differences here, and that it would be helpful to partition them and examine them distinctly [separately]" (Angier, 1995).

Required

1. Is Professor Emlen trying to prove the theory of evolution to be true, or is he testing its predictions for the behavior of families? What difference does this make? *Hint:* Would the theory of evolution be put into serious doubt if his predictions about families turned out not to be true?

2. To study families, Emlen had to define what a family is. What are some possible definitions? What is his definition, and how does it differ from some others? How does his definition help us understand interactions among generations within a family?

3. Show how Emlen used the theory of evolution to explain two different phenomena (laws) that previously had not been seen as belonging together.

4. Freud's theory of the Oedipal conflict says that the son tries to displace the father to mate with the mother. How does the theory of evolution make a different prediction?

5. How did the theoretical orientation of most other researchers in the field lead them to do their research in a way that made it hard for Emlen to test his hypothesis?

Reading Between the Lines

One of the most important goals of an experimental psychology course is to develop skills in critically evaluating published studies and other claims made on the basis of evidence. Any set of data always has alternative explanations, but some are more plausible than others are. Students need to develop a healthy skepticism for claims made about data. The problems that will be presented in this section contain conclusions that are questionable. Study each one to see what other hypotheses might account for the data.

Some of the problems are fairly easy; others are very difficult. Because all involve actual cases, they also involve questions of interpretation that authorities of one sort or another have differed on. Most of these examples have been published in the scientific literature, passing through the peer-review process with their original interpretations. In some cases, the problem of interpreting was so difficult that scientists worked for years to find the proper interpretation of the results. In other cases, the results are still debated. So don't feel discouraged if you cannot see immediately what is questionable about the interpretation of the data. Study each problem to see what other interpretations might be possible. Begin to learn to read between the lines. The answers are given in Appendix C.

1.1 Guns Don't Kill People; People Kill People

The gun lobby says that guns don't kill people; people kill people. This argument is used to refute the desirability of stricter gun control laws. However, it is known that the presence of a gun makes it more likely that a given situation will result in a death. Analyze the gun lobby's slogan. What assumption does it make about the causes of human behavior? What would you suggest as an answer to the slogan?

1.2 Is Prayer Effective?

Sir Francis Galton wanted to know whether prayer changes things. He reasoned that more people would pray for royalty and royalty should therefore live longer than average. He found, instead, that on average, royalty lived 64 years, intellectuals lived 68, and gentry lived 70 (Webb, Campbell, Schwartz, & Sechrest, 1999). What do you think of Galton's reasoning? What way or ways of knowing about behavior did Galton use?

1.3 Imagine that Precognition Does Occur

One way to evaluate the hypothesis of the existence of precognition, or fortune telling, is to imagine what the world would be like if precognition existed. What does this exercise tell you about precognition? What goals and assumptions of science are violated in such a claim as the existence of precognition?

1.4 Reincarnation

Many people believe in reincarnation because, under the effects of hypnosis, they have recalled past lives. They may have had vivid recollections of being a soldier in the Trojan War or of being King Solomon's favorite concubine. How would you test such a claim? How would you suggest an alternative explanation?

Web-Based Workshops on Research Methods and Statistics

 Wadsworth Publishing Company maintains Web-based workshops on research methods and statistics. These workshops give a different slant on the material in this book.

www.cengage.com/psychology/workshops

For this chapter, see the Research Methods Workshops: *What Is Science?*

Exercises

1.1 Identify Facts, Laws, and Theories

After Ken left his dirty socks on the floor for the seventh time in the same week, Barbie went ballistic [___]. "You always leave your socks on the floor [___]. Men really want mothers, not partners [___]. If I didn't pick up after you, the mice would be nesting in them [___]. They can pile up until you can't cross the floor, for all I care [___]."

Required:

Assuming Barbie was not exaggerating, indicate the type of statements by putting the appropriate letter in each blank. Use each letter only once: (a) data, (b) law, (c) hypothesis, (d) theory. One blank should not be filled.

1.2 Identify Facts, Laws, and Theories

One theory of hunger motivation says that the brain acts as a feedback mechanism, something like a thermostat, that has a set point, or ideal weight, which our body strives to maintain. Rats that are starved below the weight that they would maintain if they could eat whatever they want will quickly return to their free-feeding weight after the period of starvation. Likewise, rats that are fed a high-fat diet will reduce their weight after they return to their normal diets. After Juan read about these ideas in his psychology book, he remembered that the weight he had put on over the Christmas holidays went away after he returned to college.

Required:

a. Identify a statement in the paragraph that refers to theory.
b. Identify a statement that may be considered a law and explain how it relates to the theory.
c. Identify one statement of fact. How is the fact explained by the theory?

1.3 Objective Definitions

A researcher plans a study to determine the extent of hostility between factory workers and their supervisors. Supervisors are classified as either autocratic or democratic.

Required:

Suggest possible operational definitions of hostility, autocratic, and democratic.

CHAPTER **TWO**

Developing a Research Question

PREVIEW

This chapter deals with the process of developing a question that can be answered by empirical research. Many students find this to be a daunting task. We try to break it down into a set of manageable steps.

Choice of a Problem

You would be surprised to learn how many scientists have chosen by accident the problem they make their life's work. Perhaps they enrolled in psychology so they would not have to walk too far between classes. They liked the course and subsequently majored in psychology, then went to the graduate school recommended by their instructor, were assigned to an adviser, and began working on whatever that person was doing. Their interest in the area grew until it consumed their working hours. Because this process is little appreciated, students become anxious when they must choose a problem for an experimental psychology class. How do they find the right project on which to spend a whole term?

Ideas are found in several likely places. Previous psychology courses may have covered topics that especially interested you. Most psychology

journal: scholarly magazine devoted to research in a particular academic discipline

textbooks, scholarly **journals**, and lectures contain statements of unsolved problems and suggestions for future research. Everyday observation is another source for research problems. For instance, you may have wondered what caused a certain type of behavior. The list of sources is perhaps endless, including such possibilities as dormitory bull sessions and newspaper articles.

A valuable source is your instructor or adviser, who has been thinking about research for a number of years and can often respond to an idea with a key reference or a suggestion. You would be wise to ask what problems your instructor is interested in and pick one that appeals to you. The advantage in this procedure is that, by virtue of background knowledge in the area, your instructor can give you sound advice and will be more motivated to do so than if you choose an unfamiliar problem.

Do not worry too much about whether your topic is the best one to study. You may feel that there are too many interesting topics, or none that interests you enough. The best solution is to pick one and dig in. You will likely find that it becomes more interesting as you get into it, or you will decide quickly that it is the wrong one. The most important thing is to get started!

Try to narrow the topic down to a manageable size. Say you start out with an interest in developmental psychology. You will find that this is a very large topic in itself. At this stage, you will probably be looking through textbooks and handbooks. If you turn to an introductory psychology text, you will find at least an entire chapter devoted to the topic. Looking through the chapter, you will find sections devoted to smaller divisions, such as Piaget's theory. Even this covers a lot of ground, so look for more manageable sections. You may find a heading on moral development that discusses Kohlberg's theory, which grew out of Jean Piaget's thinking. Reading that section, you will find that Carol Gilligan has suggested that Kohlberg's theory does not apply to women. So you may narrow your interest to gender differences in moral development. If possible, make your topic a specific question: Does the moral thinking of women depend more on social responsibilities than that of men? It is hard to make your question too narrow: You need to ask a question that you can answer with the resources you have at hand, and that includes time as well as money.

The Literature Review _____

Before you can design a study that will contribute to psychological knowledge, you need to have a good idea of what is already known. Newcomers to a field often tend to display one of two opposite tendencies. The first is to act as though he or she were the first intelligent person ever to have contemplated this particular problem and to plunge right into designing the study. The second tendency is to be overwhelmed by the number of books in a particular field and conclude that every conceivable study must have been thought of already.

How do you steer a course between these two extremes? Avoiding the first involves realizing that for thousands of years thoughtful people have considered most of the important issues that we confront, albeit, until recently, without the benefit of modern methods to guide them. Discovering the results of their labors may be difficult, however. As someone has said, "More is known than is known is known." There is, in fact, a considerable amount of information in libraries that has been forgotten or overlooked. It happens with some regularity that someone with a historical bent will show that a researcher many years ago found the same thing that is now being presented as brand new. It takes hard work to keep knowledge from being forgotten and to ensure that scientific knowledge actually is cumulative. This is the purpose of conducting research literature reviews.

Avoiding the opposite extreme of being overwhelmed by the sheer bulk of what is known requires knowing some techniques for cutting the literature down to manageable size. If you pick a problem suggested by your adviser, that person no doubt will suggest a few references with which you should begin your search of the literature. If you select a problem of your own, you may be able to start with a reference from a textbook you have studied. Otherwise, you may have to start from scratch in the library. The first source to check for books in your area of interest is the library catalog. If you do not find any books on your topic, consult one of the many textbooks and handbooks that provide broad coverage of most areas. Review articles have been published in many journals that will also give you an idea of the previous research that is relevant to your own. These sources should give you access to the literature you need. Skim through as many of these books or articles as are available to you in order to get an overview of your topic. After you have an initial idea of the scope of what is known in your field, you are ready to dig a little deeper. You can look up the references suggested by the articles and books to get firsthand knowledge of the important research on your topic.

Using the Internet

The usefulness of the Internet for research is undeniable, yet it suffers from some drawbacks, too. This section deals with the Internet as a research tool. Because the possibilities are so great, and the technology is changing so rapidly, we can give only some basic suggestions and guidelines.

URL: uniform resource locator, a Web address

A Note on URLs (Web Addresses). Every Web page has an address known as a **URL** (which stands for *uniform resource locator*). These are often very long and contain numbers, letters, punctuation, and infrequently used characters. Typing these can result in errors. Sometimes, for various reasons, you get an error message even when you have typed the address properly. You can often get to your target page by truncating the address from the right and trying again until you succeed. Sometimes this process leaves you with only the main section of the address, which takes you to a main page from which you can navigate to the page you are looking for. Persistence and inventiveness pay off in this process.

peer review: a prepublication process in which work submitted for publication is evaluated for quality by other experts in the field

The Internet Is Not a Library. The Internet is something like a library in that it contains a great deal of information. And libraries provide access to the Internet. But it is necessary to realize that there is a big difference between the two. All the information in libraries was put there by a person *other than the author* who made a decision to do so. Further, the books and journals that are selected by the librarian have editors. Many of these resources are **peer reviewed**, meaning that other professionals in the field felt that the work was worthy of publication. The Internet has none of these filters. Anybody and their cousin can put information on the Net, and they do! Web site creators range from cranks and jokers, through well-meaning amateurs of varying competence, to highly professional organizations. Crackpots and jokers can set up Web pages that look every bit as good as those of professional societies and government agencies. Some even make their sites seem to be those of reputable organizations.

Sometimes people who oppose the message of some book in the library will slip a pamphlet inside the book that attempts to refute it. The Internet is more like a library where a large portion of the shelf space is taken up by pamphlets put there by their authors. So, here more than ever, let the buyer beware! How can you separate the nuggets from the noxious? One always useful rule is to consider the source. Is the Web site sponsored by a university, professional society, reputable private organization, or government agency? If so, you can have some confidence that the author of the material has some credibility and has followed professional and ethical guidelines.

Library Material May Be Available Through a Web Interface. Because of the differences between the Internet and a library, your instructor may ask you to limit your use of Internet material. Some people think this restriction applies to any material accessed through an Internet interface. The resources of most libraries, however, are available through an Internet interface. In other words, you may gain access to library materials through a Web server. This is not the same as finding materials via the Internet because the materials are selected and supported by the particular library.

Guidelines for Evaluating Information from the Internet

A number of libraries have developed guidelines to help people separate the wheat from the chaff of the Internet. One of the best is by Elizabeth Kirk (1996) and is available on the Johns Hopkins University Library Web page:

http://guides.library.jhu.edu/content.php?pid=198142&sid=1657518

The following checklist is a summary of her main points:

Authorship

☐ Is the author of the page a well-known authority?
☐ If not, is the author's work cited approvingly by a known authority?
☐ If not, can you find biographical information that would validate the author's credentials?

The Publishing Body

☐ Who sponsors the site?
☐ Is the site linked to a respected organization?
☐ Information that exists only on a personal Web site should be considered highly suspect.

Point of View

☐ Does the organization sponsoring the Web site have a biased point of view? Information provided by corporations should be considered advertisements.

Be especially wary of information provided by political organizations and advocacy groups.

Connection to the Literature

☐   Are there references to other works in the field?
☐   Are the appropriate theories discussed?
☐   Are controversies acknowledged?

Verifiability

☐   Is there information that would allow you to verify methodology?

Currency

☐   Is there a date on the document that would allow you to evaluate the timeliness of the information?

How the Search Engine Determines Order of Hits

☐   Much of the information obtained on the Internet is found by using search engines such as Google or Bing (see section below). Some search engines sell space to advertisers. How does the search engine you use determine the order of information listed?

In general, you want to follow the same principle as with any information search: Be critical.

Government and Organizational Web Sites

Certain organizations have highly useful Web sites that will help you find information on your topic. These include the U.S. government's Web site

www.fedstats.gov,

which lists statistical information provided by the federal government from more than 100 agencies, including the census bureau and the Center for Disease Control.

The Canadian government agency Web sites may be found at

canada.gc.ca/depts/major/depind-eng.html,

which includes a link to the Canadian Institutes of Health Research:

www.cihr-irsc.gc.ca

The major psychological organizations have excellent Web sites:

American Psychological Association (www.apa.org)
Association for Psychological Science (www.psychologicalscience.org)
Canadian Psychological Association (www.cpa.ca)

Some Individual Web Sites for Psychology

Following are some psychological Web sites maintained by individuals:

Psych Web (www.psychwww.com)
Mega Psych (www.tulsa.oklahoma.net/~jnichols/bookmarks.html)

Search Engines

Search engines, such as Google, Yahoo!, Ask, and Bing, are tools that permit you to search the Web using keywords, proper names, and phrases. Each one has special features that allow you to tailor the search to your specific interests. Be aware that some search engines sell space to advertisers, so the listing may be biased. Each search engine also has its own strengths and weaknesses. So just because you found nothing using one engine (like google.com) doesn't mean that another (like maybe yahoo.com) won't find just what you want. This problem is alleviated somewhat by using a meta-engine, such as Metacrawler (metacrawler.com). These meta-engines essentially search the output of several other search engines. Although meta-engines are very useful, they do not allow you to use the special features of the engines they search.

General-purpose search engines are highly useful for popular (rather than scholarly) material. Consequently, using them to blindly search for peer-reviewed information may not yield very much information. Using search engines targeted for academic literature, such as Google Scholar (scholar.google.com), will help you to uncover some scholarly material. The problem, however, is that it is not clear which journals, books, or Web sites Google Scholar uses to find its information, and it includes some nonscholarly information from things like student handbooks. Google Scholar also covers a wide range of disciplines, so you may or may not find information relevant to your specific topic.

Proprietary Web Sites

Access to the Web sites just listed is free. They are provided as part of the mission of the organizations sponsoring them, or for an individual's own motives, which may not always be pure. Making information available is expensive, of course, so it is not surprising that access to some of the most useful sites is limited to those willing to pay in one way or another. These sites are known as proprietary and can be thought of as analogous to magazines to which you must subscribe so you can read them. Most colleges and universities subscribe to a number of proprietary sites and provide their students, faculty, and staff with free access to them as a benefit. These are generally available through the library system, which is linked to the institution's home page. When you access the library's home page via the Internet, your username and password give you access to these proprietary sources. Terminals wired to the institution's network also have access. If you try to access these same home pages from outside the subscribing network, you will not be recognized as an authorized user and will not be able to use them. This is why you may find these databases on the Internet, but when you click on them they do not work for you.

Although you are able to access these databases through your institution's library home page, assuming you are authorized to do so, they can be a little hard to find. Databases may be organized alphabetically at some institutions, while others tend to group them by discipline. And then there is the fact that the screens are constantly being revised (*improved*), which can be another source of frustration. Your librarian will probably be essential in helping you find the databases you need.

Another advantage of an institutional Web page is that some of them provide links between databases. Once you find a source or citation, for example, you may be able to see immediately if it is available in your local library. Some also provide full text. This means that in addition to finding the citation and abstract of a paper, you can read the entire article right on your screen.

PsycINFO

The APA sponsors a database that provides citations and abstracts of the world's literature in psychology and related fields. This database, PsycINFO, has rendered a previous book version, *Psychological Abstracts*, obsolete. PsycINFO and PsycARTICLES are two versions of this database. PsycARTICLES contains only full-text articles, while PsycINFO contains many more citations, including references for dissertations and technical reports. We discuss PsycINFO, but almost everything we say about one applies to the other.

PsycINFO permits searching by author, title, keyword, or phrase (text word or words). You should consider PsycINFO your default source because you will find almost every relevant psychological source here. Virtually everything you come across in PsycINFO can be considered a scholarly source because it does not cover popular magazines and newspapers.

PsycINFO has two features that are especially useful. (1) It permits you to move *backwards* in time, by listing all of the references cited by a particular article. Just find publication information for an article in PsycINFO and then click on *Cited References* to get a list of the references cited by that article. The process is similar to reading a key article and then looking up the articles in its reference list to learn what was already known when the article was written. (2) PsycINFO also permits you to *forward* in time, following the development of a field by tracing the influence of particular articles on later ones. You can start with any article from any date. PsycINFO will then tell you whether anyone has referred to that article in a particular year or span of years. Using PsycINFO, you can find any other article that was published after the article you started with, and that cites your starting article in its reference list. Thus, you can follow pertinent articles only and are not distracted by the many articles that may sound relevant to your topic but are not.

Example: Chapter 1 of this book cites the following article:

Hoffman, R. E., et al. (2005). Temporoparietal transcranial magnetic stimulation for auditory hallucinations: Safety, efficacy and moderators in a fifty patient sample. *Biological Psychiatry*, 58, 97–104.

After entering PsycINFO, look under *Search*, and click on *Find Citation*. Then fill in some of the fields (not all are necessary) and click on *Search*. The next screen will give you, among other information, the publication information of your target article. When you click on the button, *Times Cited in This Database*, you will get a list of articles that cite your target article. There were 62 as of January 2012; there may well be more by now.

In a later section, we give an example of a PsycINFO search. The main thing to remember is that you may have to exercise some ingenuity to get a useable list of citation hits. For example, typing in "Hoffman and schizophrenia" without selecting a field to search in gave us 172 hits. The same words as a text-word search gave 192 hits. "Hoffman and hallucinations" as a text-word search gave 71 hits.

Web of Science

The Web of Science (Science Citation Index, Social Sciences Citation Index, and Arts and Humanities Index) is another very powerful database that covers a wider range of scholarly journals than PsycINFO. Like PsycINFO and a similar database called Scopus, it also allows you to find other articles that have cited a particular paper, and has links to full-text articles.

E-mail

Electronic mail is rapidly replacing the postal service as the preferred means of written communication at a distance. Most scientists now receive far more messages via e-mail than snail-mail. Early editions of this book did not suggest that a student simply write a letter to a psychologist for information, although there would be nothing wrong with doing so. But the advent of e-mail has changed the customs of communicating. It is easier to reach someone by e-mail than by telephone because the recipient need not answer the message instantly. Second, the e-mail does not put the recipient on the spot in the way a telephone call does. But people seem to respond to e-mail much more promptly than to either a phone message or a letter—so, e-mail has encouraged communication between students and scientists. Many scientists are flattered by the attention. Most authors include their e-mail addresses in all publications. E-mail addresses are generally easily obtained by logging into the person's institution and doing a search for his or her name. The first author of this book once called a colleague several times and got no answer. When he asked the colleague's secretary for his e-mail address, she said, "Oh, I can't give you that over the phone." So he thanked her politely, logged on to the institution's home page, and found the colleague's home page, which listed the e-mail address. He sent a message, which the colleague answered within a few minutes.

Psychology Databases

A number of organizations are beginning to make large data sets available on the Internet. Some of these include actual data of experiments conducted by various investigators. The data may be analyzed for relationships not considered by the original researchers. The Henry A. Murray Research Center maintains an archive of more than 125 terabytes of data on human development and social change at

http://www.murray.harvard.edu/frontpage,

which is fully searchable. The functional Magnetic Resonance Imaging Data Center at Dartmouth College maintains an archive of fMRI experiments and their data.

www.fmridc.org

Numerous data sets in many different areas are maintained by the Inter-University Consortium for Political and Social Research.

www.icpsr.umich.edu/index.html

The database of the National Longitudinal Study of Adolescent Health is located at www.cpc.unc.edu/addhealth

These databases constitute a gold mine of information. We can expect more research data to be made available in the future.

An Extended Internet Search Example: Waist-Hip Ratio and Attractiveness

As an extended example of database searching, we consider the question of the effect of waist-hip ratio (WHR) on the attractiveness of human females. WHR is the circumference of the waist divided by that of the hip. Devendra Singh (1993) proposed that the WHR was an honest signal of fertility, that is, a measure that reliably differentiated young, healthy women from older or sick women. He found that men and women judged a woman with a low (0.7) ratio as the most attractive. His paper has become both widely cited and controversial. We discuss the results of database searches on this topic using PsycINFO.

Since there are many interfaces for PsycINFO, depending upon the vendor, we'll give you an idea of how the search is performed. Keep in mind that screens may differ from this example. First, we do a keyword search using "waist hip ratio." Click on *Basic Search* to make the search easier, and then enter "waist hip ratio" into the search box, and click on *Search* (Figure 2.1).

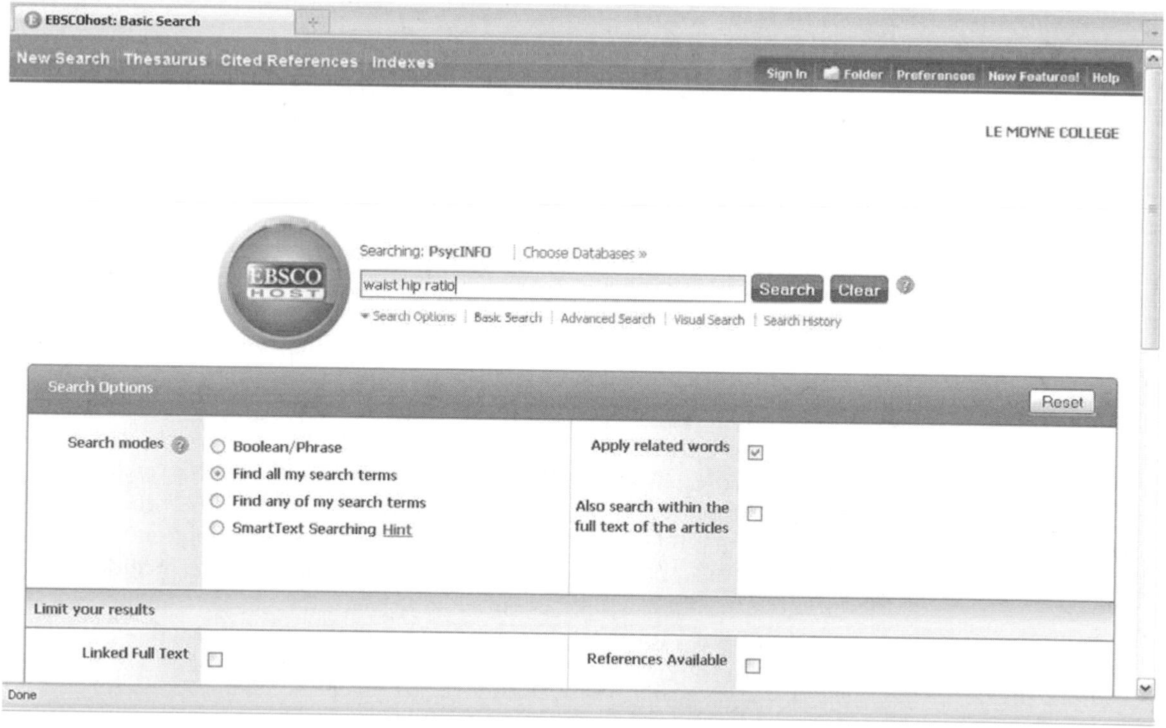

FIGURE **2.1** Simple PsycINFO Search

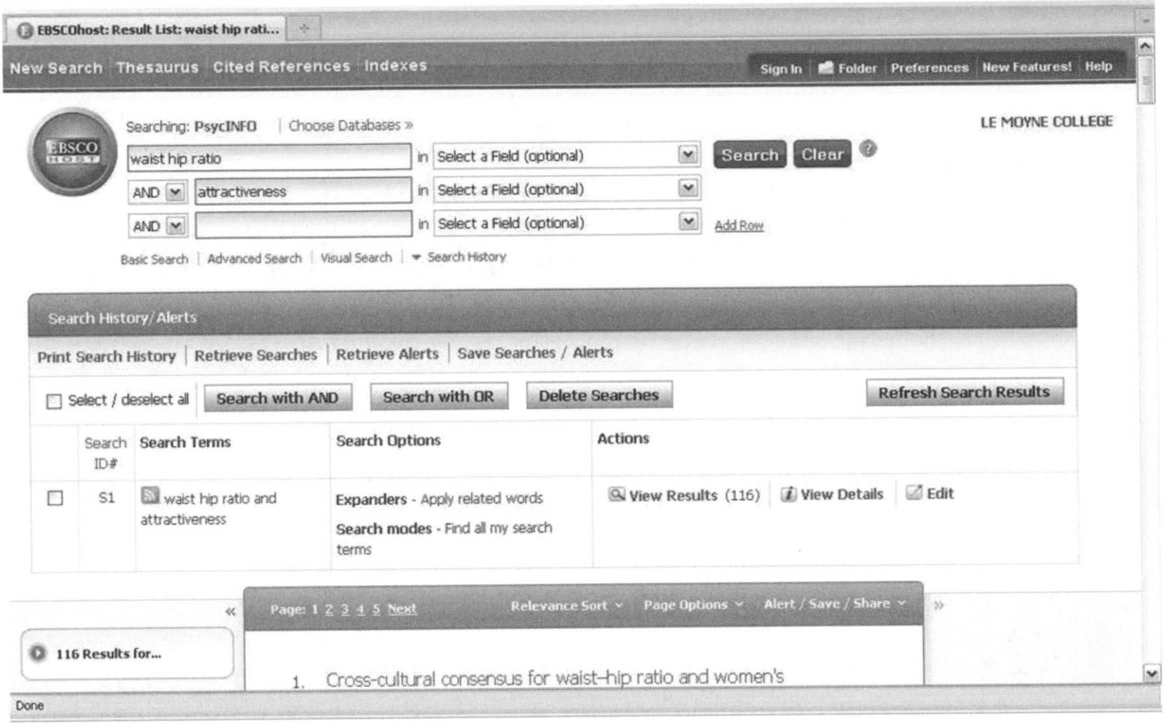

FIGURE **2.2** PsycINFO Search, Combining Terms

PsycINFO finds 426 publications that used the term. Six of the first 10 hits are relevant to Singh's hypothesis.

Now, let's do a search using "attractiveness." We find 6,820 publications on that topic: obviously too many to look at. It looks as though we are going too far away from our main interest. But we can find those publications that match both criteria by clicking on *Advanced Search* (Figure 2.2). In this search screen, PsycINFO allows us to combine both search terms by typing them in separate boxes that are combined with *And* (*Or* and *Not* are also available options). We then find that we have narrowed our search to 116 hits. Perusal of this list shows that the entries are all relevant to our search.

Next, let's try a different tack. We will find articles that cite the 1993 Singh article that started this area of research. In PsycINFO, we first locate the article by Singh (1993). We need to enter enough information to uniquely identify the article that we're starting with, which in this case includes part of the title, the author's name, and the date. Once the citation to the article is found, click on *Times Cited in This Database* (Figure 2.3), and we that find 257 articles have referred to Singh's (1993) paper. We know that all of these articles will likely be important to our search. This *Times Cited in This Database* search has given us more articles, and they are all relevant.

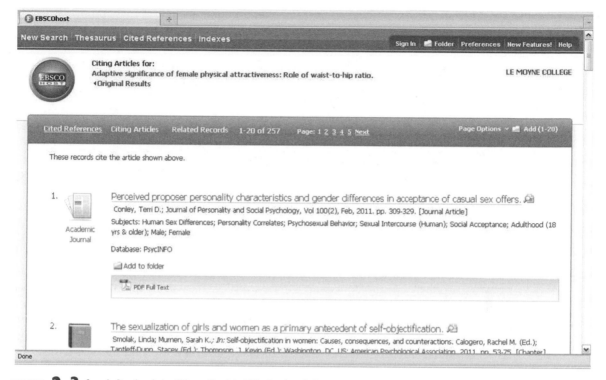

FIGURE **2.3** Search Result of the "Times Cited in This Database" Feature in PsycINFO

Locating Important Articles _____

Once you have found a list of the books and journal articles relevant to your topic, you need to search out copies of them. Many of the databases that you have just used now have direct links to many journal articles. Furthermore, many libraries now subscribe to journals online and have electronic copies of books. It may be tempting for you to restrict your search to full-text articles, such as those found in PsycARTICLES, since you can quickly locate these resources. However, a thorough literature search will probably have articles and books that are not yet available online. Although these articles are often older, they form the foundation for newer research because of the progressive nature of science. It is well worth the effort to go to the library to keep you from reinventing the wheel and to help you to understand the full range of literature related to a problem.

Inter-Library Loan

Whereas some smaller libraries may not have computerized database capabilities, Inter-Library Loan is a service that all libraries provide. If you find a reference to a book or journal that your library does not have, your librarian can generally obtain a copy within a few days. The combination of database searching with Inter-Library Loan can make a small library almost as useful as a large one and save a long trip.

After You Locate the Important Articles

Once you have identified and found most of the key articles in your field, you should begin to read them. Pay particular attention to the introductions to the articles: What was known at the time the authors began their work? What are the major theories? What are the major unsolved problems? At this point, do not worry about the details of the methods and results. Read the abstract and the conclusion, if there is one, to learn the basic results. Skim the rest. Check the reference list for articles you may have missed. In this way, you will begin to get a grasp of the subject area. You will find that certain studies are the key ones in the field.

After this initial review, you can begin to focus on the methods of these key experiments. What are their strengths and weaknesses? Remember that well-trained scientists can make mistakes and sometimes overlook important problems of design. Some of these problems will be pointed out by other authors; some you may think of yourself. All experiments are not created equal. The fact that they are published in major journals does not make them perfect. In addition to the author, as few as three people may have read a particular paper: the editor and two reviewers. In any case, you will find that there are unsolved problems, theories to be tested, and conflicting results to be resolved. These may give you an idea for your own study.

The Research Question

Let us say you have been working on a general research problem. For example, why do people in large cities fail to help the victim of a crime? You have developed some ideas, and you feel ready to test them. You must narrow down the larger research problem to a specific, testable question. You may want to test the idea that people in large groups feel less responsible for other individuals. Your hypothesis, which is a specific prediction of a relationship between variables, might be this: As group size increases, the members feel less responsibility for the other people in the group.

The rest of the experimental process is an empirical test of your hypothesis. It is essential that your hypothesis be as specific as possible. In the hypothesis about group size and responsibility, do you mean that the subjects feel less concern for other persons, or do you mean they feel just as concerned but they believe that someone else will do something? (See Darley & Latané, 1968.) The more precise you can be in stating the hypothesis, the better you can design a cogent and straightforward test of it. If the hypothesis is vague, the experiment is likely to be difficult to interpret. When the hypothesis is stated in vague terms, the temptation arises to develop a kitchen sink design—to throw in every variable that might bear on the phenomenon. As you develop the hypothesis and then design the experiment, you must keep asking yourself, "Exactly what am I trying to find out?" All efforts should be bent toward that question, and care should be taken to pare ancillary questions from the experiment unless the added cost of answering them is negligible.

The Proposal

proposal: preliminary statement outlining the literature review, statement of the problem, research design, and expected results and their significance

Your instructor may ask you to prepare a proposal before you proceed with your research project. This proposal is often called a *prospectus*. Proposals are required in various situations. Graduate students usually prepare proposals that are presented to the committee that oversees master's thesis or dissertation research. Proposals are also required by some agencies, including universities, before research is permitted in their institution. Thus, although the proposal is not logically necessary in designing research, it is often a practical necessity, and it has the advantage of getting the researcher to think through the issues before proceeding.

The proposal is a statement of everything necessary to evaluate the adequacy of the research before the research is conducted. As such, the proposal serves some of the same functions as the published report that will result from the research. For this reason, you will find it convenient to follow the same outline and style in the proposal as in the final report (see Chapter 4). You may then be able to take much of the final report from the proposal, especially the introduction and the method section.

The introduction section of a research proposal should explain your reasons for wanting to perform the experiment. Why is the study important? The introduction should explain the relevant theories and background literature as they relate to your specific problem. How does the previous literature suggest that your experiment is a good idea? What would each of the theories predict as the answer to your hypothesis?

The method section explains the way in which you want to test your hypothesis. One of the key questions to ask at this point is whether the experimental results from this particular study will truly answer your research question. That is, can you actually find a solution to your problem by testing the hypothesis in this particular way?

The results section of the proposal indicates the expected results and the ways in which you intend to analyze and display them graphically. This function of the proposal is particularly useful. It is embarrassing to conduct a study and then find that you have to use some unconventional statistic to analyze the data simply because you overlooked an elementary design consideration. You can usually avoid this problem by deciding in advance what statistics you will use, obtaining advice when necessary.

The discussion section of the proposal is short and indicates the significance of your expected results. Both the results and discussion sections will need to be completely rewritten for the final report! Although the proposal, when it is approved, serves as a sort of contract between the student and the adviser or committee, this does not mean that it must be adhered to slavishly. When a problem arises, as often happens, the researcher should solve it in the best way possible, with the approval of the adviser or committee.

Summary

1. A research topic must be narrowed down to a manageable size.
2. The literature review is essential to help you understand what is currently known about a problem.
3. The Internet has become a valuable tool in research, but it is not a library.
4. Internet sources should be used carefully, following guidelines that help one assess the credibility of sources.
5. Many organizations and governmental agencies maintain useful Web sites.
6. Proprietary databases, such as PsycINFO, PsycARTICLES, and Web of Science, are extremely useful and generally accessible through a library.
7. A number of organizations make large data sets available on the Internet.
8. The research question is a very specific hypothesis that can be answered empirically.
9. The proposal is a statement of everything necessary to evaluate the adequacy of the research before it is conducted.

Suggestions for Further Reading

DOCHARTAIGH, N. (2007). *Internet research skills: How to do your literature search and find research information online* (2nd ed.). Thousand Oaks, CA: Sage Publications. This book will help you to avoid some of the common mistakes that can occur as you search for articles.

PAN, M. (2008). *Preparing literature reviews* (3rd ed.). Glendale, GA: Pyrczak Publication. This book guides the novice through the process of searching for ideas and information to synthesize results into a reasonable review of the literature.

Web-Based Workshops on Research Methods and Statistics

Wadsworth Publishing Company maintains Web-based workshops on research methods and statistics. These workshops may be helpful as a review, in planning your study, or give you a different slant on the material in this book.

www.cengage.com/psychology/workshops

For this chapter, see *Getting Ideas for a Study* in the *Research Methods Workshops*.

Exercises

2.1 Using PsycINFO

The purpose of this exercise is to enable you to learn to use the PsycINFO to do a library search.

a. Choose a topic to research. (See the earlier discussion about choosing a topic and

narrowing it down to a manageable size.) Go to PsycINFO. For example, you might search for "Kohlberg," "Gilligan," and "moral development" as keywords. (If you search for Kohlberg or Gilligan as authors, you would get only works by those authors, not works that discuss their ideas.) When you combine those searches, you will find several dozen relevant papers. Some specifically compare and contrast the ideas of Kohlberg and Gilligan. Pick several that look most relevant. Click on the abstracts to decide which you should read.

b. Now look up the articles or books that are on your list. Skim them to see if they are actually relevant. Make up a list of about 10 references in APA style (in alphabetical order). Turn them in, together with a statement of the question or topic that you are researching.

Required:

Turn in the references to the articles you found. At the top of the page, state your topic and the keywords and author names you used. Append printouts of the abstracts to the articles and a photocopy of the first page of at least one of them.

2.2 Using the *Times Cited in This Database* Feature in PsycINFO

It is good to do this exercise after the PsycINFO exercise above. If you do so, you may use one or more of the references from that search as the starting reference. In that way, you will see how this information can supplement the PsycINFO search. (But note that if the starting reference you chose is too recent, you may find that it has not yet been cited by anyone.)

a. Take an article or book referred to in some standard psychology text. (So that students will use different articles, you should choose one whose author's name starts with the same letter as yours.) We will call this the starting reference.

b. Find references to several articles or books that refer to the starting reference. We will call these citing articles. Continue until you have at least five citing articles referring to your starting reference. You may have to use more than one starting reference to get five citing articles.

c. Put the list into APA style. Generally, all the information needed for APA style is present in the PsycINFO information.

Required:

Turn in an alphabetical list containing the complete reference to the starting article (cited in a book) and complete references to five articles that cite it, all in APA style. (If there aren't five articles that cite the one starting reference, you may use two or more starting references.)

2.4 Reading a Research Paper

Read the sample paper in Chapter 4 of the text, and answer the following questions.

Required:

Answer the following questions. (Some of the questions concern material not yet covered in the book.) Because of the variety of articles published in psychology, not every question is applicable to any one paper.

General

1. What kind of a publication did the paper appear in (e.g., newspaper, popular magazine, trade publication, professional journal, edited book)?
2. What kind of paper is it (e.g., empirical report, review article, theoretical article, tutorial)?

Introduction

3. What problem, question, or observation led to this study?
4. What is the theoretical context of the paper (if it is explicitly mentioned)?
5. What was the current status of the problem before this paper?
6. What will the paper contribute to the understanding of the problem? (Questions 7–18 apply in the case of an empirical report.)
7. What hypotheses are being tested?

Method

8. What was the general type of study (e.g., survey, naturalistic observation, experiment, quasi experiment)?
9. Who were the participants or subjects, and how were they selected?
10. How were participants or subjects assigned to conditions (in case of a true experiment)?

11. If an experiment, was it between subjects or within subjects?
12. Were participants run blind or double blind?
13. Was there a manipulation check (to see if the instructions were effective in setting up the appropriate conditions, in social-psychological experiments)?
14. What equipment or other materials were used?
15. What were the independent variables and levels of each?
16. What were the dependent variables?
17. What was the logic (design) of the experiment?
18. Were the participants debriefed?

Results

19. Were any transformations performed on the data?

20. How were the results analyzed (i.e., what statistical analyses were used)?
21. Were the data collapsed over any independent variables? If so, why?
22. Was the manipulation check effective (if applicable)?
23. What were the principal findings?
24. Were there any interactions? If so, describe them.

Discussion

25. Were the hypotheses supported? Be specific.
26. How do the results relate to what was already known, or what are the implications of these findings?
27. What are the weaknesses or limitations of the study?
28. What are the implications for further research?
29. Are practical applications stated?

CHAPTER THREE

Ethics in Research

PREVIEW

Chapter 3 discusses ethical issues in psychological research according to the structure of the APA ethics code. Particular attention is paid to the treatment of ethics in scientific writing, the ethical treatment of human research participants, and the ethics of research on animals.

The concern for ethics in psychological research may be seen as part of the historical trend in civil and human rights. Before World War II, research ethics were considered a matter for the individual researcher to worry about. However, the Nuremberg trials of Nazi war criminals led to a consciousness of the need for ethical controls in scientific research. In addition, the growth of all types of research, fueled by increasing government funding, prompted concern with research ethics. As a result, research ethics are in a state of rapid evolution. Some practices that were considered acceptable and routine a few years ago are considered unethical today. For this reason, we must present our discussion of research ethics as tentative, rather than chiseled in stone. What will be acceptable practice 10 or 20 years from now cannot be predicted.

The APA Ethics Code

The American Psychological Association (APA) has developed an extensive document known as the "Ethical Principles of Psychologists and Code of Conduct"

(2010), which is available online at **http://www.apa.org/ethics/code/index.aspx**. This is a substantial revision of an earlier document in an effort to keep pace with the changing challenges of scientific ethics. The ethical principles addressed by the APA cover all of the professional activities of psychologists, including teaching and therapeutic situations, as well as engaging in research. A number of the principles, such as those on sexual harassment, nondiscrimination, and the like, concern all professional activities, not just research. Discussion of all the statements that could bear on research would take us too far afield. Instead, we quote those sections that are most directly relevant to ethical concerns in the conduct of research, and then follow the quotes with commentary on each ethical concern.

The APA ethics code represents the consensus of the psychology profession about what is considered acceptable practice. In addition, the federal government and certain other jurisdictions have passed laws governing the conduct of research. So, the federal government requires institutions that receive federal funds to establish an institutional review board (IRB) to approve virtually all research on human participants. IRB committees must have a minimum of five members, at least one of whom is not a scientist, and one member must be unaffiliated with the institution (Swerdlow, 2000). The IRB committee is charged with ensuring that the studies present as little risk to subjects as possible and have scientific merit (Puglisi, 2001); thus many proposals require a full review from the IRB. However, it is also possible to seek an expedited review from the IRB. The expedited review does not require approval from the full IRB committee (only a few of the committee members) and is thus completed more quickly than a full review. Research that represents minimal risk to the participants and falls into one of nine specified categories is eligible for expedited review. At least three of the categories are of interest to psychologists. Expedited Category 5 involves data collected for solely nonresearch purposes (e.g., demographic data that were collected as part of an incarceration procedure), whereas Category 6 concerns the collection of data from recordings made for research purposes. Category 7 entitles research employing surveys and a wide range of other low-risk research activities to an expedited review (Puglisi, 2001).

It is possible to create a research project that is exempt from the regulations governing research, and thus does not require IRB approval. As a student, you should consult your instructor, department chairperson, or school's IRB before you initiate any research to familiarize yourself with the applicable regulations on research. William Langston (2010) discusses the IRB in his lab manual in "Appendix A: Institutional Review Boards."

APA Guidelines on Responsibility and Protection from Harm

APA Code Section 2.01: Boundaries of Competence

A. Psychologists provide services, teach, and conduct research with populations and in areas only within the boundaries of their competence, based on their education, training, supervised experience, consultation, study, or professional experience.

B. Where scientific or professional knowledge in the discipline of psychology establishes that an understanding of factors associated with age, gender,

gender identity, race, ethnicity, culture, national origin, religion, sexual orientation, disability, language, or socioeconomic status is essential for effective implementation of their services or research, psychologists have or obtain the training, experience, consultation, or supervision necessary to ensure the competence of their services, or they make appropriate referrals, except as provided in Standard 2.02, Providing Services in Emergencies.

C. Psychologists planning to provide services, teach, or conduct research involving populations, areas, techniques, or technologies new to them undertake relevant education, training, supervised experience, consultation, or study.

D. When psychologists are asked to provide services to individuals for whom appropriate mental health services are not available and for which psychologists have not obtained the competence necessary, psychologists with closely related prior training or experience may provide such services in order to ensure that services are not denied if they make a reasonable effort to obtain the competence required by using relevant research, training, consultation, or study.

E. In those emerging areas in which generally recognized standards for preparatory training do not yet exist, psychologists nevertheless take reasonable steps to ensure the competence of their work and to protect clients/patients, students, supervisees, research participants, organizational clients, and others from harm.

F. When assuming forensic roles, psychologists are or become reasonably familiar with the judicial or administrative rules governing their roles.[1]

APA Code Section 2.03: Maintaining Competence
Psychologists undertake ongoing efforts to develop and maintain their competence.

Commentary on Responsibility

The decision to conduct research often presents a conflict between two sets of values. In general, the conflict is between (1) the commitment of the psychologist to expanding our knowledge of behavior and the potential benefit the research may have for society and (2) the cost of the research to the participants. It is not possible to resolve this conflict in terms of moral absolutes or by a set of prescriptions that will cover all cases. The conflict is faced continually by researchers who must consider themselves responsible for deciding to conduct their research. Researchers who do not review ethical problems carefully are negligent toward society. From another viewpoint, a researcher who refrains from doing an important study because of an excessively tender conscience is also failing to keep a commitment to the same society that supports behavioral research with the hope that it will provide important social benefits.

---

[1] *All Ethical Principles of Psychologists and Code of Conduct* (2002, amended June 1, 2010) material used in this chapter is reproduced with permission. Copyright © 2010 by the American Psychological Association. No further reproduction or distribution is permitted without written permission from the American Psychological Association.

The investigator—the person who is in overall charge of the research—has the greatest responsibility to see that ethical principles are followed. In most cases, students work in the capacity of experimenters or assistants under the supervision of the investigator. All people working on a research project, however, should consider themselves bound by the APA ethics code, even if they are not professional psychologists or members of the APA.

Investigators should discuss their research with colleagues and seek advice about the ethics of the research procedures. This helps to curb the bias that we all have of thinking that our research is more important than it really is, that we are morally superior, and therefore will act ethically. Most institutions have committees that review all research on human participants. Before investigators begin any research, they should be certain that they are complying with institutional procedures. Students should initiate research only under the sponsorship of a faculty member, who is in turn subject to professional sanctions.

Commentary on Protection from Harm

It is impossible to avoid risk of harm entirely in behavioral research because any new situation by definition is stressful and conceivably could be harmful. Some experiments, though, have subjected people to the threat of shock, to being told that they have latent homosexual tendencies, or to being locked in a room that appears to be on fire. Today, these situations are considered unduly stressful. Stress in an experiment may be either physical or psychological. In judging the acceptability of stress, the researcher must assess how stressful the situation is likely to be compared with activities of everyday life. Would people willingly put themselves into this situation? What special groups must be considered, such as heart patients, epileptics, or borderline schizophrenics? Researchers must also consider the idea that participants may resent being treated merely as objects, even if there is no other direct harm to the person. Informed consent and thorough debriefing can help with this concern.

consent: legally given permission to participate in a study

APA Guidelines on Informed Consent

APA Code Section 3.10: Informed Consent

A. When psychologists conduct research or provide assessment, therapy, counseling, or consulting services in person or via electronic transmission or other forms of communication, they obtain the informed consent of the individual or individuals using language that is reasonably understandable to that person or persons except when conducting such activities without consent is mandated by law or governmental regulation or as otherwise provided in this Ethics Code. (See also Standards 8.02, Informed Consent to Research; 9.03, Informed Consent in Assessments; and 10.01, Informed Consent to Therapy.)

B. For persons who are legally incapable of giving informed consent, psychologists nevertheless (1) provide an appropriate explanation, (2) seek the individual's assent, (3) consider such persons' preferences and best interests, and (4) obtain appropriate permission from a legally authorized person, if such substitute consent is permitted or required by law. When consent by a legally authorized person is not permitted or required by law, psychologists take reasonable steps to protect the individual's rights and welfare.

C. When psychological services are court ordered or otherwise mandated, psychologists inform the individual of the nature of the anticipated services, including whether the services are court ordered or mandated and any limits of confidentiality, before proceeding.

D. Psychologists appropriately document written or oral consent, permission, and assent. (See also Standards 8.02, Informed Consent to Research; 9.03, Informed Consent in Assessments; and 10.01, Informed Consent to Therapy.)

APA Code Section 8.01: Institutional Approval

When institutional approval is required, psychologists provide accurate information about their research proposals and obtain approval prior to conducting the research. They conduct the research in accordance with the approved research protocol.

APA Code Section 8.02: Informed Consent to Research

A. When obtaining informed consent as required in Standard 3.10, Informed Consent, psychologists inform participants about (1) the purpose of the research, expected duration, and procedures; (2) their right to decline to participate and to withdraw from the research once participation has begun; (3) the foreseeable consequences of declining or withdrawing; (4) reasonably foreseeable factors that may be expected to influence their willingness to participate such as potential risks, discomfort, or adverse effects; (5) any prospective research benefits; (6) limits of confidentiality; (7) incentives for participation; and (8) whom to contact for questions about the research and research participants' rights. They provide opportunity for the prospective participants to ask questions and receive answers. (See also Standards 8.03, Informed Consent for Recording Voices and Images in Research; 8.05, Dispensing with Informed Consent for Research; and 8.07, Deception in Research.)

B. Psychologists conducting intervention research involving the use of experimental treatments clarify to participants at the outset of the research (1) the experimental nature of the treatment; (2) the services that will or will not be available to the control group(s) if appropriate; (3) the means by which assignment to treatment and control groups will be made; (4) available treatment alternatives if an individual does not wish to participate in the research or wishes to withdraw once a study has begun; and (5) compensation for or monetary costs of participating including, if appropriate, whether reimbursement from the participant or a third-party payor will be sought. (See also Standard 8.02a, Informed Consent to Research.)

APA Code Section 8.03: Informed Consent for Recording Voices and Images in Research

Psychologists obtain informed consent from research participants prior to recording their voices or images for data collection unless (1) the research consists solely of naturalistic observations in public places, and it is not anticipated that the recording will be used in a manner that could cause personal identification or harm, or (2) the research design includes deception, and consent for the use of the recording is obtained during debriefing. (See also Standard 8.07, Deception in Research.)

APA Code Section 8.04: Client/Patient, Student, and Subordinate Research Participants

A. When psychologists conduct research with clients/patients, students, or subordinates as participants, psychologists take steps to protect the prospective participants from adverse consequences of declining or withdrawing from participation.

B. When research participation is a course requirement or an opportunity for extra credit, the prospective participant is given the choice of equitable alternative activities.

APA Code Section 8.05: Dispensing with Informed Consent

Psychologists may dispense with informed consent only (1) where research would not reasonably be assumed to create distress or harm and involves (a) the study of normal educational practices, curricula, or classroom management methods conducted in educational settings; (b) only anonymous questionnaires, naturalistic observations, or archival research for which disclosure of responses would not place participants at risk of criminal or civil liability or damage their financial standing, employability, or reputation, and confidentiality is protected; or (c) the study of factors related to job or organization effectiveness conducted in organizational settings for which there is no risk to participants' employability, and confidentiality is protected or (2) where otherwise permitted by law or federal or institutional regulations.

Commentary on Informed Consent

The APA guidelines require researchers to "obtain the informed consent of the individual" (see 3.10 on page 54). This is to ensure that the participant is taking part voluntarily and is aware of what is about to happen. Participants must be given all the information necessary about factors that might affect their willingness to participate, such as risks or adverse effects. Some participants in a psychological experiment could be legally incapable of giving informed consent, because of age or other considerations. In those cases, researchers must still explain the situation and consider the person's best interest. It is necessary to obtain permission for research participation from a guardian or legally authorized person, and it is advisable to obtain the individual's assent, or willing participation. The participant's informed consent should be documented in writing. Depending on the nature of the procedures that are to be followed, it may be advisable to have participants sign a form that describes the procedures that will be followed and the potential risks involved. In most psychological research, however, the written protocol of the study constitutes sufficient documentation. Whether or not a signed form is required should be determined by consulting your department or institutional procedures.

assent: willingness to participate in a study

Medical researchers have developed a concept of informed consent, according to which patients have the right to know exactly what is being done to them and for what reasons. The APA ethics code differs from this medical view of informed consent by saying that participants need be informed only of aspects of the research that might be expected to influence their decisions to participate. The assumption of the APA ethics code is that participants in psychological experiments ordinarily do not care what the hypothesis or purpose of the experiment is. For example, most participants would want to know if their intelligence or mental health were being evaluated before they agreed to participate, but the fact that an experiment concerns whether memory is scanned by serial or parallel processes would probably not influence their decision to participate.

APA Guidelines on Coercion

APA Code Section 8.06: Offering Inducements for Research Participation

A. Psychologists make reasonable efforts to avoid offering excessive or inappropriate financial or other inducements for research participation when such inducements are likely to coerce participation.
B. When offering professional services as an inducement for research participation, psychologists clarify the nature of the services, as well as the risks, obligations, and limitations.

Commentary on Privacy and Freedom from Coercion

coercion: compelling or influencing a decision to participate in a study

The idea of freedom from coercion is part of the larger question of civil rights and the right to privacy in particular. The legal concept of a right to privacy is a development of the last hundred years or so. It is agreed that people have the right not to be disturbed, as well as the right not to reveal certain information about themselves. Although psychologists respect this right to privacy, it must be balanced against the welfare of society as a whole. The solution to many thorny social problems may require information that people are reluctant to reveal. How does one weigh the value to society of understanding and controlling the behavior of criminals and tax evaders against the rights of law-abiding citizens to be left alone? The reluctance of many people, particularly undocumented immigrants, to respond to the 2010 US census is an indication of this tension. Although the Census Bureau stated that its information would not be made available to other government agencies, the Internal Revenue Service in particular, many people refused to answer the questions.

The experimenter must remember at all times that the participant is doing a favor by taking part. The freedom to refuse to participate or to withdraw at any time without penalty should be made clear to the participant at the beginning of the research if it has not already been explained during the recruitment of participants. The researcher should realize that many people are apprehensive about participating in research. The role demands of the situation, however, will cause them to tolerate considerable discomfort without complaint. This tendency of participants increases the researcher's obligation not to exploit the participant.

The most likely problem of coercion that you as a reader of this book will face is the decision to use introductory psychology students as *volunteers*. In many colleges, introductory psychology students are commonly asked to serve as research participants as part of the course requirements. The APA guidelines require departments to alleviate the problem of coercion by allowing students extra credit for participation or by providing alternative means of satisfying the requirement. In favor of the research requirement is the educational value of serving in an experiment; unpublished data collected by the University of Pittsburgh Psychology Department indicate that most students enjoy their participation and learn something from it. Coercion may be subtle, however, if a student feels that participation may lead to a chance for a better grade. Most students do not seem especially concerned about this degree of coercion. In the experience of the Pittsburgh researchers, only about 1% of students who are required to participate either in research or in an alternative experience request the alternative. Serving as participants appears to be as acceptable to them as other course requirements.

Issues of coercion become more serious if substantial sums of money are offered for participation or if people are induced to participate with promises to "improve your relations with the opposite sex" or "gain valuable insights into your personality." The APA's *Ethical Principles of Psychologists and Code of Conduct* (American Psychological Association, 2010) contains a list of guidelines for departments that want to set up experimental participation requirements for students.

The concern for the privacy of the participants continues after the data are collected. People who participate in psychological studies have the right to expect that their data will never be made public in a way that would permit their identification, unless they agree to such publication. Problems have arisen when researchers have written up actual cases in a thinly disguised fashion. In other instances, courts have subpoenaed information from social scientists about their clients or research participants who are involved in cases of alleged criminal activities. This situation is particularly problematic when a scientist has studied members of deviant groups or individuals who engage in illegal activity and has promised them confidentiality. Social scientists are not granted the legal protection that lawyers and physicians have against being forced to reveal information about their clients. In one case, a rape counselor was ordered to reveal information that the victim had given as part of the counseling process following the rape.

To protect privacy, data from cases that involve sensitive material should be coded so that all information that would permit identification of the individual is destroyed. This process may not be possible in some types of case-study work because of the continuing nature of the data collection.

APA Guidelines on Deception

APA Code Section 8.07: Deception in Research

A. Psychologists do not conduct a study involving deception unless they have determined that the use of deceptive techniques is justified by the study's significant prospective scientific, educational, or applied value and that effective nondeceptive alternative procedures are not feasible.

B. Psychologists do not deceive prospective participants about research that is reasonably expected to cause physical pain or severe emotional distress.
C. Psychologists explain any deception that is an integral feature of the design and conduct of an experiment to participants as early as is feasible, preferably at the conclusion of their participation, but no later than at the conclusion of the data collection, and permit participants to withdraw their data. (See also Standard 8.08, Debriefing.)

Commentary on Deception

So many experiments require participants to be naive about the hypothesis that deceiving participants about the true purpose of their research participation has almost become standard practice. The APA ethics code requires that a participant who has been deceived be provided with a sufficient explanation of the deception as soon afterward as feasible. Some researchers, however, feel that deception is always objectionable. They note that the prevalence of deception in psychological experiments is common knowledge among college students and that most subjects routinely assume that the story they are given at the beginning of an experiment is false. The effects of this pollution of the participant pool are not known.

Yet, to foreswear deception would rule out the study of many important questions. To handle this problem, some departments inform people at the time they join the subject pool that certain experiments in which they participate may use deception. Other experimenters have used role playing instead of deception to induce behaviors of interest. The subjects are asked to act as if they were in a certain situation or to tell what they would do in such a situation. The disadvantage of role playing is that it assumes that subjects can tell what they would do in a situation by just adopting a role. Evidence for this assumption is quite weak.

The simple term *deception* covers a wide range of actions by experimenters. Relatively innocuous deceptions routinely involve setting up false expectations of the processes under investigation. More serious deceptions include giving subjects false information about their performance on a task. Some research has shown that the initial false feedback may be believed even after debriefing (Ross, Lepper, & Hubbard, 1975). Deception that presents subjects with a negative self-evaluation should be avoided.

APA Guidelines on Debriefing

APA Code Section 8.08: Debriefing

A. Psychologists provide a prompt opportunity for participants to obtain appropriate information about the nature, results, and conclusions of the research, and they take reasonable steps to correct any misconceptions that participants may have of which the psychologists are aware.
B. If scientific or humane values justify delaying or withholding this information, psychologists take reasonable measures to reduce the risk of harm.
C. When psychologists become aware that research procedures have harmed a participant, they take reasonable steps to minimize the harm.

Commentary on Debriefing

As soon as feasible after the individual participants have completed their part in the experiment, they should be informed about the nature of the study and have any questions answered and misconceptions removed. This process is known as debriefing. Debriefing is an extremely important part of the experiment. Participants must be told the purpose and expected results of the experiment so that their experience has as much educational and personal value for them as possible.

When deception has been employed, the experimenter has a touchy situation. A blunt admission of deception can make participants feel foolish, stupid, or abused. Because many investigators additionally use the debriefing to ascertain whether the deception was effective, their explanation requires great subtlety. Sometimes, participants, in an effort not to embarrass the experimenter, may be reluctant to admit that they saw through the deception. This response is part of the good-subject role that they tend to adopt. The degree of awareness of deception varies greatly with the phrasing of the question. A simple "Any questions about the experiment?" may elicit no response, whereas "Was there anything that might lead you to suspect that the experiment was not exactly what it seemed on the surface?" is more likely to yield a statement indicating awareness of the deception. For this reason, any estimate of the effectiveness of the deception is highly uncertain.

Some investigators delay the debriefing so that other potential participants will not learn the purpose of the study. In this case, the investigator could take participants' addresses and send them an explanation when the experiment is completed. This delayed debriefing is less effective because people may move away or lose interest in the study over time.

Role of the Research Participant

The debate on research ethics has raised questions about the role that the participant plays in psychological research. According to the traditional view, the participant contributes behavior to the experiment in much the same way that a participant in a medical experiment might contribute a urine specimen. The very term *subject* is believed by some to imply that the participant is made an object of study and, necessarily, is dehumanized.

This objectification is held to be a consequence of the traditional view of science that requires a separation between the observer/scientist and the observed/subject.

Another view of the research participant is popular with feminist and humanistic psychologists, who hold that the participant is a colleague who cooperates in providing the data. In some examples of this process, the participants take a role in designing the experiment and may have a degree of control over the conditions in which they are tested. Similarly, some psychologists have argued in the Marxist tradition that the participant should be considered part owner of the data by virtue of having helped to create them.

This view reminds us that the research participant may have valuable insights and suggestions that could improve the study. Another advantage of looking at the participant as a cooperator in the research effort is that the

---

debriefing: the process of informing participants after the session of the experiment's true purpose to increase their understanding and to remove possible harmful effects of deception

researcher becomes more understanding of the viewpoint of the participant. In addition, this viewpoint reminds us to treat participants with dignity and respect and to make them know that they are doing the experimenter a favor. Minority groups in particular have become resentful of being endlessly studied when they perceive that the only apparent result is to promote the careers of the already advantaged scientists.

Then again, although this view of research may increase cooperation by the participant, it also increases the risk of sloppy experiments. The humanistic view of research is popular among parapsychologists and has led to many poorly conducted and uninterpretable experiments. Although certain types of research may profit from the insights and opinions of the participants, the scientist bears the ultimate responsibility for the results and must make the final decisions about the research.

APA Guidelines on Scientific Writing

APA Code Section 8.10: Reporting of Research Results
A. Psychologists do not fabricate data.
B. If psychologists discover significant errors in their published data, they take reasonable steps to correct such errors in a correction, retraction, erratum, or other appropriate publication means.

APA Code Section 8.11: Plagiarism
Psychologists do not present substantial portions or elements of another's work or data as their own, even if the other work or data source is cited occasionally.

APA Code Section 8.12: Publication Credit
A. Psychologists take responsibility and credit, including authorship credit, only for work they have actually performed or to which they have substantially contributed. (See also Standard 8.12b, Publication Credit.)
B. Principal authorship and other publication credits accurately reflect the relative scientific or professional contributions of the individuals involved, regardless of their relative status. Mere possession of an institutional position, such as department chair, does not justify authorship credit. Minor contributions to the research or to the writing for publications are acknowledged appropriately, such as in footnotes or in an introductory statement.
C. Except under exceptional circumstances, a student is listed as principal author on any multiple-authored article that is substantially based on the student's doctoral dissertation. Faculty advisors discuss publication credit with students as early as feasible and throughout the research and publication process as appropriate. (See also Standard 8.12b, Publication Credit.)

APA Code Section 8.13: Duplicate Publication of Data
Psychologists do not publish, as original data, data that have been previously published. This does not preclude republishing data when they are accompanied by proper acknowledgment.

APA Code Section 8.14: Sharing Research Data for Verification

A. After research results are published, psychologists do not withhold the data on which their conclusions are based from other competent professionals who seek to verify the substantive claims through reanalysis and who intend to use such data only for that purpose, provided that the confidentiality of the participants can be protected and unless legal rights concerning proprietary data preclude their release. This does not preclude psychologists from requiring that such individuals or groups be responsible for costs associated with the provision of such information.

B. Psychologists who request data from other psychologists to verify the substantive claims through reanalysis may use shared data only for the declared purpose. Requesting psychologists obtain prior written agreement for all other uses of the data.

APA Code Section 8.15: Professional Reviewers

Psychologists who review material submitted for presentation, publication, grant, or research proposal review respect the confidentiality of and the proprietary rights in such information of those who submitted it.

Commentary on Ethics in Scientific Writing

Although Chapter 4 will address the issue of scientific writing in psychology in more detail, the ethics related to the publication of research reports are discussed here. The APA guidelines specifically address several aspects of the publication process. Essentially, the APA charges psychologists with the responsibility of publishing only data that have been legitimately obtained and with giving appropriate credit to all those who contributed to the project. To fabricate or make up data strikes at the very heart of science because it stands in the way of science's progressive nature. Future researchers who attempt to base their experimental ideas on someone else's false results will fail, and science will eventually self-correct. But that correction may come only after many years of futile work and many wasted research dollars for other scientists. The following section on fraud gives several examples of data fabrication. One of the safeguards against the fabrication of data is the APA's mandate to share data with other psychologists after a report has been published. This requirement means that the original data can be confirmed and that any errors in the original study can be corrected. As noted in Chapter 2, many organizations have made data sets available online, partially to allow any interested psychologist to inspect both the data and their analysis.

The APA also requires that writings by psychologists be their own ideas presented in their own words, with appropriate credit given to ideas from other people. Attempting to pass someone else's work off as your own is called **plagiarism**. Because the empirical testing of ideas is the foundation of science, plagiarism is essentially scientific theft because it is stealing ideas. Plagiarism is treated as seriously in the scientific community as the theft of gold or diamonds would be in the wider community. For that reason, it is discussed in more detail in Chapter 4.

plagiarism: attempts to present another person's work as your own

Fraud in Research _____

Fraud is an unpleasant topic that no one likes to talk about, but fraud occurs in science just as in all other human activity. Psychologists have long known that honesty is not a unitary trait. People may be scrupulously honest toward their employers but fudge on their income taxes. An intriguing question is why fraud in science seems to strike us as so much worse than, say, fraud in banking. One answer lies in the nature of a scientist's data. Bank records can be verified in internal and external ways, but scientific data are creations that can easily be concocted. This means that often we are utterly dependent on the scientist's honesty for the truthfulness of the data.

The honesty of the scientist is a prerequisite for the very existence of science. Because of the progressive nature of science, the path of scientific discovery is thrown off course by fraudulent data. Many thousands of research dollars can be wasted following up on a research result that doesn't exist. Likewise, there can be public health consequences, such as when Andrew Wakefield and colleagues published a paper that fraudulently claimed an association between autism and vaccines (Wakefield et al., 1998). Though the article has now been retracted, many research dollars have been wasted following up on the result and many children have gone unvaccinated, leaving them at risk for damage from measles, mumps, or rubella (Eggertson, 2010).

Another reason that fraud in science seems so shocking is the priestly function that scientists serve in our society. Because of this role, we tend to expect scientists to have higher morals, and we are more apt to be scandalized when we find them to be human.

Cases of fraud in psychology have not been many, but some have been spectacular. In 1974, a scandal that rocked the field of ESP occurred in the parapsychology laboratory of J. B. Rhine. Walter Levy, a young physician and director of the Institute for Parapsychology in Durham, North Carolina, was caught cheating in an experiment.

The experiment involved testing rats in an apparatus that was designed to allow them to use either precognition or psychokinesis (a kind of psychic ability) to increase the number of pleasurable brain stimulations they received. An assistant noticed that Levy seemed to be loitering needlessly about the automated apparatus. From a hiding place, the assistant and two others observed Levy during a session and saw him tamper with the apparatus. Suspicions confirmed, they rigged up a second recorder that would not be affected by the tampering. Later, the first recorder showed the rats receiving stimulation 54% of the time, but the second one showed a chance level of 50%.

Confronted with the evidence, Levy confessed and resigned. The scandal shook Rhine, who had considered Levy the best hope for the institute's future, as well as for the field of parapsychology, because Levy's evidence had seemed the strongest yet for the existence of ESP.

The most spectacular case of apparent fraud in psychology was perpetrated by Sir Cyril Burt, an eminent British psychologist, who was knighted for his work. He published much work on the IQs of identical twins reared apart. This work purportedly showed a high degree of correlation between twins, and hence suggested that heredity was the dominant contributor to intelligence. Around 1974, Leon Kamin noticed that the correlations reported were identical to the third decimal place in several different reports, over which the number of twin pairs supposedly increased from 15 to 53, a mathematical impossibility. This lead was followed up by a journalist, Oliver Gillie, who discovered that at least two of Burt's coauthors either did not exist, or had never worked for him. Although leading scientists such as H. J. Eysenck defended Burt against "a determined effort on the part of some very left-wing environmentalists determined to play a political game with scientific facts" (Gould, 1979, p. 104), the consensus now is that Burt was guilty of a conscious fraud over the course of many years. Burt's life and career are the subjects of a biography by Leslie Hearnshaw (1979). Although Hearnshaw began his work as an admirer of Burt's, he became convinced that Burt was undoubtedly a fraud. He attributes the deviation to serious setbacks in Burt's life: a marriage gone sour, the loss of his papers in the bombing of London, and a serious illness. These blows caused an exaggeration of a tendency to paranoia and led him to cheat as a way of vindicating his ideas (Hawkes, 1979).

The Burt case remains controversial. Robert Joynson (1989) was able to find some evidence for the existence of Burt's mysterious coauthors. William Tucker (1997) concludes that Burt is guilty beyond a reasonable doubt, but the authors of a book edited by Nicholas Mackintosh (1995) argue that both sides have made serious errors in presenting their cases, although Burt was not totally innocent.

Parallels between the Levy and Burt cases and with other famous frauds suggest that few scientists start out as frauds. They seem to cheat when early successes are followed by failure. The need to build on past successes, whether motivated internally or by external career pressures, can provide a strong temptation to cheat.

The same need to achieve can also been seen in the case of Marc Hauser, a psychologist at Harvard who has been found guilty of eight counts of scientific misconduct (Wade, 2010). Hauser studied cognition in animals, and was interested in whether the animals would remember sound patterns. The experiments were videotaped, so that two different investigators could independently code each animal. His research assistant at Harvard became suspicious of fraud when he tried to pressure her to change her coding of the videotapes to match his (Bartlett, 2010a). The research assistant reported him to the University's Ombudsman, who began a three-year investigation into the allegations. In addition to the original allegations of data falsification, Hauser was unable to produce raw data to substantiate some of the experiments that he had published. As a result of the investigation, three of his papers have been retracted or corrected to date, and Hauser has taken a leave from Harvard. Full details of the sanctions that Harvard has taken against him have not been made public (Bartlett, 2010b). Because Hauser received federal grant money, the Office of Research Integrity of the U.S. Department of Health and Human Services has launched its own formal investigation. Like other fraud cases, this case has resulted in considerable discussion about the manner in which universities and the granting agencies monitor research. Some have proposed that the federal government should audit research results, similar to the way that companies' records are audited.

Why are there so few frauds? The biggest factor seems to be the knowledge that successful experiments, particularly the more startling ones, frequently are replicated. This knowledge provides motivation for honesty. When word gets around that several laboratories could not replicate a certain person's experiment, that person loses credibility. Eventually the work is quietly forgotten, and the person fades into oblivion.

The problem of fraud also points to the need for good record keeping so that an author's claims can be backed up with data sheets and protocols. Even though data sheets can be faked, they can be checked for internal consistency. Nevertheless, replication is the ultimate test for the reality of a finding and thus is the ultimate deterrent to fraud.

Ethics and Animal Experimentation _____

Not all psychological research involves human participants. A quick look at the literature will show that many types of animals are also the subjects of psychological research. Like humans, however, the APA is concerned that animals are treated ethically and has created guidelines for dealing with them in research. Like the guidelines for humans, the *APA Guidelines for Ethical Conduct in the Care and Use of Animals* are available online at www.apa.org/research/responsible/guidelines.pdf

APA Guidelines on Animal Experimentation

APA Code Section 8.09: Humane Care and Use of Animals in Research

A. Psychologists acquire, care for, use, and dispose of animals in compliance with current federal, state, and local laws and regulations, and with professional standards.

B. Psychologists trained in research methods and experienced in the care of laboratory animals supervise all procedures involving animals and are responsible for ensuring appropriate consideration of their comfort, health, and humane treatment.

C. Psychologists ensure that all individuals under their supervision who are using animals have received instruction in research methods and in the care, maintenance, and handling of the species being used, to the extent appropriate to their role.

D. Psychologists make reasonable efforts to minimize the discomfort, infection, illness, and pain of animal subjects.

E. Psychologists use a procedure subjecting animals to pain, stress, or privation only when an alternative procedure is unavailable and the goal is justified by its prospective scientific, educational, or applied value.

F. Psychologists perform surgical procedures under appropriate anesthesia and follow techniques to avoid infection and minimize pain during and after surgery.

G. When it is appropriate that an animal's life be terminated, psychologists proceed rapidly, with an effort to minimize pain and in accordance with accepted procedures.[2]

Commentary on Animal Experimentation

Research involving animal participation should not be taken lightly. As with experiments involving human subjects, psychologists should have a reasonable expectation that the results of an experiment involving animals will yield results that increase scientific knowledge of people or the species involved in the research. Psychologists should assume that stimuli that are painful to people are also painful to animals, so care should be taken to minimize the number of animals involved in the research or to consider nonanimal research alternatives. Psychological research on animals should be carried out by trained personnel under the supervision of an institutional animal care and use committee. The animal care and use committees usually include a veterinarian, and the committee members generally ask researchers to remember the three Rs in conjunction with animal research: reduction, refinement, and replacement. In other words, try to reduce the number of animals used, see if the experiment can be refined, or if the study can be executed without animal involvement (Goldberg, Zurlo, & Rudacille, 1996). If animals must be involved in experimentation, they should be treated with humane consideration of their well-being in conjunction with research goals.

Despite the considerations given to the care of animals in research, there is a vigorous animal rights movement that would ban or severely restrict the use of animals in research. Although many people find the message of the animal rights movement appealing, it actually has serious implications for human welfare, as well as for the conduct of psychological research.

Animal Rights and Animal Welfare

animal rights: the notion that animals have the same sort of rights as people, including legal rights; not generally accepted

Because the term animal rights has become so widely used in connection with the use of animals in research, it is necessary at this point to make a distinction between *animal rights* and *animal welfare*. Some authors have claimed that animals should have the same sort of rights as people, including legal rights (e.g., Regan, 1983, 2001). According to this view, it is unethical to use animals for research, for food, as pets, for recreation, for work, or for any other human-serving purpose. Ethicists, however, generally ascribe rights to members of a community who share moral standards and can be held to moral responsibilities. An individual who has rights has a moral claim on other members of the community to accept certain responsibilities with respect to that individual, who, in turn, takes on responsibilities. If an individual has the right of free speech, both the individual and other members of the community have the responsibility not to endanger (as by shouting "Fire!" in a crowded theater), defame, or unduly annoy one another (disturbing the

---

[2] This section is essentially a condensed version of the *Guidelines for Ethical Conduct in the Care and Use of Nonhuman Animals in Research* (APA Committee on Animal Research and Ethics, 2010). These guidelines should be studied by any researcher using animals.

peace). Animals do not belong to a moral community: You cannot take a dog to court for barking at night; a cat is not guilty of murder when it kills a bird.

If animals had the same sort of rights as people, we would be involved in murder by eating a hamburger, we would be guilty of slavery by keeping a dog as a pet, and we would be stealing when we collect eggs from a chicken. Although it is not impossible that some society might decide to give animals legal rights, ours does not.

animal welfare: the generally accepted term for concerns about the care and use of animals

The generally accepted term to use in discussing the appropriate use of animals in research is animal welfare, or humane treatment of animals. As members of a moral community, humans are responsible for the welfare of animals that are under their care. Because mistreatment of animals reflects on the person who does the mistreating, it is called *inhumane treatment.* Although only a minority of those who would limit research on animals hold to the position that animals have the same legal rights as people, the term *animal rights* has become so widely used that it is necessary to make this distinction clear. The research community clearly supports humane treatment of animals but rejects the notion of animal rights.

Some people raise an objection to this position on animal rights by pointing out that infants and individuals who are severely retarded, senile, or brain damaged are not capable of being held to the same moral standards as normal adult humans and thus would not have rights according to that argument. First, it should be noted that not all humans have the same rights. Infants may not be elected president of the United States, and prisoners cannot vote. But, more importantly, we do make ethical distinctions on the basis of a larger class to which an individual belongs. No person under 35 years of age may be elected president, no matter how mature, and no nonhuman animal has legal rights, no matter how intelligent.

Speciesism?

speciesism: term used by analogy with racism and sexism by those who claim that it is unethical to treat animals differently from humans, particularly in research

Another claim that needs to be discussed is that use of animals in research is a manifestation of speciesism, a term that was chosen to parallel racism and sexism. The claim is that researchers, as well as those who eat meat, wear animal products, and so forth, are guilty of discriminating against animals simply on the basis of their species membership. Although the concept has a certain plausibility, especially with those who eschew racism and sexism, it leads to a logical and ethical thicket. We can agree that it is wrong to discriminate against women or minorities on the basis of their gender or race because all humans share their essential humanity with us. But nonhuman animals are manifestly not like ourselves in certain important characteristics. To our knowledge, no monkey can contemplate its own mortality, and no cat has ever expressed moral ambivalence over killing a mouse.

Further, practical considerations require everyone to draw the line somewhere in applying the doctrine of speciesism. Higher animals are like us in some respects, especially primates, dogs, and cats. But it is hard to consider a lobster just like us. For example, if we believe that doing research on a chimpanzee constitutes speciesism, what about ridding a house of termites or inadvertently stepping on an ant while walking in the yard?

Finally, the concept of speciesism explicitly invokes the common evolutionary ancestry of all animals, including humans, and rejects any special moral status for humans. If that is taken seriously, then either a cat is guilty of speciesism when it kills a bird, or neither the cat nor the human is guilty whenever each does what it has evolved to do. There is no reason based on logic whereby the concept of speciesism can be used to support including animals in our moral system instead of permitting humans to act like other animals (Stafford, 1991).

Although animal rights activists devote most of their concern and activities to the use of animals in research, it should be noted that research and teaching are responsible for less than 1% of animals killed annually by humans. And more than 90% of those used in research are rats and mice (Miller, 1984). By contrast, more than 96% of animals killed by humans are used for food (Nicholl & Russell, 1990).

The animal rights activists also try to convey the idea that most animals used in research suffer pain. The fact is that about 94% of animal research involves no use of pain. Most of us have seen the gruesome pictures of research animals being operated on. What the pictures do not convey is that the animals have been anesthetized and so feel no pain. The small number of animals that do experience pain in research are contributing to the knowledge of human diseases such as arthritis that cause pain to millions of humans every day. The opposition to the use of animals in research cannot be justified by the amount of suffering that is being experienced by animals. The regulations on housing of research animals are more stringent than those for human habitation, and there is far more pain, abuse, and cruelty caused to animals by pet owners and farmers than by researchers (Miller, 1984).

There are compelling reasons to use animals in research. First, it should be noted that much animal research has led to an improvement in the welfare of animals themselves, from vaccines against feline leukemia, rabies, and distemper to nonlethal methods of pest control.

Second, although younger people find it difficult to appreciate the fact, there has been tremendous improvement in health care in the past century, much of it in the past few years. About a hundred years ago, around 25% of the US population died by age 25, and half were dead by 50. Today, only 3% fail to live to 25, and only 10% die by age 50 (Committee on the Use of Animals in Research, 1991). Research on animals has been essential to this progress. Some have suggested that we should substitute computer models, tissue cultures, bacteria, or even humans for animals in research and teaching. The simple fact is, however, that computers depend on the information and programs put into them. We often don't know enough about a process to be able to model it on the computer. Bacteria cannot be used to test systems that are found only in animals. Behavioral research in particular must be done on whole animals; and to test procedures on humans before testing them on animals would place many volunteers at grave risk. There simply is no substitute for live, intact animals in much research.

To eliminate or restrict use of animals in research would mean little or no progress against AIDS, Alzheimer's, cancer, arthritis, birth defects, traumatic injury, mental illness, and many other diseases and conditions that cause pain and suffering to millions of people each year. Whenever you see a picture of a lab animal that appears to be suffering, think of the millions of people who would continue to suffer dreadfully if there were no more medical progress.

Neal Miller (1985) has demonstrated how important behavioral research has been in this medical progress. To mention only two applications, behavioral techniques have made it possible to cure infants who suffer from a life-threatening condition that prevents them from keeping food down and to cure anorexia nervosa, another life-threatening eating disorder. Restricting the use of animals in research would bring this progress to a crawl.

Those who object that we should not use animals for research should consider that animals have been, and still are, used for work, for food, and as pets. None of these animals volunteers for these services. It may be useful to consider the research animals as draftees in a cause that helps society as a whole, much as men have historically been drafted for military service.

Finally, although the viewpoint presented here is the view of most scientists, we must acknowledge that ethics in general, and the ethics of animal experimentation in particular, is a difficult issue. Many are bothered by the use of animals in research but do not want to restrict it altogether. The general position of researchers, like that of most people, is that it is permissible to cause a certain amount of suffering to a few animals to reduce the suffering of many millions of people. However, researchers have developed alternatives to the use of animals where possible and have been more careful in the use of their animals as a result of the increasing concern about animal welfare in our society.

The Georgie Project

Gordon Lark, a biologist at the University of Utah, adopted a stray Portuguese Water Dog that he named Georgie. After Georgie died of an autoimmune disease, Dr. Lark began research (called the Georgie Project) to investigate the genetics associated with Portuguese Water Dogs (Davis, n.d.). He worked with owners, breeders, and veterinarians to examine the pedigree records, autopsy results, and DNA of these purebred dogs. Dr. Lark's work benefits both animals and humans, by providing information that would result in more informed breeding and perhaps information applicable to human diseases. For example, the Georgie Project has provided clues to the cause of Addison's disease, which is prevalent in both Portuguese Water Dogs and in humans. (For example, former President John F. Kennedy had the disease.) The Georgie Project is now supported by the National Institute of Health, and is a good example of how animal research provides valuable health information across species.

NUTS & BOLTS

Almost every chapter in this book has a section titled *Nuts & Bolts*. These sections are intended to bridge the gap between the material in the earlier part of the chapter and the carrying out of research—that is, between theory and practice.

Recommended Practices in the Use of Animals in Research

Pressure from animal welfare groups and pet owners has led to a tightening of practices in animal experimentation and to the promulgation of federal standards for the care of experimental animals. Fortunately, the days are over when researchers obtained their experimental cats and dogs by prowling the streets dragging a piece of meat. In general, acceptable practice in animal experimentation consists of ensuring that the scientific benefit of the study warrants whatever discomfort is caused and that the animals are kept in comfortable and sanitary conditions. Furthermore, the decision to use animals in an experiment involves a commitment to their care. Many species cannot tolerate the extremes of temperature common in academic buildings, and animals cannot be left uncared for during weekends or holidays. A researcher cannot initiate an experiment using animals without considering a host of logistical problems. For example, many people are allergic to rats. If a special facility with separate ventilation is not available, a number of people who share the building likely will suffer allergic reactions.

Ordinarily, a student who uses animals in research will be joining an ongoing laboratory with well-established animal care procedures. All institutions that conduct animal research must have an animal care committee that oversees the operation of the animal facility. Such a committee is required for nearly all institutions that receive federal research grants. The Institute of Laboratory Animal Resources Commission on Life Sciences National Research Council has prepared a publication, *Guide for the Care and Use of Laboratory Animals* (1996), which summarizes guidelines for animal research. This document lists standards for food, sanitation, and health, including size of cage and recommended institutional policies on veterinary care and personnel. In addition, the document has a valuable bibliography on animal care and lists federal laws that relate to animal experimentation. Among recommended practices is the responsibility to make sure that the animals are kept in adequate-size cages and that they are warm, dry, and well fed and watered at all times, unless the experiment legitimately requires other conditions. Their health must be maintained, and they must be disposed of properly after the experiment. Any experiment that causes pain should employ anesthetics if possible. The animals should be as well cared for as a pet would be. These provisions are not just idealistic notions. Much of the impetus for the restriction of animal research has come from pet owners.

These principles are summarized in another document (National Institutes of Health, 1996) that incorporates changes required by the Health Research Extension Act of 1985, Public Law 99–158.

© Cengage Learning

Summary

1. All psychological research should be guided by the APA ethics code.
2. The decision to conduct research often presents a conflict between the commitment to expanding knowledge and the potential cost to the research participant.

3. Although it is impossible to avoid all risk to research participants, researchers should consider whether people would willingly put themselves into such a situation in ordinary life.

4. There should be some documentation showing that the participant gave informed consent to participate.

5. The APA position on informed consent differs from medical practice in that subjects need be informed only about aspects of the research that might be expected to influence their willingness to participate.

6. Although some researchers hold that deception is always objectionable, the APA code permits deception, provided that the participant is provided with a sufficient explanation as soon afterward as is feasible.

7. Researchers should respect the right of privacy of their participants and be careful about the possibility of coercion.

8. Participants should be debriefed as soon after their part in the study as feasible.

9. Although the traditional and dominant view is that the researcher maintains control over the experimental situation and the participant in the interest of objectivity, humanistic psychologists consider the participant to be a colleague who cooperates in providing the data.

10. Fraud in science is a matter of serious concern because data are easily faked and scientists have so much influence in our society. Although not many documented cases of fraud have occurred in psychology, the Levy and Burt cases are instructive in their parallels.

11. The major deterrent to fraud seems to be the realization that important experiments are likely to be replicated and making data public for verification purposes.

12. Acceptable practice in animal experimentation consists of ensuring that the scientific benefit of the study warrants whatever discomfort is caused to the animals and that they are kept in comfortable and sanitary conditions.

13. It is important to distinguish between the terms *animal rights* and *animal welfare*. Psychologists support the concept of animal welfare.

14. Most psychologists hold that there are compelling reasons to use animals in research.

15. The Georgie Project illustrates the way that animal research produces benefits across species.

16. Most institutions doing animal research have animal care committees that oversee the operation of animal facilities.

Suggestions for Further Reading

American Psychological Association. (2002). Ethical principles of psychologists and code of conduct. *American Psychologist*, 57, 1060–1073. Ethical principles of research and therapy are presented, along with discussion of issues.

Baird, R. M., & Rosenbaum, S. E. (Eds.). (1991). *Animal experimentation: The moral issues*. Buffalo, NY: Prometheus Books. This reasonably balanced discussion of moral issues behind the use of animals in research provides arguments by representatives of both sides of the debate.

Broad, W., & Wade, N. (1983). *Betrayers of the truth*. New York: Simon & Schuster. This is an important examination of fraud in science.

COHEN, C., & REGAN, T. (Eds.). (2001). *The animal rights debate*. Lanham, MD: Rowman & Littlefield. This book presents both sides of the debate.

COMMITTEE ON THE USE OF ANIMALS IN RESEARCH. (1988). *Use of laboratory animals in biomedical and behavioral research*. Washington, DC: National Academy Press. This is a discussion of the benefits that have resulted from animal research and addresses concerns for animal welfare.

COMMITTEE ON THE USE OF ANIMALS IN RESEARCH. (1991). *Science, medicine, and animals*. Washington, DC: National Academy Press. This is an excellent summary of the case for the use of animals in research, prepared for the Councils of the National Academy of Sciences and the Institute of Medicine.

COOK, S. W. (1991). Ethical implications. In C. M. JUDD, E. R. SMITH, & L. H. KIDDER (Eds.), *Research methods in social relations* (6th ed., pp. 477–528). New York: Holt, Rinehart & Winston. This excellent discussion is somewhat broader than the issues covered in the APA principles.

KOOCHER, G. P., & KEITH-SPIEGEL, P. (1998). *Ethics in psychology: Professional standards and cases* (2nd ed.). New York: Random House. This book provides commentary on the APA ethics code and a number of cases that illustrate particular ethical problems. These cases make worthwhile subjects for discussion.

KORN, J. H. (1988). Student's roles, rights, and responsibilities as research participants. *Teaching of Psychology*, 15(2), 74–78.

STOLZ, S. B., et al. (1978). *Ethical issues in behavior modification*. San Francisco: Jossey-Bass. This book is the report of the Commission on Behavior Modification of the American Psychological Association. It considers ethical and legal issues surrounding behavior modification in outpatient settings, institutions, schools, prisons, and society at large. The presentation is balanced and well reasoned.

WILLIAMS, J. (Ed.). (1991). *Animal rights and welfare*. New York: Wilson. This collection of reprints of popular articles on animal welfare is balanced and accessible.

A CASE IN POINT

Professor D. Lemma and Informed Consent

Professor D. Lemma has developed a new method of therapy for depressed patients, based on his theory of depression. Informal observation of several of his patients suggests that his method is more effective than the current standard therapy for depression. He wants to perform an experiment to test his therapy in which there will be three groups: a no-treatment control group, a standard-therapy group, and the Lemma-treatment group. Participants in the no-treatment control group would be told that they are being placed on a waiting list for inclusion in a later phase of the study. The two experimental groups would be treated according to the respective methods.

Professor Lemma believes that it is necessary to assign participants randomly to the three groups to have a valid research design. He knows, however, that depressed patients are at risk of suicide. He is concerned that some of his control participants might commit suicide while they wait for the treatment. Also, he is bothered by the fact that if his new treatment actually is better than the standard treatment, he will be giving some of the depressed subjects a treatment that is less effective than his new treatment.

Lemma's proposed protocol involves informing the participants that they will be randomly placed in the various groups. He knows, however, that research has shown that many subjects in such experiments actually do not understand what randomization involves, even when it is explained carefully to them. Appelbaum, Roth, Lidz, Benson, and Winslade (1987) found that even though participants are able to state the principle of random assignment, they often simultaneously hold to the erroneous belief that the researchers will somehow manage to place them in the condition that will be best for them individually.

Professor Lemma is preparing to present his protocol to the institutional review board (IRB) that must approve all experiments using human participants at his university. He intends to argue that the use of a no-treatment control group is justified because he will be treating as many patients with this design as he would if there were no such control group: He can treat only 20 participants in his study; he could not handle 10 extra participants in the two treatment groups. So the maximum possible number of depressed people will be treated. He intends to offer treatment to

(continued)

the control group after the experiment proper is completed.

Mr. Softheart is a nonscientist member of the IRB and is reading Professor Lemma's protocol in preparation for the IRB meeting. He thinks there should be only one group of participants, all of whom would get the new treatment. The improvement shown by the participants could be compared with that in other published studies. In any case, he is opposed to random assignment. He believes that participants should be able to choose which treatment they prefer because one treatment might appeal to certain participants and another might appeal to other participants. Softheart is also afraid that the participants in the control group will be even more depressed at being put on the waiting list than they were to begin with.

Dr. Caring is another member of the IRB and has also read the Appelbaum, et al. article. She is concerned that participants will not comprehend that a psychologist will sometimes put a participant in a condition that is not the best for him or her for scientific purposes. Caring holds that the participants will believe that Lemma will have their own best interest in mind when he assigns them to conditions.

Professor Weary is an anthropologist on the IRB. She believes that this business about informed consent is in reality a ritual whose purpose is to legitimize experimental procedure as much as to inform the participant. She believes that it is sufficient to explain the procedure and not to worry too much about what the participants really believe in their hearts. It is all right with her if the participants all think they are getting what is best for them.

Professor Upbeat is in the education department. He wants Lemma to spend three hours teaching each participant the theoretical basis of randomness, with a mathematical treatment of probability and examples of coin flipping, until each one is able to understand the true nature of the process.

Required

Write the report of the IRB, including the main arguments for and against Lemma's proposed protocol and your suggested solution. Cite the relevant parts of the APA ethics code.

Scientific Misconduct and Conflict of Interest

Professor Jaspers, a psychologist at Northern State University, has done a study that found that Dreckium contributes to the onset of Alzheimer's disease. Dreckium is a heavy metal commonly occurring in the soil that is taken up by certain vegetables and, when eaten, is concentrated in brain tissue.

Although it has been known for many years that Dreckium is toxic in large quantities, Jaspers' research found that it is harmful at much lower doses than previously believed.

Publication of his study led to a determination by the Environmental Protection Agency (EPA) that Dreckium constitutes a public health threat and has been instrumental in the outlawing by several states of the growing and selling of the offending vegetables.

Professor Weeble is a psychologist in the Psychology Department at Southern State University who has done a good deal of research on intellectual functioning in older adults, but he and Jaspers have not been fond of each other after Jaspers once wrote an unfavorable review of Weeble's research. Weeble served on the EPA committee that found Dreckium to be a health threat. At that time, he thought some of the procedures in Jaspers' study were questionable. He couldn't figure out exactly how Jaspers had matched his high- and low-Dreckium subjects for education, socioeconomic status, and other variables that could be correlated with measured intelligence. Weeble wrote an article in which he questioned the validity of Jaspers' work. In that article, he suggested that the amount of money spent by the vegetable industry in changing over to production of different foods would better be spent on research to reverse the effects of Alzheimer's.

The Consolidated Amalgamated Vegetable Producers Association (CAVPA), which represents the interests of the vegetable industry, accuses Jaspers of being biased against the vegetable industry ever since his mother forced him to eat

(continued)

broccoli as a child. They note that Jaspers receives large fees for testifying in court on the dangers of Dreckium. They offer Weeble money to do research on Dreckium and ask him to testify as a paid expert witness before a legislature that is considering weakening Dreckium standards. He accepts.

The Office of Research Integrity (ORI) at the National Institutes of Health (NIH) requires all universities that receive research grants from the federal government to have procedures in place to investigate allegations of research misconduct. Weeble next writes to ORI that he suspects that Jaspers had not properly reported how he did his study and that the results may be invalid. Congressman Diddle represents a farming district in Pennsylvania. He has been a keynote speaker before CAVPAs annual winter convention in Acapulco, Mexico. He also chairs a congressional committee that investigates waste and fraud in federal spending and is particularly critical of what he sees as the lack of accountability in the use of NIH research grants. ORI requests Northern State to investigate and report back.

Professor Berger is the Research Integrity Officer at Northern State. It is her responsibility to investigate accusations of research impropriety made against faculty at State. An internal investigation of Jaspers' work has already been conducted, but its report was inconclusive. Berger knows that Northern State has been criticized for covering up scientific misconduct in the past and realizes that NIH could cut off all federal funding to Northern if it is found that they do not properly investigate allegations of misconduct. Berger appoints a hearing board to investigate. The chair of the hearing board is Professor Marshall, the professor at NSU who knows the most about research on intelligence in older populations. She has known both Jaspers and Weeble for many years, having served on various committees with both and having cited their research in her papers. After a long investigation that includes a complete reanalysis of Jaspers' data, the hearing board finds that Jaspers' results are valid, although a detailed reading of his original protocols shows that he did not accurately report exactly how he chose his

subjects. Specifically, his criteria for placing subjects into the high- and low-Dreckium groups changed over time, so some subjects were included who, according to what he said in his published paper, should have been excluded, and vice versa. Nevertheless, the data from the disputed subjects did not alter the conclusions because the statistical analyses were significant whether the disputed subjects were included or excluded. The board finds Jaspers not guilty of scientific misconduct but concludes that he deliberately misrepresented his methods.

Required
You are the provost of NSU, to whom all academic officials report, including Berger. Write a letter that is to be sent to all parties in the conflict. Deal with the various conflicts of interest. Discuss the role of free speech.

Alternative
Arrange a panel discussion of the issues involved in this case, with a member of the class taking the role of each named person or agency. Each participant is to justify his or her actions while espousing the values of academic freedom, free speech, and fair play.

Note: This case study is entirely fictional.

Doris Diligent and the Runaway Participant
Doris Diligent was a student experimenter in Professor Casual's laboratory. Casual was performing an experiment on the effect of failure at a certain task on subsequent performance of that task. Half of the participants were to be given impossible anagrams to solve. The other half were to receive anagrams that had obvious solutions. After working on the anagrams for five minutes, the participants were to be told that the time was up and that most participants had solved them in the time allowed. Next, they would be given another set of anagrams that had solutions. The dependent variable in the experiment was the number of problems solved in the given period of time. The participants were not to be informed that the first set of anagrams was insolvable until afterward.

Doris asked how to go about getting approval from the institutional review board. Casual said that

(continued)

he felt that the research came under the category of *minimal risk* and that no IRB approval was necessary. This did not sound right to Doris, but she did not say anything.

Participants were to be recruited from the class of one of Casual's colleagues, thus bypassing the necessity of going through the department's rather involved subject pool procedures. After the experimental sessions, those participants who expressed an interest in learning about the experiment would be told about the deception. Casual said that in his experience, most participants just wanted to leave and get on to their next activity.

One day when Doris was running a group of four subjects, one participant became upset at his failure to solve the problems and said that he did not want to continue.

Doris wanted the student to realize that the problems were impossible, but she could not say so in front of the other participants. Before she knew what had happened, the student had left the room in a huff. She ran after him and tried to explain that the anagrams were insolvable and that he had no reason to be upset. When she put a hand on his arm to urge him to return, he threatened to call campus security and have her reported. He said that he had trusted her to tell him the truth, that it was just like psychologists to deceive people, and that he was fed up with this college and would probably change majors or even quit college.

By this time, Doris was upset and confused as to what she should do. She let the student leave and returned to her remaining participants. After discussing the matter with her roommate, she decided not to tell Professor Casual about the incident and recorded the runaway participant as a no-show.

Required

List the violations of the APA ethics code that were involved in this situation. Cite specific sections.

Optional

What should Doris have done with the upset participant? What problems did she face in trying to prevent him from leaving? What should she tell the other participants? Could this situation have been anticipated and thus prevented; and, if so, how?

© Cengage Learning

Reading Between the Lines

3.1 The Causes of Child Abuse

The causes of child abuse have long been a topic of experimental interest. Researchers have found that child abuse is reported more frequently in poor families than in middle-class or wealthy families. Some researchers believe that poor families do not abuse their children any more than do other social classes, but that they are unable to cover up the abuse as well as middle-class and upper-class families are. Leroy Pelton (1978) believes there may be political bias behind the objection to the class differences theory of the amount of child abuse. Can you think why Pelton would object to a conclusion that child abuse is more common in poor families?

Research Methods Laboratory Manual

 William Langston (2010) has prepared a laboratory manual that contains many suggestions for research activities that work well with this book. Many chapters in this book contain a section that refers the reader to appropriate sections of the Langston book.

Appendix A of Langston (2011) is titled *Institutional Review Boards*. It contains a good discussion of the questions that one needs to keep in mind when applying for approval for research from an IRB, along with a completed sample form.

Exercises

3.1 Joe Eager and the Dating Survey

Joe Eager was a graduate student in social psychology at State University. He was taking a course in the psychology of social relations at the same time that he was a teaching assistant in an undergraduate research methods course. He thought that a survey of the dating and sexual experiences of his students would be a valuable and interesting example of questionnaires. He took it upon himself to develop, administer, and score such a questionnaire using the 15 students in his section.

Joe included an item in the questionnaire based on a theory he learned in his class. This item was designed to determine whether certain past experiences would predict various types of sexual activity. He did not discuss this hypothesis with the students either before or after they completed the questionnaire. The results were so interesting that he decided to publish a paper on them.
Sue Nice was embarrassed by the questions and said that she did not wish to participate. In front of the other students, Joe joked that Sue must have something to hide. Sue was so upset that she went to the department chair. She said that even though Joe had announced that participation was voluntary, she felt obligated to complete the form because she was afraid it would affect her grade.

Required:

What ethical violations was Joe guilty of? Cite specific parts of the APA ethics code. Note that there may be other problems not specifically addressed by the ethics code.

3.2 Identify the Researcher's Responsibilities

A researcher designs a study to determine how truthful college students are in answering personality surveys. He designs the study in a way that makes it possible to detect certain lies that could not generally be detected under normal conditions. At the conclusion of the study, several participants become furious when they learn that they have been deceived and caught in lies.

Required:

a. Discuss the responsibility the researcher has to his participants in this experiment.
b. What steps or procedures would you take to meet this responsibility?

3.3 Identify the Researcher's Responsibilities

A researcher plans a study to determine the role of heredity and environment in determining individual differences in intelligence. As part of the study, she plans to administer an IQ test to a large sample of Native Americans, blacks, and whites from all over the United States. She reasons that because most people do not understand the nature of research procedures and methodology, she needs to inform principals and teachers, but not parents and pupils, only about the general purpose of her research project. She decides that the parents and pupils need not be informed of such specifics as the IQ test to be administered, the number of students to be involved, and how, when, and where the results will be reported.

Required:

c. Do you agree or disagree with the researcher's position? Explain.
d. What responsibilities does the researcher have in conducting this study?

3.4 Ethics of Scientific Writing

A professor assigns a research paper to her students in which they must develop a hypothesis that is supported by evidence from the psychological literature. Anita Clue, a student in the class, decides to write her paper on altruism, and finds two journal articles about it. The articles are hard to read, though, and Anita doesn't really understand them. She completes the assignment by copying from one of the articles verbatim and tries to make the copied text look like her own ideas. What ethical violation has Anita committed? Which specific parts of the APA ethics code applies in this situation?

3.5 Ethics of Animal Research

You are a professor whose research is on humans, although you have no objection to the use of animals in research. At a party, you meet a person you would like to get to know better socially. This person is opposed to the use of animals in research. How would you defend animal research?

3.6 Ethics of Animal Research

You are a professor who is opposed to animal research, although you have colleagues whom you respect who do use animals in their research. At a party you meet a person whose child is hospitalized with schizophrenia. What do you say to him when he asks you to justify your opposition to animal research?

CHAPTER **FOUR**

Writing in Psychology

PREVIEW

Chapter 4 discusses how to communicate research results in American Psychological Association (APA) style. A sample paper illustrates the main principles. We also give guidelines for poster presentations.

Of all the steps in the research process, the most crucial may be communicating the findings to others. The most perfect experiment in the world makes no contribution to science if the results are not reported to the scientific community. As we discussed in Chapter 1, science is a social enterprise. It grows by the public discussion and assimilation of knowledge contributed by individual scientists.

Scientific communication takes place in different ways. We think of books and articles published in scholarly journals as the standard form of scientific communication. This form is known as **archival publication**, because these journals and books are publicly available in places such as libraries. Archival publication is the permanent record of science. As such, it clearly serves a vital function, but it is not the only way scientific findings are communicated.

Another important type of communication goes on informally over the telephone, by e-mail, by visits to laboratories, and at professional meetings. The people who communicate about their research in this way are said to

archival publication:
written record of scientific progress

invisible college: informal communication network of people having common scientific interests

form **invisible colleges:** informal networks of people with common scientific interests. New ideas and results are usually first discussed through this informal communication. Published papers typically appear one or two years after the information is available to the invisible college. Informal communication not only allows scientists to keep up with what is happening in other laboratories but also permits researchers to present their ideas in a tentative form before committing themselves in archival publications. For these reasons, it is important for scientists to be aware of the role of the invisible college and to become part of the one that operates in their areas of research. Many young scientists have been frustrated by the difficulties of *breaking into the club* by relying on archival communication. Therefore, in this chapter we discuss how to present findings at scientific meetings as well as via the standard article in an archival journal.

No matter how you choose to present your data, keep your audience in mind. When you write a letter to a friend, you take account of that friend's interests and knowledge in deciding what you need to say and what you can leave unsaid. When you sit down to write your psychology laboratory report, you should also have an audience in mind. This audience consists of the people in the invisible college that we just talked about. It is convenient to consider your audience as a **discourse community:** a group of people who share a common goal, a public means of exchanging information, a body of common knowledge, and a specialized language.

discourse community: a group of people who share common goals, a public forum, common knowledge, and a specialized language

In our case, the discourse community consists of psychologists. When we sit down to write our report, we assume that our reader will know certain things about psychology and will expect us to use the style of writing common to psychologists: APA style. Our report won't read like a letter to a friend because it belongs to a different type of writing and is intended for a different discourse community.

The Written Report

Articles in scientific journals are usually reports of empirical research, review articles, theoretical articles, methodological articles, or case studies. In this section, we discuss the writing of a formal report of an empirical study as it would be submitted to a scientific journal. We follow APA format because it is used by most psychological journals as well as by other publications. Once you are familiar with APA format, you will find that it makes reading and writing professional literature more convenient. A full discussion appears in the *Publication Manual of the American Psychological Association* (2010), which you can reference for details and additional information when writing other types of articles. Another way to learn how to prepare a paper for publication is to look through a recent issue of the journal to which you want to submit your paper and study its format.

General

Writing a scientific report is not easy. From reading a few research articles, many students get the feeling that writing one should be easy: Just use a lot of big words and long sentences, stick with the passive voice, and above all, sound dull and pompous. Sometimes these attributes, unfortunately, do characterize scientific writing. The purpose of scientific writing, though, is the same as that of all good writing: to convey a message clearly, concisely, and interestingly. It is true that scientific writing must conform to a certain format in the interest of economy. Yet every writer should try, within that format, to write as well as possible, and this takes effort. Many scientists with reputations as good writers testify that they must work hard to make their writing seem effortless.

Scientific writing, like other expository writing, aims to persuade as well as to inform (Sternberg, 2003). If you simply throw your results and theory down on paper and let them "speak for themselves," you will be disappointed with the outcome. Young scientists sometimes underestimate the importance of good writing in gaining acceptance for their ideas. Repeatedly in the history of science, the person who wrote more clearly and persuasively was remembered and the one who wrote poorly was forgotten.

argument: a set of reasons in support of a proposition

thesis: the proposition that is supported by an argument

In some respects, a scientific report is one form of presentation of an **argument.** Although we tend to think of an argument as a disagreement between two people, it has the technical meaning of a set of reasons that support a proposition that one wants to prove. This proposition is known as the thesis of the argument. The term *thesis* is commonly used to refer to a scholarly paper, such as a master's thesis. It is helpful to think of your paper as a presentation of an argument in support of a proposition as a way of focusing your writing. Keep in mind your purpose (what you are trying to convince your reader of) and the support that you are providing for your propositions.

Because the scientific paper is an argument, it is worth considering each part of the article in that light. The abstract of the paper is an overview of the entire argument. The introduction section gives the premises of your argument, the method section tells how you obtained your evidence, and the results section presents the evidence itself. The discussion section draws conclusions from the evidence, and the references tell the reader where you got your premises.

We can capture the essence of good report writing in three words: clarity, brevity, and felicity. The first two terms are familiar; the term *felicity* means pleasing style.

Clarity

The most important element of writing a scientific paper is to say exactly what you mean as directly as possible. You must look at each sentence and ask whether someone could mistake its meaning. Sometimes this approach means avoiding common usages, such as writing *hopefully* when you mean to say *it is hoped*. Consider the following sentence: "Hopefully, the subjects followed the instructions." Does it mean that the author hopes the subjects followed the instructions, or that the subjects followed the instructions eagerly or full of hope?

This use of *hopefully* illustrates the difference between ordinary conversation and formal writing. Some things that are acceptable in one place are not in another. Recognizing and eliminating such problems requires work and practice. Ask someone else to read a draft of your paper to suggest places where the meaning is unclear. It is not cheating to do so, as long as the person makes suggestions and doesn't actually write the paper for you.

A number of words are commonly misused in scientific writing; Sternberg (2003) has an excellent discussion of many of them. One pair of words is particularly troublesome in psychology because they are so similar, and their meanings can be confused. They are *affect* and *effect*. The problem is compounded because both can be either nouns or verbs. As a noun, *affect* means *emotion*, but as a verb it means to *influence*. *Effect* as a noun means *result* or *outcome*, but as a verb it means to *accomplish*. The meanings of the two as verbs are similar. If you say that the hurricane affected the demolition of the building, you mean that it influenced the demolition, which presumably was being carried out by workers. If you say, however, that the hurricane effected the demolition of the building, the hurricane accomplished the destruction by itself.

Make use of the available tools to check spelling and grammar. If you are using a computer, use its dictionary, thesaurus, grammar checker, and spell checker. These are useful, although they should not be considered a substitute for standard reference books. Most notoriously, spell checkers don't know which word you are trying to write, and so will not notice when you write *their* for *there* or *no* for *know*. You should always have a dictionary at hand when you are writing a paper.

Brevity

Next, work at brevity. Does every word, phrase, and sentence contribute to the paper? Years ago, research papers were long and discursive. Today, because of space shortage in journals, papers must be as brief as possible. The need for brevity can sometimes lead to an unfortunate terseness of style, which should be avoided if at all possible (see Felicity, below). Still, brevity can also be an aid to good communication. Pascal once apologized to a correspondent: "I have made this letter longer than usual because I lack the time to make it shorter." Writers sometimes attempt to clarify by repeating information, rather than revising material so that it is clear in the first place. Remember that your intended reader is a busy person whose time you are competing for. If you had an appointment with your reader in person, you would be careful not to waste his or her time.

Felicity

Felicity, or a pleasing style, may seem out of place in scientific writing, but scientific reporting, too, needs liveliness and grace. How you express your ideas is important to how well they are accepted (Sternberg, 2003). Although many forms of humor are best avoided because they can distract from the message or even backfire, there is a place for wit. A well-known paper in vision research was titled, *What the Frog's Eye Tells the Frog's Brain* (Lettvin, Maturana, McCulloch, & Pitts, 1959). The title conveys the topic of the paper in such a way that people want to read it. This paper has become a classic in its field, helped in part by its catchy title.

Avoiding Bias in Writing

The APA style reflects recent changes in our culture by requiring that authors avoid bias in their writing. This includes biased language related to gender, sexual orientation, racial or ethnic identity, disabilities, or age. This is not easy to do. Long-lived attitudes and traditions have become built into our language. We have terms such as *manpower, mailman,* and *manhole cover.* It may be easy to replace *manpower* with *personnel,* and *mailman* with *letter carrier,* but it is harder to think of a replacement for *manhole cover.*

The *Publication Manual of the American Psychological Association* (2010) suggests three guidelines for avoiding biased language. First, precision should be used in describing people. In other words, be as specific and accurate as possible when describing people; using the term *man* to refer to all humankind is simply inaccurate in that it ignores half the population. The second guideline suggests that writers should take care to be respectful in labeling people. Instead of "the schizophrenics," the phrase "people with schizophrenia" is preferred. The third guideline involves writing about people in a way that acknowledges their participation in a study and avoids a passive voice in writing.

In the following section, we consider two common problems with biased language, following the discussion in the *Publication Manual of the American Psychological Association* (2010). First is ambiguity of referent; the second is stereotyping by labeling.

Ambiguity of referent occurs when a masculine term is used when it is not clear that only males are in view. It is very common to read something like the following:

(Poor) The participant was asked to indicate his preference…

Unless the subjects were all male, this should be reworded to avoid the ambiguity by making clear that both sexes are being referred to:

(Preferred) Participants were asked to indicate their preference…

When only one person is being discussed, it becomes somewhat awkward to avoid sexist language. Some writers solve this problem by creating another:

(Poor) The participant placed their preferred hand on the button.

Here the noun is singular and the pronoun is plural, but both refer to the same person. Without making the noun plural, there are at least two solutions to this problem. One is to indicate both sexes explicitly:

(Preferred) The participant placed his or her preferred hand on the button.

The other is to alternate gender, one time saying his and another time her. Neither of these is completely satisfactory: The first is wordier, and the second can be distracting.

Writing can stereotype people by choosing examples that imply limitations on sex roles, social status, and so forth, even though those limitations may be accurate on a statistical basis. Although many professors are men, to refer to an unspecified professor as *he* implies that all are men. The remedies are the same as those just discussed: Reword the sentence to make the noun plural so that you can use *they*, use *he* or *she*, or use some alternate language.

In the matter of group biases, one should avoid labeling people whenever possible so as to avoid stereotypes. Referring to people by race, gender, disability, age, or sexual orientation marginalizes the person's individuality. When labeling cannot be avoided, be aware that preferred ways of referring to groups change over time and should be respected. One should be careful not to use a term that may have been acceptable at one time but has been replaced by another. The appropriate term should be determined by the members of the group, not by your own sense of style.

The Parts of a Paper

The parts of a paper reporting an empirical study are (1) title, (2) author names and their affiliations, (3) author note, (4) abstract, (5) introduction, (6) method, (7) results, (8) discussion, (9) references, (10) footnotes, (11) tables with notes, (12) figures with captions. We have listed them in the order that they appear in a typescript submitted for publication in a journal. In the published form, the footnotes, tables, figure captions, and figures are placed appropriately throughout the paper.

Each part of the paper serves a specific function, which we will consider in order. As you begin to write a paper, consult a recent issue of the journal for which you are writing to see its style for a typical article.

On pages 94–103, we show a manuscript in the appropriate form for submission to a journal. You should study this manuscript carefully for style. The numbers in the annotations refer to paragraphs in the sixth edition of the *Publication Manual of the American Psychological Association*.

Following are some guidelines for typing the manuscript: Use a computer or word processor. Use a 12-point font, preferably Times New Roman. Leave 1-inch margins all around. Double space everything. Start every section on a new page except for the method, results, and discussion sections (the headings for these sections are also in bold). Together with the introduction, these sections form the body of the paper, which is typed straight through.

Title

The title is your chance to gain the attention of the desired audience. It should convey the main idea of the paper in a few words. The title should contain keywords that will catch the eye of a person scanning the table of contents of the journal or that will come up on computerized searches of the literature. Avoid words that do not contribute directly to the idea of the paper, such as *An experimental study*.

Author Names and Their Affiliations

Authors are usually listed in order of the importance of their contributions to the paper. Authorship on papers is relevant when researchers are seeking grants, jobs, or promotions, and first authorship is generally preferred. Because psychology is a collaborative science, it can be difficult to determine name order (Domjan, 2008), and thus who gets credit for an article can sometimes be contentious. To make this easier, discuss the order of authorship clearly as early in the process as possible. When you settle on authorship, you will want to list your name in a form that you will be comfortable with for the rest of your career to avoid having your work listed under several different names in bibliographic sources.

Author Note

An author note is the appropriate way to provide a mailing address for reprints, acknowledge financial support or technical assistance, and the like. The author note appears on the first page of the document, under the title, author names, and affiliations.

Abstract

The abstract is a brief (less than 250 words) synopsis of the paper. It should summarize the problem, method, results, and conclusion and contain elements of each major part of a paper. The abstract must be self-contained because it will be reproduced verbatim in the PsycINFO database and other publications. Because of its condensed form, the abstract is the most difficult part of the paper to write, and thus is often written last.

Introduction

The introduction sets the stage for the rest of the paper. First, state the general problem examined in the paper. Then briefly discuss the relevant literature in a way that shows the present theoretical status of the problem and places your experiment in context. Although you must acknowledge the sources of the ideas you discuss, you do not need to give an exhaustive history of the problem. Finally, state how your study will contribute to understanding the problem. Indicate your hypothesis and expected results.

Method

The method section is the heart of the paper, and many authors write this section first. Because the method section describes what you did in the experiment, everything in this section should be stated in the past tense. The method section has two purposes. First, having read your method section, someone else should be able to repeat the experiment exactly in all essential details. Second, another person should be able to judge the validity of your conclusions by comparing them with the method section. For example, in what exact ways did you induce a certain theoretical state, such as hunger, in the subjects? How did you measure their responses? The following subsections can be convenient for organizing the method section.

   Participants.[1] Tell how many participants you used and how they were obtained. Describe any characteristics of your participants that are important

---

[1] APA style now requires that human subjects be referred to as *participants* where possible. (One exception is when describing statistical results; e.g., a condition X subject interaction.) We have followed APA style in this book, although the reader should note certain situations where *subject* works better. Following common usage, we talk about *between-subject* designs and so forth. In addition, we use *subject* in discussing animal research. When we discuss design principles in general, and either animals or humans could be the subjects, we use *subject*.

to the study, such as their age, gender, student status, and any compensation. State that IRB approval was obtained and that APA ethical guidelines were observed for the study. In the case of animal subjects such as rats, you should name the strain and supplier as well as the species.

Materials. Indicate the materials used in the study, including the type of apparatus. Describe the stimuli and give the associated values.

Design. State the logic of the experiment, including the variables (e.g., The design was a 2×2 factorial in which sex and instructions each varied between subjects). Give information as to the order in which variables were presented by stating which variables were randomized, which were counter-balanced, and so forth. Tell what the dependent variables were.

Procedure. Although procedure does not need to be a distinct subsection from design, it is helpful to remember that the design is a logical construction in your head, whereas the procedure is the sequence of steps you followed in putting the design into effect. How were the subjects assigned to conditions? What instructions were they given? You may find it helpful to think of the design subsection as what you did and the procedure subsection as the details of how you did it. Both aspects are fundamental to understanding the method.

Results

The main function of the results section is easy to state: What did you find? Results are usually described in the past tense (e.g., The rats bar-pressed more when they were hungry). First indicate any data transformations that you made before analyzing the data. Then state what you found. Usually you will refer the reader to a table or graph of the data. Indicate which results were statistically significant and what tests of significance you used.

A common problem in the results section is to get bogged down in describing the inferential statistics and lose sight of the results that you are trying to present. You should not spend time presenting results that were not statistically significant or, except in rare cases, raw data. Remember that the focus of the results section is on what you found; the statistics assure the reader that results are not likely to have been a fluke. More information on preparing a results section can be found in Appendix C of Langston's (2010) laboratory manual.

Although neither is actually presented in the results section directly, usu-ally you summarize the results in either a table or a figure or graph (see Chapter 14) that is discussed in this section of the paper. Tables have the advantage of being economical of space, precise, and easy to coordinate with the statistical analysis. Figures, however, allow the reader to get a better idea of the size of the effects and any interactions among variables. Our preference is for figures because they seem to make it easier for the reader to grasp and retain the main features of the results.

Discussion

The discussion section builds on the results by interpreting them and relating them to the literature. The focus of this section is on the theoretical contri-bution of the study. Start by clearly stating the relationship between your findings and the original hypothesis. Describe similarities and differences between your results and those of others. Do not introduce further data from your study unless they are incidental to a comparison with other published data. The following questions are appropriate to address: What weaknesses are there in your data? What qualifications must be made to your conclusions? What has your experiment contributed to the understanding of the problem stated in the introduction? Whereas the method and results sections are written in the past tense, conclusions found in the discussion section are stated in the present tense (e.g., Hunger increases bar-pressing rate).

References

The reference section contains the documentation of points made in your paper. It serves the essential function of tying your paper to the literature. Many readers will turn to the references immediately after reading the title and the abstract to see whom you cite. Be sure to reference all sources that you have drawn on for specific ideas. Remember, however, that the reference list is not a bibliography of background material; it should list only papers specifically cited in the text.

Footnotes

There are two types of footnotes: content and copyright permission. Footnotes to the content of the paper should be avoided. When essential, content footnotes are numbered and will appear in the journal at the bottom of the page on which they are cited. Copyright permission footnotes are used for reprinted tables or figures.

Tables

Put data into a table when doing so will help make the data clearer than having them strung out in lines of text. The best way to learn how to set up a table is to look in a journal to see how tabular material is handled. Table 4.1 shows a typical table and offers some suggestions. Tables should not duplicate material presented in the text or in figures, but should supplement that material. Refer to the table in the text (usually in the results section) and explain its significance.

Figures

Although you can describe and refer to figures in the text, the figures themselves appear last in a typewritten manuscript submitted for publication. Each figure has its own page in the manuscript. Figures that are to be published in a journal should be created professionally, generally using a computer. Frequently the standard, or default, choices in the graphics package must be altered to conform to APA guidelines (see example on pages 378–379 of Chapter 14). Avoid color coding in graphs because colors do not photocopy. Instead, different symbols should be used to indicate groups and conditions. The axes should be clearly labeled. Make the symbols and lettering large enough (between 8-point and 14-point font) that the figures can be easily read. Each figure should have a caption that briefly describes the contents of the figure. The caption should be understandable by itself, but should

TABLE **4.1**

Significance of Numbers and Variables

© Cengage Learning

Mean Number of Correct Responses as a Function of Sex and Amount of Reinforcement						
Variable B	Reinforcement ← Variable A					
	Low ← A_1			High ← A_2		
Sex	M	SD	N	M	SD	N
B_1 → Female	43	5.1	8	52	5.4	9
B_2 → Male	19	2.4	10	27	3.2	8

Note: Maximum score = 100. ← Footnote explains features that may not be obvious.

avoid repeating material from the body of the paper. The figure caption is placed directly below and on the same page as the figure.

See the checklist in the *Nuts & Bolts* section of this chapter for further details on style and Chapter 14 for further discussion of tables and figures.

Documenting Your Paper

An essential feature of scientific writing is that certain types of statements must be documented, or cited, appropriately.

What to Document

First, you must give credit to ideas that are not your own by citing the appropriate source. Second, you need to show where your ideas fit into a larger framework, and so cite several sources to give your reader a feel for the existent work in an area. By doing so, you allow your reader to find out where to go for further information about the theory, methods, or data you discuss, which is a third purpose for documenting in an article. It is not necessary to document statements that are common knowledge among your audience. For example, you do not need to document a reference to the concept of short-term memory or Freudian theory. Beyond this generalization, however, one cannot give a clear rule on what to document. Perhaps one way of answering the question is to recall what it is like to read about scientific topics in popular literature. When scientific claims are made but not documented, readers who want to learn more, but are unable to do so. Who found this phenomenon? What methods were used? Under what conditions does it occur? What theories does it relate to? What do other scientists think of these ideas? All these questions are unanswerable without adequate documentation.

Avoid Plagiarism

Students sometimes plagiarize other authors' work without realizing it. Some students do this because they do not understand that citing another author's work is part of the process of building one's own argument. Others may plagiarize simply because they do not know the proper way of giving credit to another author.

Basically, plagiarism is presenting another person's work as your own. Plagiarism is a serious matter that can result in dismissal from college or even a lawsuit if plagiarized material is published. The basic principle is simple: Always give credit when you discuss another person's work or idea. For example:

> The ancient Greek philosopher Plato (translated 1995) said, "[The goal of this method is to] cut up each kind according to its species along its natural joints, and to try not to splinter any part, as a bad butcher might do." (p. 64)

This quotation encloses the original author's exact words in quotation marks and gives the proper reference. Words that are not the original author's, but are added for clarification, are enclosed in brackets.

You may paraphrase, or put another person's ideas into your own words, but you must still give credit for the ideas. For example, the previous quotation is often paraphrased in words such as the following: Plato (translated 1995) said that we should try to carve nature at the joints.

The line between plagiarism and paraphrase can be hard to draw because a paraphrase seeks to put the same idea in different words. How different is different? Basically, a paraphrase uses different terms or phrases to describe the same idea. The following is too close to the original to be considered a paraphrase: Plato (translated 1995) said that we should carve nature along its natural joints, and not splinter it like a bad butcher.

As a rule of thumb, if you use three or more consecutive words in a sentence that are the same as the original author's, revise your sentence in your own words or use an exact, direct quote. Whether you quote exact words or use a paraphrase, however, you should always include a reference citation to the original author.

Unintentional plagiarism can occur when you write something that you think is your own words, but you are unconsciously influenced by having read someone else's work. This can happen all too easily. The way to prevent unintentional plagiarism is to take good notes when you are doing your library research.

Self-plagiarism can also easily occur, when you submit previously published work as though it were new. Because of the progressive nature of science, many researchers are modifying past work in order to create new experiments. Care must be taken to clearly document work that has already been published (yes, you must cite yourself!) and to delineate this work from new scholarship.

Don't Cite a Source You Haven't Read

When you cite an author, you are claiming that you have actually read the work you cite. If you have not laid eyes on it yourself, you can't cite the work directly. Instead, you must give a **secondary citation** for the work. Suppose you want to cite the Plato reference but you know of it only by reading this book. Then you may cite it as follows:

secondary citation: documentation of an idea from one work that is reported in another one

> Plato (as cited by White & McBurney, 2012) said that we should try to carve nature at the joints.

The appropriate details of the secondary source (this text, in our example) would then appear in your reference list. You would be surprised how many errors get repeated in books because the authors cite an original source, even though they actually read a secondary source whose author has mixed up the original author's idea.

APA Style of Documentation

In APA style, there are two main techniques for citing or documenting other works. In the first technique, the authors of the work you are citing are named in the text, followed by the date of the publication:

Jones and Smith (2006) found that...

In the second technique, you refer to the authors of the work and the date of publication parenthetically. You may say:

Recent work (Jones & Smith, 2006) shows that...

Note that when the names appear outside of the parentheses, you use the word *and,* but when they are inside the parentheses you use the ampersand (&). If there are two authors, always list both names whenever you cite their work in the text. If there are three or more authors, list all names the first time you refer to the work:

Jones, Smith, and Brown (2006) found that...

Thereafter, list only the first author, followed by the term *et al.* and the year of publication:

Jones et al. (2006) found that...

The reference list will contain an entry for each work cited in the paper. There must be no entries in the reference list that are not cited in the paper, and vice versa. A reference has four major parts: (1) author(s), (2) date, (3) title of article or book, and (4) publication information (including name of journal in the case of periodicals, and Digital Object Identifier or URL in the case of electronic sources). Each part is separated by a period. Other information is separated by commas. The first line of the reference has a hanging indent of five spaces. For example:

Miller, G. A. (1956). The magical number seven, plus or minus two: Some limits on our capacity for processing information. *Psychological Review, 63,* 81–97.

This particular example is of a journal article. The author data appear in the same form for all kinds of references (that have individual authors). Titles of books and names of journals are italicized, but titles of articles are not. The publication data may differ from one type of publication to the next, as the following examples show.

A reference to the hard copy of a journal article contains the following information: author(s), date, title, journal (italicized), volume (italicized), page range. Most journals number all pages of a volume consecutively, even though each volume may have several issues. Some journals, however, begin each issue with page 1. For such publications, it is necessary to give the issue number, as follows:

> Parks, A. B. (1990). Delinquency and social class. *Journal of Social Issues*, *48*(3), 118–135.

Citations of electronic copies of journal articles that are exact duplicates of a print source should follow the same basic format as that of a journal article, with a couple of exceptions:

1. References to journal articles should always include the issue number. This is not always the case for print-based citations.
2. Readers should be directed as closely as possible to the online source. Many publishers have begun assigning Digital Object Identifiers (DOI) to journal articles. If the DOI is available, it is preferable to the URL in the reference. The DOI or URL should follow the rest of the reference.

Digital Object Identifiers (DOI): a unique alphanumeric code that identifies and provides a persistent link to information on the Internet

An example of a reference to a journal article that appears online and has been assigned a DOI is below.

> Carey, G. (2006). Race—social, biological, or lemonade? *American Psychologist*, *61*(2), 176. doi: 176. 10.1037/0003-066X.61.2.176a

The following information is given for a book: author(s), date, title (italicized), city in which it was published, publisher. Here is an example of a reference to a book:

> Gaulin, S. J. C., & McBurney, D. H. (2004). *Evolutionary psychology* (2nd ed.). Upper Saddle River, NJ: Prentice Hall.

Note that when the book is not published in a major city, you must give the state or country also. Note too that the publisher is identified as briefly as possible; nonessential words such as *Publishing Company* or *Inc.* are eliminated.

Electronic books are now readily available in a variety of formats. Final versions of electronic books require that you include the source location in your citation as in the following reference entry:

> O'Keefe, E. (n.d.) *Egoism & the crisis in Western values*. Retrieved from http://www.onlineoriginals.com/showitem.asp?itemID=135

When the work cited is an article or chapter in a book to which different authors have contributed, the book is considered an edited volume. The following information is given for an article or chapter in an edited volume: author(s), date, title of article or chapter, editor(s), book title (italicized) and article or chapter page numbers, city of publication, publisher. Here is an example of a reference to a chapter in an edited volume:

> Tooby, J., & Cosmides, L. (1992). The psychological foundations of culture. In J. H. Barkow, L. Cosmides, & J. Tooby (Eds.), *The adapted mind: Evolutionary psychology and the generation of culture* (pp. 19–136). New York, NY: Oxford University Press.

Note that the editors' names and initials are listed in forward rather than reverse order.

Like journal articles and books, electronic copies of book chapters are also cited slightly differently than their print sources. If it is available, the DOI should be cited at the end of the reference. If it is not available, though, the URL where the book can be located should be included with the citation.

gray literature: scientific literature that falls outside the peer review process

Some scientific literature published on the Internet falls outside the peer review process, yet is valuable scholarly work. This literature is called gray literature, and citing it requires attention to two relevant guidelines:

1. You should direct readers to a URL as close to the cited information as possible (rather than to a home page or menu page).
2. If the content that you are citing is likely to be changed or updated, give the date that the information was retrieved. The date isn't important in content that is unlikely to change, like a book or journal article, but it is highly relevant in citing some gray literature. An example of a citation to an article on a pharmaceutical company's Web site (which is gray literature) follows:

GlaxoSmithKline. (1997). *Welcome to depression.* Retrieved August 19, 2010, from http://www.depression.com/

These four forms are the most common types of references, but they are by no means all of them. Refer to the *Publication Manual of the American Psychological Association* (2010) (Chapter 7) for other examples.

Steps in the Publication Process

In this section, we describe the steps that a paper goes through in becoming an article in a typical journal. Our discussion provides an overview of the publication process, rather than a detailed description. Refer to the APA *Publication Manual* for details.

Before you begin writing a manuscript for publication, you should decide to which journal you are going to submit your paper. You should make sure that your manuscript fits the mission and length of the journal that you are considering. Each journal may have slightly different requirements for style, length, and so forth that you should consider. Consult a recent issue of the journal for such information, or visit the journal's Web site.

Deciding which journal to submit a paper to is not always an easy task. You want your paper to appear in a journal with wide circulation. You also want it to appear in a journal that is read by specialists in the area that the paper concerns. Other considerations include prestige of the journal and likelihood of acceptance. As you might expect, these last two considerations generally involve a trade-off. Two guidelines are helpful. First, choose a journal that has published other articles on the same topic. Second, choose the journal that you have cited most frequently in your reference list.

Before you submit your manuscript, consult the journal's Web site (usually this information is located in a recent issue of the journal) to double-check the requirements for submission. Prepare a cover letter addressed to the editor, giving the title of your paper and some details about it, such as the number of pages, tables, and figures. Tell the editor whether it has been presented at a meeting, and whether portions of the information have been published elsewhere. Even though many journals now require online submission, give your return address, your telephone number, and your e-mail address in your cover letter, so that the editor can get in touch with you if needed.

On receiving the manuscript, the editor reads it for an initial screening and sends it out for review, usually to two other people in the field. After the reviews are received, the editor decides either to accept the paper as is (rarely), to accept it pending certain revisions, to reject it with the suggestion that it be resubmitted with certain revisions, or to reject it outright. It would be nice if every paper was accepted right away, but that is generally not the case (Tamashiro, 2003). The editor's letter gives an overall evaluation of the paper, interprets the reviewers' comments, and suggests how you should proceed. These rejection letters can be helpful in improving your final manuscript. If you are going to revise the paper, you should study the comments of each reviewer. You need not accept each suggestion, but you must give a good reason if you do not. If a reviewer is completely off base, you may say so—carefully. In extreme cases, an editor will get additional reviews if you can show that the reviewer did not do a competent job. Generally, however, papers are much improved as a result of the review process.

After you have revised the paper, submit the new copy with a new cover letter that tells how you have accounted for the reviewers' comments. At this point, the editor usually makes a final decision to accept or reject. If accepted, you can often wait a considerable amount of time while the article is scheduled into one of the journal's upcoming issues. This period is sometimes referred to as *in press*. The exact sequence of events varies from journal to journal, but the following is typical. You receive the copyedited version of your manuscript, with editorial changes in grammar, spelling, and style, but not in substantive matters. Any corrections you want to incorporate into the manuscript should be made at this point. After the copyedited manuscript is returned to the editor and set in type, you receive page proofs, which show how your paper will actually look in the journal, along with your original manuscript. Read the page proofs carefully for typographical errors and compare them with your manuscript. Also check the beginning and end of each page to see that nothing is out of order or lost. Shortly after you return the page proofs, your paper appears in the journal. The whole process may take a year or more. The editor usually requires somewhere between one and three months for the initial review process; after final acceptance, the publication delay may be another nine months. Many journals print a note indicating when a paper was accepted for publication. You can consult recent issues to estimate when your article will appear.

405 Langley Hall
University of Pittsburgh
Pittsburgh, PA 15260
Phone: 412 555 3257
Fax: 412 555 3258
Email: ST4529@vms.cis.pitt.edu

17 May 2012

Professor Amy Butler, Editor
Langley Hall Journal of Psychology
420 Langley Hall
University of Pittsburgh
Pittsburgh, PA 15260

Dear Professor Butler:

The enclosed manuscript, "The effect of capsaicin on burn in tasters and nontasters of PTC," is submitted for publication in the *Langley Hall Journal of Psychology*. The manuscript contains 10 pages, one table, and one figure.

The data described in the manuscript have been presented at the 2011 Undergraduate Research Fair at the University of Pittsburgh, but they have not been previously published or submitted for publication.

The participants were treated in accordance with the ethical principles of the American Psychological Association and the regulations governing treatment of human research participants of the University of Pittsburgh.

Thank you for your consideration of this manuscript.

Sincerely,
Joanna M. Goodrich

Running head: CAPSAICIN BURN   1

The Effect of Capsaicin on Burn in

Tasters and Nontasters of PTC

Joanna M. Goodrich

University of Pittsburgh

Author Note

Joanna M. Goodrich, Department of Psychology, University of Pittsburgh.

Joanna M. Goodrich is now at the Neuroscience Department, Yale University, New Haven, Connecticut.

I thank Prof. Carey Ryan for statistical and editorial advice, Prof. Philippa Benson for helpful comments, and Prof. Donald H. McBurney for making up the data, which are entirely fake, as well as inventing me.

If I did exist, and the paper was real, correspondence should be addressed to Joanna M. Goodrich, Department of Neuroscience, 33 Cedar Street, Yale University, New Haven, Connecticut 06510. E-mail: ST4529@yale.edu

Number every page (8.03).

Running head will go at top of each page in journal but the words "Running head" only appear on the first page. Do not exceed 50 characters (8.03).

Position title in upper half of the page (2.01).

Title may be up to 10–12 words (2.01).

Use the form of your name you will be comfortable with for your entire career.

The institution where research was conducted.

The four parts of an author note (2.03).

Do not indent abstract. Type it in a single paragraph (2.04).

Write out word to be abbreviated first time and put abbreviation in parentheses (4.23).

Abbreviate scientific measurement (4.27).

Set word processor for a 6½ inch line; margins should be 1 inch.

Length of abstract should not exceed the word limit of the journal, usually between 150–250 words (2.04).

Cite the source of ideas.

CAPSAICIN BURN   2

Abstract

Tasters and nontasters of phenylthiocarbamide (PTC) rated the burn caused by either 100 or 300 ppm capsaicin, the active ingredient in chili peppers, applied to the tongue. Tasters rated the burn higher than nontasters, and 300 ppm was rated higher than 100 ppm. Contrary to prediction, the effect of concentration was greater for nontasters than tasters. Stevens's theory of psychophysical scaling (1975) suggests that the failure to find greater reactivity to capsaicin in tasters may have resulted from the high concentrations tested, and the use of a limited rating scale.

Keywords: capsaicin, PTC, taste

CAPSAICIN BURN   3

Capsaicin Burn in Tasters and Nontasters of PTC

This study concerns the sources of individual differences in response to capsaicin, the chemical that gives chili peppers their characteristic burning quality. Although millions of people throughout the world consume foods containing capsaicin daily, individuals differ widely in their reaction to it. One source of the difference appears to be experience with chili peppers; Rozin (1990) has shown that the taste for capsaicin is acquired by repeated exposure.

Another source of the differences may be a person's status as a taster or nontaster of phenylthiocarbamide (PTC). The response to PTC differs greatly; some people find it intensely bitter whereas others can barely taste it (Blakeslee, 1932). Thresholds for PTC are strongly bimodal and approximately 30% of the population are nontasters. Taster status is highly stable within an individual, and its genetic basis is well understood. Tasters of PTC rate the burn of capsaicin greater than do nontasters (Karrer & Bartoshuk, 1991).

Previous studies of the relation between PTC status and capsaicin burn have not considered the effect of PTC status on the burn of different concentrations of capsaicin. It is possible that the effect of PTC status may depend on concentration of capsaicin. In particular, capsaicin may not simply cause a greater burn in tasters than nontasters, but stronger concentrations may cause an increasingly greater burn in tasters than nontasters. In other words, tasters may not simply be more sensitive to capsaicin, they may react more to increasing concentrations of it.

The present study examined the amount of burn caused by two concentrations of capsaicin for tasters and nontasters of PTC. I expected to find that (a) a stronger concentration of capsaicin would burn more than a weaker concentration, (b) tasters would rate the burn of capsaicin stronger than nontasters, and (c) the effect of concentration of capsaicin on burn would be greater in tasters than nontasters.

Type the complete title at the beginning of the introduction. The introduction, which opens the main body of the paper, is not labeled (2.05).

Indent five spaces for every paragraph except the abstract, block quotes, titles and headings, table titles, and figure captions (8.03).

Period goes outside parentheses, unless entire sentence is in parentheses.

Do not leave extra lines between paragraphs (8.03).

Use ampersand (&) when reference is within parentheses (6.12).

For seriation see 3.04.

Center a main heading and use initial capitals, in bold (3.03).

Spell numbers that begin sentences.

Use numerals for 10 and above, except to begin sentence (see 4.31–4.38).

A second level of heading is typed in bold, flush left, and upper- and lower-case letters are used (3.03).

Do not abbreviate "participants", "subject", or "experimenter" (4.25).

Note spacing.

First person permits use of active voice and greater clarity (3.18).

Italics for scale anchors (4.21).

CAPSAICIN BURN   4

Method

Participants

Sixty introductory psychology students (32 women and 28 men, mean age = 20.3 years) participated in the experiment to meet a course requirement. Recruitment material requested people who did not find the taste of chili peppers, Tabasco™ sauce, Buffalo wings, and similar foods aversive.

Materials

Capsaicin (Sigma, 98%) was dissolved in alcohol to make a stock solution of 1000 ppm. This stock was further diluted in alcohol to either 100 ppm or 300 ppm. Solutions were stored at −10°C. Twenty-five µl of solution was pipetted onto 1.27 cm diameter filter paper disks and allowed to dry.

PTC stimuli were prepared by dipping the same type of filter paper disks into a saturated solution of PTC and allowing them to dry.

Design

Participants rated the burn of either 100 ppm or 300 ppm capsaicin and were either tasters or nontasters of PTC, yielding a 2 (levels of capsaicin concentration) $\times$ 2 (taster vs. nontaster) between subjects design. Participants were randomly assigned to capsaicin concentration.

Procedure

All participants were run individually. They tasted the PTC first because I did not want any residual burn from the capsaicin to mask the taste of PTC. They were asked to rate the bitterness of the PTC on a scale of 0 (*no taste*) to 9 (*the most bitter taste imaginable*) on an index card and place it in an envelope. Then they rinsed their mouths with water ad libitum. I left the room while they rated the PTC so that I would be blind to their PTC taster status.

CAPSAICIN BURN   5

Next, with a pair of forceps I placed the filter paper containing capsaicin
on the participant's outstretched tongue. The participant held the filter paper in
the mouth. At the end of one minute, signaled by a computer, the participant
wrote the rating of the burn on a file card and turned it over. Participants rated the
burn caused by capsaicin on the same scale they used for PTC. I removed the filter
paper and immediately replaced it with another. This procedure continued for 15
minutes, resulting in 15 ratings of capsaicin for each participant. I debriefed the
participants, answered any questions, and thanked them for their participation.

Results

The distribution of PTC ratings is shown in Figure 1. The data are strongly
bimodal. Following Bartoshuk, Duffy, and Miller (1994), participants who rated
the PTC 0, 1, or 2 were categorized as nontasters. There were 23 nontasters, 11
men and 12 women.

The mean rating of burn over the 15 minutes was computed for each
participant. Table 1 shows the ratings of capsaicin as a function of concentration
and taster status. A 2×2, between-subjects analysis of variance showed that the
following effects were significant at the .05 level or greater: Three hundred ppm
capsaicin was rated stronger than 100 ppm, $F(1, 56) = 7.12$ $p = .01$. Tasters
rated capsaicin stronger than did nontaster, $F(1, 56) = 7.76$, $p = .01$. The effect
of capsaicin concentration was less for tasters than nontasters, indicating an
interaction, $F(1, 56) = 4.10$, $p = .05$.

Discussion

The proportion of PTC tasters found in this study is consistent with
previous studies (e.g., Bartoshuk et al., 1994; Wooding et al., 2006). Also
consistent with previous research (Karrer & Bartoshuk, 1991) is the finding that
tasters rated capsaicin higher than nontasters.

Use words for numbers 0–9, with certain exceptions (see 4.31–4.34).

Do not begin a new page when a heading occurs within the main body of the paper (8.03).

List all authors the first time they are cited if there are five or fewer. List only the first, followed by "et al." if there are six or more (6.12).

Note spacing.

Give exact p value (4.44).

See 4.44 for how to present statistics.

Results are in past tense.

Compare results to previous studies.

CAPSAICIN BURN   6

Contrary to my hypothesis, however, the effect of capsaicin concentration on
burn was less in tasters than in nontasters.

    Two possible reasons for such a ceiling effect interaction suggest
themselves. The first concerns the scale. Because the tasters' ratings of the lower
concentration were so high, the closed-ended scale effectively limited the
participants' ability to rate the stronger concentrations much higher. Stevens
(1975) argues that open-ended scales give more valid measures of sensory
magnitude than closed-ended scales. Nevertheless, I chose the closed-ended scale
for this study because I believed it would be easier for participants to use than
Stevens's scale.

    The second possible reason for the ceiling effect is saturation of the burn
sensation. By definition, every sensory system has a maximum response beyond
which it cannot increase. It is possible that the concentrations I chose caused
close to the maximum possible burn. In fact, some participants spontaneously
reported that they had never tasted any chili products as hot as the stimuli they
experienced in this experiment. A wider range of stimuli, including much weaker
concentrations, might reveal two kinds of interactions: the synergistic one
originally predicted for lower concentrations, and a ceiling effect for stronger
concentrations.

    Future research might profitably compare the effect of concentration on
the burn comparing closed-ended scales with Stevens's open-ended scale, using
a wider range of concentrations.

Use hyphens with compound adjectives only if meaning is unclear without.

Capitalize first word after a colon only if it starts a new sentence, except in a title.

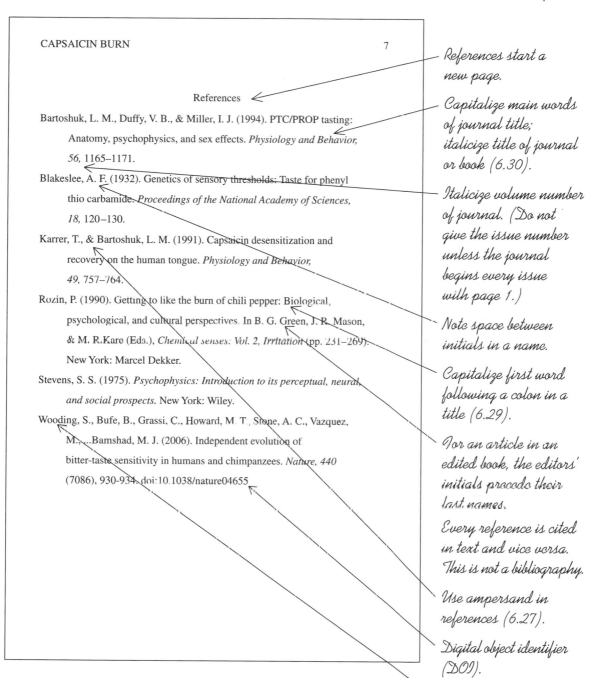

CAPSAICIN BURN   7

References

Bartoshuk, L. M., Duffy, V. B., & Miller, I. J. (1994). PTC/PROP tasting:

Anatomy, psychophysics, and sex effects. *Physiology and Behavior,*

56, 1165–1171.

Blakeslee, A. F. (1932). Genetics of sensory thresholds: Taste for phenyl

thio carbamide. *Proceedings of the National Academy of Sciences,*

18, 120–130.

Karrer, T., & Bartoshuk, L. M. (1991). Capsaicin desensitization and

recovery on the human tongue. *Physiology and Behavior,*

49, 757–764.

Rozin, P. (1990). Getting to like the burn of chili pepper: Biological,

psychological, and cultural perspectives. In B. G. Green, J. R. Mason,

& M. R. Kare (Eds.), *Chemical senses: Vol. 2, Irritation* (pp. 231–269).

New York: Marcel Dekker.

Stevens, S. S. (1975). *Psychophysics: Introduction to its perceptual, neural,*

and social prospects. New York: Wiley.

Wooding, S., Bufe, B., Grassi, C., Howard, M. T., Stone, A. C., Vazquez,

M., ...Bamshad, M. J. (2006). Independent evolution of

bitter-taste sensitivity in humans and chimpanzees. *Nature, 440*

(7086), 930-934. doi:10.1038/nature04655

References start a new page.

Capitalize main words of journal title; italicize title of journal or book (6.30).

Italicize volume number of journal. (Do not give the issue number unless the journal begins every issue with page 1.)

Note space between initials in a name.

Capitalize first word following a colon in a title (6.29).

For an article in an edited book, the editors' initials precede their last names.

Every reference is cited in text and vice versa. This is not a bibliography.

Use ampersand in references (6.27).

Digital object identifier (DOI).

More than seven authors requires ellipses (7.01).

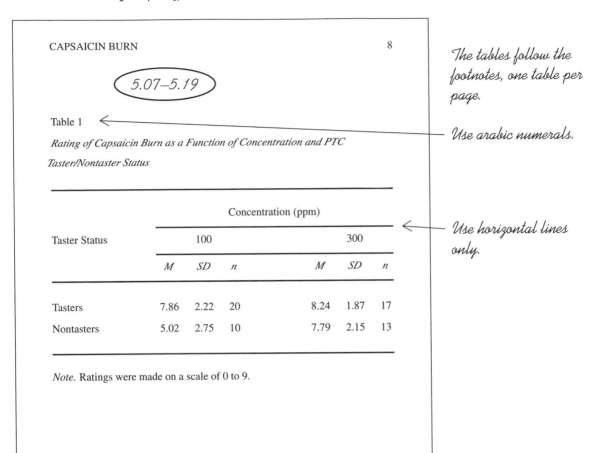

CAPSAICIN BURN   8

5.07–5.19

Table 1

Rating of Capsaicin Burn as a Function of Concentration and PTC

Taster/Nontaster Status

	Concentration (ppm)					
	100			300		
Taster Status	*M*	*SD*	*n*	*M*	*SD*	*n*
Tasters	7.86	2.22	20	8.24	1.87	17
Nontasters	5.02	2.75	10	7.79	2.15	13

Note. Ratings were made on a scale of 0 to 9.

The tables follow the footnotes, one table per page.

Use arabic numerals.

Use horizontal lines only.

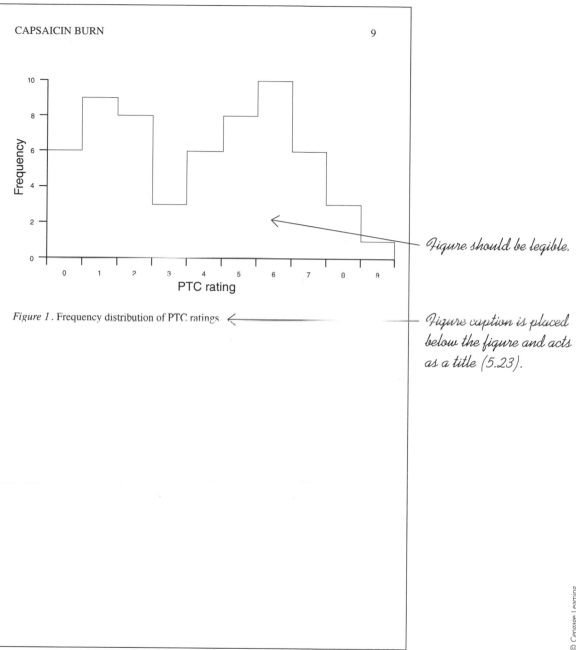

CAPSAICIN BURN   9

Figure 1. Frequency distribution of PTC ratings ←

Figure should be legible.

Figure caption is placed below the figure and acts as a title (5.23).

Oral Presentations

The oral presentation is an important means of scientific communication. Numerous regional, national, and international meetings are held each year in which the primary formal means of communication is the oral presentation of short research papers. For the student, presenting a paper toward the end of a course in experimental psychology is an excellent learning experience. Many regional student psychology conferences are also held, at which papers are presented.

Although the parts of an oral presentation are the same as for a research report, simply reading the manuscript of a paper prepared for publication is a mistake. The oral format requires several changes. First, the paper must be shorter because in the 10 or 15 minutes that are usually allotted, presenting all the material in a typical paper is physically impossible. Second, simplify the material so the audience can digest the ideas as they are presented. Third, listening to written material read aloud tends to be boring. If you choose to write out your talk so you feel prepared, focus on how it will sound when spoken. Then, leave the written version at home or in your pocket, and speak from an outline.

Organize your talk according to the main parts of a paper: introduction, method, results, and discussion. Make only one or two points in each section of the talk. Your introduction should set the stage in a few sentences. The method section should stick to the essential elements of design, assuming that your audience is generally familiar with how such research is done. Most of your time should be spent on the results. Be sure to emphasize the main findings. Also, keep the discussion section brief, simply pointing out some of the implications of the research. Always summarize your results at the end.

Visual aids are a key element of any oral presentation. Ordinarily, visual aids are slides or overhead transparencies. In practice, it is surprising how often visual aids are the weakest part of a presentation. When you use slides (either conventional or Microsoft PowerPoint™), preview them to make sure they will be legible under the conditions that are typical of a convention. Also, see that conventional slides are not placed upside down in the projector. Complicated tables are not as useful when viewed on a slide because they are difficult to read. If you are talking to a small group, you may choose to distribute a handout that describes the results.

Practice the talk in front of sympathetic peers. This technique helps you to know if you are on the right track, and have the timing right. It also allows you to modify rough spots. An additional benefit is having most of the potential questions asked first by your friends instead of by strangers, who may be less forgiving.

Poster Presentations

Posters have become a popular way of presenting research at meetings. They present the same abbreviated material as a talk, but in a static graphic format. The advantages are that people can browse among many posters, spending time on the ones that interest them, and can discuss the material in as much depth as desired with the author of the poster. Poster sessions are also ideally suited to class projects.

Typically at scientific meetings, a vertical surface of 3 by 6 feet or 4 by 8 feet will be available for the presentation. You bring the poster and assemble it on the board with tacks. Increasingly, authors are creating posters with graphics software, such as PowerPoint™. A major advantage of this is that the entire poster may be printed on a single sheet of paper, which is easily set up (see Figures 4.1 and 4.2). If a single printed sheet is not possible, a poster can still be constructed using graphics software by using separate, smaller sheets of paper. Place a strip of paper across the top of the board with the title and the author's name in letters at least an inch high. Position the abstract of the paper in the upper left corner on a single sheet of paper. Place the rest of the material in columns so that people can read from top to bottom of one column, then move from left to right, without having to move back and forth. Your figures should also help to tell your research story, so make sure that they are appropriately ordered. Because people have to be able to make sense of your poster, it is important that it be well organized. Use a large type font, usually 30 to 45 point, and make all tables and figures about 8 by 10 inches. Remember that a poster should contain much less text than a journal article and keep in mind that your poster should be readable from a distance of several feet. Place copies of the paper or of the abstract in a pocket on the board so that interested people can take one with them.

During the poster session, stand near the poster to answer questions and discuss the material with people who stop by. Many people who have

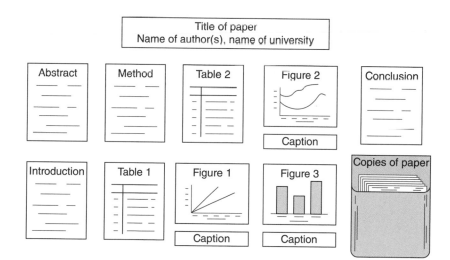

FIGURE **4.1** Typical Layout of a Poster Presentation
© Cengage Learning

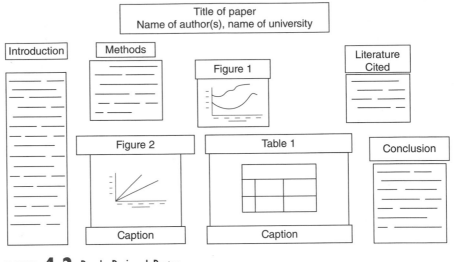

FIGURE **4.2** Poorly Designed Poster

© Cengage Learning

presented posters at meetings find they prefer the personal give-and-take of the poster format to the usual oral presentation. Additional information about preparing a poster presentation can be found in Appendix C of Langston's (2010) laboratory manual.

NUTS & BOLTS

Checklist for Manuscripts in APA Style

The following checklist gives general guidelines. Not all items apply to all papers, and there are some exceptions. The checklist is intended to call attention to things you should watch for. Read the chapter in the text and use the sample paper as a model.

General:
- ☐ Paper is typed, or printed by a computer.
- ☐ Everything is double spaced.
- ☐ Allow at least 1-inch margins on both sides, top and bottom.
- ☐ Don't right justify. Text is aligned on the left, but not the right.
- ☐ Type is 12-point serif font, such as Times New Roman.

Abstract:
- ☐ Includes aspects of all parts of paper: Introduction, Method, Results, and Discussion.
- ☐ Is self-contained.
- ☐ Reader can tell from abstract alone what paper is about and decide whether to read rest of paper.
- ☐ Is between 150 and 250 words.

Introduction:
- ☐ States the problem the paper addresses.
- ☐ Puts the problem in theoretical context.
- ☐ Cites earlier work on the problem.

(continues)

NUTS & BOLTS *(continued)*

❑ States what the study will contribute to understanding the problem.
❑ States the hypotheses of the study.

Method General:
❑ Another person could replicate your study based only on a reading of your method section.
❑ A reader could evaluate your study well enough to tell whether your conclusions are valid.
❑ Everything is in the past tense.
❑ Covers the following: participants, materials, design, procedure. (Label the paragraphs for the various subsections.)

Participants:
❑ Describes the participants and their characteristics.
❑ Tells how the participants were selected.
❑ States what inducements were offered for participation.
❑ Lists species, strain, supplier, age, and other specifics of nonhuman subjects.

Materials:
❑ Lists equipment, computer programs, questionnaires used.
❑ If apparatus is specialized, refers to articles that describe it.
❑ Describes custom equipment, programs, and the like.

Design:
❑ This subsection appears only in a report of an experiment, not in a survey, observational study, or the like.
❑ Describes the logic of the experiment.
❑ Lists variables and levels of independent variables.

Procedure:
❑ Describes steps in carrying out design. (Procedure subsection may be incorporated into design.)
❑ Lists methods of control, such as randomization or counterbalancing.
❑ Summarizes or reproduces verbatim any specialized instructions to participants, such as how to do magnitude estimation.

Results General:
❑ Uses only past tense.

How the Data Were Handled:
❑ Describes any transformations made on the data.
❑ Explains any data that were eliminated from analysis.

What Was Found:
❑ States principal findings clearly.
❑ Avoids description of individual subjects or individual data points.
❑ Refers reader to table or figure, if applicable.
❑ Doesn't repeat detailed information found in table or figure.

(continues)

NUTS & BOLTS *(continued)*

Statistics:
- ❑ Doesn't let description of statistics substitute for a description of results.
- ❑ Names any statistic used, and gives statistical significance of result (value of statistic, degrees of freedom, significance level).
- ❑ Generally avoids describing trends or data points that are not statistically significant.

Discussion:
- ❑ Clearly states whether hypotheses were supported.
- ❑ Interprets results.
- ❑ Avoids introducing further results, except incidental to comparison with other published results.
- ❑ Relates results to those of others.
- ❑ Cites other work discussed.
- ❑ Relates results to theory.
- ❑ Discusses limitations and weaknesses of results, when appropriate.
- ❑ Avoids ad hoc explanations of difficulties.
- ❑ Discusses implications for further research.
- ❑ Suggests applications of findings, when appropriate.
- ❑ Avoids undue speculation.
- ❑ States conclusions in the present tense.

References:
- ❑ Starts on a new page.
- ❑ Includes every citation in text, and vice versa.
- ❑ Does not include any references not cited in the text of the paper.
- ❑ Are in alphabetical order.
- ❑ Uses a hanging indent of five spaces.

Figures:
- ❑ Reflects awareness that the purpose of a figure is to communicate information. The reader will be able to understand clearly the information you are trying to convey.
- ❑ Professionally computer drawn, including axes, histograms, and line graphs.
- ❑ Places only one figure per page. Figure captions are below figures on the same page.
- ❑ Uses black pencil or ink only. (Do not use color because journals generally do not reproduce color graphics.)

Size of Letters and Symbols:
- ❑ Uses letters and symbols large enough to be legible when the figure is reduced in size. (A good test is to see if you can read your graph from about 15 feet away.)

Axes and Their Labels:
- ❑ Generally, size graphs about two-thirds as high as they are wide.
- ❑ Exceptions include scattergrams, which are usually square.
- ❑ Ordinarily, has the origin (where the *x* and *y* axes cross) at zero. If this would result in excessive white space, indicate a nonzero origin with a break. The origin of the *y*-axis must be zero for a cumulative frequency distribution, or the

(continues)

NUTS & BOLTS *(continued)*

slope will be meaningless. Labels both axes with the appropriate variables. (Do not label them *x* and *y*.)

❑ Indicates units.

❑ Uses uniform increments.

Plotting Data Points:

❑ Locates data points exactly where they belong. You may offset them slightly if they would otherwise overlap completely. On a scattergram, when two or more data points fall on a given spot, print that number instead of the usual symbol.

❑ Plots data points that fall at zero.

Different Symbols, Legends:

❑ Uses different symbols for data points that do not belong together and are not connected by the same line.

❑ Labels two or more types of symbols in a figure or defines them in a legend. The legend appears somewhere in the white space inside the figure.

Connecting Data Points:

❑ Connects all data points using straight lines only, unless they represent a theoretical function (such as linear regression). Does not draw curved lines unless they represent theoretical equations that you have computed.

Drawing Theoretical Lines:

❑ Does not treat the dots used to locate theoretical lines as data points. (These dots are not shown in publications.)

❑ Does not have lines that extend past data points. Exception: Frequency polygons and cumulative frequency polygons must start at zero.

Captions:

❑ Provides a descriptive caption below each figure (describes, doesn't interpret). The caption should explain everything in the figure (so the reader does not need to turn to the text of the paper), but contain no data.

Reporting Statistics in the Text of a Paper

In writing your results, you should be careful to focus on describing the data, not the statistics. Nevertheless, you need to report certain information about the statistical tests you performed, particularly the significance level of effects you found. State that the effect of variable X was significant, followed by the abbreviated name of the statistic, the number of degrees of freedom in parentheses, the value of the statistic, and the probability—for example, $F(1, 117) = 4.71$, $p = .03$. Following is an example:

> The short hallway had the greatest proportion of social behavior, 58.0%; the long, interrupted hallway had the next most, 56.8%; and the long hallway had the least, 43.7%. Analysis of variance showed that the effect of hallway was significant: $F(2, 177) = 4.32$, $p = .03$.

Other examples are given in the sample paper reproduced in this chapter.

Summary

1. Scientific communication takes place in many ways, including archival publication in scholarly journals and informal communication among groups of scientists, known as invisible colleges.
2. Most psychology journals follow the *Publication Manual of the American Psychological Association*, which should be consulted for detailed matters of style.
3. Scientific writing can be considered one form of argumentation, which is the presentation of a set of reasons in support of a thesis, or proposition.
4. A scientific report requires the same attention to good writing as does any other form of written persuasion. Key concepts are clarity, brevity, and felicity.
5. Authors should be careful to avoid sexism and ethnic bias.
6. The parts of a paper are (1) title, (2) authors and their affiliations, (3) abstract, (4) introduction, (5) method, (6) results, (7) discussion, (8) references, (9) author notes, (10) footnotes, (11) tables, and (12) figures with captions.
7. The title should convey the main idea of the paper in a few words.
8. The authors of your paper are listed in the order of the importance of their contributions.
9. The abstract is a brief summary of the paper and includes elements from the introduction, method, results, and discussion sections.
10. The introduction states the general problem the paper deals with, discusses the relevant literature, and states what the paper will contribute to the understanding of the problem.
11. The method section tells what you did in the experiment in such a way that another person can evaluate the validity of the conclusions of the study and can repeat it in all essentials. The method section describes the participants, materials, design, and procedure.
12. The results section describes the results and their statistical analysis. Graphs and tables are described here.
13. The discussion section interprets the results and relates them to the literature. It states the contributions that the study makes to the understanding of the problem posed in the introduction, and it deals with any weakness in the data or any qualifications of the conclusions.
14. Documentation is used in a paper to give credit to the work of other authors, to show the larger framework in which your ideas belong, and to point the reader to sources of further information. Avoid plagiarism.
15. References are cited in the text by author name and date of publication.

16. The reference list contains an entry for each work cited in the text, and no others.

17. The steps in the publication process include choosing the journal, submitting the final manuscript along with a cover letter, revising the paper to account for reviewers' comments, resubmitting the paper, reviewing the copyedited manuscript, and reading the page proofs.

18. Oral presentations include most of the elements of the written paper in a simplified format. Practicing the talk before a sympathetic audience, preparing good visual aids, and speaking from an outline rather than reading the paper directly are keys to a good presentation.

19. Poster presentations are a popular form of communicating results at scientific meetings. The various parts of the paper are reported succinctly and placed on a vertical surface in such a way that they can be read from a distance of several feet. The author remains near the poster to discuss the results with passersby.

Suggestions for Further Reading

AMERICAN PSYCHOLOGICAL ASSOCIATION. (2010). *Publication manual of the American Psychological Association* (6th ed.). Washington, DC: Author. This publication is an indispensable guide for anyone writing in the field of psychology.

BARRASS, R. (2003). *Scientists must write: A guide to better writing for scientists, engineers, and students* (2nd ed.). London: Chapman & Hall/New York: Wiley. This book covers all aspects of scientific writing.

ROSNOW, R. L., & ROSNOW, M. (2006). *Writing papers in psychology* (7th ed.). Belmont, CA: Wadsworth. This book provides concise coverage of all aspects of writing in psychology.

STERNBERG, R. (1992, September). How to win acceptances by psychology journals: 21 tips for better writing. *APS Observer, 5*(5), 12–18. This is an excellent brief overview of writing a psychology paper.

STERNBERG, R. (2003). *The psychologist's companion: A guide to scientific writing for students and researchers* (4th ed.). New York: Cambridge University Press. This book specifically covers psychology papers and APA style.

STRUNK, W., Jr., & WHITE, E. B. (2000). *The elements of style: With index* (4th ed.). Englewood Cliffs, NJ: Prentice-Hall. This is a basic writing guide.

A CASE IN POINT

On the following pages is a manuscript of an entirely fictitious paper. It contains many errors of style, grammar, and spelling, as well as some problems of design. Correct the paper, noting the design problems.

Behavior Modification: An Alternative to Drug
Therapy in Treating Hyperactive Children

ABSTRACT

The purpose of this study is to determine whether application
of behavior modification methods can be an effective and safe
alternative to amphetamine therapy in the treatment of hyperactive
school children. Sixty elementary age school children who were
identified as hyperactive were randomly assigned to one of three
treatment groups. It was concluded that additional research is needed
to determine the generalize ability of the findings to larger groups
and to non-special education classes.

In recent years, the use of amphetamines in treating hperactive
children, has caused much controversy and concern. According to
some researchers, an estimated 400,000 hyperactive school children
are presently being treated with these drugs. Much of the public's
concern has to do with the way in which children are diagnosed.
Many children, for example, are being treated with amphetamines
solely on the recommendations of school authoritys. Despite the
fact that many teachers mistake the normal restlessness of childhood
for hyperkinesis. Anohter cause for concern stems from a lack of
follow-up studies on the long-term affects of amphetamines.

As an alternative to drug therapy, researchers have begun to
focus on behavior modification techniques that are believed to be
more safer and more effective over time (Strong, 1974). Strong (1974)
conducted a two-year study with an autistic boy and found thast
positive reinforcement was significantly more effective than drug
therapy in reducing facial grimacing. In another study, this same
researcher found token reinforcement to be more effective then
medication in increasing adaptive behavior in retarded women.

Behavior modification techniques have also been studied in
classroom settings. Smith (1969), for example, was able to reduce ina
pproriate classroom behavior of a ten-year old hyperactive girl by

using these techniques. In another study, Nixon (1969) tested the effects of behavior modification in increasing the "on-task performance" of 24 boys who had been diagnosed as hyperactive by there teachers. In the Nixon (1969) study, their was four treatment groups which consisted of various reinforcement techniques and control. Results of a one-way analysis of variance indicated no significant differences between the groups. Although it was reported that some of the children in each gorup made great improvement in staying on task in learning situations. The Nixon study, however, contained possible sources of error: (1) treatment groups only contained 6 subjects each; (2) there were only 8 treatment sessions; (3) no instruments were used to evaluate children's performance; and (4) the children knew they were participating in a study.

Widespread use of amphetamines in treating hyperactive children may be a dangerous practice. Moreover, behavior modification techniques have shown to be just as effective in reducing hperactive behavior in children in certain settings.

The sample group for this study will be selected from the population of North Side Educational Center for behaviorally disturbed, elementary-age children. Those children who were diagnosed as "hyperactive" or "hyperkinetic" by the school's psychologist were cosnidered the population. The stratified random sampling method is to be used to insure that children ages 6 through 12 were represented in the study.

METHOD

Subjects will be assigned to three treatment groups. Each group will be pre-tested using the Swan Maze Test as the pre-test instrument and the Winsand Child Observation System as teh post-test instrument. After they were classified by age, subjects will be randomly assigned to one of three treatment groups. During the semester, group 1 received amphetamine therapy, group 2 received behavior modification techniques, and group 3 received regular classroom instruction, thus serving as a control group. Each of the treatments took place in the regular classroom setting. The pre-test means revealed that the three groups were essentially equal at the beginning of the study (see figure 1). As figure 1 shows, levels of hyperactivity were extremely high in all three groups. At the end of the six month treatment period, all subjects were administered the Swan Maze Test. A one-way analysis of variance was used, to compare the post-test means of the three groups.

RESULTS

It was found that the groups differed significantly ($F = 66.15$, $df = 2/57$, $p < .05$). At t-test comparison of the group means revealed that while the behavior modification and amphetamine therapy groups did not differ significantly, both treatment groups did differ significantly from the control group (See Figure 1). The control group maintained essentially the same level of hyperactivity during the treatment period (16.0 versus 15.7).

Insert Figure 1 about here

DISCUSSION

The level of hyperactivity was reduced in both experimental groups from 15.8 to 5.9 and from 15.4 to 5.5 (See Table 1). Based on these results, it was concluded that behavior modification techniques and amphetamines treatment was equally effective in reducing hyperactivity in elementary-aged children.

Since this study utilized classroom groups of size 15, and teachers who had prior experience in handling behaviorally disturbed children, results cnanot be generalized to regular classroom situations. However, in vies of the results, it appears that research investigating the feasibility of using behavior modification techniques with larger groups of hyperactive children and with regular elementary teachers, is warranted. If regular teaachers could be trained to recognize and modify some of the behavioral symptoms of hyperactivity, perhaps the widespread use of amphetamine drugs with these children could be minimized.

REFERENCES

Smith, Judy L. (1972). *The use of ritalin for treatment of minimal brain dysfunction and hyperkinesis in children,* Baltimore: Simpson Publishers.

Ladd, E.G. (1971). "Pills for classroom peace?" *Education Digest,* 36, 1-4.

Nixon, S. B. (1965). Increasing the frequency of attending responses in hyperactive distractable youngsters by use of operant and modeling procedures, *Dissertation Abstracts,* 26, 6517.

Woody, R. (1969). *Behavior Problem Children in the Schools.* New YOrk: Appleton-Century-Crofts.

Figure 1. Means and standard Deviations for the Behavior Modification, Amphetamine Therapy, and Control groups on the Pre- and post-test measures.

Pre-Test
  Mean
   SD
Post-Test
  Mean

----

*n = 15

Reading Between the Lines

4.1 The Authoritarian Personality

After World War II, a group of researchers (Adorno, Frenkel-Brunswik, Levinson, & Sanford, 1950) were concerned to find the causes of anti-Semitism and German compliance with Hitler's policies. The researchers hypothesized that a personality type existed that lent itself to authoritarianism, antidemocratic beliefs, and racism. Using specially developed questionnaires, they gave tests of *authoritarianism* to a large sample of people. Those receiving especially high or low scores were interviewed about their childhood experiences. People with high scores were more often found to come from families with high status concern and repressive discipline procedures. According to the authors, children in these families learned to repress their faults and to project them onto minority groups. They also repressed feelings of anger and of hatred toward their parents, and these feelings also were projected onto the minority groups. Therefore, the authoritarian people had a tendency to be prejudiced against Jews, blacks, and so forth, and to show discrimination toward them.

Can you think of another explanation of the causes of the correlation between authoritarian attitudes and childhood experiences?

4.2 Life Events and Illness

A large amount of research exists indicating that life events can cause illness. The life events may be obviously stressful, such as the death of a family member, or they may be desirable events, such as marriage, birth of a baby, or a new job. Many illnesses have been studied, including depression and schizophrenia. The studies ask people who have suffered the illness to list the life events they have experienced in a period before the illness. A control group of people who have not experienced the illness are asked the same questions. The results show that people who suffered the illness had experienced more stressful life events than had the control people. What problems of interpretation can you think of in such retrospective research?

Research Methods Laboratory Manual

LAB William Langston (2010) has prepared a laboratory manual that contains many suggestions for research activities that work well with this book. Many chapters in this book contain a section that refers the reader to appropriate sections of the Langston book.

Appendix B of Langston contains a useful discussion of considerations in writing a results section of a research report, focusing on the description of statistics in a research paper.

Appendix C has a helpful discussion of how to prepare poster presentations and oral presentations. Langston gives many useful hints on what to do and what to avoid doing in an oral presentation.

Web-Based Workshops on Research Methods and Statistics

 Wadsworth Publishing Company maintains Web-based workshops on research methods and statistics. These workshops give a different slant on the material in this book.

www.cengage.com/psychology/workshops

For this chapter, see Research Methods Workshops: APA Style.

Exercises

4.1 Reporting References

Put the following information into APA-style references:

a. Herkimer Alphonse Smith wrote a book titled "The Psychology of Passing Exams." It was published by the Fullcourt Press, 3500 Forbes Avenue, Pittsburgh, PA 15213 on the 10th of July, 1993.

b. Jones, A. P., and Riddle, R. A. "Knowns and Unknowns of Family Therapy" (1992). In Handbook of Group and Family Therapy, edited by A. D. Thurman and B. D. Munson (pp. 719–740). Grover Press: Boston.

c. White, Theresa L. and McBurney, Donald H. "Research Methods." (9th ed.) Belmont, California: Cengage, 2012.

d. In his article, Science or Pseudoscience, John Neal provides a brief history of the role that introspection has played in science (1963). It is found on pages 25–42 of the New Age Journal of Psychology, volume 2.

4.2 Tabular versus Textual Presentation of Data

Read the following excerpt:

The mean reaction times reported for the four subjects were 5.7, 5.9, 4.9, and 5.3, respectively, for the low-resolution screen; 4.7, 4.6, 5.0, and 4.9, respectively, for the medium-resolution screen; 3.8, 3.6, 3.5, and 3.0, respectively, for the high-resolution screen; and 2.2, 2.4, 2.3, and 2.1, respectively, for the super-resolution screen.

Required:

e. Present these data in a table.
f. Give the table a brief but explanatory title.

Optional:

g. In a sentence or two, describe the data in the table.

4.3 Clarify Research Titles

Rewrite the following research titles to make them brief yet descriptive:

h. "A Preliminary Investigation into the Effectiveness of the Key Image Method of Vocabulary Development in First-, Second-, and Third-Grade Primary School Children."

i. "A Study Investigating the Relationship Between Anxiety and Low Reading Achievement Scores."

4.4 Identify the Parts of a Research Report

Prepare an outline of the major parts of a research report.

4.5 Evaluate a Research Report

Use the checklist on pages 106–109 to evaluate a published report. (*Suggestion:* Choose a journal such as *Psychological Science* that publishes brief reports.)

CHAPTER FIVE

Variables

PREVIEW

This chapter introduces independent and dependent variables and the different kinds of each. We continue to discuss how variables are measured and the concepts of the reliability and validity of measurements.

In Chapter 1, we discussed how scientists develop laws and theories to explain the phenomena they observe. To do this, we must move from general statements about broad classes of behavior to specific examples of that behavior. The phenomenon we want to study can be any event in all its complexity and variety. When we begin to study the event experimentally, however, we must strip away some of this complexity. Essentially, we take the phenomenon and turn it into one or more variables.

A **variable** is some aspect of a testing condition that can change or take on different characteristics with different conditions. Reducing a phenomenon to variables focuses the researcher's attention on specific events out of the many that may be related to the phenomenon. In the example of pain perception discussed in Chapter 1, the phenomenon of interest was social pain. To study this phenomenon, it was necessary to designate certain classes of events as the variables to be measured and to ignore other events. DeWall and his colleagues (2010) measured students' daily level of hurt feelings, daily level of positive emotions, and so forth. They recorded whether the students had

variable: aspect of a testing condition that can change or take on different characteristics with different conditions

been assigned to the Tylenol® group or to the placebo group. The researchers ignored the students' grades, year in school, and socio-economic situation.

In this chapter, we study some topics related to variables. First, we make several distinctions that are important for psychology among types of variables, and then we discuss the concept of measurement.

Before we discuss types of variables, we must show how the variables of a study relate to the theoretical concepts, as discussed in Chapter 1. Because the variables exist in the world but the theory is an idea, you must make certain assumptions to relate the two. These assumptions are guide ropes that tie a theory to the real world. The variables are tangible: duration, frequency, rate, or intensity of bar presses; items checked on a questionnaire; murders committed; books written. The theoretical concept is intangible: hunger, love, motivation, anxiety. The variables are related to the theoretical concepts by means of the operational definitions used to measure the concepts.

Suppose your theory says that increasing anxiety will increase the affiliation motive. To test this theory, you must take the theoretical concepts of anxiety and affiliation motive and relate them to variables in the real world by means of operational definitions. The theory is an abstract statement. You must bring it down to cases. You can measure anxiety by the Taylor Manifest Anxiety Scale and affiliation by how close people sit to each other in the experiment. These two measures constitute the variables of the study. The scores on the variables of anxiety and distance apart are related to one another as tests of the hypothesis. The relationship between the variables is taken as providing support for or against the particular theory that generated the experiment.

Types of Variables

To understand how variables are used and discussed in psychological research, you must understand several distinctions that are made among types of variables.

Dependent and Independent Variables

The most basic distinction among variables is between dependent variables and independent variables. The **dependent variable** is a measure of the behavior of the subject. The dependent variable is the response that the person or animal makes. This response may be a score on some sort of test, or it may be a behavioral response that can be measured using at least one of several different dimensions (Alberto & Troutman, 2006). For example, suppose that we were interested in whether the presence of music would change the running behavior of a participant named Yolanda. We could measure this behavior in several different ways or dimensions. If we were to measure her running using **frequency**, we would count the number of times that Yolanda went running, or perhaps the number of times that her foot hit the ground, because frequency is the number of times that a particular behavior occurs. If we measured the miles per hour that Yolanda traveled when running, we would actually be measuring the **rate** of her behavior, because rate is the

dependent variable: a measure of the subject's behavior that reflects the independent variable's effects

frequency: the number of times that a behavior is performed

rate: the number of times that a behavior is performed relative to time

duration: the amount of time that a behavior lasts

latency: the amount of time between an instruction and when the behavior is actually performed

topography: the shape or style of the behavior

force: the intensity or strength of a behavior

locus: where the behavior occurs in the environment

independent variable: the condition manipulated or selected by the experimenter to determine its effect on behavior

ratio of frequency to time. If we were to measure the length of time that Yolanda spent running on any given location, we would be measuring the **duration** of her run. Although these three dimensions are perhaps the most obvious ways to measure running, it could also be measured in four other ways. If, for example, we asked Yolanda to run and then measured the time until she started running, we would have measured **latency**. We could also more closely examine the way that Yolanda runs, including the length of her stride, to measure the shape of her behavior, or **topography**. When the intensity with which Yolanda's feet hit the ground is measured, it is called **force**. If we wanted to describe the environment or area where Yolanda's running took place, we would measure the **locus**. We call these types of measurements dependent variables because they depend (we hope) on the value of another variable (the independent variable). In Chapter 1, we said that one goal of science is to find lawful relationships among events in the world. These relationships are sought between the dependent and independent variables.

The **independent variable** is one that is believed to cause some change in the value of the dependent variable. In our example above on running, the independent variable is the music; it is what we hope will affect Yolanda's running behavior. In the example on social pain, from Chapter 1, the independent variable was the pill that the students were given; the researchers hoped that the Tylenol® would reduce the social pain, while the placebo would not (DeWall et al., 2010).

The independent variable is the stimulus of stimulus-response psychology. The term *stimulus*, in its most general use, is equivalent to a cause. As another example, consider frustration in the following example. According to the famous frustration-aggression law, frustration causes aggression. We could test the frustration-aggression law by promising students a reward for completing a certain task, such as coloring. The students would be divided into two groups. We could give one group the reward but give the other group some excuse why they wouldn't get the promised reward, which presumably increases frustration. If the frustrated group rated the task less fun than the nonfrustrated group, then we would confirm the hypothesis. (Both ethical and practical considerations should lead you to give both groups the promised reward after the dependent variable is measured!) Here, the independent variable is whether students were given the promised reward. The dependent variable is their rating of how much fun the task was.

levels: the different values of an independent variable

Every independent variable has at least two values; otherwise, it wouldn't be a variable. These values are commonly called **levels**. In the example on the frustration-aggression law, there were two levels of the independent variable: frustrated and not frustrated. The example on social pain (DeWall et al., 2010) also had two levels to the independent variable: Tylenol® and placebo.

Although it is useful to think of the independent variable as a cause and the dependent variable as an effect, it is not always that simple. Sometimes we have trouble deciding which of two variables in a study is the cause and which is the effect. Suppose, for example, there is a relationship between violent behavior and television watching. We may have a hard time deciding whether watching violent television programs causes violent behavior or whether a predisposition to violence causes people to watch violent shows.

variable of interest: a variable for which its role in the cause and effect of an observed relationship is not clear

In such investigations, variables are often called **variables of interest**, because the cause and effect of an observed relationship between the variables is not clear. This problem is typical of the nonexperimental research discussed in Chapters 8 and 9.

The independent variable can often be thought of as what the researcher does to the subject, and the dependent variable as what the subject does back. Although this rule is true in many cases, sometimes there are independent variables that the researcher does not manipulate. These are called **subject variables**.

subject variable: a difference between subjects that cannot be controlled but can only be selected

Examples of subject variables are poverty and the sex, age, or intelligence quotient (IQ) of a person. These independent variables cannot be controlled by the researcher. We will devote Chapters 8, 9, and 13 to studies that use such nonmanipulated independent variables. Precisely because they are not manipulated, they require more care in their interpretation, as we will see in those chapters.

Confounded Variables

confounded variable: one whose effect cannot be separated from the supposed independent variable

A confounded variable is one that varies with the independent variable. Suppose Professor Marshall wanted to study gender differences in color preference. If all the male participants in his study had always been dressed in blue as babies and all female participants had always been dressed in pink, then the color of clothing worn as a baby would be confounded with gender. Professor Marshall could not determine whether a difference in color preference between males and females in his study was the result of biology or past experience. So, in Professor Marshall's study, the subject variable of gender is unfortunately confounded with past experience. You can easily see that gender differences could result from all sorts of differences in the way boys and girls are treated. Confounding is a large problem in research using subject variables, such as gender, because males and females vary on many dimensions.

Not All Details of a Study Are Independent Variables

To be a variable, something has to, well, vary. To make sure that unintended variables do not confound a study, many potential variables are kept constant, or the same, across conditions. For example, in the DeWall et al. (2010) study on social pain, the color of paper that the Hurt Feelings Scale was printed on, the lighting of the room, and all the other incidental details of the study were not variables because they did not vary between conditions (between those who took Tylenol® and those who took the placebo). Instead, they were controlled, or held constant, across conditions. Obviously, the paper had to be some color, they had to use some type of light in the room, and so forth. But unless the investigators varied the color of the paper, or the type of room lighting, these details are not variables. Such a detail may be essential to the success of the experiment, but was held constant instead of included as a variable for this particular study. Now, some later investigator may turn these details into variables in a follow-up experiment, but they were not variables in this study.

Quantitative and Categorical Variables

quantitative variable: one that varies in amount

categorical variable: one that varies in kind

The distinction that some variables are quantitative whereas others are categorical is easy to state, even though it may be difficult to apply to particular cases. A quantitative variable is one that varies in amount, whereas a categorical variable varies in kind. Examples of quantitative variables would be speed of response and loudness. College major and gender would be categorical variables.

The distinction between quantitative and categorical variables can become important when we start to build theories. For example, theorists debate about taste, asking whether there are distinct basic tastes—salty, sour, sweet, and bitter—or whether all tastes fall along a continuum, with the four basic tastes being merely convenient but arbitrary categories (McBurney & Gent, 1979). For the same reason, keeping in mind the distinction between quantitative and categorical variables is necessary in making graphs, as we shall see in Chapter 14.

Continuous and Discrete Variables

continuous variable: one that falls along a continuum and is not limited to a certain number of values

discrete variable: one that falls into separate bins with no intermediate values possible

Some quantitative variables can take any value on a continuum. They are called continuous variables because they are not limited to a certain number of values, such as whole numbers, or to discrete bins. In principle, you can measure latency, duration, or force of a bar press with any desired precision; in practice, the fineness of the measure is limited by the ability of the measuring instrument. Discrete variables, by contrast, fall into distinct bins, as the word *discrete* suggests. The number of marriages contracted, murders committed, or books written are all discrete variables.

Although a variable may be continuous, its measurement is often discontinuous. Although height is a continuous variable, we generally measure it to the nearest inch. Similarly, knowledge of psychological research methods may be a continuous variable, but it is often measured by the number of items correct on a test, a discontinuous measure. This does not make knowledge a discrete variable because it would be possible in principle to measure knowledge as finely as one wished.

real limits: the interval defined by the number plus or minus half the distance to the next number

apparent limits: the point indicated by a number

Because continuous variables are commonly measured in a discontinuous fashion, it is necessary to distinguish the real limits of a measure from the apparent limits. The apparent limits of a score on a Research Methods test are an infinitely small point: a score of 1, 2, or some other whole number. But that score represents an estimate of the knowledge of the material, which is a continuous variable. The real limits are that score plus or minus half the distance to the next score: 0.5 to 1.5, 1.5 to 2.5, and so on. This distinction is important when one graphs data and performs certain statistical computations, as we will see in Chapter 14.

Measurement _____

All the variable types we have been discussing must be measured on some scale. Often we don't give much thought to this process, assuming that it is obvious. However, when we say that a person is an 8 on a scale of 10, we are making assumptions about the scale on which the measurements are made. For example, would a 10 be twice as good looking as a 5?

On the other hand, students may shy away from the mathematics involved in measurement. Some may be uneasy about numbers, whereas others may be turned off because to them, numbers make the subject drier and less human. We cannot escape entirely the mathematics needed to do experimental psychology. The reason is simple. As has often been said, an indication of the scientific progress of a field is the extent to which it states its laws quantitatively.

The ability to state laws quantitatively means that two things are true. First, the phenomenon is regular enough to make a reasonably precise statement of it. Data that are too variable can obscure any underlying law; they change too much to observe any relationship. It is true that many ingenious techniques exist to uncover the regularities that can lurk in data, but the scientist always strives to make the regularity of the phenomenon as apparent as possible, so that the law may be stated precisely.

The second implication of stating a law mathematically is that the law is simple enough to write an equation describing it. If the law contains many qualifying statements and special conditions, it follows that the equation will be complicated in order to be accurate. Complicated equations are difficult to test. For this reason, scientists seek simplicity in the laws they use to describe their data. This fact is one of the reasons why Einstein's famous $E = mc^2$ captures the imagination: His theory is simple and elegant. In psychology, an example of an elegant law is Stevens's law of sensation magnitude: $R = kS^n$. This law says that R, magnitude of response, is equal to k, an arbitrary constant, times S, stimulus intensity, raised to a power, n. Stevens's law has spurred much research and has greatly influenced the field of sensory processes, largely because of the elegance with which the law is stated.

What Is Measurement?

measurement: the process of assigning numbers to events or objects according to rules

Measurement is the assignment of numbers to events or objects according to rules that permit important properties of the objects or events to be represented by properties of the number system. The key to this definition is that properties of the events are represented by properties of the number system. The rules by which the numbers are assigned to the events determine how useful the measurement is. For example, if we called every psychologically normal person a 0 and every disturbed person a 1, we would have done a kind of measurement: We would have assigned numbers to people according to a rule. The rule permits us to count numbers of people that fall into the two categories and to determine the percentage of psychological abnormalities in the population.

We could not do much more with this set of numbers, however. The reason is that the particular measurement permits us only to express an all-or-nothing difference between people. It is not possible, for instance, to state severity of abnormality, duration of problem, and so forth. To do this, we would need to assign numbers according to a different rule. Perhaps we might use a scale of severity from 0 to 10, with people falling along the scale according to their symptoms. Then we could say that one person was twice as disturbed as another or that the average level of disturbance in Group A was three times that of Group B.

Types of Measurement Scales

The rule by which you assign numbers determines the kinds of conclusions you reach. For this reason, it is common to distinguish four types of measurement scales according to the rules by which numbers are assigned to objects or events.

Nominal Scales

nominal scale: a measure that simply divides objects or events into categories according to their similarities or differences

A **nominal scale** is one that classifies objects or events into categories. Suppose that Ulf is a foreign exchange student in the United States. He is learning the English names for vegetables: asparagus, broccoli, corn, green beans, and peas. He must learn that fresh peas, frozen peas, and canned peas are the same vegetable whether they are steamed, creamed, or stir-fried. What Ulf is doing is learning a simple scale of vegetables that gives each example of a kind of vegetable one name and each member of other vegetable classes a different name. We will develop this rather elementary example of a nominal scale as we progress to the other types of scales.

A nominal scale is the simplest kind of scale because its rule for assigning numbers (or other labels) to objects or events is the simplest. The rule is that objects or events of the same kind get the same number and objects or events of a different kind get a different number. A nominal scale, as the name implies, is a classification system. Each individual event or object, vegetables in this case, has been assigned to a class.

People sometimes think that a nominal scale is too primitive to be considered a proper scale. It seems to have little mathematics in it. In fact, in the vegetable example, words can be used instead of numbers to identify classes. Such an attitude overlooks the importance of classification for the development of science. As we discussed in Chapter 1, defining classes of behavior is the first step in developing laws of behavior.

Ordinal Scales

ordinal scale: a measure that both assigns objects or events a name and arranges them in order of their magnitude

An **ordinal scale** is one that ranks objects or events in order of their magnitude. Suppose Jessica's mother tells her there are five vegetables in the freezer and asks her to list them in the order of her preference for them, with 5 standing for the most preferred. Jessica might give her mother the following ranking:

5 peas
4 corn
3 green beans
2 broccoli
1 asparagus

We have an ordinal scale of Jessica's preference for vegetables. The rule for assigning numbers on an ordinal scale is that the ordinal position (rank order) of numbers on the scale must represent the rank order of the psychological attributes of the objects or events. Notice that the scale does not tell *how much more* Jessica prefers green beans to broccoli. Perhaps she loves peas, corn, and green beans, but is totally indifferent to broccoli. The scale gives only the order of preference, not the difference in preference among items.

Interval Scales

interval scale: a measure in which the differences between numbers are meaningful; includes both nominal and ordinal information

An interval scale is one in which the differences between the numbers on the scale are meaningful. Let us suppose that Nico's mother says to him, "I know you like peas the best and asparagus the least. On a scale of 1 to 7, with 1 standing for asparagus and 7 standing for peas, how do you rate broccoli, corn, and green beans?" Suppose Nico gives the following data:

7.0 peas
6.5 corn
6.0 green beans
5.0 broccoli
4.0
3.0
2.0
1.0 asparagus

From these data, we are able to infer that Nico's liking of green beans is halfway between that of broccoli and peas. Also, there are 5 units of difference between green beans and asparagus but only 0.5 unit of difference between corn and green beans. Nico's mother knows more about his liking for vegetables than Jessica's mother does about Jessica's vegetable preferences. Nico's mother has developed an interval scale of his liking for vegetables. The rule for assigning numbers to events or objects on an interval scale is that equal differences between the numbers on the scale must represent equal psychological differences between the events or objects.

Ratio Scales

ratio scale: a measure having a meaningful zero point as well as all of the nominal, ordinal, and interval properties

A ratio scale is one that has a meaningful zero point as well as meaningful differences between the numbers on the scale.[1] Suppose that Jasmine's mother says to her, "If your feeling toward green beans is 10 on an open-ended scale, how do you feel about broccoli, corn, and so forth? If you are neutral about a vegetable, give it a zero. If you like one twice as much as you like another, give it a number twice as large. If you dislike a vegetable, give it a negative number. A rating of −10 would indicate that you disliked a vegetable as much as you liked green beans. You may use any number that

---

[1] The term *meaningful* is used in the sense of nonarbitrary. The zero point in the Celsius scale of temperature is arbitrarily set to the freezing point of water. The zero point of the Fahrenheit scale is arbitrarily set to the coldest mixture of salt, ice, and water (the temperature of an old-fashioned ice cream freezer). These zero points do not reflect the absence of temperature. The Kelvin scale (which is obtained by adding 273 degrees to the temperature in Celsius) has a meaningful zero point, known as absolute zero. Thus, of the three, only the Kelvin scale is a ratio scale of temperature. As in the example in the text, a ratio scale can have both positive and negative numbers; the zero point need not be the lowest value on the scale.

seems appropriate; there is no upper or lower limit to the numbers you may use." Now, suppose Jasmine gives the following data:

      30
      20 peas
      15 corn
      10 green beans
       0 broccoli
     −10
     −20
     −30
     −40 asparagus
     −50

The scale developed by Jasmine's mother contains the most information of the scales we have discussed. First, this scale has a meaningful zero point, which none of the other scales had. Therefore, we can know that Jasmine is indifferent to broccoli. Second, the ratios between numbers are meaningful. We can say that Jasmine likes peas twice as much as green beans or that she hates asparagus four times as much as she likes green beans.

The rule for assigning numbers to events or objects on a ratio scale is that the ratios between the numbers on the scale must represent the psychological ratios between the events or objects. For example, if you measured the time it took for three people to press a button in response to a question, their times may be 50 milliseconds, 100 milliseconds, and 75 milliseconds. Because reaction time is a ratio scale, you can with accuracy tell that the second person took twice as long to press the button as the first person. Like the vegetable scale developed above, reaction time has a true zero and the ratios between the numbers are meaningful.

Comparison of the Scales

As we go from nominal to ordinal, interval, and ratio scales, we are able to gain more information from the data. The nominal scale gives information only about whether two events are the same or different. The ordinal scale does that too, but also gives us a ranking on some variable. The interval scale conveys nominal and ordinal information, and also allows us to make quantitative statements about the magnitude of the differences between events. The ratio scale contains all the information of the other three scales, as well as conveying information about ratios of magnitudes. For this reason, we strive to make our scales of variables ratio scales, if possible. Failing that, we try for an interval scale, and so forth.

You may have noticed as we went along that each person's rating of the five vegetables was consistent with all of the others' ratings. In other words, knowing Jasmine's data on the ratio scale, we could derive all of the information in the other three scales. This was done purposely to show that the ratio scale is the most powerful scale, with the other scales being less powerful in the following order: interval, ordinal, nominal. Thus, Jasmine's mother knew the most about her liking for vegetables and Ulf's hostess knew the least about his. Specifically, Jasmine's mother knows that her daughter likes peas twice as much as green beans, is indifferent to broccoli, and dislikes asparagus twice as much as she likes peas. Jessica's mother, on the other hand, knows only her rank order of preferences, not the differences between them or the zero point. All that Ulf's hostess knows is that he knows one vegetable from the other.

Another way to look at the differences among types of scales is to ask, *how* could we have altered the assignment of the numbers to the events without violating the rule governing the type of scale? The ways that we can alter the assignment of numbers to individual events without distorting the scale are called *permissible transformations*. Transformations of data can be performed in order to aid in interpretation, or to meet the assumptions of a statistical test. The permissible transformations become fewer as we go from nominal to ratio scales. In the nominal scale example, we could have called asparagus 1, broccoli 2, and so forth. Or we could have done the reverse. On the other hand, we could also label them 37 and 59 and so forth; any five numbers will do. We would not have lost any information about Ulf's ability to identify the vegetables if we had changed the labels because we were using the numbers only to put vegetables into classes.

For the ordinal scale, we can change the numbers any way that would preserve the order of preference for the vegetables. We could have called Jessica's favorite vegetable 59, the second one 14, the third 13, and so forth. We would still know Jessica's order of preference for the vegetables.

We can do less to change the numbers of the interval scale because we must preserve the meaningfulness of the differences between items. But we could add or subtract a constant from all numbers, or we could multiply them by a positive constant. Thus, we could add 10 to all of Nico's answers or multiply them by 100 without changing any of our conclusions about his preferences for vegetables.

In the ratio scale, we can change little without distorting it. The only thing we can do is multiply all the numbers by a positive constant. If we were to add a constant, we would destroy the significance of the ratios between numbers; we could no longer say that Jasmine likes peas twice as much as green beans.

Table 5.1 summarizes the points we have been making in this section. The types of scales are listed in order in the first column. The second column indicates the properties of the number system that must be represented in the rule used to assign numbers to events or objects. The third column gives the permissible transformations. The fourth column gives common examples of psychology scales.

The various psychological defense mechanisms are good examples of nominal scales. No order of severity is implied by the names for the defense mechanisms: projection, denial, intellectualization, and so forth. Common examples of ordinal scales would include any preference data of the sort we have already used in our discussion. IQ is a good example of an interval scale. The IQ tests are designed so that the amount of the differences between people can be meaningfully represented by the IQ score. However, IQ is not a ratio scale because it would be meaningless to say that a person with an IQ of 120 is twice as smart as someone with an IQ of 60. The most common

TABLE **5.1**

Summary of Information on Scales of Measurement

© Cengage Learning

Scale	Number System Properties Represented by Assignment Rule	Permissible Transformations	Example
Nominal	Similarities and differences	Any substitution of a number for another number that preserves similarities and differences, including all below	Types of defense mechanisms
Ordinal	Similarities and differences, rank order	Any change that preserves order among members, including both below	Preferences
Interval	Similarities and differences, rank order, magnitude of differences between individuals	Addition of a constant, multiplication by a positive constant	IQ
Ratio	Similarities and differences, rank order, magnitude of differences, ratios of properties between individuals, meaningful zero point	Multiplication by a positive constant only	Stevens's law of sensation magnitude

example of a ratio scale is given by Stevens's scale, as in the example of Jasmine's liking for vegetables. She was told to use numbers to represent ratios of differences between vegetables.

Understanding the type of scale that the data are measured on is important to avoid drawing incorrect conclusions. We already said that it would be meaningless to say that a person with an IQ of 120 is twice as smart as someone with an IQ of 60. Similarly, even though many teachers, when computing grade-point averages, consider an A to be worth 4 points, a B to be worth 3 points, and so forth, no one would conclude that a person who received an A had learned twice as much as someone who received a C. In reality, there are relatively few psychological inventories that are measured on ratio, or even interval, scales, though many dimensions of behavior (such as reaction time or frequency) are measured with ratio scales. Therefore, we must know what kind of scale our data are measured on before we compare the magnitudes of differences between numbers.

Measurement and Statistics?

It is a widespread notion among psychologists that the scale on which a variable is measured determines the type of statistics that can appropriately be performed on the data. Thus, many hold that it is not appropriate to use the usual parametric statistics unless the data are measured on an interval or ratio scale. (Parametric statistics are those that make assumptions about the population from which the data are drawn—namely, that the data are normally distributed and each group has the same variance.) Parametric statistics include the usual Pearson correlation coefficient, the t test, and analysis of variance. Nonparametric statistics include various tests that are based on rank order of the data or on the sign of the differences between subjects.

Nonparametric tests are relatively infrequently used because they lack power compared with the corresponding parametric test. The reason is technical, but in a nutshell, parametric tests use all the information present in the data, whereas nonparametric tests use only a portion of it.

Without going into the history of the controversy over scales and appropriate statistics, suffice it to say that the notion that parametric tests are limited in use to data measured on an interval or ratio scale originated with psychologists, and statisticians do not agree with it. Statisticians hold that it is appropriate to use parametric statistics on nominal, ordinal, interval, or ratio data (Gaito, 1980). Most psychologists have come to accept the position of the statisticians, although some statistics books written by psychologists still teach that the scale on which data are measured determines the appropriate statistics.

Reliability and Validity of Measurements _____

reliability: the property of consistency of a measurement that gives the same result on different occasions

validity: (of a measurement) the property of a measurement that tests what it is supposed to test

For a measurement to be of any use in science, it must have both reliability and validity. These are two different concepts, as the following example illustrates. Suppose we tell you that we have a one-item intelligence test: We measure your hat size. Now you immediately realize that this would be a lousy intelligence test because there is a very limited relationship between IQ and size of head. Nevertheless, we argue that our measurement is **reliable** because it gives the same result every time we measure the size of your head. Circumference of your head does not change from day to day. The reason our hat-size test of intelligence is no good is that it does not give **valid** results because the measurement has nothing to do with the concept that we are trying to measure.

Now, suppose that we try a different one-item test of intelligence: What did the Dow Jones Industrial stock average close at yesterday? This test would be valid because the answer is something that can be considered general knowledge. (You might argue that it would be biased toward people with money to invest, but all tests of general knowledge have this problem of cultural bias to some extent.) On average, people who know the value of the Dow Jones average are more intelligent than others. But it would not be a very reliable measurement. It would not give consistent results, either with the same person from time to time or from one person to another. So our two tests would be bad, but for different reasons: The hat-size test yields data that are reliable but not valid, and the Dow Jones average test yields data that are valid but not reliable. Good measurements of intelligence or anything else have to be both reliable and valid. (This example is somewhat oversimplified: Strictly speaking, a measurement should be reliable before it can be valid. So the Dow Jones measurement might be considered potentially valid if it were reliable, which it isn't. In practice, intelligence tests solve the problem of unreliability by including many items. Averaging across all items tends to cancel out the errors.)

We talk about validity of measurement next. The validity of research as a whole is a rather broader concern, so we will deal with it at length in Chapter 6. We consider reliability of measurements later in this chapter.

Variability and Error

Every study deals with variability of measurements. Both the dependent and independent variables will vary—otherwise, they wouldn't be variables. Broadly speaking, the task of research is to find relationships between independent and dependent variables; that is, to find how the dependent variable changes with changes in the independent variable—so, as in one of the earlier examples, how enjoyment of coloring varies with rewards. So variability in the dependent variable is good when it is associated with changes in the independent variable.

error variance: variability in the dependent variable that is not associated with the independent variable

But there is a bad kind of variability known as error variance, or random error (see p. 132). (Variance is a technical way of measuring variability, as in the analysis of variance or ANOVA. See Chapter 15.) Error variance (or simply, error) is the variability in the dependent variables in a study that cannot be shown to be associated with changes in the independent variables. We will devote Chapters 6 and 7 to the problem of identifying and controlling sources of error variance.

Validity of Measurements

The following types of validity of measurements are commonly defined: construct validity, face validity, content validity, and criterion validity.

construct validity (of a test): a test that the measurements actually measure the constructs they are designed to measure, but no others

There are several ways to determine whether a test yields data that have construct validity. First, the test should actually measure whatever theoretical construct it supposedly tests, and not something else. A test of leadership ability should not actually test extraversion, for example. Second, a test that has construct validity should measure what it intends to measure but not measure theoretically unrelated constructs. A test of musical aptitude should not require too much reading ability, for example. Third, a test should prove useful in predicting results related to the theoretical concept it is measuring. A test of musical ability should predict who will benefit from taking music lessons, should differentiate groups who have chosen music as a career from those who haven't, should relate to other tests of musical ability, and so on. We will encounter the concept of construct validity again in Chapter 6, when we discuss the validity of a particular study, or piece of research, as a whole.

The other kinds of validity discussed in relation to tests and measurement—face validity, content validity, and criterion validity—are actually different ways of talking about construct validity, although it is useful to give each one its own name for pedagogical purposes.

face validity: idea that a test should appear superficially to test what it is supposed to test

Face validity is the idea that a test should appear to any person to be a test of what it is supposed to test. Many a person who has been given a Rorschach test has wondered what a bunch of inkblots has to do with personality. (Actually, projective tests have other serious problems of validity besides face validity.) Face validity, however, is more a problem of public relations than of true validity. A test may have a high or low degree of validity, regardless of its face validity.

content validity: idea that a test should sample the range of behavior represented by the theoretical concept being tested

Content validity is the notion that a test should sample the range of the behavior that is represented by the theoretical concept being measured. An intelligence test, for example, should measure general knowledge, verbal ability, spatial ability, and quantitative skills, among others. An intelligence test that measured only spatial ability would not have sufficient content validity.

criterion validity: idea that a test should correlate with other measures of the same theoretical construct

Criterion validity is the idea that a valid test should relate closely to other measures of the same theoretical construct. A valid test of intelligence should correlate highly with other intelligence tests. It should also correlate with behaviors that are considered to require intelligence, such as doing well in school. If the criterion of an intelligence test is whether it correlates with how well a child is doing in school at the time the test is given, it is called *concurrent validity*. If the criterion of an intelligence test is how well the test can predict some future performance of the child, such as graduation from college, then it is called *predictive validity*.

Questions involving the various kinds of test validity are technical ones; for further discussion, refer to any standard text on tests and measurements (e.g., Anastasi & Urbina, 1997). As you can tell from this brief discussion, however, the concept of correlation is closely intertwined with that of validity.

A good test of leadership, for example, should not correlate too highly with a test of extraversion. However, a good test of intelligence should correlate highly with other tests of intelligence and with how a child performs in school.

Types of Measurement Error

There are two basic types of measurement error: systematic (or constant) error and random error. Consider my (D.M.) weight, which changes from time to time, as everyone's does. I notice that it decreases about 2 pounds overnight, it increases temporarily about 3 pounds if I eat salty foods such as pizza, it increases temporarily over holidays, and it has increased reasonably steadily in the years since I was a college student. All this variability can be accounted for by independent variables: loss of water during the night, thirst induced by salt, overeating, and the process of aging. This variability, then, would not be considered error at all because it is associated with independent variables.

But my scales also register variation in my weight that I cannot associate with these variables. If I get on the scales and don't like what I see, I sometimes try again and get a lower reading, or even a higher one. This variability could be called random error (or error variance) because it is not associated with any known independent variable. Some of this random error may be caused by exactly where I place my feet on the scales, how I lean, whether I just had a drink of water, and so forth. But if we don't measure these other independent variables, we can lump them all into random error.

I find, however, that I weigh less in the morning, wearing my night clothes, and if I stand on a certain spot on the scales. But this isn't necessarily

systematic error: measurement error that is associated with consistent bias

my true weight because now I have introduced systematic error. However, even though I have introduced systematic error by weighing myself in this standardized way that also gives the lowest reading, this weighing method is not such a bad idea because it allows me to track trends in my weight with greater consistency, measure the effects of pigging out, and the like. But when I go to the doctor and weigh in, I always weigh 5 pounds more on those scales than on my own, even if I go straight there after weighing myself at home.

Systematic error is never desirable in research, but it may not be such a serious problem if the error is the same for the entire study—that is, all groups or conditions of the study are equally affected by the systematic error. Suppose you did an experiment on weight loss under two different conditions using scales with a systematic error. The results of the study would not be affected by that particular error.

Systematic error can be very serious, though, if it is associated with the independent variable, because it can confound your experimental results. The systematic error may be present for one level of the independent variable and not for another level. If I were to go on a diet and at the same time I changed my routine of weighing myself, using all my little tricks of lowering the reading on the scales, then the systematic error would be associated with the diet, the independent variable. I would find my weight to be lower at least partly because of the systematic error that I introduced at the same time I started on the diet.

Random error is always a serious problem in research because it can reduce the precision with which you assess the effects of the independent variable. It is a threat to the reliability of measurement.

Types of Reliability Measures

test-retest reliability: the degree to which the same test score would be obtained on another occasion

Here, we discuss two types of reliability of measures: test-retest and internal consistency. Test-retest reliability concerns whether the same measure would yield the same result on another occasion. I am concerned with test-retest reliability when I try the bathroom scales immediately after getting a reading I don't like. Other examples are retaking the SAT or GRE. A good test gives a similar score on two occasions.

internal consistency: the degree to which the various items on a test are measures of the same thing

Internal consistency concerns whether the various items on a test are measures of the same thing. There are several tests of internal consistency of dependent variables; we consider one of them. Split-half reliability is determined when the items on a test are divided into two sets as if they were two separate tests. Then the scores on the two halves are correlated to see how closely the various individuals' scores agree on the two halves. If the test is a good test, it will have a high split-half correlation.

A widely used measure of internal consistency is the Kuder-Richardson-20, which the first author's university's testing service routinely computes on all multiple-choice tests that it scores. The K-R-20 can be thought of as computing all possible split-half correlations on a set of data and taking the average. The value of the K-R-20 can vary from 0.0, meaning complete disagreement, to 1.0, perfect agreement.

Choosing the Levels of the Independent Variable

NUTS & BOLTS

Many experiments involve only two conditions, such as presence or absence of a variable. In other experiments, the number of conditions is strictly limited by practical or theoretical considerations. This section concerns experiments that call for several stimulus conditions. Because you probably want to keep your experiment as simple (few levels) as possible, selecting the levels of the independent variables can be very important to assessing your hypothesis. We can state four principles that apply to most such experiments.

First, the stimuli should cover as much of the range as practicable. Relationships between the variables will be better understood if the limits of the system are explored. Figure 5.1 shows how too short a stimulus range can be misleading. If the middle three stimuli were chosen, the experimenter probably would conclude that no relationship exists between the stimulus and the response. Adding more stimuli above and below the middle three, however, shows clearly that there is a U-shaped function relating stimulus and response. The middle three stimuli are not sufficient to provide an accurate picture of the functional relationship between stimulus and response.

The second principle is that the stimuli should be close enough together that overlooking any interesting relationship between the stimuli is unlikely (see Figure 5.2.). Here, the range of stimuli is wide enough, but the wrong conclusion could be drawn if the middle stimuli were not included.

The third principle is that in within-subjects designs, when a participant is to experience all stimuli in a single session, at least seven stimuli should be presented if possible. If fewer than seven are experienced, participants can identify and remember each stimulus. In that case, responses may not be based on the stimulus itself, but may be related to the memory of stimuli from previous trials. With seven or more stimuli, participants respond to the stimulus itself because they are not able to identify it (Miller, 1956). Of course, using seven stimuli may not be possible because doing so may make the experiment too long.

The fourth principle of choosing stimuli concerns the spacing of quantitative variables—those that vary in amount along some continuum. If you plan to use only two stimuli, you simply pick those that seem the most appropriate. If you have more than two, you are faced with a choice of spacing sizes. Should you make the intervals between stimuli equal, or should you use some other spacing pattern? You might wonder why you would ever use anything but equal intervals.

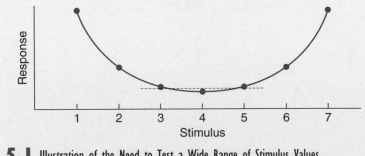

FIGURE **5.1** Illustration of the Need to Test a Wide Range of Stimulus Values

(continues)

NUTS & BOLTS (continued)

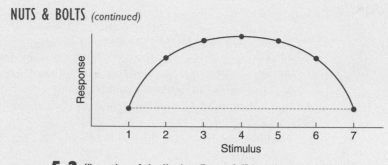

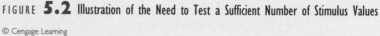

FIGURE **5.2** Illustration of the Need to Test a Sufficient Number of Stimulus Values

© Cengage Learning

Suppose your experiment involves the effect of number of rat pellets on the speed at which a rat will run a maze. You want to use 1 pellet as the fewest and 81 as the most. You are going to have five groups of rats, each of which receives a different number of pellets. If you wanted to space the stimuli evenly, you would use 1, 21, 41, 61, and 81 for the various groups. However, you suspect that the difference in effect on the rat's running speed between 61 and 81 pellets may not be as great as the difference between 1 and 21. An alternative would be to space pellets logarithmically. With logarithmic spacing, the stimuli are spread out evenly according to ratios between number of pellets, which would work out to 1, 3, 9, 27, and 81. Here, each condition has three times as many pellets as the one before. A great many stimulus dimensions— perhaps most—are such that most action takes place at the lower end of the scale. In these cases, stimuli should be spaced so that equal ratios fall between stimuli.

The difference in spacing is illustrated in Figure 5.3. Running speed is plotted as a function of number of pellets given as reinforcement. Notice that the difference in running speed between 1 pellet and 21 pellets is 2.75 units, whereas the difference between 61 and 81 is only about 0.25 units. If you had used equal-difference spacing, you would have missed most of the "action," which occurs between conditions that present 1 or 21 pellets. Then again, by spacing pellets according to equal ratios, you have found equal effects on the running speed between each number of pellets used. Of course, this example was created so that this would be the case.

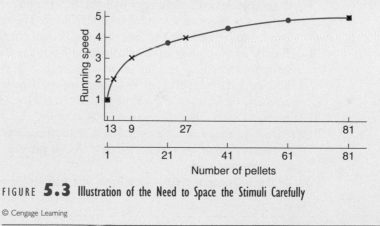

FIGURE **5.3** Illustration of the Need to Space the Stimuli Carefully

© Cengage Learning

Summary

1. A variable is some property of an event in the world that has been measured.
2. A dependent variable is a measure, either results of a test or of the behavior of a subject on one of several different dimensions.
3. An independent variable is one that is believed to cause some change in the value of the dependent variable.
4. The different values of an independent variable are called the levels of the variable.
5. A subject variable is an independent variable that the researcher does not manipulate, but measures instead.
6. A confounded variable is one that varies with the independent variable.
7. Quantitative variables vary in amount, whereas categorical variables differ in kind.
8. A continuous variable is one that is not limited to a certain number of values.
9. A discrete variable is one that falls into a certain number of distinct bins.
10. The apparent limits of a number are the point indicated by the number itself; the real limits are the interval defined by the number plus or minus half the difference to the next numbers.
11. Measurement is the assignment of numbers to objects or events according to rules that permit important properties of the objects or events to be represented by properties of the number system.
12. Four scales of measurement are distinguished according to the rules by which numbers are assigned to objects or events: nominal, ordinal, interval, and ratio.
13. A nominal scale is one that classifies objects or events into categories. Objects or events of the same kind get the same number and different objects or events get different numbers.
14. An ordinal scale is one that ranks objects or events in order of their magnitude. The ordinal position of the numbers on the scale must represent the rank order of the psychological attributes of the objects or events.
15. An interval scale is one in which the differences between the numbers on the scale are meaningful. Equal differences between the numbers on the scale must represent equal differences between the event or objects.
16. A ratio scale is one that has a meaningful zero point as well as meaningful differences between the numbers on the scale. The ratios between the numbers on the scale must represent the ratios between the events or objects.
17. We are able to gain more information from the data as we progress from nominal to ordinal to interval to ratio scales.
18. Knowing the type of scale that data are measured on (nominal, ordinal, interval, or ratio) is important to avoid drawing incorrect conclusions from the data.
19. Although many psychologists hold that parametric statistics may be performed only on variables measured on interval or ratio scales, statisticians do not agree.
20. Measurements must be both reliable and valid.

21. Four types of validity of measurements are commonly recognized: construct validity, face validity, content validity, and criterion validity.
22. Error variance (or random error) is variability in the response that is not associated with the independent variable.
23. Systematic error is caused by a measurement bias.
24. The choice of stimulus values is guided by four principles:
    a. The stimuli should cover as much of the range as possible.
    b. They should be close enough together to prevent overlooking interesting effects between stimuli.
    c. In within-subjects studies, at least seven stimuli should be presented if possible.
    d. If the continuum is quantitative, logarithmically spacing the stimuli may be advisable.

Suggestions for Further Reading

GUILFORD, J. P. (1954). *Psychometric methods*. New York: McGraw-Hill. This book contains a good discussion of scales of measurement as well as a mathematical introduction that covers much of the material in this chapter.

MILSAP, D., & MAYDEU-OLIVARES, A. (2009). *The Sage handbook of quantitative methods in psychology*. Thousand Oaks, CA: Sage. This text provides valuable mathematical background for this chapter.

A CASE IN POINT

Class Size and Learning

State University is concerned about the effect of class size on learning. There are more students each year, but the legislature has not increased the instructional budget. The dean would like to find out if students in large classes learn as much as students in small classes do.

Approximately 1,500 students take introductory psychology classes each term. The largest classroom available has 500 seats. The smallest classes generally have about 20 students. The psychology department will be able to staff eight sections of the course next term.

Professor Chips in the psychology department is coordinating the study. He believes that more highly motivated students will learn the same amount regardless of class size because they will compensate for any differences in teaching methods or other factors by studying hard enough to learn the material. Less motivated students may learn less in larger sections. Mr. Chips will administer a standard test of motivation on the first day of class to all students and use the results to separate each class into highly motivated and less motivated students for the purpose of evaluating the data.

Required

1. Decide how many sections of introductory psychology should participate in the study and what size each should be. (Assume that you have complete control over class size, within the limits on room size.)
2. Identify the variables of interest and independent variables in the study.
3. Sketch a graph that shows the kind of data that Mr. Chips expects to find.

Reading Between the Lines

5.1 Testing for Independence of Dimensions

William Pelham and his colleagues (2005) wanted to test whether a stimulant drug to treat attention deficit hyperactivity disorder (ADHD) would be better than behavioral therapy or whether the two treatments would have a combined effect when presented together. The researchers observed children in a double-blind study that took place within the context of a summer program. All children received the medication (each of three levels of the drug and a placebo) as well as behavioral therapy (present or not) during the time in which they were enrolled in the program. The two dimensions were the strength of the drug and the frequency of therapy. Although both treatments produced effects, the combination of treatments was superior to either treatment alone. Can you think of a reason why behavioral treatment and medication treatment might not be independent of one another?

Web-Based Workshops on Research Methods and Statistics

Wadsworth Publishing Company maintains Web-based workshops on research methods and statistics. These workshops give a different slant on the material in this book.

www.cengage.com/psychology/workshops

For this chapter, see Research Methods Workshops, Experimental Methods, and Reliability and Validity.

Exercises

5.1 Identify Types of Variables

A researcher administers an intelligence test to 30 college students. After gathering information on subjects' age, sex, height, weight, political preference, college major, career goals, and socioeconomic status, the researcher administers an attitude survey on current world issues to all 30 subjects.

Required:

Identify examples of the following types of variables in the paragraph:

a. discrete
b. continuous
c. categorical
d. quantitative

Identify examples of variables that would be measured on the following types of scales:

a. nominal
b. ordinal
c. interval
d. ratio

5.2 Identify Independent and Dependent Variables

The following is modified from the abstract of an article (Debono & Klein, 1993).

Subjects who were high in dogmatism read a message from either an expert or nonexpert source who supported his position with either strong or weak arguments. Strong arguments were more persuasive than weak arguments. Subjects were persuaded by strong arguments when the source was not an expert, but they were equally persuaded by strong and weak arguments when the source was an expert.

Required:

a. What was (were) the independent variable(s) and levels (of each)?

b. What was (were) the dependent variable(s)?

5.3 Identify Variables

Following is an abstract of an article. Read it and answer the questions that follow.

This study examined the effects of psycholegal knowledge on a mock jury decision-making task. Psycholegal knowledge was obtained by completion of a university course on psychology and law focusing on jury decision-making. It was predicted that psycholegal knowledge would enhance juror competence, motivation, and satisfaction with participation in the legal process. Mock jurors who had taken the course were compared with those who had not. Both groups were shown a videotape of a rape trial and participated in jury deliberations. Jurors trained in psycholegal knowledge voted for acquittal more often than those who were not. Additionally, trained jurors were more satisfied, were more confident that their jury reached a correct verdict, and believed more that their jury's decision was based on the evidence presented than did untrained jurors. (Shaw & Skolnick, 2005)

Required:

a. What is (are) the independent variable(s)?

b. What were the levels (conditions) of the independent variables?

c. What is (are) the dependent variable(s)?

d. Which sentence states a hypothesis?

5.4 Identify Variables

The following is a slightly modified abstract of an article. Read it and answer the questions that follow.

Two experiments examined the effects of a number of motivated encoding strategies (anticipated interaction, friend comparison, and memory instructions) on the recall and cognitive organization of information about multiple target persons. As in past research on the motivated encoding strategies on the cognitive processing of information about a single target, memory instructions produced the lowest levels of recall. However, in contrast to past research, no [other] instruction set produced evidence of higher cognitive [organization] of targets than [did] memory

instructions. The results are discussed in the context of two alternative models of person memory—the associative network model and the elaboration model. (Sedikides, Devine, & Furman, 1991)

Required:

a. What is (are) the independent variable(s)?

b. What were the levels (conditions) of the independent variables?

c. What is (are) the dependent variable(s)?

d. Which sentence concerns a theory?

5.5 Identify Variables

Read the following abstract (von Hippel & Gonsalkorale, 2005).

An experiment explored the hypothesis that inhibitory ability helps people stop themselves from engaging in socially inappropriate behavior. All participants completed a Stroop color-naming task, after which half of the participants were asked to remember an eight digit number (inducing divided attention). Participants were then offered an unfamiliar and visually unappetizing food product (a chicken foot) under conditions of either low or high social pressure to pretend that it was appealing. Participants who had full attention available and were under pressure to pretend the food was appealing were least likely to emit a negative response, and performance on the Stroop task predicted the degree to which they successfully restrained negative responses. These results suggest that the cognitive ability to inhibit unwanted information facilitates socially appropriate behavior.

Required:

a. What is (are) the independent variable(s)?

b. What were the levels of the independent variable(s)?

c. What is (are) the dependent variable(s)?

d. What hypothesis was tested?

e. What were the results?

5.6 Identify Independent and Dependent Variables

Read the abstract in Exercise 11.2.

a. Identify independent variable(s) and levels (of each).

b. Identify dependent variables.

5.7 Identify Independent and Dependent Variables

Same as 5.6 for Exercise 11.3.

5.8 Identify Independent and Dependent Variables

Same as 5.5 for Exercise 11.4.

5.9 Identify Independent and Dependent Variables

Same as 5.5 for Exercise 13.4.

5.10 Identify Independent and Dependent Variables

The following questions are adapted from Walker (1982). For each of the following research reports, indicate the following:

a. the independent variable(s)
b. the dependent variable(s)

A Rolling Stone Gathers No Moss

Researchers took 10 stones varying in color and size and rolled them down the stairs of their laboratory and then down a little slope on the laboratory grounds. None of the stones gathered any moss.

I Know Which Side My Bread is Buttered On

Researchers gave a panel of 14 volunteers whole slices of bread with butter spread only on one side. No matter what kind of bread researchers used (white, whole wheat, or pumpernickel), all of the volunteers were able to identify which side of the bread was buttered. This was the case when the subjects were blindfolded, had their hands tied behind their backs, and had their noses pinched by clothespins.

An Apple a Day Keeps the Doctor Away

A panel of 10 volunteers was divided into two groups. Five of the volunteers were given an apple a day for 14 days. The other five were not given apples at all but were given other edibles. The researchers then instructed a doctor to approach each of the 10 volunteers every day. Researchers found that the doctor did successfully approach each of the 10 volunteers every day and that the apples did not keep the doctor away. Whether the apples had been eaten or not, were being eaten at the moment of approach, or were hidden on the persons of the volunteers or at some distance away in metal footlockers, apples were completely ineffective in warding off the approach of the doctor.

CHAPTER SIX

Validity

PREVIEW

Chapter 6 discusses the concept of validity of research. We consider the various types of validity and the threats to each. We discussed validity as it pertains to a test or measurement instrument in Chapter 5. This chapter discusses the broader concern of validity of research as a whole.

Most research is designed to permit the researcher to draw conclusions about cause-effect relationships among variables. As we discussed in Chapter 1, the ultimate goal is to develop a theory that explains the relationships found among variables. This chapter concerns the various problems that can threaten the validity of conclusions drawn by a researcher. By validity, we mean simply that the researcher's conclusion is true or correct—that it corresponds to the actual state of the world. You probably realize that achieving the truth about the world is asking a great deal.

validity: an indication of accuracy in terms of the extent to which a research conclusion corresponds with reality

Some validity problems threaten the conclusion that a cause-effect relationship exists among the variables at all; some threaten the theoretical explanation of the kind of relationship obtained. We discuss, first, the various kinds of research validity and, second, the many threats to validity. In Chapter 7, we will consider the methods available to the researcher to control for these threats.

Types of Validity

William Shadish, Thomas Cook, and Donald Campbell (2002) list four types of validity that must be considered in designing and evaluating a piece of research: internal validity, construct validity, external validity, and statistical conclusion validity.

Internal Validity

internal validity: extent to which a study provides evidence of a cause-effect relationship between the independent and dependent variables

Internal validity is the most fundamental type because it concerns the logic of the relationship between the independent and dependent variables. An experiment has internal validity if there are sound reasons to believe that a cause and effect relationship really is present between the independent and dependent variables. In other words, in an experiment with high internal validity, it really was the independent variable that caused the dependent variable to change.

Suppose you did an experiment on the effect of informational feedback on a motor learning task, such as learning to fix a laser pointer on a moving target. Group A received a tone whenever they hit the target; Group B did not. So far, so good. But you tested all the people in Group A on Monday and all in Group B on Tuesday. Now, besides differing in feedback, the two groups also differed in the time that they took part in the experiment. It is impossible to decide whether any differences in behavior should be attributed to feedback or to time of testing. This experiment lacks internal validity because you cannot conclude that feedback caused any differences between the groups. This problem is known as **confounding**. In this case, time was confounded with feedback because its possible effects were not tested separately from the effects of feedback. We say that time is correlated with feedback. When some condition co-varies with the independent variable in such a way that their separate effects cannot be sorted out, the two variables are confounded. You can easily imagine a number of potentially important variables that could affect performance on a motor skills task. The Monday could have followed fraternity rush weekend, with some of the subjects feeling a bit shaky as part of the aftereffects. Perhaps on Tuesday, the barometric pressure was high, or the experimenter had just learned that her boyfriend was going to break up with her. Notice that none of these confounded variables enter into any theory of motor learning, even though some of them might affect behavior.

confounding: error that occurs when the effects of two variables in an experiment cannot be separated, resulting in a confused interpretation of the results

Confounding is one of the biggest threats to validity in experimentation. Great care must be taken that no important variable is confounded with the independent variable. Much of the rest of this book concerns techniques used to avoid confounding.

Considering all of the possible incidental variables associated with an experiment, making sure that none of the other variables are confounded with the independent variable is not feasible. For example, among the possible confounded variables in the previous example is phase of the moon. Although some people have suggested that strange behavior occurs during a full moon, the evidence for this conclusion is weak. Most investigators therefore feel justified in ignoring lunar phase.

If day of the week is an important confounding variable but lunar phase is not, how do experimenters decide which variables to worry about? The fact is that many value judgments are made as an experiment is designed. For example, many taste researchers take care that no smokers serve as subjects or that no participants smoke within one hour of the experiment. McBurney, one of the authors of this text, used to eliminate smokers routinely from his taste experiments, despite the fact that no persuasive evidence existed that smoking affects sensation for college-age people. In one experiment that he did with an undergraduate student, he concluded that there was no discernible effect of smoking on taste thresholds in the college-age participants. These results, together with the fact that other experiments in the literature were inconclusive, led him to quit paying attention to whether his participants are smokers.

The problem of confounding is particularly acute in research in which the experimenter cannot control the independent variable—when participants are selected according to the presence or absence of a condition and not selected simply to have a condition assigned to them. Such variables are called subject variables.

> **subject variable:** a difference between subjects that cannot be controlled but can only be selected

A good example of a subject variable is gender. Participants cannot be assigned to one gender, but must be selected from preexisting groups. When gender is one of the independent variables of an experiment, as it often is, we have a quasi experiment (see Chapter 13) and a much greater probability of confounding. Take, for example, the lively debate about the extent of the differences in psychological processes between men and women. This debate results from the greatly differing influences in our society on males and females that begin when they leave the hospital in their blue or pink clothes. All the innumerable experiences and the resulting learned attitudes and skills are confounded in the simple term *gender differences*. The extent to which these confounded variables contribute to the sex differences found in research is the crux of the sex difference controversy. Similarly, in research on race and IQ, we find many variables confounded with race that are known to influence IQ, such as parents' level of education, family income, and quality of available schooling.

We continue our discussion of confounding in a later section when we consider threats to internal validity. Each of the threats is a possible source of confounding.

Construct Validity

We discussed construct validity of measurements previously in Chapter 5. Recall that the construct validity of a measurement concerns whether it measures what it is intended to measure and nothing else. So, for example, does an IQ test actually measure intelligence, rather than economic status or some other variable? Here we discuss another kind of construct validity. Construct validity of research concerns the question of whether the results support the theory behind the research. In other words, can you generalize from the specific operations of your experiment (including people and settings) to the general theoretical construct about the population in question? Would another theory predict the same experimental results? You can see

> **construct validity:** extent to which the results support the theory behind the research

that the two types of construct validity are related. Both are concerned with how well the underlying idea (or theory) is reflected in the measurement. If the measurement used in some research lacks construct validity, the research as a whole will also lack construct validity.

Every study is designed to test some hypothesis; yet a hypothesis cannot be tested in a vacuum. The particular conditions of a study constitute auxiliary hypotheses that must also be true so that you can test the main hypothesis. Suppose your hypothesis is that anxiety is conducive to learning. You may select your participants on the basis of whether they bite their fingernails and test to see how fast they can learn to write by holding a pencil in their toes. If you find no difference in the rate of learning between fingernail-biting and non–fingernail-biting groups, you might conclude that your hypothesis is false. However, you did not test just the one hypothesis that anxiety is conducive to learning. Whether you meant to or not, you also tested two auxiliary hypotheses: that fingernail biting is a measure of anxiety and that writing with one's toes is a good learning task. If either of these auxiliary hypotheses is false, you could have found negative results. In other words, your main hypothesis that anxiety is conducive to learning might actually be true, but your experimental results wouldn't show that if you chose a bad way to measure either anxiety or learning.

How can you ensure construct validity? Actually, you cannot, but you can plan your research so that it is more plausible. To improve the validity of your experiment, you might have used a **manipulation check**, such as including the Beck Anxiety Inventory (Beck, Epstein, Brown, & Steer, 1988) as a way to make sure that the fingernail biting was a good way to classify your subjects on anxiety. Manipulation checks aim to see that a variable (usually the independent variable) is working in the way that you think that it is, and these checks are often built right into the experimental design. In this particular experiment, you also could have used a more standardized learning measure, such as learning a list of unrelated words, to improve your construct validity. These techniques, although not perfect, have been used many times. We have more faith that they are valid than that fingernail biting alone and writing with the toes are valid.

Another example of the problem of construct validity can be taken from psychobiology. Destruction of a particular part of the brain (the hypothalamus) will cause a rat to become obese if it is allowed to eat all it wants. Researchers initially believed that the rat was hungrier than normal as a result of the operation. Later they learned that the rat would eat more only if the food was tasty and if the rat did not have to work hard for it. The conclusion was that the rat really was not hungrier; it simply lacked the ability to tell when it had eaten enough.

Experiments that used destruction of a rat's hypothalamus as a way of increasing hunger, then, were actually decreasing satiety. Any research using this method to increase hunger in rats would lack construct validity because the manipulation did not increase hunger as measured by other manipulations such as food deprivation. A later study (Friedman & Stricker, 1976) suggested that the injury to the brain may not be influencing either hunger or satiety directly, but may be changing the rat's metabolism. The rat gains

manipulation check:
aspect of an experiment designed to make certain that variables have changed in the way that was intended

weight because it has a greater tendency to store fat, even if its food intake is restricted.

Construct validity is similar to internal validity. In internal validity, you strive to rule out alternative variables as potential causes of the behavior of interest; in construct validity, you must rule out other possible theoretical explanations of the results. In either case, you may have to perform another study to rule out a threat to validity. For internal validity, you may find it possible to redesign the study to control for the source of confounding. In the case of construct validity, you must design a new study that will permit a choice between the two competing theoretical explanations of the results. When the researchers suspected that rats with brain damage were not really hungrier, they designed tests to find out how the rats responded when the food was unpalatable or harder to obtain or when their exposure to food was limited. In each case, the brain-damaged rats ate less food than normal rats, making the hypothesis of greater hunger less tenable than the alternative theory.

External Validity

external validity: how well the findings of an experiment generalize to other situations or populations

External validity concerns whether the results of the research can be generalized to another situation: different subjects, settings, times, treatments, observations, and so forth. Strictly speaking, the results of a piece of research are valid only for other identical situations: 18 sophomores at State University on a rainy 13th of April 2012 in a room with green walls and an experimenter with a beard. Such literalness is ridiculous, of course, but which variables are trivial to the validity of the experiment, and which are important?

In an influential experiment in perception conducted by Elliott McGinnies in 1949, people were asked to read words that were flashed on a screen. The results showed that taboo (socially unacceptable) words had to be displayed for longer before people reported them correctly. These results were interpreted as showing that a person's threshold for seeing taboo words was higher than the threshold for seeing ordinary words. Today researchers would interpret the data as reflecting people's reluctance to utter the taboo words rather than a truly higher perceptual threshold for them. We mention this experiment because of the particular taboo words used. You may be surprised and skeptical to learn that people would hesitate to say the words *belly*, *bitch*, and *rape* aloud in an experiment. We must remember, though, that this experiment was reported in 1949. The use of language in public has changed a good deal since then, though the status of some words as taboo has remained (Jay, 2009). Today, it is unlikely that if the experiment were conducted in the way that it was in the 1940s it would yield the same results. This experiment could not be generalized to today's world; it would lack external validity.

ecological validity: extent to which an experimental situation mimics a real-world situation

As you read about the experiment on taboo words, you may wonder whether the results might have been different, even in 1949, if there had been a way to examine the question that was more true to everyday life. The idea that experimental results obtained in a laboratory setting might be different from those obtained in a natural setting reflects a question about ecological validity. This type of validity is closely related, but not identical, to external validity, and is concerned with how close an experimental situation is to the real world. So, in order to increase ecological validity in this language study, the participants would have to experience all of the words, including the taboo ones, in a way that words might normally be encountered, such as reading a story out loud.

Statistical Conclusion Validity

statistical conclusion validity: extent to which data are shown to be the result of cause-effect relationships rather than accident

Statistical conclusion validity is similar to internal validity. Here the question is, *did the independent variable truly cause a change in the dependent variables, or was the result accidental, and thus caused by pure chance?* It also asks how strong the relationship is between the independent and dependent variables. To establish statistical conclusion validity, appropriate sampling and measurement techniques must be used, and inferential statistics must be used properly, in keeping with their underlying assumptions. So, for example, imagine that you have randomly assigned people to one of two groups, each of which will eventually be evaluated with a memory test. One group will be given a large amount of caffeine, while the other group will be given a placebo instead. In order for your study to have statistical conclusion validity, and for you to be certain about the effects of caffeine on memory, you must be certain that you have tested enough people, so that your statistical test will have adequate power. You must also be sure that your measure of memory is accurate. Further, you must be certain that the inferential statistic (see Chapter 15) that you chose for analysis is appropriate for data from independent random samples (such as an independent groups t-test). When statistical tests are used improperly, a lack of validity is reflected in the old saying that there are three kinds of lies: lies, damn lies, and statistics.

Even when statistics are used properly, as you may recall from your previous studies, a statistical test establishes only that an outcome has a certain low probability of happening by chance alone. The low probability of chance indicated by the statistical test does not guarantee that the change in the dependent variable was the result of a true cause-effect relationship with the independent variable; there is still a chance that it might instead be the result of random error in sampling or measurement. For that matter, there is no way to guarantee any of the types of validity of a research result; all methods of judging validity simply increase confidence in the conclusion that has been drawn from research. Nevertheless, inferential statistics are an essential tool in judging the validity of a research outcome.

power: the probability of rejecting the null hypothesis when it is, in fact, false

We review inferential statistics in Chapter 15. One question involved in judging the statistical conclusion validity of a study is whether enough observations were made to make it likely that the null hypothesis could have been rejected if it were false. This is the question of **power** (see Chapter 15). If an experiment suffers from lack of power, the experiment may appear to show that the null hypothesis is supported; when in reality, it should be rejected. In that case, the result suffers from a lack of statistical conclusion validity.

effect size: strength of the relationship between the independent and dependent variables

Another question involved in evaluating the statistical conclusion validity of a study is **effect size** (see Chapter 15), or the strength of the relationship between the independent variable (cause) and the dependent variable (effect). The magnitude of the cause and effect relationship goes beyond simply saying that the relationship is "significant" (see Chapter 15) and can help to establish whether a significant result is of practical importance.

Threats to Validity _____

We have been talking about kinds of validity. Now we consider some problems that constitute threats to validity. These threats are valuable aids that help researchers to anticipate potential problems with experiments.

Threats to Internal Validity

In essence, guarding against threats to internal validity consists of learning to avoid the confounding of potentially important variables with the independent variable or variables of interest. The major sources of confounding are considered in turn.

Ambiguous Temporal Precedence

ambiguous temporal precedence: although two variables are related, it is not clear which one is the cause and which one is the effect

As we discussed in Chapter 1, temporal precedence is important in determining whether one thing caused another. The cause must always come before the effect, but in some cases, it is unclear in **ambiguous temporal precedence**. This often happens in correlational studies (see Chapters 8 and 9), in which two things are clearly related, but which one caused the other is not obvious. Take, for example, poverty level and level of performance in school, which are related constructs. To assume that one causes the other, however, could decrease internal validity as there is confusion as to which one is really the cause and which one is the effect.

Events Outside the Laboratory (History)

history: events that occur outside of the experiment that could influence the results of the experiment

Whenever an experiment is conducted in such a way that different experimental conditions are presented to subjects at different times, it is possible for events outside the laboratory to influence the results, and this type of confound is called **history**. If you studied the effects of success and failure on feelings of depression, and all of the participants experienced the failure condition on Monday and the success condition on Wednesday, you can imagine that the results would be difficult to interpret if it rained on Monday and was sunny on Wednesday. This situation may sound like a threat to external validity, but it is not. External validity concerns whether the results of an experiment would generalize to another time, place, or set of participants. Instead, the weather on the two different days confounded the experimental conditions by possibly influencing the dependent variable, feelings of depression.

Maturation

maturation: a source of error in an experiment related to the amount of time between measurements

Subjects may change between conditions of an experiment because of naturally occurring processes. This is particularly a problem in studies that involve children. Certainly, they get older between testing sessions. If the experiment involves a significant lapse of time, changes may occur in motor coordination, knowledge, and the like that could influence the results. Suppose you were interested in studying the effect of *Sesame Street* on children's reading skills. You would want to have a control for the improvement in reading that would occur over time in children not exposed to *Sesame Street*.

Maturation is a more critical problem in research involving children because they change more rapidly over time than do adults. Yet the fact that adults change with age is now becoming widely appreciated. Take, for example, a hypothetical long-term study of attitudes toward alternative lifestyles as a function of age. To separate out changes caused by shifting attitudes in society from changes in individual people as a result of the aging process is not easy. In Chapter 13, we discuss designs that are intended to separate the effects of maturation from experimental manipulations in studies of psychological development.

Effects of Testing

effect of repeat testing: performance on a second test is influenced by simply having taken a first test

Simply being in an experiment or being tested will influence people's performance in a later experiment or administration of the test. The participants may become sophisticated about the testing procedure or may learn how to take tests so that there is an effect of repeat testing and their later behavior is changed by the earlier experience. We have noticed that students as a group generally perform better on the second and later tests in our courses after they have had experience with our styles of testing. This phenomenon is similar to maturation in that the subjects are changed over time, but it is different in that the change is caused by the testing procedure itself, rather than by processes unrelated to the test.

Regression Effect

regression effect: tendency of subjects with extreme scores on a first measure to score closer to the mean on a second testing

The regression effect, one of the most insidious threats to validity, arises in many situations. The regression effect operates when there is less than a perfect correlation between two variables. Individuals who performed at the extremes on one test tend to score closer to the mean on the other test.

The regression effect may occur when two different variables are correlated, such as SAT score and college GPA. It may also occur when the same variable is measured twice, such as when a student repeats the SAT. When two different measures are correlated, we are not surprised when the correlation is less than perfect. But we often get imperfect correlations when the same variable is measured twice. This situation arises when there is error associated with the measurement of the variable. Notice that when we say there is error in the measurement, we do not mean that recording errors are made. We mean that the test itself is not a perfect measure of the construct that is being measured. For example, on a multiple-choice test, students will know some answers and make some lucky or unlucky guesses on the rest, resulting in a score that is not a perfect indicator of what they know. Instead, their score on the test represents the student's level of knowledge plus some level of random error.

random error: that part of the value of a variable that can be attributed to chance

The classic example of the regression effect is that of a teacher who notices that students who scored highest on the first test usually do worse on the second, whereas those who did the worst improve. The teacher often concludes that the ones who did well the first time rested on their laurels for the second test, whereas the ones who did poorly worked harder. In reality, this is not what happened. Whenever random error exists in the measurement of a variable, individuals will deviate from their true score by chance. Some will be lucky; others will be unlucky. Many of the extreme scores, both high and low, will be more extreme than their true value. On the retest, the errors will tend to average out, and the scores of these previously extreme individuals tend to return toward their true value, closer to the mean.

The regression effect can lead to some unfortunate conclusions. A parent may notice that praising a child for good behavior is followed by a decrease in the desired behavior, whereas the child's behavior improves after he or she is punished for bad behavior. If the bad behavior is unusual, generally it will improve anyway. The good behavior also may have been a random event that would decrease with or without praise. The parent wrongly concludes that praise is useless and that the way to teach children is to punish bad behavior and ignore good behavior. Collecting numerous data points, as in the single-subject designs described in Chapter 12, may allow a parent to make a more appropriate judgment about effective management of a child's behavior.

Selection

selection: a confound that can occur due to assignment of subjects to groups

Many studies compare two or more groups on some dependent variable. Any bias in the selection of the members of the groups can undermine internal validity. In Chapter 7, we will discuss the foolproof remedy of randomly assigning individuals to groups. Often this is not possible, however, particularly in research in which it is necessary to study existing groups. You can easily imagine that the local chapter of the Veterans of Foreign Wars would not be a good group to compare with the local chapter of the Society to Protect Baby Seals. Most people would not make as poor a choice as this. But would the Veterans of Foreign Wars from Detroit, Michigan, be a good choice to compare with the chapter from Tuscaloosa, Alabama? You must exercise care and ingenuity to choose or create groups that can be considered truly comparable.

Mortality

mortality: the dropping out of some subjects before an experiment is completed, causing a threat to validity

Mortality is sometimes called *selective subject loss* or *attrition*. Even if there is no bias in selecting participants and you are able to constitute groups that are the same in every respect, your study may be invalid if all subjects do not complete all phases of it. Mortality is a threat to validity because the participants who drop out of a study may be different from those who complete it. Biases can result if particular kinds of participants drop out.

Suppose you are studying two methods of behavior modification on weight control. Group 1 is given a diet to follow. In addition, group members are to keep a diary of everything they eat, weigh all foods to the nearest gram, and estimate all calories consumed. Group 2 is simply given the diet to follow. If more people in the group with the more demanding tasks drop out, by the end of the experiment that group will contain a higher proportion of highly motivated participants who will, in turn, be more likely to succeed in losing weight. You then might falsely conclude that the first condition was more effective than the second.

Another example concerns whether intelligence declines with age in older people. Here, the difficulty is in obtaining equivalent groups to compare across age. If you use the same group at two different ages, some individuals will become unavailable the second time because of illness or death, thus raising the possibility of mortality as a threat to validity. If you consider only those people who are available on both occasions, you may find little or no decline. Are these the appropriate people on which to base your conclusion, or should you make a concerted effort to retest people who are now in hospitals and institutions for the aged? The harder you try to locate participants for retest, the more likely you are to get people who will perform poorly because of sickness rather than old age, per se, which is another confounding variable. Thus, it is difficult to decide whether a true age effect on intelligence exists or whether all decline results from illness.

Threats to Construct Validity

Construct validity is perhaps the most difficult type of validity to achieve because of the indefinite number of theories that may account for a given lawful relationship. The general strategy for obtaining construct validity in a piece of research is to ask whether alternative theoretical explanations of the data are less plausible than the theory believed to be supported by the research. We discuss two areas that pose threats to construct validity.

Loose Connection Between Theory and Method

The experiment described earlier for testing the effects of anxiety on learning was an extreme example of a loose connection between a theoretical construct and method. Nail biting is a poor method of measuring anxiety, and writing with the toes is likely to be a poor measure of learning. Much psychological research suffers from poor operational definition of theoretical concepts. For example, aggressive behavior can be defined as both hunting and fighting in cats. These two theoretical concepts would not be validly tested in a situation in which an example of one class of behavior was taken to belong to the other.

Take an example of behavior that might be called aggressive. We might say that Philip aggressively attacked his job of weeding the garden. Philip's aggressive weeding may simply reflect his desire to get on with more interesting activities. Alternatively, someone familiar with the frustration-aggression law may conclude that he was showing displaced aggression. Perhaps his sister had provoked him to hit her and then made it appear to be his fault, so that their father made Philip weed as punishment. Just as it would be difficult to know which of these two situations actually caused Philip's aggressive behavior, it would be difficult to compare theoretical constructs with behavior that could be ascribed to either concept.

Ambiguous Effect of Independent Variables

An experimenter may carefully design an experiment in which all reasonable confounding variables seem to be well controlled, only to have the results compromised because the participants perceive the situation differently than the experimenter does. Because some participants may see the situation in the same way as the experimenter, but others understand it differently, the experimental circumstances are ambiguous and the independent variable may be affected differently in the participants.

For example, some of the second author's research has involved measuring taste thresholds to chemicals flowed over people's outstretched tongues. The situation seemed perfectly straightforward to him. Occasionally, however, when the session was over, someone would say to him, "What was the experiment really about? You weren't interested in how all that junk tasted, were you?" What those people had done was conduct an experiment of their own instead of the one the researcher thought he was conducting. Fortunately, in research of this type, the participants' ideas about what is supposed to happen are not likely to influence the results in which the experimenter is interested.

Often, though, in psychological research the effect of participant expectations can be devastating. Whenever people are aware that they are participating in an experiment, their behavior may be different from their everyday behavior. A commonplace example is the reaction of people to having a movie camera directed toward them. The solution to this type of problem is to keep the participants from becoming aware that they are participating in an experiment. We look at the pros and cons of this technique in Chapter 8, when we discuss observational research.

The ambiguous effect of the independent variables results from the fact that any psychological experiment for which a person has volunteered must be considered to be a social situation in which both the participant and the experimenter have preconceived ideas about what is expected. The "Nuts & Bolts" section of this chapter details ways in which both experimenter and participant bias may influence an experimental outcome.

Threats to External Validity

Even if an experiment has internal validity, statistical conclusion validity, and construct validity, it may not be generalized to other situations. There are as many threats to the external validity of research as there are dimensions along which one experiment can differ from another. Here we consider the most important differences between experiments that may constitute threats to external validity.

Other Subjects

A common indictment of psychological research is that it uses mainly college students and white rats as experimental subjects. The reasons psychologists rely on these two species is their accessibility to researchers and presumed representativeness. The problem is that millions of species of animals exist, most of them insects. However, if you accept that psychologists are interested primarily in human behavior, then the attention to rats and college students is not as unfortunate as it might seem at first. The degree to which common principles of behavior operate across species is impressive. Many years ago, Skinner (1956) presented data showing that the behavior of a pigeon, a rat, and a monkey under certain experimental conditions was identical in all of the most important respects.

Then again, we must not assume that any animal can be substituted for any other in all situations. Keller Breland and Marian Breland (1961) give many examples of the need to choose the response one wants to study and then to manipulate the variables, paying careful attention to the animal's natural behavioral repertoire. It is easy to teach a chicken to dance, for example, because dancing is similar to its normal behavior of scratching for food. It would not be easy to train a rat to dance, however, because dancing is not close to its natural behavior.

Human participants should be chosen with equal attention to their representativeness relative to some larger population. If you are doing an experiment with college students on bargaining and negotiation, will the results validly predict what a secretary of state or a general would do?

Other Times

Would the same experiment conducted at another time produce the same results? We mentioned this problem earlier in introducing the concept of external validity. The *dirty word* experiment almost certainly lacks external validity today, at least as far as the original words are concerned. Many historical trends render particular research findings invalid, whether they concern use of language, attitudes toward foreign countries, or perception of deviant groups.

Other Settings

A pervasive problem that can hinder external validity involves the question of how the phenomenon observed in one laboratory can be related to a similar phenomenon observed in another laboratory or in the real world. Many psychologists have given up laboratory work altogether in favor of field research, or even armchair speculation, for this very reason. Though laboratory research ensures a higher level of control, it is sometimes not easy to decide if a certain effect is simply a laboratory effect or whether it would survive transplantation to the world outside the laboratory.

Suppose you are interested in whether letting students work at their own pace produces better learning than giving schedules, assignments, and tests. A school that would permit its students to be experimented on might be more open to innovation in general. Likewise, students, teachers, and administrators in such a school might respond more favorably to the self-paced condition than to the more regimented procedure. So your results may not be valid for more traditional schools.

Threats to Statistical Conclusion Validity

Threats to the statistical conclusion validity arise from improper use of statistics in analyzing the data. Because we do not discuss statistics in detail in this book, we mention only two of them here: the problem of power and inaccurate effect size estimation. In the problem of power, the major threat may be the conclusion that the independent variable had no effect, but if your study employed too few subjects or made too few observations, your conclusion may be erroneous. In either of those cases, a difference that is real but small may be lost in the statistical noise. Chapter 15 discusses this problem in more detail under the topic of statistical power.

In the second threat to statistical conclusion validity, inaccurate effect size estimation, the size of the relationship is measured poorly. For example, outliers that change the shape of a distribution can increase or decrease the estimated effect size (Shadish, Cook, & Campbell, 2002). In other words, you might believe that the independent variable caused a much smaller effect than it actually did, and your conclusions about your study would be incorrect. Effect size is discussed in more detail in Chapter 15.

Summary Note on Validity _____

Our review of the many threats to validity should make you aware of the kinds of problems that may arise in research. Not all of the problems discussed here will be as serious in all areas of psychology. From the examples we have used in this chapter, you may have surmised that the problems are acute in the social areas. It is true that most of the literature on validity has been contributed by social psychologists. An area such as visual perception is much less subject to these problems. For example, as long as participants have normal acuity and are not color-blind, one person is much like another for the purpose of measuring visual thresholds.

In Chapter 7, we will consider how to cope with the various threats to validity.

**NUTS
&
BOLTS**

The Social Psychology of the Psychology Experiment

Over the past several decades, much attention has been paid to the biases that can enter into an experiment as a result of the interaction between the participant and the experimenter. This concern comes from the realization that an experiment is a social situation with its own set of rules. Both the participant and the experimenter have expectations about how they should behave in an experiment. The biases that result from the interactions between participant and experimenter can unintentionally influence experimental results and possibly lead to ambiguous effects of the independent variables and suggest some ways of overcoming them.

Role Demands

The participants' knowledge that they are participating in an experiment constitutes a set of expectations about how they are to behave. These expectations are called **role demands**, or demand characteristics, of the experiment. In one experiment, McBurney, one of the authors of this book, had people smell dirty t-shirts and judge them for unpleasantness and other attributes to examine body odor's relationship to socially undesirable traits (McBurney, Levine, & Cavanaugh, 1977). Halfway through the series of t-shirts, one person looked up and said, "You know, I don't believe I am doing this." Nevertheless, she continued. This illustration is just one of the apparently pointless or socially unacceptable behaviors that people will engage in when they believe that they are in a psychological experiment.

role demands: participants' expectations of what an experiment requires them to do

good-subject tendency: tendency of experimental participants to act according to what they think the experimenter wants

Perhaps the most prevalent type of role demand is the **good-subject tendency**. Participants act the way they think the experimenter wants them to act. They may deliberately feign a naive attitude about the expected results even though they can guess the true purpose of the experiment. Perhaps they have heard about the experiment or have learned of similar experiments conducted elsewhere. You may have observed this phenomenon among participants recruited from introductory psychology classes in which many types of experiments are discussed. The participants may pretend to be fooled by the instructions to be *good subjects*.

evaluation apprehension: tendency of experimental participants to alter their behavior to appear as socially desirable as possible

Another kind of participant expectancy is the concern that the experimental procedure in some way measures the participant's competence. Some participants are convinced that the experiment is a carefully disguised measure of intelligence or emotional adjustment. This expectancy gives rise to **evaluation apprehension**, in which participants tailor their behavior to make themselves look as normal as possible. Another name for this problem is social desirability. Researchers who develop attitude scales take care to ensure that various responses appear equally socially desirable so that participants will not damage the results by concealing their true attitudes.

Suppose you are conducting an experiment on the effects of pornography on sexual behavior. Participants are asked to keep a diary of all sexual activity for a week before and after they are shown a pornographic movie. You can imagine that

(continues)

NUTS & BOLTS *(continued)*

people would hesitate to volunteer information about deviant activities. Even if they were honest in their reporting, they might modify their behavior during the experiment in the direction of social desirability. You can see how evaluation apprehension could have the opposite effect of the good-subject tendency.

The role demands of an experiment can cause serious problems with interpreting the results. In hypnosis, for example, people have been concerned that they or others might be induced to perform antisocial acts while hypnotized. In one experiment, hypnotized participants threw a concentrated acid at someone's face at the experimenter's request. (The person was protected by an invisible glass pane.) Interpretation of the results has been controversial. Did the hypnosis cause the compliance, or would nonhypnotized people do the same thing? Martin Orne and Frederick Evans (1965) replicated the study with several new control groups. The experimental group was hypnotized and asked to throw acid at the assistant, which they did. One control group was instructed to pretend to be hypnotized. Five out of six of these faking participants complied with the request to throw acid. They later said they had thought that some safety precaution had been taken to prevent injury to the other person. Orne and Evans decided that no conclusions could be drawn about the likelihood of people performing antisocial acts under hypnosis because people could so easily be induced to perform the same acts without hypnosis.

One of the most extreme examples of the effects of role demands is the well-known Milgram study (1963), in which participants were led to believe they were delivering electric shocks to others over the vigorous protests of those being "shocked." The participants later said they did believe that the other person was being shocked. The fact that they were participants in an experiment in which the experimenter projected an air of authority led them to obey the experimenter and to engage in behavior that people have since found surprising and disturbing.

These general role demands for the experiment together with the good-subject tendency may cause people to play dumb about the purpose of the experiment even if they can figure out the hypothesis or see through a deception. Getting people to admit that they have learned the purpose of the experiment from someone else is difficult because they don't want to make the experimenter feel bad.

Much ingenuity has been devoted to keeping the influence of role demands from undermining the validity of experiments. The most obvious and seemingly simplest solution is to deceive the subject about the experiment's purpose. A cover story is devised that provides a plausible rationale, and the true hypothesis is not revealed. This ploy often works but has several drawbacks, not the least of which involves ethics, as we discussed in Chapter 3. In addition, developing a satisfactory cover story that will not affect the behavior being studied is often difficult. The story may cause participants to behave in a way that interacts with the true hypothesis. Inevitably, too, people hear that many psychological experiments are not what they seem to be on the surface. This knowledge increases the difficulty of devising a believable cover story and may even influence the results of experiments that do not use deception. Another approach is to divide the experiment in such a way that parts of the data are obtained in another setting. This design makes it less likely that participants will put two and two

(continues)

NUTS & BOLTS *(continued)*

together and surmise the hypothesis. For example, people are first given a test of anxiety. Later, those who scored either high or low on the test are requested to take part in an experiment without knowing the basis for their selection.

An additional method of counteracting bias is to use a measure that is unlikely to be influenced by participants' guesses about the hypothesis. Some examples might be such nonverbal behavior as how close people sit to one another or whether they look a person in the eye. Finally, we will mention the tactic of keeping the participant unaware that an experiment is being conducted. Chairs may be rearranged in a public room to study the influence of seating arrangement on social interaction, for example. These and other methods of avoiding bias from role demands are discussed by Aronson, Wilson, and Brewer (1998).

Experimenter Bias

A large number of studies indicate that the experimenter can unintentionally bias the results of an experiment (Rosenthal, 1976). In one study, experimenters were given rats to train. Some were told that their rats had been specially bred for intelligence; others were told that their rats were particularly dull. Those experimenters who were told that they had "bright" rats found faster learning than did the others (Rosenthal & Fode, 1963). The mechanism of the bias in this case was that the experimenters who had the bright rats handled them more than did those who had the dull rats. Some of these studies of bias have become controversial (Barber, 1976). Experiments are often designed to allow bias to operate freely. In some studies, evidence exists that the experimenters may simply have fudged the data rather than biasing them. Nevertheless, there is widespread agreement that an experimenter's biases can subtly influence experiments.

The effects of experimenter bias are so ubiquitous that a standard procedure in many disciplines is for the experimenter to be "blind" to the condition a subject experiences. This method of preventing experimenter bias is excellent and foolproof, but it is not always possible in a psychological experiment. In an experiment in the laboratory of McBurney, we were interested in whether smokers had lower taste sensitivity than nonsmokers. Instead of asking each participant whether they smoked, which would alert the experimenter as to who might have elevated thresholds, participants were met by an additional experimenter who asked them to empty their shirt pockets (to remove cigarettes or lighters). Only after the experiment did we inquire about smoking habits. This technique was probably effective in most cases, but it could not make the experimenter blind to obvious tobacco stains or tobacco odor. So, as you can see, trying to blind an experimenter isn't always easy. Blind experimenters may also devise their own hypotheses about experiments and thus unintentionally bias the participants in the direction of their concocted hypotheses.

Another basic strategy for reducing experimenter bias is to standardize or automate experiments as much as possible. In some experiments, testing participants in all conditions at the same time may be possible. The various conditions can be induced by written instructions given to each subject. If participants must be tested individually, instructions can be tape-recorded or presented via computer, so that each subject receives the same experience. Variations on these basic strategies can be constructed for use in particular situations.

Summary

1. A conclusion based on research is valid when it corresponds to the actual state of the world.
2. Four types of research validity are commonly recognized: internal validity, construct validity, external validity, and statistical conclusion validity.
3. An investigation has internal validity if a cause-effect relationship actually exists between the independent and dependent variables.
4. Confounding occurs when the effects of two independent variables in an experiment cannot be separately evaluated.
5. Construct validity concerns the question of whether the results support the theory behind the research.
6. Every experiment tests auxiliary hypotheses in addition to the main hypothesis. These auxiliary hypotheses are that particular conditions of the experiment are valid measures of the theoretical concepts the experiment is testing.
7. External validity concerns whether the results of the research can be generalized to another situation: different subjects, settings, times, and so forth.
8. Statistical conclusion validity concerns the proper usage of statistics. It addresses whether the observed relationship is a true cause-effect relationship or is accidental.
9. Threats to the internal validity of an experiment include ambiguous temporal precedence, events outside the laboratory, maturation, effects of testing, regression effect, selection, and mortality.
10. The regression effect occurs when subjects are tested on related measures and there is error in the measurement. Individuals who performed at the extremes on one measure will tend to score closer to the mean on the other.
11. Threats to construct validity include a loose connection between theory and experiment and the ambiguous effect of independent variables.
12. Among the problems that cause an ambiguous effect of the independent variables is the tendency for participants to interpret conditions differently from the experimenter.
13. Threats to external validity include problems arising from generalizing to other subjects, other times, or other settings.
14. Threats to statistical conclusion validity include problems arising from a lack of power and inaccurate estimation of effect size.
15. Certain of these threats to validity are more prominent in particular types of research than in others.
16. Psychology experiments may be considered social situations with their own role demands that may interfere with the purpose of the study, eliciting effects such as the good-subject tendency and evaluation apprehension.
17. Ways of preventing role demands from biasing experimental results include inventing a cover story that deceives the participant about the purpose of the experiment, dividing the experiment in such a way that part of the data are collected in another setting, using measures that are

unlikely to be influenced by the participant's expectations, and keeping the participant unaware that an experiment is being conducted.

18. Experimenter bias can be reduced by keeping the experimenter from knowing the conditions in the experiment or its purpose and by standardizing the procedure as much as possible.

Suggestions for Further Reading

ARONSON, E., WILSON, T., & BREWER, M. (1998). Experimentation in social psychology. In D. GILBERT, S. FISKE, & G. LINDZEY (Eds.), *Handbook of social psychology: Vol. 1* (4th ed., pp. 99–142). New York: Oxford University Press. This chapter is a major revision of an earlier chapter by Aronson and Carlsmith (1968) and discusses validity and realism in experimentation.

CARLSMITH, J. M., ELLSWORTH, P., ARONSON, E., & GONZALEZ, M. H. (1990). *Methods of research in social psychology* (2nd ed.). New York: McGraw-Hill. This book focuses on mundane and experimental realism.

SHADISH, W., COOK, T. D., & CAMPBELL, D. T. (2002). *Experimental and quasi-experimental designs for generalized causal inference*. Boston, MA: Houghton Mifflin Company. This book focuses on establishing causality between two events, including evaluating various threats to validity.

A CASE IN POINT

The Effectiveness of Tutoring Sessions

Professor Morgan was interested in helping the less motivated students in his social psychology class learn the material. After the first test, he divided the class into high and low performers based on their test scores. Low performers were invited to attend special tutorial sessions. High-scoring students were not permitted to attend the extra sessions. In these tutorial sessions he covered the same material as in class, but he spent time discussing methods of studying, presented outlines of his lectures, and gave students hints about how to take notes.

On the second test, the experimental group (those who received the tutorials) improved noticeably. The control group did as well as they had on the first test. Professor Morgan concluded that his study proved that the tutorials improved the performance of less motivated students. The results are shown in Figure 6.1.

Professor Frass, however, had some doubts about the validity of the study. She felt that several problems made it impossible to conclude that the experimental condition was, in fact, responsible for the results.

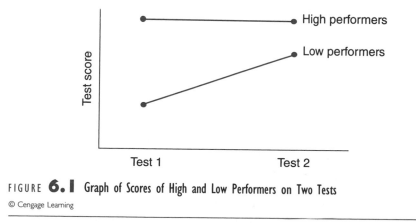

FIGURE **6.1** Graph of Scores of High and Low Performers on Two Tests

© Cengage Learning

(continued)

Required

Prepare a memo that Professor Frass might send to Professor Morgan discussing the problems of validity in his study.

Cognitive Dissonance

Michael and Natsumi designed the following experiment as a project for Dr. Jones's research methods course. They wanted to replicate the classical experiment on cognitive dissonance originally performed by Festinger (1957).

The basic plan of the experiment had participants perform the long and boring task of mating nuts and bolts. Then, the participants were asked to tell other students who were outside waiting their turns to serve as subjects in the experiment how interesting the experiment had been. Some of the participants were offered $1 for talking to the other students, and the others were offered $50. The subjects were to tell the other students that the task was actually fun and interesting.

Festinger's theory predicted that people who agreed to talk to other students for only $1 would experience cognitive dissonance because they would be telling the others that something was interesting when it was actually boring. One way members of the first group might reduce their cognitive dissonance would be to change their minds and decide that the task actually was interesting. Thus, these students, who were paid $1, would actually come to believe that the task was more interesting than would those who were paid $50. (The participants who were well paid would not experience cognitive dissonance because they had an obvious reason for doing what they did.)

Michael and Natsumi recruited their participants from a social psychology class whose instructor was very interested in Festinger's theory. After they ran the participants in the nut-and-bolt mating task, they found that about a third of their participants were grumpy and wouldn't even stay around long enough for the next phase, in which they were going to ask them to talk to the waiting students. Of the ones who did stay, most were polite but made excuses why they couldn't do it. Because

they were having difficulty getting people to agree to the next phase, they decided to get their quota of participants in the $50 group before they started doing the $1 group. Their reason was that they were afraid that the term might be over before they finished their project, and they wanted to have at least some data so they could write it up. They found that 85% of the participants they asked to be in the $50 group agreed to do it, but only 25% of those they asked to be in the $1 group ever agreed, and it took 20 minutes on the average to talk them into it. Most of those in the $50 group agreed right away.

Eventually, however, they found 10 participants who agreed to recruit others in the $50 condition, and 10 for the $1 condition. Five of the $50 participants were males, and two of the $1 participants were males.

Because most of the participants came from the same social psychology class, Michael and Natsumi decided to measure the participants' attitudes toward the experimental task by including the attitude survey on the final exam for the course. The professor agreed to let them add it on to the end of the exam. They found that six of the students who had been in the experiment didn't fill out the survey, but those who did said, on the average, that the experiment was very interesting and a valuable learning experience in relation to the course. Two of the remaining six participants were tracked down and given the survey individually.

The average interestingness scores were 5.5 for the $50 group and 6.0 for the $1 group, on a 7-point scale.

Their research methods professor was quite chagrined to read their report. Dr. Jones thought that he had done a better job of teaching than was reflected in their project. He told them they had violated just about every type of validity mentioned in their text.

Required

Write Professor Jones's critique of the way they conducted their experiment.

Reading Between the Lines

6.1 Do Younger Infants Prefer Simpler Patterns?

Wendy Brennan, Elinor Ames, and Ronald Moore (1966) showed infants cards with black-and-white checkerboard patterns on them. All cards were the same size, and the number of squares per card was 4, 64, or 576. They found that 3-week-old infants looked longest at the simplest card, that 8-week-olds preferred the middle card, and that 14-week-olds preferred the most complex card. They concluded that there was a developmental trend in preference for complexity. Can you think of another interpretation of these results?

6.2 Is There a Bias Against Men?

Martin Fiebert and Mark Meyer (1997) divided male and female college students into small groups. While someone in the group recorded the responses, the students then responded orally to the following verbal cue: "A man [woman] is ___" (Fiebert & Meyer, 1997). All participants responded to both cues. Fiebert and Meyer scored the resulting sentences for themes that reflected positive, negative, or neutral stereotypes. Fiebert and Meyer found that 57% of the sentences reflecting stereotypes about men were negative, whereas only 20% of the sentences about women were negative. They interpreted the data as indicating a large negative cultural stereotype against males. Can you think of alternative hypotheses to account for these results?

Web-Based Workshops on Research Methods and Statistics

Wadsworth Cengage Publishing Company maintains Web-based workshops on research methods and statistics. These workshops give a different slant on the material in this book.

www.cengage.com/psychology/workshops

For this chapter, see Reliability and Validity, as well as Confounds—Threats to Validity.

Exercises

6.1 Find the Confound

Dr. R. A. Rabinoff, professor of physics at the Maharishi International University, claims scientific proof that transcendental meditation (TM) can influence the weather. According to Franklin Trumpy (1983–1984), the university was building a domed structure for the practice of levitation. They were rushing the construction throughout the cold Iowa winter and needed to pour concrete on days when the weather would permit.

According to the university's architect, the concrete was poured whenever the schedule called for it and was obtained from a company that supplied ready-mixed concrete. If the company agreed to supply the concrete the next day, the students at the university were instructed to meditate that evening for favorable weather.

According to Rabinoff, the weather was favorable six out of eight times that the students meditated, proving the effectiveness of meditation. Trumpy's analysis of the actual data for the area revealed that the weather was favorable on less than half of the days during the period covered by the project, showing that there was a considerable difference in the weather on the days when concrete was scheduled to be poured.

Let us assume that the data are statistically significant and that the results were not a fluke (a Type 1 error; see Chapter 15).

Required:

What possible source of confounding can you think of in this study? Is there some other variable that might explain the correlation between the practice of TM and the occurrence of good weather? (Hint: Think about the role of the concrete supplier. Remember that concrete tends to set up within a short time after it is mixed and thus cannot be stored for any length of time.)

6.2 The *Sports Illustrated* Jinx

Sports Illustrated magazine often puts outstanding athletes on its cover. It is widely believed that this exposure jinxes these athletes because their performance often takes a nosedive afterward. However, this phenomenon is not limited to those who make the cover of *Sports Illustrated*. Between 1924 and 1986, only eight National League batting champions and 13 American League batting champions repeated their feats the next year. Similarly, there were 32 Cy Young Award winners between 1956 and 1986, and only three of them repeated the next year: Sandy Koufax of the Los Angeles Dodgers, 1965 and 1966; Denny McLain of the Detroit Tigers, 1968 and 1969; and Jim Palmer of the Baltimore Orioles, 1975 and 1976.

Besides a jinx, other causes of failure to repeat an outstanding athletic performance have been suggested: Perhaps the athletes are distracted by all the attention they receive, or they choke in trying to repeat, or they become complacent.

Required:

What principle in this chapter can explain this phenomenon? Explain in detail how the principle applies to these situations.

6.3 Identify the Source of Invalidity

An educational psychologist is asked to conduct a study to determine if class size has any effect on academic achievement. The psychologist identifies a large fifth-grade classroom in one inner-city school and a small fifth-grade classroom in another inner-city school. Principals from each school agree to participate in the study and select the teachers and classes. At the end of the school year, the researcher obtains achievement test scores from students in both schools and compares the mean achievements of the two groups.

Required:

a. Based solely on the preceding description, what threats to internal or external validity exist in this study? Explain.
b. Can you think of an alternative method that would strengthen the internal and external validity of this study?

6.4 Control and Validity

A psychology professor designs a study to determine whether alcohol consumption causes poor grades in an introductory experimental methods course. She believes that students who have higher levels of alcohol consumption will have lower grades in the class. There are a total of 104 students enrolled in four introductory experimental psychology classes, and all four classes are taught by this same professor. The students in each class are surveyed as to the amount of alcohol they intake each week, and their grades are also recorded.

Required:

a. Identify the threats to validity that may be present in this study.
b. Can you think of a different way to ask the same question that might have a higher level of internal validity?

6.5 Finding the Source of Invalidity

Ms. Hardnose and Mr. Goodheart are managers at Universal Widget, Inc. They make annual evaluations of their employees, but their evaluation methods are very poor. In fact, all differences in evaluations from one employee to another and from one time to another with the same employee are caused by random fluctuations. Hardnose fires all employees whose performance is unsatisfactory, whereas Goodheart usually gives them another try and works with them to help them improve. Hardnose finds that the replacements for the fired employees generally perform better than the ones fired. Goodheart finds that the unsatisfactory employees generally improve on their next evaluation.

Thus, Hardnose has empirical evidence supporting her position that one should always fire someone who is doing poorly, whereas Goodheart finds empirical evidence that it pays to give unsatisfactory employees a second chance. How is this possible?

CHAPTER SEVEN

Control

PREVIEW

Chapter 7 discusses the ways that scientists control for the threats to validity identified in Chapter 6. We first consider general strategies, such as experimental control, which reduces the amount of variability in a situation. Then we discuss specific strategies, such as assignment of subjects to conditions, which rule out alternative causes of outcomes.

The Concept of Control

control: any means used to rule out threats to the validity of research

Control is the other side of the validity coin. The heart of the experimental approach to knowledge is to ask the following two questions: (1) What are the threats to the validity of a contemplated piece of research? (2) What means are available to neutralize those threats? This approach is so basic that anyone who is acquainted with research has heard of control groups. Every experiment must have a control group, right? Wrong.

It *is* true that you must have some method of countering every plausible alternative explanation of the results of your experiment. It is also true that this often involves the use of a group of participants who do not experience the manipulation—that is, a control group—to serve as a standard against which to compare the effect of the variable of interest.

Many experiments are performed, however, in which the use of a group that does not receive the independent variable makes no sense at all. Suppose you are interested in the effect of teaching methods on learning. You might arrange for some students to receive only lectures and others to receive only discussion. You conclude that one method of teaching is better than the other, and you do so without having a third group that never went to class.

We define *control* as any means used to rule out possible threats to the validity of a piece of research. The concept of control is essentially a way of establishing that two individuals (or groups, or conditions) are identical except for the variable of interest. When that is the case, the research is internally valid. In psychology, the concept of control is used in two rather different ways: first, as standard of comparison, and second, as a way of reducing variability.

Control Provides a Standard of Comparison

The first and fundamental meaning of the term *control* is that of providing a standard against which to compare the effect of a particular independent variable. If two experimental conditions differ on only one independent variable, then any difference between the two conditions following the treatment may be attributed to the operation of that variable. All other explanations except those that might occur by chance are ruled out by the existence of the second, or control, condition.

The *standard of comparison* meaning of the term *control* is illustrated in Table 7.1. Two groups of participants are tested on a dependent variable. Group 1 receives Treatment A (say, 5 mg of caffeine); it is the experimental group. Group 2 receives no treatment; it is the control group. The control group serves as the basis of comparison for the experimental group. If the two groups were equal before the experimental treatment, then any post-experimental difference between them can be attributed to the treatment.

Although a control group is an effective way of achieving control of extraneous variables, it is not the only way. We said earlier that control can be achieved without a control group. Table 7.2 illustrates this point. We still have two groups, both of which are tested after receiving treatment. However, instead of Group 1 experiencing A (caffeine) and Group 2 experiencing the absence of A, both groups experience some value of A. So, A_1 (5 mg) and A_2 (10 mg) could be two different caffeine levels. Assuming the groups were equal before treatment, we can attribute any difference between Group 1 and

experimental group: subjects in an experiment who receive treatment

control group: subjects in a between-subjects design experiment who are like the experimental group in every respect except that they do not receive treatment

TABLE **7.1**

Use of a Control Group

© Cengage Learning

Group	Treatment
1 (experimental group)	A present
2 (control group)	A absent

TABLE **7.2**

Control Without a Control Group

© Cengage Learning

Group	Treatment
1	A1 (e.g., 5 mg caffeine)
2	A2 (e.g., 10 mg caffeine)

TABLE **7.3**

Use of a Control Condition in a Within-Subjects Experiment

© Cengage Learning

(All Subjects) Condition	Treatment
1 (experimental condition)	A present
2 (control condition)	A absent

Group 2 on the test to the difference between caffeine levels in Condition A_1 and Condition A_2. Although we do not have a control group as such, each group serves as a control for the other. We have as much control in this situation as we did in the previous example, in which we had a control group.

Let us consider one further point. Instead of having different subjects experience each condition, in some experiments each subject experiences every condition. In such an experiment, instead of having a control group, we have a control condition, as illustrated in Table 7.3. When each subject experiences every condition, we say that each subject serves as his or her own control. An experiment of this kind is called a within-subjects experiment because the differences between conditions are tested within individual subjects. An experiment in which different groups of subjects experience different conditions is a between-subjects experiment because the differences between conditions are tested between different subjects.

Control Reduces Variability

A second meaning of the term *control* is distinct from the first but closely related—namely, the ability to restrain or guide sources of variability in research (Boring, 1954, 1969). Why is it important to reduce variability? Limiting the things that change to those mandated by the experimental design (such as the independent variable) reduces the chances of confounding variables or measurement error and increases our confidence in the experimental results. Keeping everything constant except the independent variable gives us confidence that it is the only thing that could have caused the change in the dependent variable. This idea of experimental control is the one brought home so convincingly by the operant conditioning work of B. F. Skinner. When one has so limited the sources of variability in an experiment that the behavior becomes highly predictable, one has achieved experimental control. We are

---

control condition: a condition in a within-subjects design experiment that does not contain the experimental manipulation

within-subjects experiment: research design in which each subject experiences every condition of the experiment

between-subjects experiment: research design in which each subject experiences only one of the conditions in the experiment

extremely impressed to observe a pigeon that has been trained to peck a key for food in the presence of a green light, but not to peck in the presence of red. When the bird is well trained, the light virtually turns the bird on and off.

Relating the Two Meanings of Control

The two meanings of *control* are related in the following way. The primary meaning allows one to conclude that a dependent variable is associated with an independent variable and not with any other variable. The second usage facilitates drawing this conclusion by so limiting the number of variables operating in the situation and their range of values that the conclusion is clearer. We can characterize the difference between the two meanings by use of the terms *control experiment* and *experimental control* (compare Sidman, 1988). When we have experimental control (secondary meaning), we have a much more sensitive situation in which to rule out alternative explanations of the experimental results (primary meaning).

Both meanings of the term *control* relate to the use of statistics in research. First, we use inferential statistics to evaluate the probability that a difference between experimental and control groups or conditions is likely to have arisen by chance alone. Second, we make enough observations or use enough subjects to reduce the variability of our estimate of the size of the experimental effect, and so make our statistical evaluation more precise.

The next section deals with the most important ways of achieving control in research. At the outset, we should note that just as all types of threats to validity do not appear in all research, so it is not necessary or even possible to use every means of control in all research. The various methods of control are tools for psychologists to employ as necessary. Some will be used almost always (general strategies), others less often (specific strategies).

General Strategies

In general, an experiment is testing a hypothesis, essentially looking for a difference between a control and an experimental condition that is caused by the independent variable. Failure to confirm a hypothesis does not necessarily mean that the hypothesis is incorrect. Yes, you read that correctly. If you don't find results that support your hypothesis, it doesn't prove that the hypothesis is wrong. Instead, other problems could have occurred during the experiment that make it *seem* as if the hypothesis is deficient (see Chalmers, 1999). For example, if the electrode recording the data in a single-cell neural recording experiment had a faulty connection, it might malfunction such that only a portion of the neural activity was recorded. In that case, the conclusion drawn about the hypothesis would be as faulty as the electrode, and we could not have very much confidence in the experimental results. To have confidence that the independent variable caused the difference, it is essential that *only* the independent variable changes and that everything else in the experiment is controlled. We discuss three general strategies for achieving control in psychological research: using a laboratory setting, considering the research setting as a preparation, and instrumenting the response. Although these strategies are closely related, we consider them separately for emphasis.

Control in the Laboratory

Laboratory research is generally preferred to field research. The reason is simple and has to do with what a laboratory is. We tend to think of a laboratory as a room with gray or black furniture, no curtains on the windows, tile floors, and workers dressed in white coats. Certainly we are describing one type of laboratory, but the description has nothing to do with the essentials of research. Basically, a scientific laboratory is a place set up to allow the most appropriate control over variables of interest in the particular research. Thus, a social psychology laboratory might well have rugs on the floor, curtains on the windows, pictures on the walls, and comfortable chairs—like any living room. Laboratory work in social psychology requires control over elements such as choice of participants, beginning and end of social interaction, and freedom from distraction. If someone's home or a storefront building meets these requirements, such a setting might be a better preparation and serve just as well or better than a sterile-looking room. The results of laboratory research depend entirely on the degree and type of control that is possible.

In Chapter 8, we will discuss some methods and advantages of field research. Here we simply say that at times field research is preferable and at times laboratory research is preferable. Much social research is done in field settings because it is not possible or ethical to manipulate certain variables in a laboratory. Most people would frown on mugging subjects to learn what determines whether they will call the police. Further, in some cases, the effect of a manipulation might not be realistic enough in the laboratory. Sometimes a nonexperimental study has more external validity than a corresponding experiment could ever have. Simulating a riot, for instance, would be difficult to do in a laboratory. But even those people who advocate field research agree that they must give up a degree of control and that problems of internal validity thus become greater. Field research is warranted when ethical or practical problems preclude the degree of control that would justify calling a certain research program a laboratory experiment. The question always is this: Which type of study will best answer the question you want to ask? Laboratory research remains the ideal when it is feasible, simply because it offers the most control. Selecting the maximum level of control possible when considered with the nature of the problem is the ideal.

The Research Setting as a Preparation

One of the first questions to be answered in designing research is to decide what type of setting or system you want to use. You may be interested in learning what determines whether people will be cooperative or competitive. You could study how children play with toys, how basketball players pass to each other, how the hippocampus encodes spatial information, or how salespeople decide who will help a customer. Any of these might be a good study, and each study would be best conducted in its own unique experimental situation.

The idea of a preparation is familiar to anyone who has studied biology. A preparation is an environment that is selected or constructed for a particular purpose. Everything that is a part of the research setting is a part of the preparation, which is really a context for data collection. So the preparation includes the experimental equipment, the method of testing, and the location of testing, as well as the subject used in the study. For example, researchers often use the giant nerve axon of the squid as a good preparation for studying nerve conduction. Because the squid nerve is much larger than those in other animals, it permits biologists to do things that they cannot do with other nerves and forms an excellent preparation for neurological exploration. Scientists can easily slip electrodes into the cut end of the neuron and record the electrical activity of the neuron in response to stimuli, as well as make other measurements that are extremely difficult, if not impossible, to make on smaller neurons. The concept of a preparation is not as familiar in psychology; yet one of the researcher's goals is to choose the most suitable preparation for studying a given problem. Some of the most important contributions to psychology have been made by people who selected an appropriate preparation. For example, Eric Kandel chose to study memory in a snail called aplysia because it was a simple system that had fewer neurons than humans (Kandel, 2007). Eventually, the work on memory in aplysia resulted in a Nobel Prize for Kandel.

People who devised a new preparation for studying a given phenomenon have also made valuable contributions to psychological research. A good example is the use of reaction time to study cognitive processes. This preparation capitalizes on the theory that cognitive processes take a certain amount of time. Differences in reaction time can indicate differences in cognitive processes. The classic example is that of Franciscus Donders, who in the 1860s measured simple and choice reaction time (Donders, 1868/1969). Simple reaction time is the time it takes to respond to a certain stimulus, such as an ace of diamonds flashed on a computer screen (using modern technology). The participant knows in advance what is coming and simply has to respond as fast as possible. In contrast, choice reaction time is the time it takes to make the correct response when the participant doesn't know in advance which response will be required. For example, the participant may have to press one key with the left hand if an ace of diamonds appears, and press a different key with the right hand if a nine of clubs is seen. The difference between simple reaction time and choice reaction time is then taken to be a measure of the time required to choose between two responses. Reaction time methodology is a mainstay of cognitive research. It is used to study widely differing topics such as mental rotation, memory, and schizophrenia. One reason it is so useful is its simplicity and the reliability of the data it yields.

Preparation in the sense of the research setting is involved in every experiment, but hardly ever is it spoken of that way in books on research design in psychology. Nevertheless, it is one of the most important considerations in designing research. *Exactly which situation will provide the most powerful relationship between the variables of interest?* is an important question to ask yourself. No amount of sophisticated design or statistical analysis will make up for a poor choice of research preparation.

Instrumentation of the Response as Control

We have discussed the research setting as a preparation that allows the sensitive analysis of a phenomenon. Another important means of increasing the sensitivity of the research is to improve the measurement of the behavior being studied. Many researchers pay little attention to the response that will be measured, but here is where a little effort can pay big dividends. In short, the precision with which you measure the dependent variable can influence your results. Just as certain preparations have become classic in psychology, so certain methods of measuring dependent variables have also had enormous impact. We have already mentioned the Beck Anxiety Inventory. The Minnesota Multiphasic Personality Inventory, functional magnetic resonance imaging (fMRI), and Stevens's direct psychophysical scaling methods are other excellent examples. These techniques have greatly improved the sensitivity of research in their respective fields. Many scientists devote their careers to developing and honing measurement devices. Most of these people do not intend to become methodologists but do so to evaluate more precisely phenomena of interest to them.

We have used the term *instrumentation* in discussing the task of improving response measurement. This use may seem strange because not all measurement methods employ mechanical means. The usage is deliberate, though. It calls attention to measurement devices as instruments for reducing behavior to forms convenient for data analysis, such as numbers. One characteristic of a good measurement instrument is that it takes the response out of the realm of casual observation and makes it reliable, giving accurate measurements time after time. Only in this way can we speak of the measurement of behavior as objective, thus meeting the requirement of interobserver reliability necessary for science. Therefore, even a measure of a subjective state, such as the pleasantness of an odor, can be considered objective, provided the instrumentation of the response is adequate.

Specific Strategies

As we mentioned previously, each experiment is distinctive in terms of the potential threats to its validity. So, just as all of the types of threats to validity are not risks in every study, all control techniques are not necessary or appropriate for every study. As such, each experiment requires careful consideration as to how to best control for its own threats. The control strategies listed below are appropriate in some experimental situations, but not in others, and are tools for the psychologist to apply as the circumstance warrants.

Subject as Own Control (Within-Subjects Control)

We are aware that each of us is unique and varies in many ways that could be important in an experiment. One of the most powerful control techniques is to have each participant experience every condition of the experiment. In this way, variation caused by differences between people is greatly reduced. The experimenter is wise to adopt the strategy of using participants as their own controls whenever possible.

This control method is common in many areas of psychology, particularly in the study of sensation and perception. For example, if you are interested in the effect of adaptation to different concentrations of salt on the threshold for salt, using different participants for each condition does not make much sense. The experimental manipulation is not likely to destroy the naiveté of the participant, who is unlikely to guess the purpose of the experiment even after experiencing it. In fact, the participant may not be aware that the experiment has different conditions. In addition, if enough time is allowed between conditions, there is unlikely to be an important carryover between conditions. The participant will recover in a few minutes from the effect of adaptation to salt and will be ready to experience the next condition.

In many experiments, however, using subjects as their own controls simply is not possible. For example, once the participant has learned something by one method, learning the same problem again by using a different method is impossible. The information cannot be unlearned, so using the subjects as their own controls is not possible.

Another situation in which using subjects as their own controls is not feasible occurs when contrast effects exist between the conditions of the experiment, so that experiencing one condition may carry over and influence the response to another condition. These contrast effects, also known as order and sequence effects, will be discussed in Chapter 10. For now, it is sufficient to note that there are situations in which conditions may affect one another. For instance, if magnitude of reward is the independent variable, subjects who experience a large reward (say, $200) first may respond less to a small reward (say, $20) than they would have if only the small-reward condition had been received.

A more concrete example is provided by an experiment involving lifting weights. Suppose you have two weights and each is lifted only once. You may think that you have controlled for order and sequence effects if half of the participants experience one order (light, heavy) and the other half the opposite order (heavy, light). Let us suppose there is a *true* response of six to the light stimulus and eight to the heavy one, as determined in a between-subjects experiment in which each participant lifted only one weight.

Now, if this weight-lifting experiment were attempted in a within-subjects experiment, we would have to be alert to the possibility of contrast effects. If there were a contrast effect between the two weights that resulted in a doubling of the true difference in the responses when the weights were presented sequentially, those who experienced light before heavy would give responses of six and 10, instead of six and eight. Those who experienced heavy before light would give responses of eight and four, instead of eight and six. The average responses for the two different orders would thus be five and nine and the difference between the stimuli would *appear* to be four, instead of the true difference of two (summarized in Table 7.4). Sometimes contrast effects can simply exaggerate an outcome that would occur between subjects, as in this example. Other times they produce outcomes that would not otherwise be found. The difference between using a within-subjects design and a between-subjects design can cause puzzling discrepancies in the results of experiments.

In summary, you should consider using subjects as their own controls whenever three conditions can be met:

1. Using subjects as their own controls is logically possible.
2. Participating in all conditions of the experiment will not destroy the naiveté of the subject.
3. Serious contrast effects between conditions will not be present.

TABLE **7.4**

The Problem of Controlling for Sequence Effects in Within-Subject Experiments

© Cengage Learning

Order	Within Subjects	
	Stimulus	
	Light	Heavy
Light, heavy	6	10
Heavy, light	4	8
Average effect	5	9
	Between Subjects	
	Stimulus	
	Light	Heavy
"True" effect	6	8

Random Assignment (Between-Subjects Control)

random assignment:
unbiased assignment process that gives each subject an equal and independent chance of being placed in every condition

Another powerful control method is random assignment of subjects to groups in a between-subjects experimental design. The term *random assignment*, or *random allocation*, is used here in a specific sense: The allocation of subjects to conditions is random when each subject has an equal and independent chance of being assigned to every condition. The advantage of random allocation of subjects to conditions is that once subjects have been randomly assigned, the only way that confounding of subject-related variables with the experimental variable can occur is by chance. Although it is often used in common speech, the statistical term *random* has a specific meaning that is not to be confused with haphazard, arbitrary, or without a plan. (See also the discussion of random selection in Chapter 9.)

At first glance, calling random allocation a method of control may seem improper because you appear to be throwing away a means of control and casting yourself on the mercies of chance. However, when you randomly assign subjects to conditions, you can be sure that only chance can cause the groups to be unequal with respect to any and all potential confounding variables associated with the group members. All sources of confounding variables are ruled out, except as they become associated with the conditions by chance. Even if some variable is confounded with the independent variable by chance alone, assessing the likelihood of this happening is possible via statistical methods.

Modern statistical analysis provides numerous ways of testing whether experimental results are likely to have occurred by chance alone. These statistical methods rely completely on random allocation of subjects to conditions. In other words, statistical tests make estimates of the probability that purely random allocation of subjects to the various experiment conditions might have produced the results obtained. If the subjects are not assigned to conditions randomly, the statistical tests are not valid. One of the biggest sins in experimental psychology is to perform an experiment that cannot be analyzed statistically. A common way to commit this error is to fail to assign subjects to conditions randomly.

Suppose you have already chosen your subjects from a population in some manner, and you have an experiment with two conditions. How do you decide which subjects will experience which conditions? There are many different ways of accomplishing this, but the following is a good way to do it.

The first step is to assign numbers to individuals. If you have 20 subjects, you assign numbers one through 20 to the individuals in a way that is nonsystematic. Then look at a random-number table, such as the one in Appendix A. You could decide that the first subject would go into Group 1 or Group 2 depending on whether a one or a two came up first in the random-number table. This, however, would require you to go through many numbers because only about a fifth of the numbers in the table are ones and twos. (Of course, if you had more than two groups, it would be most efficient to use this strategy and consider the numbers in the table to be the number of the group.)

An alternative would be to consider Group 1 to be odd and Group 2 even. You would then put a subject into Group 1 if an odd number came up and into Group 2 if an even number came up. Turn now to the portion of a random-number table that appears as Table 9.1 (on page 233).

Because the first two columns appear to have been used, we might as well begin with Column 3. The first four digits are all even, so the first four subjects will go into Group 2. Then there is one odd number followed by two more even numbers, matching: control procedure to ensure that experimental and control groups are equated on one or more variables before the experiment one odd number, and then four more even numbers. By this time, we have allocated 12 subjects to conditions: two into Group 1 and 10 into Group 2. Because we want 10 per group, the last eight must all go into Group 1. Does this sound like a random assignment—to have eight of the first 10 subjects go into Group 2 and all of the last eight go into Group 1? It may not look random, but it was the result of a random process. Some researchers would be tempted to throw out this particular result as not representative and start over again, but the statistical model says we should go with it. (We would probably do another random assignment if we had some reason to believe that the numbers assigned to the subjects were systematic in any way—for example, if the assignment seemed to follow the order in which the participants had signed up for the experiment.)

Computer generated randomizations may or may not be truly random, depending upon the process by which they are calculated. Some programs use the time of request as a "seed" to generate the numbers, while others use different techniques. While the appropriateness of a random number generator depends heavily on the application, at least one Web site, www.randomizer.org, provides access to people seeking random numbers for research purposes.

Using the procedure of randomization requires care. Students may be asked to volunteer for an experiment by signing up on a sheet for available times. The experimenter might be tempted to assume that the times are

TABLE **7.5**

Steps in Conducting a Randomized-Groups Experiment

© Cengage Learning

1. Randomly assign subjects to groups

Group A	Group B
S_1	
	S_2
	S_3
	S_4
S_5	
S_6	
S_7	
	S_8
S_9	
	S_{10}

2. Administer experimental conditions

3. Examine differences between groups

selected randomly and might place the first half of the students in one condition and the last half in the other. However, you can easily think of a number of ways in which the two groups could differ. The people who sign up for the early times may be more highly motivated to serve as participants, or all may have jobs requiring them to leave campus in the afternoon. Either of these possible differences between those who sign up early and those who sign up late (or one we haven't thought of yet) has the possibility of affecting the experimental outcome and threatening the validity of the experiment. To control for these potential threats to validity, the experimenter must randomly assign participants to conditions after they have signed up. Another example of a mistake in allocating subjects is to pull rats from a group cage and place the first batch selected in Condition A, the second batch in Condition B, and so forth. A little reflection will make it clear that the order in which the rats will be picked depends on their tendency to approach or avoid the experimenter's hand. This difference could be relevant for many experiments in learning, motivation, or social behavior. Table 7.5 summarizes the steps in a randomized-groups experiment.

Matching (Between-Subjects Control)

matching: control procedure to ensure that experimental and control groups are equated on one or more variables before the experiment

Experimental precision can sometimes be improved by matching subjects on a pretest before randomly allocating them to conditions. When the subjects differ among themselves on an independent variable known or suspected to affect the dependent variable of interest, matching may be necessary. For example, suppose you are studying the effect of two different instruction techniques on mathematical performance. You might expect that children who were more mathematically competent to begin with would continue to gain more math knowledge regardless of the way they were taught. If participants were allocated randomly to conditions, the possibility exists that more of the brighter children could wind up in one condition than in the other. By testing the children before the experiment, you can allocate them in such a way that the average mathematical competence in the two groups is the same.

The first requirement to justify matching is a strong suspicion that there is an important variable on which the subjects differ that can be controlled. Further, you must believe that a substantial correlation will be present between the matching variable and the dependent variable. In our example of the math knowledge experiment with children, you would find the two children with the poorest math skills and randomly place one in Group A and the other in Group B. You would repeat this procedure until you had paired off all the children. If you found that, in fact, those children who initially had more math knowledge tended to gain skills regardless of the group they were in, you would have been justified in matching on prior math knowledge. By correlating gain in mathematical performance with starting math knowledge, you would have found that math gain correlated with beginning math knowledge despite the effect of the teaching technique, the variable of interest. If you found that there was little or no correlation, however, you would have wasted your effort in matching the participants, and may have actually weakened the power of your experiment.

It is possible to weaken your experiment by matching the subjects if the matching variable is not substantially correlated with the dependent variable. This effect results because the statistical test appropriate for a matched-groups design considers the data from pairs of subjects, whereas the randomized-groups test considers individual subjects. You can see that there are twice as many subjects as pairs of subjects, so the randomized test has more numbers to work with and therefore is more powerful. You can also see that it is important to make certain that matching is necessary before using this control technique.

A second condition necessary to justify matching is that it must be feasible to present a pretest to the subjects before assigning them to the conditions. For example, testing math knowledge before an experiment is a simple matter, but giving a full IQ test to every prospective student in an experiment on learning may not be feasible. The experimenter's time would probably be better used in simply testing more subjects, unless the IQ data can be obtained readily and ethically or unless the experiment is long enough to allow time for IQ testing.

Some bases for matching are better than others. Generally, you try to match on the basis of some variable that has the highest possible correlation with the dependent variable. Normally, the highest correlation is between the dependent variable and itself. In other words, if you are doing an experiment using reaction time, matching subjects according to their reaction times makes the most sense. You could present some practice trials and then allocate subjects to conditions based on their performance in the trials. If you are doing an experiment on learning and you want to control for intelligence, however, matching according to socioeconomic status (SES) would be a poor choice, even though there is some correlation between SES and intelligence scores. Your choice would be poor because the correlation between SES and IQ is weak. The slight control achieved by matching would be offset by the lower statistical power of a matched-groups design.

Let us emphasize a final point about the mechanics of matching. Even when you have matched your subjects, you must still randomly allocate the members of the pairs to conditions. If you have 10 pairs of rats matched for weight, you must flip a coin or follow some procedure that will ensure that the members of each pair are allocated to groups randomly. Otherwise, your procedure for placing them into groups could introduce confounding results. Table 7.6 summarizes the steps in a matched-groups experiment.

Building Nuisance Variables into the Experiment

nuisance variable: a condition in an experiment that cannot easily be removed and so is made an independent variable as a means of control

In addition to random assignment or matching, another way to handle variables that cannot easily be removed from the experiment is to design the experiment so that these nuisance variables become independent variables in the study. Nuisance variables are known or suspected to affect the dependent variable, but variables in which you have no theoretical interest. Left uncontrolled, these variables may affect the dependent variable so strongly that they hide the true effects of the independent variable. Building these nuisance variables into your study allows you to measure their effects and to examine the effects of your independent variable.

Suppose your participant pool consists of both day-school and night-school students in introductory psychology. These people may differ in several ways that could relate to psychological variables. Night-school students may be older, may have more family and work responsibilities, and so forth. If you suspect that your participants are dissimilar on some dimension related to day- versus night-student status that may affect the dependent variable, you have two choices. The first is to use only day or night students. This solution has the advantage of reducing the variability, but it also reduces the participant pool and the generality of the results. The second choice is to build the nuisance variable—in this case, when the students attend class—into the experiment.

Figure 7.1 shows the results of a hypothetical experiment in which night- or day-student status was designed into the experiment as a nuisance variable. If we do not consider day or night status, we find considerable overlap between the results of conditions A and B. We might not be willing to conclude that the conditions had a differential effect on the dependent variable. (We are ignoring the possibility of using inferential statistics to help in this decision.) But let us consider day or night classes as a nuisance variable; that is, let us analyze the data separately for day and night students.

We find now that no overlap exists between Group A and Group B for night-school students considered alone or for day-school students considered alone. We have increased the sensitivity of the experiment by building a nuisance variable into the study. Note that the nuisance variable need not have any theoretically important role in the experiment. Though we may not have cared why night-school students scored higher initially, the nuisance variable may now suggest new theoretical questions for another experiment.

TABLE **7.6**

Steps in Conducting a Matched-Groups Experiment

© Cengage Learning

1. Administer pretest
2. Rank subjects on pretest

S_1

S_2

•

•

•

S_{10}

3. Form pairs on the basis of ranking

S_1
S_2 ⎫⎬⎭ First pair

S_3
S_4 ⎫⎬⎭ Second pair

•

•

•

S_9
S_{10} ⎫⎬⎭ Fifth pair

4. Randomly assign members of pairs to groups

Group A	Group B
S_1	S_2
S_4	S_3
S_5	S_6
•	•
•	•
•	•
S_{10}	S_9

5. Administer experimental treatments
6. Examine differences between members of pairs

S_1	—	S_2
S_4	—	S_3

•

•

•

What is the average difference between pairs?

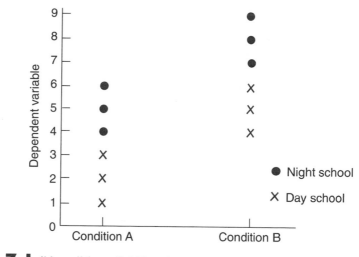

Nuisance variables should not be confused with confounded variables. A confounded variable is one that varies with the independent variable. A nuisance variable is treated as a second independent variable that is varied separately from the first one.

Statistical Control

Except for randomization, all the control methods described so far can be classified as methods of achieving experimental control; they aim to reduce variability as much as possible. Sometimes these techniques can be spectacularly effective, and a very few observations on a single subject can be used to draw firm conclusions. Usually, however, that old devil variability cannot be completely exorcised from the experiment. Then it is necessary to use **statistical control**. Statistical control in the broad sense is synonymous with inferential statistics, the branch of statistics that deals with making decisions in the face of uncertainty.

statistical control: mathematical means of comparing subjects on paper when they cannot be equated as they exist in fact

Suppose you have a difference between two groups on some dependent variable in an experiment. Was the effect real, or did it happen by chance? The point behind these questions is that statistical control is not just involved in the analysis; it is involved in designing an experiment. Are there enough subjects? How many trials should there be? Can the experiment as designed be analyzed properly by accepted statistical methods? Such considerations are important enough to merit courses that specialize in the statistical analysis of experimental data. For now, because you are not taking such a statistical design course, you will have to answer questions of statistical control with general knowledge about statistics and with advice from your instructor. Remember that in the end, the question of statistical control comes down to whether you and others believe the data. If you have enough subjects to look convincing, and if you have avoided the pitfalls discussed in this chapter, you probably have a good experiment. Although you may be fooled into thinking that some effect was caused by the independent variable when it was actually random—especially when you look at your own data—at this stage of your career, the important thing is to aim to design an experiment that will convince yourself and others.

In the narrower sense, statistical control refers to a means of equating subjects on paper when they cannot be equated in fact. Suppose you are studying the effect on grades of two different styles of PowerPoint presentations in the classroom, one of which has very few words and one of which is text intensive. Because randomly constituting the classes is not feasible, you must work with existing classes. If the students in the two classes do not have the same average IQ, you will have a problem in attributing the difference in grades to the teaching styles. But if you know the relationship between IQ and grades in the class, you can find out how much the students' grades differed from what you would have expected, based on the prediction of the IQ–learning relationship.

This approach is illustrated in Figure 7.2, which represents the relationship between grades and IQ. Each data point represents a single individual, the X being placed at the intersection of the person's grade (measured on the y-axis) and his or her IQ (on the x-axis). The slanting line shows what grade would be predicted for persons having particular IQs. (In other words, this is the regression line that predicts grade from IQ.) The data points that are circled each represent a single subject's position on the two axes. You can see that Student 1 earned a higher grade than would have been expected from the relationship shown by the slanted line. Student 2, however, earned a lower grade than predicted by the line. Notice that both students received the same grade.

The basic idea of statistical control as applied to this example is that it enables you to compare students not on their absolute grades, but on the difference between grade and what would have been expected from the line that predicts grade from IQ. Student 1 would be scored as earning a grade of plus-so-many points and Student 2 as earning minus-so-many points. You could

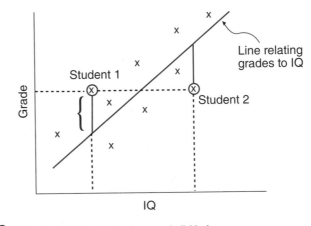

FIGURE **7.2** Using Statistical Control to Compare Individuals

© Cengage Learning

conclude that 1 had benefited more from the condition than had 2. This technique makes it possible to compare groups that are made up of subjects who differ on IQ. The technical term for this comparing process is analysis of covariance, a topic beyond the scope of this book. Be aware that this method is available as a means of controlling for variability in an experiment. You may refer to one of the standard books on statistics, such as Kirk (1994), for a description.

Replication, Replication

replication: repeating an experiment to see if the results will be the same

A method of control seldom described as such is replication—the repeating of an experiment to see if the same results are found the second time. Laypeople sometimes assume that once a result has been found by a scientific experiment, the conclusions are fixed permanently. The truth is that an experiment seldom stands by itself, particularly if the results are surprising. In fact, an unusual result remains in a kind of limbo until other experimenters have successfully replicated the experiment. If other experimenters obtain the same results, they become part of our scientific knowledge. If the replication is not successful, the supposed facts found in the original experiment are invalid and are forgotten. Many examples of this process have occurred throughout the history of psychology as well as in the other sciences.

A particularly good example of how dubious phenomena get weeded out is provided by the history of research on transfer of memory by injecting material from a trained animal into an untrained animal. The line of research began with the finding that feeding trained planaria (flatworms) to untrained planaria resulted in a transfer of memory to the untrained worms (McConnell, 1962). Eventually a similar experiment was tried on rats (Babich, Jacobson, Bubash, & Jacobson, 1965), except that instead of feeding the trained rats to untrained ones, the experimenters injected extracts of their brains. The resultant finding created much interest in the scientific community because of its enormous implications for the mechanisms of memory and for the storage of information in the nervous system in general. A number of positive replications were published (see W. L. Byrne, 1970, for a review). However, it soon became clear that all was not well with this supposed phenomenon. Not all investigators could replicate the finding. Within a few years of the original research, an article was published by 23 authors from seven laboratories (Byrne et al., 1966) reporting that all of these scientists had failed to replicate the original finding. They stated their conclusions cautiously: "Our consistently negative findings ... indicate only that results obtained with one method of evaluating this possibility are not uniformly positive" (p. 658).

In the intervening years, the phenomenon has not been firmly established despite continued work. One textbook (Cotman & McGaugh, 1980) summarizes the situation as follows:

> In general the findings are extremely conflicting, and as a consequence no firm conclusions can be drawn. Research has not as yet specified either optimal or reliable procedures for producing a transfer effect. Further, it is not at all clear

what type of molecule might be responsible for producing the effect.... Should such experiments be reproducible, it should be possible to determine the basis of the effects. At the present time, the memory transfer effect must be regarded as not yet convincingly demonstrated. (p. 313)

The history of the research on the transfer of training by injection followed a typical pattern. The first reports created a great deal of interest and many attempts at replication. Some of these attempts were successful, and the investigators naturally published their results. Those who did not find the effect were reticent about admitting their failures and, additionally, may have had difficulty getting negative results published. Enough negative results eventually accumulated, however, to overcome biases, and the literature began to reveal a preponderance of negative results. Such a scenario has occurred repeatedly in science, with the result that those research effects that are not repeatable are discarded.

Two types of replication are commonly distinguished: direct and systematic. Direct replication occurs when someone repeats essentially the identical experiment in an attempt to obtain the same results. Systematic replication occurs when Researcher B says, "If A's theory is correct, then the following should happen." Then B performs an experiment different from A's but based on it. If A's results and theory are correct, B should find a result that supports the theory.

Direct replication is seldom carried out because finding exactly the same thing as someone else did brings little glory. More specifically, it is difficult to get grants for replications, journals tend to avoid publishing such research, and professors who spend time replicating other people's work do not get promoted. Direct replication is usually attempted only when systematic replication has failed. Investigators then go back and repeat the original method more exactly to pinpoint the source of the difference in results.

Systematic replication is the usual way that experiments are replicated. Researcher B will do an experiment similar to Researcher A's but with different types of subjects, with different values of the stimulus, or with different ways of measuring the theoretical concepts. All of these approaches are considered systematic replication. As long as results consistent with A's are found, A's original experiment is supported by B's work. You will notice that systematic replication tests external validity by using different subjects, species, or situations. Construct validity is tested when different ways are used to measure the theoretical concepts. Statistical validity is tested in all replications, both direct and systematic.

The need for replication is sometimes downplayed in favor of showing that a given result would be unlikely to occur by chance alone. Believers in ESP point out that particular experiments produced results that would have happened only once in billions of experiments by chance alone. The ESP believers' statistics are usually impeccable, but their understanding of the methods of science is faulty. Innumerable ways exist in which an experiment can fail to be valid, giving results that are caused neither by chance nor by the particular hypothesis. Calculating long odds is impressive, but it is only one of a number of considerations in evaluating the experiment. Generally, experiments in ESP fail to replicate. Although believers in ESP may propose reasons for this failure, scientists will pay little attention to ESP until someone devises an experimental situation that gives consistent results in its favor. R. A. Fisher, who largely invented modern statistical methods, said, "Very long odds ... are much less relevant to the establishment of the facts of nature than would be a demonstration of the reliability of the phenomena" (as quoted in Crumbaugh, 1966, p. 527).

Experimental Design as Problem Solving

The next six chapters of this book consist largely of examples of good research design. We do not discuss all possible designs for the simple reason that doing so would be impossible. Rather, we give a list of some of the most common designs for you to use as models in designing similar experiments of your own. Experimental designs should be tailor-made for each experimental problem. Sometimes an existing design will fit the problem perfectly. More often, alterations must be made. Therefore, it is better to create the design from the beginning.

Designing an experiment is a matter of solving particular problems of validity by applying particular methods of control. When every problem has been solved, the experimental design is complete, and it is time to look in books on experimental design to see if your design can be analyzed according to accepted statistical procedures. To look in the books first is to put the cart before the horse and to forget that the essence of experimental design is solving threats to validity in the best way possible. Nevertheless, it is important to create an experiment that can be analyzed.

Two of the general strategies listed at the beginning of this chapter— using the setting as a preparation and instrumentation—are not usually discussed as such in experimental design books. They are the guiding principles of design, however. Use the specific strategies we have discussed as tactics in applying these general principles.

The Elegant Experiment

The goal of every scientist is to design the best possible experiment. How is such a concept put into practice, though? Do you keep testing more and more subjects until the conclusion is inescapable? Do you keep adding variables until every possible source of confounding is taken into account? We find the concept of the elegant experiment helpful in thinking about such questions. In everyday usage, the term *elegance* implies richness combined with tasteful simplicity. In mathematics, the term emphasizes simplicity. An elegant proof draws a powerful conclusion in the simplest possible way. This idea is what we mean by the elegant experiment: the simplest experiment that will make a clear and convincing test of a hypothesis.

It is possible to include so many variables in a study that not enough measures are made on any one to draw firm conclusions. It is possible to have such a complicated design that you lose sight of the forest for the trees.

Consequently, it is important to realize that many trade-offs must be made in the course of designing an experiment and that this process requires hard decisions. Do you spend more time and effort at the outset testing pilot subjects and refining your experimental procedure? Or do you decide to test more subjects in the main experiment to make up for the uncontrolled variability? We cannot tell you what to do in any particular case. Paying careful attention to these questions, though, will result in experiments that are convincing tests of hypotheses.

In selecting the word *elegance*, we have deliberately chosen a term that has an aesthetic connotation. Designing experiments is an art that requires creativity and that reflects the tastes of the experimenter. Such activity can be both challenging and rewarding.

NUTS & BOLTS

How to Use the Rest of This Book

By now, you have an idea of what science is. We have talked about the basic principles of research design, as well as about the principles of validity and the basic means of controlling for threats to validity. We might stop here and tell you to begin designing your own research based on these principles. Obviously, we have not done that, and for a good reason. Important as the principles are, probably no one could become a successful researcher by reading a book on the principles of research.

One learns to do research by studying examples of research and, better yet, by doing research. Scientific research is one of those activities that is best learned by working with someone who serves as a guide in a hands-on situation. In this respect, the way to become a scientist parallels the way an apprentice becomes skilled by working under the direction of an experienced person. The importance of this process can be seen in the many famous scientists who were students of other learned scientists. Firsthand experience in the laboratory of a good scientist has no substitute when it comes to learning how to do science. Myriads of attitudes, skills, and techniques are assimilated in such a situation. No book, including this one, can do more than serve as a pale substitute

Our goal in this book is to present those concepts that we spend the most time explaining when we talk with students about research. Although we cannot anticipate all questions, we have tried to answer those that are most common and most important. Your instructor, along with this book, will guide you as you learn to do research.

Choice of Methods

Once you have a question that you want to investigate, you are faced with many decisions: what kind of subjects, what task, what apparatus, what kinds and values of independent variables? By the nature of this book, we must deal with these questions in a rather general fashion. Nevertheless, certain principles can be stated.

(continues)

NUTS & BOLTS *(continued)*

Your review of the literature will reveal standard tasks, apparatus, subjects, and so forth that are generally used in studying a certain problem. For practical and theoretical reasons, it makes sense to follow the standard practice as much as possible and to deviate only when there is good reason to do so. You may feel that a different task, for example, might be more appropriate. What you want to find out will dictate many of these choices. Recall our earlier discussion of the research setting as a preparation. You should make your choices of subjects, apparatus, and so forth with the following question foremost in mind: Which alternative will permit the most sensitive test of the hypothesis? Above all, you must choose a design that will yield data that you can analyze statistically.

Choice of Subjects

Here we make only general statements about the choice of subjects because many considerations are specific to particular studies. The allegation that the college sophomore and the white rat have been studied too often is true. The reasons become obvious when you start to consider your own alternatives.

If the problem lends itself to study with animals and other experimenters have used the rat, those facts become good reasons for you to do so. Changing strains of rat or even the supplier of the rats can make comparing results between experiments difficult. In addition, using another species of animal may require you to solve new housekeeping problems. For example, can you keep another species of animal healthy in a laboratory? If you are studying humans and you want to use a population other than the college student, what problems will you face with recruitment and payment of volunteers, standardization of techniques on the population, and so forth? Such considerations help to explain the extensive reliance on these two classes of subjects. Of course, if you have good reason to use a different population, a little care and effort in designing the study around other subjects often pays big dividends.

Selection of Participants

Ethical and practical considerations enter into the selection process. With the exception of naturalistic observation and certain other types of research, the consent of the participants must be obtained before they participate. We discussed the ethics of research in Chapter 3, but let us note again that people in psychological research ordinarily should participate voluntarily.

Ideally, participants should be a random sample of the population to which you want to generalize the results of your study. For example, to generalize the results of an experiment on college students to the entire adult population of North America, the students ought to be a random sample of that population. Obviously they cannot be, but they should be at least a random sample of college students.

In actuality, most experiments on humans draw participants from introductory psychology classes. Furthermore, participants usually volunteer under coercion, for a course requirement, to meet a departmental requirement, or for extra-credit in a course. Under these circumstances, you can see that students who sign up for experiments early in the

(continues)

NUTS & BOLTS *(continued)*

term may be different from those who wait until the last week of class to volunteer. Even going into a class and asking for volunteers will produce a biased sample. For example, women are more likely to volunteer for an experiment when they are in the ovulatory phase of their menstrual cycle and less likely to volunteer when they are menstruating (Doty, 1975). If this variable were important in an experiment, atypical results would be found using women who volunteer spontaneously. Calling women randomly from a list of potential volunteers and asking them to come in at a particular time can minimize the problem. In this situation, they are less apt to participate differentially than if they have volunteered spontaneously.

Your college is likely to have standard procedures for recruiting participants. In fact, all details of the experiment must be approved by the appropriate authorities through the IRB. You should follow these procedures carefully. For example, if all introductory psychology students must participate in a certain number of hours of experimentation as a course requirement, and if they are supposed to sign up through a central office, then going directly to the classroom to seek volunteers is not fair to other experimenters.

However participants are recruited—in class, by poster, or through newspaper ads—make sure they know the exact building, room, date, and time of the experiment. You should give them a way to contact you if they must cancel, and you should be able to contact them, in case you must cancel.

Random assignment of participants to conditions is essential. You must decide in advance your procedure for achieving this. If the experiment is a between-subjects design, you should have a random order made up before the participants arrive. Then you will follow the assignment as the participants show up: The first one will receive the condition that is scheduled first, and so forth. Leave no room for subjectivity when you assign subjects to conditions. If subjects are to be tested in pairs, flip a coin to determine which one is assigned to which condition.

How many subjects should you test? There is a rational way of deciding how many participants to use in an experiment, provided you know how much variability to expect in your data. In ordinary laboratory experiments, however, almost nobody uses this basis for deciding the number of participants. The reason is simple and practical. Suppose you want to achieve a particular degree of precision in your results. Of course, the more participants you have, the less the means of your data will deviate from their true values. The usual way of representing this error of measurement is called the *standard error of the mean*. The following equation shows how the standard error of the mean decreases with increases in the number of subjects:

$$\sigma_{\overline{X}} = \frac{\sigma_x}{\sqrt{N}}$$

In this equation, sigma represents the standard deviation of the scores, and *N* is the number of subjects. You can see from the equation that to cut the standard error of the mean in half, you must double the square root of *N*. To double the square root of *N*, you must quadruple *N*.

(continues)

NUTS & BOLTS *(continued)*

How the number of subjects affects the precision of an experiment is illustrated in Figure 7.3, which shows how the standard error of the mean decreases with N. In this figure, we assume that the standard error of the mean is 1 unit when there are 10 subjects. To reduce the standard error of the mean to 0.5 units, we must increase the number of subjects to 40. If we want to reduce the standard error of the mean again by a factor of 2, to 0.25, we must use 160 subjects. Thus, you can see that increasing the number of subjects does not decrease the error of measurement in a linear way. Doubling the number of subjects reduces the standard error of the mean by only 30%. (Not all experiments will use the standard error of the mean in data analysis, but the effect is the same for other statistics.) The law of diminishing returns operates. For this reason, most experiments use a minimum of about 10 subjects—or, if they have more than one condition, a minimum of 10 subjects per condition. Examine the literature to find out how many subjects have been used in experiments similar to yours and how much precision was obtained. If you want more precision, ask yourself if using more subjects will make a significant improvement. If not, try to increase the precision of measurement experimentally.

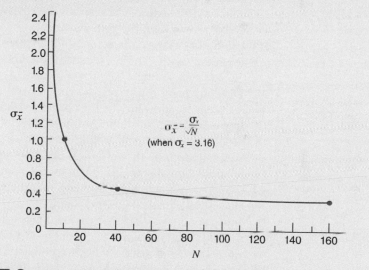

FIGURE **7.3** Relationship Between the Standard Error of the Mean and the Number of Subjects in an Experiment

© Cengage Learning

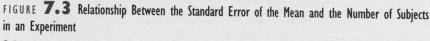

Summary

1. The fundamental meaning of the term *control* in psychology is that of providing a standard against which to compare the effect of a particular variable.

2. Experiments in which different groups of subjects experience different conditions are known as between-subjects experiments. Those in which

each subject experiences every condition are known as within-subjects experiments.

3. The group in a between-subjects experiment that receives the treatment is called the experimental group; the group that does not receive the treatment is called the control group.

4. In within-subjects experiments, the condition that does not contain the experimental manipulation is called the control condition.

5. It is not necessary to have a control group or a control condition in an experiment as long as there is some group or condition that can serve as a comparison for a particular experimental manipulation.

6. A failure to confirm a hypothesis does not necessarily mean that the hypothesis is incorrect. It may indicate problems with the way that the experiment was carried out.

7. All variables should be held constant across groups or conditions except for the manipulation of the independent variable.

8. A second meaning of the term *control* is the ability to restrain or guide sources of variability in research. This meaning is captured in the term *experimental control*.

9. There are three general strategies for achieving control in research: using a laboratory setting, considering the research setting as a preparation, and instrumenting the response.

10. Laboratory research is defined not by the use of a particular kind of room but by the ability to control the important sources of variability in the research setting.

11. The concept of a preparation emphasizes choosing the best possible research situation in which to test a hypothesis.

12. Instrumentation of the response refers to the means of measuring the dependent variables. Careful measurement renders responses objective and may even be thought of as creating responses.

13. Specific control strategies include using subjects as their own controls, randomizing, matching, building nuisance variables into the experiment, and using statistical control.

14. Subjects may be used as their own controls when doing so is logically possible, when serving in all conditions will not destroy their naiveté, and when there will not be serious contrast effects between conditions.

15. The allocation of subjects to conditions is random when each subject has an equal chance of being assigned to every condition.

16. Matching may be used when an important variable on which subjects differ is correlated with the dependent variable and where it is feasible to present a pretest to the subjects.

17. Nuisance variables that cannot easily be removed from the experiment may be controlled for by making them independent variables in the experiment.

18. Statistical control may be thought of broadly as synonymous with inferential statistics. More narrowly, statistical control involves equating subjects on paper by means of the analysis of covariance.

19. One of the most important means of control is the replication of an experiment. Direct replication is repeating essentially the same experiment. Systematic replication is doing a different experiment in which certain results should be found if the original experiments were valid.

20. Controlling the sources of invalidity is essentially a matter of solving problems. When the problems are solved, the experiment is designed. The goal of a researcher is to design the most elegant experiment that will answer the questions of interest and will deal with the problems of validity.

21. The choice of method is dictated by factors such as the exact hypothesis to be tested, the methods that are standard in the particular field, and practical considerations.

22. The number of subjects to be used depends on the size of the effect and the anticipated variability of the data. The power of the experiment increases proportionately with the square root of the number of subjects.

Suggestions for Further Reading

SIDMAN, M. (1988). *Tactics of scientific research: Evaluating experimental data in psychology.* Boston: Authors Cooperative. This book presents a classic discussion of experimental control from the Skinnerian perspective.

A CASE IN POINT

Vision in Babies

To illustrate the considerations involved in deciding on the number of subjects to test in an experiment, consider the following example. Professor Strauss studies vision in babies. She wants to find out if they can recognize their mothers' faces. Her experimental situation involves having a baby look at a pair of faces projected on a screen for five minutes. She measures how long a baby looks at the mother's face compared with a control face. Previous studies have shown that if babies recognize their mothers' faces, they will look longer at the mother than at the control woman. From pilot work, Professor Strauss estimates that a baby will look 10 seconds longer at the mother's face. The standard deviation of time spent looking is 100 seconds.

Professor Strauss has a budget of $1,000 for this experiment. It costs her $10 to run a single baby. Her apparatus has some problems, however. She believes that a new projector would make the pictures much clearer, increasing the difference in a baby's viewing time for the mother's face to 20 seconds. A new projector would cost $250. Also, her method of recording the babies' preferences has some problems because it is hard to see where the baby is looking. An automatic recording device would reduce the standard deviation of the responses from 100 to 50 seconds but would cost $500.

Professor Strauss scratches her head and wonders what to do. If she uses her old equipment, she can run 100 babies. If she buys both the projector and the recording device, she can run only 25. Of

(continued)

course, she could buy just one or the other. What should she do? For this example, the *t*-test is the appropriate statistic. The question then becomes what combination of effect size, standard deviation, and number of subjects will give the largest predicted *t*.

$$t = \frac{\overline{X}}{\sigma/\sqrt{N}}$$

Consider the effects of the various alternatives on this equation.

First, let us use our intuition. Increasing the effect size, decreasing the variability of the response, and increasing the number of subjects should all increase the predicted level of significance of the study.

Now, let us look at the equation and see how this works. Increasing the number of seconds that a baby looks at the mother's face compared with the control face will increase the numerator, *X*. So increasing the effect size will increase *t*. The denominator of the fraction is itself another fraction. The numerator of the bottom fraction is the standard deviation of the number of seconds by which the babies prefer the mother to the control. Decreasing the standard deviation will increase *t* because it affects the denominator of the main fraction. Increasing the number of subjects will increase the value of *t*, however, because it is the denominator of the lower fraction. Increasing the square root of *N* will decrease the value of the ratio. Because $\sigma/\sqrt{N}$ forms the denominator of the main fraction, *t* is increased. Determining which alternative is best requires Professor Strauss to work out the value of *t* for each alternative.

Reading Between the Lines

7.1 Brain Damage Sometimes Produces Obesity in Rats

Lesions in a part of the brain known as the ventromedial hypothalamus have been known to produce obesity in rats. Some investigators, however, were unable to find the effect as reliably as others and proposed that the lesion itself did not produce the obesity. Rather, the scar tissue that resulted from the lesion stimulated a nearby area that actually controlled eating. Experiments were done to produce more or less scar tissue and, therefore, more or less irritation to the nearby area of the brain. These experiments showed that the manner in which the lesion was produced did not matter as much as which laboratory did the experiments. One group of investigators consistently found that the lesions produced obesity, whereas others tended to find no effect. Eventually, a simple difference in methods between the successful and unsuccessful experiments was found. Can you guess what it was?

7.2 Mozart Effect–Shmozart Effect

In 1993, Francis Rauscher and colleagues published a paper in the prestigious journal, *Nature*, reporting on an experiment in which 36 students were given three sets of spatial reasoning tasks, each of which followed a 10-minute listening task that was filled with one of three things: silence, a relaxation tape, or an upbeat piece of music composed by Mozart. Results showed that students performed more highly on the spatial task after they had listened to Mozart's music as compared to the other two conditions (Rauscher, Shaw,

& Ky, 1993). The authors concluded that the complex music enhanced spatial reasoning (thus the "Mozart effect"). Can you think of any reason other than "complex music" per se for these authors' findings? (*Hint:* What else was different between the groups?)

Later, the experiment was attacked in a number of research papers (e.g., Pietschnig, Voraceka, & Formann, 2010), because many papers failed to replicate the effect. Can you think of a reason that this result might not be replicated?

Web-Based Workshops on Research Methods and Statistics

Wadsworth Cengage Publishing Company maintains Web-based workshops on research methods and statistics. These workshops give a different perspective on the material in this book.

www.cengage.com/psychology/workshops

For this chapter, see Controls.

Exercises

7.1 Random Assignment

You are designing an experiment in which 10 subjects will experience the experimental condition and another 10 will be given the control condition. A total of 20 subjects has signed up for the experiment. Randomly assign them to the two groups. Describe your steps.

7.2 Matching Participants

You are designing an experiment to investigate the effect of odor on alertness. In this experiment, 10 subjects will experience the experimental condition (smelling peppermint) and another 10 will be given the control condition (odorless). You know that age significantly affects the sense of smell, with people over the age of 60 showing a decreased ability to identify odors. A total of 20 subjects of all ages (18–80) have signed up for the experiment. How would you assign them to the two groups using a matching technique? Describe your steps.

CHAPTER **EIGHT**

Nonexperimental Research, Part 1: Observational, Archival, and Case-Study Research

PREVIEW

Chapter 8 begins the discussion of nonexperimental research —that is, research in which an independent variable is not manipulated. The researcher does not have complete control over the conditions of the nonexperimental research study. We discuss observational research, in which the researcher simply measures behavior that takes place in uncontrolled settings, and archival research, which involves examining already existing records. Case studies typically use a number of methods of studying some immediate situation, such as a psychiatric patient or an outbreak of mass psychogenic illness.

As we saw in Chapter 7, experiments provide the most powerful means of studying behavior because they permit the greatest control. Many questions cannot be studied experimentally, however. It would probably not be possible to study Mardi Gras under highly controlled conditions. Even if it were possible, you certainly wouldn't want to attempt it.

As you can tell from the term, *nonexperimental research* is defined by exclusion: research that is not experimental. This requires us to define *experiment* before we go on. The distinction between experimental research and nonexperimental research is based on the degree of control that the researcher has over the subjects and the conditions of the research. Key words here are **manipulation** and **assignment** versus **observation**.

manipulation: in an experiment, conditions or variables assigned or presented to a participant

assignment: in an experiment, pairing a subject with a condition or variable, according to the experimenter's plan

observation: the record of a behavior

An experiment is a kind of investigation in which some variable is manipulated. The researcher has enough control over the situation to decide which participants receive which conditions at which times. Suppose you were interested in the differences in learning between students who only studied a book and students who read the book and also attended lectures. A researcher who is able to perform an experiment would set up the conditions (manipulate a variable) and assign subjects to them. As we will see in later chapters, this assignment of subjects to conditions makes it possible to determine with more certainty whether the differences between conditions actually caused any differences in behavior. If the researcher cannot assign subjects to groups but must only observe how students in two already existing classes at a college learn according to the same two methods, we do not have a true experimental study. In this case, we would find that many things could have caused any differences in learning between the classes. For example, the students may have signed up for one class or the other on the basis of their preference for the instructor, the teaching method, or the time of day. Any of these factors could cause differences in learning.

A second characteristic of nonexperimental research is that the data collection procedure often must forfeit some degree of control in return for obtaining the data. For example, we might decide to study public records that may be almost, but not exactly, in the form we desire, or we might have to keep a questionnaire short to help gain the cooperation of subjects.

qualitative research: nonexperimental research that asks questions regarding how people make meaning out of the world

A third characteristic of some nonexperimental research, called **qualitative research**, concerns the questions that are typically asked by the research. The questions that are asked by qualitative research differ from those of experimental research. Qualitative research is much less interested in the cause and effect of behavior than is research based on experimentation. Instead, qualitative research is interested in how individuals understand themselves and make meaning out of their lives.

correlational research: nonexperimental research that measures two or more variables to determine the degree of relationship between them

Nonexperimental research is often called **correlational research** because it seeks causes of behavior by looking for correlations among variables.[1] (See Chapter 14 for a discussion of correlation, and Langston's [2010] laboratory

---

[1] Some students and reviewers of this book have objected to the statement that correlational research seeks causes of behavior. It is our opinion that they have taken too literally the caution that you cannot prove causation from correlational data. Of course this statement is true. However, it remains the case that correlational research is widely used to infer causation when experimental data are not available. The evidence that smoking causes lung cancer used to be entirely correlational. Most people, however, were convinced it was true, and this finding has been subsequently demonstrated experimentally.

manual for additional examples of correlational research.) The term is somewhat misleading, however, because all research is correlational to the extent that it seeks functional relationships between variables (compare Cook & Campbell, 1979). Calculating correlations among variables does not make the research correlational in the strict sense. We often compute correlations among variables in the truest of experiments. What makes research correlational in the common usage is the inability to manipulate some variable independently. In correlational research, relationships are studied among variables, none of which may be the actual cause of the other. For example, doctors have noticed that people who drink red wine have better health. This does not necessarily mean that red wine improves health, or that healthy people prefer to drink red wine. The two items are merely related; we do not know which one caused the other. Either one could actually be caused by some third variable. Perhaps people with enough money to drink red wine can also afford healthy diets. One can only speculate as to the causes of the relationship. This is why all statistics books emphasize, "correlation does not prove causation." We demonstrate causation when we can decide which variable caused the other, and this is best done in an experiment.

Nonexperimental research is often a first step in starting to answer theoretical questions by empirical methods. Experimental research frequently is done as a follow-up to previous nonexperimental observations. For example, experimental research on physiological and behavioral factors in alcoholism has followed from the nonexperimental observation that alcoholism tends to run in families.

It is convenient to distinguish several varieties of nonexperimental research. The first may be called **observational research**—that is, research in which the researcher simply observes ongoing behavior. Examples are field observation of ducks from a blind or television monitoring of people in a store.

The second category is **archival research**; in this method, existing records are examined to test hypotheses about the causes of behavior. For example, a researcher might study crime statistics in different countries to see if there is a relation between capital punishment and the murder rate.

The third category we call the **case study**. This category is different from the others in that the researcher investigates a particular situation that has come to his or her attention. The situation may be a practical problem that must be solved as soon as possible, or it may be an event, person, or animal that intrigues a researcher. An investigator might study the victims of a natural disaster (such as the oil spill in the Gulf of Mexico) to determine its effects on their psychological health (Grattan et al., 2011), or the impact of severe social isolation on an individual's ability to learn language (Jones, 1995). Case studies are typified by the varied nature of the methods used to study the problems and intensive description of a single individual or a single group of individuals.

The fourth category of nonexperimental research is the **survey**; in this method, participants are requested to cooperate by responding to questions. Nearly everyone has taken part in a survey. This chapter considers observational, archival, and case-study methods. Chapter 9 will discuss survey research.

observational research: study method in which the researcher observes and records ongoing behavior but does not attempt to change it

archival research: study method that examines existing records to obtain data and test hypotheses

case study: exploratory study of an existing situation as a means of creating and testing a hypothesis

survey: assessing public opinion or individual characteristics by the use of questionnaire and sampling methods

The Hermeneutic Approach _____

Before we begin studying the various nonexperimental methods, we need to take a short detour to discuss what it is that scientists using these nonexperimental techniques are trying to accomplish. You may be inclined to wonder why this detour is necessary because all psychologists try to understand behavior. In fact, Chapter 1 discussed methods of finding causes as a way of understanding behavior. The problem, however, is that causality is more difficult to determine in correlational research. It is often difficult to decide which variable caused the other, or whether both variables are caused by a third (see Chapter 14). This problem has led some social scientists to consider their task to be the discovery of the meaning of a behavior rather than the causes of the behavior.

These scientists consider their task to be the attempt to understand and interpret behavior rather than search for its causes. So, essentially, the question being asked is not *why did the behavior happen?* but rather, *what did the behavior mean?* Social scientists have adopted the term hermeneutics to describe methodology that looks more at interpretation than causation. The concept of hermeneutics was borrowed from the field of biblical interpretation, where the task of the scholar is to find out what the original meaning of a text was to the people originally meant to read it. Psychologists who use the hermeneutic approach may try to interpret the meaning of two people who are holding hands. If we attempted to explain the behavior in terms of cause and effect, we would have to try to determine what caused hand holding on that particular occasion for that particular couple. This attempt to explain the interaction in terms of cause and effect would be much clumsier than to interpret its meaning to the individuals as a public indication of a close relationship (Goffman, 1971). As we proceed through this chapter, we will find that in some places the traditional cause–effect approach seems more appropriate, and in others the hermeneutic approach is more natural.

hermeneutics: the principles of interpretation of a text's meaning

Observational Research _____

Observational research involves recording ongoing behavior without attempting to influence it. This method takes two general forms: naturalistic observation and participant-observer research.

Naturalistic Observation

naturalistic observation: observational research of subjects in their natural environment carried out to disturb the subjects as little as possible

Naturalistic observation is research conducted in such a way that the subject's behavior is disturbed as little as possible by the observation process. The observation is made in the environment where the behavior naturally occurs. You have probably seen films showing naturalists observing birds or other animals from within a blind, a device for screening the observers from the view of the animals being studied.

unobtrusive research: another term for naturalistic observation, commonly used in the social sciences

In the social sciences, naturalistic observation is often called **unobtrusive research.** The term *unobtrusive* simply refers to the effort that researchers make not to influence, or obtrude on, the behavior being studied. Still

nonreactive research: another term for naturalistic observation in the social sciences, emphasizing that the subjects are unaware that they are being studied

physical trace: unobtrusive measure of behavior that uses physical evidence

another term for naturalistic observation is nonreactive research. The term *nonreactive* emphasizes that the subjects are unaware that they are being studied and therefore do not react to the presence of the observer.

Methods of observational research are as varied as the subject matter being studied. Researchers have been very ingenious in devising unobtrusive measures of behavior (e.g., Webb et al., 1999). One broad category of unobtrusive measures is known as physical trace measures. These measures make use of physical evidence of some behavior. For example, researchers have studied graffiti in school restrooms to discover attitudes toward racial integration of the school, smudges on pages of library books to see which pages are most read, and grease prints on display cases in museums to see which displays are most interesting to children. Your instructor may look at the number of times the reading materials on reserve for his course have been stamped for checkout to see if the class is studying the material. Incidentally, this example illustrates that the behavior of a group of individuals can sometimes be studied quite effectively by naturalistic observation even though it may be unethical to observe an individual's behavior. (It is illegal to obtain a person's borrowing record from a library.)

Although much has been made of the cleverness of social scientists in using physical traces of behavior, naturalists have for many years used scratches on trees to study territoriality in bears, droppings to study the eating habits of owls, and similar physical traces of animal behavior.

Observational research has begun to play a more prominent role in psychology as more social scientists are becoming influenced by the methods and theories of animal behaviorists. Traditionally, however, research psychologists have not used observational methods very much. Perhaps the fact that psychologists and their favorite objects of study are of the same species accounts for the difference. We tend to assume, often incorrectly, that we have a great deal of insight into the important categories of human behavior and their causes. However, several areas of psychology, such as developmental, school, or clinical, now use observational methods regularly. Careful observation of naturally occurring behavior might suggest many fruitful hypotheses for research and might help prevent half-baked experiments.

An excellent example of the use of naturalistic observation is found in the work of Erving Goffman (e.g., 1971). He has described such naturally occurring behavior as how people avoid bumping into each other on public sidewalks. He found that people engage in rituals of looking at each other and giving signals to indicate their intention to pass on one side or the other. Many people would not be aware that they engage in these behaviors. Because Goffman's studies do not include the kind of objective records that would allow one to evaluate the generality of his findings, we should probably classify them as casual observation rather than strictly objective naturalistic observation. However, his insights have led other investigators to conduct more objective tests of his ideas.

A particularly good example of how Goffman's suggestions have led to more rigorous work is provided by a naturalistic observation study by Peter Collett and Peter Marsh (1974). They placed a videotape recorder on the seventh floor of a building overlooking a busy pedestrian intersection. They recorded and later analyzed instances when two people met in such a way that both had to move to avoid collision. They noticed a striking difference in the way men and women maneuvered in passing. Men tended to turn to face the other person, whereas women tended to turn away. The differences were large. Of the men, 75% passed in the facing orientation, compared with only 17% of the women. Collett and Marsh hypothesized that the women turned away to avoid brushing the other person with their breasts. This hypothesis was confirmed by examining the frequency with which men and women held an arm across their bodies as they passed. Women used the arm cross more often than men, particularly in those instances when they were turned toward the other person as they passed. This occurrence was not related to whether they were carrying anything in their hands.

Another example of naturalistic observation is provided by Don Zimmerman and Candace West (1975). They were interested in whether patterns of speech would reflect power through dominance of the conversation. In particular, they were interested in looking for sex differences in interruptions and other turn-taking behavior in conversations. They tape-recorded conversations between sets of two persons in public places around a university, such as a coffee shop. They chose conversations that could be overheard easily in the normal course of being in a public place. They studied 10 female–female pairs, 10 male–male pairs, and 11 cross-sex pairs. Whenever possible, they obtained the permission of the conversationalists to use their recordings. Sometimes, however, people left before the researchers could approach them. All personal identifications were edited out of the transcripts of the recordings. (For a discussion of informed consent, privacy, and debriefing, see Chapter 3.)

Zimmerman and West found that the males made 96% of interruptions in the cross-sex pairs. These investigators decided to learn whether this finding was limited to the type of setting or to people who might be already acquainted. They brought pairs of people into the laboratory, where they were asked to chat and get acquainted "before the experiment begins" (1975). In five conversations between males and females, all of the males did more interrupting, with the men doing 73% of the interrupting on the average. The amount of interrupting was unrelated to which person talked first.

The Zimmerman and West research illustrates a typical and admirable progression in observational research from idea to naturalistic observation to laboratory. This move to the laboratory allows researchers to rule out sources of confounding that would occur in the original naturalistic situation. It also illustrates that observational research is not limited to field settings but often occurs in the laboratory where it is called **laboratory observation**.

laboratory observation:
a type of observation that occurs in the laboratory rather than in the field

As we mentioned earlier, naturalistic observation has been a popular method with biologists. Although additional examples of observation can be found in Langston's (2010) laboratory manual, perhaps the most famous examples of naturalistic observation come from scientists who work in ethology, the branch of biology that deals with the study of behavior. Although ethology is synonymous in many people's minds with naturalistic observation of animal behavior, ethology concerns itself with behavior as a product of natural selection and as a tool in studying the evolution of species. Much important ethological work is observational; yet an increasing amount of ethological work is conducted in the laboratory.

An example of naturalistic observation by ethologists is the work of Konrad Lorenz (e.g., 1958) on the courtship behavior of ducks. Most people who watch ducks in a pond or zoo simply see a mass of random activity. After observing the behavior of ducks for countless hours and taking motion pictures, Lorenz was able to identify about 20 different specific behaviors. One of these is the grunt-whistle, described here by Roger Sharpe and Paul Johnsgard (1966) for the mallard and pintail: "The male flick[s] its bill backward and upward through the water, throw[s] a shower of droplets toward the 'courted' bird, then rear[s] up and back in the water, and finally shak[es] the tail after settling back to the normal position.... A whistle is uttered during the display, followed by a low grunt" (p. 263).

By studying these behaviors in many species of ducks, Lorenz was able to clarify the evolutionary relationships among them. The assumption is that species of ducks that share more specific behaviors are more closely related. The validity of the behavioral method is confirmed if the animals that share similar behaviors can be crossbred and the behavior of the resulting offspring studied. Behaviors that both parent species share should appear in the offspring, but behaviors that only one parent displays should be absent or present in a weakened or distorted form.

Sharpe and Johnsgard (1966) successfully crossbred mallard and pintail ducks for two generations. The second generation (F2) offspring varied among themselves in the degree to which they resembled the two parent species. Some looked much like mallards and some looked mostly pintail, but the majority fell somewhere in between. Observation of the offspring showed that their behavior was closely related to their appearance: Those that looked mostly mallard showed mostly mallard behavior, and vice versa. According to the prediction, behaviors present in only one of the parent species were weakened or absent. Thus, the importance of heredity in behavior was demonstrated, and the predictions of ethological theory were confirmed.

The Sharpe and Johnsgard study is an interesting blend of observation and experiment. The researchers manipulated the genetics of the animals but did not present stimuli to them. They simply observed the natural behavior of their subjects after having created them to specification.

A final example of observational research illustrates the importance of having a coding system to aid in observation, and the amount of work that can be involved in developing one. Paul Ekman and Wallace Friesen have devoted many years to studying the expression of emotions in the human face (e.g., Ekman & Friesen, 1975; Ekman, Friesen, & O'Sullivan, 1988). By a combination of observation and experiment, they demonstrated that emotions are expressed by the face in the same way in different cultures and are likewise interpreted universally.

An essential part of this research has been the development of a scheme to code the movements of the face, whether caused by emotion or other reasons, such as voluntary actions (Ekman & Friesen, 1976). Before their work, no one had systematically studied the effects of moving the various muscles of the face. Ekman and Friesen spent the better part of a year in front of a mirror, armed with anatomy texts and cameras. They taught themselves to move each muscle independently. (Remember trying as a child to move one eyebrow by itself, or learning to wink?) When they were able to move the intended muscle, they photographed the effect it had on the appearance of the face. Occasionally, when they were unable to determine which muscle was being moved, they had a neuroanatomist insert a probe into the muscle and record the electrical activity to be sure that the intended muscle was the one that moved.

As a result of their work, they were able to identify dozens of movements, which they called Action Units. These were mostly the action of a single muscle. For example, Action Unit 15 is the Lip Corner Depressor:

> The muscle underlying AU 15 emerges from the side of the chin and runs upwards attaching to a point near the corner of the lip ... [This Action Unit] pulls the corners of the lip down; changes the shape of the lips so they are angled down at the corner, and usually somewhat stretched horizontally; produces some pouching, bagging, or wrinkling of the skin below the lips' corners ...; may flatten or cause bulges to appear on the [end of the] chin, may produce depression medially under the lower lip. If the [furrow extending from ... the nostril wings down to ... the lip corners] is permanently etched, it will deepen and may appear pulled down or lengthened. (Ekman & Friesen, 1976, p. 66)

Detailed descriptions such as these, along with photographs and other instructions, constitute the Facial Action Coding System (Ekman & Friesen, 1978). As you can imagine, the many Action Units can be produced in hundreds of combinations. Someone who wants to code facial movements must spend many hours learning the coding system and a considerable amount of time applying it to a sample of videotape.

The availability of the system for coding facial movements made it possible for Ekman, Friesen, and O'Sullivan (1988) to distinguish experimentally between truthful smiles and those that hid lies. In a nutshell, a truthful smile involves not only the corners of the mouth, but also the muscles around the eyes. In dishonest smiles, the muscles of the eyes may not move and muscles that signal negative emotions such as disgust or fear are activated. You may have heard of these findings before, as the results of the Ekman, Friesen, and O'Sullivan (1988) study on truthful smiles were the basis for a recent television show called *Lie to Me*.

Naturalistic observing has few hard-and-fast rules. Three that should be mentioned are careful record keeping, the use of a variety of types of measures, and care for privacy of the participants. Careful record keeping is what separates naturalistic observation from casual impression formation. The observer should keep a record of all behaviors of interest and the times at which they occur. A check sheet may be used when all or most of the categories of behavior under observation are known in advance. The recording of information is facilitated by using cameras, video or audio recorders, or other devices. Many times, using slow-motion or speeded-motion recording is helpful to make behavior patterns easier to see; stop-action recording can freeze critical moments. In the study of pedestrian passing, motion was frozen at the instant of passing. In the study of conversations, all tape-recorded utterances were transcribed to paper for analysis. Using a variety of measures helps ensure that the observations are representative and not dependent on one measure only. The concern for privacy will be discussed briefly in the section that follows and was discussed at greater length in Chapter 3.

Participant-Observer Research

participant-observer research: observational research in which the observer participates in a group to record behavior

One kind of observational research that has yielded important results is participant-observer research, in which investigators participate in groups and record their observations. One of the most famous of these studies was that of Leon Festinger, H. W. Riecken, Jr., and Stanley Schachter (1956), who joined a group that believed the world would come to an end at a certain time. Group members believed that they would be rescued by a flying saucer. The psychologists carefully observed interactions among group members and the effect the disconfirmation of their prediction had on their behavior. Surprisingly, when the world did not end, the group members began to be more open and less analytical about their beliefs. This research was instrumental in the development of Festinger's theory of cognitive dissonance, which predicts how people deal with conflicting beliefs. We should note that careful records and diaries are crucial in evaluating participant-observer studies because of the increased possibility of subjectivity in these situations.

When Is Participant Observation Appropriate?

The usefulness of participant-observer research is limited to certain types of situations (Jorgensen, 1989). It is most useful in studying a small group that is separated from the population as a whole, when little is known about a group, or when the group's activities are not generally available to public view. Groups studied in this way have included new religious movements, nude beachgoers, criminals, hoodlums, and gays. The doomsday cult studied by Festinger and associates represents the type of situation to which participant observation is ideally suited.

You should not get the impression that participant observation is done only on groups that are generally considered out of the mainstream of society. Though we have discussed examples in which there may be ethical problems involved in participant observation, the method is applicable to a wide variety of groups, including jazz musicians, athletes, and college fraternities.

Further, the researcher must be able to gain access to the group. For the study of a nude beach, it helps to be able to shed your inhibitions; to study an ethnic or racial group, it helps to be able to pass; to study a group of jazz musicians, it helps to be able to play an instrument.

Taking the Point of View of Those You Are Studying

Participant observation is characterized by the effort to view some behavioral activity from the viewpoint of an insider to a situation. The methodology must be open-ended, flexible, and opportunistic. The approach to theory is often hermeneutic, emphasizing interpretation and understanding. Some participant observers will take the role of a central participant because it would be impossible to learn much without doing so, as in studying the people who hang out in a bar in a poor section of town. Other times, a researcher can stay more in the periphery, as in studying an organization such as a church.

By definition, participating in a group leads to problems of objectivity. The researcher must strike a balance between taking the viewpoint of the group members and maintaining scientific objectivity. A researcher who is studying police officers tries to take the point of view of the officers. But he may find that his attitudes toward criminals, and toward society as a whole, start to match those of the police, who happen to be more prejudiced and authoritarian than the population as a whole. It is not unheard of for researchers to be converted by the religious group that they were studying. Some researchers maintain their objectivity by regular contact with other researchers who debrief them about their experiences (Jorgensen, 1989).

Gaining Access to the Group

Sometimes it is possible to be open about the fact that you are there to study the group, as when a person openly enters a fundamentalist church for the purpose of research and is welcomed as a potential convert. This is known as undisguised participant observation.

By contrast, certain groups are hostile to the larger society and suspicious of anyone who shows an interest in them. Admitting that you are there to study them might result in your being kicked out or worse. In that situation, the researcher would use disguised participant observation to hide his or her true purposes from the people being observed. In addition, it is often unrealistic to expect a researcher to inform each and every member of a group the first time they meet that he or she is there for the purpose of research. It would be highly artificial to begin every interaction with a new person by saying that you are a researcher. There is no hard-and-fast rule about whether to inform the group. From an ethical perspective, it is best to be truthful where possible and to adopt a disguised strategy only when necessary.

Problems in Observational Research

Two important problems are present in participant-observer research. First, by entering the group, the observer (by definition) changes it to some extent. Therefore, the act of observing the behavior changes the behavior to be observed. A large group may not be influenced much by an observer's presence, whereas a small group may be influenced considerably. In general, participant-observer research is done in unusual groups that can absorb an observer whose presence would have little effect.

The second problem is the ethical question of invasion of privacy. Participant observers cannot always obtain informed consent from the people they study. Some researchers hold that participant-observer research is therefore always unethical. Others point out that professionals such as journalists are permitted to engage in this type of practice. They argue that if psychologists do not perform participant-observer research, they are withholding the application of psychological techniques and insights to important social problems.

Concern for the privacy of participants is discussed in Chapter 3. Here we only note that naturalistic observation techniques (not just participant-observer research) may involve recording behaviors that, even though conducted in public, may still be of a private nature. For example, in one study, a researcher feigned homosexuality to study the behavior of homosexuals. He gained their confidence by serving as a lookout in a public washroom while they engaged in sex. Later, having noted the license numbers of their cars, he obtained their identities from the department of motor vehicles by subterfuge. Then, in disguise, he joined a research team and interviewed his participants as a public health worker (Holden, 1979). Although the investigator did not reveal the identities of the participants and his conclusions are supposed to be sympathetic to homosexuals, he did obtain the data under false pretenses and subjected the persons he studied to risk. This study was later discussed at a conference on research ethics as a prime example of research that should not be conducted (Holden, 1979).

Archival Research

archival data: factual information in existing records

The term *archival research* refers to research conducted using data that the researcher had no part in collecting. Archival data are those that are present in existing records, or archives. The researcher simply examines or selects the data for analysis.

Archival research is appropriate in many instances. Data that bear on the hypothesis may already exist, and collecting new data would be wasteful. Or ethics or logistics may make it infeasible to conduct an experiment relating the variables of interest. In a moment, we will consider archival research on suicides and sex crimes, both topics inappropriate for experimental research.

Archival research has limitations, however. First, most archival data are collected for nonscientific reasons. Governments and private agencies collect the data for their own purposes, and such data often do not suit the purposes of the scientist. Even when the data were collected for scientific purposes and made publicly available (see some examples in Chapter 2), for archival data to be useful to your investigation, the agency collecting the data must ask questions similar to yours or must inadvertently collect data that are valuable to your research question. Second, because archival research is by nature carried out after the fact, ruling out alternative hypotheses for particular observed correlations may be difficult.

A researcher who relies on archival data is at the mercy of any biases that may have occurred in collecting the data. Police records are notoriously subject to bias. Many categories of crime are seldom reported to the police. It is estimated, for instance, that only roughly half of all rapes are reported in the United States (Truman & Rand, 2010). A 200% increase in rapes would suddenly seem to have occurred if every one were reported. In addition, police must use their best judgment in determining whether to record a particular incident as a criminal act. Accordingly, crime statistics can vary because of differences in individual officers.

A successful use of archival research can be seen in Irene Blair, Charles Judd, and Kristine Chapleau's (2004) analysis of the influence of racial stereotypes in the sentencing of people convicted of a crime. Previous research had already shown that people with more African facial features were subjected to more negative stereotypical interpretations of their behavior. Blair, Judd, and Chapleau hypothesized that if people with African features were more likely to face unfavorable stereotypes, then they should be given harsher sentences following a criminal conviction. They studied the criminal records and photographs of 216 inmates (roughly half of whom self-reported as black) in the Florida Department of Corrections System who had committed similar crimes. All of the photographs were rated as to whether the people shown them had facial features typical of an African American on a scale of 1–9. Then, Blair, Judd, and Chapleau looked in the criminal records and compared the sentences that the inmates had received. They found that although no difference in sentencing was seen between people who self-reported as white or black, inmates with more African features (regardless of their race) received harsher sentences. These data suggest that although race as a category has been eliminated as a source of sentencing bias, the facial appearance of the offender is a type of racial bias that still exists in our courtrooms.

One of the challenges of performing archival research is finding the specific archives that have the information relevant to your research needs. Once you locate and gain access to an archive that has a good deal of material on your topic, preparation is vital before you actually visit the archive itself (Faye & Bazar, 2007). If you have done as much research as you can before you arrive, your work can concentrate on the information that can only be found in the resources of the archive, rather than on information more readily available.

Case Studies

Case studies constitute a category of research that is difficult to characterize with a simple definition. Because case studies often include the use of observation and archival methodologies, the distinctions among them are not always clear. Nevertheless, it is possible to say that case studies tend to involve a situation that presents itself for investigation.

The principal characteristic of case studies is that they examine individual instances, or cases, of some phenomenon. Sometimes this is an individual person, as in a psychiatric or neuropsychological case. Other times it is an individual town or institution, as in a case of mass hysteria reported after a meteorite crash in Peru (Thompson, 2007). Or it can be an individual method or treatment, such as the effectiveness of a new surgical intervention on a patient's health. The individuality of the situation, or case, characterizes the case study.

Robert Yin (2008) defines a case study as "an empirical inquiry that investigates a contemporary phenomenon within its real-life context when the boundaries between phenomenon and context are not clearly evident … The case study inquiry copes with the technically distinctive situation in which there will be many more variables of interest than data points, and as one result, relies on multiple sources of evidence … and benefits from the prior development of propositions to guide data collection and analysis" (p. 18). According to Yin's definition, the multiple approaches distinguish a case study from other nonexperimental methods.

Many case studies result from problems that present themselves to researchers as opportunities that must be grasped quickly or lost. Little time may be available for planning, and the study often must be conducted under difficult conditions. An example of case-study research is the study of unilateral visual-spatial neglect reported in a seven-year-old boy by Rebecca Billingsley and her colleagues (2002). In this neuropsychological disorder, patients ignore stimuli in one-half of space. So patients will draw a flower with petals only on one side, or only eat the food on one-half of their plates. Frequently, this disorder is observed after a stroke in an elderly person, but in this case, it was observed in a young child.

When the little boy first visited the medical team, he had experienced difficulty in moving his right hand, but he had no trouble paying attention to anything in his environment. A magnetic resonance image (MRI) of his brain revealed the presence of a cancerous tumor near the ventral thalamus of the brain. After surgery to remove the tumor, the child began to exhibit symptoms of unilateral neglect, such as leaving off the beginning few letters when attempting to read long words and drawing a clock with numbers only on the right side. Fortunately, six months after his surgery, he was able to overcome these difficulties and again attended to space somewhat normally. This case assists in demonstrating specific brain regions that are tied to unilateral neglect and the development of visual-spatial attention.

This study of visual-spatial neglect is typical of case studies. The efforts of the physicians and psychologists were directed toward a practical problem. The case appeared unpredictably and required prompt attention. A multidisciplinary team approach was used to elucidate the problem. Members of each discipline used several techniques to rule out various explanations and narrow the possible causes.

narrative case study: a viewpoint expressed by telling and listening to stories that communicate meaning

Closely related to the concept of a case history is that of a narrative case study. A narrative is essentially a story told firsthand, and it reflects the meaning experienced by the teller. In other words, one hears directly from the participant in a narrative, such as this passage from a woman named Jill who has an amazing memory: "I am never absentminded. I've never lost a single key. In fact I still have the house key my parents gave me when I was 10 years old, which I used until I was 37, when we moved. I've never lost an ATM card or credit card, and I had the same driver's license until I was 27, when I had to renew it. I never find my mind wandering in this way; to the contrary, it's always crammed full of remembering. There are never times when the 'film' isn't running and I can focus exclusively on the present moment" (Price & Davis, 2008). Jill's experiences were also reported in the literature as a narrative case study by Elizabeth Parker, Larry Cahill, and James McGaugh (2006). Jill is called AJ in the article, which reports not only her own experience of her amazing memory, but also the results of various neurological tests, and performance on a variety of memory tests. Jill's evaluation of her own memory, and its limits, is framed and substantiated by the quantitative testing.

Other case studies are quite varied. In fact, one of the few generalizations possible about case studies is that it is difficult to generalize about them.

Theory Development and Testing in Observational and Archival Research

Because of the ad hoc nature of observational and archival research, the process of theory development and hypothesis testing must be rather flexible. We are familiar with the model of hypothesis testing commonly used in the statistical analysis of experiments, in which the researcher states a null hypothesis and alternative hypothesis before the research is conducted. Hypothesis testing by this model involves attempting to reject the null hypothesis in favor of the alternative hypothesis. (See Chapter 15 for a discussion.) In observational research, however, the investigator may not even have particular problems in mind before beginning the research, let alone any specific hypotheses.

For this reason, observational researchers use one of two techniques: either a mathematical approach toward combating threats to internal validity (see, e.g., West, 2009) or a more flexible, inductive process of developing and testing hypotheses (see, e.g., Campbell, 1979). In the latter case, a hypothesis may be tentatively stated based on existing observations. Predictions are made based on the hypothesis, which are tested against new data. The hypotheses and theory are continuously modified to take account of new data. When a hypothesis is contradicted by the data, the hypothesis is abandoned or modified. When the data are what the hypothesis predicted, confidence in the hypothesis is increased.

This cycle of hypothesis development, prediction, testing, hypothesis modification, and so on, illustrates a number of characteristics of science as stated in Chapter 1, particularly that concepts must be falsifiable. Those that are not falsifiable are not scientific. But some scientists tend to get so wrapped up in their ideas that they look mainly for evidence that confirms their hypothesis and ignore evidence that contradicts it. Any good researcher, but particularly those doing observational research, needs to be critical of his or her theory and look carefully for evidence that would prove it wrong.

Philosophers point out that there are an unlimited number of incorrect theories consistent with any particular set of data. Evidence that seems to favor your theory also favors many other theories, all of which may be wrong. You know you have made progress when you have rejected an incorrect theory, but you have not necessarily made any progress if your data support your theory, because it may still be incorrect.

This process of hypothesis generation and modification is well illustrated in a study by Donald Cressey (1971), who investigated men who were in prison for embezzlement. His study was a combination of observation (interview) and archival research. Cressey's first hypothesis was that embezzlers believed that what they had done was merely a technical violation rather than a crime. It became evident from talking to a few men, however, that the embezzlers knew all along that what they had done was really wrong. After this first hypothesis was proven wrong, Cressey formulated a second hypothesis: that they embezzled when they had emergency needs that could be met by violating their trust and taking the money. He abandoned that hypothesis, however, when he found men who said they had had emergencies before that did not lead them to embezzle. Hypothesis number three was that they became embezzlers when they had incurred financial obligations that they felt they could not reveal to others, such as a gambling debt that could be met by embezzlement. This hypothesis was abandoned, in turn, because some of the men did not need the money for actual obligations but had a situation that could be considered a financial problem. For example, a man might be maintaining a mistress, which would incur a financial burden without being an actual obligation, like a debt. The fourth hypothesis, then, was that a person embezzled when he had a nonshareable financial problem that could be met by embezzlement. This hypothesis, too, had to be abandoned when he found some men who had fit this criterion at some earlier point but had not embezzled at that time.

Cressey's fifth, and final, hypothesis was that a person embezzled when he had a nonshareable problem that could be met by embezzlement and he could rationalize to himself that he was still a trusted person despite the illegality. An example might be a salesperson who receives an initial payment toward a new life insurance policy. Because the first payment largely goes to pay the salesperson's commission, he may convince himself that he can safely spend his share because the sale has been made and he will get it eventually anyway. The salesman would come to grief, however, if the client backed out of the sale or if the salesman could not come up with the cash to turn in to the company when he needed to deposit the first payment.

Whenever he found a single case that contradicted it, Cressey abandoned each hypothesis and developed a new one. Eventually, he found that his final hypothesis covered all the cases he could find. This method illustrates the ad hoc, cyclical nature of hypothesis testing and theorizing in observational and archival research. It may, however, raise too high a standard that cannot always be met. It is unusual to find a single explanation that will cover every single case of a phenomenon that one is trying to explain.

Generally, researchers are faced with evidence that points to conflicting hypotheses. Their job is to find the theory that gives the best explanation for the bulk of the evidence, taking into account that some evidence may be crucial and other evidence may be peripheral to the situation.

NUTS & BOLTS

Recording Methods in Nonexperimental Research

As we have seen, nonexperimental research encompasses a wide range of methods. This fact makes it impossible to provide a complete inventory of recording techniques used. It is important, nevertheless, to discuss recording methods in nonexperimental research because they present some challenges that are generally not present in experimental research. These problems stem from a number of factors. First, it may not be obvious to you what you should record because you don't know exactly what you are looking for. This is especially true for naturalistic observation, participant observation, and case studies. Second, you may know what you are looking for but not know how to define instances of it. This problem is particularly acute in archival research. We discuss these two problems under the headings of field notes and content analysis, respectively.

(continues)

NUTS & BOLTS *(continued)*

Field Notes

Researchers using observation and case-study methodologies often start with some general questions in mind, but without specific categories of behavior defined. In fact, this characterizes much observational research.

Be Systematic

You should keep a notebook of all of your observations and their interpretations. Make certain that you think about the categories of behavior that you are concerned with and clearly define your behaviors of interest. You should also decide the length of your total observation period and observation intervals. Checklists can help considerably in keeping clear records. This documentation may sound like a daunting task, and it is. You may be so busy observing that you don't have time to take notes. Or you may be in a social situation where note taking is impossible, either because it will inhibit the behaviors you are observing or because you are taking part in the situation. In such cases, you should consider inconspicuous recording devices (with due consideration to ethical issues), or at least write up your observations as soon as you leave the situation. You will be tempted to skimp on writing up your notes because you are tired or you think you will remember what was important later. If you think you won't forget, you are probably wrong. Just try to remember everything you did one week ago. What did you wear, eat, say, and do? Your notes should include as much detail as possible, including the time and the setting. Later on, the significance of these details may make sense in a way that they don't as you take the notes.

You may want to write your notes in stages. You can jot down brief notes as you work, and elaborate on them later at leisure. You may also need to develop shorthand codes to help in your note taking.

Be Selective

The problem of having too much to observe can often be solved by taking samples of behavior. Instead of watching television all day long for a week to observe the content of commercials, you might watch only the first batch of commercials after the top of the hour. Instead of watching all channels, you might focus on only one. Instead of watching everything that all the children in a day-care center do for a whole day, you might watch for instances of one kind of behavior, such as fighting, or attend only those behaviors that are on your prepared checklist. Instead of watching all the children, you might focus on just one or two. Instead of watching constantly, you might record what they are doing at 10-minute intervals. Selecting the particular behavior and time interval for observation will help in managing your data.

Make Use of Recording Devices

Nowadays, recording devices such as video and audio recorders are inexpensive enough that most researchers can afford to record their observations electronically.

(continues)

NUTS & BOLTS *(continued)*

The main problem is that you generally must review your records in real time; that is, it takes the same amount of time to review your tape as it did to record it. This problem can be reduced by viewing videotape in fast-forward mode or employing a voice-activated audio recorder or motion-sensitive video camera. In addition, commercial event recorders allow you to press defined keys to indicate particular events. In many situations, however, the problem is just the opposite: A great deal happens quickly. In such situations, the tape can be played in slow motion to permit coding of subtle and transient phenomena.

Content Analysis

Content analysis involves evaluating the pictures and language in publicly available texts to evaluate a hypothesis. The main questions of content analysis are: "Who says what, to whom, why, to what extent and with what effect?" (Lasswell, 1951).

When dealing with textual or photographic materials, you don't have to take field notes because the material is already in a permanent form. The problem remains, however, that of deciding how to deal with what may be a large body of material. Suppose you are investigating the sexual content of magazines. How do you decide what to record? There are two basic approaches to content analysis. The first one is based on counting the frequency of some objective measure, such as frequency of certain sexual words. This is known as coding the **manifest content** of the text. Because it is relatively simple to count the number of times the word *kiss* or *love* appears in a body of text, the coding of manifest content is very reliable. There may be a problem, however, if words are used in different ways. The word *love* appears many times in a certain chapter of the Bible where it has nothing to do with sex. You would draw the wrong conclusion about the point of the chapter if you just counted the word *love*.

The alternative method of analyzing the content of a text or photograph is coding its **latent content**. With this method, the researcher reads a passage of text, or looks at a photograph, and interprets the presence of a particular theme. That same passage of the Bible would easily be seen to be about what might be called brotherly love, rather than sexual love.

Because latent content analysis is inherently subjective, it runs the risk of being less reliable than manifest content analysis. It is a good idea to do both manifest and latent content analysis and compare the results. If the results turn out the same by both methods, you have strong evidence of the validity of your results. If they differ, you can look for the reasons why they differ.

Reliability of Content Analysis

Whichever method of content analysis you use, there is a problem of reliability. If you use latent content analysis, another researcher might interpret the same passage differently. Even with manifest content analysis, there is the possibility of a coder making mistakes when going through large amounts of data. Thus, to establish the reliability of your coding scheme, it is important to use at least two coders.

manifest content: the content of a text or photograph as indicated by measuring the frequency of some objective word, phrase, or action

latent content: the content of a text or photograph as measured by the appearance of themes as interpreted by the researcher

(continues)

NUTS & BOLTS *(continued)*

Various techniques based on statistical correlation are available to quantify the reliability of coders and coding schemes.

Example of Content Analysis

Golder and Macy (2011) used content analysis to study Twitter messages (140-character micro-blogs called "Tweets") in order to find out how moods change across the course of a day. The researchers analyzed Tweets from 509 million messages from people in more than 84 countries authored over a two-year period. Messages were coded for time, date, and season, as well as whether they contained positive affect (words such as *enthusiasm* or *delight*) or negative affect (words such as *distress* or *anger*). These affective categories were based on a lexicon of emotion-related words developed by previous investigations. Using an automated text-search program, the researchers counted the number of words across all messages that appeared in the positive and negative word lists for each hour. The authors found that on average, people begin the day in a good mood (positive affect), but that it tends to decrease throughout the day.

Suggestions for Nonexperimental Research: Important Guidelines

Observe the American Psychological Association (APA) ethics guidelines (see Chapter 3). Do not break any laws, violate privacy, or do anything that will embarrass or annoy anyone. If you do a natural observation study, do not observe any behavior that is not normally observable in public. Obtain approval in advance from your instructor for any study you conduct. Be sure to follow any guidelines he or she may have. Thank anyone who cooperates in research.

Procedure

Procedure is different from method. *Method* is a broader term that encompasses all aspects of the study, including the logic of the design and the steps for carrying it out.

Procedure refers only to the latter—what the researcher does in translating the design into action. The design, for example, may be an experiment with two conditions that are both experienced by each subject. Procedural concerns include whether each condition is tested on the same day or on different days. Procedure also involves instructions and how they are given, the debriefing, and so forth. Many details must be worked out in the course of translating a design into practice.

The step of going from design to procedure can be a difficult one for students because it involves going from a logical plan in the mind to a practical plan of action in the lab. After the design is completed, you should develop a clear idea of the exact procedure, or protocol, you will follow. A **protocol** is a list of the exact steps needed to test a subject from start to finish. Will you be greeting the participants? Giving them a written debriefing form? What part of the experiment will the participants do first? All of these things may be part of a protocol. A written protocol is helpful for beginning researchers, especially when more than one researcher will help run a given study.

protocol: list of all the steps that a subject goes through in a study

(continues)

NUTS & BOLTS *(continued)*

The Pilot Study

pilot study: tentative, small-scale study done to pretest and modify study design and procedures

Once a protocol has been developed, you should do a **pilot study** to find the bugs in the procedure. There are almost always problems to be smoothed out. One of the researchers, your adviser, or a friend should be run through all steps of the study exactly as it will be carried out. Although the temptation to skip the pilot phase may be great, you should resist it. Nearly every experiment we have performed without testing some pilot subjects has been disappointing. Here is where a little effort can greatly increase the precision of a study.

Researchers with reputations for excellent design are often those who do extensive pilot research. Some researchers will not proceed to the main study until they have a good idea of what they will find in the full experiment, based on pilot work. This preliminary step is not always possible, but it is an aid to careful research. It also emphasizes that research is not a one-step process. When a pilot study has been done, followed by a main study that has been run once and replicated once or twice, the credibility of the finding is increased tremendously over a single study that was not preceded by pilot work. The phase in which the design is translated into procedure and then to a pilot study often takes longer than the study proper. You may have difficulty understanding what took all the time and effort. It is not unusual for the literature search and design phase of an undergraduate project to require three-fourths of the term. Running the subjects may take only a week.

Guarding the Integrity of the Data

All of the care expended on designing and conducting a study is wasted if the data are compromised by carelessness in recording and handling. Before the study begins, the researcher must have a plan for recording and handling the data. A good procedure is to keep all data and other research details, such as dosages, stimulus settings, and the like, in a notebook. All pages should be dated and identified in such a way that they can be replaced if any sheets become lost. Often it is convenient to reproduce a blank set of data sheets with spaces for all necessary information, so that nothing will be overlooked. Data should be placed in a file and kept in a secure place, where the participant's privacy can be maintained. They should never be carried around in a briefcase from which they can be lost. Too often data have been eaten by the dog, scribbled on by the baby, or left on the bus. Making photocopies of any data that must be taken out of the laboratory is a good practice.

After it is collected, the raw data will be transferred from the data sheets to a summary form in an electronic spreadsheet. (See Chapter 14 for more detail.) Preparing the format of the summary data sheet ahead of time is a good idea. The summary sheet should allow space for doing simple manipulations of the data, such as taking the logarithm or means, before the statistical analysis is performed. Any information necessary to re-create the summary data from the data sheets should be carefully recorded, such as the random order of stimuli that

(continues)

NUTS & BOLTS (continued)

were used for each subject. Records of the study should be set up in such a way that another person could decipher the design and procedure from the records alone. Essential features of studies can be forgotten, especially if the researcher has conducted a number of them.

The data sheets should be kept for as long as anyone is likely to want to reanalyze the data. It is becoming more popular to make data publicly available in an archive (Johnson, 2001, 2002), so that it will be available to future scientists for meta-analyses (see Chapter 13 for more detail) or archival research. In addition, although fraud in research is not a welcome topic, it does happen (see Chapter 3 for some examples). The existence of original data sheets may be the only proof that the data were collected as claimed. The original data sheets should be locked up after the data have been transferred to a tabular form, before data analysis is begun. This procedure protects the researcher from the temptation to fudge data to make them fit the hypothesis.

(The raw data often do not permit ascertaining whether the hypothesis was confirmed.) Recording the original data in ink is advisable, as is backing up the data if it is collected electronically. A modicum of compulsiveness in guarding data is a good idea.

© Cengage Learning

Summary

1. Nonexperimental research has two main characteristics: No attempt is made to manipulate an independent variable, and some degree of control often must be forfeited during the data collection procedure.

2. Although nonexperimental research is called correlational research, all research is correlational in that it seeks to find relationships between variables.

3. Nonexperimental research methods include observational, archival, case study, and survey.

4. The hermeneutic approach to understanding behavior attempts to discover reasons for behavior, rather than causes. It is based on techniques of textual interpretation.

5. Observational research involves recording a subject's behavior without attempting to influence it.

6. Naturalistic observation involves recording a subject's behavior in such a way that the behavior is not disturbed by the process of making the observation. Other terms for this are *unobtrusive research* and *nonreactive research*.

7. Physical trace research is a kind of naturalistic observation that uses physical evidence of behavior.

8. Participant-observer research is useful in studying small, little-known groups that are not generally open to public view. Observers join the group, take the point of view of the members, and record their observations.

9. Invasion of privacy poses an ethical problem in participant-observer research. A practical problem is the likelihood that the researcher may influence the group as well as observe it.

10. Archival research involves the examination of existing records. Advantages are that the data do not need to be collected by the researcher and that the research afforded may be on problems not amenable to experimentation. Disadvantages are that the researcher is limited to the types of questions asked by the agency that collected the data and by any biases present in the collection procedure.

11. Case studies are ad hoc studies of existing situations that are based on a single individual or group of individuals. Case studies take many forms and cannot be neatly classified.

12. Theory development and testing are more flexible and inductive in observational and archival research than in experimental research.

13. Observational and case-study researchers must be systematic in making field notes but often need to be selective in what they record.

14. Manifest content is the objectively measurable content of a text. Latent content is the content as interpreted by a researcher.

15. The procedure of a study consists of the steps taken to carry out the method and design of the study.

16. It is advisable to conduct a pilot study before doing the main study.

17. The data should be carefully managed so that they can be understood long after the study is completed.

Suggestions for Further Reading

JORGENSEN, D. L. (1989). *Participant observation: A methodology for human studies.* Newbury Park, CA: Sage. This book provides thorough discussion of methods for participant-observer research.

ROSENBAUM, P. R. (2010). *Design of observational studies.* New York: Springer. This book, particularly the first three chapters, points out the statistical problems associated with considering an observational study as if it were a fully randomized study.

WEBB, E. J., CAMPBELL, D. T., SCHWARTZ, R. D., & SECHRIST, L. (1999). *Unobtrusive measures.* Thousand Oaks, CA: Corwin Press. This book contains thought-provoking discussions of observational and archival research, with emphasis on methods that do not cause people to be aware that they are being studied.

YIN, R. K. (2008). *Case study research: Design and methods* (4th ed.). Newbury Park, CA: Sage. Yin gives many examples of case-study research.

A CASE IN POINT

Is Group Size a Function of Sex?

Sociobiology predicts that females will travel in larger groups than males (Burgess, 1984). At a shopping mall, observe same-sex groups of teen-agers, and record the sizes of the groups. Analyze your data using the chi-square method. (Some problems of design you may encounter are defining "group" and "teenager".) You might observe groups of various ages to see if there are trends.

Styles of Carrying Objects by Males and Females

Females tend to carry books and similar objects across their chests, whereas males tend to hold them in one hand at the side (Jenni & Jenni, 1976). At a shopping mall, observe methods of carrying as a function of sex. (*Problems*: How do you define small package? What about packages with handles? What is the appropriate statistic?)

Seatbelt Use as a Function of Sex

While standing at a stoplight, record your observations of the passengers in the first car in the nearest lane only. Do males or females use seatbelts more often? You might hypothesize that females will conform more. (*Problems*: Because females are smaller, it may be more difficult to see the belt. Would seatbelt use differ between two-door and four-door cars because of difficulty of reaching belts in two-door cars? Do men and women tend to drive the same type of car?)

Smoking as a Function of Whether Parents Smoke

Interview some friends about whether they smoke and whether their parents smoke. Your hypothesis might be as follows: Smoking is more likely if both parents smoke than if one smokes or if neither smokes. (*Consideration*: how to define smoking.)

Success in Quitting Smoking

Interview several former smokers. Ask how many times they quit and relapsed before succeeding. Did they use any programs to help them stop, or did they do it on their own? (*Considerations*: how to define smoking, quitting, relapse.)

Cohort Effects in Smoking

Interview people of different ages about their smoking history. Find out how many never smoked and how many once smoked but have quit. At what age did the smokers begin? Look for trends as a function of when they were born. (*Considerations*: distortion of memory, social desirability.) If you study members of the same family, the data will not be independent.

Naturalistic Observation of Nonverbal Flirtation

You are a social psychologist who is interested in the development of romantic relationships. You would like to know whether the man or the woman tends to take the initiative in developing a relationship and whether the initiative shifts during the early phase of a relationship. Researchers used to assume that the male takes the initiative. There is new evidence, however, that the female may tend to control the relationship early in the interaction. Later in the flirtation episode, the male may initiate the escalation of more intimate behavior.

A previous researcher has classified behaviors into two categories: those that escalate the relationship and those that de-escalate it.

Escalation

Gaze toward. Move closer. Open posture (relaxed, facing toward partner). Positive facial expression (smiling, laughing, grinning). Self-grooming (smoothing hair, thrusting chest, licking lips). Brief touching (such as shoulder, arm, hand, hair, for a few seconds). Continuous touching (such as

(continued)

holding hands, arm around shoulder, leaning on). Intimate touching (kissing, hugging, rubbing, hand on sexual areas).

De-escalation

Gaze away. Move away. Closed posture (arms/legs crossed, facing away). Negative facial expression (frowning, yawning, grimacing).

Considerations

A number of bars near campus are frequented by young adults. Some are hotel lounges, some restaurants with bars, some strictly bars, and some have live entertainment.

You decide to observe heterosexual couples for a period of 15 minutes each. You would like to have 10 couples in both the early- and later-phase groups. Perhaps 10% of the couples will turn out to be married. You can spend five hours per night on Thursdays, Fridays, and Saturdays for four weeks.

You are concerned that the couples might notice they are being observed, but you need to take notes of the behavior so you can be objective. You want to have two observers so that you can determine the interobserver reliability, but you are concerned not to appear to be together or be obviously communicating with each other. You need some method of signaling that will permit you to coordinate whom to observe and when to

begin and end. Further, you need to develop a protocol for deciding which couple to observe, and how to avoid spending time observing couples who may interact for only a minute or two.

After the observation period is over, you want to be able to discard data from married couples. The remaining couples are to be divided into early- and later-stage groups on the basis of how long they interacted that particular evening. Some may have just met, and others may have been interacting for hours.

You are concerned about the ethics of observing behavior that may be intimate, but you understand that the couples realize they are in a public place.

Required

Design the study. Describe your procedure in detail, taking account of the preceding considerations. Provide mock data showing interobserver reliability, behavior of males and females, and behavior during early and later stages of interaction.

Optional

Describe what statistical analyses would be appropriate for these data. The study on which this material is based is referenced in the Instructor's Manual.

Reading Between the Lines

8.1 Aggression and XYY Males

Some males have a genetic abnormality that results in an extra Y chromosome. One study found that these XYY males, as they are known, were overrepresented in a prison population and concluded that the XYY condition caused persons to be overly aggressive. This finding gave rise to speculation and research into the possible causes of the apparent connection between the XYY condition and aggression.

One such study was conducted at the Boston Hospital for Women, which is connected with Harvard University. Between 1965 and 1975, more than 16,000 male infants born at the hospital were screened for chromosome abnormalities as part of a large study funded by the Center for the Study of Crime and Delinquency, a federal agency. Before giving birth, the mothers were presented with a booklet that contained the following paragraph: "In this hospital all male infants are undergoing chromosome analysis. This new and simplified test allows the doctors to do an accurate screening examination of your baby's chromosomes and if any serious abnormalities are found, you will be so informed. It is hoped that in time this test ... will become a universal test on all infants" (Chorover, 1979, p. 176). Another paragraph of the booklet referred to the chromosome test as a service and pointed out that there was no charge for it.

The study identified six male infants with the XYY condition out of the more than 16,000 babies tested. A pediatric psychiatrist visited the homes of all of the XYY children and informed the parents that "their children have extra chromosome material" and that the baby's pediatrician was "fully informed about the child's variation" (p. 186).

What ethical and design problems can you find with this study?

Research Methods Laboratory Manual

William Langston (2010) has prepared a laboratory manual that contains many suggestions for research activities that work well with this book and require minimal materials. Many chapters in this book contain a section that refers the reader to appropriate sections of the Langston book.

In Chapter 2, Langston describes a naturalistic observation study involving the detection of people who are staring at them, and makes several suggestions for replicating and extending the study.

In Chapter 4, Langston describes a correlational study of belief in paranormal activity and mathematics ability, and suggests extensions of the study.

Web-Based Workshops on Research Methods and Statistics

Cengage Learning Publishing Company maintains Web-based workshops on research methods and statistics. These workshops give a different slant on the material in this book.

www.cengage.com/psychology/workshops

For this chapter, see Nonexperimental Approaches to Research in the Research Methods Workshops section.

Exercises

8.1 Identify Types of Nonexperimental Research

For each of the following research questions, indicate the following: (1) the type of research that would best answer the question, (2) an appropriate sampling method, and (3) the best method of collecting the data.

a. How do the minority groups at a certain university view the student counseling program?

b. What are the daily classroom activities of the children participating in the Head Start program?

c. What trends exist in the growth of population in American prisons from 1900 to 1988?

d. What is the relationship between intelligence and creativity?

8.2 Identify Potential Problems of Validity in a Case Study

Mr. E was an elderly man who gradually began having problems in speaking and understanding speech. When he could no longer talk over the telephone, Mr. E was tested by a neurologist, but no brain damage was detected at that time. Later Mr. E went to a speech clinic, which tested his hearing, speech, and intellectual function and made some recommendations for therapy. Eleven years into the course of his problem, his family called in a researcher, who interviewed Mr. E and his family. She began to develop a history of his case based on her continuing interviews, their recollections, and his letters and personal notes. An autopsy performed when he died a year later found widespread evidence of brain damage, particularly in the speech areas (Holland, McBurney, Moossy, & Reinmuth, 1985).

Required:

a. Identify the different types of research that went into this case study.

b. What problems of interpretation are presented by the fact that the researchers did not begin their study until Mr. E's problem had progressed for 11 years?

8.3 Physical Traces of Shoppers

Market researchers have recently begun observing the Web sites that people visit. Facebook, for instance, has used an ad system called "Beacon" that reports back to Facebook on a member's activities when the member visits any other site that also uses the Beacon system (Perez, 2007). So, even after a member has signed off from Facebook and left the site, Beacon keeps track of the other sites that the member visits for Facebook.

Required:

List some advantages and disadvantages that this type of research might have over surveys of consumer attitudes.

CHAPTER NINE

Nonexperimental Research, Part 2: Survey Research

PREVIEW

Chapter 9 continues the discussion of nonexperimental research by considering surveys. We discuss how to design a valid survey and how to administer it to a representative sample of respondents. Chapter 3 of Langston's (2010) laboratory manual also gives information about survey research.

Surveys are a widely used method of gathering scientific information. Often the purpose of a survey is simply to determine how people feel about a particular issue, such as gun control or the performance of the president of the United States. Other surveys may attempt to find out the effect of some event on people's behavior. For example, surveys conducted before the presidential election in 2012 attempted to determine the effect of the economy on voter opinion. In addition, surveys provide an opportunity to examine correlations among the participants' responses and to look for possible patterns of cause and effect, such as showing that bullying in childhood is related to internalizing problems later in life (Arseneault et al., 2008).

A major function of surveys is to dispel myths. One such myth is that women whose children have grown up and left home suffer a kind of depression called "the empty nest syndrome." Lillian Rubin (1979) surveyed 160 women in this situation and found that, rather than being depressed, virtually all of them experienced a sense of relief. The results of other surveys surprise us, such as by indicating how highly related physical punishment and aggression are in children. An international survey of mothers and children from six different countries showed that in general, as physical punishment increased, so did anxiety and aggression in the children (Lansford et al., 2005).

Because survey research is technical and complex, we give only a brief overview here. Nevertheless, it is important to have an idea of the techniques because survey research is used so often.

How a Questionnaire Is Designed

Designing a questionnaire is a surprisingly complex procedure that involves a great many considerations. It shares many of the other considerations of research design in addition to the concerns that are inherent in any written or oral form of communication. Frequently, researchers use existing questionnaires, rather than designing their own instruments. Thus, they avoid redesigning the wheel and they can compare their results with those of previous studies using the same instrument. For example, one useful source is the Mental Measurement Yearbook™ (Buros Institute of Mental Measurements), which reviews more than 2700 standardized tests, including many questionnaires. The Measures of Social Psychological Attitudes series (e.g., Robinson, Shaver, & Wrightsman, 1991) also reviews and lists numerous measures of subjective well-being, self-esteem, social anxiety, depression, and so forth. The considerations listed in the following sections will be helpful, whether you design your own questionnaire or select an existing one.

Determine the Purpose of the Questionnaire

The first question to ask when designing a questionnaire is the same as for any research: What do I expect to accomplish? We mention this here because beginning researchers sometimes tend to design and administer a questionnaire without thinking through the purpose of doing the survey in the first place.

Suppose the students at your college are concerned about campus security. Someone might design and administer a questionnaire that shows that students are, in fact, concerned about the problem. This is not particularly useful information. What would be useful is information about what specific things could be done to improve campus security: increasing the frequency of patrols by police, providing an escort service, reducing the number of entrances to buildings, or installing an electronic security system, for example. In this way, the administration would know what changes would be acceptable to the college community and be given some guidance in deciding how best to allocate resources to improve campus security.

You should try to anticipate questions of interpretation that may arise when you have the data. If you think that women will see things differently from men, or commuters differently from dorm students, you need to include questions that will help you to address these concerns.

Determine the Types of Questions

open-ended question:
one that the respondents answer in their own words

closed-ended question:
one that limits the respondents to certain alternatives

Survey questions can be divided into two basic categories: open-ended and closed-ended. An open-ended question permits the respondents to answer in their own words. A closed-ended question limits the respondents to alternatives determined in advance by the questionnaire's designers. Each type of question has advantages and disadvantages.

The open-ended question permits respondents to answer more completely and to reveal the reasoning behind their answers. Using open-ended questions makes it more likely that the questionnaire will discover something not anticipated by its designers.

Open-ended questions are harder to code, however, because the answers are in narrative form. (See the discussion of content analysis in Chapter 8.) It is necessary to categorize responses in some way to summarize the data after the survey is complete. This type of categorization makes data analysis a messy job and makes it likely that you will have to break a cardinal rule of research by not deciding in advance how you are going to analyze your data. In addition, open-ended questions require more effort from the respondents and are more difficult for less articulate respondents to answer.

The advantages and disadvantages of open-ended questions make them more useful for smaller and preliminary studies. Coding a small number of open-ended surveys may be manageable, whereas hundreds would not. In addition, trying out a preliminary version of a survey with open-ended questions can determine the range of likely answers, permitting you to standardize the alternatives into a closed-ended format that will be easier to deal with in the larger administration.

Closed-ended questions have complementary advantages and disadvantages to open-ended ones. They are easier to code and analyze, and there are fewer off-the-wall responses. The alternatives are presented to the respondents, so they do not have to think as hard. The respondents do not need to be as articulate to formulate their answers as they do with an open-ended question.

The disadvantages of closed-ended questions are that the issues being studied may be too complex to reduce to a small set of alternatives, or the respondent may not agree with any of them, resulting in simplistic answers. Closed-ended questions tend to put words into the mouths of respondents, suggesting alternatives that respondents might never come up with themselves. Furthermore, errors can creep into the closed-ended questionnaire: If a respondent misinterprets the question or a clerical error is made in coding the data, there may be no way to discover the fact. To reduce errors, many questionnaires require that each response be recorded in two places, so the responses can be tested for consistency.

In summary, the flexibility of open-ended questions makes them more useful for small-scale and preliminary studies, whereas the standardization of closed-ended questions makes them more suitable for large studies. Often, the two types of questions are mixed in a single study, when respondents may be offered the opportunity to expand on the answers to a closed-ended question. This permits the data to be coded and analyzed easily but gives some insights into respondents' reasons for choosing the alternative they did.

Write the Items

We outline some basic principles of questionnaire construction so that you will be aware of the major pitfalls.

Address a Single Issue Per Item

The principal concern is that the questionnaire items be unambiguous. Each item should address a single question and do so in a clear manner. The following item is ambiguous because it is double-barreled: *College students should receive grades in their courses because this prepares them for the competitive world outside of college.* This item contains both an opinion about grading and a reason for grading. A person might agree with giving grades but disagree with the reason stated for grading students. It would be better to phrase the item: *College students should receive grades in their course work.* Another item could address the desirability of preparing students for a competitive society.

Avoid Bias

The next consideration is to write the question in a way that will not bias the results. Two members of Congress may survey their respective constituents on attitudes toward abortion. The first one's newsletter asks, *Do you believe in killing unborn babies?* The second one's newsletter asks, *Should women be forced to bear unwanted children?* Even if the people in the two congressional districts had identical attitudes toward abortion, the survey results could indicate dramatically opposite attitudes.

A good example of the importance of phrasing (and its potential for bias) can be seen in the questions that the Gallup Poll uses to gain information about the way that Americans feel about the death penalty (Newport, 2001). In one reported comparison, 65% supported the question: *Are you in favor of the death penalty for a person convicted of murder?* Support for the death penalty drops down to 52% if the question is reworded so as to include an alternative punishment: *If you could choose between the following two approaches, which do you think is the better penalty for murder—the death penalty or life imprisonment, with absolutely no possibility of parole?* Support for the death penalty rose to 81% when the concept was assessed with a specific criminal example in the question (that of Tim McVeigh, the Oklahoma City bomber). These results do not indicate that Americans are confused about how they feel about the death penalty. Instead, the different results from these questions show that the way that a question is asked is very important and can easily become a source of bias.

Bias can come from unexpected sources, such as the general context of the survey. For example, when patients in a doctor's office questionnaire are asked for their level of pain and fatigue without a specified reporting period, they report levels similar to their current pain. If a reporting period, such as "within the last month" is included, the reported pain levels are much higher (Stone, Broderick, Schwartz, & Schwarz, 2008). So carefully constructing the survey questions, such that the frame of evaluation is clear, helps to avoid bias.

Make Alternatives Clear

mutually exclusive: categories defined so that membership in one rules out membership in another

There is a particular need to write closed-ended questions in such a way that the options are distinctly different from one another and that they cover all possibilities. A philosopher would say that the answers must be **mutually exclusive** and exhaustive. Categories are mutually exclusive if no individual case could belong to more than one category at a time. The categories—*undergraduate* and *graduate*—are mutually exclusive because you cannot be both at the same time. But *scholarship recipient* and *undergraduate* are not mutually exclusive: You could be both an undergraduate and receiving a scholarship.

exhaustive: categories defined so that all possible cases will fall into one of them

For the categories to be exhaustive, all cases must fall into one or another of the alternatives. Using only *graduate student* and *undergraduate student* leaves out the possibility that someone has a bachelor's degree but is taking undergraduate courses to prepare for application to graduate school. We might define the category *nondegree student* for this type of individual. Because of the difficulty of thinking of all the alternatives, questions sometimes include the category *other*. This category should be used with care, however, because your interpretation of the question is in trouble if *other* turns out to be a popular answer.

Beware of the Social Desirability Tendency

social desirability: a characteristic of certain responses that causes people to choose that response even if it does not represent their true tendency or opinion

Bias often enters when respondents perceive one alternative as more socially acceptable than the other—a phenomenon called social desirability. Researchers avoid this problem by wording questions so that each alternative appears equally socially desirable. The question on abortion might be better structured as follows: *Women should be permitted to decide for themselves whether to continue a pregnancy.* To balance people's natural tendency to agree with any item, an experimenter might also include a question that presents the matter the other way: *Abortions should be restricted by law.* Some personality tests include a set of questions designed to detect if a person has a tendency to be overly influenced by social desirability. A collection of such items designed to detect dishonest responses is sometimes called a verification key. The Minnesota Multiphasic Personality Inventory (MMPI)—a widely used personality test—has a verification key called the *lie scale.* One question on the lie scale might ask whether a person has ever stolen anything, no matter how small. Most people, to answer truthfully, would have to say that they had. People who say they have never done so would raise suspicions. These scales can be quite sophisticated, so it may be hard to make yourself look better than you really are without scoring high on a lie scale.

verification key: a collection of items on a questionnaire designed to detect dishonest answers

Beware of Acquiescence

acquiescence: the tendency to agree with a statement on a questionnaire, regardless of its content

Although it may be tempting to format a questionnaire entirely with binary closed-ended questions such as Agree/Disagree or True/False because they are easy to administer, these formats are highly susceptible to bias caused by acquiescence (Krosnick, 1999). Participants exhibiting acquiescence will have a tendency to agree to any statement on the inventory, regardless of its content. The effect of this bias is that participants will agree with both a statement and its opposite, so, for example, will respond *yes* to both *I like fish* and *I don't like fish*. It is estimated that the effect accounts for approximately 10% of responses (Krosnick, 1999).

Determine the Format of the Item

visual analogue scale: a question that asks for a response by marking a line between the minimum or maximum value for the statement

Answers can take various formats, depending on the type of question, such as true/false, multiple-choice, or ratings. Often respondents are asked to indicate their degree of agreement or disagreement with a particular position. This may be achieved with a **visual analogue scale** (VAS), which is often a single line, labeled at either end in terms of the minimum and maximum levels of a statement or sensation (Hetherington & Rolls, 1987), as follows:

Women should be permitted to decide for themselves whether to continue a pregnancy.

Agree ——————————————————— Disagree

Likert scale: a question that asks for a rating of the extent of agreement or disagreement with a statement; a rating scale

Rating scales, often called Likert scales after the person who made them popular, may also be used. Rating scales are used a great deal because they measure the magnitude of opinion, not simply its direction.

Attitudes elicited by questionnaire items are frequently measured on a 7-point scale or 9-point scale. Seven categories of agreement are the maximum that can be distinguished on most dimensions, though. The item might be laid out as follows, with instructions for the respondent to circle the number that most closely corresponds with his or her attitude:

Women should be permitted to decide for themselves whether to continue a pregnancy.

Agree   Disagree
  1   2   3   4   5   6   7

Though a full discussion of scaling is well outside the scope of this book, it is worth noting that scales are measurement instruments, just as thermometers or EEG (electroencephalogram) machines are. Using an appropriate scale to measure a response is as important as having an accurate ruler to measure the length of a line. Particularly when creating questionnaires that concern sensations (such as pain or taste intensity), the usage of Likert or VAS scales may produce less valid results than using the general Labeled Magnitude Scale (gLMS; Bartoshuk et al., 2002), which takes into account the idea that past experiences form a context for judging strength and thus allows the comparison of sensations between people (Bartoshuk et al., 2004). Essentially, choosing a particular scale should be made with the care that you would give to any other measurement instrument.

branching items: a set of questions that enable the respondent to move through a survey in different ways, depending upon the responses

When constructing questions, often it is convenient to write branching items that permit the respondent to skip inappropriate items and move through a questionnaire more efficiently.

If you have ever had to fill out a federal financial aid form (FAFSA) or complete income taxes in a paper format, you have experienced branching questions directly. These are the items that begin with one question, and then, depending upon how you answer, send you to a different question. An example might be a question that looks similar to the following:

1. **Are you single?**
    Yes .... ☐ ——————➤ *CONTINUE TO QUESTION 2*
    No .... ☐ ——————➤ *SKIP TO QUESTION 25*

If you answered "Yes" to the question above, you would be sent to other questions about single individuals, such as whether or not you live with your parents. If you answered "No," you would be sent to other questions that were appropriate for married people. There are other examples in Box 9.1, which gives an extended example of a branching questionnaire concerning dining out. This example is particularly useful because it has a number of branching points. In addition, note that the terms used—*dine out, weekday, weekend*—are carefully defined. Although these terms may seem clear to you, they need to be defined in this context because different people use them differently. For example, some people consider Friday to be a part of the weekend.

If you have only experienced the computerized version of the FAFSA or income tax preparation, you have still experienced a branching question. However, the computer is able to do the branching for you, so it automatically puts the correct next question on the screen.

Sequence the Items

Care should be given to sequencing the items in a questionnaire. Answers to some questions may be biased if they were to follow some others. The Campus Security Survey, which is found at the end of this chapter, for example, asks a number of questions of different types. The first group of questions concerns demographics. If you are taking a survey of students on your campus, the first thing you want to determine is whether the participant actually is a student.

Before you ask questions about campus security, you would want to know if security is even an issue with the students. If you were to start out asking about safety, the respondents might say that they felt unsafe. But if you begin with an open-ended question about things they dislike about the campus, they might not even list safety as a concern. Next, the survey asks them to rank safety among a set of other concerns they might have; here you get another idea of its importance to them. Finally, you move on to specific questions about safety.

BOX 9.1

Dining Out Questionnaire

1. How often would you say that you dine out (pay to eat in a restaurant)?
   A. [ ] I have never dined out ————————→ SKIP TO QUESTION 7
   B. [ ] I very rarely dine out ————————→ SKIP TO QUESTION 7
   C. [ ] I dine out regularly

2. Which answer best describes how often you dine out?
   A. [ ] less than once per week ————————→ SKIP TO QUESTION 7
   B. [ ] 1 or 2 times per week
   C. [ ] 3 or 4 times per week
   D. [ ] nearly every day
   E. [ ] every day

3. On how many weekdays (Monday, Tuesday, Wednesday, and Thursday) do you usually dine out?
   A. [ ] 0 days ————————→ SKIP TO QUESTION 5
   B. [ ] 1 day
   C. [ ] 2 days
   D. [ ] 3 days
   E. [ ] 4 days

4. When you dine out on a weekday, how much money do you usually spend at a single restaurant?
   A. [ ] less than 10 dollars
   B. [ ] $10.01 – $20.00
   C. [ ] $20.01 – $50.00
   D. [ ] $50.01 – $100.00
   E. [ ] More than $100.00

5. On how many days of a weekend (Friday, Saturday, and Sunday) do you usually dine out?
   A. [ ] 0 days ————————→ SKIP TO QUESTION 7
   B. [ ] 1 day
   C. [ ] 2 days
   D. [ ] 3 days

6. When you dine out on a weekend, how much money do you usually spend at a single restaurant?
   A. [ ] less than 10 dollars
   B. [ ] $10.01 – $20.00
   C. [ ] $20.01 – $50.00
   D. [ ] $50.01 – $100.00
   E. [ ] More than $100.00

7. [Questionnaire continues with other questions.]

The dining out questionnaire in Box 9.1 provides another reason to consider the sequence of items. The first question asks whether the participant dines out at all. If not, he or she is instructed to skip to the next section of the questionnaire.

Determine How the Data Will Be Analyzed

Another question to consider is how the questionnaire is to be scored and analyzed. Once again, this should be done in advance of collecting data for any research project. See Chapter 14 for a discussion of data reduction techniques and the coding guide.

If you think that women will respond differently than men, commuters differently than dorm students, first-year students differently than other students, and so on, you need to include questions to permit the classification of students on these dimensions.

You also need to decide what statistics will be used. Will you be able to draw proper conclusions from the data? It is an excellent idea to devise the form on which you will code your data as a way of checking to see if your questionnaire is well designed.

Administering the Questionnaire _____

Determine the Method of Administration

There are essentially four different modes of administering surveys: face-to-face, written, computerized, and by telephone. Each one has its advantages and disadvantages, as we shall see. The one that is best depends on the circumstances. For example, it might be a relatively simple matter to survey the members of a local fraternity face-to-face. The alumni of that fraternity, however, could best be reached by mail.

The typical survey tries to obtain responses from a large group of individuals who are difficult to locate and whose cooperation may be difficult to obtain. Frequently, however, questionnaires are administered as part of a program in which people come to an office or a laboratory on a routine basis. A questionnaire may be administered to all patients in a doctor's office or all participants in a large study, for example. In such situations, obtaining cooperation may be less of a problem. The following discussion largely assumes the usual situation in which finding and gaining cooperation of the participants is a major consideration.

Face-to-Face

Personal interviews have the advantage that the interviewers can establish rapport with the people being interviewed. Interviewers can direct the attention of the respondents to the material and motivate them to answer the questions carefully. Interviewers can guarantee the order in which questions are administered, thus making sure that people answer the survey in the order intended. In addition, interviewers may be able to notice when respondents seem to misunderstand a question and explain its meaning and can probe for more complete answers when a respondent gives a brief answer or one that does not respond to the question. Visual aids can also be presented to clarify a survey question in a face-to-face testing situation that may be impractical to present with other methods of survey administration.

The main disadvantage of face-to-face interviewing is the flip side of its main advantages: The presence of the interviewer creates a social situation that may result in biased responses. Respondents say what they think interviewers want to hear. The potential for interviewer effects is greater with face-to-face interviewing than with any other method.

Face-to-face interviewing also has several practical problems. First, interviewing is much more expensive than conducting computer-based, telephone, or mail surveys because of the need to travel to the respondents' locations. Second is concern for the safety of the interviewers. With so many people away from home during the day, it is often necessary to conduct interviews in the evening. Interviewers are understandably reluctant to go from house to house after dark. Finally, personal interviewing has the problem that it is more difficult to supervise the interviewers. It is not unheard of for interviewers to look at the list of addresses they are to reach and decide to fake the data, thus saving themselves a great deal of travel and interview time.

Written Responses

Written administration of questionnaires can take several forms: The questionnaires may be administered to a group, they may be dropped off at a particular location, or they may be mailed to the respondents.

Group administration is familiar to you if you have completed course evaluations in college. Group administration is a very efficient use of time and money and can have a very high response rate if attendance by group members is high, as in a class. Drop-off administration is often done by an organization, such as a church, that has many members who attend a particular location over some period of time but may not all be present at one time. Copies of the questionnaire are dropped off in a particular location to be picked up at some later time. Mail administration is familiar to all. We frequently receive questionnaires in the mail, sometimes as part of another mailing or in a magazine.

The main advantage of written questionnaires is their low cost. There is no monetary cost of group or drop-off administration other than the duplication of the materials. Even postage is relatively cheap compared with many of the alternative methods of administration. Except for group administration, respondents can complete the questionnaire at their leisure, and they have greater anonymity in their responses, reducing interviewer bias.

response rate: in survey research, the percentage of individuals in the sample who return the completed survey

The main problem with written questionnaires is response rate. We discuss the consequences of different response rates later in this chapter. At this point, we simply note that low response rates may invalidate the results because of differences between individuals who respond and those who don't. Drop-off and mail administration may have very low rates of responding, often less than 50%.

Written questionnaires have other drawbacks as well. There is no possibility of clarifying questions that might be misunderstood. Some individuals in the sample may be illiterate or have vision problems. Illiterate participants are frequently embarrassed to admit their problem and sometimes respond to questions they do not understand, compromising the reliability and validity of the data. It is impossible to determine how seriously the respondent took the survey. Perhaps a survey of attitudes toward consumer products intended for the person who does the household shopping has been given to a child in the family to fill out for the fun of it.

Computerized Administration

As the Internet continues to rise in popularity, it may be convenient to administer a questionnaire by computer. The questionnaire may be distributed via e-mail, posted as a Web-based survey that is open to the general public, or administered in a laboratory setting. The computer has the advantage of being impersonal, so social desirability may be reduced. The computer is also absolutely consistent. The investigator can be sure that all the questions were asked in order, and none were skipped. The computer can check for invalid responses and prompt the interviewer to recheck implausible answers, such as the presence of 20 children in the home. More importantly, the computer can control the sequencing and branching of questions so that, for example, people who do not drive will not need to be asked about how many miles they drive to work. In addition, Internet surveys are available to people 24 hours a day, making a high level of participation possible without the costs of photocopying or postage.

Computerized administration suffers from some of the same problems as the written response method. Illiterate or uncooperative participants will provide meaningless data. True measures of response rates are difficult, particularly if a link to the survey is simply posted on a Web site, but response rates to Web-based surveys are typically rather low (Skitka & Sargis, 2006). Further, because they are totally unmonitored, people taking an anonymous Web-based survey might not be honest about their ages or genders. A truly random sample of respondents may also be difficult to obtain because people participating in a Web-based survey are self-selected (Azar, 2000). It is also unlikely that people who do not own a computer will even be aware of the Web-based study, much less able to participate, so a participant selection bias may be present.

In addition to the problems faced by written response methods, computer-administered surveys have additional challenges. For example, if the questionnaire is Web-based, security of responding is vital. Further, storage of survey information obtained electronically must be ensured (via backups, etc.) without violating the privacy of the person responding to the questionnaire.

Although programming the computer to administer the survey can be difficult, the cost savings, speed of collection, and high response rate (Azar, 2000) make Internet-based surveys a viable alternative to other data collection measures. The quality of the data is comparable, and Internet respondents seem to have more diversity that those seen with the traditional pen-and-paper type of survey (Lewis, Watson, & White, 2009). Further, there are some indications that Internet surveys have higher predictive validity than data collected by telephone without sacrificing measurement reliability (Chang, 2002).

Telephone Administration

The main advantage of the telephone as a method of administering surveys is low cost. Nowadays the percentage of people who can be reached by telephone is about as high as the percentage that can be reached by other means. Even unlisted numbers are not a problem when random-digit dialing is used. This method involves choosing an exchange and then randomly selecting the last four digits from a random-number table. Although it may take as many as five calls on the average to reach a working number that is a residence instead of a business, this may still involve less effort than some other methods of administration. Like Internet surveys, telephone interviews can be conducted rapidly, without having to wait for interviewers to travel to many locations or for respondents to mail back their completed surveys.

Another advantage of telephone surveys is the possibility of using a computer-assisted interview. Although computer-assisted interviewing is by no means limited to telephone administration, it is probably most widely used in conjunction with the telephone. The interviewer reads the questions from a computer screen and types the answers onto the keyboard. This method has many of the previously noted advantages of computerized interviewing.

Finally, telephone surveys can be conducted from a central location where the interviewers can be supervised. This careful supervision can reduce slippage and ensure that they administer the survey as it was designed.

On the negative side, the external validity of telephone surveys is reduced by the fact that only people who have a home telephone and are willing to put up with the intrusion can be sampled. Since more and more people are giving up their home phones in favor of cell phones, some particular problems can arise. Since cell phone users pay for their minutes, they are somewhat disinclined to spend them on answering a questionnaire (American Association for Public Opinion Research, 2008). So the calculation of response rate (see the next section) is more complicated and less reliable with cell phone–based surveys. Some states prohibit using auto-dialers (a way of rapidly calling telephone numbers) with cell phones, so calling these individuals can be more expensive for the agency conducting the survey. Lastly, since a person with a cell phone can be physically located almost anywhere, sampling appropriately from within a specific location, such as everyone who may live within a particular town, is extremely difficult. Despite the difficulty, there is no reliable evidence that the data collected from cell phone–based studies are poorer in quality than landline-based surveys (American Association for Public Opinion Research, 2008).

In addition, telephone surveys are less anonymous than mail or Web-based surveys and introduce the possibility of interviewer bias. It is more difficult to ask complicated or open-ended questions over the telephone than with a written questionnaire. Compared with face-to-face interviews, it is harder to establish rapport or to judge the degree of seriousness with which the respondent is taking the interview, and it is impossible to use visual aids. Telephone surveys must also be relatively short to get participants to finish the survey.

The Problem of Response Rate

A principal concern with all methods of administering surveys is the problem of response rate. We are all bombarded by surveys from a great variety of sources; many of them are actually sales pitches disguised as surveys. More than a third of the American population may refuse to participate in surveys (Neuman, 1999). Further, the response rate varies significantly among methods of administration. Surveys printed in magazines may have a 1% or 2% response rate. Mail surveys often have return rates between 10% and 50%, telephone surveys 80%, and face-to-face surveys 90% (Neuman, 1999).

Magazines and radio stations often publish questions for their audiences to respond to, but these broadcast surveys lack reliability. One station says, "Our poll is not a scientific survey but a rough estimate of the views of our listeners." All of the data come from people who are motivated to respond. Most people feel only moderately one way or the other about an issue such as gun control, but a few are strongly, perhaps violently, opposed. A survey with a low response rate will be biased in the direction of the more vocal people.

The British magazine, *New Scientist*, polled its readers on their attitudes toward ESP (Evans, 1973). The results showed that 67% of those responding considered ESP to be either *an established fact* or a *likely possibility*. This sounds like impressive evidence in favor of the scientific credibility of ESP until one discovers that the return rate on this questionnaire was only about 2%. People who believe in ESP would likely be more motivated to respond than nonbelievers, thus giving biased results.

The quality of the data is a direct function of the return rate, although lower response rates do not necessarily translate into less accurate results (Krosnick, 1999). Most researchers require at least 50% and prefer 90%, although many will accept a lower rate if ways of increasing return rate are not practical. Refusal to cooperate, failure to return a questionnaire, or unavailability of target respondents should be recorded. Possible biases thereby introduced should be kept in mind when the research is evaluated.

Sampling

Types of Samples

Surveys differ greatly in value according to how the respondents are sampled. Depending upon the type of sample, the potential to come to an erroneous conclusion can be dramatically increased. We discuss four types of samples: haphazard samples, purposive samples, convenience samples, and probability samples.

Haphazard Samples

haphazard sample: population subgroup for whose selection the researcher uses hit-or-miss methods

Sometimes the surveyor has control over whom to sample but uses haphazard methods of obtaining people. A television station may send a crew out to interview 11 people on the street with instructions to include five women, two black people, three teenagers, and one adorable little girl. These **haphazard samples** are almost worthless. Perhaps the most famous haphazard survey was conducted by the now-defunct *Literary Digest*, which obtained respondents from telephone books and automobile registration lists. This survey predicted that Landon would win the 1936 presidential election over Roosevelt by a landslide. It overlooked the fact, however, that during the Great Depression people who could afford telephones and automobiles were more likely to vote Republican.

Purposive Samples

purposive sample: a nonrandom sample that is chosen for some characteristic that it possesses

Frequently, researchers will base a survey on a sample that is chosen to meet some particular definition. A **purposive sample** is not selected randomly, but for some particular reason. A researcher may survey the opinions of the presidents of several leading colleges about desirable changes in the college curriculum. The opinions of these people may be more valuable than those that would be obtained in a random sample of all college presidents.

Purposive samples can almost be considered to constitute a population—for example, all presidents of leading colleges. In practice, of course, a researcher frequently does not have access to an entire population, even one as small as the presidents of the top 50 colleges, nor will there necessarily be agreement on which are the top 50 colleges. Nevertheless, a purposive sample is frequently preferable to a random sample.

The main problem with purposive sampling is that an error in judgment by the researcher in selecting the sample may influence the results. A list of leading colleges composed by a researcher is more likely to contain the researcher's own college than would a list compiled by someone at a different college. Another problem is that the presidents of leading colleges might not know what the most desirable curriculum would be for students at the colleges that constitute most of the population of colleges.

Convenience Samples

convenience sample: a nonrandom sample that is chosen for practical reasons

Another kind of sample that is quite acceptable is similar to the purposive sample in that it selects a desirable group of people but differs in that it may not come close to sampling all of a population. This is the convenience sample. A researcher may want to study the effects of integration on social development in schoolchildren. There may be many appropriate schools to choose among, but it is much more convenient to study one in the researcher's own city. Even though such selection is not random, one would usually be willing to generalize the results to other similar schools and similar children. Most research in psychology is done using convenience samples: students enrolled in introductory psychology courses.

Probability Samples

The most satisfactory surveys generally obtain their respondents in some manner such that the researcher knows the probability that any given individual will appear in the sample. Whereas the other three types of samples permit only subjective evaluation of the validity of the results, probability samples permit one to apply various statistics. Our focus, therefore, is on probability samples.

Probability Samples and Random Selection

Most probability sampling methods rely on random sampling, although there are important exceptions, as we shall see shortly. Before we go further, therefore, it is necessary to discuss the concept of random selection.

Although you may have an idea of random selection, the concept is not a simple one. First, it is necessary to realize that the term *random* as used in science is a technical one, very different from our everyday use, where we might say that we picked the socks we wore today "at random." In that usage, *random* means you picked the first pair of socks that fell to hand; most likely it implies that you would wear those same socks much more than some of your other pairs. That would happen if you always replaced the laundered socks in the drawer on top of the previously laundered ones and pulled them out again from the top of the pile.

As a first approximation, selection is random when it is controlled by chance alone. A common example is selecting a state lottery number. The authorities want to be sure that no one will be able to predict the number better than chance. Another way to define a **random sample** is to say that a selection process is random if every member of the population has the same probability of being selected, and selection of one individual is independent of the selection of any other. The equal-probability-of-selection part may seem obvious, but the necessity of independent selection of individuals requires some comment.

Suppose John and Marsha, Bob and Carol, and Ted and Alice attend a party at which there are to be two door prizes awarded. If the host puts each couple's names on a slip of paper and pulls one paper out of a hat, then it is obvious that if John's name is chosen, Marsha's will be also. Marsha's selection, then, was dependent on John's (and vice versa). John and Marsha each had a one in three chance of winning, but because only both or neither could win, their selection was not random. If the host put all the names on separate pieces of paper and pulled two names, however, then the selection would be random. Both John and Marsha would have a one in three chance of being selected, as before, but Marsha's chance of selection would not depend on John's.

This example is a bit contrived, but it is quite possible for structure to exist in some ordering of individuals. You may have been in a group that was being divided into two smaller groups by counting off. If people tended to sit together in pairs, then counting off would result in each member of the pair winding up in a different group. This may be the desired result, but it is not random. Random selection would result in separating some, but not all, pairs. Thus, any method of selection other than a true random method could result in some nonindependence among members of the groups.

The Sampling Frame

To take a probability sample of a population, it is necessary to define the population. Suppose you want to take a survey of 10% of your research methods class. The population in this case is the class. The class, however, contains some individuals who have not yet officially registered for the course or who will drop before the end of the term. You must develop a definition of the population for the purposes of the survey, and this may be different from the actual population. For example, you may define the population for the purposes of the study as those whose names appear on the official class roster as of a certain date. Any who have not yet registered will not be considered, even if they are attending class. The population that you will work with for your particular study is called the **sampling frame**. To take another example, the sampling frame for the purpose of studying the population of Allegheny County, Pennsylvania, might exclude those who are in jails or mental institutions.

Each individual who falls within the sampling frame is called an element. You would sample a number of elements from the sampling frame.

random sample: a sample in which every member of the population has an equal and independent chance of being selected

sampling frame: a population as it is defined for the purposes of selecting subjects for a study

element: individual member of a sampling frame

Systematic Samples

systematic sample: a
probability sample that is
not randomly selected

A systematic sample is a probability sample but not a random sample. It involves selecting elements from an ordered sampling frame.

As an example, suppose you want to select a sample of 20 students from your research methods class of 80 students. Your first step would be to obtain the class roster from the instructor. Then you would need to identify each element. You could use the students' names, but this would require you to have some way of randomizing their names. Because it is much more convenient to work with numbers, you would identify each element by a number. If there were 80 students in the class, they would be numbered from 1 to 80. If you were to choose every fourth name from the class roster, you would have a probability sample, because 25% of the class would have been selected. The sample would not be random, however, because those whose names were in positions one, five, nine, and so on, had a 100% chance of being selected, and everyone else had a zero chance. This method fails the equal-probability part of the definition of random selection. Suppose, however, that you randomly chose which of the first four positions you started counting from. This method would meet the equal-probability-of-selection criterion, but it would still be nonrandom because the very first choice would determine the selection of all subsequent elements.

It should be noted that although systematic samples are not random, they may be perfectly good for practical reasons. Taking every nth individual from a roster is much less work than the random method we are about to describe. If there is some structure to the list, as we have seen, the results will be nonrandom. For example, a list of couples might be structured such that the man's name always followed that of his partner. Choosing every tenth person on the list would result in the selection of all men or all women.

If the list has no structure to it, however, the results will be as good as random in practice. A list of names in alphabetical order is unlikely to have any structure that would affect a sample drawn by selecting every nth name. (If names were selected in bunches, however, structure could easily arise: Selecting all the M's would result in a high proportion of Scottish names that begin with Mc and Mac.) Therefore, systematic sampling is commonly done in survey research because it is so easy.

Simple Random Samples

simple random sample:
group chosen from an
entire population such
that every member of the
population has an equal
and independent chance of
being selected in a single
sample

Exactly how to select elements randomly from a population may require considerable thought and ingenuity. As we have seen, some methods that may seem random actually are not. The basic simple random sample is used when we believe that the population is relatively homogeneous with respect to the questions of interest.

Let us continue with the same example of selecting 20 students from your class of 80. After you have obtained the roster and assigned each student a number as before, you would next obtain a list of random numbers. Random-number tables are available in many books about research methods and statistics, or you can generate a list of random numbers with a computer. (A program to generate random numbers is given in the Instructor's Manual.)

TABLE **9.1**

Portion of a Random-Number Table

© Cengage Learning

0	9	8	3	5	8	0	6	9	9
5	6	0	5	3	7	2	6	6	4
9	6	2	7	1	7	0	0	0	2
3	1	6	9	2	7	1	8	5	8
3	6	3	2	0	4	9	6	4	0
5	0	4	7	3	2	4	6	9	4
7	7	4	6	6	7	1	5	3	4
0	9	3	0	8	0	6	6	4	1
4	9	6	5	1	9	7	0	7	1
5	5	6	6	5	3	8	4	5	3
5	2	8	8	7	2	2	6	1	0
1	4	0	5	4	4	8	2	5	7
0	9	7	8	3	9	1	0	4	6
5	9	5	8	4	5	8	9	8	8
0	5	0	2	5	8	6	4	2	5
6	6	6	7	8	7	2	7	9	7
4	1	4	1	8	6	0	8	5	6
7	1	1	2	0	4	2	5	2	0
4	5	7	4	8	6	1	0	7	0
5	4	6	2	7	2	2	9	8	9
3	1	7	7	6	5	6	7	8	2
1	5	5	2	2	2	4	5	8	9
8	4	0	2	6	4	4	3	3	8
6	7	8	5	1	5	0	8	7	6
9	6	7	1	1	5	6	6	6	1
1	6	2	5	8	7	9	9	2	6
9	8	3	3	5	5	4	0	7	2
3	6	6	5	9	6	3	2	0	6
8	5	7	2	9	7	0	6	9	0
8	1	9	3	4	2	5	6	7	3
1	7	4	4	3	9	9	7	0	3
2	9	8	4	7	0	1	9	7	2

Table 9.1 shows part of a matrix of random numbers. This table presents columns of one-digit numbers. For our example, you need numbers between 1 and 80. This requires that you have a list of two-digit numbers. To accomplish

this, simply rule the table into two-digit columns. Next, go down the list of numbers, looking for numbers between 1 and 80. Each time you see number 1, write it down on a list until you have found 20 numbers. These become the identification numbers of the people who are selected for the sample. Occasionally, a number will repeat before you have completed your sample. Simply ignore such numbers because the people they represent are already in the sample. In this example, ignore the repeat occurrence of numbers 31 and 9 (twice). Also ignore the numbers 84 and 96 (twice) because they are outside the desired range.

Stratified Random Samples

If you are surveying a population that has identifiable subgroups that are likely to differ markedly in their responses, you can improve the validity of your study by obtaining a stratified random sample.

stratified random sample: a random sample in which two or more subsamples are represented according to some predetermined proportion, generally in the same proportion as they exist in the population

Suppose you know that the college has 55% women and 45% men and you have reason to believe that males and females may respond differently on your dependent measure. If you took a simple random sample, the ratio of males to females would probably not match the population exactly. By stratified random sampling you can ensure that the proportion of men and women in the sample matches that in the college population.

Stratified random sampling essentially treats the population as two or more separate subpopulations and creates a separate random sample of each. In this case, you take one sample from the female subpopulation and one from the male subpopulation. First, you determine how many of each you need. Because you want your sample to contain one-fourth of the population of 80 students and have the same-sex ratio as the population, you need one-fourth of the females and one-fourth of the males. If there are 48 females and 32 males in the class, you will require 12 females and eight males. Next, you number the females from 1 to 48 and select from the random-number table in the same manner as before. Then you number the males from 1 to 32 and repeat the process. Now you can be sure that the sample exactly matches the population with regard to sex ratio. The procedure is still random, however, because every member of the population had an equal and independent chance of being selected.

Sometimes stratified random sampling is used to oversample some subgroup of the population—that is, to purposely include some group at a greater frequency than it is represented in the population. Suppose you are interested in comparing the opinions of black people and white people on some matter. You would want to include the same number of black people and white people in the survey to get as reliable an estimate of the attitudes of black people as of white people, even though black people may constitute only 10% of the population. You would stratify on race and include 50% black people and 50% white people in your sample. The sampling would still be random within the subpopulations.

Random samples can be extremely accurate. A sample as small as 1,000 individuals will allow a survey researcher to estimate within plus or minus 3.2% the attitude of a population as large as that of the United States (Weisberg & Bowen, 1977).

Cluster Samples

Many populations would be impossible or impractical to number. For instance, making a list of every person in the United States would be impossible. Even random sampling of all the students in a college may be difficult. Suppose there is no student directory. You may decide to obtain the students from classes. Rather than taking one-tenth of the students in each class, sampling every student in one-tenth of the classes would be more efficient. You would obtain a list of all classes at the college. From this list you would randomly select one-tenth of the classes to study. This method would produce a cluster sample. Even though the students whom you sample by clustering would probably be more alike than those in a purely random sample (because students within classes are likely to be similar in background), the ease of obtaining the sample would permit you to study more individuals and therefore offset the disadvantages of not having a purely random sample.

cluster sample: group selected by using clusters or groupings from a larger population

If you wanted to make sure your sample contained the same proportion of students in particular categories as the college as a whole, you could stratify your clusters. You might separate the classes into sciences, humanities, and so forth, as well as into lower- and upper-division courses. Then you would randomly select one-tenth of the classes in each category.

multistage sampling: a form of cluster sampling in which clusters are further broken down by taking samples from each cluster

A sophisticated form of cluster sampling is known as multistage sampling. Commercial polls, such as the Gallup Poll, use multistage sampling. First, they may randomly select several ZIP codes. From these ZIP codes, streets are selected randomly; from the streets, addresses are selected randomly. For practical reasons, it is common to select a number of individuals from within a given cluster.

An example of multistage sampling can be seen in a study of the motivations for nonmedical use of drugs among high school seniors in the United States. Sean McCabe, Carol Boyd, James Cranford, and Christian Teter (2009) first selected a number of geographical areas. Next, they selected one or more high schools within each geographical area. Then they selected senior students within each high school. This method was much more efficient than trying to make a simple random selection from all high school seniors. It is likely that no single list of all such individuals exists. Even if it did, it would be very inefficient to try to study one or two students in a given school. Obtaining access to the students and administering the test is vastly more efficient in groups. In contrast to cluster sampling, this study used only certain students from each school. If they had studied all students in a given school, they would have had more individuals than they needed by the time they had obtained enough clusters to be representative of different types of schools and regions of the country.

Although cluster sampling is not as accurate as random sampling—because each stage of sampling introduces another source of sampling error—it can be very accurate. Cluster samples are able to determine attitudes with a margin of error of plus or minus 4% with a sample size of 1,000 (of the entire U.S. population), compared with 3.2% for a simple random sample of the same size (Weisberg & Bowen, 1977).

Note on Using Random-Number Tables

Strictly speaking, it is necessary to choose in a random manner the place to begin using a random-number table; otherwise, each member of the population will not have an equal chance of being selected. As you can see, this involves an infinite regress (an endless chain of steps), because how do you choose your random starting place? In practice, there are two ways in which researchers commonly handle this problem. The first way is to start by pointing blindly at some point in the table and starting at that point. The second, and preferable, method is to start at the beginning of the table and use any part of the table only once. This method is feasible if you have access to a computer to generate new lists as necessary.

Summary of Sampling Procedures

Random Sampling

1. Define and identify the sampling frame.
2. Determine the desired size of the sample.
3. Compile a list of all members of the population, and assign each member on the list a number from zero to the required number.
4. Group the columns of digits according to the required number of digits—for example, three digits for numbers up to 999.
5. Arbitrarily select a number in the random-number table by closing your eyes and pointing.
6. If the selected number corresponds to the number assigned to any member of the identified population, that member is in the sample.
7. Repeat Step 6 by running down the table until the desired number of subjects has been selected.

Stratified Random Sampling

1. Identify the sampling frame.
2. Determine the desired size of the sample.
3. Determine the subgroups, or strata, for which you want equal or proportional representation.
4. Identify each member of the population as a member of one of the subgroups or strata.
5. For each of the population subgroups or strata, assign each member a number from zero to the required number.
6. Use a random-number table to select the appropriate number of subjects from each of the subgroups or strata.

Cluster Sampling

1. Identify the sampling frame.
2. Determine the desired sample size.
3. Identify and list all appropriate clusters.
4. Assign all clusters on the list a consecutive number from zero to the required number.
5. Determine the average number of subjects in each cluster of the population.

6. Determine the number of appropriate clusters by dividing the desired sample size by the estimated size of a cluster.
7. Use a random-number table to select the appropriate number of clusters.
8. Either select randomly from the clusters or use the entire cluster.

NUTS & BOLTS

Tips on Interviewing

As is the case with those who conduct any type of research, interviewers must be properly trained to avoid slippage between the protocol designed by the principal investigator and what actually takes place. Arthur Kornhauser and Paul Sheatsley (1976) give a number of suggestions for conducting interviews.

The first principle is to create a friendly but professional atmosphere. A face-to-face interview may start with some pleasantry about the weather or the dog but should get right to the point to avoid arousing suspicion. A telephone interviewer may start out by saying "Good evening, I am conducting a survey and would like to get some of your ideas. For instance ..." followed by the first question.

Interviewers should keep the interview on track, without getting into discussions of subject matter. Interviewers are basically reporters who should avoid giving any of their own opinions so they do not bias the results.

It is very important to read the questions exactly as written; otherwise, different respondents will be answering essentially different surveys. The interviewer should not rephrase questions, even if the respondent is confused about the meaning of the words. Similarly, the questions must be asked in order, without skipping questions, unless a branching questionnaire is being used.

If a respondent gives an incomplete or too brief answer to an open-ended question, it is permissible to use probe questions to get the respondent to complete the answer. You might say, "That's interesting; could you explain that a little more?" It is very important not to put words into the respondent's mouth. Usually it is safer to simply repeat all or part of the question.

Sometimes people will say, "I don't know," when they are reluctant to reveal their opinion or are confused as to the meaning of the question. Then you might say, "Well, I just want your own opinion; no one actually knows the answer to many of these questions." The number of questions that elicit unsatisfactory answers can be reduced by careful writing and by piloting the questionnaire on a number of people before beginning the actual administration.

The responses should be written down verbatim while the interview is in progress; don't wait until it is over because you will forget or give biased answers. People will be patient with a few pauses as you write. Then, the whole questionnaire should be reviewed for omissions and errors immediately after the interview is completed, but before leaving or hanging up, if possible.

Obtaining True Answers to Questions

Sometimes people may not give honest answers on questionnaires. For example, it is likely that people will be influenced by social desirability when answering questions about behaviors that are criminal, antisocial, or unusual. Research on the prevalence of drug use, tax evasion, or condom use would likely encounter this type of problem.

(continues)

NUTS & BOLTS *(continued)*

randomized response method: a survey technique that encourages honesty by introducing a random variable that makes it impossible to identify whether an answer is true of a particular individual

A method that encourages honest answers is called the **randomized-response method** (Kolata, 1987). With this technique, the person answering the question is guaranteed anonymity because he or she uses some random device to determine how to answer. Suppose you want to know how many people cheated in a course last term. You ask the participants a question that has a true or false answer and have them flip a coin. If the answer to the question is true (if they cheated), they are instructed to answer no, regardless of what the coin says. If the answer is false (if they did not cheat) and the coin is heads, they are to say yes. If the answer is false (if they did not cheat) and the coin is tails, they are to say no (see Figure 9.1).

It can be shown that the actual probability of the behavior in question is given by the following equation:

$$P(T) = 1 - [2 \times P(Y)]$$

That is, the probability of the behavior is 1 minus twice the probability of a yes response.

Because the person answering the questionnaire is the only one who knows whether the coin was heads or tails, there is no way of knowing whether that answer is true for that person (whether the person actually cheated). Also, a person for whom the answer is true will always say no. (The cheaters will always say no.) Further, all the people who say yes actually did not cheat.

There are two drawbacks to this procedure. First, the person answering the questionnaire must understand the instructions and believe that there is no trick to them. As people will not always believe that the experimenter is being honest, variations of this technique have been developed that take into account the possibility that some participants will lie, rather than give a potentially socially unacceptable answer (Moshagen, Musch, & Erdfelder, 2011). Second, because flipping a coin introduces randomness into the process, the results have more variability than a direct question. Nevertheless, the randomized-response method can be useful when one wants to investigate a behavior about which people are likely to lie.

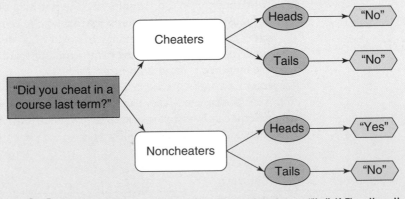

FIGURE **9.1** Randomized-Response Method—Participants Only Answer "Yes" If They Have Not Cheated and If Their Coin Is "Heads"

© Cengage Learning

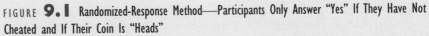

Summary

1. Surveys are useful ways to determine the attitudes of people on particular questions, to determine the effect of some natural event, or to look for patterns of cause and effect among many variables.
2. Designing a survey is a complex procedure that shares components of research design and written communication.
3. The first step in designing a questionnaire is to determine its purpose.
4. Questions may be open-ended or closed-ended. Each has advantages and disadvantages.
5. Questions should address a single issue per item, avoid bias, offer clear alternatives, and take into account the tendency toward social desirability and acquiescence.
6. Common response formats are the VAS, the Likert scale, and the gLMS, each of which asks for ratings of the level of a sensation or of agreement with a statement.
7. Before collecting the data, the researcher should decide how the data will be analyzed.
8. Methods of survey administration include face-to-face, written, computerized, and by telephone. Each has advantages and disadvantages.
9. Written surveys may be administered in groups, dropped off for individual completion, or mailed.
10. Most researchers require at least a 50% return rate before they consider a survey representative.
11. Surveys may use haphazard samples, purposive samples, convenience samples, or probability samples.
12. Random sampling has a particular scientific meaning and requires considerable care to perform.
13. The sampling frame is the population that is available and actually sampled. Each individual who falls into the sampling frame is called an element.
14. Probability samples include systematic samples, simple random samples, stratified random samples, and cluster samples. Systematic samples use a probability rule for sampling that is not random. Simple random samples are feasible only with relatively small populations. Stratified random samples permit the researcher to ensure that various segments of the population are represented proportionately in the sample. Cluster samples are commonly used with large surveys.
15. Interviewing is a complex skill that requires considerable training.
16. The randomized-response technique, in which it is impossible to identify whether an answer is true of a particular individual, can be used to reduce the social desirability bias.

Suggestions for Further Reading

BIRNBAUM, M. H. (2000). *Psychological experiments on the INTERNET*. San Diego, CA: Harcourt. This edited text contains chapters that discuss ethical issues particular to Web-based research.

FINK, A. & KOSEKOFF, J. (2005). *How to conduct surveys: A step-by-step guide* (3rd ed.). Beverly Hills, CA: Sage. This is a clear, practical guide to designing and conducting surveys.

GROVES, R. M., FOWLER, F. J., COUPER, M. P., LEPKOWSKI, J. M., & SINGER, E. S. (2009). *Survey methodology*. Hoboken, NJ: Wiley. A concise description of survey and questionnaire techniques, as well as information on ongoing surveys.

JUDD, C. M., & HOYLE, R.H., HARRIS, M.J. (2001). *Research methods in social relations* (7th ed.). New York: Holt, Rinehart & Winston. This book has several chapters devoted to nonexperimental tech-niques: observational methods, questionnaires and interviews, archival research, and sampling of individuals from a population.

NEUMAN, W. L. (2003). *Social research methods: Qualitative and quantitative approaches* (5th ed.). Toronto: Allyn & Bacon. This book contains helpful discussion of advantages and disadvantages of various types of questionnaires and other issues of survey design.

A CASE IN POINT

Campus Security Survey

The following is a survey of campus security. Adapt it to your campus. Are the questions unambiguous? Do they cover the appropriate alternatives? What is the purpose of asking students to rank various aspects of campus life that they dislike in this survey? Should there be open-ended as well as closed-ended questions? In what order should the questions be? Are there any other items that should be included to classify respondents? How should the questionnaire be administered: by interview, to individuals or groups, by mail? How should the respondents be chosen: randomly, all students in randomly chosen classes, all students in the population? Will the questionnaire yield information that will be useful? What should be done with the information when gathered?

Campus Security Survey

We are taking a survey of things about the campus that students like and dislike. Are you a student at Pitt?

Yes ____ No ____ (If answer is no, STOP HERE and return the questionnaire.)

If answer is yes, please check the appropriate box.
Year in school:

    1. Freshman ....[   ]

    2. Sophomore ....[   ]

    3. Junior ....[   ]

    4. Senior ....[   ]

    5. Graduate/Professional ....[   ]

    6. Other(1) ....[   ]   (1) _____

Sex:

    1. Male ....[   ]

    2. Female ....[   ]   (2) _____

What are your living arrangements?

    1. Live in a Pitt dorm ....[   ]

    2. Live off campus, but within walking distance ....[   ]

    3. Commute by car or public transportation ....[   ]   (3) _____

(continued)

Please list some things that you DISLIKE about the Pitt campus.

1. _____

2. _____

3. _____

4. _____

5. _____

6. _____

7. _____

Following are some things you may DISLIKE about the Pitt campus. Please rank them from 1, meaning dislike most, to 9, meaning dislike least. (Use each number only once.)

Not enough community activities _____   (4) _____

Not enough campus activities _____   (5) _____

Too far between classes _____   (6) _____

Parking problems _____   (7) _____

Concerns about personal safety _____   (8) _____

Difficulty in finding place to relax between classes _____   (9) _____

Inconvenient library hours _____   (10) _____

Not enough restaurant choices _____   (11) _____

Not enough recreational facilities _____   (12) _____

Please answer the following questions on the accompanying scales.

I feel safe walking on the campus at night.

Agree 1 ___ 2 ___ 3 ___ 4 ___ 5 ___ 6 ___ 7 ___ Disagree   (13) _____

I expect to be a victim of a crime on campus this term.

Agree 1 ___ 2 ___ 3 ___ 4 ___ 5 ___ 6 ___ 7 ___ Disagree   (14) _____

I am considering transferring to another school because of the likelihood of being a victim of crime.

Agree 1 ___ 2 ___ 3 ___ 4 ___ 5 ___ 6 ___ 7 ___ Disagree   (15) _____

I feel safe inside campus buildings.

Agree 1 ___ 2 ___ 3 ___ 4 ___ 5 ___ 6 ___ 7 ___ Disagree   (16) _____

My parents are concerned about my safety while I am at school.

Agree 1 ___ 2 ___ 3 ___ 4 ___ 5 ___ 6 ___ 7 ___ Disagree   (17) _____

I feel that my safety is threatened most by students, as opposed to persons from off campus.

Agree 1 ___ 2 ___ 3 ___ 4 ___ 5 ___ 6 ___ 7 ___ Disagree   (18) _____

Following are some possible ways of increasing campus security. Please rank them from 1, indicating most preferred, to 8, indicating least preferred. (Use each number only once.)

Involve local police in investigating campus crime _____   (19) _____

Increase patrols by campus police _____   (20) _____

(continued)

Provide an escort service_____   (21) _____

Reduce the number of entrances to buildings_____   (22) _____

Require identification for entering buildings after a certain hour_____   (23) _____

Lock all buildings after a certain hour _____   (24) _____

Have a curfew for female students _____   (25) _____

Have a curfew for male students _____   (26) _____

Which of these alternatives, if any, would be UNACCEPTABLE to you?
(Be specific.) _____

If you have a suggestion that is not listed above, please list it here.
(Be specific.) _____

Reading Between the Lines

9.1 Red Wine Reduces Heart Attacks

A study found that men who drink red wine with dinner have fewer heart attacks on average and concluded that the wine somehow reduces the risk of heart disease. The important factor could be the alcohol or the particular type of grapes or the combination of the two. Can you think of any other explanation for the reduction in heart disease associated with men who drink red wine with dinner?

Research Methods Laboratory Manual

William Langston (2010) has prepared a laboratory manual that contains many suggestions for research activities that work well with this book and require minimal materials. Many chapters in this book contain a section that refers the reader to appropriate sections of the Langston book. In Chapter 3, Langston discusses how to conduct a survey, as well as the implications of the Barnum Effect in obtaining data from surveys.

Web-Based Workshops on Research Methods and Statistics

Wadsworth Publishing Company maintains Web-based workshops on research methods and statistics. These workshops give a different slant on the material in this book.

www.cengage.com/psychologys/workshops

For this chapter, see The Research Methods Workshops: Nonexperimental Approaches to Research, Surveys, Sampling Methods, and Designing a Survey.

Exercises

9.1 Choosing Research Methods

For each of the following research problems, choose the method that would be most appropriate for studying it: (1) questionnaire, (2) naturalistic observation, (3) participant observation, (4) experiment. Use each method once.

a. Relation of eating, talking, and restlessness during a movie to age, sex, size, and composition of groups in a movie theater.

b. Effect of altering seating arrangements in a library on the amount of studying, socializing, and sleeping done by patrons.

c. How a psychologist uses a psychotherapy organization as a cover for her authoritarian political agenda.

d. The relationships among age, income, and other demographic factors and watching rented videos at home.

9.2 The Effect of Sample Size on Sampling Error

Before doing this exercise, you should read the section of Chapter 15 on sampling distributions. This exercise is based on the computer program given in the Instructor's Manual.

The program takes samples from one of two populations. Both populations have what are called *rectangular distributions*; that is, the distribution has the same height at all locations, so a graph of the distribution will be rectangular. The mean of the first distribution is 17, and the standard deviation is 9.7 (see Figure 9.2a). The second distribution has the same shape and the same standard deviation, but its mean is 22 (see Figure 9.2b).

The computer program will draw samples of various sizes from the distributions. These samples are actually being drawn randomly by the computer from the population. So the first point to notice is that the sampling distributions will not conform exactly to the shape predicted by the theory. They will differ from the theoretical shape because of chance factors.

At first you will be given a sample of size 1; that is, a single individual will be sampled from the distribution. The values will be built up into a sampling distribution. Notice that the first sampling distribution will look more or less rectangular. Any difference between your distribution and a perfectly rectangular distribution is purely the result of chance.

Next, you will see another sampling distribution from a rectangular population with a mean five points higher than the first. It will overlap the first one. Where the distributions overlap, the data points will be indicated by a plus sign. Notice that if you were given a score based on a single individual you would not be able to predict very well which distribution it came from.

The next two sampling distributions will be based on samples of size 4. (Figure 9.2c shows the theoretical shape of these distributions.) You will note two things about these distributions. First, they are beginning to look like normal (bell-shaped) distributions. Second, their standard errors are smaller. Because the sample size is four times as large, the standard error will be half as large. (As discussed in Chapter 7, the standard error is inversely proportional to the square root of N. The square root of 4 is 2, and the square root of 1 is 1.)

Successive pairs of distributions will have sample sizes four times as large as the previous pair and thus will have standard errors half as large. Notice that the overlap between the distributions becomes less and less as sample size increases (see Figures 9.2d and 9.2e). The important point to be derived from this demonstration is that if you know that you have sampled from one of two distributions that have different means but don't know which one, your ability to guess which distribution your sample comes from increases as sample size increases.

Required:

a. Define sample mean, sampling distribution, and standard error of the mean.

b. How does the standard error of the mean vary with sample size? (Describe in words and with an equation.)

c. What importance does the concept of sampling distribution have for doing experiments?

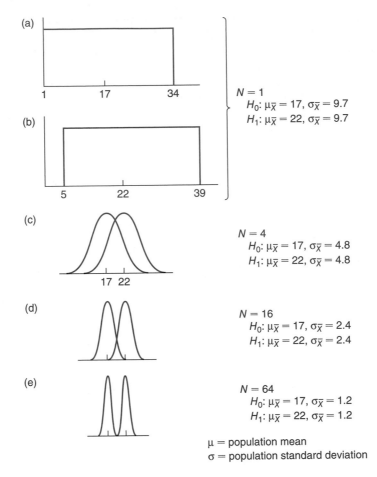

FIGURE **9.2** Effect of Sampling Size on Sampling Error

9.3 Randomized-Response Questionnaire

The following exercise illustrates the randomized-response method of obtaining information about behaviors for which social desirability is likely to influence the results.

This exercise should be done only with the supervision of your instructor. Administer the following questionnaire to two groups of students using the following control instructions and randomized-response instructions.

Control Instructions:

The purpose of this questionnaire is to determine the frequency of certain types of cheating. Please indicate which, if any, of the following you did during the last term. Your answers will be analyzed anonymously.

Randomized-Response Instructions:

The purpose of this questionnaire is to determine the frequency of certain types of cheating. Please indicate which, if any, of the following you did during the last term. The procedure we are asking you to follow will make it absolutely impossible for anyone, including the person scoring the answers, to determine whether you actually cheated.

1. Take a coin from your pocket and cup it in your hands.
2. Shake the coin up and down for a while until you are sure that you cannot predict whether it is

heads or tails. Then peek at it so that no one else can see it. Remember whether it is heads or tails.

3. Read the next question.
4. If the answer is *true*, say *no*, regardless of whether the coin is heads or tails.
5. If the answer is *false* and the coin is *heads*, say *yes*. Otherwise, say *no*.
6. Go back to Step 2 and repeat the procedure until you have answered all of the questions.

If you have any questions, please ask the person administering the questionnaire.

Cheating Questionnaire:

Answer the following questions with respect to last term.

1. I used a crib sheet during an exam. (Y/N)
2. I looked at someone else's paper during an exam. (Y/N)
3. I received a copy of a test before it was given. (Y/N)
4. I turned in a paper that someone else had written. (Y/N)
5. I received help on a take-home exam. (Y/N)
6. I had someone else take an exam for me. (Y/N)
7. I turned in homework that someone else had done. (Y/N)

Coding the Answers

For the randomized-response method, the true probability of cheating can be calculated by means of the following equation:

$$P(T) = 1 - [2 \times P(Y)]$$

That is, the probability of cheating is 1 minus two times the probability of a yes response. For example, if there were 23 yes responses on the first question out of 54 students answering, then the true probability of cheating is

$$P(T) = 1 - [2 \times 23/54]$$

or

$$P(T) = 1 - (2 \times .43) = 1 - .86 = .14$$

The principal drawbacks to this method are that the instructions are more difficult to understand and flipping a coin introduces

randomness, making the answers less statistically reliable.

Question:

Which is more important in this case, maximizing statistical reliability or reducing the effect of social desirability?

9.4 Random Sampling

Required:

a. Using the procedures outlined in this chapter, draw a random sample of size 10 from the population data set in Appendix B. List the identification numbers for each subject in the order obtained.
b. Using the corresponding data in Column A for each subject selected, calculate the sample mean and standard deviation.

Optional:

c. Compare the sample mean and standard deviation with the population mean and standard deviation (listed in the Instructor's Manual). What do you conclude?

9.5 Stratified Random Sampling

Required:

a. Using the procedures outlined in this chapter, draw a stratified random sample of size 20 from the population data set in Appendix B. Include 12 females and eight males in your sample. List the identification numbers for each subject in the order obtained.
b. Using the corresponding data in Column F for each subject selected, calculate the sample mean and standard deviation.

Optional:

c. Compare the sample mean and standard deviation with the population mean and standard deviation (listed in the Instructor's Manual). What do you conclude?

9.6 Proportional Allocation in Stratified Sampling

The population of undergraduate college students in a small state college is divided into four strata: 1,156 freshmen, 918 sophomores, 748 juniors, and 578 seniors. A sample size of 100 is to be selected using stratified random sampling with proportional allocation.

Required:

Distribute the sample among the four classes, or strata, using proportional allocation.

9.7 Sample Size and Sample Error (Manual Version)

Required:

a. Draw ten random samples of size 1 from the population data set in Appendix B. For each subject selected, list the corresponding data from Column G.
b. Draw ten random samples of size 4 from the population. For each subject selected, list the corresponding data from Column G.
c. Calculate the mean for each sample selected in Steps a and b.
d. Group the ten sample means from Steps a and b into side-by-side histograms. Which sampling distribution has less variability? Why?
e. The mean and standard deviation of the population are listed in the Instructor's Manual. What are the theoretical means and standard deviations for each of your sampling distributions? How do they compare with the actual data?

9.8 Bias in Questionnaires

The following is a questionnaire item from a Democratic Party mailing:

Republicans have proposed a new budget plan that would provide large tax cuts for the rich, large increases in defense spending, and cuts in social programs and entitlements.

Republicans claim that their plan will reduce the deficit. What is your opinion?

☐ The Republican plan would raise the national debt.
☐ The Republican plan would lower the national debt.
☐ The Republican plan would make no difference.

Required:

a. Identify sources of bias in the wording of the question.
b. Reword the question as if you were a Republican sending out similar campaign material.
c. Reword the question so that it does not favor the Republicans or the Democrats.

True Experiments, Part 1: Single-Factor Designs

PREVIEW

Chapter 10 begins the discussion of true experiments, in which the researcher has complete control over the research situation. First, we consider single-factor experiments—those that manipulate one independent variable. Then, we consider some designs to be avoided because they lack adequate controls.

As we saw in Chapter 7, a key concept in designing experiments is that of control. The experimenter seeks to control as many of the potential threats to validity as possible. When a sufficient number of these are under control, the study is a true experiment. A true experiment is one in which the experimenter has reason to believe that he or she has control over both the assignment of subjects to conditions and the presentation of conditions to subjects. When a study does not meet the requirements of a true experiment, it is called a *quasi experiment*. We discuss quasi experiments in Chapter 13. We begin this chapter by defining true experiments. Then, we define the basic elements of a valid experimental design, describe some representative experimental designs, and, finally, mention some designs that should be avoided.

True Experiments

true experiment:
research procedure in
which the scientist has
complete control over
all aspects

In a true experiment, the experimenter has complete control over the experiment: the who, what, when, where, and how. Control over the *who* of the experiment means that the experimenter can assign subjects to conditions randomly. Recall that random assignment is preferred because it allows one to conclude that any other variable could be confounded with the independent variable only by chance. No other method of assignment of subjects to conditions permits such a conclusion. Control over the what, when, where, and how of the experiment means that the experimenter has complete control over the way the experiment is to be conducted. The conditions of a true experiment allow the researcher to infer causality, or to say that the changes in the dependent variable were caused by the independent variable. By contrast, a **quasi experiment** (see Chapter 13) is an experiment in which the investigator lacks the degree of control over the conditions that is possible in a true experiment. Because of this reduced level of control, inferring causality in a quasi-experimental design cannot be achieved with the same level of certainty as a true experiment.

quasi experiment:
research procedure
which does not meet the
requirements of a true
experiment

Factors, Levels, Conditions, and Treatments

Until this point, we have simply used the term *independent variable* to talk about what the experimenter manipulates in an experiment. Now we need to introduce some other terms that are often used in discussing independent variables.

factors: the independent
variables of an experiment

The independent variables of an experiment are often called the **factors** of the experiment. Suppose we are doing an experiment on the effect of human handling on the socialization of tiger cubs. Tiger cubs would be either handled or not handled by people as they were reared. We would say that handling was an independent variable, the factor of this experiment. An experiment always has at least one factor, or independent variable; otherwise, it wouldn't be an experiment. As we discuss more completely in Chapter 11, it is possible for an experiment to have more than one independent variable. To have an experiment, it is necessary to vary some independent variable, or some factor.

level: in an experiment,
a particular value of an
independent variable

The independent variable in our example has two levels. A **level** is a particular value of an independent variable. An independent variable always has at least two levels—if it didn't, it wouldn't be a variable. The two levels of handling in this example would be handling versus no handling. It is possible for an independent variable to have any number of levels, of course: The tigers could be handled for 0, 10, 20, 30, or any other number of minutes per day, giving that many different levels of the independent variable of handling. But for the example at hand, let's just stick to two levels, and focus on tigers that were either handled or not handled.

condition: a group or
treatment in an
experiment

The term **condition** is the broadest of the terms used to discuss independent variables. It refers to a particular way in which subjects are treated. In a between-subjects experiment, such as the present example on tiger handling, the experimental conditions are the same as the groups. Any one tiger in this example was either handled or not handled. In other words, each tiger experienced only one treatment or condition. In the present example, we might speak of a particular tiger as being in the non-handled condition or group. When it is possible for each subject in an experiment to experience every condition, then we speak only of various conditions, not groups, because there is only one group of subjects and that group experiences all conditions. There would be as many conditions as there are different ways in which subjects are treated. Thus, there could be many conditions in a complicated experiment.

treatment: another word for a condition of an experiment

Treatment is just another word for condition. You should be aware of this usage, however, as you may run across the term *treatment effect* in statistics. It is a statistical test of the effect of various conditions of the experiment.

The Basic Elements of a Valid Experimental Design

Chapter 6 discussed types of validity and the many threats to validity that exist, and Chapter 7 discussed methods of control that are available to improve the validity of an experiment. In this chapter, we begin to consider some specific experimental designs as examples of ways of achieving control over threats to validity. You should keep in mind a point made previously: Designing an experiment is an exercise in problem solving. When threats to validity are adequately controlled for, the experiment has been designed. At the same time, you should realize that no design can rule out all threats to validity for all time. For example, as we said in Chapter 6, societal changes since the "dirty word" study was conducted have reduced the external validity of that experiment.

Even though there can be no perfect experiment, two particular elements of design provide control over so many different threats to validity that they are basic to good experimental designs: (1) the existence of a control group or a control condition and (2) the random allocation of subjects to groups. (If the experiment is a within-subjects design, each subject experiences all conditions, so random allocation of subjects to conditions is not applicable. In such experiments, the subjects should experience the conditions either in random order or in counterbalanced order.) Both of these methods of control were discussed in Chapter 7.

These two basic elements of good experimental design are illustrated in Table 10.1, which represents a simple experiment with two conditions. Note that participants may be either randomly allocated to conditions or all subjects may experience both of the conditions. If this is taken to represent a between-subjects experiment, then different participants would be randomly allocated to the two conditions. This allocation ensures that the groups will be equal in all respects, except as they may differ by chance. If this is a within-subjects experiment, then all participants experience both conditions: A participant's behavior in one condition is compared with his or her behavior in another condition. Either way, we have reason to believe that the participants in both conditions were equal to begin with, and that enables us to compare their performance between experimental and control conditions.

TABLE **10.1**

Basic Elements of Good Experimental Design

© Cengage Learning

Condition	Allocation	Treatment	Test
1 (or experimental)	*Either* Random assignment of subjects to conditions *or* All subjects experience both conditions	Yes (or A₁)	Yes
2 (or control)		No (or A₂)	Yes

Any difference in behavior can be attributed to differences between the two conditions.

Within-Subjects Designs

Recall that Chapter 7 discussed, as a specific strategy of achieving control, using a subject as his or her own control. Recall also that this strategy is desirable when the effect of one condition will not carry over to, or contaminate, the other condition or conditions of the experiment to a serious degree. The recommended designs we discuss in the rest of this chapter use this strategy. Because the same subjects experience all conditions in within-subjects designs, it is often necessary to exercise some ingenuity in controlling for possible carryover effects.

Controlling for Order and Sequence Effects

In within-subjects experiments, because a subject experiences more than one experimental condition, the possibility exists that some variable may influence the data as a result of the repeated testing. The outcomes as a result of these variables are called carryover effects, and there are two types: Order and sequence effects. Some of these possible variables are related to the subjects; others are related to the conditions of testing. The participants may get fatigued during the session, or the first condition may be tested before lunch when participants are hungry, and the second after lunch when they are sleepy. Ordinarily, experimenters avoid within-subjects designs if they believe that carryover effects will be substantial. In that case, a between-subjects design is probably more appropriate.

order effects: changes in a subject's performance resulting from the position in which a condition appears in an experiment

sequence effects: changes in a subject's performance resulting from interactions among the conditions themselves

Before we discuss ways of controlling for these problems, let us note the distinction between order effects and sequence effects. Order effects are those that result from the (ordinal) position in which the condition appears in an experiment, regardless of the specific condition that is experienced. The best example of an order effect is the warm-up or practice effect that often occurs in experiments on learning. Whichever condition is presented first will show poorer performance than later conditions simply because the subjects had not warmed up to the task. Sequence effects, by contrast, depend on an interaction between the specific conditions of the experiment. For example, in an experiment on judging the heaviness of lifted weights, there is likely to be a contrast effect such that a light weight will feel even lighter if it follows a heavy one, and vice versa. Order effects are more general and result from warm-up, learning, fatigue, and the like. Sequence effects are the result of interactions among the conditions themselves.

The difference between order and sequence effects can be seen by referring to page 254, where the six possible ways of ordering three different conditions—A, B, and C—are presented. Note that Subjects 1 and 3 experience Condition C in the same ordinal position—namely, third—and so have the same order effect for C. Subjects 2 and 3, however, both experience Condition C following A, and so have the same sequence effect for C (with respect to A).

In general, one controls for order effects by arranging that each condition occur equally often in each ordinal position—first, second, third, and so on. This is known as counterbalancing. Sequence effects are generally controlled for by arranging that each condition follow every other condition equally often. Note that these controls are not the same. You should also note that the various methods of controlling for order and sequence effects are effective only under certain conditions, which we discuss shortly. However, if you are using a within-subjects design, you are wise to control as effectively as possible for order and sequence effects.

Two basic strategies are available for controlling order and sequence effects. The preferable one is to arrange the order of conditions in such a way that order and sequence effects are controlled within subjects. When this is not possible, you must control for order and sequence effects between subjects. (It should be noted that controlling for order and sequence effects between subjects does not result in a between-subjects experiment. As long as each subject experiences each condition, it is still a within-subjects experiment.)

Within-Subjects Control of Order and Sequence

Controlling for order and sequence effects within subjects is possible when each subject receives each condition. Randomization can be used when each condition is given several times to each subject or when a sufficient number of subjects will be tested such that one particular sequence is unlikely to have much influence on the outcome. Experiments in learning or perception typically involve presenting each stimulus many times to the subject. The best procedure is to randomize the order of conditions for each subject. Although you might prefer to be told a magic number of subjects or repetitions that are sufficient for randomizing to be effective, this determination remains a matter for your judgment.

A useful variation on randomizing to control for order and sequence effects is block randomization. Block randomization means that the order of conditions is randomized, with the restriction that each condition is presented once before any condition is repeated. If there are four conditions and each one is to be represented twice, block randomization might give you the following sequence: BCAD, ADCB. Here, each of the four conditions is presented once in random order within each of two blocks. Thus, there is less

counterbalancing:
controlling for order and sequence effects by arranging that subjects experience the various conditions in different orders

block randomization:
control procedure in which the order of conditions is randomized but with each condition being presented once before any condition is repeated

chance that unwanted sequence effects would be produced by orders of the following type: AABDBCCD. Block randomization is particularly useful if you want to present each condition at least twice and your experiment requires two or more sessions. So block randomization is most useful when conditions are presented several times to each subject.

When relatively few subjects will be tested and you have several conditions that can be presented only a few times, you must begin to exercise ingenuity. A typical example is the instance in which you have three conditions, each presented twice. In this situation, it is common to use reverse counterbalancing to control for order effects. The three conditions are presented in order the first time and then in reverse order. This technique is known as ABCCBA sequence, or ABBA for short. An example of this type of presentation technique can be found in the work of Irene Harris and Carlo Miniussi (2003), who wanted to look at which area of the brain contributed to the mental rotation of asymmetrical letters, like "F" or "P". Harris and Miniussi already knew that the parietal lobe was involved in mental rotation, but they decided to use repetitive transcranial magnetic stimulation (rTMS) to find out which hemisphere of the brain was most involved in this activity. TMS is a way of electrically stimulating the brain through the skull by inducing a rapidly changing magnetic field at the scalp that disrupts any pattern of brain activity that occurs during the stimulation. While each person in the study attempted to mentally rotate the letters, these researchers interfered with processing in one of three specific brain areas with rTMS: left parietal lobe, right parietal lobe, or a sham stimulation at the midline of the left and right hemispheres that served as a control. The order in which the rTMS was administered to the parietal lobe was left, right, control, control, right, left. Reverse counterbalancing was an important part of the design, in order to make certain that carryover effects, such as boredom or task familiarity, did not affect brain activation. Harris and Miniussi found that performance on the mental rotation task was only disrupted when the activity of the right parietal lobe was interrupted with the rTMS, which suggests that this part of the brain is crucial in rotating letters mentally.

Because some experiments have effects that may carry over from one condition to the next, such as task familiarity in the example above, it is important to take steps to control them. Reverse counterbalancing works well as a control technique when you suspect that the possible confounding variables will act in a linear manner over conditions. Figure 10.1 gives an example of ABCCBA order in which there is a linear effect. Conditions A, B, and C are presented in order (lower line) and then repeated in the order C, B, A (upper line). The dotted line represents the average effect of each condition. The order effect produces a large increase in the dependent variable that, because the effect is linear, averages out. The counterbalancing has done its job.

Then again, suppose a variable has a large effect in the early part of the experiment but a smaller effect later on. The best example is a warm-up, or practice, effect that may occur in the early part of an experiment and be less important later. Figure 10.2 shows an example in which there is a large practice effect. Here, you can easily see that counterbalancing has not been effective

reverse counterbalancing: method of control in which conditions are presented in order the first time and then in reverse order

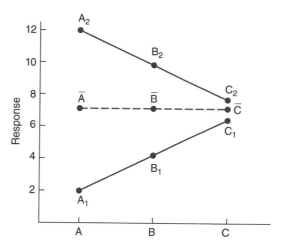

FIGURE **10.1** Using Reverse Counterbalancing to Control for Order Effects (see text for details)
© Cengage Learning

in eliminating the order effect. One way of improving such an experiment is to provide enough practice beforehand that the practice effect is eliminated.

Note that reverse counterbalancing may do an incomplete job of controlling sequence effects in an ABCDDCBA experiment: The B condition follows A once and C once, but never follows D or itself.

Between Subjects Control of Order and Sequence

If presenting each condition enough times to randomize the order is not possible, or if counterbalancing within subjects does not seem appropriate, you must leave order and sequence confounded with conditions within subjects. Then you must control for order and sequence between (or across) subjects, essentially within the group. For example, suppose you have three conditions and each

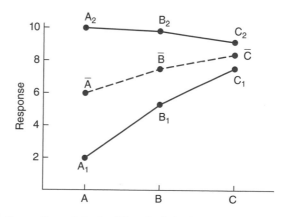

FIGURE **10.2** Reverse Counterbalancing When the Order Effects are not Linear
© Cengage Learning

one is to be presented only once to each subject. Then if you have six subjects, or 6N subjects, you can control for order and sequence in the following way:

SUBJECT	ORDER
1	ABC
2	ACB
3	BAC
4	BCA
5	CAB
6	CBA

Both order and sequence are completely counterbalanced within the group because each condition occurs an equal number of times in each rank-order position and follows every other condition an equal number of times. Thus, you have controlled for order and sequence within a group of subjects, even though every subject experiences a biased sequence. The disadvantage of this method of counterbalancing is that as the number of conditions increases, the number of orders required increases geometrically. You have two possible orders of two conditions (AB and BA), six orders of three conditions (as in the previous example), 24 orders of four conditions, and 120 orders of five conditions! Even for only four conditions, you would need 24 subjects to control for order and sequence using complete counterbalancing.

You can control for the order in which each condition occurs with fewer subjects than would be required by complete counterbalancing if you give up the requirement that each condition follow every other condition an equal number of times. You would be controlling for order, but not for sequence, of conditions. This type of incomplete counterbalancing is called the Latin square technique, after the ancient puzzle of finding ways to arrange a number of letters in a matrix such that each letter occurs once and only once in each row and column:

Latin square: control procedure in which each subject experiences each condition in a different order from other subjects

SUBJECT	RANK ORDER			
	1	2	3	4
1	A	B	C	D
2	B	C	D	A
3	C	D	A	B
4	D	A	B	C

If the letters represent conditions, the columns represent order, and the rows represent subjects, you are controlling for order effects with the Latin square counterbalancing technique.

A disadvantage of the Latin square technique is that sequence is not controlled. Notice in the previous example that B always follows A, C always follows B, and so forth. Thus, sequence is always perfectly confounded with order in this particular Latin square. If there were a carryover effect between conditions, this design would not control for it. However, you can control for sequence effects of the immediately preceding condition by using particular sets of Latin squares known as balanced squares. In the balanced Latin square, each condition is immediately preceded once by every other condition (W. A. Wagenaar, 1969), as in the following example:

SUBJECT	RANK ORDER			
	1	2	3	4
1	A	B	C	D
2	B	D	A	C
3	C	A	D	B
4	D	C	B	A

When you can assume that the carryover effects are primarily between pairs of conditions, the balanced Latin square will be effective.

The advantage of the Latin square technique over complete counterbalancing is that it permits greater flexibility in choosing the number of subjects to be tested. Instead of needing 24 or 48 subjects in a four condition experiment, for example, you can use only four or eight. This advantage is great enough to outweigh the disadvantage of leaving small sequence effects uncontrolled.

We turn now to some representative within-subjects designs that offer typical solutions to the problems of validity and control discussed in Chapters 6 and 7. The designs presented here do not constitute all that are possible because an indefinite number of designs exists. These designs are simply the most common solutions to common experimental problems.

Two Conditions, Tested Within Subjects

two-conditions design: the simplest research design, involving only two conditions

The two-conditions design is the simplest possible true-experiment design because it has only two conditions and each subject serves as its own control. This design is illustrated in Table 10.2. The two conditions are labeled Condition 1 and Condition 2, although one of them may be considered the experimental condition and the other the control condition. All subjects experience both conditions in counterbalanced order. Despite its simplicity, this design is not used as often as one might expect, for two reasons. First, many experiments involve more than two conditions. Second, there is the possibility of carryover effects from one condition to the other.

TABLE **10.2**

Two-Conditions Design, Tested Within Subjects

© Cengage Learning

Condition	Allocation	Treatment	Test
1 (or experimental)	All subjects experience both conditions in counterbalanced order	1	Yes
2 (or control)		2	Yes

An experiment that serves as an example of this design is one by Leila Reddy, Naotsugu Tsuchiya, and Thomas Serre (2010) on the phenomenon of mental imagery. Research has shown that it is possible to decode what a person is looking at, just by examining the pattern of brain activation (e.g. Kay et al., 2008). Reddy and her colleagues wanted to know whether objects that were imagined could also be decoded, and whether imagined objects were processed in the brain in the same way as objects that were truly perceived. In other words, would it be possible to tell what people were thinking by looking at the pattern of their brain activity? To answer this question, they had their participants undergo a series of functional magnetic resonance imaging (fMRI) scans. In fMRI, changes in blood flow related to the level and area of brain activity can be measured in a person while they are taking part in a study. The participants in this study were scanned while they were either viewing pictures of four object categories (food, tools, faces, or buildings) or imagining an object from the same object categories (see Figure 10.3). Each type of task, viewing pictures or imagining, was presented twice. The resulting four conditions were presented in a counterbalanced fashion: "pictures", "imagine", "imagine", "picture".

The researchers found that the human ventral temporal cortex was active in both the picture and the imagine tasks, but primary visual cortex was only active in the real picture condition. They also found that they could discriminate between the categories of objects in both tasks and that the pattern of activation in temporal cortex for each category was similar in the picture and imagine tasks. So it is likely that some of the same brain areas involved in the visual perception of an object are involved in the mental imagery of that object, while others are not. These results also show that it is now possible to look into the mind's eye and decode the information there.

Thus, from a design point of view, having scans while people were both viewing pictures and imagining allowed each person to be used as his or her own control. By using each person as their own control, the experimenters were able to say that the ventral temporal cortex reacted to both real and imagined images, and that the pattern of activity created by that reaction was similar.

Multiple Conditions, Tested Within Subjects

multiple-conditions design: research design that involves more than two conditions

Psychology experiments generally employ more than two conditions. The first reason researchers choose a **multiple-conditions** design is that seldom do they want to ask a simple *yes* or *no* question. Usually they want to compare several variables or treatments for effectiveness. For example, the question may be which of three different types of psychotherapy is most effective.

A second reason for conducting multiple-conditions experiments is to determine the shape of the function that relates the independent and dependent variables. When experimenters want to know how the sensation of brightness increases with the physical intensity of a light, they present each of several intensities of the light to a group of subjects. From the responses to the various intensities, researchers can plot the relation between intensity and brightness. Each intensity level is a condition of the experiment.

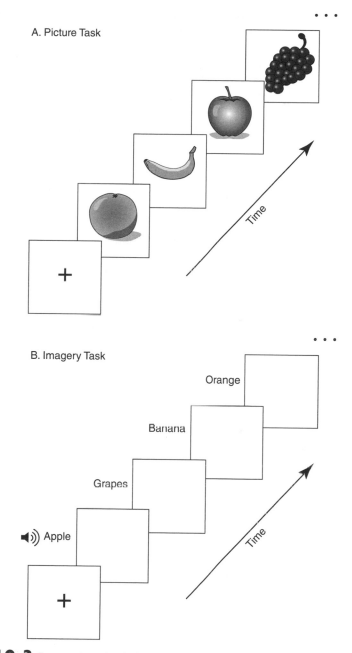

FIGURE **10.3** Two experimental tasks in the example for the ABBA design. A). In the picture task condition (P), people viewed different exemplars of 4 categories of objects (tools, food, faces and buildings). B). In the imagery task condition (I), people were given auditory instructions with the names of the stimuli and asked to imagine images corresponding to these names. Each task was given twice, in an ABBA order

A third reason for doing multiple-conditions experiments is the presence of more than one rival hypothesis that must be ruled out. Suppose a child has a favorite toy that is fuzzy, colorful, and noisy. If you want to find out which of the three characteristics is responsible for the child's attachment to the toy, you could make up three versions of the same toy, as follows:

A: FUZZY, not colorful, not noisy
B: not fuzzy, COLORFUL, not noisy
C: not fuzzy, not colorful, NOISY

Toy A tests for fuzziness, B for colorfulness, and C for noisiness, as the independent variable causing attachment. Because Toys A and B are not noisy, they control for noisiness. Similarly, A and C control for colorfulness, and B and C control for fuzziness. To accommodate the three hypotheses, you would need three conditions (toys). Each toy serves as a partial control (condition) for the other hypotheses. In this example, we have varied three conditions in a single factor (toy) in one experiment. Notice that this experiment does not test for the possibility that two or more of the attributes are necessary for the child to like the toy. We will discuss experiments that could address this problem in Chapter 11.

Many multiple-conditions experiments are between-subjects experiments because it is often impossible or inappropriate to expose all subjects to the various conditions. Within-subjects experiments are also fairly common, however.

One such experiment is a classic study by Fergus Craik and Endel Tulving (1975), which examined whether different strategies of processing words would affect memory. They flashed words on a screen. Before each word appeared, they asked the participant a question: "Is the word in capital letters?" or "Does the word rhyme with 'train'?" or "Does the word fit in this sentence: 'The girl put the _____ on the table'?" Each of these questions was designed to induce the subjects to adopt a different strategy of processing the word. The first strategy focused on the visual properties of the word, the second on the acoustic properties, and the third on the semantic properties. Craik and Tulving theorized that each successive type of strategy would induce greater depth of processing. Their theory predicted that increasing depth of processing increases memory for words.

Each subject in their study experienced all three types of questions, making this a within-subjects design. The experimenters believed that subjects could adopt different strategies of processing on different trials. The various questions were the independent variables in the study. The questions were randomly varied for each trial. After the words were all presented, the experimenters unexpectedly gave the participants a list that contained all of the words the experimenters had presented, along with an equal number of words they had not presented. They asked the participants to indicate which words they recognized from the list. The percentage of words recognized varied as a function of the depth of processing induced by the questions. The participants recognized only 18% of the visually processed words, but they recognized 78% of the acoustically processed and 96% of the semantically processed words.

TABLE **10.3**

Multiple-Conditions Design, Tested Within Subjects

© Cengage Learning

Condition	Allocation	Treatment	Test
1	All subjects experience *all* conditions	1	Yes
2	in either random or	2	Yes
3	counterbalanced order	3	Yes

Table 10.3 shows schematically the general design of a multiple-conditions, within-subjects experiment.

Between-Subjects Designs

As indicated previously, subjects cannot be used as their own controls in many situations because of the possibility of carryover effects. As with within subjects designs, between-subjects experiments may have two conditions, or more than two.

Two Conditions, Tested Between Subjects

The experiment by Reddy and colleagues (2010) described previously was a within-subjects experiment because each person served as their own control. This design may not be desirable when the possibility of large order or sequence effects is present. Such was the case in an experiment on the effect that an advertisement can have on memory conducted by Kathryn A. Braun, Rhiannon Ellis, and Elizabeth Loftus (2002). They hypothesized that the ads that use nostalgia to sell a product could possibly create a false memory and cause people to believe that they had actually experienced the events described in the ads. In their two-session experiment, Braun and colleagues investigated whether people could be persuaded that they had actually visited a Disney theme park and shaken hands with Mickey Mouse just by seeing a nostalgic ad. In the first session, people were asked to rate how sure they were that they had experienced each of 20 childhood events. People who were certain that they had met and shaken hands with a favorite character at a theme park were excluded from participating in the rest of the study, so the only remaining participants were either sure that they hadn't or unsure about whether or not they had ever shaken hands with Mickey. When the remaining participants returned for the second session, all of them saw advertisements and were asked to imagine experiencing the event depicted by the ad. Those in the experimental group, a random half of the participants, saw an ad for Disney theme parks. The Disney advertisement depicted a child meeting and shaking hands with Mickey Mouse during a visit to a Disney park. Those in the control condition saw a different ad. Otherwise, they were treated the same as the experimental participants were. The experimenter then pretended that there was a problem with the data collected in the first session and asked all of the participants to repeat the task, essentially rating the childhood events again. The people who saw the Disney ad became more confident that they had visited a theme park and shaken hands with a favorite character compared to the people who saw the other advertisement. Simply by seeing and thinking about the Disney ad, they experienced a bigger increase in confidence in their memory than did the other group.

You can see that this experiment had to be conducted as a between-subjects experiment. Once participants had experienced one of the conditions, they would no longer be naive about the situation. If they had been asked to serve again in the other condition, the cover story surrounding the reason for collecting the data in the experimental condition would not have had the same effect. They would have noticed the repetition of the task and would have begun to suspect the experiment's purpose. Only by having a separate group in each condition could Braun and her colleagues (2002) test the effect of the advertisement on the dependent variable, memory confidence.

Multiple Conditions, Tested Between Subjects

The design of a multiple-conditions, between-subjects experiment is illustrated in Table 10.4.

A good example of such an experiment is the following. Electroconvulsive shock (ECS) is the application of a brief electrical current to the scalp to cause a seizure. It is used in the treatment of severe depression, but one of its side effects is amnesia for events that precede the shock. John Pinel (1969) wanted to see if ECS could be used to estimate how long it takes for experiences to be laid down in memory. For five days in a row, Pinel allowed thirsty rats 10 minutes to explore a box that had a small cubbyhole in it. The purpose of this manipulation was to habituate the exploratory behavior that rats show on entering a novel environment. On Day 6, he put a bottle of water in the cubbyhole and allowed the rats to drink for a while after they found the water. Then, he took the rats out of the box and gave them ECS at varying intervals. The next day he put them back into the box, but this time there was no water bottle in the cubbyhole. If they remembered about the water, they would explore the cubbyhole looking for it. If they didn't remember the water, they would ignore the cubbyhole, providing they remembered exploring the box during the first five days.

Pinel used five different experimental groups of rats, one for each interval of time between the learning and the ECS: 10 seconds, 1 minute, 10 minutes, 1 hour, and 3 hours. (He also used three control groups that we will not con-

TABLE **10.4**

Multiple-Conditions Design, Tested Between Subjects

© Cengage Learning

Group	Allocation	Treatment	Test
1		1	Yes
2	Random allocation of subjects to groups	2	Yes
3		3	Yes

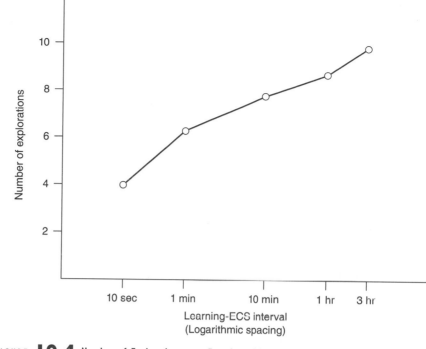

FIGURE **10.4** Number of Explorations as a Function of Learning-ECS Interval

(Adapted with permission from "A Short Gradient of ECS-produced Amnesia in a One-Trial Appetitive Learning Situation," by J. J. Pinel, Journal of Comparative and Physiological Psychology, 68, pp. 650–655. Copyright © 1969 American Psychological Association.)

sider here.) The results are shown in Figure 10.4. We can see that the 10-second group made the fewest explorations and the 3-hour group made the most. The number of explorations increased steadily up to a 3-hour delay, indicating that the memory consolidation process took as long as 3 hours to complete.

This experiment illustrates the use of a between-subjects design to study the effects of several levels of one independent variable (in this case, time between learning and ECS). Thus, Pinel determined the shape of the function relating time between learning and ECS and the amount learned as measured by number of explorations of the cubbyhole.

An interesting feature of the experiment is the way Pinel chose his various intervals between learning and ECS. The intervals were not spaced evenly, apparently because Pinel believed that the rate of memory consolidation might not be linear but, rather, faster in the earlier part of the three hours. Then again, he did not quite choose a logarithmic spacing. See the discussion of spacing of stimuli on page 134.

Some Designs to Avoid

In this chapter, we consider a number of examples of designs that are appropriate to the particular problem they address. However, we should also look

TABLE **10.5**
One-Group Posttest-Only Design
© Cengage Learning

	Treatment	Test
Single group	Yes	Yes

at some designs that should be avoided. These undesirable designs are weak because they do not control for various alternative explanations of the results. They all fail to control for certain threats to validity, discussed in Chapter 6.

The One-Group Posttest-Only Design

one-group posttest-only design: research design that measures the behavior of a single group of subjects after they are given a treatment.

The one-group posttest-only design is a simple one in which a group of subjects is given a treatment and then tested on some dependent variable (see Table 10.5).

Suppose you wanted to test the effectiveness of one of the popular motivational programs where people attend a retreat during which they engage in several group activities, some of which are humiliating and exhausting. To evaluate the effect of the training, you decide to survey the participants. You find that most of them say that the experience was worthwhile and that they feel better about themselves than they did before the training. After a little reflection, you realize that the results of your survey are nearly worthless. Although the people report that they feel better than they did before the training, you have no measures of how they felt before. Therefore, you cannot determine if they changed. Furthermore, even if they did change, you have no assurance that the training itself caused this change. Perhaps the interruption in their routine caused the change. Or perhaps they would have felt better if they had gone to the movies for several evenings and then gone camping for a weekend.

Such a one-group posttest-only design leaves so many threats to validity uncontrolled that it is nearly worthless. Nevertheless, you can certainly recall people who have recommended a product or practice to you on the basis of their own experience. Many people in everyday life, as well as some scientists, have used this design.

The Posttest-Only Design with Nonequivalent Control Groups

nonequivalent control group: a group of subjects that is not randomly selected from the same population as the experimental group

Suppose you wanted to improve the study of the effectiveness of a motivational retreat by comparing people who had gone on the retreat with a control group that had not. You might try to find a group of people who matched the retreat group on as many variables as possible: age, income, education, and so forth. Table 10.6 illustrates this design. Although the design is an improvement over the one-group posttest-only design, it still has a serious flaw: The control group is not equivalent in every way to those who took the training. The most important difference is that the test group members selected themselves for the training and the control group members did not. Thus, we have a **nonequivalent control group** because the two groups were not randomly constituted from the same population.

TABLE **10.6**

Posttest-Only Design, with Nonequivalent Control Groups

© Cengage Learning

Condition	Allocation	Treatment	Test
1 (or experimental)	Any method that is	Yes (or A$_1$)	Yes
2 (or control)	NOT random	No (or A$_2$)	Yes

A nonequivalent control group is better than no control group, but you would have to consider this study a quasi experiment at best because the subjects were not randomly assigned to groups. The only way you could construct a control group that was equivalent to the motivational retreat group would be to ask the organization that runs the retreat to provide a list of all people who applied for the retreat. Then, you would randomly place half of them into a control group that would not be allowed to attend the retreat.

The One-Group Pretest-Posttest Design

one-group pretest-posttest design: research design that measures the behavior of a single group of subjects both before and after treatment

Another way of improving on the one-group posttest-only design is to take a measure of behavior before the treatment that can be compared with behavior after the treatment. This approach is called the one-group pretest-posttest design. In the example of the motivational retreat study, you might obtain responses of the participants before they attended the retreat to compare with responses after the retreat. Such a design is illustrated in Table 10.7. If you were to use this design in the motivational retreat study, you would probably find a change in the subjects' reports of their moods, feelings of self-worth, and so forth. You would still have the problem of determining what caused the changes: the retreat or some unrelated event. Even if the retreat did cause the changes, you wouldn't know what aspect of it was responsible. You still wouldn't know if going on a camping trip might have been equally beneficial. The following example discusses these problems in the context of a different situation.

Suppose a company introduced a new work schedule whereby its employees put in four 10-hour days a week instead of five eight-hour days. If output increased, management would probably credit the new schedule. This conclusion represents an improvement over one that might have resulted from a one-group posttest-only design because, in this case, you know that a behavior change did follow the treatment. However, you have not considered other potential causes of the increase in output and hence other threats to validity. Workers may have responded to the attention paid them by management

TABLE **10.7**

One-Group Pretest-Posttest Design

© Cengage Learning

	Pretest	Treatment	Postest
Single Group	Yes	Yes	Yes

when the change was initiated. Or any number of events may have led to increased productivity: favorable weather conditions that allowed the workers to get to work on time, a change in seasons that made the plant more comfortable, or a favorable response to a new supervisor. These occurrences represent threats to internal validity: The change was caused by a variable other than the one management thought to be responsible. Threats to external validity could arise from the possibility that these workers are young and like long hours, whereas older workers might have preferred shorter days.

This study would have been better designed by forming two groups through random allocation of workers to different schedules so that one group would remain on the old schedule as a control group. This control would have eliminated the threats to internal validity. Random allocation of workers to two groups may not be possible, however. In that event, if the company had two plants, one could be switched to the four-day week while the other was kept on the five-day week. Productivity in the two plants could then be compared. This example is a nonequivalent-control-group design. Differences between the workers at the two plants or in the plants themselves may account for the results instead of the work schedule. The addition of a nonequivalent control group to a pretest-posttest design improves the control sufficiently that the design may be considered a quasi experiment. Chapter 13 will discuss a number of quasi-experimental designs.

Summary

1. In a true experiment, the experimenter has complete control over the experiment. A quasi experiment is one in which the experimenter lacks some degree of control. The most important difference is that in a true experiment, the subjects are assigned to conditions, whereas in a quasi experiment, the subjects are selected for conditions from previously existing groups.

2. The independent variables of an experiment are sometimes called factors, each of which has at least two levels.

3. In one-factor experiments, the levels of the variables are sometimes called treatments or conditions.

4. The two basic elements of good experimental design are the existence of a control group or a control condition and the random allocation of subjects to various conditions (for between-subjects experiments).

5. Order effects are those that result from the ordinal position in which the condition appears in an experiment, regardless of the specific condition that is experienced. Sequence effects are those that depend on an interaction between the specific conditions of the experiment.

6. Within-subjects control of order and sequence effects may be achieved by randomization, block randomization, or reverse counterbalancing.

7. When it is not possible to control for order and sequence effects within subjects, the Latin square technique may be used.

8. The simplest possible true experiment has two conditions tested within subjects. All subjects experience both conditions in counterbalanced order.

9. Multiple-conditions experiments are conducted when the hypothesis is not a simple *yes* or *no* question, when determining the shape of a function is desirable, or when multiple rival hypotheses must be ruled out.
10. Multiple-conditions, within-subjects experiments are common in perception research, as when one scales the brightness of different intensities of a light.
11. A between-subjects design is used when a significant interaction between conditions would occur if tested within subjects.
12. Some designs to avoid are the one-group posttest-only design, the posttest-only design with nonequivalent control groups, and the one-group pretest-posttest design.

Suggestions for Further Reading

For advice on true experiments, the best place to look is in journals or books on particular research areas. Analyze the methods of actual experiments to see how problems of validity were controlled in experimental situations.

A CASE IN POINT

Intensity of Tone and Reaction Time

Professor Stevens is designing an experiment to determine the effect of intensity of tone on reaction time. He believes that participants will respond more quickly to more intense tones. He wants to use five intensities of tone: 10, 30, 50, 70, and 90 dB.

He expects there will be a practice effect such that participants will get faster during the first 20 or so trials. (A trial is a presentation of a single tone.) He is able to present a trial every 10 seconds. Participants will be available for one hour, including the time taken in introducing them to the experiment, practicing, and debriefing. He estimates that he may be able to collect data for as long as 30 minutes. He has reason to believe that reaction time might differ between the left and right hand. It is likely that people are faster with their preferred hand. About 5% of people are left-handed, but left-handedness is more common in men than in women. He has no theoretical interest in differences between left and right hand, the effects of handedness, or gender differences.

Professor Stevens wonders whether to use a within-subjects or between-subjects design. The within-subjects design would require him to decide which order of presenting the stimuli to the subjects would be best. If he used a between-subjects design, he would not have that problem, but he would require more participants to complete the experiment.

If he uses a between-subjects design, each participant would experience only one intensity level. He thinks that he would need at least 20 different individuals at each intensity level to control for individual differences between subjects.

If he uses a within-subjects design, he could use reverse counterbalancing, a Latin square, random order, only increasing order, or only decreasing order. He realizes that each one has certain advantages and disadvantages.

If he randomizes the order or uses a Latin square, loud tones will follow soft ones, and vice versa, in an unpredictable manner. This might startle the participants, causing them to be possibly faster on the loud tones, or slower, depending on whether the startle reaction is compatible with pressing the key on the computer. Then again, presenting the tones in a predictable sequence might make the participants "tune out," or habituate to, the effects of intensity.

He believes that he needs 100 trials per stimulus in the total experiment to obtain reliable results.

Required: Decide

a. whether to do the experiment within or between subjects.

(continued)

b. what sort of order to use, if it is to be done between subjects.

c. whether to control for hand and handedness, and if so, how.

d. how many participants to use.

Justify each of your decisions. Summarize your decisions by showing the total number of stimulus presentations, how they are distributed across participants, and in what order. (It is not necessary to list the exact order for all trials and participants—just give the schema.)

Psychological Reactance

Brehm's theory of psychological reactance (1966) predicts that people will desire an object more when some barrier is introduced that prevents them from obtaining it. Suppose you want to test this theory with small children. Your specific hypothesis is that two-year-olds will choose to play more often with toys that are visible but more difficult to reach than with toys that are equally far away but unobstructed. You have available to you the following resources.

Participants

The names of one hundred two-year-olds are available from the files of the laboratory. Their mothers are willing to bring them in for an hour's observation. Half are boys. The expenses connected with observing the toddlers, including parking and paying the mothers, come to $20 per child.

Apparatus

You have an observation room with a one-way mirror, and you have a reception room. A collection of toys is available to use as choice objects. You know from earlier research that several of these toys are approximately equally preferred by two-year-olds. You have clear Plexiglas available that would be suitable for making barriers that the toddlers could see through but that would make it more difficult for them to reach the toys.

Personnel

Two female fellow students have volunteered to help you run the experiments. At the present time, they are unaware of Brehm's theory or your hypothesis.

Considerations

You are inclined to test the toddlers with a pair of toys, one in plain view behind a barrier that they could easily get around and one that is an equal distance away without a barrier.

If you give instructions to the child, the order in which you show the toys might influence their desirability because your holding one toy first might itself cause reactance by leading the child to think that you are trying to persuade him or her to take that one and not the other.

You have thought of three possible types of dependent variables. First, you could measure the amount of time spent playing with the toys. Second, you could measure which toy the child played with first. Third, you could measure how long they took to start playing with the toys.

Questions of design include whether to test both boys and girls, how many conditions to have, and whether to test each child on all conditions or to test different children on each condition.

Procedural questions include whether to have the mother in the room with the child and, if so, where she should sit and what she should be told. Should the child be put in a certain place to start? Should the experimenter go into the room with the mother or mother and child? What should the experimenter say to the child? Should the experimenter stay to observe the child or go outside? Who should record the data? Your budget for subjects is $1,000.

Required

Design the study. Include your hypothesis, method, and expected results. Justify your decisions, including why you rejected alternatives. Be sure to describe how you will analyze your data. Provide data sheets with mocked-up data. Make a table or graph of expected data.

Optional

What is the appropriate statistical analysis?

The experiment on which this case study is based is cited in the *Instructor's Manual.*

Reading Between the Lines

10.1 Subliminal Seduction

In his popular book *Subliminal Seduction* (1973), Wilson Bryan Key describes many ways by which, he claims, the advertising industry attempts, by subliminal advertising, to motivate people to purchase products. One example concerns an ad in *Playboy* for subscriptions to that magazine. The two-page spread shows a naked woman kneeling and holding a large Christmas wreath. Key says that of the approximately 100 men who had read the entire magazine, more than 95% remembered seeing the ad. He states further that "over 70 percent specifically remembered the wreath, but could provide only vague ideas about the blonde's description. Over 40% of those who recalled the ad were not even certain that she was a blonde" (p. 40). Key's explanation for why the men remembered the wreath better than they remembered the woman is that the wreath was made of nuts, which on close inspection of an enlargement are seen to resemble male and female genital parts. What alternative explanations can you think of for why the men would remember the wreath better than they remembered the woman?

Research Methods Laboratory Manual

William Langston (2010) has prepared a laboratory manual that contains many suggestions for research activities that work well with this book and require minimal materials. Many chapters in this book contain a section that refers the reader to appropriate sections of the Langston book.

In Chapters 7 and 8, Langston discusses two-group experiments and multiple-condition designs. Chapter 7 discusses experiments in which there is one independent variable and two groups. Chapter 8 talks about experiments in which there is one independent variable and more than two groups.

Web-Based Workshops on Research Methods and Statistics

Wadsworth Publishing Company maintains Web-based workshops on research methods and statistics. These workshops give a different slant on the material in this book.

www.cengage.com/psychology/workshops

For this chapter, see: True Experiments and Between Versus Within Designs.

Exercises

10.1 Two Independent Groups

An aspirin manufacturer claims that its brand of aspirin produces faster pain relief than the leading brand. To test this claim, a team of independent researchers identifies 20 people who suffer from chronic headaches. Participants are randomly divided into two groups of 10 each. One group receives Brand C aspirin, and the other group receives Brand E aspirin. Participants in each group are given one aspirin when they experience a headache, and the researcher records the amount of time it takes before each person experiences relief. The reported times are rounded to the nearest minute.

Required:

a. *Option A*: Use participants 21–40 from the population data set in Appendix B. Participants 21–30 use Brand C aspirin, and Participants 31–40 use Brand E aspirin. Data for participants using Brand C are in column C, and data for participants using Brand E are in column E. *Option B*: Using the procedures outlined in Chapter 9, draw a random sample of size 20 from the population data set in Appendix B. Randomly assign 10 subjects to the Brand C condition and 10 subjects to the Brand E condition. Data for subjects using Brand C are in column C, and data for subjects using Brand E are in column E.

b. Calculate the means of the two groups.

c. What tentative conclusions can you draw?

Optional:

d. Test the null hypothesis versus the alternative hypothesis at the .05 level of significance with the independent t test. Interpret the results.

10.2 Two Related Measures

A research methods professor has developed two equivalent forms of a test designed to measure students' conceptual knowledge of hypothesis testing. Both tests are intended to be equally difficult. On Monday, the professor administers both forms of the test to the population of undergraduate students enrolled in the introductory research methods class.

Required:

a. *Option A*: Use participants 11–20 from the population data set in Appendix B. Column A contains participants' scores on Form A of the test, and column B contains participants' scores on Form B of the test. *Option B*: Using the procedures outlined in Chapter 9, randomly select 10 participants from the population data set in Appendix B. Column A contains the scores on Form A of the test, and column B contains the scores on Form B of the test.

b. List the corresponding paired scores on Forms A and B of the test for each participant selected.

c. Calculate the group means of the two tests.

d. What would you tentatively conclude?

Optional:

e. Test the null hypothesis versus the alternative hypothesis at the .05 level of significance with a related t test. Interpret your results.

10.3 Multiple Conditions

A number of recent commercial airline crashes are tentatively attributed to errors made by air traffic controllers. The Federal Aviation Administration (FAA) believes that a relationship exists between fatigue and errors made by air traffic controllers. To study the effects of fatigue on the performance of air traffic controllers, FAA researchers randomly select 25 air traffic controllers from the union roster, all of whom agree to participate in the study. The researchers randomly assign participants to one of five groups of five individuals each. Participants in each group are given a simulated vigilance task to perform on a radar screen after a designated number of hours at work. Listed next are the number of hours each group worked before performing the simulated task.

Treatment Group	Number of Hours of Work	Corresponding Columns in Population Data Set
1	0	B
2	2	D
3	4	E
4	6	F
5	8	G

Required:

a. *Option A*: Use participants 40–64 from the population data set in Appendix B. Participants 40–44 comprise Group 1, participants 45–49 comprise Group 2, participants 50–54 comprise Group 3, participants 55–59 comprise Group 4, and participants 60–64 comprise

Group 5. Obtain each participant's score from the column corresponding to the treatment group as indicated previously.

Option B: Using the procedures outlined in Chapter 9, draw a random sample of 25 participants from the population data set in Appendix B. Randomly assign five participants to each of the five treatment groups, and obtain each participant's score from the column corresponding to the treatment group.

b. Calculate and graph the group means.
c. What tentative conclusions can you draw?

Optional:

d. Test the null hypothesis versus the alternative hypothesis

H1: not all the means are equal

at the .05 level of significance with a one-way analysis of variance. Present an analysis of variance (ANOVA) summary table, and interpret the results.

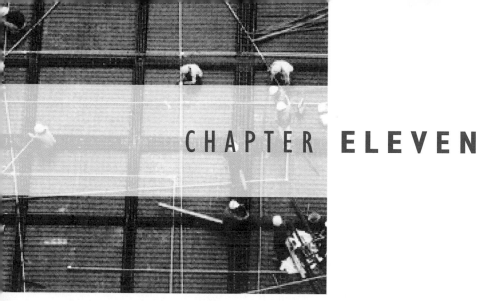

CHAPTER ELEVEN

True Experiments, Part 2: Factorial Designs

PREVIEW

Chapter 11 continues the discussion of true experiments with factorial designs—experiments that manipulate more than one variable at a time. A major reason to use factorial designs is to see how two or more independent variables interact with each other.

Until now we have primarily discussed experiments in which the researcher studied the effect of one independent variable. Often, however, you will want to examine the effect of two or more variables in a single experiment. One reason is efficiency: As long as you are designing an experiment, building another independent variable into the design may not require much additional effort. But we have already seen a second reason for having more than one variable in a single experiment: You might have more than one alternative hypothesis to rule out, as in the fuzzy, colorful, noisy toy example in Chapter 10. In order to achieve this, sometimes simply varying levels of a single factor is not enough, and multiple variables are necessary to answer the question.

Suppose, for example, that the child did not like the toy at all if it was only fuzzy. Instead, the child liked the toy only if it was both fuzzy and colorful, and was indifferent to a toy that was only fuzzy or only colorful. A simple three-condition experiment would not be able to reveal that preference because the only toy that was fuzzy would be neither colorful nor noisy, and no fuzzy, colorful, not-noisy toy would be presented. To solve this problem, we could design an experiment that included all possible combinations of these attributes and treated them as individual conditions to discover which combination the child preferred. Thus, the third reason for studying two or more variables in the same experiment is to reveal interactions among variables.

factorial design: research design that involves all combinations of at least two values of two or more independent variables

A factorial design is one in which two or more variables, or factors, are employed in such a way that all the possible combinations of selected values of each variable are used. In the simplest case, we have two variables, each of which has two values, or levels. This is known as a two-by-two (2×2) factorial design because of the two levels of each variable. The 2×2 design gives rise to four combinations, as shown on the front surface of Figure 11.1. (Table 11.1 also represents a 2×2 factorial design.) If there were two levels of one variable and three of another, we would have a 2×3 factorial experiment.

In the fuzzy, colorful, noisy toy example discussed in Chapter 10, there were three conditions, which was the minimum number necessary to find out which attribute was responsible for the child's attraction to the toy. If we

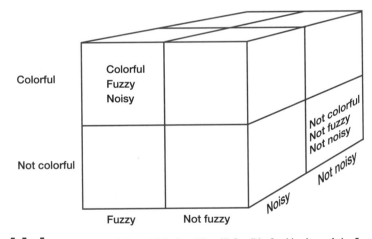

FIGURE ▌▌.▌ A $2 \times 2 \times 2$ Factorial Design Using All Possible Combinations of the Fuzzy, Colorful, Noisy Toy Example

© Cengage Learning

TABLE ▌▌.▌
A 2×2 Factorial Design

© Cengage Learning

Factor B	Factor A	
	A_1	A_2
B_1	A_1B_1	A_2B_1
B_2	A_1B_2	A_2B_2

were to consider all possible combinations of these variables, we would need to consider two levels of fuzziness times two levels of colorfulness times two levels of noisiness equals eight conditions. This $2 \times 2 \times 2$ factorial design is illustrated in Figure 11.1. Such a design would permit us to determine if some combination of variables, instead of one acting alone, is responsible for the child's attraction to the toy.

Of course, you can have as many factors and levels as you desire, but with increasing complexity you will require much more time to conduct the experiment. In addition, considering a large number of interactions taxes the mind, defeating the purpose of doing the experiment in the first place. Most experiments use two or three factors, with two to six levels on the various factors.

A Simple Factorial Design

Suppose you are interested in the physical characteristics of an accused criminal that influence verdicts of guilt made by a judge. You hypothesize that a smiling person may be judged as less guilty than a person who displays a neutral expression. You also hypothesize that physical attractiveness of the accused may influence the judge's opinion. (This example is adapted from an experiment by Forgas, 1987. Data have been modified slightly for illustrative purposes.)

Thus, you are interested in two independent variables: facial expression and attractiveness. Your dependent variable is judgment of guilt. You could do two separate experiments, one in which you varied his or her facial expression and another in which you varied the attractiveness of the person being judged. The first experiment could be diagrammed as in Table 11.2. This table shows that the independent variable facial expression has two levels: (1) neutral and (2) smiling. The second experiment could be diagrammed as in Table 11.3,

TABLE **11.2**

Design of an Experiment on Facial Expression

© Cengage Learning

Facial Expression (A)	
Neutral	Smiling
A_1	A_2

TABLE **11.3**

Design of an Experiment on Attractiveness

© Cengage Learning

Facial Expression (B)	
Unattractive	Attractive
B_1	B_2

TABLE **11.4**

Design of an Experiment on Attractiveness and Facial Expression

© Cengage Learning

Attractiveness (B)	Facial Expression (A)		Row Means (Effect of B)
	Neutral (A_1)	Smiling (A_2)	
Unattractive (B_1)	A_1B_1	A_2B_1	
	88	24	56
Attractive (B_2)	A_1B_2	A_2B_2	
	16	32	24
Column Means (Effect of A)	52	28	

where we see that the independent variable of attractiveness has two values, or two levels: (1) unattractive and (2) attractive.

Now, suppose you have the idea of studying the effects of the two different independent variables at the same time. You have two independent variables, each with two levels. This gives you four combinations of the various conditions, as shown in Table 11.4. The upper left cell combines the first level of the variable of facial expression (neutral) with the first level of the variable of attractiveness (unattractive). This is indicated by the notation A_1B_1, showing that you are combining the first level of Variable A with the first level of Variable B.

If you want to study the effects of the two variables of facial expression and attractiveness at once in a factorial design, you need to have one stimulus face that is attractive and smiling, one that is attractive and neutral, one that is unattractive and smiling, and one that is unattractive and neutral. Let us say that you had four different groups of participants, each of which judged the guiltiness of one face after reading a description of an alleged crime. Your results might be as shown in Table 11.4. The number in each cell indicates the mean judgment of the face in that condition.

You can see that the data in the two left cells are the judgments of Condition A_1: the two neutral faces. The data in the two cells on the right side are the judgments of Condition A_2: the two smiling faces. Therefore, we can average the data in the two left cells and find the average response to neutral faces to be 52, as shown in the left column. Similarly, averaging the data in the two right cells gives us the average response to the smiling faces: 28. Because 52 and 28 were obtained by averaging the columns of the table, they are called the *column means*. Looking at the column means shows us that neutral-stimulus faces were judged as more guilty than smiling faces were, so we conclude that smiling reduces judged guiltiness.

The effect of attractiveness of the faces can be seen by looking at the rows of the table. The two upper cells show the judgments of Condition B_1, the two unattractive faces. The two lower cells show the responses to Condition B_2, the two attractive faces. Averaging across the rows, we find that the average judged guiltiness of the unattractive faces was 56, but the average for the attractive faces was 24. Because 56 and 24 are obtained by averaging across the rows of the table, they are called *row means*. From the row means, we conclude that unattractive faces are judged as guiltier than attractive faces.

Main Effects

main effect: in a factorial experiment, the effect of one independent variable, averaged over all levels of another independent variable

At this point it is necessary to introduce the technical term main effect. Because we have two independent variables, we are able to examine two possible main effects. Because this term can be misleading, we will say first that *main effect* does not mean the principal effect of a variable. It means simply the effect of a variable averaged over all values of another variable (or variables). We have already talked about main effects, except that before we simply called them the effects of facial expression and attractiveness. In other words, we found the main effect of facial expression by averaging effect of facial expression over the two levels of attractiveness when we looked at the column means. Similarly, we found the main effect of attractiveness by averaging the effect of attractiveness over the two levels of facial expression when we looked at the row means.

Interactions

The conclusions based on the main effects of the two independent variables are actually very misleading, however, and are incorrect if we do not qualify them. Compare the top two cells of Table 11.4 with the bottom two. Smiling does reduce the judged guiltiness of the unattractive faces (from 88 to 24), but it increases the judged guiltiness of the attractive faces (from 16 to 32). So the conclusion that smiling reduces judgment of guiltiness is true only for the unattractive faces. The correct conclusion is that an unattractive face is judged less guilty if it is smiling, but an attractive face is judged less guilty if it has a neutral expression.

interaction: when the effect of one independent variable depends on the level of another independent variable

This outcome is an example of an interaction between two variables. Two variables interact if the effect of one variable depends on the level of the other. We have an interaction here because the effect of smiling depends on attractiveness. Whenever it is necessary to say something like the following, you are looking at an interaction: The effect of smiling on judged guiltiness depends on the attractiveness of the faces; specifically, smiling reduces the judged guiltiness of unattractive faces, but increases the judged guiltiness of attractive faces.

The concept of interaction is a difficult one for students to understand. So far, we have presented the data in a tabular format. Some people, however, find the idea easier to understand when it is presented graphically. Figure 11.2 shows the same data as Table 11.4. Judged guiltiness is plotted as a function of facial expression, with attractiveness as a parameter. The two solid lines show the effect of facial expression separately for attractive and unattractive faces. You can see that smiling decreases the judged guiltiness of unattractive faces but increases the judged guiltiness of attractive faces. This simply states the interaction, as we have already done. The dashed line shows the effect of

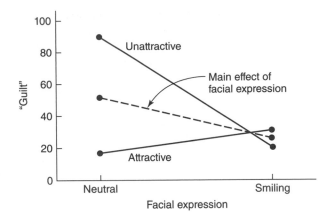

FIGURE **11.2** Judged Guiltiness as a Function of Facial Expression, with Attractiveness as a Parameter
© Cengage Learning

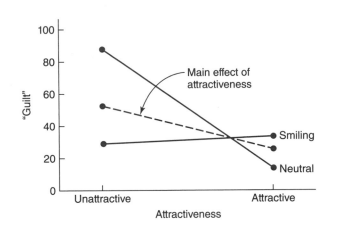

FIGURE **11.3** Judged Guiltiness as a Function of Attractiveness, With Facial Expression as a Parameter
© Cengage Learning

smiling on judged guiltiness averaged over levels of attractiveness. This simply restates the main effect of facial expression. The main effect of facial expression is that smiling reduces judged guiltiness.

Now refer back to Table 11.4. Notice that the table is completely symmetrical in its layout: The columns represent facial expression, and the rows represent attractiveness. We could just as easily represent attractiveness over the columns and facial expression over the rows; that is, we could simply rotate the table by 90 degrees. Similarly, in Figure 11.2, we could have plotted guiltiness as a function of attractiveness, with facial expression as the parameter, as shown in Figure 11.3. Here we see that the main effect of attractiveness is to reduce judged guiltiness.

If interactions are concerned, we prefer graphical presentation of data for a simple reason: If the graphical representation of a factorial experiment shows curves that are not parallel, there is an interaction between the variables.

The two curves in Figure 11.2 are not parallel; therefore, there is an interaction between facial expression and attractiveness. If you could slide one of the curves up or down so that it matched another, there would be no interaction because they would be parallel; if you cannot slide them up or down so that they match, then there is an interaction. This is true no matter how complicated the curve may be. Of course, small differences may be the result of chance, so statistical evaluation may be necessary.

In this example, we talked about the main effects before we discussed the interactions; we did this for pedagogical reasons. Whenever there is an interaction in the data, the main effects cannot be interpreted without discussing the interactions. Some authorities hold that main effects are meaningless when interactions are present, but this seems extreme; however, main effects can be misleading when interactions are present, as in this example.

Interactions and Main Effects

In our example, there was an interaction in the data and both independent variables showed main effects: Smiling and attractiveness both reduced judged guiltiness. It is entirely possible, however, to have an interaction if one or the other independent variable has no main effect, or even if neither independent variable has a main effect. So a possible outcome of the smiling and attractiveness experiment could have been that when smiling and attractiveness occur together, they affect a judge's decision, but otherwise, they do not influence it at all. Any of the independent variables may or may not have an effect, and an interaction between the variables may or may not be present. In other words, the example of smiling and attractiveness had at least eight possible outcomes, which you can see in Table 11.5.

TABLE **11.5**

Possible Outcomes of a 2 × 2 Factorial Experiment. A "+" indicates the presence of an effect; a "−" means that the effect is absent

© Cengage Learning

	Main Effect of Smiling	Main Effect of Attractiveness	Interaction Effect
Possible Outcome 1	−	−	−
Possible Outcome 2	+	−	−
Possible Outcome 3	−	+	−
Possible Outcome 4	−	−	+
Possible Outcome 5	+	+	−
Possible Outcome 6	+	−	+
Possible Outcome 7	−	+	+
Possible Outcome 8	+	+	+

So, with a 2×2 factorial experiment, you could obtain any of these eight patterns of results with your data. As you can imagine, as the number of independent variables in your experiment increases, the number of possible outcomes increase as well.

To further illustrate the point that main effects may be present without interactions and interactions may be present without main effects, we should consider an example: an experiment with two independent variables with two levels each. Suppose you are intrigued by the apparent contradiction between the following two proverbs: "Absence makes the heart grow fonder" and "Out of sight, out of mind." Certainly they appear contradictory, and they are often cited by psychologists as examples of the limitations of common sense. You decide to do an experiment in which you study the degree of attraction between members of couples who are either near to each other (operationally defined as living within one mile of each other) or separated by distance. You also suspect that whether the people are truly in love might make a difference in their mutual attraction. So you use the Partner Relationship Scale (Hoskins, 1988) and determine a cut-off score that will serve as your operational definition of whether they are truly in love or merely having a flirtation.

Although there are eight possible experimental outcomes, let us assume that after you run your experiment, you actually find the results shown in Table 11.6. From the column means, you see that distance has no main effect on measured attraction. The presence of a main effect of true love is shown by the row means in the table. Further examination of Table 11.6 reveals that there is an interaction between true love and distance: Attraction increases as a function of distance for members of couples who are truly in love, but it decreases for those who are only having a flirtation. With this set of results, it turns out that both proverbs are true, under particular circumstances. Absence makes the heart grow fonder for couples truly in love, but out of sight, out of mind is the case for those who are not. In other words, there is an interaction between the two variables.

Let us now look at the graphical representation of the same data in Figure 11.4a. Here we see again that distance increases attraction for the true-love condition, but decreases it for the not-true-love condition. The fact that the lines are not parallel indicates the presence of the interaction. Furthermore, the dashed line showing the data averaged over the variable

TABLE **11.6**

Relationship Between Attraction Within Couples and Distance

© Cengage Learning

	Distance		
True Love	Near	Far	Row Means (Effect of True Love)
Yes	8	12	10
No	6	2	4
Column Means (Effect of Distance)	7	7	

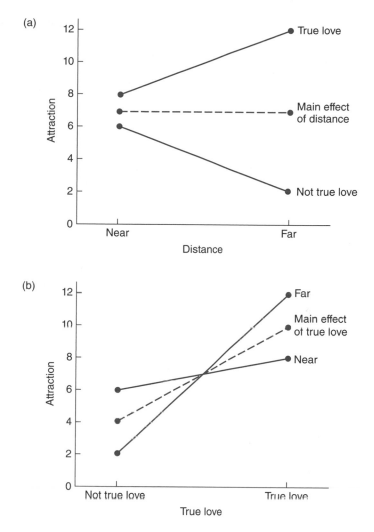

FIGURE **11.4** Outcome of Example Experiment. (a) Relationship Between Attraction Within Couples and Distance, with True Love as a Parameter. (b) Relationship Between Attraction and True Love, with Distance as a Parameter.

© Cengage Learning

of true love indicates that there is no main effect of distance. Now, let us re-plot attraction as a function of true love with distance as the parameter, as shown in Figure 11.4b. Here we see that true love increases the attraction between members of the couples, but the increase is greater for distant couples than for near couples. In other words, there is still an interaction. (There had better be, because all we did was rearrange the same data we had before.) The main effect of true love is seen by the dashed line in the graph. By comparing Figure 11.4a with Figure 11.4b, we can see that we have one variable (distance) that does not produce a main effect, and one (true love) that does produce a main effect.

Types of Interactions

In addition to a number of possible outcomes, experiments that show an interaction can vary in terms of the type of interaction that is found. There are at least three types of interactions: antagonistic, synergistic, and ceiling effect.

antagonistic interaction: interaction in which the two independent variables tend to reverse each other's effects

The type of interaction that is not accompanied by any main effects is called an **antagonistic interaction:** The two independent variables tend to reverse each other's effects. This situation is shown in Table 11.7. The row and column means indicate no main effect of either variable, A or B. Looking at the cells, however, shows that there is an interaction, as we can also see from Figure 11.5. In Figure 11.5a, we see that A increases the response for condition B_2, but decreases it for B_1. The fact that the lines are not parallel indicates the presence of an interaction. Furthermore, the dashed line showing the data averaged over the variable B indicates that there is no main effect of A. Now, if we re-plot the data from Table 11.7 with A as the parameter, as shown in Figure 11.5b, we see an almost identical graph. In other words, there is still an interaction. (Because all we did was rearrange the same data we had before!) We see that B increases the response for condition A_2, but decreases it for A_1. The dashed line tells us that there is no main effect of variable B.

TABLE **11.7**

Data Illustrating an Antagonistic Interaction

© Cengage Learning

B	A_1	A_2	Row Means (Effect of B)
		A	
B_1	10	2	6
B_2	2	10	6
	6	6	

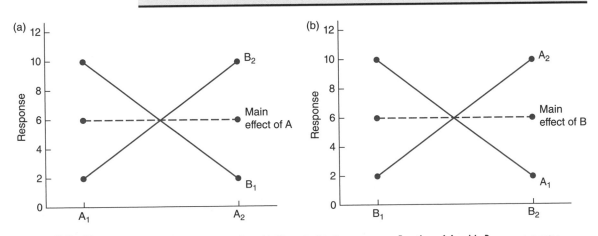

FIGURE **11.5** Graph of an Antagonistic Interaction. (a) Plotted with Response as a Function of A, with B as a parameter. (b) Plotted with Response as a Function of B, with A as a Parameter.

© Cengage Learning

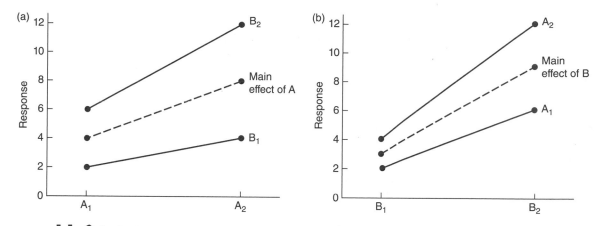

FIGURE **11.6** Graph of a Synergistic Interaction. (a) Plotted with Response as a Function of A, with B as a Parameter. (b) Plotted with Response as a Function of B, with A as a Parameter.

© Cengage Learning

synergistic interaction: interaction in which the two independent variables reinforce each other's effects

The interaction shown in Figure 11.6 can be called a **synergistic interaction** because the higher level of B enhances the effect of A, and vice versa. This relationship is shown in Figure 11.6a, where the slope of the line relating the dependent variable to A is steeper when B is larger. Figure 11.6b shows the same data re-plotted with B as the independent variable, and A as the parameter. The same type of interaction is seen either way.

ceiling-effect interaction: interaction in which one variable has a smaller effect when paired with higher levels of a second variable

Figure 11.7 shows a **ceiling-effect interaction**: The higher level of B reduces the differential effect of A on the dependent variable. As you can see in Figure 11.7a, Variable A has a smaller effect when it is paired with the higher level of B. Likewise, in Figure 11.7b, which shows the same data re-plotted, Variable B has less effect when paired with the higher level of A.

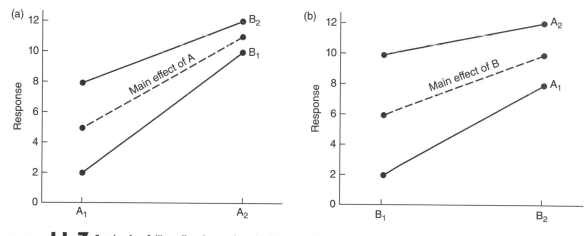

FIGURE **11.7** Graph of a Ceiling-effect Interaction. (a) Plotted with Response as a Function of A, with B as a Parameter. (b) Plotted with Response as a Function of B, with A as a Parameter.

© Cengage Learning

All of these types of interactions are common in psychological research. Others are possible, but these are the principal kinds.

Within-Subjects, Between-Subjects, and Mixed Designs

Factorial experiments may be conducted either within subjects or between subjects, although between-subjects factorial designs may be more common. In fact, sex of subject, a between-subjects variable, is one of the most common variables in factorial designs. Here, we give examples of both within-subjects and between-subjects experiments, as well as an example of a mixed design. A mixed factorial is one that has at least one within-subjects variable and at least one between-subjects variable.

Within-Subjects Factorial Experiments

Table 11.8 illustrates a factorial experiment in which Factors A and B are the two independent variables. Each independent variable has two values, or levels (e.g., A_1 and A_2). The two levels of the two variables give us four possible combinations of the independent variables (A_1B_1, A_1B_2, A_2B_1, A_2B_2). Thus, we have a 2×2 factorial design. The letters J, K, L, M stand for the four conditions of the experiment, with J standing for the combination A_1B_1, and so forth. If Table 11.8 is taken to represent a within-subjects

TABLE 11.8
A Within-Subjects Factorial Design

© Cengage Learning

TABLE **11.9**

Possible Sequence of Conditions Experienced by Eight Subjects in the Factorial Experiment Illustrated in Table 11.8

© Cengage Learning

Subject	1	2	3	4
S_1	J	K	L	M
S_2	K	M	J	L
S_3	L	J	M	K
S_4	M	L	K	J
S_5	K	J	L	M
S_6	M	L	J	K
S_7	J	M	K	L
S_8	L	K	M	J

experiment, then each subject experiences each condition in some particular order.

Table 11.9 shows the same information, indicating that the same group of subjects—eight in this case—experiences all conditions and shows one way that eight subjects could experience the four conditions in counterbalanced order. Subjects S_1–S_4 together constitute a balanced Latin square, because each condition occurs once in each ordinal position and follows every other condition once (see Chapter 10). Subjects S_5–S_8 constitute another balanced Latin square. This example is only one way of showing how eight subjects could experience the four conditions. In this illustration, the experimenter winds up with eight responses to each of four conditions using eight subjects.

An experiment by Joseph Stevens and Lee Rubin (1970) provides an elegant example of a within-subjects factorial design. Stevens and Rubin studied the size-weight illusion, a well-known effect in which large objects feel lighter than small objects when both have the same weight. You may have noticed that a large empty suitcase feels lighter than a full handbag even though both weigh the same. Table 11.10 provides a schematic of the essential features of

TABLE **11.10**

Simplified Design of the Stevens and Rubin Experiment

© Cengage Learning

Weight	Size (Volume)		
	Small	Medium	Large
Heavy	X	X	X
Medium	X	X	X
Large	X	X	X

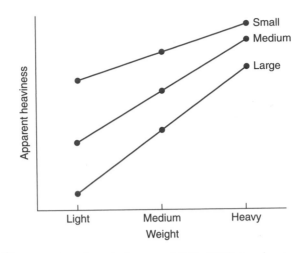

FIGURE **11.8** Idealized Data from the Stevens and Rubin (1970) Experiment

the experiment. Participants were asked to lift containers that varied in both volume and weight.

Figure 11.8 shows idealized data from the experiment. Apparent heaviness is plotted against physical weight, with volume as a parameter. You can see that containers having the same weight seem lighter the larger they are, thus showing the illusion. Because the curves are not parallel, you conclude that there is an interaction between volume and heaviness in the size: weight illusion.

Control in Within-Subjects Factorial Experiments

Controlling for order and sequence effects over all of the independent variables can require considerable ingenuity in within-subjects factorial experiments. A 3 × 3 × 3 factorial, for example, has nine conditions to consider, even if each one is presented to a subject only once. If there are multiple presentations of each condition, the situation can become very complex. Sometimes, things may be somewhat simplified in that one of the variables may permit, or even require, that all the conditions of one variable (B) be tested first under one condition of the second variable (A_1) and then tested under the other condition of the second variable (A_2).

Take, for example, an experiment on the effect of light adaptation on visual acuity. Suppose you wanted to measure the visibility of four targets (B_1, B_2, B_3, B_4) under both dark adaptation (A_1) and light adaptation (A_2). Varying the adaptation state between each pair of targets would be extremely time-consuming because 30 minutes is needed to achieve a state of complete dark adaptation. Table 11.11 shows a sample design for such an experiment. The four targets are abbreviated 1234 and so forth. The order of stimuli (conditions of Variable B) has been block randomized for every subject, and the state of adaptation (conditions of Variable A) is reversed for half of the subjects. Often this type of control for order and sequence is successful.

TABLE **11.11**
Design of Experiment on Light Adaptation and Visual Acuity
© Cengage Learning

Subjects	Dark Adapted	Light Adapted	Dark Adapted
S_{1-5}	2143, 4321	1342, 1243	
S_{6-10}		4123, 3214	3241, 1243

Factorial, Between-Subjects

Just as in single factor experiments, there are occasions when subjects cannot act as their own controls in factorial designs, and a between-subjects design is needed. A between-subjects factorial design is illustrated in Table 11.12. This example is also a 2 × 2 design. Separate groups containing eight subjects experience each condition, thus requiring 32 subjects to get eight responses to each of four conditions. Table 11.13 shows another way of representing the information from Table 11.12, so that you can easily see the groups, or which conditions each subject experiences.

An interesting example of a between-subjects factorial experiment is provided by Brian Wansink and Junyong Kim (2005). They studied the conditions that affected the amount of food that people ate by offering free popcorn at a movie theatre. Since most people would tell you that the reason that they eat food is because of the way that it tastes, the researchers varied the palatability of the popcorn by making some of it stale and some of it

TABLE **11.12**
A Between-Subjects Factorial Design
© Cengage Learning

		A_1	A_2
		S_1	S_{17}
		S_2	S_{18}
B_1		•	•
		•	•
		•	•
		S_8	S_{24}
		S_9	S_{25}
		S_{10}	S_{26}
B_2		•	•
		•	•
		•	•
		S_{16}	S_{32}

TABLE **11.13**
Between-Subjects Factorial Design (Table 11.12), in Summary Form
© Cengage Learning

Subjects	Group
S_{1-8}	A_1B_1
S_{9-16}	A_1B_2
S_{17-24}	A_2B_1
S_{25-32}	A_2B_2

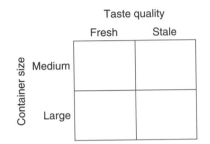

FIGURE **11.9** Design of the Wansink and Kim (2005) Study
© Cengage Learning

fresh. The researchers suspected that container size played a big role in the amount of food that people ate, so they varied the size of the container to be either medium or large. Thus, the researchers had a 2 × 2 design, with popcorn freshness and container size varied between subjects. Participants were randomly assigned to one of four groups: large stale popcorn, large fresh popcorn, medium stale popcorn, or medium fresh popcorn. At the end of the movie, the containers were weighed to see how much had been consumed by each group.

The design of the experiment is summarized in Figure 11.9. As you might expect, more of the fresh popcorn was eaten than the stale popcorn. However, container size also had an effect. People ate more popcorn when the container size was bigger, even if it was stale. An interaction also occurred between the two independent variables, such that people ate most when the food was both fresh and in a large container.

mixed factorial designs: designs containing at least one variable that is presented in a within-subjects fashion and one other variable that is presented in a between-subjects fashion

Mixed Factorial Designs

A factorial design offers an opportunity for design not available in single-factor experiments, namely combining within-subject variables and between-subject variables in a single experiment. A mixed factorial design is illustrated in Table 11.14. Variable A is the within-subjects variable, and Variable B is the between-subjects variable. Subjects either experience B_1, once with A_1 and also with A_2; or they experience B_2, once with A_1 and also with A_2. The way the 16 participants would experience the conditions is illustrated in Table 11.15.

TABLE **11.14**
A Mixed Factorial Design
© Cengage Learning

Between-Subjects Variable	Within-Subjects Variable	
	A_1	A_2
B_1	S_1	S_1
	S_2	S_2
	•	•
	•	•
	•	•
	S_8	S_8
B_2	S_9	S_9
	S_{10}	S_{10}
	•	•
	•	•
	•	•
	S_{16}	S_{16}

TABLE **11.15**
Mixed Factorial Design (Table 11.13), in Summary Form, Including Order
© Cengage Learning

Group	Subjects	Group
B_1	S_{1-8}	A_1B_1 then A_2B_1
	S_{9-16}	A_2B_1 then A_1B_1
B_2	S_{17-24}	A_1B_2 then A_2B_2
	S_{25-32}	A_2B_2 then A_1B_2

Suppose that the A variable is two types of smells, either peppermint or citrus, and the B variable is the cover story told to participants: Some are told that the smell of peppermint increases energy and health but that citrus does not, while others are told the same story in reverse: that citrus smells increase health but peppermint does not. The dependent variable is degree of liking. Individual participants would indicate their degree of liking for the two types of smell, A_1 and A_2. Individual participants, however, could experience only two conditions: Those with the peppermint health instruction (B_1) could rate their preference for smell A_1 (Condition A_1B_1), and they could rate their liking for smell A_2 (Condition A_2B_1). Those with the citrus health instruction would respond likewise (Conditions A_1B_2 and A_2B_2). An individual participant could not provide data in all four conditions.

This example shows a situation in which you would have to use a mixed design because doing otherwise would be physically impossible. Mixed designs are also used when using the same participants in all conditions is possible but not desirable. Suppose the A factor is two different mood induction techniques. The B factor might be two different questions asked during the experimental session. Because inducing a mood effectively takes time, the A factor would be studied better between subjects, but the B factor could easily be studied within subjects.

An interesting example of a mixed factorial design with one between-subjects variable and one within-subjects variable is given in the work of David Strayer, Frank Drews, and William Johnston (2003). Their research examined the effects of hands-free cell phone conversations on driving. Participants in this study were put into a driving simulator, and told to follow a pace car in front of them. Half of the participants found themselves driving in heavy stop-and-go traffic in the simulator, while the other half were in the same situation in lighter traffic. This formed the between-subjects variable. Strayer and his colleagues measured how quickly each participant was able to apply the brakes when the car in front of them stopped under two different conditions that formed the within-subjects variable: When they were involved in a cell phone conversation on an interesting topic and when they were not on the telephone. The results of this experiment showed a synergistic interaction. Even though people were using a hands-free cell phone, they were much slower to apply the brakes in a heavy traffic situation (see Figure 11.10).

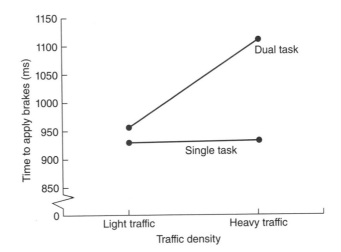

FIGURE **11.10** Relative Time to Apply Brakes in Light Traffic and Heavy Traffic While Talking on a Cell Phone (Dual Task) or Not (Single Task)

(Based on Data from Experiment 1 in "Cell Phone-Induced Failures of Visual Attention During Simulated Driving" by David L. Strayer, Frank A. Drews, and William A. Johnston, *Journal of Experimental Psychology: Applied*, 2003, 9, 23–32.)

Considering Number of Subjects When Selecting Factorial Designs

Comparing Tables 11.8, 11.12, and 11.14 shows one of the advantages of the within-subjects design. The within-subjects design requires only eight subjects to obtain eight responses in each of the four conditions. The mixed design requires 16 subjects to obtain the same number of responses. The between-subjects design is the least efficient, requiring 32 subjects. Whenever it is possible to present each condition to every subject, the within-subjects design should be considered, as long as order and sequence effects are not expected. This choice is especially applicable if recruiting enough subjects is a problem.

Summary

1. A factorial design uses all combinations of two or more independent variables, each having at least two levels.
2. Factorial designs are employed when one wants to study the joint effect of two or more independent variables.
3. A factorial design may save time by studying more than one condition per experiment, or it may be used when ruling out more than one rival hypothesis, or when one is interested in possible interaction between the independent variables.
4. In a factorial experiment, the main effect of one variable is the effect of that variable averaged over all the levels of the other variable(s).
5. An interaction exists between two independent variables when (independent) Variable A has a different effect on the dependent variable when it is combined with one level of (independent) Variable B than with another level of B. If the graph of a factorial experiment has nonparallel lines, there is an interaction between the variables.
6. If there is an interaction, the main effect is uninterpretable unless the nature of the interaction is taken into account.
7. Types of interactions include antagonistic, synergistic, and ceiling effect.
8. Factorial designs may be conducted as either within-subjects or between-subjects experiments, or they may be used in mixed experiments that have one within-subjects variable and one between-subjects variable.
9. The within-subjects variable of a factorial design is experienced at all levels by each subject. In contrast, each subject experiences only one level of a between-subjects variable.
10. Controlling for potential sequence and order effects is important when including a within-subjects variable in a factorial experiment.
11. The within-subjects factorial design requires the fewest subjects to achieve a particular degree of power, the mixed design the next fewest, and the between-subjects design the most.

Suggestions for Further Reading

For advice on true experiments, the best sources are journals or books on particular research areas. Analyze the methods of actual experiments to see how problems of validity were controlled for in experimental situations.

A CASE IN POINT

Within or Between?

You are interested in the role of mental images in memory. Your hypothesis is that children tend to use imagery more than adults do when they retrieve information from memory. In other words, you believe that to recall whether a tiger has spots, a child will first recall an image of a tiger, then look at the image and see that it has stripes instead of spots. An adult, however, might simply recall facts about tigers and know directly (without the use of images) that tigers have stripes.

You will use reaction time as the dependent variable. It is known that it takes longer to recall information from an image than to recall it directly.

Your first independent variable will be age. You have first-graders, fourth-graders, and adults available for your study.

Your second independent variable will be whether participants are instructed to use imagery in deciding whether an animal has a certain property. In the no-imagery condition, they will simply be asked to respond as quickly as possible whether, for example, a tiger has spots. They will be instructed to think about the properties of the whole animal, not just a part of it. In the imagery condition, they will be asked to form an image of the animal when they hear its name and then examine the image for the property in question.

Required

Design the study, and provide mock summary data in a table or graph. Decide which, if any, of the independent variables you would test between subjects and which, if any, you would test within subjects. Give the rationale for each of your choices.

Considerations

Your theory predicts that children will always tend to use imagery, whether you instruct them to or not. Adults, by contrast, will use imagery when instructed to do so but may or may not use imagery when they are not instructed to do so. Therefore, you predict an interaction between age and instruction: Children will always be slow (because they will use imagery), but adults will be slow when they use imagery and fast when they don't. (It will help to graph your expected results at this point.)

You expect adults to be faster at this task than children, even when they use imagery.

In thinking about whether to study the imagery-versus-nonimagery variable within subjects, you realize that it may be inadvisable to randomize the order of conditions, because once a participant has received imagery instructions it may be difficult for him or her not to use imagery. Thus, there may be a sequence effect of imagery on the nonimagery condition.

Then again, you are not so concerned with how much slower the participants will be in the imagery condition as with the interaction between age and imagery versus nonimagery. The prediction you are making is that adults will show a greater difference in reaction times between imagery and nonimagery conditions than children will.

There may be order effects between the first and second condition, regardless of which condition participants experience first because of either practice or fatigue.

The experiment on which this case study is based is cited in the *Instructor's Manual*.

Reading Between the Lines

11.1 Thirst in Brain-Damaged Rats

Normal rats respond to an intraperitoneal (into the body cavity) injection of salt solution with a marked increase in water drinking to restore their normal salt balance. Elliott Blass and Alan Epstein (1971) reported that rats with lesions of a part of the brain known as the lateral preoptic area did not drink in response to this stimulus. The result was not surprising given considerable other evidence that this brain area is involved in regulating drinking in response to salt levels. Christopher Coburn and Edward Stricker (1978), however, suspected that another interpretation of the data might be possible. They knew that these brain-damaged rats also respond abnormally to other ways of making rats drink that should not have anything to do with the supposed function of the lateral preoptic area. First, they repeated the experiment of Blass and Epstein and found the same results. Then Coburn and Stricker showed that the brain-damaged rats responded normally to several other ways of changing salt balance. Additional research has also indicated that various types of lesions may induce or reduce drinking behavior (Saad, Luiz, Camargo, Renzi, & Manani, 1996). What might be some plausible explanations for the difference between the brain-damaged rats and the normal rats in their response to the intraperitoneal injections and the other ways of inducing thirst?

Research Methods Laboratory Manual

William Langston (2010) has prepared a laboratory manual that contains many suggestions for research activities that work well with this book and require minimal materials. Many chapters in this book contain a section that refers the reader to appropriate sections of the Langston book. Chapters 9 and 10 of Langston's book discuss factorial designs.

Web-Based Workshops on Research Methods and Statistics

Wadsworth Publishing Company maintains Web-based workshops on research methods and statistics. These workshops give a different slant on the material in this book.

www.cengage.com/psychology/workshops

For this chapter, see the Research Methods Workshops: True Experiments and Between Versus Within Designs.

Exercises

11.1 Factorial Designs

Professor Hyde studies the effects that two or more drugs have on animal activity when the drugs are administered simultaneously. She designs a study that involves two factors. Factor A consists of two levels of Drug A (3 cc, 6 cc). Factor B consists of two levels of Drug B (2 cc, 4 cc). The experimental subjects are white rats, and the dependent variable is amount of activity, as measured by the number of times each rat revolves an exercise wheel (in hundreds of revolutions, rounded to the nearest 100). The results of the study are given in Table 11.16.

Required:

a. Calculate and graph the cell means.
b. Is there an interaction between Factors A and B? If so, explain the nature of the interaction.
c. Is there a main effect of Factor A? Explain.
d. Is there a main effect of Factor B? Explain.

TABLE **11.16**

Data from the Study of the Effects of Two Drugs on the Activity of White Rats

© Cengage Learning

	B_1	B_2
A_1	1	11
	6	16
	3	11
	3	12
	5	14
A_2	6	11
	8	10
	7	9
	8	7
	4	9

OPTIONAL:

e. Analyze these data with a two-way fixed-effects analysis of variance, using $\alpha = .05$ for all tests performed.

f. Present an ANOVA summary table. What do you conclude?

11.2 Read an Abstract

The following is from the abstract of an article (Kernis, Zuckerman, & McVay, 1988, p. 535): Subjects were led to attribute success on a two person maze test either to their own actions (internal locus) or to the actions of their partner (external locus). Subsequently they worked either on another maze or on a completely different task. Performance on these tasks served as the ... dependent measure. Level of self-awareness was manipulated by having half of the subjects work on the test task while facing a mirror.... Internal-success subjects performed better [than external-success subjects] when tested on the maze task, but worse when tested on a novel task. The self-awareness manipulation did not reliably affect performance.

Required:

a. Is this a true experiment or a quasi experiment?
b. Describe the design.

c. Was there a main effect of locus (internal vs. external)?
d. Was there a main effect of task (maze vs. novel)?
e. Was there a main effect of self-awareness (mirror vs. no mirror)?
f. Was there an interaction? What kind of interaction was it?

11.3 Read an Abstract

The following is from the abstract of an article (Mollenauer, Bryson, & Phillips, 1991, p. 217): After 5 weeks of voluntary wheel running ... mice [of a certain strain] were significantly resistant to the sleep-inducing effects of [alcohol]. Sixty-four mice, 32 males and 32 females, were assigned to wheel (free access to a running wheel in the home cage) or no wheel conditions. At the end of the training period, the animals were removed from the exercise cages and tested for sensitivity to [alcohol] ..., assessed by [the time it look them to fall asleep]. Exercised animals [took significantly longer before they fell asleep and had] shorter duration of sleep time [after falling down]. Exercise caused a significant decrease in body weight in male, but not in female, mice. The present results suggest that exercise training may be effective in reducing [alcohol]-induced sleep.

Required:

a. What was (were) the independent variable(s)?
b. What was (were) the dependent variable(s)?
c. What was the design of the study? (List each independent variable, and indicate the levels of each.)
d. Was this a true experiment or a quasi experiment, or partly both? Explain.
e. Was there a main effect of sex on time before the mice fell asleep?
f. Was there a main effect of running on time before the mice fell asleep?
g. Was there an interaction with regard to time to fall asleep? If there was, describe it.
h. Was there an interaction with regard to weight loss? If there was, describe it.

11.4 Read a Description of a Study

Ilene Bernstein (1978) wanted to test whether the conditioning of taste aversion to novel foods experienced just before a gastrointestinal illness, known as the Garcia effect, occurred in humans. Children who were receiving chemotherapy were randomly assigned to three groups. Mapletoff is an unusual flavor of ice cream that the children would not have experienced before. Group 1 received Mapletoff ice cream and then chemotherapy. Group 2 received chemotherapy only, and Group 3 received Mapletoff ice cream only. Later, all three groups were given a choice of eating Mapletoff ice cream or playing with a game. It was found that 21% of Group 1, 67% of Group 2, and 73% of Group 3 chose Mapletoff ice cream.

Required:

a. What was the hypothesis?
b. What type of study was this?
c. What was (were) the independent variable(s)?
d. What was (were) the dependent variable(s)?
e. What was (were) the control group(s)?
f. What did it (they) control for?
g. What was the design?
h. What were the results?
i. What statistic would be appropriate?

11.5 Read an Abstract

Reread the abstract in Exercise 5.2 and answer the following questions:

a. Was this a true experiment or quasi experiment?
b. What was (were) the independent variable(s), and levels (of each)?
c. What was the design?
d. Was it a between-subjects or within-subjects design?
e. What was (were) the dependent variable(s)?
f. Were there any main effects, and if so, what were they? (If none are mentioned explicitly, assume there were none.)
g. Was there an interaction? If so, describe it.
h. What statistic would be appropriate? (*t* test, ANOVA, chi square, or can't tell from the information given)?

CHAPTER TWELVE

Single-Subject Experiments

PREVIEW

Not all experiments use groups of subjects. This chapter discusses advantages and disadvantages of research using single subjects and basic strategies of control in this area.

So far, we have talked as if the only way to do research is to use groups of subjects. Although most psychological research does involve groups of subjects, this approach is not the only way to do research. This chapter deals with strategies for achieving control in experiments using single subjects.

Research using single participants is common and has a long tradition. In fact, scientists have used single participants in research for longer than they have used groups. Gustav Fechner, who some historians say is the founder of experimental psychology, worked extensively on individual participants—himself and his brother-in-law. Beginning in 1860, Fechner invented the basic psychophysical methods that are still used to measure sensory thresholds and discovered principles of psychophysics that are still taken seriously. Twenty-five years later, inspired by Fechner's work, Hermann Ebbinghaus did his experimental work on memory. Following Fechner's example, Ebbinghaus used himself as his own participant. Wilhelm Wundt, who is credited with founding the first psychological laboratory in 1879, conducted experiments measuring various psychological and behavioral responses in individual participants. Wundt's famous student, E. B. Titchener, espoused the use of introspection, which is the careful reporting of one's own experience. Because this procedure required a great deal of training, much of his work was done using one or a few individuals. Finally, I. P. Pavlov did his pioneering work on conditioning with individual dogs as subjects. The list of psychologists who relied on individual participants is long and includes most of those working before about 1930, when modern statistical methods were developed.

These early researchers used single subjects in the time-honored scientific tradition. In any case, modern statistical methods did not then exist. The solutions of these researchers to the problems of reliability and validity were extensive observations and frequent replication of results. A traditional assumption of researchers doing single-subject experiments has been that individual participants are essentially equivalent and that one should study additional participants only to make sure the original participant was not grossly abnormal.

The modern statistical methods that have become an integral part of present-day research grew out of a different tradition. A Belgian astronomer, Adolphe Quételet, discovered that human traits followed the normal curve. From this, he concluded that nature strove to produce the "average man" (Barlow & Hersen, 1984). The variability around the mean that is always found was considered to be a result of nature's failure to achieve the ideal average person in every case. The individual-differences tradition of Sir Francis Galton and Karl Pearson grew out of this thinking. According to the individual-differences tradition, variability between participants is inevitable. The task then becomes how to separate the effect of the experimental manipulation from this inherent variability. During the 1930s, statistician R. A. Fisher, a mathematician working on problems of genetics, invented many statistical methods such as the analysis of variance (ANOVA) that have become standard in psychological research. These techniques dominated psychological research to such an extent that the single-participant tradition almost disappeared for several decades.

Nevertheless, certain psychologists continued to work in the single-subject tradition during that period, notably B. F. Skinner. Skinner disdained the use of statistics, claiming that he would rather study one animal for 1,000 hours than study 1,000 animals for an hour each. Skinner's philosophy of research is described in the classic book by Murray Sidman (1988). Sidman makes the difference in attitude between the single-participant approach and the groups approach to research very clear. The single-participant tradition assumes that most variability in the participant's behavior is imposed by the situation and therefore can be removed by careful attention to experimental control. The individual-differences, group-research tradition assumes that much of the variability is intrinsic and should be statistically controlled and analyzed.

We cannot settle the debate between these two positions. Psychologists began using statistical methods to evaluate the results of experiments in which removing all sources of variability was not feasible. A set of data may look so regular that it is hard to believe that they could be the result of chance, especially when one has a large personal investment in getting a certain result. The use of statistics is one way to avoid being fooled into thinking that data are more reliable than they really are. Then again, using statistical methods does not guarantee that you will draw the right conclusion about the data; that is why we talk about type I and type II errors (see Chapter 15 for more detail). In addition, we should note that employing single-participant methods is not completely incompatible with statistical analysis inasmuch as statistical methods are being developed to handle data from individual participants (e.g., Kratochwill & Levin, 1992).

Advantages of the Single-Subject Approach

Although we acknowledge that the group-comparison approach has a rightful place in psychology, in this section we point out several advantages of the single-participant approach. We should keep these advantages in mind whenever we are designing research.

Focusing on Individual Performance

People or animals in a single-participant design act as their own controls, similar to a within-subjects design (Morgan & Morgan, 2001). This avoids the possibility that the average picture is a distortion of the behavior of the individual participants, which is a potential problem whenever data are averaged over many participants. Consider Figure 12.1. Suppose this represents a learning curve of a group of participants on some task. Because the curve is a smooth ogive (S-shaped curve), we might conclude from the group data that learning was a gradual, continuous process. However, look now at Figure 12.2. This graph shows the individual data for the five participants who make up the group in the previous graph. Here we get a different picture. Each participant learns suddenly, going from *no* to *yes* on a single trial. Participants learn on different trials, however. Participant 1 goes from *no* on Trial 6 to

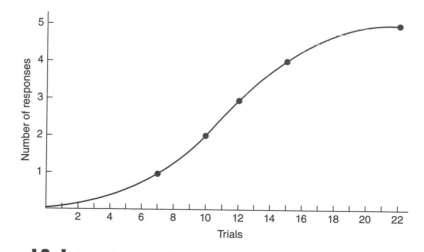

FIGURE **12.1** Hypothetical Learning Data for a Group of Participants

© Cengage Learning

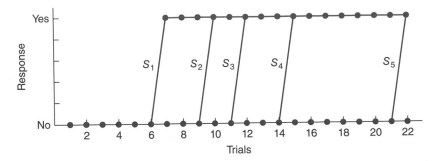

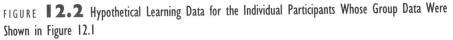

FIGURE **12.2** Hypothetical Learning Data for the Individual Participants Whose Group Data Were Shown in Figure 12.1

© Cengage Learning

complete mastery on Trial 7; Participant 2 goes from *no* on Trial 9 to complete mastery on Trial 10; and so forth. When the data of the whole group are averaged, though, the learning appears gradual. Although this example is extreme, it occurs fairly often in laboratory situations.

Focusing on Big Effects

An experiment that employs large groups of participants will be likely to discover that an independent variable has an effect even if the effect is a minor one. For example, given enough participants, it might be possible to show that a clinical treatment produced improvement in 55% of the participants, whereas 50% of the control participants improved spontaneously. A therapist is not likely to adopt a treatment that shows such a marginal difference in success rate. The experiment would have little clinical significance even if it had plenty of statistical significance (Barlow & Hersen, 1984).

clinical significance: the practical importance of a result

Some researchers in nonclinical situations feel this same reluctance. They would rather not spend time investigating the effects of variables that produce small effects but would rather find the powerful variables that produce large effects. In a single-participant experiment, the effect of a minor variable is less likely to be discovered so the experimenter will not be distracted by it. In addition, the researcher can spend time reducing variability so that the effect of a given variable will be maximized, instead of spending time testing more participants.

power: the probability that a statistical test will find a significant difference when a difference actually exists in the population

Statisticians use the term power to refer to the probability that a statistical test will find a significant difference when there actually is a difference in the population from which the data are drawn. The power of a test depends on the size of the difference that exists in the population and the size of the sample drawn from the population. Therefore, a researcher has two ways of increasing the probability of finding a significant result in an experiment: increasing the size of the effect or increasing the size of the sample (the number of participants or the number of observations per participant). In Chapter 7, we discussed how increasing the number of participants decreases the variability of the data. The other tactic, and the one favored by single-participant researchers, is to increase the size of the effect. (See Chapter 15 for a discussion of effect size in a statistical context.)

Suppose that you are interested in whether the students at Alma Mater College are smarter than those at Rival College. The larger the number of students sampled from each college, the greater the likelihood of finding a difference in intelligence between the groups. Eventually, if you include every student from both colleges, any difference you find is *statistically significant* because it is not based on a sample at all: You have measured the whole population. You are not performing an inferential statistic, but measuring the population value itself. This statement is true even if the difference between the students at the two colleges is barely measurable.

Suppose that two researchers work on the same problem, and each measures the correlation between the same two variables. Researcher A uses 10 participants and finds a correlation of 0.765. Researcher B uses 50 participants and finds a correlation of 0.361. Both researchers find that their correlations are significant at the 0.01 level. That is, there is one chance in 100 that the correlation either researcher obtained does not reflect a true correlation between the two variables in the populations studied. The question is: In which researcher's findings should you have greater trust? Should you put more confidence in Researcher B's results because more participants were used?

The answer is that you should feel more confident with Researcher A's results because the same level of significance was obtained with fewer participants. Remember that each had the same probability that the results were spurious: one in 100. To get the same level of significance with fewer participants, Researcher A had to obtain a larger effect. This fact is shown by A's having found a correlation that is larger than B's. The square of the correlation coefficient gives us the percentage of the variance in the data that is accounted for by the independent variable. Researcher A's correlation of 0.765 accounts for 58.5% of the variance, whereas Researcher B's correlation of 0.361 accounts for only 13% of the variance. Researcher A obtained a larger correlation, and the independent variable accounts for a greater percentage of the variance, even though fewer participants were used. Researcher A must have had better control over the sources of variability in the study.

Avoiding Ethical and Practical Problems

Whenever research involves testing the efficacy of a treatment that is expected to benefit the participant, an ethical question arises over placing some participants into a control group that will not receive treatment or that will receive inferior treatment. In clinical psychology, this area is particularly touchy when the client's situation can be life-threatening, as with suicide-prone persons. One solution is to treat all the participants and to evaluate them from a single-participant standpoint.

Another situation that calls for a single-participant experiment is when the researcher cannot locate enough participants to constitute a group to study. Perhaps the researcher is testing the efficacy of a clinical treatment. If there are not enough people suffering from the same condition, participants will have to be studied on a single-subject basis.

Flexibility in Design

An experiment on a group of subjects must be designed so that all subjects receive the same experience and can be compared. This necessity can result in a design that is not the best one for all subjects. During an experiment on behavior modification, an experimenter may discover that a subject does not respond to a reinforcer (or reward) that has worked on previous subjects. If the design is a single-subject one, the experiment can be modified on the spot by switching reinforcers or by altering the instructions.

Another problem that can be solved by a design modification is when a large change occurs in the participant's behavior that the experimenter suspects is caused by an outside event rather than by the experimental manipulation. The experimenter can immediately switch the conditions to see if the behavior changes correspondingly. A group experiment, however, would call for continuing all participants in the same procedure and hoping that the outside events would cancel each other out.

Disadvantages of the Single-Subject Approach

We should also mention some disadvantages of the single-subject approach. If there were none, after all, no multiple-subject experiments would ever be done!

First, some effects are small relative to the amount of variability in the situation. It may be impossible to control the other sources of variability sufficiently to observe the experimental effect in one subject. This is why modern statistical methods were developed in the first place. For example, the only way to decide if having been abused as children causes adults to be child abusers themselves is to compare large groups of individuals. It is no surprise that group experiments and statistical analysis are discussed together so often. Statistical procedures for analyzing single-subject data are not as well developed.

Second, some experimental effects are by definition between-subjects effects. It is impossible to have a participant who simultaneously receives two opposite sets of instructions in a social psychology experiment, or who is taught the same material by two different methods.

Basic Control Strategies in Single-Subject Research

Just as there are standard ways of controlling for rival hypotheses in group experiments, there are standard strategies in single-subject experiments as well. We discuss the most important of them. Others are discussed in the work of David Barlow, Matthew Nock, and Michel Hersen (2008).

Obtaining a Stable Baseline

When you are using a group design, you compare one group of subjects against another, or a group of subjects in one condition against the same subjects in another condition. The assumption that the groups were equal before the treatment is the basis of your attributing the effect to the manipulation rather than to something else. This assumption can be tested by statistically analyzing the differences between the groups. When you have only one subject, however, you must use a different strategy to compare outcomes between conditions. That strategy is to compare the behavior that occurs before and after the introduction of the experimental manipulation. The behavior before the manipulation must be measured over a long enough time span to obtain a stable baseline against which the later behavior can be measured. The baseline serves two purposes: It measures the current level of the behavior, and it predicts what the behavior would be in the future if no treatment were administered. Evaluation of a treatment's effect can occur only if a baseline measurement shows the behavior to be either remaining at the same level or changing in the direction that is opposite to the predicted treatment effect.

baseline: the measure of behavior before treatment that establishes a reference point for evaluating the effect of treatment

Suppose you want to measure the effectiveness of a treatment for anorexia nervosa, a disorder characterized by voluntary self-starvation. You would need to measure the patient's weight and food intake for a period of time before initiating the treatment so that you could show that the weight was stable and that the patient had not begun gaining weight spontaneously. How long this baseline measure should be continued is difficult to say. The judgment of stability is a subjective one. However, the experiment would be useless unless it was evident that the patient had not begun gaining weight before the treatment. A declining baseline may be acceptable because the treatment in this example is expected to cause an increase in the behavior. A decrease in weight in the absence of treatment is not unusual for a patient with anorexia nervosa, so a weight loss would constitute an acceptable baseline for comparison with a treatment. This example illustrates another consideration in obtaining baseline measures: Sometimes the existing condition is harmful to the subject, or even life-threatening, so the goal of a stable baseline may be overridden by other factors.

Comparison (AB Designs)

If you simply measure the baseline behavior (usually referred to as "A" in single-subject designs) and introduce a treatment (usually called "B"), it is called a **comparison design** or an AB design. Marteinne Steinar-Jonsson and Keren Fisher (1996) report a case of phantom pain that was treated effectively with an AB design. The 63-year-old woman in this study had lost her leg below the knee, yet was still experiencing pain sensations that seemed to come from the part of the leg that had been amputated (baseline). During a single session, the woman was taught a strategy for diverting her attention from the pain (treatment). After the treatment, the woman reported that the pain had substantially decreased. But can we be sure that the treatment really led to pain relief? No. The difficulty with an AB design is that you will not know whether other variables that may have coincidentally changed at the same time that the treatment was administered actually produced the change in behavior. In fact, you would have the single-participant equivalent of the quasi-experimental design called the *one-group pretest-posttest design*. (See Chapters 10 and 13.)

AB design: also called a comparison design; single-participant research design that consists of a baseline followed by a treatment

Withdrawal of Treatment (ABA Designs)

Although an AB design may be appropriate in some clinical situations, the argument that the treatment is the cause of the change is considerably strengthened if the treatment is withdrawn after a period of time and the behavior shows a return toward the baseline. This use of treatment withdrawal is often referred to as an **ABA design.**

ABA design: research design that includes a baseline period, a treatment period, and a subsequent withdrawal of treatment

Two principal problems are associated with an ABA design. First, the effect of the manipulation may not be fully reversible. If the treatment were a lesion of the brain that causes obesity, clearly it would be impossible to reverse. If a learning procedure causes a more or less permanent change in a participant's behavior, that, too, would not be reversible.

The second problem with the ABA design is that you may want to leave the participants in the new condition rather than return them to their original state. Treatments involving weight control, phobias, and compulsive behaviors are typical examples in which it would be unethical and undesirable to withhold treatment until the patient returned to the original state. In such cases, the experimenter may withdraw the treatment temporarily before the behavior change has reached the desired level. After the behavior shows some reversal of the trend toward improvement, he or she reinstates the treatment. In any case, experimenters in behavior modification seldom end an experiment with the baseline, or withdrawal, condition. Rather, they reintroduce the treatment to produce maximum benefit for the client.

Repeating Treatments (ABAB Designs)

In the examples just discussed, the treatment was repeated after the withdrawal phase to leave the participant with the full benefit of the training. This repetition of treatment also has the advantage of providing another opportunity to evaluate the effect of the treatment and its reliability. This kind of ABA design experiment in which treatment is repeated is called a **repeating treatments design,** an ABAB design or a **replication design.** Repeated presentation and withdrawal of a variable can produce strong evidence for the validity of the independent variable's effect. Anyone who watches a pigeon that has been trained in a Skinner box to respond in the presence of a light and not to respond in its absence is impressed by the control that the light exerts over the animal's behavior. The light appears to turn the behavior on and off as though by a switch.

ABAB design: also called a repeated treatments or replication design; an ABA design with treatment repeated after the withdrawal phase

An interesting example of an ABAB design is provided by the work of Matthew Wallenstein and Matthew Nock (2007). They wanted to treat Mrs. A, a 26-year-old woman who had a long history of self-injurious behavior, including hitting herself and banging her head, despite her ongoing counseling treatments. Wallenstein and Nock hypothesized that if self-injury was pleasurable to Mrs. A because it caused the release of endorphins in her brain, then giving her an appropriate alternative way of generating the endorphins, such as exercise, would decrease Mrs. A's tendency to hurt herself. Figure 12.3 shows the number of times that Mrs. A hurt herself over the entire experiment. Before she began the treatment, Mrs. A reported the number of times that she had hurt herself each week for a month in a baseline period. Then treatment began: Mrs. A was asked to exercise for at least 60 minutes three times per week, as well as any time that she felt the urge to injure herself. As you can see in Figure 12.3, the number of times that she hurt herself decreased dramatically. After five weeks, Mrs. A decided for herself to

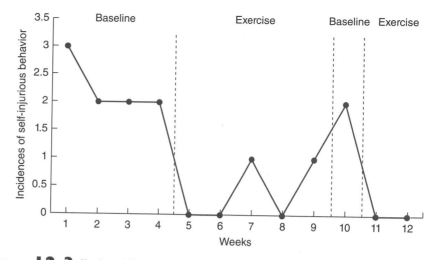

FIGURE **12.3** Number of Incidents of Self-Injurious Behavior per Week

(Based on "Physical exercise for the treatment of non-suicidal self-injury: Evidence from a single-case study" by M. B. Wallenstein and M. K. Nock, 2007. *American Journal of Psychiatry, 164,* 350–351.)

discontinue the exercise, instituting essentially a second baseline measurement period. During this time, her self-injurious behavior increased to the level of the first baseline. Following this reversal, treatment was continued, and Mrs. A did not harm herself for the remainder of the monitoring period. You can see that the number of times that Mrs. A hurt herself decreased steadily during treatment, increased during the reversal, and decreased again during the second treatment to such a low level that it was essentially eliminated. The reversal feature of the design strengthens the conclusion that the exercise had the effect of decreasing the self-injurious behavior.

Changing Only One Variable at a Time

An important rule of single-participant research is to vary only one thing at a time. If two variables are changed simultaneously, it is impossible to decide whether the change in behavior was caused by one or the other, or by the two together. On occasion, however, it may be important to evaluate the effects of two or more different treatments to assess which one would be the most effective. For example, Michael Mozzoni and Stephanie Hartnedy (2000) were interested in ways that therapeutic rehabilitation sessions could be more effective for people with brain injuries. Many of the therapeutic activities are frustrating or difficult, and brain injury patients often have difficulty in remaining on task. Mozzoni and Hartnedy wondered which of three different treatments would be most effective in helping patients stay on task: allowing the patient to earn short breaks, giving praise for cooperation, or displaying the progress of the rehabilitation. To meet the requirement that only one variable at a time be changed in a single-participant design, they alternated the treatments across sessions with a 15-year-old male patient in a speech therapy session; this

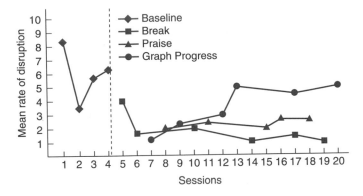

FIGURE **12.4** Alternating-treatments Design. Based on Results of Mozzoni and Hartnedy (2000) in a Behavioral Intervention with a 15-Year-Old Acquired Brain Injury Patient

© Cengage Learning

alternating treatments design: a type of single-participant design that allows the comparison of two different independent variables

method is called an alternating-treatments design. Behavior was observed during the first baseline phase; then the three treatments were administered. One of the three alternating treatments was chosen in each session. If a strict alternation had been followed, then the type of treatment would have been confounded with time of day or day of the week, so it was important that the treatments were randomly allocated. It is possible that attention might be lower in the afternoon than in the morning, for example. The patient was told which of the three treatments (or consequences) would be in effect for each session before it began. The results showed that allowing the patient to earn short breaks was the most effective of the three treatments (see Figure 12.4).

The first part of the alternating-treatments design answers the question of which is the more effective treatment. It does not, however, necessarily show that the behavior change was the result of that treatment, as the baseline might have been changing anyway. Evaluating whether the treatment caused the behavior changes would have required some sort of repetition within the design. One way would have been to remove all three of the treatments, then measuring baseline performance for a period of time. When the baseline was again stable, the more effective treatment could have been reintroduced. Essentially, this design is similar to an ABAB design, with the proviso that more than one type of treatment is administered during the first non-baseline condition. However, Mozzoni and Hartnedy did not want to withhold treatment from the patient, because they were afraid that the therapeutic gains might be reversed. Instead, they continued to implement the most effective treatment, earning short breaks from speech therapy somewhat like a changing-criterion design. So they gradually increased the amount of time that the patient would have to concentrate in order to earn a break from two minutes to 30 minutes.

Using Multiple Baselines

Another effective way to demonstrate that the manipulation caused the behavior change is to introduce the manipulation at different times for each of several different behaviors to see if the onset of behavior change coincides with the manipulation. For example, suppose a researcher is trying to determine if rewarding a mentally retarded child for doing certain personal tasks is effective. If the researcher begins rewarding tooth brushing, face washing, hand washing, and hair combing all at the same time, it is possible that the presence of the experimenter, the attention received, or a spontaneous decision to turn over a new leaf was responsible for the change. The researcher, however, could begin rewarding only tooth brushing the first week, tooth brushing and face washing the second week, and so forth until, after four weeks, all behaviors were being rewarded. This sequence would make it possible to see whether the increase in behavior coincided with the reward.

This design is known as a **multiple-baseline design**. Multiple-baseline designs are especially useful if the expected behavior change is irreversible, because you don't have to remove the treatment to demonstrate causality. Each untreated situation acts as a second baseline for the treatment conditions.

The separate experimental baselines in a multiple-baseline design may occur one of three different ways. In **multiple-baseline across behaviors**, different behaviors in the same individual in the same setting, as in the example on personal hygiene, are assessed. In **multiple-baseline across individuals**, the same behaviors in the same setting in different individuals is assessed. An example of this type of design would be a novel system to improve balance in six people with cerebral palsy (Shumway-Cook, Hutchinson, Kartin, Price, & Woollacott, 2003). The system would be introduced to each person, one at a time. If the new system caused improvement in balance, changes in the person's balance wouldn't be seen until the system was introduced. Notice that even though there are several subjects involved, each individual's performance is evaluated separately and acts as a control for the performance of the other children. A third possibility, called **multiple-baseline across settings**, is to test the same behavior in the same individual but in different behavior settings, as can be seen in the example that follows.

Nirbay Singh, Maryan Dawson, and Paul Gregory (1980) used a multiple-baseline across settings design with withdrawal of treatment to stop an 18-year-old female with profound mental retardation from hyperventilating (see Figure 12.5). This problem, in which a person breathes too deeply, can have serious medical consequences. Several treatments, including reprimand and medication, had been attempted on the participant without success.

Singh, Dawson, and Gregory decided to punish episodes of hyperventilation by briefly presenting ammonia (smelling salts) to the participant every time she hyperventilated. The design was a multiple-baseline design, with the withdrawal of treatment as a test probe.

Baseline recordings were made for five days in each of four different settings (classroom, dining room, bathroom, and dayroom). Experimental sessions lasted 2 hours per day (30 minutes in each of the four settings). During this time, all instances of hyperventilation were recorded but not punished. Then the baseline recordings were continued in three of the settings, and punishment was administered to any episodes of hyperventilation that occurred in the classroom. After five more days, punishment was instituted for episodes

multiple-baseline design: research design that introduces different experimental manipulations to see if changes coincide with manipulation. Three types of manipulation: behaviors, subjects, and settings

multiple-baseline across behaviors: design that measures the effects of implementing a treatment following baseline measurement to multiple behaviors in the same subject sequentially, so that each untreated behavior's baseline acts as a control for those that have been treated

multiple-baseline across subjects: design that measures the effects of implementing a treatment following baseline measurement to multiple subjects sequentially, so that each untreated subject's baseline acts as a control for those that have been treated

multiple-baseline across settings: design that measures the effects of implementing a treatment following baseline measurement of a subject's behavior in multiple settings sequentially, so that each untreated setting's baseline acts as a control for those that have been treated

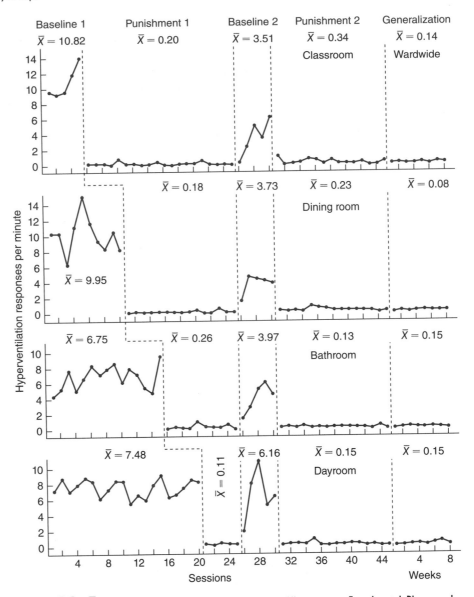

FIGURE **12.5** Number of Hyperventilation Responses per Minute across Experimental Phases and Settings

(From "Suppression of Chronic Hyperventilation Using Response-Contingent Aromatic Amonia" by N. N. Singh, M. J. Dawson, and P. R. Gregory. *Behavior Therapy*, *11*, 561–566. Copyright © 1980 by Elsevier. Reprinted with permission.)

occurring in the dining room as well as in the classroom, and baseline recording continued in the bathroom and dayroom. After five more days, punishment was extended to the bathroom, and after another five days, to the dayroom.

The data from this experiment are indicated in Figure 12.5. You can see that frequency of hyperventilation did not decrease in any of the baseline conditions. In each situation, when punishment was initiated, however, hyperventilation decreased dramatically. After punishment had been continued for five days in the last setting, punishment was withdrawn but the episodes of hyperventilation were still recorded. You can see that the participant began hyperventilating again in all situations but ceased abruptly when punishment was reinstated. After 15 more days of punishment for any instance of hyperventilation in the four settings, the procedure was generalized. Instead of having one experimenter administer punishment in the four settings during a two-hour session, all nurses in the ward were to administer punishment whenever they observed hyperventilation in any setting during an eight-hour day. This practice was instituted to consolidate and maintain the previous gains.

The study illustrates how to test the effectiveness of an experimental manipulation on a single participant in an unambiguous manner. Because the manipulation was instituted at four different times in four different settings, the researchers would otherwise have had to use four different alternative hypotheses to account for the decreases in hyperventilation that occurred. The increase in hyperventilation that occurred following the removal of punishment, and the abrupt decrease when punishment was reinstated, give further evidence of the effectiveness of the treatment.

Employing a Changing Criterion

Another way of showing that the manipulation caused the behavior change is to change the criterion for reward over time. After a baseline measurement, a reward can be given for meeting a lax criterion of the behavior. After the behavior stabilizes at that level, the criterion can be raised until the behavior stabilizes again, and so forth. If the behavior begins to change after each change in the criterion, then the conclusion that the reward is the cause of the improvement is rather convincing.

Suppose that a child is unable to sit still in class. The teacher may reward the child for sitting still for five minutes at a time until the performance becomes stable. Then the criterion may then be increased in steps, perhaps to 10 minutes, later to 15, and so forth. The behavior at each criterion becomes the baseline against which to evaluate the effect of the manipulation at the next criterion. It is important to note that if a participant cannot attain the next criterion, one must step back to a lower level of effective performance. A less substantial increase in criterion can then be implemented.

changing-criterion design: research design that introduces successively more stringent criteria for reinforcement to see if behavior change coincides with the changing criteria

Like the multiple-baseline design, a **changing-criterion design** is useful when the behavior change is irreversible or when a return to the initial baseline is not desirable, as in a case involving the reading skills of a man with schizophrenia named Craig (Skinner, Skinner, & Armstrong, 2000). Craig was able to read at the beginning of the experiment, but only read on average one page per day. In an effort to increase the amount of time that Craig spent reading, a program was developed that included the number of pages read per day as the dependent variable and the opportunity to earn a soft drink as the treatment. Craig had demonstrated during baseline that he could read one page per day, so this was set as the initial criterion level. After Craig achieved the criterion level three days in a row, the criteria would be raised by one page per day. At the end of the program, Craig was reading on average eight pages per day, a change in behavior that persisted for at least seven weeks after the program ended.

Two Examples from Psychophysics

All the examples that we have discussed so far reflect clinical applications of operant-conditioning principles. As we stated at the beginning of this chapter, however, the single-participant design has a rich tradition in other areas of psychology. We mentioned earlier that Gustav Fechner, the founder of psychophysics, used single subjects extensively. This practice is still common in psychophysical experiments, which tend to show less variability and larger effects than some other types of experiments. There are a wide variety of types of single subject designs. The following examples are elegant experiments that illustrate two ways in which single-subject evaluations are conducted in this area.

Visual Thresholds in Humans

Brian Wandell and E. N. Pugh, Jr. (1980) measured the threshold for detection of a flash of colored light seen against a background of a different color. They were interested in whether the color of the background made any difference in the threshold for the flash in their situation. Their theory predicted that it would not.

The threshold for detection of the flash was measured at each combination of several background colors and intensities. The flash was presented in one of two temporal intervals, and the subject was to guess in which interval it occurred. The intensity of the flash was varied from trial to trial depending on whether the subject had been correct or incorrect on the previous trial, thus giving a type of staircase method. A typical staircase sequence is shown in Figure 12.6. The intensity was increased after an error and decreased after two correct responses in a row. The staircase procedure continued until 12 reversals in the staircase had been made. The threshold was taken to be the average intensity of the combined reversals. This procedure was repeated for each combination of background intensity and color.

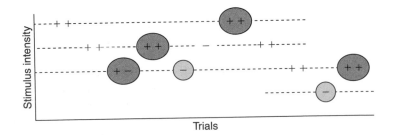

FIGURE **12.6** Typical Sequence of Responses Obtained When Measuring Thresholds by the Staircase Method

No report is made of the order in which combinations were tested. This omission, common in psychophysical research, stems from the fact that the likelihood of finding significant order or sequence effects in such a study is minimal. Wandell and Pugh used two subjects in their experiment, a paid participant and one of the experimenters. This practice of using an experimenter as a subject is also common in psychophysical research inasmuch as the methods used make it unlikely that knowledge of the hypothesis will influence the outcome.

The design is a factorial experiment in that all combinations of selected background intensities and colors were used. It differs from most factorial experiments because it used only two participants whose data were considered separately, thus making it a single-subject design.

The results of the experiment for one subject are shown in Figure 12.7. The x-axis shows the intensity of the background against which the flash was seen. The y-axis shows the threshold for seeing the flash. Each curve is for a different color of background. To allow us to see the effects of the background color more clearly, the curves for each color background have been displaced vertically by 0.5 unit on the y-axis. In other words, each curve has been moved up by a certain amount so that the data from different curves will not overlap. The bottom curve shows what the data look like when they are not separated in this way. The curves drawn through the data points were derived from the pooled data.

From the curves, the authors concluded that the color of the background did not affect the threshold for detecting the flash under their conditions. Note the impressive regularity of the data. The data points fit the line well with little variability. There is little doubt that Wandell and Pugh's conclusions are supported by the data from this participant. In addition, the data from the other participant were similar.

Visual Thresholds in Pigeons

Our previous example concerned vision, but the participants were humans who could be instructed to look at a light, tell when they saw it, and so forth. Imagine trying to get an animal to give you information about what it can see! Nevertheless, one of the classic single-subject studies was conducted by Donald Blough (1956) on the dark-adaptation curve of the pigeon.

Blough used a variation of the familiar operant-conditioning paradigm in which a pigeon pecks a key to obtain reinforcement. He arranged two keys that controlled the intensity of light in the operant chamber. Pecking on the first key drove the intensity of the light lower. Pecking on the second key drove the intensity up and also led to occasional reinforcement. Blough wanted the birds to peck the first key until they could no longer see the light, then switch to the second key until they could see it, then go back to the first key, and so on. In this way, the birds would drive the intensity of the light up and down across their visual threshold.

But how to get the pigeon to peck on the first key when pecking this key did not lead to reinforcement? Blough used the fact that animals will perform one task to have a chance to perform a second one that will lead to food. Being able to perform the second task becomes a reinforcer for performing

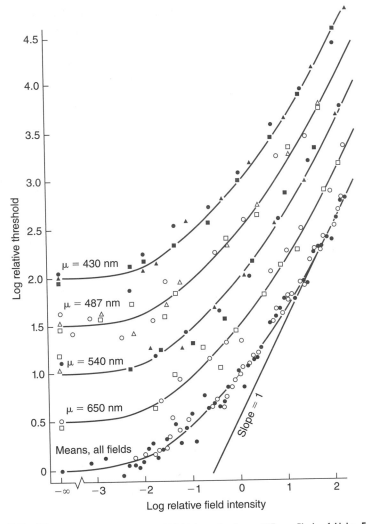

FIGURE **12.7** Threshold as a Function of Field Intensity for a 667-nm Flash of Light. Each Point Represents 50–70 Forced-Choice Trials for One Subject

(From "A Field-Additive Pathway Detects Brief-Duration Long-Wavelength Incremental Flashes" by B. A. Wandell and E. N. Pugh, Jr.. *Vision Research, 20,* 613–614. Copyright © 1980 by Elsevier. Reprinted with permission.)

the first one; it becomes a secondary reinforcer. So the birds will peck the first key to drive the light so low that they cannot see it, which signals them that they are then able to peck the second one for food.

The next question was how to keep the pigeons from simply pecking awhile at the first key and then switching to the second key even though they could still see the light. Blough's problem was that he wanted the pigeon to switch from pecking the first key and go to the key that drove up the light (and produced food) only when it could not see the light. But how could Blough know when the light was not visible to the pigeon? That was, after all, what he was trying to find out. He solved this problem in a most ingenious way: Every so often, pecking the first key would cause the light to go completely dark; only at such times was pecking on the second key reinforced. Therefore, Blough was sure that the pigeon would switch to the second key only when it could not see the light.

So most of the time the bird would peck away on the first key until the intensity of the light was below its threshold and switch to the second key when it could not see the light. On those occasions when the pigeon was pecking on the first key and the light actually went completely dark, the pigeon would switch to the second key and get reinforcement.

In this way, Blough trained the pigeons using a changing criterion design, and was able to track a pigeon's dark-adaptation threshold and determine how it was affected by various manipulations. Notice that in this example the main questions of design did not concern control groups, counterbalancing, and the like, but did concern ways of achieving control over the pigeon's behavior. This is consistent with the positions of Skinner and Sidman that we discussed earlier.

Summary

1. Experiments using single participants have been performed for as long as psychology has existed.
2. The single-participant tradition assumes that variability is imposed by the situation and therefore can be removed by careful attention to experimental control. The individual-differences, group-research tradition assumes that much of the variability is intrinsic and should be statistically analyzed.
3. Single-participant research has several advantages over group research: It focuses on individual performance that may be obscured by group research, and it focuses on big effects, avoiding ethical and practical problems in forming control groups and permitting greater flexibility in design.
4. Averaging the data from group experiments may obscure individual performance because the average data may not resemble the performance of any single individual.
5. Group experiments that find small but significant effects may have little clinical or practical significance.
6. The term *power* refers to the probability that a statistical test will find a significant difference when there actually is a difference in the population from which the sample is drawn. A researcher can increase the power of an experiment by increasing the sample size or by increasing the size of the effect. The single-participant tradition prefers to focus on increasing the size of the effect.
7. Basic control strategies in single-participant research include obtaining a stable baseline, using withdrawal of the treatment, repeating treatments,

changing only one variable at a time, using multiple baselines, and employing a changing criterion.

8. A comparison design is often called an AB design, and a design that includes withdrawal of the treatment is called the ABA design. Two major difficulties with the ABA design are that the treatment may be irreversible or that the experimenter wants to leave the participants in the new state rather than return them to the original condition.

9. When treatment is repeated, the experiment is called an ABAB design. The ABAB design removes one of the objections to the ABA design in that it leaves the participant in the trained state.

10. When a single-participant experiment has several variables, only one variable should be changed at a time.

11. The alternating-treatments design allows the evaluation of more than one treatment without violating the rule that only one variable is changed at a time. One treatment is given first, then the other, in an alternating fashion.

12. The multiple-baseline design is an effective way of demonstrating that the manipulation caused the behavior change. The manipulation is introduced at different times for different behaviors to see if the onset of behavior change coincides with the manipulation for each behavior.

13. Multiple-baseline designs can be used across participants, across settings, or across behaviors.

14. The changing-criterion design introduces successively more stringent criteria for reinforcement over time. It is useful when the behavior change is irreversible.

15. Psychophysical research often employs single-participant designs.

Suggestions for Further Reading

BARLOW, D., NOCK, M. & HERSEN, M. (2008). *Single case experimental designs* (3rd ed.). Boston, MA: Allyn & Bacon. The emphasis in this book is on clinical research.

JOHNSTON, J. M., & PENNYPACKER, H. S. (1993). *Strategies and tactics of human behavioral research* (2nd ed.). Hillsdale, NJ: Erlbaum.

SIDMAN, M. (1988). *Tactics of scientific research: Evaluating experimental data in psychology.* Boston: Authors Cooperative. Sidman discusses the step-by-step planning of experiments.

A CASE IN POINT

Reducing Dangerous Behaviors in Infants

Infants and toddlers frequently injure themselves around the home with electrical devices and outlets, hot stoves, and the like. You are interested in testing a program for teaching parents to reduce such injuries by means of a variety of behavioral techniques: childproofing the home by removing dangerous objects from the baby's reach, giving positive attention to the infant for safe behaviors, and giving time-outs for unsafe behavior. A time-out is defined in this case as saying *no* and placing the baby in a playpen with only soft toys to play with until he or she remains for 10 seconds without crying.

You have 16 mothers of infants 10–12 months of age available from the files of the laboratory.

(continued)

Sessions will take place in the infant's home. Some time will be needed with each mother to instruct her in how to childproof the home, how to pay positive attention to the baby, and how to administer a time-out.

Considerations

With 16 infants available, you have enough participants for a complete 2 × 2 × 2 factorial design, with 2 participants per condition. Because you need to travel to the homes, it would take a lot of time to study all 16 infants. Some mothers may already have childproofed their homes, and some

may already use positive attention or time-outs with their babies.

Required

Design the study. Decide whether a group-based design or a single-participant design should be used. Should you study the three conditions separately or as one combined condition? If you study the conditions separately, how will you control for random events that might influence the data? The study on which this case is based is cited in the instructor's manual.

Reading Between the Lines

12.1 Electrical Inhibition of Aggression in a Charging Bull

Jose Delgado (1969) received a great deal of publicity for a demonstration in which he entered an arena with a bull that had an electrode implanted in a part of the brain known as the caudate nucleus. The electrode was connected to a radio receiver attached to the bull's horn. When Delgado pressed a button, an electrical stimulus would be transmitted to the bull's brain. First, Delgado induced the bull to attack him. Then, while the bull was charging him, Delgado pressed the button, which caused the bull to turn sharply to one side and stop. Delgado claimed that he had stopped the charge by inhibiting the part of the brain that was involved with aggression. What other reason could account for the bull's sudden change of heart about goring Delgado?

12.2 Clever Hans

In the early 1900s in Germany, a horse with amazing intellectual abilities caused a sensation. Although horses are not usually known for their intelligence, Mr. von Osten's horse, Hans, was able to add, subtract, multiply, and divide. Hans could tell all the factors of a number and could even add fractions. He could tell the day of the week on which a certain date would fall. In addition, he had perfect pitch and could identify chords played on a musical instrument. If the notes played did not constitute a pleasing chord, he would indicate which notes should be removed. He could read German but not Latin or French. In short, Hans was able to do many things that a college graduate might well have trouble doing.

Hans answered questions by tapping with his hoof to indicate number and by moving his head for yes, no, and various directions. He demonstrated his ability to read either by choosing one card that contained the desired word out of several or by tapping to indicate the rows and columns of a specially prepared table of the alphabet. When asked a question, Hans would first nod if he understood or shake his head if he did not. No wonder he was called Clever Hans and was the subject of numerous newspaper and magazine articles. Hans was studied by many people, including zoologists, a circus manager, an animal behaviorist, a sensory physiologist, and a psychologist, all of whom were prominent in their fields. They concluded that no trick was involved and that Hans was genuine. What could these well-educated people have overlooked that would explain Hans's amazing abilities?

Research Methods Laboratory Manual

LAB William Langston (2010) has prepared a laboratory manual that contains many suggestions for research activities that work well with this book and require minimal materials. Chapter 1 of the Langston book discusses single-subject designs.

Exercises

12.1 Identify the Research Design

A teacher designs a study to test the hypothesis that praise as a positive reinforcement will improve the behavior of a hyperactive boy in her third-grade class. Figure 12.8 contains results from the study.

Required:

a. Identify the design.
b. Describe the initial baseline stability.
c. What is the independent variable?
d. What is the dependent variable?
e. What is the effect of the independent variable on the dependent variable?

12.2 Identify the Research Design

A psychologist designs a study to test a new drug that is supposed to reduce the frequency of hallucinations among schizophrenic patients. Figure 12.9 contains the results from the study.

Required:

a. Is the baseline stable? Explain.
b. What is the independent variable?
c. What is the dependent variable?
d. What is the effect of the independent variable on the dependent variable?
e. What type of design is this?

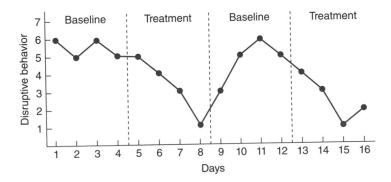

FIGURE **12.8** Frequency of Disruptive Behavior Before, During, and After Treatment

© Cengage Learning

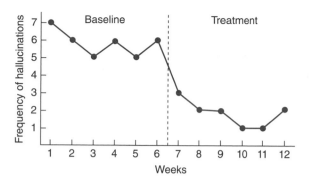

f. What major threat to internal validity is evident in this design?

g. How could you modify this experiment to strengthen its conclusions?

12.3 Identify the Research Design

Read the following abstract: Physical therapists were interested in whether a contoured foam (CF) seat would improve the way that a baby with neuromotor impairment interacted with the environment. A 9-month-old girl who was unable to sit independently because of congenital hypotonia (a birth condition that involves poor muscle tone) was evaluated as to her engagement with toys. The percentage of time that the child spent with her hands on her toys over three days was measured and found to be quite low. Then, the percentage of time that the child spent engaging with the toy was measured under three different seating conditions each day for five days: (1) a regular highchair, (2) a regular highchair with a thin foam liner, and (3) a CF seat used as an insert in a regular highchair. The order of the seating conditions was randomized each day. Results showed that the little girl interacted with the toy most in the CF seat condition. (Based on Washington, Deitz, White, & Schwartz, 2002.)

a. What is the independent variable?

b. What is the dependent variable?

c. What is the effect of the independent variable on the dependent variable?

d. What type of design is this?

e. What major threat to internal validity is evident in this design?

f. How could you modify this experiment to strengthen its conclusions?

12.4 Who to Believe?

Dr. Black and Dr. Jones are both working on the same problem; they are both interested in the relationship between eating disorders and major depression. Each psychologist measures these two variables in a different way, then finds a correlation between the two. Dr. Black uses 15 participants and finds a correlation of 0.831. Dr. Jones uses 60 participants and finds a correlation of 0.359. Both researchers find that their correlations are significant at the 0.01 level.

a. Which researcher has likely shown the stronger effect?

b. What percentage of the variance is accounted for by each result?

CHAPTER THIRTEEN

Quasi Experiments

PREVIEW

This chapter discusses methods known as quasi experiments that fall between true experiments and nonexperimental research. Typically, researchers using these methods have some degree of control over the independent variable but not enough to qualify the method as a true experiment. Although quasi-experimental research faces more problems with validity than true experiments do, it is some of the most interesting and creative research in psychology.

quasi experiment: research procedure in which the scientist must select subjects for different conditions from pre-existing groups

Experiments are powerful ways of answering research questions. Sometimes, however, it is not possible to meet the requirements of conducting a true experiment. This chapter discusses research that does not meet the definition of a true experiment.

The Principal Difference Between Quasi Experiments and True Experiments

As you may recall from Chapter 10, a true experiment is one in which the experimenter has complete control over the *who*, *what*, *when*, *where*, and *how* of the experiment. A quasi experiment, by contrast, does not permit the experimenter to control the assignment of subjects to conditions. The word *quasi* means "as if" or "to a degree." Thus, a quasi experiment is one that resembles an experiment but lacks at least one of its defining characteristics. Whereas it is possible to *assign* subjects to conditions in a true experiment, often in a quasi experiment it is necessary to *select* subjects for the different conditions from previously existing groups.

For example, you may want to study the effect of number of food pellets on the rate at which rats learn a maze. This situation would permit the design of a true experiment because you could arbitrarily assign some rats to the large-reward condition and others to the small-reward condition. Assume that before the experiment the rats belonged to a homogeneous population of rats. For experimental purposes, you assign the rats to groups that you create according to your needs.

However, suppose you suspected that there were sex differences such that the maze running of male rats might be affected differently than female rats by the number of food pellets. In that case, you would have to conduct a quasi experiment because you cannot assign participants to the two conditions, male and female; the rats already belong to those groups naturally. In this situation, the researcher cannot create groups of males and females, but instead selects members from preexisting groups.

The independent variable in a quasi experiment is often called a *subject variable* if it is a characteristic of the subjects on which they have been selected, such as sex of participants.

Quasi experiments are sometimes called *ex post facto*, or *after the fact*, experiments because the experiment is conducted after the groups have been formed. In the case of a quasi experiment with the subject variable of sex as the independent variable, the experiment takes place long after the subjects become males or females. If you performed an experiment using preexisting classes of students, the two classes would be ex post facto variables because the classes were formed before you did the experiment.

Another way to look at the difference between true experiments and quasi experiments is to note that in true experiments we manipulate variables, whereas in quasi experiments we observe categories of subjects. When we take two preexisting groups and consider a difference between them to be the independent variable, we are not manipulating a variable, but simply labeling groups according to what we think is the important difference between them. The true difference between them for our experiment may be quite different from what we think it is. If we find that two different socioeconomic groups differ on some measure, the difference may be caused not by the socioeconomic difference itself but by cultural differences between the two socioeconomic groups. By calling the difference *socioeconomic*, we may obscure the fact that the difference is actually a difference in the level of need for achievement, or perceived helplessness, or religion, or some other variable that we have yet to consider.

When we present some independent variable to two preexisting groups, more is involved than measuring the effect of the variable on their behavior. We have the additional problem of not knowing whether the difference in behavior was caused by differences between the groups that existed before the experiment started or by the independent variable. For example, if we studied the effects of two different teaching methods on learning in two pre-existing classes, we would not be sure whether any differences in learning resulted from the teaching methods or from some other preexisting differences between the classes.

A true experiment, then, permits the experimenter the greatest degree of control in ruling out alternative hypotheses, or alternative independent variables, as being the cause of the difference between two groups or conditions. Thus, a true experiment permits the most powerful control for confounding because all other potential independent variables have been eliminated by randomly assigning subjects to conditions. A quasi experiment leaves open the possibility that other differences exist between the experimental and control conditions and thus permits other potential differences to remain.

It is possible to have one experimental variable and one quasi-experimental variable in an experiment. For example, in studying the effects of two different teaching methods on classroom learning, we might be interested in whether slow learners differ from fast learners in their response to the teaching methods. The two teaching methods would constitute a true experimental variable, assuming we assigned students to sections, and the classification into slow and fast learners would constitute a quasi-experimental variable.

Other Features of Quasi Experiments

In addition to not being able to control the *who* of an experiment, the experimenter in a quasi experiment in some instances cannot completely control the *what, when, where,* and *how.* Often data must be collected at a particular time or not at all. For example, an experimenter who wants to study the effects of changing work schedules on productivity must do so when the management of the plant decides to make the changes. The problem with such an experiment is that productivity may already have been changing because of some outside variable. Similarly, the experimenter may want to do parts of the experiment in certain ways but cannot because of practical limitations. Any of these considerations may lead us to regard a piece of research as a quasi experiment. The boundaries between true and quasi experiments are not always distinct. If the experimenter has good control over all aspects of the experiment, we can call it a true experiment. If enough compromise of experimental control takes place, the research is considered a quasi experiment.

The presence of uncontrolled or confounded variables reduces the internal validity of a quasi experiment but does not necessarily render it invalid. Recall that the presence of randomization in true experiments permits the greatest degree of control. Because quasi experiments lack randomized groups by definition,[1] they also provide weaker application of the method of differences. The inability to randomly allocate subjects to groups reduces the internal validity of the experiment. The experimenter must evaluate the likelihood that the confounding variables are responsible for the outcome. This appraisal involves the use of the experimenter's judgment, as does the evaluation of all research.

---

[1] When the experimenter has no control over the presentation of the independent variables and can only record what happens in a certain situation, we call the research nonexperimental.

Nevertheless, the external validity of a quasi experiment may be higher than that of a true experiment done on the same problem if the quasi experiment studies subjects or settings that are more appropriate to the question of interest than a true experiment could do. For example, if you wanted to know the effects of changing the size of work groups in a widget factory on productivity, an experiment using college students working at solving anagrams would probably not apply. It would have little external validity. Quasi-experimental research allows the examination of natural experiments, which are formed when real-world events divide people into two groups for comparison. So it is possible to examine the effect of the presence of a large new supermarket in a neighborhood on the health and diet of nearby residents (Petticrew et al., 2005).

In general, the true experiment is preferable to the quasi experiment, but many situations exist in which randomly assigning subjects to conditions is not possible. Then a quasi experiment is performed simply because doing it is better than doing no experiment at all. For example, does the disadvantage of using two preexisting classes to study the effects of different teaching methods outweigh the fact that it is virtually impossible to randomly constitute two new classes? In designing a piece of research, the experimenter must weigh the costs and benefits of each choice.

Which Is the Best Research Method?

It never fails when we lecture on the difference between true experiments and quasi experiments that a student asks which one is better. We suspect that they think we are wasting their time on inferior methodology when we discuss quasi experiments. The degree of control is less in a quasi experiment; however, the fact that we discussed true experiments first does not mean that true experiments are necessarily better than other types of investigations. Rather, discussing true experiments first reflects the fact that as the degree of control that the researcher can exercise decreases, the threats to the validity of the conclusions increase.

Other things being equal, one would choose a true experiment over a quasi experiment and a quasi experiment over a nonexperimental method. Things are seldom equal, though. Many social-psychological phenomena are difficult to bring into the laboratory in a realistic fashion. Therefore, a field study may be preferable to an experiment because the advantage of realism and ecological validity outweighs the loss of control. Nevertheless, you should try first to design a true experimental study and use the other designs only when you believe that the gain in validity will be worth the loss of control. But the crucial point is this: The best research method is the one that best answers your research question. If a quasi experiment best answers your question, it is the best method.

nonequivalent control-group design: research design having both an experimental and a control group wherein subjects are not randomly assigned to groups

Nonequivalent-Control-Group Designs _____

If both an experimental and a control group are part of an experiment but subjects have not been allocated randomly to the two groups, we have a **nonequivalent-control-group** design. Of the variety of quasi-experimental designs, this is the most typical. The problem with this design is in determining how to compare results between the experimental and control groups when the two groups were not equivalent to begin with.

Recall the discussion in Chapter 10 of designs to be avoided. In the example of the company that wanted to evaluate the effect of a new work schedule, we said that the study would be improved by having a second factory as a control group. Any change in productivity at the experimental factory that followed the switch in work schedule could be more confidently attributed to the new work schedule if a second factory showed no change over the same time interval. This example of a nonequivalent-control-group design with pretest and posttest is a typical quasi-experimental design and is diagrammed in Table 13.1. Because the participants already worked at the factories and thus were not randomly allocated to the two groups, we do not have good reason to believe that they were equivalent before the experimental manipulation was performed. Therefore, we must consider the likelihood that alternative hypotheses may account for the results. For example, the workers in the experimental factory may have been less experienced on the average than those in the control factory. The increase in productivity in the experimental factory may have been caused by the experience those workers gained between pretest and posttest. The control subjects, by contrast, might already have been working at their maximum.

Quasi experiments that employ nonequivalent control groups with pretest and posttest may be interpretable or they may not. Whether they can be interpreted depends on whether the pattern of results obtained can be accounted for by possible differences in the groups or by something else in the experiment. The pattern of results we would like to see from this design is shown in Figure 13.1. Here the two groups showed the same performance on the pretest. The experimental group improved on the posttest, but the control group did not change. Although the experimental and control groups were not equivalent in all respects because they were not randomly constituted, their performances can be compared and the results interpreted because their behavior as measured by the dependent variable was the same at the beginning.

The pattern of results from quasi experiment with nonequivalent control groups with pretest and posttest is not always interpretable, however, as you can see from Figure 13.2, which shows one kind of uninterpretable pattern of results. These results could be those of the factory study we just discussed. In this example, the experimental group improved but the control group did not. Notice that

TABLE **13.1**

Nonequivalent-Control-Group Design with Pretest and Posttest

© Cengage Learning

	Allocation of Subjects and Groups	Pretest	Treatment	Posttest
Group 1	Any method that is not random	Yes	Yes	Yes
Group 2		Yes	No	Yes

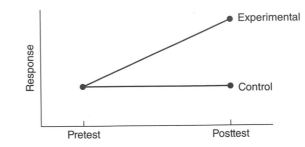

FIGURE **13.1** Desired Pattern of Results for a Nonequivalent-Control-Group Design with Pretest and Posttest

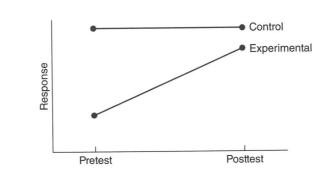

FIGURE **13.2** One Kind of Uninterpretable Pattern of Results in a Nonequivalent-Control-Group Design with Pretest and Posttest

the control group was superior to the experimental group on both occasions. This difference could result from the operation of a ceiling effect. If it was not possible for the control group to perform any better, then we cannot attribute the improvement in the experimental group to the experimental manipulation.

Another pattern of results that may be uninterpretable is shown in Figure 13.3. These results could represent a learning experiment in which the experimental group performed better than the control group on the pretest. Both groups showed improvement on the posttest, but the experimental group showed twice as much improvement. Can we attribute the difference in rate of improvement to the experimental manipulation? No, we cannot, because although the experimental group improved more, both groups showed the same proportional improvement. On the posttest, both doubled their previous performance. Although it is possible that learning was twice as fast in the experimental group, their improvement likely was caused by some other variable that had nothing to do with the experimental manipulation.

A pattern of results that usually is interpretable is shown in Figure 13.4. Here the experimental group was lower than the control group on the pretest but higher than the control group on the posttest. Finding a rival hypothesis

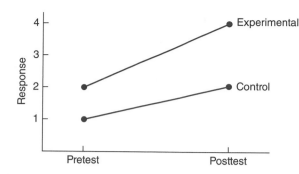

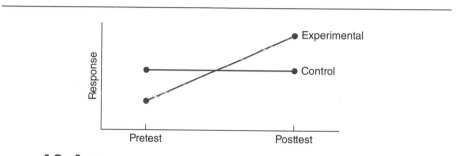

for this pattern of results is difficult. You might suppose that the experimental participants were as good as the control participants to begin with and did worse on the pretest simply by chance. In that case, you would expect them to do the same as the control group on the posttest if the experimental manipulation were not effective. You would have no reason, however, to expect them to do better than the control group on the posttest by chance alone. Therefore, it is usually safe to conclude that a pattern of results such as those in Figure 13.4 shows the effectiveness of the experimental manipulation.

Mixed Factorial Design with One Nonmanipulated Variable

An example of a nonequivalent-control-group design—a mixed factorial design with one nonmanipulated variable—can be found in an experiment on pain perception. Edmund Keogh and Gerke Witt (2001) thought that caffeine intake might influence the perception of pain, and that the effect might be different in men than in women. They tested this theory by having 25 men and 25 women take part in two sessions separated by a week. In one of the sessions, participants drank a cup of coffee that contained caffeine and in the other session the coffee was decaffeinated. In each session, participants put their nondominant hand in an ice-water bath and were instructed to indicate the point of just noticeable pain.

TABLE **13.2**

Design of the Keogh and Witt Study

© Cengage Learning

| | Beverage | |
Sex	Decaffeinated	Caffeine
	S_1	S_1
	S_2	S_2
WOMEN	•	•
	•	•
	•	•
	S_{25}	S_{25}
	S_{26}	S_{26}
	S_{27}	S_{27}
MEN	•	•
	•	•
	•	•
	S_{50}	S_{50}

The design of this experiment is a mixed factorial because it has one between-subjects variable and one within-subjects variable. The between-subjects variable is sex because participants were either male or female and this is a quasi-experimental variable. The within-subjects variable is caffeine because participants experienced both conditions at different times. The design is illustrated in Table 13.2. Keogh and Witt found that caffeine generally produced a higher pain threshold, and that women both had a slightly higher pain threshold than men and showed the greatest increase related to caffeine. The data are shown in Figure 13.5.

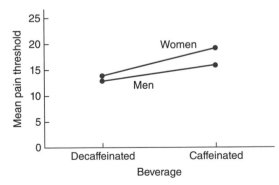

FIGURE **13.5** Mean Pain Threshold Scores for Male and Female Participants After Drinking a Decaffeinated Beverage and After Drinking a Caffeinated Beverage. Based on the Results of Keogh and Witt (2001)

© Cengage Learning

Designs Without Control Groups _____

Sometimes no control group can be obtained that can be considered comparable enough to be useful. Then a design that allows the same group to be compared over time can be used. We discuss two such designs: the interrupted time-series design and the repeated-treatments design.

Interrupted Time-Series Designs

In Chapter 10, when we discussed designs to be avoided, we said that measurement of a single group before and after the manipulation is not a good design. One way to improve on the one-group before-after design is to consider the trend of the data before and after the manipulation, rather than simply comparing the average data before and after. For example, the manager of a factory that is changing its work schedule might keep a weekly record of output for the years preceding and following the change. Management could then look not only for average differences between the two periods but also for trends that might appear. Seasonal changes or other cyclical changes in output may be important, as well as any overall trend toward higher or lower productivity that occurred around the time of the change.

The ideal situation would be a flat and stable baseline before the change, followed by either an abrupt change to a new level or a gradual change to a new level. However, a baseline that is changing in the opposite direction from the predicted influence of the manipulation would still produce a valid comparison. Evaluation of such time series is a difficult procedure that requires different statistical tools from those generally used for analyzing group data. Instead, **interrupted time-series experiments** are quasi experiments that are similar in design and interpretation to some single-subject designs and to the nonexperimental methods, topics discussed in Chapters 8, 9, and 12.

interrupted time-series design: research design that allows the same group to be compared over time by considering the trend of the data before and after experimental manipulation

Although the following study is presented as an example of the interrupted time-series design, the authors of the study examined existing records to obtain their data rather than manipulating some independent variable, thus making them technically examples of nonexperimental research rather than quasi-experimental study. Nevertheless, this study presents good examples of the advantages and disadvantages of interrupted time-series research. In addition, similar nonexperimental studies are commonly described under the heading of quasi experiments in books on design (e.g., Cook & Campbell, 1979).

Thomas Niederkrotenthaler and Gernot Sonneck (2007) were interested in the effect that the media coverage of suicides has on the suicide rate. They knew about some work that had been done in the 1970s (Phillips, 1974) showing that people had a tendency to perform "copycat" suicides if a suicide was prominently featured in a popular newspaper. As a result of this early work, the country of Austria had implemented strict media guidelines in 1987 that mandated toning down the reporting of suicides. Niederkrotenthaler and Sonneck wanted to know if the guidelines had been successful in reducing the rate of suicide and whether this decrease could be attributed to the change.

Niederkrotenthaler and Sonneck (2007) used the interrupted time-series design to answer their question. They examined data from 1946 until 2005, paying close attention to what happened after 1987, which is when the

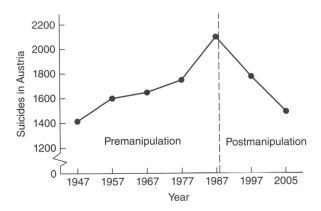

FIGURE **13.6** Number of Suicides in Austria Before and After Media Guidelines, 1946/1947–2004/2005

(Based on Information in "Assessing the impact of media guidelines for reporting on suicides in Austria: Interrupted time series analysis" by T. Niederkrotenthaler and G. Sonneck, 2007. *Australian and New Zealand Journal of Psychiatry, 41,* 419–428.)

media guidelines went into effect. Figure 13.6 is based on the data that Niederkrotenthaler and Sonneck found, with the dotted line indicating the implementation of the media guidelines. They found that while the rate of suicide prior to the date that the guidelines were implemented seemed to be increasing, the rate after that date seemed to decrease. This finding supports the idea that changing the way that suicides were reported in the media helped to decrease the number of suicides.

Still, it was possible that the results were caused by some factor other than a change in reporting guidelines. Niederkrotenthaler and Sonneck therefore divided the country of Austria into three media markets, based on areas that purchased the most newspapers. Their thinking was that if the change in suicide rate was due to a change in the way that suicides were reported in the newspapers, then areas that were low-impact media markets should not show any effect of the change in guidelines. Their results reflected the hypothesized difference in media markets, giving more support to the idea that media guidelines caused the decrease in suicide rates.

Even after checking for differences in media markets as another means of supporting their case that the media guidelines were effective, Niederkrotenthaler and Sonneck acknowledge that other factors might account for their results. They explore the idea that changes in unemployment levels or in the rate of prescriptions for antidepressants might be related, but reject each of these possibilities based on statistical analyses. Thus, although there is good support for the hypothesis that the implementation of media guidelines decreased suicide rates in Austria, like all quasi-experimental data, the possibility exists that other as yet unconsidered factors may contribute to the findings.

Repeated-Treatment Designs

As the name implies, repeated-treatment designs attempt to improve the validity of the experiment by presenting the treatment more than once. The subject's response is measured before and after the introduction of a treatment, then the treatment is withdrawn and the whole process is begun again. Table 13.3 shows the general design. This design has an obvious limitation: The treatment must be one that can be withdrawn without causing complications in the analysis of data.

Suppose an instructor is going to give four hour-long tests in a course. She wants to find out if giving extra credit for turning in homework will improve grades on the tests. If she instituted the extra credit between the first and second tests, she would then have a pretest and a posttest to permit her to examine the effect of the treatment. To repeat the treatment, she would have to stop giving the extra credit after the second test (Posttest$_1$). The third test then could be considered Pretest$_2$, after which she would reinstitute the extra credit and look for improvement between Pretest$_2$ and Posttest$_2$. This design might be a good one, except that the students would likely rebel at having the extra credit taken away. If the instructor went ahead with the plan anyway, the students might be demoralized enough that their performance would suffer on the later tests.

Whatever change is found between Pretest$_1$ and Posttest$_1$ should be in the same direction as that between Pretest$_2$ and Posttest$_2$. A reversal in any previous trend of response between Posttest$_1$, when the treatment is withdrawn, and Pretest$_2$ is desirable to rule out the possibility that there would have been a continuous change in performance over the four tests regardless of treatment. Like the interrupted time series design, the repeated-treatment design is similar to one that is used in single-subject experiments (the ABAB design discussed in Chapter 12).

A good example of the repeated-treatment design can be found in the study of the effects of a ban on alcohol consumption in a small Alaskan community (Chiu, Perez, & Parker, 1997). Barrow, Alaska, is an isolated town of about 4,000 people, most of whom are indigenous to the area. When oil was discovered near Barrow in 1967, prosperity increased and many non-native Alaskans came to the area. Although previously rare, alcohol became widely available with the increased cash economy. Many residents disapproved of the increase in drinking, and in 1994, possession of alcohol was made illegal in the town of Barrow. This ban was repealed in 1995, and then reinstated in 1996 after a lawsuit alleging flaws in the referendum that ended the ban. To assess the impact of alcohol policy changes on medical problems related to alcohol consumption, the number of outpatient alcohol-related visits to Barrow's hospital was examined over a 33-month period, spanning 1993 to 1996. As Figure 13.7 demonstrates, the number of alcohol-related outpatient

TABLE **13.3**

A Repeated-Treatment Design

© Cengage Learning

Pretest$_1$	Treatment	Posttest$_1$	Withdraw treatment	Pretest$_2$	Treatment	Posttest$_2$

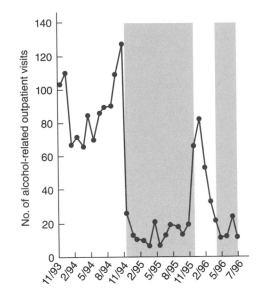

FIGURE **13.7** Impact of Banning Alcohol on Outpatient Visits

("Impact of Banning Alcohol on Outpatient Visits in Barrow, Alaska" by A. Y. Chiu, P. E. Perez, and R. N. Parker, 1997. *Journal of the American Medical Association 278* (21), 1775–1777. Copyright 1997 by JAMA. Reprinted by permission of the publisher and author.)

visits was much higher during the periods of time that alcohol could be legally possessed than when it was illegal in Barrow.

Designs to Test Developmental Changes

Many of the quasi-experimental designs we have discussed in this chapter have involved time as a variable, and others have involved nonequivalent control groups. An area of psychological research that has to deal with both characteristics is developmental psychology. We use developing the ability to program a DVR as a way of introducing the problems of developmental research deign.

A few years ago, one of the authors (McBurney) bought a DVR and decided to hook up the TV to play through the stereo system. After studying the manuals that came with the stereo amplifier, the TV, and the DVR for several hours, he gave up in frustration. Then he called his teenage nephew, who hooked it up in about 10 minutes without so much as a glance at the manuals. The author's chagrin at having to turn to his nephew was somewhat reduced when he learned that the average person needs some level of instruction in learning to operate a DVR. This led him to wonder about the developmental aspects of learning to program a DVR.

We could take two simple approaches to determining the effects of age on ability to program a DVR. We could do a cross-sectional study, taking samples of people at different ages and testing them for ability to program a DVR at the same general time. The advantage of the cross-sectional approach is that all the age groups can be tested at the same general time. The disadvantage,

cross-sectional study: in developmental research, a study that tests different age groups at the same time

however, is that the people at different ages were all born at different times, so age is confounded with date of birth. Because every group was born in a different year, cohort effects are likely. A cohort is a group that has some characteristic in common, and so people with this characteristic are treated as a group. Everyone born in 1990 could be considered part of the 1990 cohort. Members of the 1990 cohort would have grown up with DVRs, whereas members of the 1960 cohort would have been in their 30s before such things even existed. It is likely that there would be a large cohort effect on ability to program a DVR.

To avoid cohort effects, you might do a longitudinal study, taking samples over time of people born in a certain year to see how many of them can program a DVR. The advantage of this approach is that all the people would have the same birthdates, so there would be no cohort effects. Longitudinal studies have two main problems—one theoretical and one practical.

The practical problem is that the researcher has to wait years to complete the study as the cohort ages. For example, the psychologists at the Minnesota Center for Twin Family Research have followed their participants for over a dozen years in an effort to find links between genetics and health issues, such as alcohol addiction (Legrand, Iacono, & McGue, 2005). Other longitudinal studies have gone on for many decades, during which time the researchers retire and new researchers take over the project.

The main theoretical problem with a longitudinal study is that it confounds age with time of testing. All the participants would be aging together, but at the same time technology would be changing. For example, a person might have been born in the same year that the DVR was invented. Over time, not only did the person age, but DVRs also became more popular and readily available. It might be the changes in technology—not the changes in age—that caused any differences in ability to program a DVR. The technological changes are an example of secular trends: general changes that take place in a society that may influence the results of your study.

Thus, both designs have important sources of confounding. The longitudinal study confounds age with time. The cross-sectional study confounds age with date of birth. It is important to realize that there is no way to eliminate this confounding: It is logically impossible for a person born in 1960 to be 10 years old in 2000.

Considerable ingenuity has been devoted to developing research designs that help tease out the various results of this confounding. One such design is the cross-sequential design. This design tests individuals from two or more cohorts at two or more times. Suppose we take four groups of people, born in 1990, 1980, 1970, and 1960, and see what percentage of each group can program a DVR. Suppose also that we test them in the years 2000, 2010, and 2020. Let's say that we obtain the data shown in Table 13.4. Any row of the table shows the data for people with the same year of birth. The top row, for example, shows the data for the 1960 cohort. Any column of the table shows the data for people tested in a given year. The first column, for example, shows the data for all people tested in 2000.

We can see longitudinal trends by following the cohorts over time (see the horizontal arrow). We can see cross-sectional effects by looking at the people tested in a given year (vertical arrow). The cross-sequential design permits us to do

cohort: in research, a group that has something in common, such as age

longitudinal study: in developmental research, a study that tests individuals in a single cohort over the course of time

secular trend: a change that is taking place in the general population over time (the term has nothing to do with religion)

cross-sequential design: design used to help separate developmental, cohort, and secular effects

TABLE **13.4**

Percentage of People Who Can Program a DVR

© Cengage Learning

	Year of Testing		
Year of Birth	2000	2010	2020
1960	10 (40)	40 (50)	70 (60)
1970	40 (30)	60 (40)	80 (50)
1980	70 (20)	80 (30)	90 (40)
1990	100 (10)	100 (20)	100 (30)

Longitudinal effect

Cross-sectional effect   Time-lag effect

Note: Numbers in Parenthesis indicate age at time of testing.

something that neither a simple longitudinal nor simple cross-sectional study would permit: to see the effect of time lag on the ability to program a DVR. By looking down one of the diagonals, we can see how many people of the same age can program a DVR at different times. Although the time-lag effect does not escape the problem of confounding, it helps to show the secular trend and to directly examine cohort effects, since different cohort groups are tested longitudinally.

time-lag effect: in a cross-sequential design, the effect resulting from comparing subjects of the same age at different times

The longitudinal, cross-sectional, and time-lag effects can be seen by displaying the data from Table 13.4, as shown in Figures 13.8 through 13.10. Figure 13.8 shows the cross-sectional data by plotting percentage of people

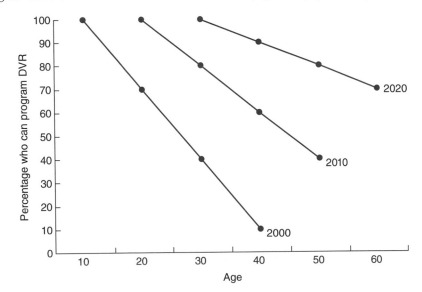

FIGURE **13.8** Percentage of People Who Can Program a DVR as a Function of Age, with Year of Testing as the Parameter

© Cengage Learning

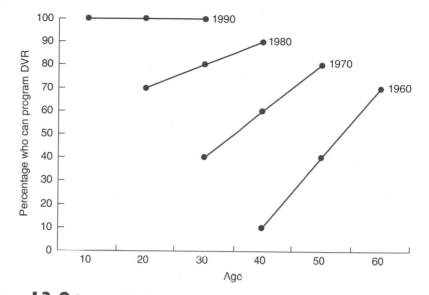

FIGURE **13.9** Percentage Who Can Program a DVR as a Function of Age, with Year of Birth as the Parameter

© Cengage Learning

who can program a DVR as a function of age (reported in parentheses), with year of testing as the parameter. As you might expect from the anecdote about the nephew, the data clearly show that older people are less likely to be able to program a DVR than are younger ones.

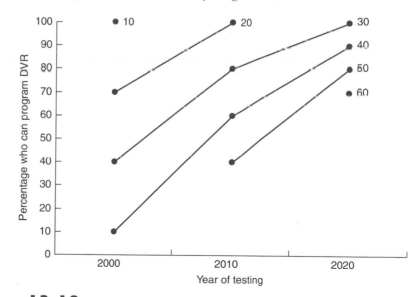

FIGURE **13.10** Percentage Who Can Program a DVR as a Function of Year of Testing, with Age as a Parameter

© Cengage Learning

The picture is very different, however, when we look at the longitudinal data in Figure 13.9. Here the same data are plotted as a function of age, with cohort as a parameter.

In other words, here we see the trend over age for people born in different years. These data show that, because the rate of change is steeper, the older cohorts learn faster. The 1990 cohort doesn't show any learning at all in these data; it appears that they were born knowing how to program DVRs! (We can suppose that they learned very fast sometime between birth and age 10.) Actually, Figure 13.10 and Figure 13.11 are the same with the exception of how the data points are connected: Figure 13.8 connects the data points that represent the same year of testing, whereas Figure 13.9 connects those points that represent the same year of birth.

The explanation for the apparent contradiction between the two graphs can be seen by looking at the time-lag data. Figure 13.10 shows the percentage of people who can program a DVR as a function of year, with age as a parameter. This graph shows that there has been a very strong secular trend in ability to program DVRs. Thus, the cross-sectional data shown in Figure 13.8 could give the wrong impression because it does not highlight the fact that people of all ages are learning to program DVRs.

This example was concocted to show how longitudinal and cross-sectional studies could come up with opposite conclusions. A more common

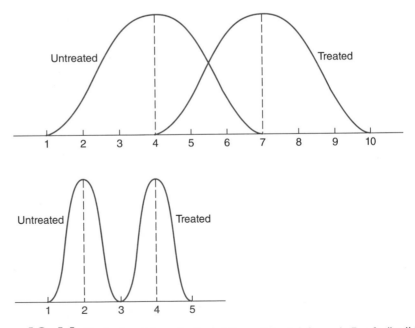

FIGURE **13.11** Distribution of Scores for Treated Versus Untreated Groups in Two Studies Using Different Scales

© Cengage Learning

situation is one in which a cross-sectional study of, say, intellectual ability shows a decline with age, but a longitudinal study shows no change. The difference can be accounted for by recognizing that there has been a secular improvement in educational levels. A cross-sectional study will have younger people who are better educated than the older cohorts, resulting in higher intellectual performance. A longitudinal study, by contrast, will follow the same person over time and find no decline in intellectual ability. A cross-sequential design will show the effect of increase in educational level by the time-lag effect.

Program Evaluation _____

program evaluation:
a set of techniques for determining the effectiveness of a social service program

Although we have emphasized the importance of research in developing and testing theory, we have noted that some research is not driven by theoretical concerns but is intended rather to determine some factual question. An important example of such an area of research in the social sciences is program evaluation, in which agencies' programs are assessed for their effectiveness. Quasi-experimental designs are often used in program evaluations, because clients of the program are more likely to be assigned, rather than to be randomly allocated, to groups for comparison. For example, clients might be matched with someone who has not been served by the program on some key variables, and then the clients and non-clients might be compared to see how well the program is working by using some variant of a non-equivalent control group design.

Although private and public agencies have always provided social services, their effectiveness was not usually evaluated systematically until the mushrooming of federal government programs as part of the Great Society of the 1960s. When the government started spending millions of dollars to achieve social ends, there was understandable concern that the money be well spent. Now all programs that provide services supported by federal grants must be evaluated (Posavac & Carey, 1997).

How to go about evaluating a social program can be more difficult than it would appear at first. Why not use the same techniques to evaluate programs that we employ in evaluating a company? You can ask what percentage of the market General Widget controls, how long their widgets last, or whether the company makes a profit. All these indices can be used to evaluate a company operating in a competitive market system.

These indicators, however, do not work very well for social service agencies. In the first place, the agencies frequently do not operate in a competitive market: There is only one public school system in a given city. Second, their product is difficult to evaluate: Should you evaluate graduates by their scores on standardized tests, by the percentage who go to college, or by the percentage who are employed? Third, profit or loss is often irrelevant to program evaluation: If there were a profit to be made in providing a social service, a company would be providing the service in the first place.

For reasons such as these, program evaluation has developed as a specialized field that uses the expertise of psychologists, among other disciplines. Many of the techniques used in program evaluation have already been discussed in this book. They range across all the research methods from true experiments to archival research, with emphasis on quasi experiments and nonexperimental methods. As you can imagine, it would be difficult to evaluate a program such as an alcohol awareness intervention at a college by experimental techniques. Because of the wide variety of techniques employed, we have included program evaluation in this chapter after all the various techniques have been discussed.

Sources of Resistance to Program Evaluations

Program evaluation is unusual among types of research projects in the extent to which it is conducted in a social context. Generally, the evaluators work either for the organization being evaluated or for the external sponsor of the program. In either case, the evaluation involves many people and affects many people. Further, the evaluation has the potential of making the people who run the program look good or bad and can directly affect their futures. These circumstances introduce a political dimension to program evaluation that is not present in most of the research methods discussed so far. People who feel threatened by the evaluation will actively or passively resist the process. Emil Posavac and Raymond Carey (1997) discuss a number of potential sources of resistance to a successful program evaluation. We discuss several of them here.

Fear That the Program Will Be Terminated

In the extreme case, a negative evaluation could result in termination of the program, although this seldom happens. Even in these days of "sunset laws," programs generally continue even following negative evaluations as a result of pressure from people who benefit from the program. More often, programs are modified as a result of the evaluation. In any case, people with a vested interest in the program, including its employees, may resist the evaluation.

Fear of Losing Control of the Program

Introduction of an evaluation procedure causes changes in the day-to-day operation of a program. The managers and personnel of the program may feel they are losing control of their projects. The evaluators should make it clear that they are there to evaluate rather than control the program.

Fear That Information Will Be Abused

Some program personnel may fear that information generated by the program could shed a negative light on their individual performances. Successful evaluators will carefully distinguish between evaluation of the program and the individual personnel and work to build trust among the program personnel.

Fear That the Wrong Measures Will Be Used

The people working in the agency may believe they have an understanding of the successful workings of the school or clinic that cannot be captured by a formal evaluation. The evaluator should try to integrate quantitative and qualitative measures into the final evaluation.

Belief That Evaluation Is Pointless

There is often cynicism about the worth of doing an evaluation because it may have no apparent effect on the program. This may be justified because the existence of programs is often subject to political considerations that are not directly related to their worth. Evaluations, however, often do accomplish their purposes.

Hopes That Are Too High

Many times programs are begun with hopes of making dramatic changes in outcomes, whether dropout rate in school, drug rehabilitation, or whatever. When the program does not live up to these unrealistic expectations, personnel may resent an evaluation that is likely to find only a modest improvement compared with some alternative program. Frequently, a new program is compared with some standard program of treatment. Usually the standard treatment will have some effect, or it would not have come into general use. It is necessary to reassure program personnel that the most successful program will not save the world.

Steps in Planning an Evaluation

Throughout this book, we have discussed a number of steps in conducting research. The political dimension of program evaluation makes it necessary to be more systematic in planning an evaluation. Posavac and Carey (1997) list six steps in planning an evaluation. The following discussion is adapted from their list.

Step 1. Identify the Stakeholders

stakeholders: people in an organization who stand to gain or lose by any change in it

You need to spend some time finding out who the stakeholders in the program are. Stakeholders are those who have a vested interest in the program and stand to gain or lose by the outcome of the evaluation. The stakeholders in a college include students, faculty, alumni, trustees, administrators, and donors. All these constituencies need to be consulted in important matters concerning the college. An evaluation that does not involve all the stakeholders in the planning phase is asking for trouble. Every stakeholder has some potential for sabotaging the evaluation.

Step 2. Arrange Preliminary Meetings

Once the players have been identified, it is helpful to meet with them to discover the answers to several important questions: (1) Who wants the program evaluated? (2) Why do they want it evaluated? (3) What type of evaluation is desired? (4) What resources are available? (5) When do they want it completed?

It makes considerable difference who wants the evaluation. The sponsors of the program need to be convinced that the evaluation would be a good use of their dollars, and the program personnel need to be made comfortable with the idea of being evaluated. Ideally, both groups should see the evaluation as having potential benefit for them. Different stakeholders may want the evaluation for different reasons. The sponsor may want to know how effective the program is; the personnel may want to know how to make it run more smoothly from their perspective; the administrator of the program may welcome the evaluation as a way of putting off making a difficult decision (let's form a committee and study it). The evaluators need to be sensitive to the political pressures that each stakeholder will be bringing to bear.

The type of evaluation desired can differ from one stakeholder to another. The sponsor may want a **summative evaluation**—one that evaluates how effective the project is in meeting its goals. The sponsor may want to decide whether to continue the project or spend its money elsewhere. The project personnel, however, may prefer a **formative evaluation**—one that focuses on how the project can be improved.

The evaluators need to know what resources they have available to them. Will the program personnel be assigned to help them, or do the evaluators need to do all their own data collection? The resources available obviously impose a limit on the scope and quality of the evaluation that can be done.

It is also necessary to have a clear understanding of when the evaluation is needed. It may be that the sponsor wants the evaluation by a certain time before making a decision, but that deadline does not allow for the development of the proper methodology for the evaluation.

Step 3. Decide Whether an Evaluation Should Be Done

Although it might seem that this should be the first step, only after you have identified the players and met with them are you in a position to decide whether it is possible to evaluate the program. The stakeholders need to agree on what constitutes program success before the program can be evaluated. If the sponsor wants to reduce drinking by college students but the project personnel want to keep students from embarrassing the college by having loud parties that result in calls to the police, then there may be some differences in how the project should be evaluated.

Another consideration in deciding to proceed is whether the program is soundly based in theory. The program leaders may believe that providing information about the dangers of alcohol will be sufficient to reduce drinking, without considering the other factors that lead to drinking by college students, such as social pressure. Until the program is grounded in current knowledge of the problem it is addressing, evaluation could be a waste of time. Notice that the program evaluation does not test the validity of the theory underlying the program; it only concerns the effectiveness of the application of the theory. Nevertheless, if the program does not have a sound theoretical basis, it is not ready to be evaluated.

Step 4. Examine the Literature

Evaluators tend to be generalists who evaluate many different types of programs. It is necessary to become familiar with the literature on evaluation in the field relevant to the program they are working on. What types of evaluation have been done in this area, and how successful were they? What methods were used, and how might they be adapted or improved? The methods of literature review discussed in Chapter 2 are useful here. Computerized databases are especially helpful in program evaluation because of the interdisciplinary nature of the field.

Step 5. Determine the Methodology

We say little here about this important step because it concerns issues dealt with throughout this book: the measures, control and comparison groups, sampling methods, statistics, and so on. The one issue that should be mentioned is the general strategy of the evaluation: What is it exactly that you want to evaluate? Is it the need for the program, the outcome of the program, and the cost-effectiveness of the program? The methodology will depend greatly on what you want to evaluate, but as we mentioned previously, quasi-experimental designs are often used in these circumstances because there are often naturally occurring groups (for example, those who benefited from the program vs. those who did not) that are compared.

Step 6. Present a Written Proposal

This step forces you to put in writing all the decisions in the previous step and permits the stakeholders to understand what is about to happen. Some issues may need to be discussed further. The proposal might have an unrealistic timetable or make assumptions about resources that are contrary to fact. It is best to have these issues ironed out before the evaluation proceeds.

Two Examples of Program Evaluation

To illustrate some of the problems and benefits of program evaluation, we consider two examples. First, we consider a case in which program evaluation failed because of organized opposition. Then, we consider a more successful case.

Implementing Alcohol Guidelines in a University

Friedner Wittman (1989) describes the experience of a large state university that attempted to implement guidelines for the use of alcohol in its fraternities and sororities. The project began as a cooperative effort among representatives of the Greek system, an independent agency known as the Prevention Research Center, the Student Health Service, and another office of the university that worked with the students in the Greek system.

The Student Health Center and the Prevention Research Center held a kickoff meeting to which a number of organizational representatives were invited, including all identified stakeholders. At the introductory meeting, it was explained that student representatives would be asked to accept a major share in planning the project and that an evaluation would be built into the project.

The effort led to the formation of the Greek Alcohol Advisory Board (GAAB), which developed a set of Party Planning Guidelines to reduce problems such as party crashing by high school students, a climate that encouraged drinking to intoxication, and the like. The GAAB, however, had little enthusiasm for the evaluation component of the project because it placed new responsibilities on students for enforcing university policy. More important, a vocal minority of the alumni advisers to the fraternities strongly objected to the evaluation. They objected to the design of the survey, complained that they had not been involved in planning the program, and feared that results might make the newspapers. The alumni advisers were successful in torpedoing the evaluation even after preliminary data had been collected for about a year on the first phase of the project. Wittman (1989) reports that the program is continuing at the university, and judging by informal observations, it seems to be successful, although it is impossible to tell for sure.

The failure of this program evaluation can be attributed to several of the potential sources of resistance listed previously. Specifically, the alumni advisers were concerned that the program would change the relationship between the Greek system and the university, that the wrong kind of evaluation was being done, and that information from the evaluation could be abused. Although the program developers followed the steps suggested by Posavac and Carey (1997) by identifying the stakeholders and arranging preliminary meetings, it appears that they were not diligent enough in actually getting stakeholders involved. The organizers invited the alumni advisers to the preliminary meeting, but they apparently did not show up. Finally, and most significantly, relations between the university and the Greek community were already strained before this program was initiated, and the main issue was alcohol.

Preventing Pregnancy at a University

William Fisher (1990) reports the results of a campaign to reduce pregnancies among undergraduate students at a large public university in Canada. For the five years before the start of the campaign, positive tests for pregnancy made by the Student Health Service were stable at a rate of about 10 per 1,000 female students. The university initiated a series of pregnancy-prevention lectures in the dormitories in 1983. The next year, a specially developed videotape and booklet on prevention of pregnancy were added to the program. The pregnancy rate dropped to about 7 per 1,000 in the first year of the program and then dropped further the next year to 6.5, after which it remained at about the same low level for the three later years reported by Fisher. As a control for a possible secular trend in unwanted pregnancies, Fisher notes that the abortion rate for Canada remained steady during the period. (It was assumed that all pregnancies that resulted in tests by the Student Health Service were unwanted.) In addition, Fisher believes that the pregnancy rate measured by the Student Health Service was a reliable measure of the pregnancy rate because he sees no good reason to expect that the program would cause pregnant women to avoid the health service. The program was purposely designed to be nonjudgmental and to increase the likelihood that pregnant women would go to the Student Health Service. It is likely that the effect of the program was, if anything, larger than the measure indicates.

One reason that this evaluation succeeded where the previous example failed was that an outcome measure was already routinely available to the Student Health Service. Although not all women who suspected they were pregnant would go to the health service for a test, enough of them would go to give a good indication of the pregnancy rate.

Meta-Analysis

What do you do when you are reviewing the literature in some area and are faced with two studies that report opposite results? Perhaps one study finds evidence that a certain psychotherapy technique is useful, and another one finds that it is not. If that's not bad enough, suppose 35 studies find the technique to be useful, and 23 conclude that it isn't. Reviewers sometimes used to rely on the box-score method: Simply count the numbers of positive and negative studies, and declare the winner to be the side with the largest number of studies. But the box-score approach clearly has its limitations. For one thing, all studies are not of equal value. Some studies may have procedural flaws in them; others may have smaller sample sizes, and so on.

In the past, reviewers who wanted to go beyond the simple box-score method would use their judgment when they considered one study better than another, but the criteria they used could not always be stated in a straightforward manner, and the whole process was subject to the reviewer's biases. There was a need for a method of reviewing that would be more up front about how the review would be conducted and what biases would be operating.

These concerns have led to the development of a methodology called **meta-analysis**. The word *meta* implies taking a larger view of a topic—something like backing away for a better perspective. Meta-analysis is actually a group of methods that permit a researcher to combine many studies with a variety of characteristics to reach a unified conclusion. Some of these methods allow a researcher to estimate whether there is a bias toward publication of only those studies with positive results—the so-called file-drawer problem. If researchers have a tendency to publish studies that favor behavioral psychotherapy and put their nonsignificant results into a file drawer, then the literature will be biased in favor of studies supporting behavioral psychotherapy.

Other meta-analytic techniques allow a researcher to give more weight to studies with fewer flaws, larger samples, or other relevant factors. All the meta-analytic methods are somewhat technical, so we discuss just one of them to provide an introduction to the area. Azy Barak and his colleagues (2008) reviewed studies of the efficacy of internet-based psychotherapeutic treatments. As you might imagine, there has been concern as to whether therapy conducted online could be effective at treating patients, particularly when compared to face-to-face therapy. To examine this question, Barak and his colleagues did not simply count which of nearly 9,764 clients found positive benefits from internet-therapy, nor did they count the number of statistically significant results found in the 92 studies reported in the review. Instead, they looked at the size of the effect produced by internet psychotherapy in each study.

The difference between effect size and statistical significance is crucial. It is possible for a study to find a large effect that is not statistically significant because there were too few subjects. Conversely, it is possible to find a trivially small effect that is statistically significant because an enormous number of subjects are studied. (Turn to Chapter 15 if you are not familiar with the statistical concept of power.) Thus, statistical significance has limitations as a criterion in determining whether psychotherapy is effective.

meta-analysis: a set of methods for combining the results of many studies

(continues)

NUTS & BOLTS (continued)

Comparing effect sizes among different experiments requires one to have a common metric, or yardstick, to measure the outcome. The problem is that different experimenters often measure their results on different scales. Suppose some studies compared improvement after psychotherapy on a 10-point scale, whereas others used a 5-point scale. Because the scales differed among experiments, it might seem impossible to have a single measure of effect size. For example, if a study using a 10-point scale found a difference of 3 points between groups, and one using a 5-point scale found a difference of 2 points, you might wonder whether 2 points on the 5-point scale meant more or less than a 3-point difference on a 10-point scale.

However, if we use the variability of the group that did not receive treatment, instead of the arbitrary scale, as the unit of measurement, we can compare different studies on a single scale. Suppose the untreated group in the study with the 5-point scale had a small standard deviation because almost all of that group scored 2, but the untreated group in the experiment with the 10-point scale were spread out on the scale. Dividing the difference between the treated and untreated groups in each study by the standard deviation of the untreated group would give a common metric by which to compare the two experiments. Figure 13.11 shows that almost all of the treated subjects in the experiment with the 5-point scale did better than the untreated subjects, whereas many of the untreated subjects in the other experiment did as well as the treated ones. Therefore, we could conclude that the effect size is larger in the experiment that measured the results on the 5-point scale.

Barak and his colleagues measured the size of the effect of psychotherapy by the standard deviation, or variability, of the results. When they did this, they found that the average client who received internet-based therapy was better off than 53% of those who did not receive therapy. When only the studies that compared internet-based therapies to face-to-face therapies were examined, no differences were seen. Thus, Barak and his colleagues were able to compare many different studies using meta-analysis and conclude that internet-based psychotherapy is effective, despite the bias against internet-based treatments.

Summary

1. The boundaries between true experiments, quasi experiments, and non-experiments are not sharp; the distinctions are based on the relative amount of control that the researcher is able to maintain.
2. Quasi experiments may be performed when a true experiment would be impossible or when the advantages of a quasi experiment outweigh its disadvantages.
3. The most common quasi-experimental situation is to have nonequivalent control groups. Such experiments are sometimes uninterpretable, depending on the pattern of results.
4. Quasi-experimental designs often have less internal validity and greater external validity than true experimental designs.

5. Interrupted time-series designs consider the trend of the data before and after some manipulation in a study with no control group. The ideal situation is to have a stable baseline before the manipulation, followed by an abrupt or gradual change to a new stable level.

6. Repeated-treatment designs improve on the validity of an experiment by presenting the treatment more than once. The ideal result is for each presentation of the treatment to produce a change in the same direction, with a reversal of the effect when the treatment is removed.

7. One prominent area of psychology that uses quasi-experimental methods is developmental, where time is a variable and nonequivalent control groups are used.

8. Cross-sectional designs study individuals of different ages at the same time but have the problem of cohort effects.

9. Longitudinal designs study the same individuals over time but have the problem of secular trends.

10. Cross-sequential designs attempt to get around the problems of longitudinal and cross-sectional designs by combining features of both. The time-lag effect compares subjects who are of a given age at different times.

11. Program evaluation is a set of techniques for evaluating the effectiveness of a social service program.

12. Some sources of resistance to program evaluation are fear that the program will be terminated, fear of losing control of the program, and fear that information will be abused or that wrong measures will be used; belief that evaluation is pointless; and hopes that are too high.

13. In planning an evaluation, the evaluators should identify the stakeholders, arrange preliminary meetings, decide whether an evaluation should be done, examine the literature, determine the methodology, and present a written proposal.

14. Formative evaluations are aimed at improving a program while it is ongoing; summative evaluations evaluate the quality of the program, often after it is completed.

15. Meta-analysis is an approach to evaluating research literature that permits one to combine many different studies to reach a unified conclusion.

Suggestions for Further Reading

Campbell, D. T., & Stanley, J. C. (1963). *Experimental and quasi-experimental designs for research*. Chicago: Rand McNally. This book is the classic reference on quasi experimentation.

Carey, R. G., & Posavac, E. J. (2006). *Program evaluation: Methods and case studies* (7th ed.). Upper Saddle River, NJ: Prentice-Hall. This book contains an accessible discussion of the area.

Cook, T. D., & Campbell, D. T. (1979). *Quasi-experimentation: Design and analysis for field settings*. Chicago: Rand McNally. This book updates the material in Campbell and Stanley (1963).

Cronbach, L. J., Ambron, S. R., Dornbusch, S. M., Hess, R. D., Hornik, R. C., Philips, D. C., Walker, D. F., & Weiner, S. S. (1980). *Toward reform of program evaluation*. San Francisco: Jossey-Bass. This is a classic discussion of the issues.

Shadish, W. R. (1993). *Foundations of program evaluation*. Newbury Park, CA: Sage. Shadish discusses differing approaches of major thinkers in the field of program evaluation.

A CASE IN POINT

Bulimia in College Women

Bulimia is a very common eating disorder in women. It consists of episodes of binge eating alternating with fasting, strict dieting, or purging (by means of vomiting, diuretics, or laxatives). As many as 15% of college women may be seriously affected by bulimia.

You are a researcher who suspects that bulimia is partially controlled by social forces: Because women desire to match cultural norms of thinness, social pressure may influence women to engage in behaviors that they believe may help them achieve lower weight. This suggests to you that you might find evidence of social pressures for bulimia among groups of women.

Participants

There are two large sororities on your campus that are very popular with the same group of women. In talking with members of the sororities, you discover that Alpha seems to have more women who engage in bulimic behavior than Beta. You confirm this by giving a survey to the women in both sororities in the middle of April, before the term ends and the sororities close for the summer. Alpha women score higher on the Binge Eating Scale (BES; Gormally, Black, Daston, & Rardin, 1982).

Materials and Measures

Besides the BES scale, you can administer questionnaires to the women. Possible questions include height and weight (the ratio of weight to height can be considered a measure of deviation from ideal weight), popularity of the other women in the sorority, their perceived deviation from ideal weight, and the Rosenberg Self-Esteem Scale (RSES). You can also physically measure height and weight. You can measure the popularity of each woman in the two sororities.

Considerations

You are concerned that the women who are recruited during the fall rush will be self-selected for bulimia to match the two patterns at the two sororities. You are able to make your various measurements once per term for two more terms. You could make the fall term measurements shortly after fall rush. The spring wave of measurements could be any time from January through April. You are concerned that bulimia may be related to proximity of holidays and special occasions on campus.

Regression to the mean may be a problem because you have chosen your groups based on their differences on the BES, which is one of your possible dependent measures.

Required

Design a study to test your theory. Discuss how you will deal with the various considerations listed here. Specify the variables of the study, and indicate expected data. (*Optional*: Specify the statistical analysis you will use.)

The experiment on which this case is based is referenced in the Instructor's Manual.

Preventing Smoking in Adolescents

Cigarette smoking is a major public health concern because of its well-documented effects on health and because of the large numbers who smoke. It is very difficult for people to quit smoking, and most smokers begin as adolescents. Therefore, there has been considerable interest in preventing young people from beginning to smoke in the first place.

Despite the importance of preventing smoking, programs to educate young people have not been notably successful. You are interested in developing and testing a program that would be successful. Research and common experience both indicate that peer pressure is an important factor in the onset of smoking. You believe that using slightly older students as counselors might be an effective method. In addition, you are aware of a technique called inoculation, in which people are exposed to pressure to conform to some behavior at the same time that they are given a means to counter the pressure. For example, a person may be shown an ad for cigarettes that has the implied message that women who smoke are more liberated. The inoculation technique would

(continued)

teach students to reason that a woman is not really liberated if she is addicted to tobacco. You suspect that the use of peer counselors and the inoculation technique will reduce the rate of smoking onset in seventh grade students.

You have the following resources at your disposal.

Participants

There are three schools whose principals are willing to let you test your program on their students. Central is located in the inner city and has the most problems with drugs and alcohol. Of the parents of students at Central, 50% are smokers. Greenfield is a suburban school. Drugs and alcohol are a problem there, but not as serious as at Central. Only 40% of Greenfield parents smoke. Millbridge is in a factory town that has fewer problems with alcohol and drugs than do the other two schools, but 45% of Millbridge parents are smokers.

Apparatus

Your materials will be primarily printed matter, slides, and videotapes. There is a machine you can purchase that will measure exhaled carbon monoxide, which is present in the breath of smokers and those who breathe automobile exhaust. If you buy this machine, it will use up half your budget, requiring you to test fewer subjects.

Personnel

You have two assistants who can go to the schools to help run the program and analyze the data.

Considerations

You are inclined to combine the inoculation technique with peer counseling because your main concern is to develop a program that works. If you had one group with peer counseling, one with the inoculation procedure, and one with both, however, you could assess the separate effects of the two variables.

You realize that to perform a true experiment you would have to randomize subjects to conditions. This would require, as a practical matter, that some students in any particular school would be in different conditions. You are concerned that students in different groups would talk among themselves and contaminate the effect of the different conditions.

Another possibility would be to use a nonequivalent-control-group design. You could use the three different schools as the groups. You are not sure which schools to use because of the differences among them. You wonder whether the school with the highest or the lowest rate of parental smoking should be the control group.

Required

Design the study. Include your hypothesis, method, and expected results. Justify your decisions, including your reasons for rejecting alternatives. Be sure to describe how you will analyze your data. Provide data sheets with mocked-up data. Make a table or graph of expected results. (*Optional*: What is the appropriate statistical analysis?)

The experiment on which this case study is based is cited in the Instructor's Manual.

Reading Between the Lines

13.1 Ulcers in Executive Monkeys

In a famous study (Brady, Porter, Conrad, & Mason, 1958), pairs of monkeys received electric shocks. One of the monkeys in a pair received a shock when it failed to press a lever at least once every 20 seconds. The other monkey received a shock according to the behavior of the first monkey; its own behavior had nothing to do with the shock it received. The monkey whose behavior determined the shock was called the *executive monkey*. Before the experimenters placed the monkeys in the experiment, they gave them a pretest on their ability to learn the avoidance response. Those monkeys in each pair that learned more quickly were made the executive monkeys, and the ones that learned more slowly became the control monkeys. Brady et al. found that the executive monkeys tended to develop ulcers, whereas the control monkeys did not. Although this experiment became well known, other researchers were unable to replicate it. Can you think of any fault in the procedure?

13.2 Memory for Words

The study of how words are remembered and later recalled is an active research area. One way this question is studied is by using the sentence verification procedure, in which subjects are asked whether statements such as "All robins are birds" are true or false. Variations in the speed of their responses between different pairs of concepts are taken to indicate how the words are related in memory. One theory says that the speed of response depends on how similar the concepts are to each other. Similarity is defined by how many characteristics the two concepts have in common. For example, a robin is a typical bird and so would share many characteristics with the concept bird: has feathers, sings, perches in trees, and eats berries. By contrast, a penguin has fewer of these characteristics, even though it is a bird. Michael McCloskey and Sam Glucksberg (1979) tested this theory, using the sentence verification procedure. Their sentences were of the type "All As are Bs." In some of the sentences, the words shared many characteristics: "All robins are birds" or "All oaks are trees." In other sentences, the concepts shared fewer characteristics: "All penguins are birds" or "All mahoganies are trees." They found that subjects responded more quickly to the sentences containing the highly related concepts, supporting their theory. Can you think of anything else about the words that could explain the differences in reaction times?

Research Methods Laboratory Manual

LAB William Langston (2010) has prepared a laboratory manual that contains many suggestions for research activities that work well with this book and require minimal materials. Many chapters in this book contain a section that refers the reader to appropriate sections of the Langston book.

Exercises

13.1 Classify a Study

This exercise is based on a study by Noll, Zeller, Trickett, and Putnam (2007). The following synopsis is based on the article.

To test the hypothesis that adverse childhood experiences such as sexual abuse may be implicated in the development of obesity, the Body Mass Index (BMI) of 84 female abuse victims and 89 comparison female subjects were tested at six different time points over the course of 19 years.

At initial testing, the ages ranged from 6 to 16 for both groups. Though obesity rates did not differ between groups in childhood or adolescence, by young adulthood, women who had been abused were significantly more likely to be obese than comparison female subjects.

Required:

a. Was this a true experiment, a quasi experiment, or a nonexperiment?

b. What was (were) the independent variable(s)?

c. What was (were) the dependent variable(s)?

d. Describe the design.

13.2 Identify the Design of a Study

Parents from MADD (Mothers Against Drunk Driving) were recruited to take part in a study, along with parents who were not members of the organization. The parents were equally assigned to one of four groups. They read a message about elevating the nonaccompanied driving age from 16 to 18 from either an expert or nonexpert source who supported his position with either strong or weak arguments. Participants then rated how likely they would be to vote for a law mandating the elevated driving age on a Likert scale. Parents from MADD were more likely to vote for the law. Strong arguments were more persuasive than weak arguments. Parents were persuaded by strong arguments when the source was not an expert, but they were equally persuaded by strong and weak arguments when the source was an expert.

a. Was this a true experiment or quasi experiment?

b. What was (were) the independent variable(s) and levels (of each)?

c. What was the design? Was it within or between subjects?

d. What was (were) the dependent variable(s)?

e. Were there any main effects, and if so, what were they? (If none are mentioned explicitly, assume there were none.)

f. Was there an interaction? If so, describe it in words.

g. What statistics would be appropriate (t test, ANOVA, chi-square, can't tell from information given)?

13.3 Data Interpretation

Figure 13.12 shows the average classroom attendance of inmate groups enrolled in adult basic education classes in a certain correctional facility. Attendance is reported for the 18-month period before a *good time* law was passed and the 18-month period after the law was passed. The good-time law allows inmates to earn three days a month off their minimum sentence for attending adult basic education classes.

Required:

a. Is the baseline stable? (*Hint:* Look for seasonal trends.)

b. What is the independent variable?

c. What is the dependent variable?

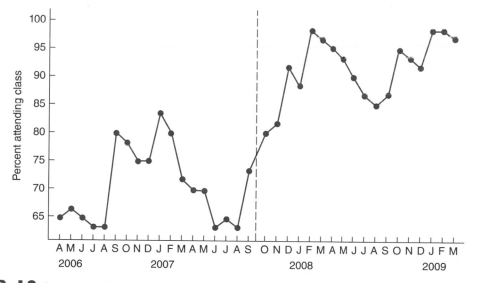

FIGURE **13.12** Percentage of Classroom Attendance for the 18-Month Period Before the Good Time Bill Was Passed and the 18-month Period After the Bill Was Passed

d. What is the effect of the independent variable on the dependent variable?
e. What type of graph is this?
f. Does the *x* axis represent the independent variable? Explain.

13.4 Identify the Design of a Study

Children who were trick-or-treating on Halloween were given an opportunity to steal candy from a bowl left in the entrance to a home. Some children came alone, and others came in groups. The adult at the home randomly asked some of the groups or individuals their names and addresses, and others were not asked. More children in groups stole candy than did children who were alone, and more anonymous children stole more than did the non-anonymous children. The effects of anonymity depended on group membership, being the greatest on children in groups (adapted from Diener, Fraser, Beaman, & Kelem, 1976).

Required:

a. Was this a true experiment, a quasi experiment, a case study, or a survey?
b. What was (were) the independent variable(s)?
c. What was (were) the dependent variable(s)?
d. What was the design of the study?
e. What was (were) the effect(s) of the independent variable(s)?
f. Was there an interaction? If there was, describe it in words.
g. Suggest a variable that could have been confounded with group membership.
h. Which statistic would be appropriate to analyze the data?

CHAPTER **FOURTEEN**

Data Exploration, Part I: Graphic and Descriptive Techniques

PREVIEW

Chapter 14 introduces ways of handling empirical data. First, we discuss data reduction, the process by which raw data are put into a form useful for statistical analysis. Then we discuss the descriptive techniques that are most common in psychology, as well as common types of tables and graphs. This chapter concerns the description of empirical data: the analysis and summarization of data in ways that make it possible to see the patterns that exist in them. This process includes presenting data in tables, graphs, and numerical summaries. Of course, description is only the first stage of the analysis process. The second stage of analysis, inferential statistics, is discussed in Chapter 15.

Preparing Data for Analysis

Beginning researchers are most likely to think about how to get their data ready for statistical analysis after the data have been collected and they are faced with a stack of raw data: the sheets on which they entered the subjects' responses. This can be a daunting prospect. If you do this, you will soon discover your first mistake: You should have decided exactly how you were going to handle your data—how to record them, how to prepare them for analysis, and which statistics to use—before you ever saw your first subject. Do not rely on your memory to remind you of the design, procedure, and intended analysis of the study; instead, record this information in a **lab notebook**. You will be amazed at the details of the study that you were sure you could never forget, but that are lost forever because they are not written down.

lab notebook: notebook for recording information important to a study, such as design, procedure, and the planned analysis

Once you have collected your data, you cannot analyze it right away. Instead, you will need to prepare the data for analysis. We can summarize the components of data handling as follows:

1. Put the data into matrix form in a summary data sheet.
2. Do preliminary statistics and plots.
3. Check for invalid data and make corrections.
4. Check for missing data and replace with missing data code.
5. Check for wild data and remove.
6. Describe data numerically, with descriptive statistics.
7. Describe data graphically.
8. Perform inferential statistics.

The first step in this process of going from raw data to statistical analysis is called **data reduction**. It involves a number of steps.

data reduction: the process of transcribing data from individual data sheets to a summary form

Data Reduction

Let's assume that you have designed your study, including your hypotheses and all the procedural steps, and the planned statistical analysis. Let's also assume that you have actually collected your data. A number of practical matters must be managed in order to go from the subjects' responses to the statistical analysis. Because the actual details of data reduction differ from one kind of study to another, we give some general principles here and one example.

The initial recording of the data is generally done on sheets (electronic or hard copy) that record the responses of a single participant. The data sheet should have spaces to record the date, time, researcher's name, condition (where appropriate, and nearly always in code), and any other necessary identifying information. (Most often, you do not want to record a participant's name on the sheet. If you need this information, you should identify the person by number and keep the person code in a separate place.)

If the data are collected as a questionnaire or in some other format that the person (rather than the researcher) fills out, it may be desirable to place a column on the right-hand side of the data sheet into which the data can be transferred as a first step in data reduction. (The Campus Security Survey in Chapter 9, pages 240–242, is an example of such a data sheet.) Each space in this column should be numbered to correspond to the column in which the data will be recorded in a summary sheet or electronic spreadsheet.

After readying the data, the next step is to transcribe it into the summary data sheet or electronic spreadsheet. This summary sheet should be, when possible, a single sheet that contains all the data from the study. Usually, the summary data sheet contains all the data in a matrix format. In other words, the data are placed into a tabular arrangement in which the rows indicate subjects and the columns indicate independent variables.

As an example, suppose that Professor Carlton teaches two classes, one that meets at 8 a.m. and one that meets at 11 a.m. He has given two 20-point tests in his classes so far, and is somewhat worried that the students in the 8 a.m. class aren't scoring as well as those in the 11 a.m. class. He decides to look at each class as a group, and the results from each of his tests are shown in Table 14.1.

For this example, it is most convenient to have a given row of the matrix refer to the data from one particular person, and each column refer to one variable. The first column (not counting the row numbers) is simply the identification number of the person. Thus, by looking in column 1, we see that the first two rows all contain information about person number 1. Columns 2 and 3 contain information about the independent variables. A number 1 in

TABLE **14.1**

Data from Dr. Carlton's First Two Tests

© Cengage Learning

Row	ID	8 a.m. Class = 1 11 a.m. Class = 2	Test	Test Score
1	1	1	1	10
2	1	1	2	11
3	2	1	1	15
4	2	1	2	1
5	3	1	1	14
6	3	1	2	19
7	4	1	1	13
8	4	1	2	18
9	5	1	1	10
10	5	1	2	12
11	6	2	1	17
12	6	2	2	13
13	7	2	1	18
14	7	2	2	19
15	8	2	1	17
16	8	2	0	18
17	9	2	1	19
18	9	2	2	18
19	10	2	1	18
20	10	2	2	20

column 2 indicates the 8 a.m. class; a number 2 indicates the 11 a.m. class. The number in column 3 indicates the test number, which is either the first or second test.

Column 4 gives the number of correct items (out of 20) on the test. Generally, all the data for a given dependent variable will appear in only one column (although that column may contain data from more than one variable). Thus, data from both classes appear in column 4. You must look at column 2 to see whether the test score listed in column 4 is from the 8 a.m. or 11 a.m. class.

The rows and columns of the matrix permit us to locate any particular test score. Suppose we want to find out the value of the second test for the third person in the 8 a.m. class. Column 1 tells us that rows 5 to 6 contain information about the third subject. Column 2 allows us to verify that she is in the 8 a.m. class. Then column 3 tells us that row 6 contains the data 19 for the second test for person 3.

In summary, even though the details of data reduction differ a good deal from one type of study to another, the general idea is to put the data into matrix form, and to identify clearly the variables that will be important for analysis.

The Coding Guide

coding guide: a record that specifies the variables of a study, the columns they occupy in the data file, and their possible values

The data matrix in Table 14.1 shows the logical arrangement of the rows and columns. Such a table is useful for hand analysis of data or for use by many of the popular statistics packages. Some computer statistics packages, however, require us to specify the arrangement of data more completely. For example, some of the data, such as test number and class meeting time, require only one digit to code their values. Other data, such as test score, require either one or two digits. For this and other reasons, it is common to devise a coding guide that specifies for each variable the number of digits, which columns in the data file they occupy, and the possible values of the variable. Further, because statistics must be done on numbers, it is necessary for nominal scale data to state which label goes with which number. The variable of class meeting time is a nominal scale variable, because the values of 1 and 2 are labels and carry no other quantitative information by themselves. We have chosen to indicate the 8 a.m. class by a 1 and the 11 a.m. class by a 2, but any other two numbers would do equally well for the purposes of data analysis. Thus, it is necessary to have a coding guide so that you will remember the arbitrary numbers that you have assigned to each label for your code at some later time. You should record your coding guide in your lab notebook, in a comment page of your data spreadsheet, and any place else that you think you may look for it in the future, as deciphering your code is critical for interpreting the results of your study.

Table 14.2 shows the coding guide for the data in Table 14.1. Table 14.2 also shows the format in which the data in Table 14.1 will appear in a data file. Note that the column number and the row number are not part of the file itself. The computer keeps track of columns and rows automatically.

TABLE **14.2**

Coding Guide for Data in Table 14.1

© Cengage Learning

Column	Variable	Values
1–2	Participant number (ID)	0–99
3	Class meeting time	1 = 8 a.m.
		2 = 11 a.m.
4	Test number	1–2
5–8	Test score	0–20

Preliminary Descriptive Statistics

inferential statistics: statistics that help us to draw conclusions about populations

descriptive statistics: statistics that summarize a set of data

Once the data have been transcribed from the raw data sheets to the summary data sheets in matrix form, we can begin to analyze them. We use descriptive statistics to summarize what was found in a set of empirical data. If we try to draw a conclusion from the data set, we need to use inferential statistics, which are discussed in Chapter 15.

After you have collected the data and performed some level of data reduction, you might be tempted to jump right into the inferential statistics that you planned to do, but you should wait. First, we should take a preliminary look at the data. Descriptive statistics give an idea of what the typical score is, how much the scores differ from each other, and can also provide a hint as to errors in the data. The most common descriptive statistics are those that concern the average (measures of central tendency) and the variability of a set of data (measures of variability).

Measures of Central Tendency

measures of central tendency: a measure of the average score in a distribution, such as the mean, median, or mode

measures of variability: a measure of the degree of difference between scores in a distribution

A measure of central tendency is a single number that is used to represent the average score in the distribution. Three common measures of central tendency are the mode, the median, and the mean. All three are actually kinds of averages although people commonly use the term *average* to refer to the mean, one of the kinds of averages. Some of the meanings commonly associated with the term *average* are these: a number that is typical of all the scores, a number that is in the middle of the scores, and a number that represents all scores. Although all three meanings are true of each measure of central tendency, each measure best captures one of them, as we see in the following sections.

Mode

mode: the most common score in a frequency distribution

The mode is the easiest measure of central tendency to define. It is the most common score in a frequency distribution. The mode has the advantage of representing the most typical score. For example, in the data shown in Table 14.1, the most frequent score on the tests for the 8 a.m. class is 10, while mode for the 11 a.m. class is 18.

In a large distribution, the mode will be fairly stable, but in a small data set, such as the one shown in Table 14.1, the mode can bounce around considerably. For example, notice that if participant one had produced a score of 19 instead of a 10 on the first test, the mode would have changed to 19 for the 8 a.m. class. The mode, therefore, is not very useful for small data sets. In large data sets, however, the mode is a good representation of the typical case. Another disadvantage of the mode is that it does not enter into any further statistical calculations. It is sort of a statistical orphan.

Median

median: the middlemost score in a distribution

The **median** is the middlemost score in a distribution. Computing the median requires you to rank-order the scores that you have collected from highest to lowest and find the middle one. The following equation tells you which score is the middle one:

$$\text{middle score} = (\text{number of scores} + 1)/2$$

For example, if there are nine scores, the middle score is:

$$(9 + 1)/2 = 5\text{th score}$$

If there is an even number of scores, then there are two middle scores. In that case, the median is halfway between the two middle scores. For example, if there are 10 scores, the middle one is:

$$(10 + 1)/2 = 5.5$$

You average the fifth and sixth scores to obtain the median.

For example, go back to Table 14.1 and find the median for each of Dr. Carlton's classes. We first count the number of scores for each type of task, and find that there are 10 scores for each class. We then put the scores for each class in order, from highest to lowest. From the last equation we know that the median is halfway between the fifth and sixth scores. For the 8 a.m. class, we find that the fifth score is 12 and the sixth score is 13, so the median is the average of these two, or 12.5. The fifth score for the 11 a.m. class is 18, and the sixth score is 18, so the median score is also 18.

The median has the advantage that half the scores in the distribution fall above it, and half fall below it. Thus, it is the middlemost score. It is not affected by how far other scores are from the median, only by how many scores fall above or below. Disadvantages of the median are that it requires ranking all the scores and counting to find the middle. This can be quite a chore in a large data set. Another disadvantage of the median is that its use in further statistical computations is somewhat limited, as we will see shortly.

Mean

mean: the common average

The **mean** is the ordinary average that you learned to compute in grade school. As you may recall, the mean is computed by adding all the scores and dividing by the number of scores:

$$\text{mean} = \Sigma X / N$$

or

$$\text{mean} = \text{sum of scores}/\text{number of scores}$$

For our example data from Table 14.1, the mean of the 10 test scores in Dr. Carlton's 8 a.m. class would be 12.3, while the mean of the 11 a.m. class would be 17.7. The main advantage of the mean is that it uses all the information in the distribution. In other words, the mean is influenced by the value of every score in the distribution. (Note that all the scores are summed and therefore enter into the value of the mean.) Thus, of the three measures of central tendency, the mean best captures the idea of the average as the quantity that represents all the scores in the distribution. The mode, by contrast, is not influenced at all by the other scores in the distribution; the median is influenced only by how many scores fall above and below it. A second advantage is that the mean is the basis of the most common and most powerful of the further statistical computations that we will discuss later.

A third advantage of the mean is that means of subgroups may be combined to obtain the mean of the entire group.[1] So, if we were interested in the mean of all the scores in Table 14.1, we could either average the means of the subgroups (8 a.m. class = 12.3; 11 a.m. class = 17.7) or simply average all 20 scores. Both techniques would produce the same answer of 15. There is no way that medians or modes of subgroups can be combined to get the median of the entire group.

The mean does have disadvantages, however. Precisely because it uses every score in the distribution, it is sensitive to the value of extreme scores, as we will see shortly.

Measures of Variability

The second type of descriptive statistic is a measure of the variability of the data. Besides knowing the typical score, we generally want to know how much the data vary, or differ from each other. To illustrate the reason that this is important, imagine that you cannot swim, and you want to wade across a river that is two feet deep on the average. It makes a great deal of difference to you whether it is two feet deep all the way across, or whether it is 10 feet deep in places. Three general types of measures of variability are those based on the range, those based on percentiles, and those based on the mean.

Range

range: difference between the highest and lowest scores in a distribution

The **range** is the simplest measure of variability: It is simply the difference between the highest and lowest score in a distribution. In Table 14.1, the range of test scores for the 8 a.m. class was $19 - 1 = 18$. The range for the

---

[1] Provided each subgroup has the same number of cases, or the subgroup means are weighted by the number of cases.

$$\text{Grand mean} = \frac{(\text{mean}_1)N_1 + (\text{mean}_2)N_2}{N_1 + N_2}$$

For example, if Group 1 has a mean of 16 and 4 cases, and Group 2 has a mean of 6 and 6 cases, the mean of all cases will be 10:

$$\frac{(16 \times 4) + (6 \times 6)}{10} = 10$$

11 a.m. class is $20 - 13 = 7$. If both classes were considered, though, the range would become $20 - 1 = 19$. Thus, although it is easy to compute, the range depends completely on the two extreme scores. For this reason it is highly unstable, as we can see. The mode and range can be thought of together, then, as descriptive statistics that depend completely on a few individual scores rather than on the entire distribution of scores.

Percentile-Based Measures

percentile: a score below which a certain percentage of the cases in a distribution fall; a percentile is a score, not a percentage

Although we defined the median as the middle score, we could have also defined it as the 50th percentile. A percentile is a score in a distribution below which a certain percentage of the cases fall. The 50th percentile is the score below which 50% of the cases fall. That score is by definition the middle score in the distribution, or the median.

We can use any arbitrary set of percentiles to describe the variability of scores around the median, but the interquartile range is generally used. This statistic is defined as the 75th percentile minus the 25th percentile. The 25th percentile is called the first quartile (Q_1), the 50th percentile is called the second quartile (Q_2), and so on.

interquartile range: measure of variability defined as the difference between the 75th percentile and the 25th percentile; it is a difference in scores, not percentages

$$\text{interquartile range} = \text{75th percentile} - \text{25th percentile}$$
$$= Q_3 - Q_1$$

The interquartile range includes half the cases in a distribution. It has the advantage over the range that it is not affected by outliers.

semi-interquartile range: measure of variability defined as half the interquartile range

A closely related measure of variability is the semi-interquartile range, which is simply half the interquartile range:

$$\text{semi-interquartile range} = (Q_3 - Q_1)/2$$

The advantage of percentile-based measures of variability is that they better represent skewed distributions than do other measures. However, they are more cumbersome to compute (as we will discuss later) and they do not enter into further statistical calculations.

Variance and Standard Deviation

variance: the average of the squared deviations from the mean

standard deviation: the square root of the variance; a measure of variability in the same units as the scores being described

The most commonly used measures of variability are the variance and the standard deviation. These measures are based on the mean. The variance, σ^2, is defined as the average of the squared deviations from the mean.

$$\sigma^2 = \Sigma(X - \bar{X})^2/N$$

Table 14.3 shows how one would compute the variance for the data[2] from the 8 a.m. class that is presented in Table 14.1. The first column contains the

---

[2] For simplicity's sake, we have used the formula to calculate the variance of a population with this data, despite the fact that the data actually represents a sample. The formula to calculate variance for a sample would be

$$\sigma^2 = \frac{1}{N-1}\sum_{i=1}^{N}(x_i - \bar{x})^2 = \frac{N}{N-1}\left(\frac{1}{N}\left(\sum_{i=1}^{N}x_i^2\right) - \bar{x}^2\right)$$

TABLE **14.3**
Variance Calculation

© Cengage Learning

X	$(X-\bar{X})$	$(X-\bar{X})^2$	X^2
10	−2.3	5.29	100
11	−1.3	1.69	121
15	2.7	7.29	225
1	−11.3	127.69	1
14	1.7	2.89	196
19	6.7	44.89	361
13	0.7	0.49	169
18	5.7	32.49	324
10	−2.3	5.29	100
12	−0.3	0.09	144
$\Sigma X = 123$	$\Sigma(X - \bar{X}) = 0$	sum of squares $= 228.1$	$\Sigma X^2 = 1741$

$(\Sigma X)^2 = 15{,}129$

$$X = \frac{123}{10}$$

$$\sigma^2 = \frac{\Sigma X^2 - \frac{(\Sigma X)^2}{N}}{N}$$

$$\sigma^2 = \frac{1741 - \frac{15129}{10}}{10}$$

$$\sigma^2 = \frac{228.1}{10}$$

$$\sigma^2 = 22.81$$

$$\sigma = 4.78$$

10 individual scores. Below that column we see that the sum of all the scores is 150 and the mean is 2. The second column indicates how much each score deviates from the mean. Notice that the sum of these deviations is zero, as required by the definition of the mean. This tells you why we do not use the average deviation from the mean as a measure of variability: If the sum of the deviations from the mean is zero, the average deviation must also be zero.

The third column indicates the square of the deviation of each score from the mean. The square of a negative number is a positive number, so the sum

sum of squares: the sum of the squared deviations from the mean

of the squared deviations from the mean is greater than zero, and thus can be used as a measure of variability. The sum of the squared deviations from the mean is often called the **sum of squares**, and it is different from the sum of the squared scores. The sum of squares is used to compute not only the variance but many other statistics as well.

The formula we have given for the variance is simple to define and is useful for conveying the idea of what the variance is, but it is somewhat cumbersome to compute because it requires one first to find the mean, then to subtract each score from the mean, and finally to square the deviation. Another formula, known as the *computational formula*, is more complicated looking but actually easier to use:

$$\sigma^2 = \frac{\Sigma X^2 - (\Sigma X)^2 / N}{N}$$

The computational formula requires each score to be squared and then summed, as in the fourth column of Table 14.3. The only other quantities required to compute the variance are the square of the sum of all the scores, and the number of scores.

The variance is useful mainly because it enters into other statistical calculations, such as the analysis of variance (ANOVA; see Chapter 15). It has the disadvantage that it is not scaled in the same units as the original scores because it is expressed in terms of squared deviations from the mean. So the variance is analogous to a square foot, which cannot be used as a measure of distance. Fortunately, it is a simple matter to convert the variance into a measure of distance by taking the square root of the variance, which would be 4.78 in the example listed in Table 14.3. The square root of the variance is known as the **standard deviation**.

The standard deviation (*SD*, or σ) has the advantage, as already mentioned, that it is related to other commonly used statistical procedures. The *SD* is widely used for this reason alone. Beyond that, the *SD* has the same advantages and disadvantages as the mean, on which it is based: *SD* represents all scores, but it is also affected by outliers.

Choice of Measure of Variability

The range is not very useful as a measure of variability because it depends completely on the two extreme scores. The interquartile range and the semi-interquartile range are useful in describing data when the median has been used as the measure of central tendency and when the data are skewed. The variance and standard deviation are the most widely used measures because they relate to the mean and other common statistics.

Tables and Graphs _____

table: a display of data in a matrix format

One thing that psychology students quickly discover is that psychologists are constantly making tables and drawing graphs. A **table** is a display of data in

TABLE **14.4**

Distribution of Test Scores

© Cengage Learning

Score	Upper Real Limit	Tally	Frequency	Cumulative Frequency	Percentage	Cumulative Percentage
20	20.5	I	1	20	5	100
19	19.5	III	3	19	15	95
18	18.5	IIIII	5	16	25	80
17	17.5	II	2	11	10	55
16	16.5		0	9	0	45
15	15.5	I	1	9	5	45
14	14.5	I	1	8	5	40
13	13.5	II	2	7	10	35
12	12.5	I	1	5	5	25
11	11.5	I	1	4	5	20
10	10.5	II	2	3	10	15
9	9.5		0	1	0	5
8	8.5		0	1	0	5
7	7.5		0	1	0	5
6	6.5		0	1	0	5
5	5.5		0	1	0	5
4	4.5		0	1	0	5
3	3.5		0	1	0	5
2	2.5		0	1	0	5
1	1.5	I	1	1	5	5
0	0.5		0	0	0	0

$N = 20$

$\Sigma = 300$

$\overline{X} = 15$

Median $= 17$

Mode $= 18$

and displayed in a clear format. We will be looking at this table in some detail later, but for now we move on to a graphical display of the same data.

Frequency Distributions

Next, Professor Carlton decides to make a graphical representation of his data. The particular kind of graph that Professor Carlton finds useful to

frequency distribution: a graph that shows the number of scores that fall into specific bins, or divisions of the variable

describe his class's performance on the test is a **frequency distribution**. This is a graph that shows how many scores fall into particular bins, or divisions of the variable. The bins used here are the number of items correct on the test.

Figure 14.2 shows the same basic information about the dependent variable as the table but in a graphical format. The *x*-axis shows the various possible scores, and the *y*-axis shows the frequency of each score. Each bar, then, represents the frequency of a given score. Some scores did not occur on any of the tests (e.g., 6 and 9) and thus are represented on the histogram by a zero frequency.

Note that the bar that indicates a given score is centered on that score: The bar goes from half a unit below the score to half a unit above the score, indicating the real limits of the score. Thus, for example, the bar that indicates a score of 15 extends from 14.5 to 15.5. Also note that the bar touches the bars representing the scores on either side, rather than being separated by a space. This use of contiguous bars represents the idea that the underlying variable we are measuring is continuous, rather than discrete. Although a student can answer only whole items, we believe that knowledge of the subject is continuous.

Both the table and the graph allow us to begin to see a number of characteristics of the data: the highest and lowest scores, the most common score, the shape of the distribution, and so on. A frequency distribution drawn with bars indicating the frequency at each particular score, like that shown in Figure 14.2, is called a **histogram**. A histogram makes it easy to find the mode, because it literally sticks out in a frequency distribution. We can see from data shown in Figure 14.2 that the mode is 18, having been earned by five students.

histogram: a frequency distribution in which the frequencies are represented by contiguous bars

As an alternative to the histogram, we could have used a dot to represent the frequency at each score and connected these points with straight

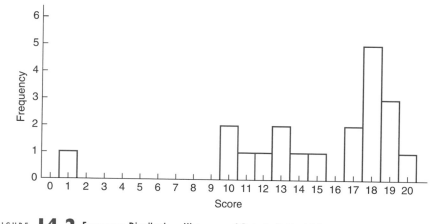

FIGURE **14.2** Frequency Distribution: Histogram of Data in Table 14.4

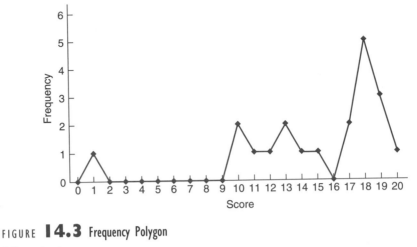

FIGURE **14.3** Frequency Polygon

© Cengage Learning

lines, as shown in Figure 14.3. This form of presentation is called a frequency polygon.

frequency polygon: a frequency distribution in which the frequencies are connected by straight lines

Notice that a frequency distribution is an exception to the usual type of graph in that the *y*-axis and *x*-axis do not represent an independent and dependent variable, respectively. The *x*-axis, or horizontal axis, of a frequency distribution represents values of a dependent variable, such as scores on a test. The *y*-axis, or vertical axis, represents frequencies, such as the number of individuals who obtain various scores on the dependent variable.

Although both histograms and frequency polygons show the same information, and both are correct, generally a histogram is more informative when there are relatively few categories, as in Professor Carlton's test scores. When there are a great many categories, the data usually begin to approximate a smooth curve, and then the frequency polygon is clearer.

normal curve: a bell-shaped curve described by a certain mathematical function

We are often interested in the shape of a frequency distribution. Many distributions are bell-shaped; that is, they are symmetrical, with most cases falling in the middle and fewer cases at either end (the tails). One particular bell-shaped curve is called the normal curve (see Figure 14.4a). This is a certain mathematical function that happens to describe many frequency distributions that occur in nature. The **normal curve** enters into a number of theoretical and practical statistical considerations.

skewed: a distribution that is not symmetrical

If a frequency distribution is not symmetrical and has a longer tail on one end or the other, we say that it is skewed. When the tail is to the low end of the distribution, it is said to be negatively skewed (Figure 14.4b); when the tail is to the high end, it is positively skewed (Figure 14.4c). If we examine the shape of the distribution of Dr. Carlton's test scores across both classes that is shown in Figure 14.3, it seems to be somewhat negatively skewed.

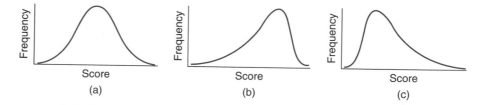

FIGURE **14.4** Normal and Skewed Curves: (a) Normal Distribution; (b) Negatively Skewed Distribution; (c) Positively Skewed Distribution

© Cengage Learning

Behavior of the Mean, Median, and Mode with Various Shaped Distributions

When data are distributed symmetrically, the three measures of central tendency will be the same. When the data are skewed, however, they will be differentially affected. Refer back to Professor Carlton's test, as shown in Figure 14.3. As is common with tests in college courses, the data are skewed to the left. Most students tend to do quite well, but a few fall at the low end of the scale. The mode is 18, the median is 17, and the mean is 15. This is what would be expected with a distribution skewed to the left: mode > median > mean. (Skewness to the right would produce the opposite order.)

The mode is not affected at all by the skewness of the data because, as we have seen, it is not affected by any other scores. The median is affected by the number of scores above and below it, so the skewness will pull it down somewhat. The mean, however, is lowest because it is affected by the distance of the low scores from the middle, as well as by the number of scores.

The effect of skewness on the various measures of central tendency can be seen by thinking about the addition of a couple of outliers to the data presented in Table 14.4. Suppose that two other students took the test late and both got a very low score of 4. The mode is not changed by the addition of the two scores of 4. The median score, however, has gone from 17 to 16, and the mean has gone from 15 to 14. These changes illustrate the differential effects of skew on the three measures of central tendency.

Professor Carlton will probably take the mode into account when assigning grades. He might decide to make the A cutoff at 19 because 18 was the most common score, and a lower cutoff would mean that an A would be the grade for the most common score. He will probably also take the median into account when trying to decide what he should consider the middle of the C range. Because of the skew of the data and the outlier, he may decide that the median is the better choice than the mean for the center of the distribution. (Then again, Professor Carlton may not grade on the curve and may pay no attention to these considerations! We are using this distribution simply to illustrate the behavior of kinds of averages, not professors.)

cumulative frequency distribution: a frequency distribution that shows the number of scores that fall at or below a certain score

Cumulative Frequency Distributions

A frequency distribution indicates the number of cases at each score. A related distribution is the cumulative frequency distribution (see Figure 14.5).

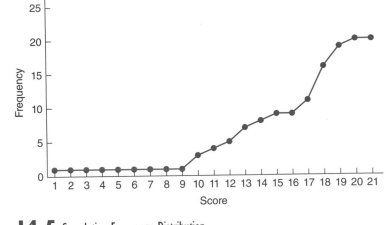

FIGURE **14.5** Cumulative Frequency Distribution

This distribution shows the number of scores that fall at or below a given score and can be seen in the fifth column of a frequency table (like Table 14.4). So, if Professor Carlton was concerned about the number of students who might have scored lower than 15 on the test, the cumulative frequency distribution would be an effective way to answer that question. Frequency polygons are generally used to indicate cumulative frequency graphically, as in Figure 14.5, although histograms can be used.

Several points should be noted about the cumulative frequency distribution. First, note that the score is represented by its upper real limit, not the midpoint of the interval. For example, the line goes from a frequency of 1 at 9.5 to 3 at 10.5. The reason is that the upper real limit is the only point in the interval that is certain to include all scores that fall in or below the entire interval.

The second point to note is that a graph of a cumulative frequency distribution always increases monotonically. That is, the graph either increases or stays horizontal as it goes from left to right; it never decreases. This follows from the definition of cumulative frequency: The number at or below a certain score can never be less than the number at or below a lower score. For example, if there are nine cases at or below a score of 15 in Dr. Carlton's data, there must be at least nine at or below 16.

Third, the shape of the cumulative frequency curve is generally sigmoidal, or S-shaped. The curve is horizontal at either end, and is steepest somewhere in the middle. If the distribution is skewed, as this one is, the steepest part of the curve will be toward the lower or higher end, because that is where most of the cases fall. Figure 14.6 shows a cumulative frequency distribution that represents a normal curve, a curve that is positively skewed, and one that is negatively skewed. Establishing that a distribution is skewed gives valuable information; for example, in Dr. Carlton's case, his data is somewhat negatively skewed, suggesting that perhaps his tests may have been a little too easy for his students.

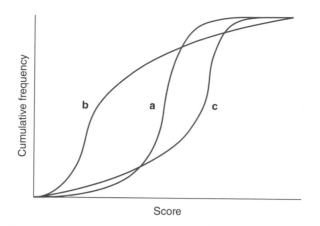

FIGURE **14.6** Cumulative Frequency Distributions: (a) Normal; (b) Positively Skewed; (c) Negatively Skewed

© Cengage Learning

Percentiles

By using a frequency table, you can find the percentiles which are indicators of variability. Look again at Table 14.4. Column 5 of the table gives the cumulative frequency, or the number of cases that fall at or below a given score. Column 7 converts these cumulative frequencies into cumulative percentages: the percentage of cases that fall at or below a given score. Looking at column 7, we find that 80% of the cases fall at or below a score of 18.5, and 55% fall at or below a score of 17.5. Therefore, the 75th percentile must fall somewhere in the interval of 17.5 to 18.5; let's call it 18 for simplicity.[3] Likewise, the 25th percentile is easily read from the Table as 12.5. Finding the 25th percentile in this example shows the importance of the concept of real limits. If you looked only at the midpoint of the interval—that is, the score—you might think that the 50th percentile should be 12 because 50% fall at or below a score of 12. Note, however, that 50% of the scores fall at 13 or higher. So, the median has to be between 12 and 13. Thus, the interquartile range is $18 - 12.5 = 5.5$.

Now we need to find the 50th percentile. Looking at column 7, we find that 55% of the cases fall at or below a score of 17.5, while 45% of the cases fall at or below a score of 16.5. The 50th percentile, or the median, must fall between those two points, at 17.

---

[3] Although we have used the middle of the interval that contains the particular score to represent a percentile, it is possible to use linear interpolation to find the exact location within the interval that represents a particular percentile. For example, the 75th percentile falls in the interval of 17.5 to 18.5. From the graph we can see that the 75th percentile is actually in the lower part of the interval and could estimate the point graphically. Alternatively, we could set up an algebraic equation by which we could calculate that the 75th percentile is exactly 18.30.

Tables and Graphs that Show the Relationship Between Two Variables

Frequency distributions show only one variable—the dependent variable—and a frequency. Other tables and graphs show the relationship between two variables. Some of these present individual data and others present group data.

Scattergrams

scattergram: a graph showing the responses of a number of individuals on two variables; visual display of correlational data

A scattergram is a graph that shows the relationship between two variables for a number of individual cases. Although the x-axis of a graph often represents an independent variable while the y-axis represents the dependent variable, scattergrams are commonly used to illustrate correlational data that illustrate relationships between two variables of interest. If we have measured only two variables and then make a scattergram, it makes no difference which variable is plotted on the x-axis and which on the y-axis. Sometimes both the x-axis and y-axis may be independent variables, or both may be dependent variables. Suppose you had a scattergram showing the relationship between the stickiness of the blacktop on the road in front of a hospital and the number of babies that die in the hospital on various days. Suppose also that the pattern of data points indicated a positive correlation, so it showed that more babies died on days when the blacktop was stickier. You might wonder whether sticky blacktop killed the babies, or whether all of the ambulances rushing to the hospital made the blacktop sticky. You should note that we often do not know whether the variables of interest in a scattergram are independent or are dependent unless we have actually manipulated one of the variables. In this instance, hot weather makes blacktop sticky and also puts stress on babies. Thus, both variables on your scattergram would be dependent variables.

Figure 14.7 shows the relationship between the grades that students in Professor Carlton's class earned on the first test as compared to the second test. The x-axis indicates the grades on the first test, and the y-axis indicates the grade on the second test. Each symbol on the scattergram represents one individual student. By dropping a line perpendicular to the x-axis from a given point, we can read the score that an individual earned on the second test. By dropping a line perpendicular to the y-axis, we can read that same individual's grade on the first test. We can see, for example, that one individual scored a 10 on the first test, and an 11 on the second test. It is important to note that the scattergram shows the scores on two variables for each individual. By looking at the pattern of the individual data points, we can get an idea that there is some relationship between scores on the first test and scores on the second test. We can determine the degree of the relationship and what the function is that relates the two variables by computing the correlation coefficient. We may also be able to predict one of the two variables from the other through the use of **regression**.

correlation coefficient: statistic indicating the strength of the relationship between two variables

Correlation and Regression

We said in Chapter 1 that one of the fundamental tasks of science is to establish that two variables are associated; for example, we may want to determine whether grades on one test are related to grades on another test. Statisticians have developed techniques to measure the strength of a relationship between variables.

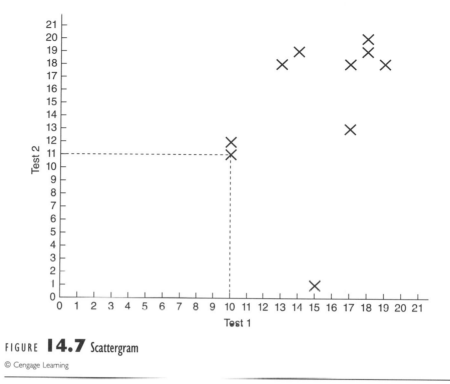

Correlation

correlation: the strength
of the relationship
between two variables

The most commonly used measure of relationship between variables is the Pearson correlation coefficient, usually referred to simply as the **correlation,** or r. The correlation is expressed as a number that can take any value between $+1.0$ and -1.0. Figure 14.8 shows five scattergrams, or scatterplots, depicting different sorts of correlations between two variables, x and y.

In Figure 14.8(a), there is a perfect correlation between x and y. The value of r is $+1.00$. Variable y increases with increasing values of x, and for any given value of x, there is only one value of y. In other words, there is a perfect straight-line relationship between x and y. This is an example of a linear function. An example of a correlation of 1.00 between two variables would be the relationship between weight in pounds and weight in kilograms. If you know someone's weight in pounds, you can predict perfectly his weight in kilograms because one is a simple linear transformation of the other.

Figure 14.8(b) shows another perfect correlation. There is a straight-line relationship between x and y, but this time high values of x are associated with low values of y. The correlation here is -1.00. Examples of perfect negative correlations are not common, but a trivial example would be the height of two ends of a seesaw.

Figure 14.8(c) shows a more usual situation in which there is a correlation between x and y, but the correlation is not perfect. High values of x tend to be associated with high values of y, but the data are scattered instead of falling exactly on a straight line. The correlation in this panel is about 0.5.

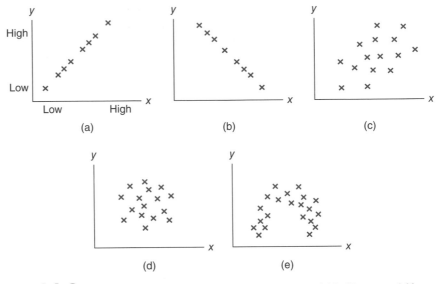

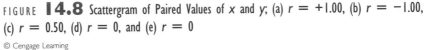

FIGURE **14.8** Scattergram of Paired Values of x and y; (a) $r = +1.00$, (b) $r = -1.00$, (c) $r = 0.50$, (d) $r = 0$, and (e) $r = 0$

There are many examples of such a correlation: height and weight of people, grades and time spent studying, education and income, and so forth.

Figure 14.8(d) shows a situation in which there is no correlation between x and y. A value of x can be associated with any value of y, and vice versa. The correlation between the two variables is 0.00. An example of a zero correlation is eye color and income. People with each eye color are equally likely to be rich, poor, or in between.

It is common to describe various correlation coefficients by adjectives to indicate the strength of the relationship they represent. Correlations less than 0.2 are considered weak; 0.2 to 0.4, moderately weak; 0.4 to 0.6, moderate; 0.6 to 0.8, moderately strong; and 0.8 to 1.0, strong.

It is important to note that the Pearson correlation coefficient is a measure of a linear (straight-line) function. It is entirely possible that there may be a close relation between two variables but the relation does not fit a straight line. If the data actually fit a curved line very closely, a straight line cannot make a good fit. As you can see, the data in Figure 14.8(e) fit a curvilinear function closely. The correlation here is 0.00 because both low and high values of x are associated with the same values of y. Thus, if the data actually fit a curvilinear function, the correlation coefficient, r, will underestimate the amount of the relationship between the variables. There are other measures of correlation appropriate for curvilinear data.

Regression

An important property of the correlation coefficient is that it measures how well you can predict the value of one variable when you know the value of

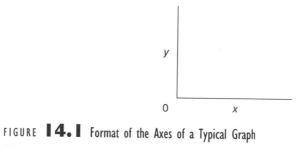

FIGURE **14.1** Format of the Axes of a Typical Graph
© Cengage Learning

graph: a representation of data by spatial relationships in a diagram

numerical form in the rows and columns of a matrix, and you have already seen several examples of them in this chapter. A **graph** is a representation of data by spatial relationships in a diagram. Graphs and tables help us summarize data and understand the relationships between variables. The old saying that a picture is worth a thousand words often is literally true of graphs and tables. So you can see why it is imperative to be able to read and understand tables and graphs.

Most graphs used in psychology have two axes plotted at right angles to one another. Figure 14.1 is an example of a basic graph. The horizontal axis is called the *x*-axis. The vertical axis is the *y*-axis. Typically, the *x*-axis represents the value of the independent variable, whereas the *y*-axis shows the value of the dependent variable. Many other possibilities exist, as we will see. A graph may have two independent variables or no independent variable. It is necessary to pay particular attention to what the axes of a graph represent.

Tables and Graphs of Frequency Data of One Variable

Frequency Tables

Before he goes any further, Professor Carlton decides to arrange the data from both of his classes in a frequency table (see Table 14.4) so that he can see how many people earned each test score. In this type of table, the rows indicate possible scores on the test. The columns represent particular information about those possible scores.

The first column of the table is a list of all the possible scores from highest to lowest. The second column shows the upper real limits of the scores. (Remember them from Chapter 5?) The third column is a tally of the scores that were obtained by the students. Each score is noted by a slash. The fourth column is simply a numerical representation of the information in the third column: the number of students who obtained a given score. We will discuss other columns of this table later.

Each row gives information about a particular score. Looking across the row that indicates a score of 15, for example, we can see how many students received a score of 15. Tables enable a considerable amount of information to be organized

the other. When the correlation is 1.00, prediction is perfect: If you know the temperature outside in degrees Celsius, you can predict the temperature in degrees Fahrenheit perfectly. When the correlation is 0.00, prediction is impossible: If you know a person's eye color, your prediction of her income will be no better than if you did not have that information.

regression: predicting the value of one variable from another based on their correlation

Regression is the technical term for the process of predicting the value of one variable from another. When we predict y from x, we use the familiar equation for a straight line:

$$y' = mx + b$$

The y has an apostrophe next to it and is read "y prime" to indicate that we are predicting y from x. The m is the slope of the line relating y' to x. The value of m depends on two things. The first is the correlation coefficient, r. Recall that if the correlation is perfect, the value of r is 1.00, and if there is no correlation, r is 0.00. Under certain conditions, r is the slope of the regression line predicting y' from x, and hence $r = m$. Return to Figure 14.8 for a moment. Notice that the value of r is the same as the slope of the line drawn predicting y' from x in each case.

Now, what else goes into the slope of the regression line besides the value of r? Recall that we said there is a perfect correlation between temperature in degrees Celsius and temperature in degrees Fahrenheit because one is a simple linear function of the other:

$$F = 9/5(C) + 32$$

But the regression equation between the two, shown here, has a slope of 9/5 rather than a slope of 1.00. The difference in slope is the result of the differing scales of measurement of the two variables. In fact, scale of measurement is all that differs between temperature in Fahrenheit and temperature in Celsius; otherwise the two are identical. So the slope of the regression line is a quantity that reflects both the correlation between the two variables and the scale of measurement of the two variables. The scale on which the two variables are measured is their variability, or standard deviation.

There is a mathematical procedure for determining the regression line, with which we will not concern ourselves here. (It essentially involves computing the correlation coefficient.) The important thing to note is that when the correlation is perfect, there will be a slope of 1.00 between the two variables (when scaled by their variability), and when there is no correlation, there will be a slope of 0.00. Values of r between 0.00 and 1.00 indicate differing slopes of the line predicting y from x.

The situation in which the correlation is 0.00 is very instructive. When there is no correlation between two variables, knowing the value of one does not help you to predict the other. If you know a person's eye color and want to predict his income, your best bet is to guess the mean income of the population. Your best guess would be the same number whether the person's eyes are blue, brown, green, or hazel. This simply puts into words the significance of a slope of 0.00 in the line predicting y from x: Always predict the same value for y no matter what the value of x.

Most of the time you will not see scattergrams in which the two variables are scaled by their variability; they are usually plotted by the units in which they are measured: IQ, GPA, cm, and so forth. Then the slope of the line predicting y and x will not be equal to the correlation coefficient.

Example of Correlation and Regression

Consider the scores of the 20 students who have taken the first two of Dr. Carlton's tests (Table 14.1). We find a correlation of 0.38 between the first test scores and the second test scores. This is a fairly low correlation, and it suggests that a high score on one test does not necessarily indicate that a student will perform well on the second test. The regression line predicting the second test score from the first is

$$\text{Test } 2' = 0.6821(\text{Test 1}) + 4.5996$$

This equation predicts that the second test score will increase by 0.6821 for every point increase in first test score. According to this equation, a student who has a first test score of 14 would be predicted to achieve a second test score of 14.149.

Variance Accounted For

An important property of the correlation coefficient is that by squaring it we obtain a measure of the proportion of the variability in y that is accounted for by x. Now, there is a certain amount of variability in the scores on variable y and also on variable x. When there is a correlation between x and y, we can predict the value of y when we know x. Another way of saying this is that some proportion of the variability of y can be explained by the effect of x. If the correlation is 1.00, we have accounted for all the variability in y when we know x because the square of 1.00 is 1.00. If the correlation is 0.00, we have accounted for none of the variability in y by knowing x because the square of 0.00 is 0.00.

When the correlation is other than 1.00 or 0.00, the proportion of variance accounted for is less than the value of the correlation. A correlation of 0.5 accounts for only 0.25 of the variance because the square of 0.5 is 0.25. To account for half the variance, you need a correlation of 0.71, because 0.71 squared is 0.5.

This concept is important to remember because researchers sometimes are impressed when they find a correlation of 0.5 in their data. They need to remember that such a correlation accounts for only one-fourth of the variability in their data. Three-fourths of the variability in y is not associated with x.

The square of the correlation coefficient, r^2, is sometimes considered a measure of the **goodness of fit** of the data to the regression line. As r^2 approaches 1.00, the data fit the regression line better and better.

goodness of fit: the degree to which data match the prediction of a regression line

Tables with One Independent and One Dependent Variable

Rather than displaying individual data in a scattergram, as in Figure 14.7, we might prefer to display the same data in summary form. Returning to our example from Professor Carlton's class, we find that it is possible to look at the average, or mean, grade earned by each class. These data are shown in

TABLE **14.5**

Test Score as a Function Class Meeting Time

© Cengage Learning

	Class Meeting Time	
Score	8 a.m.	11 a.m.
Mean	12.30	17.70
Standard deviation	5.03	1.89

the first row of Table 14.5. As with all tables, we have a matrix format. Notice that the independent variable, class meeting time, becomes the columns of the matrix. The dependent variable, test score, becomes the elements of the matrix. This table demonstrates that the values of the dependent variable become the elements of the matrix and the values of the independent variable become the columns. So you might keep in mind that a table that shows a dependent variable as a function of one independent variable could have only one row.

Tables become more complicated, and more informative, when there is more than one independent variable and more information is provided. For example, suppose we want to show the variability of the data, as well as the mean. In Table 14.5, the two rows show different aspects of the same dependent variable: mean and standard deviation. Thus, although there is more than one row in this table, both rows refer to aspects of the same dependent variable, score. Alternatively, if there had been more than one dependent variable, the different dependent variables could have become rows of the table. We might have measured the score on the test and the length of time spent taking the test, for example, and then each of these would be reflected in a separate row of the table.

Graphs of Functions (Line Graphs)

Probably the most typical graph in psychology is the graph of a function. The y-axis represents some dependent variable as a function of an independent variable. Generally, functions that we graph involve a response that varies continuously with changes in the level of a quantitative independent variable. For example, we might graph the number of error-free words a person can type per minute as a function of the number of cups of coffee consumed during the previous hour. Figure 14.9 is a **line graph** that shows these hypothetical data. You can see that the speed of typing increases as the amount of coffee increases up to about two cups, after which more coffee is associated with slower typing speeds. The line graph also allows us to predict what the speed of typing might be like if a person were given 2.5 cups of coffee.

line graph: a graphical representation using lines to show relationships between quantitative variables

The fact that we have drawn lines between the data points implies that we could find a particular mathematical function that would describe the data if we tried to do so. Note that the data points in this graph are connected by straight lines. You should always connect data points by straight lines rather than drawing a smooth curve through the points, unless you can

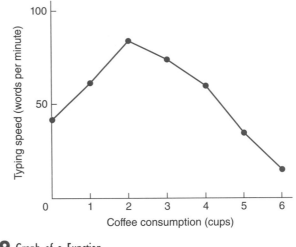

FIGURE **14.9** Graph of a Function

© Cengage Learning

write the mathematical equation that describes the curve. Drawing a smooth curve implies a particular mathematical function and generally means that there is a theory that describes the exact shape of the function. Data points connected by straight lines indicate only an empirical, rather than a theoretical, function.

Bar Graphs

bar graph: graphical representation of categorical data in which the heights of separated bars, or columns, show the relationships between variables

Bar graphs are used when the independent variable is categorical rather than quantitative. If the independent variable in an experiment is gender, for example, the data can be represented only by a bar graph (see Figure 14.10). Because people are either male or female, the independent variable is categorical; it is impossible to have data points that fall between the two points (M and F) on the x-axis. Note that the individual bars on a bar graph are drawn so that they do not touch each other, emphasizing that they represent different categories of behavior. A line graph would be incorrect in this case because it would imply the possibility of data points anywhere along the line. If the independent variable is masculinity-femininity as measured by a test, however, we can draw a line graph because individuals can, in principle, fall anywhere along the x-axis (see Figure 14.11).

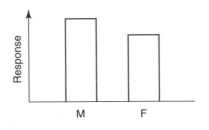

FIGURE **14.10** Bar Graph Used to Represent Categorical Data

© Cengage Learning

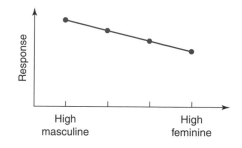

FIGURE **14.11** Line Graph Used Correctly to Represent Continuous Data

© Cengage Learning

Relation Between Frequency Distributions and Other Graphs

Recall that a frequency distribution differs from other graphs in that the y-axis represents a frequency, not the value of a dependent variable. Instead, the x-axis represents a dependent variable, such as number of correct responses on a test. However, frequency distributions and other graphs can often be related to one another.

Table 14.5 showed the mean number of correct responses as a function of class membership. If we plot the two mean scores—12.3 for those students in the 8 a.m. class and 17.7 for those in the 11 a.m. class—we have a graph of this function (Figure 14.12).

Figure 14.13 is a frequency distribution that combines the information in Table 14.4 with that provided by Table 14.5. Compare Figure 14.13 with the frequency distribution shown in Figure 14.2. In Figure 14.13, we have superimposed two separate frequency distributions on the same axes. The boxes are shaded differently for the two groups: those in the 8 a.m. class and those in the 11 a.m. class. The distribution looks a little different than it did in

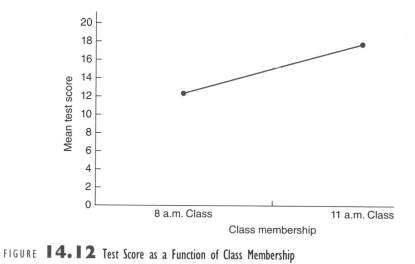

FIGURE **14.12** Test Score as a Function of Class Membership

© Cengage Learning

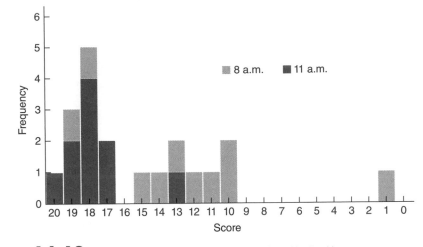

FIGURE **14.13** Frequency Distribution of Test Scores by Class Membership

© Cengage Learning

Figure 14.2 for two reasons. First, we have reversed the direction of the numbers on the *x*-axis. Second, data in the two conditions can overlap; see, for example, the two scores of 13, one from each group. Thus, we see that frequency distributions are different from other graphs but can be related to them. Remembering this distinction will help you when you are reading graphs.

Time-Series Graphs

time-series graph: a graph in which the abscissa (*x*-axis) represents time

A **time-series graph** is one in which the *x*-axis represents the passage of time. Suppose an instructor who gives six tests in her course notices in the middle of the third test that a student's eyes are wandering to the paper of the person next to him. She moves the student to the front row and makes sure that the two students are separated for all subsequent tests. Because she kept a seating chart on the test days, she knows that the suspect sat next to the same person for the first three tests. Then she computes the percentage of identical answers on each test, as shown in Figure 14.14. This is an example of a time-series graph because the various tests took place over time in the order shown on the graph. From these data, the instructor concludes that the student whose eyes were wandering had been copying answers from the other student, and she goes to the dean with her evidence.

Another type of time-series design in psychology is the cumulative record (see Figure 14.15) commonly used in operant conditioning research and in behavioral research involving a changing criterion design (see Chapter 12). The *x*-axis shows time, as in all such graphs. The *y*-axis, however, shows the cumulative number of responses since the beginning of the session. The data shown in Figure 14.15 reflect a mouse learning to press a bar, with responses that are automatically noted by a recorder. Each response causes the recorder to make a small vertical movement. If the detail of the graph were fine enough, you could see that each response made the pen move a step up and then move horizontally until the next response. (See detail insert.) The slope of the graph

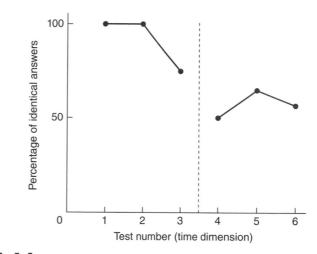

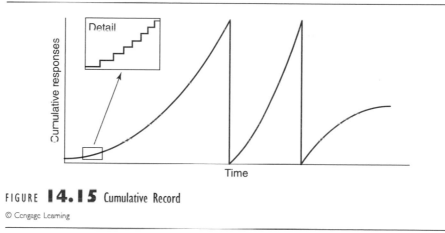

shows the rate of responding. When the animal is making no responses, the graph is flat because the pen does not move vertically as time passes horizontally. When the animal responds rapidly, the graph becomes steep. (The vertical line shows the recorder resetting to zero after reaching the top of the graph.)

Chapters 12 and 13 discuss a number of examples of research using time-series designs.

Indicating Variability of the Data in a Graph

error bars: in a graph, vertical lines that indicate plus or minus one standard deviation of the data or, less frequently, the standard error of the mean

Often a researcher will want a graph to show the variability of the data, as well as the averages. This is commonly done by drawing **error bars** above and below a data point to indicate plus or minus one standard deviation, or sometimes the standard error of the mean.

Figure 14.16 is an example of a bar graph with error bars. Suppose we asked males and females to rate their liking of an action movie. We can see from the

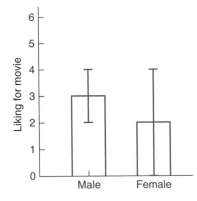

FIGURE **14.16** Bar Graph with Error Bars

© Cengage Learning

graph that males liked the movie more than females did. The error bars tell us, in addition, that females were more variable than males in their responses.

Although error bars can be helpful, they also can be misleading. One standard deviation on either side of the mean of a normal distribution will include 68% of the cases. How is it possible, then, that the error bar for females touches the origin of the graph—a rating of zero? Such a rating implies that some women rate the movie less than zero, which is impossible.

box-and-whisker plot:
a type of graph based on median and percentiles rather than mean and standard deviation

This problem can be resolved by using a different method for indicating the variability of the data. This technique, known as a box-and-whisker plot, is illustrated in Figure 14.17. A box-and-whisker plot is based on median and percentiles, rather than on the mean and standard deviation. The box for females extends from the 25th to the 75th percentiles. A horizontal line through the box indicates the median (50th percentile). The lower vertical line, or whisker, extends to the 10th percentile, and the upper one to the 90th. It is clear from this graph that the two distributions are skewed: The median woman did not like the movie, but there were a few who liked it

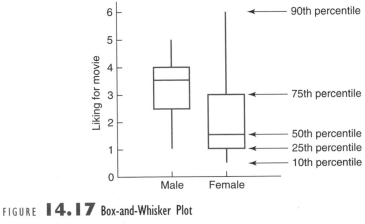

FIGURE **14.17** Box-and-Whisker Plot

© Cengage Learning

quite a lot. The reverse is true for the men. The box-and-whisker plot shows clearly how skewed the data is, whereas the bar graph with error bars does not. Box-and-whisker plots are very useful whenever the data are skewed, as well as in other situations in which the median is appropriate for the data.

Box-and-whisker plots are seen more often in other disciplines than they are in psychology, but they deserve much more use in psychology. A little thought will reveal that they are useful for any type of graph we have discussed so far, including frequency data. Because the box-and-whisker plot is based on percentiles, it can be used in place of a frequency distribution.

Checking for Invalid Data, Missing Data, and Outliers

After you have had a preliminary look at the data using descriptive statistics, tables, and graphs, it is possible that you may have to clean up the original data a bit. Mistakes can be made in transcribing the data to the matrix, or there may be some wild data that you might be justified in excluding. You could simply scan the data sheets, but some data sets are too big to scan efficiently. For those large data sets, it is easiest to check for errors by looking at some of the preliminary statistics and graphs that we have just discussed.

Invalid data: data points that fall outside the defined range for that variable of data

Let's return to data from Dr. Carlton's test scores that were presented in Table 14.1, and look at it closely. First, let's consider invalid data. Many times either the independent or dependent variables can take only certain values. The independent variable of class meeting time, for example, can only take one of two values: 8 a.m. or 11 a.m., which we have coded as 1 or 2. Any other number is clearly an error. Likewise, the variable of test can only be the first or second one, which we have also coded as a 1 or a 2. If the dependent variable is a score on a 20-point test, any value other than 0 to 20 will be invalid. If you have a sharp eye, you may have noticed that the test number in row 16 in Table 14.1 is 0, which is invalid. There can be no test 0.

missing data: empty cells in a data matrix

Second, missing data are simply what the name implies. A cell in the matrix may contain no data point. Perhaps a subject did not complete every part of the study. We would have missing data in this example if a subject only took one of the two tests in Dr. Carlton's class. Missing data are common in questionnaires when a respondent skips an item or refuses to answer.

outliers: data points that are highly improbable, although not impossible

Third, we can have outliers. These are data points that are not invalid but are highly improbable. Potential outliers can arise for two basic reasons. First, they may simply be extreme scores from a normal distribution. Recall that a normal distribution does not reach zero probability; it only approaches zero. Any valid score has some theoretical probability, however small. Generally, we do not want to exclude responses that actually come from the distribution of interest. Second, potential outliers can come from a different distribution than all the other scores. If we have a distribution of test scores, an outlier could come from a distribution we might call *Oops, I wasn't paying attention* responses. We do want to exclude these types of responses as they are not truly indicative of test performance. The best reason for excluding an outlier is obvious: gross failure to follow instructions. For example, someone may fill out a questionnaire in a fraction of the time that the other people take, and give the exact same response to most of the items instead of answering them thoughtfully.

Sophisticated statistical procedures are available for evaluating outliers (e.g., Hawkins, 1980), but most researchers rely on informal analyses to exclude them. These informal methods include visual and numerical analysis of distributions to spot them. One criterion might be to perform some descriptive statistics and to eliminate any response that falls three or more standard deviations from the mean of the data.

We must emphasize that we do not eliminate wild data casually. It is all too easy to eliminate data in such a way as to bias the results in our favor. Wild data should be eliminated only after a process such as we have followed; then it is necessary to report that data were eliminated and describe the criteria that were used to do so. It is wise to perform the statistical analysis on all the data, including the wild data, and report what difference excluding the wild data made in the results. Not to do this can be an ethical violation. Elimination from analysis has resulted in ethical investigations of researchers.

Returning now to Table 14.1, we see that row 4 shows a test score of 1, which seems highly improbable. Row 20 also seems to stand out as unusual because it is the only data point that reflects a perfect score. We will keep these data points in mind as candidates for exclusion as wild data.

The simplest and most systematic way to search for invalid data, missing data, and outliers is to do some preliminary statistics on the matrix. Table 14.6 shows part of the output of one popular statistics package as applied to these data. The rows of the table show the variables in the study. (These were the columns in our summary data matrix.) The columns are the various statistics on the variables.

We could look for many things in such a table. For example, it is possible that all the data for some variable were recorded in the wrong column. Errors like this are not rare and can be caught by looking for obviously incorrect means. For example, if the mean ID were 15, instead of 5.500, we would suspect that we had recorded the test scores in the ID column. No such error was made in these data, so we go on looking for other potential problems.

We can check for missing data by noting the numbers in the first column. Each row of this column (N) shows 20 data points; therefore, there are no missing data (ten students, two tests = 20). If there were missing data, we would place a missing data code in the blank cell. Some computer statistical packages have a specified **missing data code**, such as an asterisk or a dot,

missing data code: a symbol, such as an asterisk (*), that is entered in a cell that has no data

TABLE **14.6**

Preliminary Summary Statistics on Test Scores

© Cengage Learning

	N	Mean	Median	Stdev	Min	Max
ID	20	5.500	5.500	0.513	1.000	10.000
Mtg. Time	20	1.500	1.500	0.513	1.000	2.000
Test No.	20	1.500	1.500	1.513	0.000	2.000
Test Score	20	15.000	17.000	4.780	1.000	20.000

that is used to indicate missing data. The computer ignores that data point and adjusts the number of cases accordingly.

The columns labeled MIN and MAX tell us the minimum and maximum score on each variable. The minimum value for test shows up as 0.000, which we can recognize as invalid. The invalid data point is easy to fix in this example because we can see that the 0 in row 16, column 3, had to be a 1. Note that we found the invalid data point by looking at a fairly small summary table (Table 14.6), rather than having to look through what could be a very large data matrix (Table 14.1).

Now we are ready to consider whether the very low minimum test score of 1 might be an outlier. The consideration of potential wild data points takes a little thought and effort. Perhaps the data are just skewed, and a few low values are to be expected. To check for possible skewed data, we can look at Table 14.6 and see that the mean test score is quite a lot smaller than the median. This makes us suspect that the data are, in fact, skewed.

To look at the possible skewed data, we can look back at the histogram of the data that is shown in Figure 14.2. Although there is some negative skew to the data, the score of 1 seems to be far away from the other scores, and seems more like an outlier than reflecting the general skew of the data.

The one test score of 1 is nearly three standard deviations below the mean. We can feel justified in assuming that this data point is, in fact, a wild point that can be eliminated. The student probably did not pay attention when they took the test. Our other potential wild data point was a perfect test score of 20. When we look at the histogram, we see that this point is actually only about 1 standard deviation above the mean, a very likely event. We will keep this data point.

We remove the one outlier from the data and treat that cell of the matrix as a missing data point. Table 14.7 shows the data after the correction of the incorrect data point and the replacement of the wild data with the missing data code. We can now proceed to inferential statistics with confidence in our data set.

TABLE **14.7**

Data from Dr. Carlton's Tests After Correction and Removal of Wild Data Point

© Cengage Learning

Row	ID	8 a.m. Class = 1 11 a.m. Class = 2	Test	Test Score
1	1	1	1	10
2	1	1	2	11
3	2	1	1	15
4	2	1	2	*
5	3	1	1	14
6	3	1	2	19
7	4	1	1	13
8	4	1	2	18
9	5	1	1	10

(continued)

TABLE **14.7**

Continued

Row	ID	8 a.m. Class = 1 11 a.m. Class = 2	Test	Test Score
10	5	1	2	12
11	6	2	1	17
12	6	2	2	13
13	7	2	1	18
14	7	2	2	19
15	8	2	1	17
16	8	2	2	18
17	9	2	1	19
18	9	2	2	18
19	10	2	1	18
20	10	2	2	20

NUTS & BOLTS

Style Guide for Figures

Figures include bar graphs, histograms, line graphs, pie charts, scattergrams, drawings, charts, and photographs. The following guidelines concern figures other than drawings and photographs, which have specialized requirements. It is assumed that you will be drawing the figures by computer, but please keep in mind that some software packages do not conform to APA guidelines.

1. Remember that the purpose of a figure is to communicate information. Plan the figure so that the reader will be able to understand clearly the information you are trying to convey.
2. Is there a clear title?
3. Computer graphs are preferred, but use graph paper for all hand-drawn graphs.
4. Use black pencil or black ink only. Do not use color, because journals generally do not reproduce color graphics.
5. Usually, graphs should be about two-thirds as high as they are wide.
6. Label both axes with the appropriate variables.
7. Make sure that the units of measurement are either in the title or data labels.
8. Provide a descriptive caption for each figure. Place the caption below the figure.
9. If there are two or more types of symbols in a figure, label them or define them in a legend. The legend appears somewhere in the white space inside the figure.
10. All letters and symbols should be large enough to be legible.
11. Connect points using straight lines only. Do not draw curved lines unless they represent theoretical equations that you have computed.
12. If the lower left-hand corner of the graph is not the origin, and there is a possibility of misunderstanding, indicate that fact by a break in the axis.

(continues)

NUTS & BOLTS *(continued)*

chartjunk: parts of a graph that aren't necessary to understand it

It might take considerable effort to find how to format a particular graph correctly. Many software packages include considerable **chartjunk** (Tufte, 2001) with their output, which includes Moiré vibrations, grids, and ducks. Moiré vibrations are any of the patterns that packages provide as a way to fill in bars. Generally, they are hard to see in print; solid bars are much clearer. Grids are the background patterns on which the bars or data are represented. These make it difficult to pick out the data from the background. Ducks are features of the data that have been dressed up to be something other than data points, such as pictures of ducks over points relating to wildlife activity. These are also distracting, and should be avoided.

© Cengage Learning

Summary

1. Data reduction is the process of transcribing data from individual data sheets to a summary in the form of a matrix.
2. Before inferential statistics are performed, you should calculate preliminary descriptive statistics and represent the data in tables or graphs or both.
3. Descriptive statistics include both measures of central tendency and measures of variability.
4. A table is a display of data in a matrix format.
5. A graph is a representation of data by spatial relations in a diagram.
6. Most graphs in psychology represent two variables and have two axes plotted at right angles to one another.
7. A frequency distribution is a graph that shows the number of scores that fall in specific bins, or divisions of the variable, rather than values of a dependent variable. A distribution may be in the form of a histogram or a frequency polygon.
8. A cumulative frequency distribution shows the number of scores that fall at or below a certain score. They tend to be sigmoidal in shape and are useful for determining percentiles.
9. A scattergram shows the relationship between two variables for a number of individual cases.
10. A line graph is a graphical representation using lines to show relationships between quantitative variables.
11. Bar graphs are used when the independent variable is categorical; otherwise, line graphs are used.
12. Although frequency distributions are different from other graphs, they are related to them in that they represent different aspects of data that could be represented in a graph of a function.
13. A time-series graph is one in which the *x*-axis represents the passage of time.
14. Variability of data may be shown graphically by error bars, which may indicate standard deviation or standard error, or by box-and-whisker plots, which represent percentile data.

15. The summary data should be checked for invalid data, missing data, and outliers.
16. Figures should conform to the style described in this chapter and in the APA *Publication Manual*. Keep in mind that the purpose of a figure is to communicate information about your data.

Suggestions for Further Reading

CLEVELAND, W. S. (1994). *The elements of graphing data* (2nd ed.). Monterey, CA: Wadsworth Advanced Book Program. Despite the title, a high-level discussion of graphing techniques.

MILLSAP, R. E. & MAYDEU-OLIVARES, A. (2009). *The SAGE handbook of quantitative methods in psychology*. Thousand Oaks, CA: Sage. Valuable mathematical background for this chapter.

MOSTELLER, F., FEINBERG, S. E., & ROURKE, R. E. K. (1983). *Beginning statistics with data analysis*.

Reading, MA: Addison-Wesley. An excellent introduction to statistics, with an emphasis on exploratory data analysis.

TUFTE, E. R. (2001). *The visual display of quantitative information* (2nd ed). Cheshire, CT: Graphics Press. An enlightening discussion of graphing with many specific hints and examples.

TUKEY, J. W. (1977). *Exploratory data analysis*. Reading, MA: Addison-Wesley. Very practical introduction to dealing with data.

A CASE IN POINT

Professor Smith's Slide Presentation

Professor Smith was about to present a paper on his research on food preferences at a psychology convention. As is customary, he gave an informal practice talk to the members of his department before going to the convention.

The slides that he presented are shown in Figure 14.18. Following is a description of the data on which they are based:

1. The ratings of preference, on a scale of 1 to 5, of 10 subjects for four foods (1 = dislike intensely, 2 = dislike moderately, 3 = neutral, 4 = like moderately, 5 = like intensely). (Figure 14.18a)
2. Frequency distribution showing how many people liked one, two, three, or four of the sample foods. (The data in this figure cannot be verified from the previous one.) (Figure 14.18b)
3. Number of people who liked this many foods, or fewer (cumulative frequency of the same data as in 2 and shown in Figure 14.18b). (Figure 14.18c)
4. Professor Smith believed that the people had never had a chance to learn to like the foods

they claimed to dislike. Therefore, he presented the most liked food and the least liked food to people alternately for lunch for six days, starting with the most preferred on Day 1, the least preferred on Day 2, and so on. He wanted to see if they would get tired of the most preferred but begin to like the least preferred over the trials. (Figure 14.18d)

5. Professor Smith took pictures of their faces when they ate the various foods. He believed their expressions could be described in terms of two variables: pleasantness and fear. Combinations of these two variables produced four different facial expressions, which he labeled happy, sad, worried, and embarrassed and showed in schematic form. (Figure 14.18e)

After the talk, Professor Avuncular took him aside and suggested that he might make a better impression if he redid his slides.

Required

Redo Professor Smith's slides so they better reflect the point he is trying to make. Pay attention to proper style.

(continued)

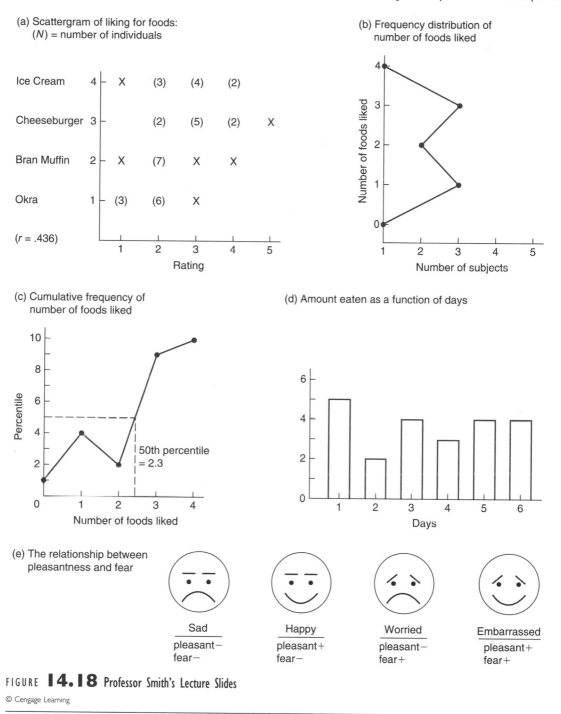

(a) Scattergram of liking for foods:
(*N*) = number of individuals

(b) Frequency distribution of number of foods liked

(c) Cumulative frequency of number of foods liked

(d) Amount eaten as a function of days

(e) The relationship between pleasantness and fear

Sad
pleasant−
fear−

Happy
pleasant+
fear−

Worried
pleasant−
fear+

Embarrassed
pleasant+
fear+

FIGURE **14.18** Professor Smith's Lecture Slides

© Cengage Learning

Reading Between the Lines

14.1 "You Can Prove Anything with Statistics"

Many cultures value a male child more than a female child; so much so, that parents in those cultures will sometimes abort a pregnancy when they learn that the child is a girl. *The Economist* published an article on the reduction in the birth of female children in India, and included the graph shown in Figure 14.19. The graph shows the girl-to-boy ratio for 11 (rather than all 35) Indian states. What is the problem in drawing conclusions from the graph? What is wrong with the formatting of the graph that makes it very difficult to interpret?

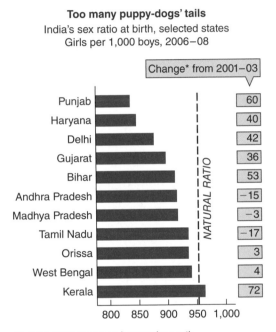

Too many puppy-dogs' tails
India's sex ratio at birth, selected states
Girls per 1,000 boys, 2006–08

*Positive value means an improved sex ratio

FIGURE **14.19** Graph Indicating India's Ratio of Births of Girls to Boys

(Reprinted with Permission from *The Economist*, April 9, 2011, Seven Brothers: An Aversion to Having Daughters is Leading to Millions of Missing Girls, pp. 45–46. Copyright © 2011 Economist Newspaper, Ltd.)

Exercises

14.1 Graph Interpretation

Researchers have administered an ability test to a random sample of subjects ranging from 10 to 60 years in age. Figure 14.20 presents results from this study.

Required:

a. What is the independent variable?
b. What is the dependent variable?
c. Explain the relationship between the dependent and independent variables.

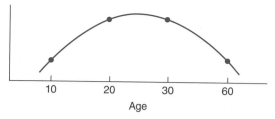

FIGURE **14.20** Relationship Between Agility and Age

© Cengage Learning

d. What kind of study was this?

e. List five things that are wrong with this graph.

14.2 Types of Graphs

Choose the most appropriate type of graph for each of the following situations:

a. Professor Jackson wants to make a graph showing the number of students who got various scores on a test.

b. The SAT publishes a graph showing how many people taking the test score at or below a certain score.

c. Jorge makes a chart of the library on which he marks every seat occupied in the library during the course of a week.

d. The university publishes a graph showing how many students are in each major.

e. Tamika wants to see if there is a relationship between the percentage gained by the stocks in her portfolio in 1998 and their price at the beginning of the year.

f. Christopher makes a graph showing the combinations of oven temperature and baking time that causes his bread to come out with a nice brown crust.

g. Heather plots the percentage of people who volunteer to serve in her experiment as a function of the size of the class from which she recruits them.

14.3 Graph Interpretation

Each of the following pairs indicates the type of variable that is on the y-axis and the x-axis of a graph, respectively. For example, *dependent, independent* means that the y-axis shows a dependent variable and the x-axis shows an independent variable. For each combination, choose the type of graph that could be indicated. Use each category only once.

a. dependent, independent

b. dependent, dependent

c. frequency, dependent

d. independent, independent

Alternatives: (1) grading distribution, (2) contour graph, (3) scattergram, (4) amount learned as a function of trials.

14.4 Creating Graphs

Use the data in Table 14.5 to make a bar graph that compares the data for Dr. Carlton's two classes. Make certain to include evidence of variability with error bars.

14.5 Creating Graphs

Use the data presented in Table 14.5 to assist you in making a box-and-whisker plot that compares the data for Dr. Carlton's two classes.

CHAPTER FIFTEEN

Data Exploration, Part 2: Inferential Statistics

Proceeding with the Analysis

Once we have displayed our data visually as well as numerically, we have a pretty good idea about them. Even though we can observe some potential effects or relationships, we cannot tell, based on the way that we have examined the data thus far, whether or not the result occurred due to chance. So, after completing the steps described in Chapter 14, finally, we are ready to perform inferential statistics on the data that have been collected.

We have found in teaching research methods that even students who have had a prior course in statistics find a review of some basic concepts very helpful. We believe that this results from the technical and abstract nature of statistical thinking. The purpose of this chapter is to review some concepts from introductory statistics in a nontechnical way to provide a starting point for thinking about analyses, as well as additional practice in understanding statistics. Because there are so many different statistical tests, and they differ among themselves, you will need to refer to a book on statistics to select the appropriate tests, and to find the formulas and steps for conducting them, for your particular study.

Some Basic Terms

empirical data: facts derived from experience

First, let us review a few basic terms. Statistics is—this is not a misprint; statistics as a field is a singular word—an area of study having to do with interpretation of empirical data. This term needs some definition. The word *data* refers to facts. As we stated back in Chapter 1, the word *empirical* means based on experience. So empirical data are facts that are obtained by observation or experiment. Now, these empirical data ordinarily exist in numerical form: Eric's IQ is 120, the average reaction time was 483 (milliseconds [ms]), and so forth. But it is important to note that not all numbers are empirical data. Mathematicians often talk about numbers in the abstract: Two plus two is four. These numbers are not empirical data because they do not refer to a specific observation or experiment; they are true by definition. It is worth noting that *data* is a plural word. The singular form is *datum*. A datum is a fact, and data are a collection of facts. Scientists say, "The data are such and such" rather than "The data is such and such." In common usage, it is often considered pedantic [picky] to treat the word *data* as plural, but scientific usage still favors treating *data* as a plural word.

population: all members of some group

As we mentioned in Chapter 9, a **population** is the entire collection of individuals being considered: all people who live in the United States (the US population), all students at State University, all college sophomores, all possible tosses of a pair of dice, and the like. Note from the last example that a population does not necessarily contain people or even animate objects. Nor is a population necessarily finite: You could toss dice forever and still be able to toss them some more. A **sample**, by contrast, is a subset of the population: 100 randomly selected people who live in the United States, every 100th student at State University, 100 tosses of a pair of dice, and so on. Statistics deal sometimes with populations and sometimes with samples.

sample: a subset of a population

statistic: a quantity computed from a sample

A **statistic** is a quantity computed from a sample: The mean number of hours worked per week is a statistic if it is based on a sample of the students at State University. (This differs from the common usage in which a statistic is any sort of empirical datum: "Drive carefully or you will become a statistic.") A **parameter** is a quantity computed from the population. The mean number of hours worked per week by students at State University would be a parameter if we had obtained the data from every student at the university. Note that the term *parameter* is used in statistics in a somewhat different sense than it is when one is talking about a function. A mean, then, can be either a statistic or a parameter, depending on whether it is based on a sample of the population or the entire population. This distinction is signified in statistical notation. A statistic is identified by a Roman letter (the ones we use every day), whereas a parameter is identified by a Greek letter. Thus, the mean of a sample is usually indicated by $\overline{X}$, called "X bar," whereas the mean of a population is indicated by μ, the lowercase Greek letter mu (pronounced "mew").

parameter: in statistics, a quantity computed from a population

As we mentioned in Chapter 14, there are two main uses of statistics: to describe a particular set of data and to use data to draw conclusions about a population. These two uses correspond to the distinction between descriptive statistics and inferential statistics. In this chapter, we are interested in inferential statistics.

Inferential Statistics _____

Now we turn to inferential statistical techniques, which allow us to draw inferences about the population by examining a sample drawn from the population.

Sampling Distributions

By definition, the mean IQ of the population is 100 and its standard deviation is 15. If you were to select a person at random and had to guess his or her IQ, you would probably guess that it was 100 because that is the mean of the population. You would not be greatly surprised, however, if that randomly selected person had an IQ of 70 or 130. After all, one person out of a population might have any score in the population. If you had a group of 100 randomly selected people, however, you would be very surprised if the mean IQ of the group was 70 or 130. If it was 70, you would probably guess that you had somehow selected a class of slow learners instead of a random sample from the population; if the mean was 130, you would likely think you had gotten the members of an honors class. This intuitive notion is related to the concept of a sampling distribution.

We know from descriptive statistics (discussed in Chapter 14) that we can describe a population by its mean and standard deviation. Now, suppose we take samples from the population and measure IQ. These samples of IQ will vary from one to another. See Figure 15.1, in which we have taken three samples of size 5 from the population.

We can do various things with these samples. First, we can find the means of the samples. Our three samples have means of 92, 99, and 104. We can also make a distribution of the means of the samples. This is a new distribution, a distribution of sample means, and it is not to be confused with the original population distribution. This distribution of the means of samples from a population is called a sampling distribution.

sampling distribution: the distribution of means of samples from a population

The sampling distribution has three important properties. First, it has the same mean as the original distribution. If the mean IQ in the population is 100, the mean of the sampling distribution will be 100. (The average sample you select will have a mean of 100.)

Second, the sampling distribution has a smaller standard deviation than the population distribution; the larger the size of the samples that are drawn from the population, the smaller the standard deviation of the sampling distribution. As noted previously, the larger the sample you draw from a population, the more you expect its mean to be close to the population mean. The standard deviation of the sampling distribution is called the standard error of the mean. The standard error of the mean is the standard deviation of the population divided by the square root of the sample size:

standard error of the mean: the standard deviation of a sampling distribution

$$\sigma_{\overline{X}} = \frac{\sigma_X}{\sqrt{N}}$$

The standard error of the mean is thus inversely proportional to the square root of the sample size: The larger the square root of the sample size, the smaller the standard error of the mean. This is true because the square root

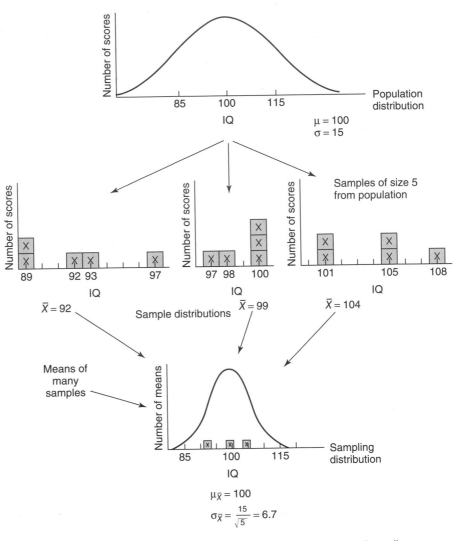

of N is the denominator of a fraction. The larger the denominator of a fraction is, the smaller the value of the fraction is; therefore, increasing the square root of N by a factor of 2 cuts the standard error of the mean in half. Putting it another way, large samples result in a smaller standard error of the mean because the means of large samples are more similar to one another. The standard error of the mean of the sampling distribution in Figure 15.1 is 6.7.

The third characteristic of the sampling distribution is that, as the sample size becomes larger, the shape of the distribution approaches a normal distribution, regardless of the shape of the population from which the samples are drawn. The population distribution in Figure 15.1 is normal because the distribution of IQ is normal. However, the sampling distribution will be normal no matter what the original population looks like. Exercise 15.1 at the end of this chapter illustrates the concept of sampling distributions and shows the effects of changing sample size. Turn there now to see the effect of sample size on the shape and variability of sampling distributions.

Testing Hypotheses

We said in Chapter 1 that virtually all scientific research has the purpose of testing a hypothesis. Usually this is a test of a theory-level hypothesis. But when we test such a hypothesis, we must state it as a particular research hypothesis. The research hypothesis is more specific than the theory-level hypothesis because it must be stated in terms of the particular way the study was carried out.

In the DeWall and colleagues (2010) study discussed in Chapter 1, the theory-level hypothesis was that social pain is processed by the brain similarly to physical pain. The theory predicts that although people can discriminate the source of their pain, all types of pain should respond to similar treatment. The research-level hypothesis was that particular people experiencing particular social pain will respond to particular pain relievers designed to reduce physical pain. But there may be many reasons why social pain could be reduced. For this reason the experiment had to be designed to take these other factors into account.

The difference between the theory-level hypothesis and the research hypothesis is that the research hypothesis must take into account other factors that the theory does not address, such things as positive or negative experiences that might have occurred during the three weeks of the study. Whether the research hypothesis does justice to the theory-level hypothesis was the subject of Chapter 6.

When we have collected the data in a study, we need to analyze them statistically, to see which unobserved population they are most likely to have come from. (The logic of hypothesis testing is the same no matter what statistic you use. The arithmetic procedure differs with the statistic—t test, analysis of variance, and so forth. We refer you to a statistics book for the details.) The statistical hypothesis is actually a restating of the research hypothesis into two different hypotheses. The first one is just the research hypothesis itself, but we are going to introduce a new name for it: the **alternative hypothesis**. It is generally written H_1 and is called "H sub one." The reason for this term will become clear in a moment. In our example, the alternative hypothesis is as follows: People who take a product shown to reduce physical pain, such as acetaminophen (the pain reliever found in Tylenol®) will experience a reduction in social pain.

The second hypothesis is the one that would be true if the alternative hypothesis were false. We call this one the **null hypothesis**. It is often written H_0 and is called "H sub oh." It is called the null hypothesis because it is an *empty* hypothesis, of no scientific interest to you. You set up the null hypothesis strictly for the purpose of rejecting it. It is a "straw man" hypothesis. In our example, the null hypothesis is as follows: People who take a product shown to reduce physical pain will *not* experience a reduction in social pain.

alternative hypothesis: statistical term for the research hypothesis

null hypothesis: the hypothesis that is of no scientific interest; sometimes the hypothesis of no difference

Notice that the null hypothesis covers all possible exceptions to the research hypothesis. We could have stated the null hypothesis as follows: People who take a product shown to reduce physical pain *will experience greater* social pain than people who do not take such a product, or both groups will experience an *equal amount of* pain. In other words, either the null hypothesis is true, or the alternative hypothesis is true. Between the null hypothesis and the alternative hypothesis, you have covered all possible states of the world. A philosopher would say that the two alternatives are mutually exclusive and exhaustive.

The hypothesis that we are trying to prove is the alternative hypothesis. (Some people object to the phrase *proving the alternative hypothesis* because it implies that you have made the correct decision when, in fact, your decision may be incorrect. We use the expression here anyway because we believe that everyone should realize that science never proves anything once and for all.) We prove this hypothesis to be true by using a roundabout method of disproving the null hypothesis. If we have disproved the hypothesis that includes all possible outcomes that could happen if the research hypothesis were false, then the research hypothesis is left standing.

Now we know the reason for calling the research hypothesis the alternative hypothesis: The logic of the test is set up so that you try to reject the null hypothesis. When you have done that, all there is left, if you have set up the hypotheses properly, is the alternative hypothesis. So the logic of hypothesis testing is to set up a straw man. When you have knocked it down, you have proven your research hypothesis.

Here is a tricky but extremely important point. Your alternative hypothesis is the one that you want to be true. However, according to the logic of the statistical test, you cannot do this directly. You can only reject the null hypothesis, which leaves you with only one alternative: to accept the alternative hypothesis. If it turns out that your results are not statistically significant, then you fail to reject the null hypothesis. Thus, you must say that your alternative hypothesis was not accepted because you could not reject the null hypothesis.

The null hypothesis is often stated in the following way:

$$H_0 : \mu_{HD} \leq \mu_{LD}$$

That is, the null hypothesis is that the mean level of social pain of the population of those who have taken the drug acetaminophen (HD) is reduced less than the pain level of those who lack the drug (LD) or that the means are equal for the two groups. The alternative hypothesis is then stated as follows:

$$H_1 : \mu_{HD} > \mu_{LD}$$

directional hypothesis: an alternative hypothesis that predicts that the results of one condition will be greater (or less) than another, rather than a prediction that they will simply differ

The alternative hypothesis is that the mean social pain of the population of those who have taken acetaminophen is reduced to a greater level than the mean of those who did not take the drug.

In this example, the alternative hypothesis was that the experimental population had a higher mean than the controls. This is called a **directional hypothesis** because we predicted that the HD people would differ in one particular direction from the LD people. This gives rise to what is called a

one-tailed hypothesis test: statistical test of a directional hypothesis

one-tailed hypothesis test. We are not interested in the case in which the reduction in social pain in HD people might be worse than the LD people.

Sometimes we predict only that the two groups will differ from each other; we don't know which group will be higher. This is a *nondirectional hypothesis*, and it gives rise to a two-tailed hypothesis test. The null and alternative hypotheses in this case would be stated as follows:

two-tailed hypothesis test: statistical test of a nondirectional hypothesis

$$H_0 : \mu_X = \mu_C$$
$$H_1 : \mu_X \neq \mu_C$$

That is, the null hypothesis is that the mean of X equals the mean of C, and the alternative hypothesis is that the mean of X does not equal the mean of C. We would use a two-tailed hypothesis if we predicted that the people who took acetaminophen would differ from the controls but our theory did not predict in which direction. When you do a two-tailed hypothesis test, you reject the null hypothesis if the experimental group is sufficiently higher or sufficiently lower than the control group.

Dealing with Uncertainty in Hypothesis Testing

One consequence of the fact that data are inherently variable is that we must be prepared to deal with uncertainty in making decisions about those data. Suppose the psychology department at your college wants to evaluate the effectiveness of its undergraduate program. To do this, the department requires a sample of majors to take the psychology section of the Graduate Record Exam (GRE). Let's say that the mean score on the latest version of the GRE is 150 for all students who take the exam. Suppose that the mean for the psychology majors at your college is 180. Does this prove that your college's psychology graduates are reliably better than the national average?

The fact that the group scored higher than the national average does not prove that the college's students are better than the national average. Although it may be that the college's program was responsible for the difference, it is not certain: The students in this year's graduating class may have been better than usual, or they may have been lucky on the test, or any of a number of other factors may have been responsible. So we are faced with a difference between our group and the population mean that we must interpret: Does an average score this high prove that your college's psychology program is actually better than the national average? This average score will have its own sampling distribution: a sampling distribution of means. Our job is to decide whether the observed average score is likely to have come from the distribution of all possible samples of means from the population of scores on the GRE. So we need to make a decision based on this observed sample mean compared with the theoretical sampling distribution.

Type I and Type II Errors

Suppose that your college's psychology majors were actually the same as the average of the population of psychology majors. What would you expect to happen? This is the same as asking what the null hypothesis is. If we are studying the effectiveness of your college's psychology program (C) compared with that of the average psychology program (X), we would say that our null hypothesis is that your college's psychology majors are not better than average:

$$H_0 : \mu_C \leq \mu_X$$

Our alternative hypothesis is that your college's psychology majors are better than average:

$$H_1 : \mu_C > \mu_X$$

These two hypotheses set up two possible states of the world: Either the mean of your college's psychology majors is better than the average for all psychology majors in the country, or it is not. Note that the two states of the world concern not the outcome of your single study, but the outcome of all possible studies using exactly the same methods, type of students, and so on, that you did. In other words, the two states of the world are statements about whether your experimental hypothesis is true or false.

Corresponding to the two states of the world are two possible decisions you could make: Either your college's psychology majors are better, or they are not. These two sets of alternatives make it possible to consider four distinct situations. First, let us suppose that your college's psychology program is better. You might decide that it is better, or you might decide that it is not better. Second, suppose instead that the psychology program is not better. Here you could also decide that it is better or that it is not better. It is convenient to summarize these four possibilities in a 2 × 2 table (see Table 15.1).

Looking at the table, you can see that if the program was better and you decided that it was better, you would be correct. You would also be correct if the program was not better and you decided that it was not better. Figure 15.2 provides the same information in the form of a decision tree.

There are two ways of making errors. One kind of error occurs when the program is not better but you decide that it is. This is called a **Type I error**; you have rejected the null hypothesis when it is true. The other kind of error is to decide that the program is not better when it actually is. This is called a **Type II error**; you have accepted the null hypothesis when it is false.

Type I error: rejecting a null hypothesis when it is true

Type II error: accepting a null hypothesis when it is false.

Alpha and Statistical Significance

These four outcomes can be related to the sampling distributions of the means for the two situations. First, let us consider the sampling distribution of the means for the psychology majors when the null hypothesis is true.

TABLE **15.1**

Four Possible Outcomes in Making a Decision Concerning Rejection of the Null Hypothesis

© Cengage Learning

		Null hypothesis is true	Alternative hypothesis is true
Decision	Accept null hypothesis	Correct decision	Wrong decision: Type II error
	Reject null hypothesis	Wrong decision: Type I error	Correct decision (power of test)

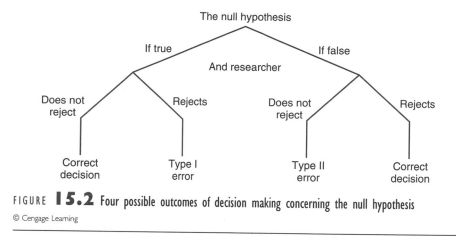

FIGURE **15.2** Four possible outcomes of decision making concerning the null hypothesis
© Cengage Learning

The curve in Figure 15.3(a) shows the relative probability of getting any particular group mean. If the null hypothesis is true, the distribution of means will have a mean of 150 and a certain standard deviation (standard error). We can see that sometimes the mean will be higher than 150 and sometimes it will be less than 150.

Figure 15.3(b) shows the distribution of means when the alternative hypothesis is true (when the program is better). Notice that the distribution of differences has a mean that is 10 points higher. Most of the time the difference is greater than zero, but sometimes it is zero or less. What we need to do is set up a criterion on which to base our decision.

The way this is done is to decide how often we are willing to say that the program is better when in fact it is not. This is the same as setting a cutoff on the dimension of scores in Figure 15.3(a) that will cause us to reject the null hypothesis a certain percentage of the time when it is true. This point is

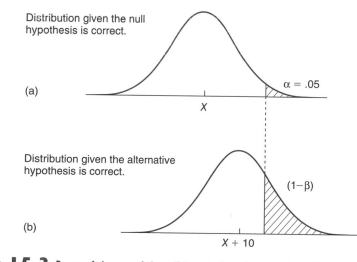

Distribution given the null hypothesis is correct.

(a)

$\alpha = .05$

X

Distribution given the alternative hypothesis is correct.

(b)

$(1-\beta)$

$X + 10$

FIGURE **15.3** Power of the test of the null hypothesis against the alternative hypothesis
© Cengage Learning

indicated by the vertical line that cuts through both curves in Figure 15.3. The line divides the curve indicating the sampling distribution given the null hypothesis into two sections. The area under the curve represents the probability of various events given that the null hypothesis is true. The area to the right of the line cuts off a certain proportion of the curve. Suppose we decide to say that the null hypothesis is false and the alternative hypothesis is true whenever the mean score is greater than a certain amount, indicated by the vertical line. The section to the right of the line on the upper curve is the probability of deciding that the null hypothesis is false when in fact it is true. This is the probability of making a Type I error and is known as **alpha**. Alpha is the probability of deciding that the null hypothesis is false when it is actually true.

alpha: probability of a Type I error.

Usually, scientists prefer to make alpha a fairly small number, such as 0.05 or 0.01. The reason is that scientists believe that to decide that an experimental finding is true when it is not is a more serious error than it is to miss a true finding.

Alpha is also called the level of significance of an effect, or the statistical significance. It is common to say that a certain experimental result was significant at the 0.05 level. This means that the effect was large enough that the probability that it happened purely by chance was 0.05, or 1 in 20.

statistical significance: the probability that an experimental result happened by chance

The Significance of Significance

Let's suppose we have found that left-handed people with hazel eyes and free earlobes are better at repeating the Pledge of Allegiance backward and that the effect is significant at the 0.05 level. What does that mean? First, there is something that it does not mean: It does not mean that the results are important. Although in common usage that is exactly what the term *significance* means, results can be statistically significant when they have no importance at all. Results may be statistically significant even when an experiment has to do with the most trivial question imaginable, as in our little example.

Statistical significance means simply that your results have a certain low probability of having been the result of chance. When a result is significant at the 0.05 level, there is a 0.05 probability, or 1 in 20, that the result occurred when the null hypothesis was true—that is, when there was actually no effect. In other words, when the alternative hypothesis is accepted with an alpha level of .05, that hypothesis is either true or a reasonably improbable fluke. The level of significance is the same as alpha, or the probability of a Type I error.

There is a second thing statistical significance does not mean: It does not mean that the effect of the independent variable was large. The reason is simple and comes from the fact that the level of significance of an effect depends partly on the number of observations on which the test was based. For a given effect size, the more observations there are, the greater the significance will be. Recall our discussion in Chapter 12 of research methods that focus on big effects. Suppose there were a true difference of 1 mm in the average height of students at two colleges. If you compared a sample of 10 students from each college you would not expect to see a statistically significant difference between the groups. The larger the samples you take, however, the more you would expect to find a significant difference. In fact, if you measured every single student in the two colleges, any difference at all would be significant by definition. The reason is that when you have measured the entire populations, there is zero probability that they do not differ (assuming no error in measuring their heights). For these reasons, the APA has recommended that hypothesis tests be supplemented by measures of effect size to help the reader interpret the results (Wilkinson, 1999).

effect size: strength of the relationship between independent and dependent variables

Effect Size

As we have just seen, the sample size and the effect size both influence the statistical significance of a result. Let us take a closer look at effect size. Effect size is a straightforward concept; it is defined as the strength of the relationship between the independent and dependent variables in a study. One common measure of effect size that we have discussed already is the correlation coefficient, which can vary from -1.0 through 0 to $+1.0$. A zero correlation indicates no relationships between variables; positive or negative 1.0 indicates a perfect relationship. Correlations less than 0.2 are considered weak; 0.2 to 0.4, moderately weak; 0.4 to 0.6, moderate; 0.6 to 0.8, moderately strong; and 0.8 to 1.0, strong.

The distinction between effect size and significance is illustrated by the fact that any of these correlations can be significant or insignificant depending on the sample size. A correlation of 0.5 can be nonsignificant if it is based on too few observations. Statistics books provide tables showing the level significance of correlations of different sample sizes. Computerized statistical packages routinely print the significance of correlations.

For some studies, effect size can be measured by meaningful units at a practical level: Group 1 ate five grams more, or solved six more problems, or smoked seven fewer cigarettes per day than Group 2 did. Measures used in other studies may be harder to interpret. For these, effect size is commonly measured as the difference between the means of the groups, measured in terms of the variability within the groups. One widely used such measure is Cohen's d, which is defined for the t test as:

$$\text{Cohen's } d = \overline{X}_1 - \overline{X}_2 / \sigma$$

where σ is the (pooled estimate of) population standard deviation. When there is a lot of variability in the data, Cohen's d will be small; when variability is low, Cohen's d is large.

Other measures of effect size can be computed for many statistics, such as F. Further information can be found in most statistics books.

Power

Looking now at Figure 15.3(b), we find that the same criterion has divided the curve that represents the situation given the alternative hypothesis into two portions. The portion to the left is the probability of deciding that the null hypothesis is true when it is actually false. This is the probability of a Type II error.

The rest of the area under the curve showing the alternative hypothesis shows us another important probability: the probability of rejecting the null hypothesis when it is actually false. This is one minus the probability of a Type II error and

power: the probability of rejecting the null hypothesis when it is, in fact, false

is known as the power of the test. This is a very important probability: the probability of deciding that you have an experimental effect when you actually do.

Notice something about the two curves. You could decide to make your alpha, or probability of a Type I error, smaller by moving the line dividing the two curves to the right. However, by decreasing alpha, you would also decrease the probability of accepting the alternative hypothesis when it is true. In other words, you would decrease the power of the test.

Three things influence the power of a test. The first is the value of alpha. The smaller your alpha level, the smaller your power. If you decide that you want to make it unlikely that you will make a Type I error, you must accept the fact that you will be more likely to make a Type II error.

The second thing that influences the power of a test is the size of your experimental effect. If you are able to make your psychology program much more effective—by giving the students more courses, better materials, higher motivation, or other advantages—you will increase their mean score. This will have the effect of moving the curve showing the alternative hypothesis to the right, making less overlap between the curves.

The third way to increase the power of a test is to increase the size of the two groups. This will have the effect of decreasing the variability of the sampling distribution, or the variability of the two curves in Figure 15.3. This will also reduce the amount of overlap between them.

Chi-Square

Chi-Square statistic: also known as the Chi-Square goodness-of-fit test or Chi-Square test for independence. Evaluates frequency data to establish whether two (or more) categorical variables are related. Null hypothesis is that the variables are independent of each other

Both in everyday life and in the course of experimentation, situations often arise in which it is important to make decisions about whether one thing has happened more often (or more frequently) than another thing. The Chi-Square statistic (X^2) helps us to make these decisions about two or more categorical variables (see Chapter 5 for more information on variables). For example, imagine that a corporation is concerned about the color of a new plastic toy product, and is torn between making it in pink or in blue. So the consumer psychologists at the corporation recruit a wide variety of children, show them the toy in both colors, and ask them to choose the one that they like best. Even though the toys are identical in every way except color, blue wins the contest by quite a bit. Is it possible that because of cultural stereotypes, the boys might have shown a reluctance to accept a pink toy? Because our question is about the frequency with which children choose the colored toys, the Chi-Square statistic is appropriate. Chi-Square wouldn't be able to answer questions about how long the children played with the toys (duration), but it would be able to evaluate our frequency question well. In order to ask the question in our example more specifically, though, one might rephrase it for testing as follows: Is it possible that significantly more boys would vote for the blue toy than girls?

The Chi-Square enables us to decide whether a relationship exists between categorical variables, which in our example are votes for the color of the blue toy and gender of the child who voted. The Chi-Square statistic works on the expectation that two variables with equal probabilities should yield equal results if they are not related. So, in the case of our toy, if cultural stereotypes were not playing a role, we would expect that equal numbers of boys and girls should have voted in roughly equal numbers for the blue toy. Thus, according to the null hypothesis (H_0), our **expected frequencies** for these preferences should be roughly similar for boys and girls. However, the real question is whether the votes that we actually obtained for the toy preferences are different from our expectations. In other words, do our **observed frequencies** differ from the values we expected? Essentially, when the votes are actually counted, did more boys vote for the blue toy than girls?

To examine the voting habits of boys and girls in this example with Chi-Square, a 2×2 contingency table must be created. First, we have to figure out our expected frequencies. If we know that the blue toy received 70% of the 200 votes cast, and also know that boys and girls voted in equal numbers, the expected frequency table will look like Table 15.2.

We also have to examine the way that the children voted by placing our observed frequencies into the contingency table (Table 15.3).

Once we have both expected and observed frequencies, we need to examine the difference between them. We make this comparison initially by obtaining the difference between the observed and expected votes (Table 15.4).

It is clear from these numbers that the blue toy received more votes from boys than girls, but it is not clear as to whether these additional votes are likely to have occurred by chance. How do we know whether this difference would be likely to occur in a random sample of voters even if there were no

expected frequencies: anticipated values of the frequencies based on probability resulting from theory

observed frequencies: actual frequencies obtained from a sample

contingency table: table designed to examine whether the rows and columns are related to each other. If the numbers in the columns show no significant relationship to those in the rows (e.g., they are not contingent on the rows), then the rows and column frequencies are not demonstrably related

TABLE **15.2**

Expected Frequencies (from null hypothesis)

© Cengage Learning

		Votes for Blue Toy		
		Yes	No	Total
Sex of Child	Boys	70	30	100
	Girls	70	30	100
	Total	140	60	200

TABLE **15.3**

Observed Frequencies (sample results)

© Cengage Learning

		Votes for Blue Toy		
		Yes	No	Total
Sex of Child	Boys	80	20	100
	Girls	60	40	100
	Total	140	60	200

TABLE **15.4**
Observed minus Expected Frequencies

© Cengage Learning

		Votes for Blue Toy	
		Yes	**No**
Sex of Child	**Boys**	$80 - 70 = 10$	$20 - 30 = -10$
	Girls	$60 - 70 = -10$	$40 - 30 = 10$

difference at all within the full population? Computing the Chi-Square statistic allows us to determine whether the sex of the voter is associated with a vote for the blue toy. The general formula is:

$$\chi^2 = \Sigma[(O - E)^2 / E]$$

where O = observed frequency and E = expected frequency in each cell of the table. (Caution: χ^2 isn't accurate if any expected value is less than five.) So each of the differences between the observed and the expected (as in Table 15.4) is squared, then divided by the expected frequency, and finally added to the results from the other cells. To get an intuitive feel for this statistic, you might notice that the greater the difference between what is observed and what is expected, the larger the Chi-Square value. Statistical tables are available in which the significance level of any Chi-Square value can be found, though most statistics software will output both a value and its significance level. Since the present example (with one degree of freedom) yielded a Chi-Square value of 5.74, the tables show that it is significant at the 0.02 level. This low level shows that it is highly likely that a voter's sex influenced whether or not they voted for the blue toy.

Analysis of Variance

Analysis of variance (ANOVA) is a powerful statistical method for analyzing experimental data. It is a flexible but complex method that can be adapted to a great variety of experimental designs. These characteristics make ANOVA difficult to summarize and to understand. Because ANOVA is so widely used, however, it is necessary to have an acquaintance with some of its basic concepts.

When one wants to analyze the data of an experiment with only two conditions, a *t* test is appropriate. Whenever there are more than two conditions, however, a *t* test is not appropriate because a *t* test can compare only two groups at a time. If there were three conditions, it would be necessary to compare the first with the second, the first with the third, and the second with the third. This would result in three separate statistical tests. Performing several tests would give you more chances to reject a true null hypothesis, so you would increase the likelihood of rejecting the null hypothesis when it is actually true.

ANOVA was developed to make it possible to test the null hypothesis that there is no difference among a number of conditions. Suppose that an experiment tested the effect of three different doses of marijuana on motor coordination. The null hypothesis would be that there is no difference among the three doses:

$$H_0 : \mu_1 = \mu_2 = \mu_3$$

The alternative hypothesis is that

$$H_1 : [\mu_1 = \mu_2 = \mu_3]$$

is not true. Note that the alternative hypothesis simply says that it is not true that all the means are equal. It does not say that all the means are unequal. For the alternative hypothesis to be true, it is necessary only that some combination of means not be equal to some other combination. For example, one situation that would make the null hypothesis false and the alternative hypothesis true could be that Conditions 1 and 2 differ significantly from Condition 3 in a three-condition experiment. It is entirely possible that neither Condition 1 nor Condition 2, considered alone, differs significantly from Condition 3, but that the participants in Conditions 1 and 2 considered together differ significantly from those in Condition 3.

ANOVA: the analysis of variance statistic tests whether the means of more than two groups are equal

Any experiment that has more than two conditions must be analyzed by ANOVA instead of a *t* test. Very simply, any ANOVA tests the significance of a difference among several conditions in an experiment by making two different estimates of the variability that you would expect to find in the data given that the null hypothesis is true. If there is no true difference among the groups, each estimate of variability should, on the average, be the same. Let us see where those two estimates of variability come from.

Two Estimates of the Variability in the Population

grand mean: mean of all the data

Suppose that the null hypothesis is true. In that case, because the experimental conditions have no effect, you would predict that all the individual data would have the same value. This value would be the mean of all the data, or the grand mean. Now, it should be obvious that all the data would not be exactly the same, because chance factors are nearly always operating to introduce variability to the data. Therefore, individual data points will vary about the mean of their respective groups. Just as the individuals will differ within a group, the means of the data from the various groups will not have the same value, for the same reason. Thus, the group means will vary about the overall mean in a random way.

We can think of the variability of the subjects within each group as one estimate of the variability in the population, and the variability of the means of the groups as another estimate of the variability of the population. Thus, we have two different ways in which chance will affect the data in an experiment when there is no experimental effect (and the null hypothesis is therefore true): by producing differences between the means of the various conditions and by producing differences among the subjects within the various groups. These are two ways in which chance affects the data that provide the basis for doing ANOVA.

Figure 15.4 represents the data from a hypothetical experiment in which motor coordination was measured in three different groups after the subjects

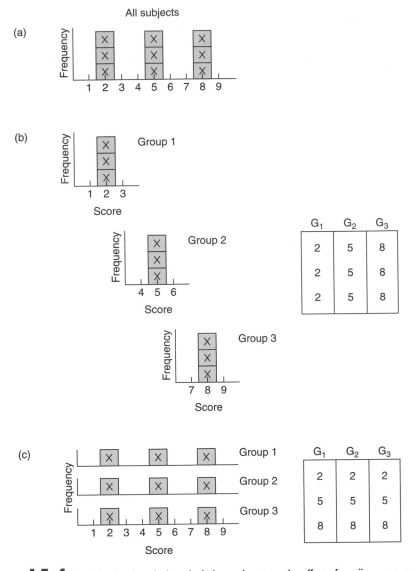

FIGURE **15.4** Possible situations in hypothetical experiment on the effect of marijuana on motor coordination

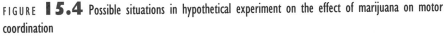

experienced three different doses of marijuana. Figure 15.4(a) represents the data from all the subjects in the experiment. We see that there was some variability among the subjects, but we don't know how the variability relates to the conditions. In Figure 15.4(b), we see one possible situation. All the subjects in a particular group had exactly the same data, and each of these groups differed from the others. Here there is variability among the groups but no variability within the groups. Figure 15.4(c) shows another way in which the variability in the experiment could be distributed. Here all the groups have exactly the same mean, and all the variability is within the groups. This example is admittedly highly artificial. Ordinarily, of course, there would be some variability within, and some between, the groups. In our example, there was either no variability within the groups or no variability among the groups. The point, however, is that we have two ways of estimating the variability in the population: one based on the variability within the groups and the other based on the variability between the groups.

The differences among the means of the groups and the differences among the subjects within the groups give us two separate estimates of the variability in the population. Sometimes one estimate will be larger, and sometimes the other will be larger. On the average, however, they should be equal if the independent variable in fact had no effect. Consider a ratio of the between-conditions variability to the **within-conditions variability**:

between-conditions variability/within-conditions variability

This ratio is called F, or the F ratio. The value of F will be 1.0, on the average.

The term *between groups* can lead to a misunderstanding if one understands it to refer to two groups, rather than more than two. As discussed earlier, the null hypothesis in ANOVA is that all the groups are equal. Recall that no two groups need be significantly different from each other for this hypothesis to be false (and the alternative hypothesis to be true). It simply means that some group *or combination of groups* differs significantly from the rest.

If the null hypothesis is false and there is an experimental effect, the between-conditions variability will be larger than expected because the variability caused by the experimental effect will add to the random variability. Then the value of the F ratio will be greater than 1.0. The F ratio is central to ANOVA. Every ANOVA has at least one F ratio. The value of F obtained in the study is evaluated statistically against the value that would be expected to occur by chance alone. If the F ratio is larger than a certain value, the experimental effect is considered to be statistically significant.

Partitioning the Variance

We need to consider one more concept before discussing how to read an ANOVA summary table. The reason this technique is called *analysis of variance* is that ANOVA makes it possible to analyze all the sources of variability in an experiment. In other words, a set of data contains a certain amount of variability. Some of this variability comes from variability among the subjects: how people differ from one another regardless of the experimental conditions. Other variability in the data is caused by the experimental conditions: The independent variable caused the subjects to behave differently.

In a simple ANOVA, there are two sources of variance: between-groups variance and within-groups variance. In Figure 15.4(a), we see a certain amount of variability among the subjects, but we don't yet know how much is between-groups variance and how much is within-groups variance. Figure 15.4(b) shows a situation in which all the variance is between groups and there is none within groups. Figure 15.4(c) shows a different possibility—all the variance is within groups and there is none between groups. Thus, in these highly artificial examples, we could say that all the variance is either

between-conditions variability: way of estimating the variability in the population based on the variability between the groups

within-conditions variability: way of estimating the variability in the population based on the variability within the groups

F ratio: statistic associated with ANOVA that is a ratio of between-conditions variability to within-conditions variability

between- or within-groups variance. Ordinarily, of course, there would be some of each.

How to Read an ANOVA Summary Table

There are many different types of ANOVA, depending on the particular experimental design. You will need to consult a statistics book to be able to perform an ANOVA. Frequently, however, you will read a description of an experiment that contains an ANOVA summary table. Fortunately, you can read and interpret an ANOVA table without knowing how to perform the ANOVA. The purpose of this section is to help you understand such a table.

It is actually possible to decipher a great deal about an experiment from an ANOVA summary table. Consider Table 15.5, which shows the analysis of a simple one-way ANOVA. The term *one-way* means that the experiment contains only one independent variable (IV).

An ANOVA summary table always contains at least two rows of information, one for each source of variance in the experiment. In addition, certain totals are shown. We see in this case that there is a row labeled "Between conditions." This row shows the information about the variance resulting from the different conditions, or levels, of the independent variable. The second row is labeled "Within conditions." This row indicates the information about the variance of the data within the conditions, or groups.

The columns indicate sum of squares (*SS*), degrees of freedom (*df*), mean square (*MS*), the *F* ratio (*F*), and probability (*p*). The sum of squares is a measure of the variability in the data. Some of the variance can be attributed to the experimental variable. This is the between-conditions variance, which has a value of 504 in this example. The rest of the variance can be attributed to the variance within each condition. This is the within-conditions variance, which is 251 in this example. Notice that the sum of these values gives us the total variability in the experiment.

sum of squares: a measure of the variability of the data; the sum of the squared differences of observations from the mean

TABLE **15.5**
ANOVA Summary Table
© Cengage Learning

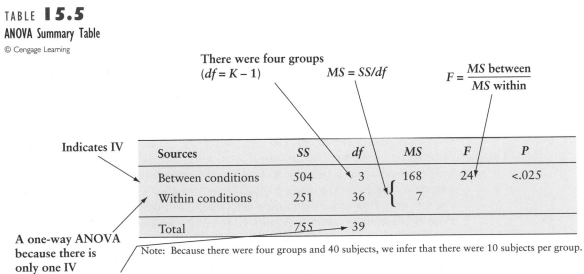

There were four groups
($df = K - 1$)

$MS = SS/df$

$F = \dfrac{MS \text{ between}}{MS \text{ within}}$

Indicates IV

Sources	SS	df	MS	F	P
Between conditions	504	3	168	24	<.025
Within conditions	251	36	7		
Total	755	39			

A one-way ANOVA because there is only one IV

There were 40 subjects
(Total $df = N - 1$)

Note: Because there were four groups and 40 subjects, we infer that there were 10 subjects per group.

degrees of freedom: number of values in a statistic that are free to vary, such as the number of groups or subjects

mean square: sum of squares divided by the number of degrees of freedom; an estimate of variance

Degrees of freedom is a quantity that depends on the number of groups, subjects, and the like. The total degrees of freedom, 39 in our example, is one less than the number of observations; therefore, we can conclude that there were 40 observations in the experiment. Because this was a between-subjects experiment, and therefore each subject contributed one observation, we know that there were 40 subjects. The number of degrees of freedom between conditions, three in this example, is one less than the number of conditions; thus, we know that there were four conditions. The mean square is the sum of squares divided by the number of degrees of freedom in the same row.

All these figures are used to determine the value of F, which is the ratio of the mean square between subjects to the mean square within subjects. Remember that if there is an experimental effect, the variance attributable to the conditions (the mean square between conditions) will be larger than the variance attributable to the subjects (the mean square within conditions). If the F ratio is sufficiently greater than 1.0, it is considered significant. This is determined by looking in a table, or it may be printed out automatically by certain statistical programs.

ANOVA summary tables differ in their structure depending on the design of the experiment. Certain things can always be counted on, however. First, there is a row in the table for each source of variance. Each independent variable is a source of variance. In Table 15.5, the first row indicates the independent variable. In a two-way ANOVA, both independent variables are sources of variance. The interaction between the two variables is also a source of variance.

Second, at least one of the sources of variance serves as an error term. The purpose of the error term is to form the denominator of the F ratio. In a simple ANOVA, such as the one summarized in Table 15.5, the within-groups variance serves as the error term. The error term is generally in the last row.

Third, there is always at least one F ratio computed from two mean squares. The numerator of the ratio is the particular effect being tested—the between-groups effect (the effect of the independent variable), for example. The denominator of the ratio is the error term. Therefore, the F ratios in the table are usually computed as the ratio of the mean square in one of the upper rows to the mean square in the last row.

Fourth, if there is a row with the word *subjects* in the label, we know that we have a within-subjects (repeated-measures) design. Table 15.6 shows such a design. Here, the numerator of the F ratio is found in the between-conditions row, as before. The denominator of the F ratio (error term) is once again in the last row, but here it is called the *residual*. Because there are only three rows of information, we know that we have a one-way, repeated-measures ANOVA. We can see that there were 30 observations because there are 29 total degrees of freedom. Also, we know that there were three conditions because there are two degrees of freedom between conditions.

Table 15.7 gives the summary information from another experiment. Here we see one row indicating the information for an independent variable A, labeled "Between conditions of A," and a second row labeled "Between

TABLE 15.6
ANOVA Summary Table: Within-Subjects Design
© Cengage Learning

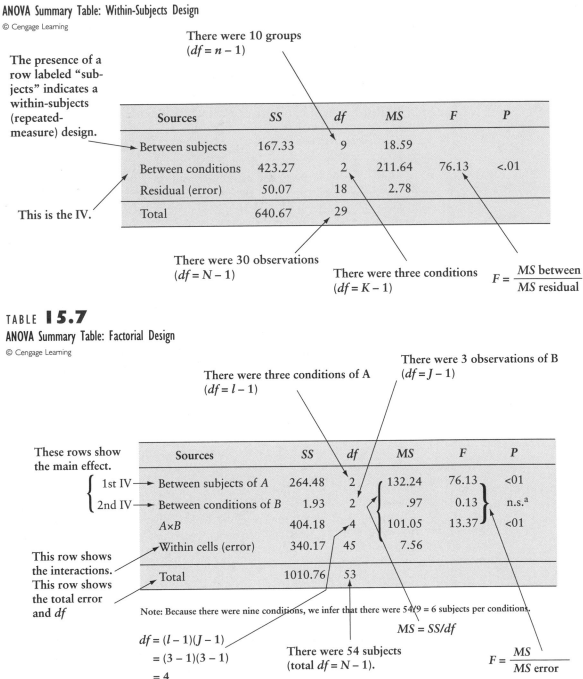

There were 10 groups
($df = n - 1$)

The presence of a row labeled "subjects" indicates a within-subjects (repeated-measure) design.

This is the IV.

Sources	SS	df	MS	F	P
Between subjects	167.33	9	18.59		
Between conditions	423.27	2	211.64	76.13	<.01
Residual (error)	50.07	18	2.78		
Total	640.67	29			

There were 30 observations
($df = N - 1$)

There were three conditions
($df = K - 1$)

$$F = \frac{MS\ between}{MS\ residual}$$

TABLE 15.7
ANOVA Summary Table: Factorial Design
© Cengage Learning

There were three conditions of A
($df = l - 1$)

There were 3 observations of B
($df = J - 1$)

These rows show the main effect.

Sources	SS	df	MS	F	P
Between subjects of A	264.48	2	132.24	76.13	<01
Between conditions of B	1.93	2	.97	0.13	n.s.[a]
A×B	404.18	4	101.05	13.37	<01
Within cells (error)	340.17	45	7.56		
Total	1010.76	53			

1st IV; 2nd IV

This row shows the interactions.
This row shows the total error and df

Note: Because there were nine conditions, we infer that there were 54/9 = 6 subjects per conditions.

$MS = SS/df$

$df = (l - 1)(J - 1)$
$= (3 - 1)(3 - 1)$
$= 4$

There were 54 subjects
(total $df = N - 1$).

$$F = \frac{MS}{MS\ error}$$

conditions of B." This tells us that there were two independent variables. This means we have a two-way ANOVA and the experiment had a factorial design. With two-way ANOVA, we see a third row for information about the interaction between the two independent variables, labeled "A X B."

Summary

1. Inferential statistical techniques enable us to draw inferences about the population by examining a sample drawn from the population.
2. A statistic is a quantity calculated from a sample, which is a sub-set of the population.
3. A sampling distribution is a distribution of means of samples drawn from a population that has the same mean as the population but a smaller standard deviation. The shape of a sampling distribution approximates the normal distribution.
4. A research hypothesis can be restated as two different hypotheses: the alternative hypothesis and the null hypothesis.
5. Hypothesis testing may be one or two-tailed, depending on whether the alternative hypothesis predicts that one group will differ from another in a specific way (one-tailed) or that one will simply differ from the other (two-tailed).
6. Errors can be made in statistical testing either by determining that there is a difference between groups when there actually isn't one (Type I error) or by determining that no difference exists when the groups are actually different (Type II error).
7. Alpha, which is also known as the statistical significance level, is the probability of making a Type I error.
8. An effect size estimate gives an idea of how strong the relationship is between the dependent and independent variables in a study.
9. The Chi-Square statistic helps us to decide whether one thing happened more frequently than another.
10. A *t* test compares the means of two groups, while an ANOVA can make comparisons between a larger number of groups.

Suggestions for Further Reading

SALSBURG, D. (2001). *The lady tasting tea.* New York: W. H. Freeman. This text illuminates the role that statistics have played in science and technology.

VICKERS, A. J. (2009). *What is a p-value anyway? 34 stories to help you actually understand statistics.* Boston: Addison Wesley. This light-hearted text illustrates basic statistical principles with interesting stories.

Reading Between the Lines

15.1 How Much Significance Should Be Placed on Significance?

In the course of an interesting article on the use and misuse of statistics, Tom Siegfried (2010a) relates an example in which two different anti-depressants were each separately evaluated to see whether they were more associated with suicidal incidents than placebos were. In the first experiment, the group given anti-depressant drug number 1 was associated with suicidal incidents at a rate that was twice as high as the placebo group. In another experiment, anti-depressant drug number 2 was associated less often with suicidal incidents than the second placebo group. Initial conclusions were that the first drug was more dangerous than the second drug, as it had a higher association with suicidal incidents. Were those conclusions correct? What else could account for these findings? (*Hint:* Think of how the experiments were performed and the comparisons that were made.)

Web-Based Workshops on Research Methods and Statistics

Cengage Publishing Company maintains Web-based workshops on research methods and statistics. These workshops give a different slant on the material in this book.

www.cengage.com/psychology/workshops

For this chapter, there are 18 workshops on various aspects of statistics.

Exercises

15.1 Hypothesis Testing and Power

This exercise uses the computer program given in the Instructor's Manual. The program takes samples from one of two distributions. The first distribution has a mean of 100 and a standard deviation of 16. The mean of the second is 101, and it has the same standard deviation. When you run the exercise, you will be presented with samples from either one distribution or the other; you will not know which.

Suppose you know that the mean IQ of the general population is 100 and the standard deviation is 16. (Actually it is 15, but 16 is more convenient for the program.) You also know that people with first names that have exactly seven letters have a mean IQ of 101 and the same standard deviation. Now, suppose you are told only the mean IQ of a sample of people, all of whom either have seven letters in their first names or have other than seven letters in their first names. Your job is to guess whether your sample has seven-letter names or other-than-seven-letter names.

Your best strategy is to guess 100 whenever the mean of the sample is less than 100.50. When it is equal to or greater than 100.50, it is at least an even bet that the sample is from the 101 population.

This exercise is an illustration of hypothesis testing. Your null hypothesis is that the sample came from the general population—those people who have names other than seven letters long and have a mean IQ of 100. The alternative hypothesis is that the sample came from the population of those who have seven letters in their names and have an average IQ of 101.

After each trial, the program will tell you whether you have made a correct guess or whether you have made an error. You can make a correct guess in two ways. First, you can guess that your sample comes from the general population when it does. This would be an example of correctly accepting the null hypothesis. Second, you could guess that the sample comes from the seven-letter-name population when it actually does. This would be an example of correctly rejecting the null hypothesis.

You could also make an error in two ways. You could guess that the sample came from the seven-letter-name population when it came from the general population. This would be a Type I error because you rejected a true null hypothesis. Alternatively, you could guess that the sample came from the general population when it actually came from the seven-letter-name population. This would be a Type II error because you accepted the null hypothesis when it was false.

You will see as you go through the exercise that you will sometimes make errors even when you make the best possible decision. This illustrates that hypothesis testing is a matter of probability—in this case, a probability of making certain kinds of errors.

At first, you will be given the mean of samples of size four; in other words, four individuals will be selected from the population. Later, you will be given the means of samples of size 400. As the sample size gets larger, the means of the samples will tend to be closer to the means of the populations from which they are sampled, and you will be able to make more accurate judgments. This illustrates the effect of sample size on the probability of making a correct decision.

The reason for this effect can be seen by examining the equation for the standard error of the mean. The standard error of the mean is the standard deviation of the distribution of sample means:

$$\sigma_{\overline{X}} = \frac{\sigma}{\sqrt{N}}$$

With a sample size of 4:

$$\sigma_{\overline{X}} = \frac{16}{\sqrt{4}} = \frac{16}{2} = 8$$

When the sample size is 400, the standard error of the mean is one tenth as large:

$$\sigma_{\overline{X}} = \frac{16}{\sqrt{400}} = \frac{16}{20} = 0.8$$

The smaller standard error of the mean means that there is less variability in the means of your sample, so they tend to fall nearer the mean of the population. Thus, you are more often able to guess correctly which population you are sampling from.

This is an illustration of the concept of *statistical power*. Remember, power is the probability of rejecting the null hypothesis when it is false, or the probability of deciding that you have an experimental effect when in fact you do. This probability is one minus the probability of a Type II error:

$$\text{power} = 1 - p(\text{type II error})$$

In the IQ example, the probability of guessing 101 when it is in fact 101 is the power of your test. Power increases as sample size increases. The theoretical power of your decision is 0.52 when

the sample size is four, but it increases to 0.73 when the sample size is 400. (These numbers assume that you guessed that the sample came from the population with a mean of 101 whenever the mean of the sample was 100.5 or greater.)

The computer will print out your obtained power. Your actual power will differ from the theoretical power because the data are empirical data subject to chance factors. If your empirical data differ markedly from the theoretical values, you may want to repeat the exercise.

Required:

a. What was your observed power when the sample size was four? When it was 400?

b. What else does power depend on?

15.2 Identify Directional and Nondirectional Hypotheses

A: $H_0 : \mu_1 = \mu_2$ D: $H_1 : \mu_1 \neq \mu_2$
B: $H_0 : \mu_1 \leq \mu_2$ E: $H_1 : \mu_1 < \mu_2$
C: $H_0 : \mu_1 \geq \mu_2$ F: $H_1 : \mu_1 > \mu_2$

For each of the following statements, identify the correct null hypothesis (A, B, or C) and the correct alternative hypothesis (D, E, or F).

a. Introductory algebra students who are taught with hand-held calculators (Group 1) for a 15-week period will have different scores on tests of computational skills (taken without the use of a calculator) from introductory algebra students who are taught without calculators (Group 2).

b. New graduate male nurses whose orientation program uses a preceptor (an individual tutor) as a major component (Group 1) will exhibit higher performance levels than will new graduate male nurses in a traditional orientation program (Group 2).

c. Kindergarten students who have a volunteer parent pool assisting their teachers (Group 1) in the classroom will show different achievement from kindergarten students whose teachers do not have extra assistance in the classroom (Group 2).

d. Students who receive key images, or pictures, with new vocabulary words (Group 1) will show greater acquisition and retention of the definition of words than will students who are left to their own strategies for learning new words (Group 2).

15.3 Does Pre-school Attendance Affect Future Mathematics Achievement?

Since many school districts are facing budget cuts, establishing the effectiveness of programs is important to determining funding. One school district's administrators wanted to know if pre-school programs affected the way that children performed later in mathematics. The administrators took a random sample of 100 eighth graders and compared the mathematics achievement levels of those who attended pre-school to those who did not. The results are in Table 15.8.

Required:
a. If mathematics achievement is independent of pre-school attendance, what should the proportions be for each cell?
b. Perform a Chi-Square analysis on the observations in Table 15.8 (*Hint*: Calculate tables for the expected frequencies and the observed minus expected frequencies) to determine if there is an association between attending pre-school and mathematics achievement.

TABLE **15.8**
© Cengage Learning

	Below grade level	At grade level	Advanced
Pre-school	15	13	12
No Pre-school	12	30	18

15.4 Interpret an ANOVA Summary Table

Required:
a. Complete the missing information in Table 15.9.
b. Is this a one-way or a two-way ANOVA?
c. Was this a within-subjects or a between-subjects design?
d. How many levels of A were there?
e. How many subjects were in the experiment?
f. How many subjects were in each group?
g. Was the effect of A significant? If so, at what level?

TABLE **15.9**
© Cengage Learning

Source	SS	df	MS	F	P
Between A	O	O	O	O	<.05
Within groups	1230	50	O		
Total	5166	54			

15.5 Interpret an ANOVA Summary Table

Required:
a. Complete the missing information in Table 15.10.
b. Is this a one-way or a two-way ANOVA?
c. Was this a within-subjects or a between-subjects design?
d. How many levels of A were there?
e. How many levels of B were there?
f. How many subjects were in this experiment?
g. How many subjects were in each group?
h. Was the effect of B significant? If so, at what level?
i. Was the interaction significant? If so, at what level?

TABLE **15.10**
© Cengage Learning

Source	SS	df	MS	F	P
Between A	160	1	160	O	<.01
Between B	160	2	O	5	<.05
A × B	O	2	12	.75	n.s.[a]
Within groups	384	24	16		
Total	728	O			

[a]Not significant.

15.6 Interpret an ANOVA Summary Table

Required:
a. Complete the missing information in Table 15.11.
b. Is this a one-way or a two-way ANOVA?
c. Was this a within-subjects or a between-subjects experiment?
d. How many levels of A were there?
e. How many subjects were in the experiment?
f. Was the F test significant?

TABLE **15.11**

© Cengage Learning

Sources	SS	df	MS	F	P
Between subjects	162	9	○		
Between A	456	2	228	○	<.01
Residual	○	○	3		
Total	672	29			

15.7 Interpret an ANOVA Summary Table

Required:

a. Based on Table 15.12, how many subjects were there?

b. How many independent variables were there?
c. How many groups were there?
d. Did each subject experience all conditions?
e. Is this a one-way or a two-way ANOVA?
f. Show where the value of F came from.
g. Were the results significant at the 0.05 level?

TABLE **15.12**

© Cengage Learning

Source	SS	df	MS	F	p
Between conditions	504	3	168	24	<.025
Within conditions	251	36	7		
Total	755	39			

EPILOGUE

Biases and Limitations of Experimental Psychology

PREVIEW

This Epilogue ends the book by discussing some ways that psychology falls short of the ideals laid out in Chapter 1. Certain features of science cause it to have both liberal and conservative effects on society at the same time. Further, science has limitations that are both theoretical and practical. We close by discussing the responsibilities of the scientist.

We have spent much of this book talking about what experimental psychology is and how psychology can be used as a method of gaining knowledge about human behavior. Before we end the book, however, we must temper our enthusiasm somewhat by discussing a few of the problems of psychological research. Science is, after all, a human activity and therefore subject to human failings. We should have a realistic idea of what science is and is not likely to accomplish.

Let us look at the place of science in relation to the fact that science has become one of the moral arbiters of our society. With the decline of the influence of traditional religions, psychologists have entered the priestly ranks in our culture. Psychologists are frequently interviewed in the media about all sorts of moral issues, from war to incest.

A need for caution arises from the tendency of people to take scientific statements about how society behaves as indications of how it ought to behave. It is easy to conclude that because 85% of the population does something, it is right to do that particular thing. By documenting what is statistically common, we contribute to the definition of what is normal. A classic example of this phenomenon is the Kinsey report on sexual behavior, but this tendency is found in studies of everything from daydreaming to cheating on income taxes. This Epilogue discusses some of the major limitations of research in experimental psychology.

Biases

In Chapter 1, we emphasized that science is a social enterprise. As such, science is subject to all the types of human bias. Some of them affect the choice of problems to work on, the theories developed, and whether particular results are reported. We consider the many sources of bias under two headings: those that cause science to be conservative and those that lead science to have a liberal influence.

Science as Conservative

As is true of any social institution, science is conservative. Editors, reviewers, department chairpersons, and deans generally are older scientists who may be slower to change than younger ones are. It is well known that new scientific ideas are adopted more readily by younger scientists. Scientists also sometimes refuse to change their positions on important theoretical issues, and thus it becomes necessary for a generation of scientists to pass before a new theory is firmly established.

Another source of conservatism is provided by science's dependence on financial support. In the latter half of the 20th century, science entered a period known as "big science." That trend has continued during the beginning of the 21st century. In 2008, $398 billion was spent on research and development in the United States, of which 26% was supported by the federal government. In the same year, more than $51 billion was spent on research at US universities and colleges, 59% of which was federally supported (National Science Board, 2010). Other developed nations also spend a considerable amount of money in support of research activities. The impact that federal spending has on psychological research is enormous. We can get some idea of its weight by noting how many journal articles report research supported by the government. For example, at least 65% of the articles published in the *Journal of Experimental Psychology: Human Perception and Performance* for 2011 acknowledged support from government grants, although only 35% of those articles received support from the US government. Many of these experiments required expensive equipment and facilities that would be beyond the reach of most universities, let alone individual researchers. The days of research conducted in spare time and funded out of the researcher's pocket are largely over.

The amount of money available for various categories of research is part of the congressional budget process and therefore is subject to political pressure. Many researchers track the types of research that are being funded and direct their grant applications accordingly. In addition, the federal government puts out periodic requests for proposals (RFPs) for projects it wants to fund. Although many of the steps in the review process involve peer review by nongovernmental scientists, the final steps include political considerations. The type of research that gets proposed and funded is subject to political pressure, even if the pressure exists only in the mind of the scientist who decides to slant a proposal to be relevant to aging, child abuse, education, or whatever is being funded at the time. One of the least subtle forms of pressure on scientists is fear of being ridiculed on the floor of the Senate if the research should be capable of sounding silly out of its proper context. The following is just one example of the kinds of pressure that scientists face from the government when doing research. One might think that political considerations have rarely had a more chilling effect on research than in 1991, when Secretary of Health and Human Services Louis Sullivan canceled a research project on teenage sexual behavior. This study was to have focused on the behavioral factors that contribute to teenage pregnancy and sexually transmitted diseases, including AIDS (Moffat, 1991). There is little basic information on adolescent sexual behavior, including the reasons teenagers engage in risky behavior, so it is difficult to know how to go about reducing the incidence of risk taking. Opposition to the project arose from conservatives who believed that it would encourage sexual activity by adolescents, and eventually money for the project was instead transferred to a "just say no" teen pregnancy prevention program. Congressman William Dannemeyer even offered an amendment to a bill that would have prevented the Department of Health and Human Services from ever supporting any national survey of human sexual behavior ("Sullivan Cancels Teen Sex Survey," 1991), which was defeated. However, even today, political arguments continue as to whether to fund peer-reviewed projects that deal with sexuality. In 2003, Representatives Patrick Toomey and Chris Chocola introduced legislation that would have prevented the funding of three projects approved by the National Institutes of Health simply because the topic of those projects was sex research. The Representatives claimed that research on this topic was morally wrong and therefore should not be supported. Although this legislation was barely defeated, legislation that second-guesses the stringent peer review process necessary for grant funding continues to be introduced ("A Political Attack," 2005). As recently as 2007, Rep. John Campbell (R, CA) ridiculed federal funding of psychological research simply on the basis of the title of the project. He attempted to block funding of a peer-reviewed project called *Accuracy in the Cross-Cultural Understanding of Other's Emotions* because he did not feel that it was up to the "standard of requiring expenditures" (Jaschik, 2008). Proposals like the one by Rep. Campbell are designed to bar the funding of particular grants. Supporting them would have essentially allowed politicians to determine what research should be funded rather than leaving the decision to trained scientists. Fortunately, in this instance, other law makers, such as Rep. Brian Baird (D, WA) stood up for the grant by stressing the importance of peer review and of knowing about a particular project in detail. But pressures like these have caused some great minds to reconsider their commitment to pursuing research.

Given that the major support for science is from the government and industry, it is not surprising that there is a great deal of research on how to make people more productive and little on how to make work more meaningful, much research on how to exercise power over subordinates and little on what having power does to the wielder of power, a great deal of interest in the personality patterns of prejudiced people and little on the social conditions that lead to prejudice, and more study of what is wrong with students who cannot read than of schools that do not teach. It is easy to make a case that research is funded by powerful groups and organizations to further their purposes.

Similarly, the results of psychological research tend to be used to control certain groups. Mental patients receive behavior modification, hyperactive children receive drugs, and prisoners receive psychosurgery. In each case, a group of powerful people finds it necessary or desirable to control the behavior of others. Needless to say, mental patients and hyperactive children need help, and society must protect itself against criminals. The controversy about psychologists participating in interrogations at Guantanamo Bay, Cuba, is a recent example of this dilemma. Since 2002, psychologists have observed the interrogation of suspected terrorists and suggested ways to exploit the weaknesses of detainees in an effort to gain information that might be crucial to national security (Ephron, 2008). Given the reports of prisoner torture coming from Guantanamo, the APA recently banned members from continuing to take part in interrogations beginning in 2009 (Tanner, 2008). So as psychologists we should be aware that our work sometimes supports a social system that oppresses people, and evaluate our own level of bias by mentally substituting ourselves for the group we are evaluating (Gernsbacher, 2006).

In discussing the influence of the social context of psychology, Kurt Danziger (1979) points out that the very origin of psychology depended on the support of conservative forces.

> In the United States [as opposed to Germany] ... control of university appointments, research funds, and professional opportunities was vested in the hands of either businessmen and their appointees, or politicians who represented their interests. If psychology was to emerge as a viable independent discipline, it would have to be in a form acceptable to these social forces.... Psychologists might become acceptable if they would reasonably promise to develop the technical competence to deal with [the problems of migration, urbanization, and industrialization]. (p. 35)

Let us not assume that scientists are swept along by forces beyond their control. As society members who have a stake in the status quo, scientists are often willing servants of power. Examples of these influences are not hard to document. Danziger quotes J. B. Watson (the founder of Behaviorism) as saying that "if psychology would follow the plan I suggest, the educator, the physician, the jurist, and the businessman would utilize our data in a practical way." Danziger suggests that "the reason his [Watson's] message found such immediate and massive resonance was that most American psychologists already accepted the premise that it was the business of their discipline to produce data to be utilized 'in a practical way' by educators, businessmen, and so on" (p. 38).

We have been discussing how government support can bias research. As great as governmental political pressures can be on research, private funding may be an even greater source of bias. Private industry now supports more than 67% of all research in the United States (National Science Board, 2010). Many psychologists work in the area of biomedical and drug investigations; in the year 2000, industry funded 62% of the biomedical research in which psychologists are studying the effects of medications (Bekelman, Li, & Gross, 2003). Others are increasingly supported by private funding coming from charitable or special interest groups. Given the trend toward corporate research funding, it is important to understand where bias could arise in these research relationships.

Corporations are in business to make money, and they cannot afford to do research that doesn't promise to increase their profits. So psychologists working for a corporate sponsor may feel pressure to produce research with specific outcomes that will benefit the company. If the psychologist doesn't produce the "right" results for the corporate sponsor, pressure may be applied to soften the discussion of the result or to suppress the publication altogether (DeAngelis, 2003; Resnik, 2007). For example, a thorough examination of the literature concerning anti-depressants suggested that many studies showing that the drugs were ineffective were not published (Turner, Matthews, Linardatos, Tell, & Rosenthal, 2008). If a psychologist's research produces results that do not benefit the company, future funding for that scientist could be in jeopardy. The tobacco company Philip Morris shut down a whole laboratory that found results not to its liking.

The researchers themselves often stand to benefit financially from their research as well. One researcher made a tidy profit by buying stock in the company that made zinc throat lozenges when his research showed that they were effective against the common cold, just before the price of the stock soared. (His later research showed that they didn't work after all.) As a reaction to potential bias due to financial incentives, most universities now require their researchers to reveal any financial interests they have in their own research, but they seldom verify these revelations beyond a researcher's disclosure statement (Greenberg, 2008). Consequently, the temptation to inappropriately or inadequately disclose conflicts of interest is not currently curbed by the threat of strong repercussions.

Even if the integrity of the results is not compromised by strong industrial suggestions as to what the outcome of the research "should be," bias associated with corporate sponsorship can also occur during the publication process. Companies that sponsor research commonly demand to see the results before they are published in the interest of keeping trade secrets. Publication is often suppressed if the findings may give some advantage to a competitor.

In an effort to protect research integrity, the APA (Pachter, Fox, Zimbardo, & Antonuccio, 2007) began a Task Force on External Funding Sources in 2002 that finished its work in 2005. The aim of the task force was to guide the

APA as an organization in determining whether or not to accept funding from particular sources, and it suggested that limits be placed on the way that private funds can be used by the APA (Pachter, Fox, Zimbardo, & Antonuccio, 2007). The APA Ethics Code (American Psychological Association, 2010) also offers suggestions that may help on institutional relationships (8.01), multiple relationships (3.05), and conflicts of interest (3.06). Some universities are also establishing specific guidelines for dealing with corporate-academic relations, and creating offices to make certain that the guidelines are followed and the integrity of research is maintained.

Science as Liberal

Although we have a clear case for science as a conservative force, we can see that science may also have a liberal influence. In fact, many people intuitively see science as a force for change directed against established institutions. This view is almost true by definition because of the objective way science operates, as discussed in Chapter 1. Because science deals only with data that can gain the assent of every person, political and other orthodoxies are frequently challenged by science. In addition, the search for truth often leads to answers that are not palatable to society as a whole and to its powerful institutions in particular. Psychological research on the adverse effects of segregated education contributed to the Supreme Court's landmark desegregation decision in 1954. The fact that the struggle for desegregation is still going on decades later is testimony to the resistance of society to liberalizing influences, psychology among them.

Funding for research in social science was reduced during the Reagan era because social science was perceived to have a liberal influence. At the same time, funding for the natural sciences was increased. The ideological nature of the spending cuts was made clear in the arguments in favor of the cuts. Congressman John Ashbrook, for example, said,

> We have seen how scholarly works have been used to launch major new government policies or programs over recent years. It was a study on the learning abilities of school-children that launched the nightmare of busing.... To avoid the risk of the government inadvertently aiding one side of an argument, many people, myself included, consider the best policy is for the government not to involve itself at all. (Association for the Advancement of Psychology, 1981, p. 3)

Efforts to reduce government funding of psychology were renewed in the 1990s. Representative Robert Walker, then chair of the committee that oversees science funding, sought to eliminate funding for "social, behavioral, and economic studies" because the National Science Foundation had "wandered into [them ... to be] politically correct" (American Psychological Association, 1995, p. 2). These and other influences have resulted in a decrease in federal funding for psychology in real (adjusted for inflation) terms during the last four decades. Between 1971 and 1996, funding of social and behavioral sciences decreased 12% in real terms, and the share of total federal science funding that goes toward social and behavioral science has been cut nearly in half, from 8% to 4.5% (Smith & Torrey, 1996), and science funding (particularly that which does not include defense-related enterprises) continues to decrease in real terms (Bennof, 2007).

It has been argued that psychology is more radical than called for by the nature of science. Donald Campbell, whose work on validity we considered in Chapter 6, observes:

> Present-day psychology and psychiatry in all their major forms are more hostile to the inhibitory messages of traditional religious moralizing than is scientifically justified....
>
> The religions of all ancient urban civilizations ... taught that many aspects of human nature need to be curbed if optimal social coordination is to be achieved; for example, selfishness, pride, greed, dishonesty, covetousness, cowardice, lust, wrath. Psychology and psychiatry, on the other hand, not only describe man as selfishly motivated, but implicitly or explicitly teach that he ought to be so. They tend to see repression and inhibition of individual impulse as undesirable. (1975, pp. 1103–1104)

This bias comes through in the topics that are studied and the way they are studied. Campbell notes further: "Conformity or suggestibility to majorities and prestige figures has been extensively studied from the beginnings of experimental social psychology ... but almost always as a popular character weakness" (p. 1107).

We could give more examples of issues on which psychologists have taken a more liberal or radical stance than prevailing public opinion, such as capital punishment, child welfare, and wife abuse. For this reason, those conservatives who believe that psychologists are a liberal influence are correct, whatever the merits of the particular issues.

Limitations of Science

When we discussed the nature of science in Chapter 1, we said that science deals with phenomena on which every person can agree. As we noted then, this premise limits the purview of science considerably. When Yuri Gagarin, the Soviet cosmonaut who was the first person to orbit the earth, returned from his historic flight, he said that there was no God because he had looked in the heavens and had not found him. To most people, it is obvious that Gagarin's method was not suited to the purpose of finding God. In this section, we discuss the limitations of science in obtaining knowledge. Some of these are essential limitations to the nature of science, and some of them are practical.

Essential Limitations

Yuri Gagarin's failure to find God in space is an example of the essential limitations of science. No matter how hard he looked, Gagarin would never find God from his spacecraft. He was using the wrong methods. Science must remain agnostic about questions that lie outside the realm of things on which every person can agree.

Science is agnostic not only concerning the existence of God but also regarding many questions of values. For example, a perennial political debate concerns whether tax rates should be directed more toward reducing the differences between the rich and the poor or toward providing incentives for people to work harder and thereby become richer. Psychology can discover that poverty leads to psychological distress and crime and that people will work hard for financial rewards, but it cannot tell which goal is more important. This question is one of values, and its answer must come from outside science. Lively debates take place in scientific organizations about the proper balance to strike between scientific objectivity and social responsibility. The American Psychological Association's decision that its annual convention would boycott states that had not ratified the Equal Rights Amendment is an example.

Closely related to the fact that values lie outside of science is the idea that much of science is culturally relative. This concept is particularly true of the social sciences. Not only is the importance of a certain question a relative matter, but also the framing of questions themselves is often relative. Years ago psychologists measured masculinity and femininity on various scales and studied the relationship of these traits to psychological adjustment and the like. It was assumed that males ought to be masculine and females, feminine. Then, in the 1970s, feminist psychologists proposed that every person should have a balance of both masculine and feminine traits and be more or less androgynous. The popular ideals of masculinity and femininity were seen as exaggerations of the norm, and it was held that a better adjusted society would contain a higher percentage of androgynous people. With a similar philosophy of cultural change, some psychologists specialized in assertiveness training for women and minorities. From another perspective, these psychologists might be viewed as encouraging defiance of legitimate authority. This type of problem, arising from cultural perspective, is common in many areas of psychology. Later developments raised doubts about the scientific validity of the concept of androgyny (Mednick, 1989), and research designed to test whether androgynous individuals were better adjusted yielded inconsistent results. Partly for this reason, and partly because of changing trends in psychology, interest in androgyny has declined in recent years.

Science is also incomplete. We know only a tiny fraction of what there is to know, particularly in psychology. As one of the youngest sciences and one that deals with nature's most complex phenomena, psychology is more incomplete than other sciences that have existed longer. We must be humble about making claims for the truth of psychological principles because of the slender base on which many of these claims rest. It is interesting to look at psychology books of 50, 25, or even 10 years ago. We find that social psychology hardly existed before World War II and that cognitive psychology as we know it dates from about 1960.

Because psychological knowledge is so incomplete, it is therefore tentative. Science textbooks are continually being revised as new information is obtained. Many times it is not simply that more becomes known about a topic but that theories are developed in areas that did not previously have theories. Also, new theories replace older ones that have been found wanting. In Chapter 1, we discussed the idea that progress in science can take place by means of revolutions that overthrow earlier theories and install new ones. One example of an earlier theory that has been discredited is phrenology— the idea that one can judge personality and intelligence from the various bumps and protrusions on the head. It is sobering to realize that some of the theories we work on today will be cited in future textbooks as examples of obvious and amusing errors of an infant science.

An excellent example of the essential limitations in psychology is provided by the work of Lawrence Kohlberg (1981) on moral development. Following Jean Piaget, Kohlberg sought to determine the course of the development of moral reasoning. He presented children with situations that posed a moral dilemma. By analyzing the reasons they gave for making particular moral choices, he found six stages of development, which may be grouped into three levels. The first level, preconventional morality, is characterized by the avoidance of punishment and gaining of concrete rewards. People in the second level, conventional morality, make decisions to gain approval of others and out of a sense of duty. People in the third and highest level have what Kohlberg calls postconventional morality. They make decisions based on agreed-upon rights and their own ethical principles. Kohlberg sees these stages as forming a ladder, with persons at a particular stage incapable of understanding the thinking of people at higher stages.

Kohlberg's theory has been criticized on several bases. Some have suggested that it represents a liberal, middle-class, secular, humanistic morality (Shweder, 1982). In fact, political conservatives do tend to score lower on Kohlberg's scale than do liberals. Further, people from non-Western societies do not seem to talk about "justice" so much as a sense of duty toward others (Shweder, Mahapatra, & Miller, 1987).

Carol Gilligan (1993) took another approach to evaluating Kohlberg's theory. She argued persuasively that Kohlberg's theory is, at best, a theory of the development of morality in males. Kohlberg based his theory exclusively on data from male subjects because he found that females did not follow the same developmental pattern as males. Females tend not to "progress" to the third level but to remain at the level of conventional morality.

In her own research, Gilligan found that women are more concerned with the effects that their actions have on personal relationships and their responsibilities to others. They are less interested in abstract principles of right and wrong than are men. Kohlberg, however, defined morality solely in terms of justice, rather than caring and interpersonal relationships. The importance these concerns have for women causes women to appear retarded on a scale of moral development that was developed by a man based on evidence from males.

Another criticism of the work on moral reasoning is that results differ between societies. One study (Skoe et al., 1999), for example, compared Canadian and Norwegian adolescents on the extent to which they based their moral reasoning on an ethic of caring. Gilligan would predict that girls would score higher than boys on this test. Canadian girls did score higher than boys, following Gilligan's prediction. The Norwegian boys and girls, however, scored equally high. We can expect interpretations of Kohlberg's and Gilligan's work to continue to change over the years.

Practical Limitations

Certain problems remain unsolved not because of any essential limitation but for reasons outside the logic and methods of science. Perhaps the most important practical limitation of science is its opportunistic nature. Science progresses where the problems are easier, where techniques of study are available, and where financial support exists. Areas that are not blessed with these characteristics will remain backward. Consider the greater understanding we have of vision compared with olfaction. The eye is amenable to analysis by well-understood techniques such as optics, and there is money available for visual research because of the handicap that blindness causes. On the other hand, the olfactory system is difficult to study for many technical reasons, and anosmia, or *smell blindness*, has not been considered to be a serious problem. Many interesting theoretical problems in psychology wait for solutions, but they will not receive much attention as long as easier ones are present for which more financial support is available.

One major practical limitation of science is the cost of research, which stems from the size and complexity of many problems and the technical difficulties of research. Physics, for example, has progressed to the point where further advances require fantastically expensive apparatus, such as the superconducting supercollider that was under construction in Texas, which was a huge engineering project in itself. It was eventually canceled in mid-construction because of its enormous cost. This one project would have consumed a major portion of the entire science budget of the country. Psychological apparatus has not reached that limit as yet, but the day may not be far off. Scientists who study the sense of balance and orientation would certainly like to have orbiting space laboratories to facilitate research under conditions of weightlessness. However, it is doubtful that such laboratories will ever be adequate to answer the many questions that could be raised. Solutions to problems of abnormal personality may require the investment of more resources than our society is willing or able to provide.

Another practical limitation of science comes from the complexity of many problems. Traditional psychological theories are developed to account for the effect of one or two variables at a time on some behavior. When we discussed the idea of interactions, we saw how complicated it is to describe behavior with only two independent variables. Adding a third independent variable can make the interactions mind-boggling. In fact, a relatively new science that has developed to account for such complicated situations is known by the somewhat fanciful name of chaos theory.

In summary, science is subject to a number of limitations resulting from its essential nature and from the practical nature of the problems that it must deal with. Awareness of the limitations of science should make us careful in making claims for science and should help put scientific knowledge in social perspective.

The Responsibilities of the Scientist _____

Our discussion of the biases and limitations of science was intended to provide perspective on our earlier discussion of the advantages of science as a way of gaining knowledge. It should not leave you with the feeling that science is so fraught with problems that you should shy away from it. Science remains one of the most magnificent achievements of civilization. This section rounds out the chapter by considering the responsibilities of the scientist as a member of society.

Scientists are given many privileges. They are permitted to work on problems that they set for themselves under conditions that they control to a large degree. They are reasonably well paid and are accorded prestige. What responsibilities accompany these privileges? First must be the goal that society will be benefited by the work. Of course, much pure research has no apparent practical significance, and one can make a strong case for satisfaction of curiosity as a valid end in itself. Nevertheless, many disciplines have struggled with the problem of balancing the uncertain long-term benefits of their work against certain near-term dangers. Atomic physics is the classic example; genetic engineering is the most recent. In psychology, debate has surrounded whether research on the genetic basis of intelligence should be done at all. What if particular groups were found to be genetically inferior in intelligence? Would it not be better if we did not know that? Most scientists have such strong commitments to the idea that knowledge is better than ignorance that they are willing to take the risks that new knowledge brings.

The role of free speech is crucial. Science flourishes only in an atmosphere of free exchange of ideas. When that atmosphere prevails, sufficient debate takes place that the necessary safeguards likely will be erected so that knowledge will be used wisely. Because of free speech, it is now, more than ever, vital to consider incoming scientific information critically, as some media sources seem to have recently developed a tendency to report rumors as though they were news. Scientific results that have not been vetted through peer review or those that simply have been misunderstood have turned up in various journalistic outlets, such as online blogs (Siegfried, 2010b), so a healthy dose of skepticism can often come in handy.

The principle of free speech also holds for scientists. They are free to study unpopular problems and propose unpopular ideas. It is up to their colleagues to refute these ideas in the open forum. Such considerations may seem hypothetical and far removed from testing rats in a Skinner box or college sophomores in a conformity study, but this philosophical arena is the larger context in which all scientists work.

Another responsibility of scientists is to educate the public about their findings. Some scientists feel that their work is done when it is published in a journal. Yet the support that society gives to science places a duty on the scientist to educate the public. It is no accident that many scientists divide their time between research and teaching. In addition, there is a long tradition of popularization of science by scientists themselves through public lectures, books, and the electronic media. Scientists must present their cases directly to the public and respond to the public's concerns. For example, many psychologists feel that answering questions about pseudosciences such as parapsychology is beneath their dignity. That attitude, though, simply allows the pseudosciences to flourish and justifies the ivory tower image of the scientist.

Summary Note on Biases and Limitations of Science

We added this Epilogue on the biases and limitations of science to balance out the enthusiasm and the promises we made for science at the beginning. In our concern to present a balanced view of science, however, we run the risk of leaving you with the wrong impression of the value and accomplishments of science. It is safe to say that science has been a spectacularly successful vehicle for human progress, arguably more so than any other human institution. The contributions of science to our everyday life need no enumeration here. Even though psychology is one of the youngest sciences, it has made important contributions, from the very early work on problems of eyewitness testimony by Hugo Munsterberg to the more recent work on the behavior of managers in organizations by Herbert Simon. These and many other investigations have resulted in immeasurable progress that is not only economic, social, and political, but also intellectual.

The contributions of psychology are likely to be even greater in the future. Certain complex systems, such as piloting and traffic control of airliners, have become so complex that their functioning has become limited by the abilities of humans to process information. Evidence for this is that human error is an increasingly large cause of plane crashes. For this and many other reasons, students such as you have a fertile and exciting field awaiting.

Summary

1. Because science is a human enterprise, it is subject to human bias. Some of these biases cause science to have a conservative influence, and some cause a liberal influence.
2. Science is conservative in the same way that any social institution is conservative, as well as in its dependence on financial support from society.
3. Much research done in colleges and universities is supported by the federal government and is subject to political pressure.
4. Individual scientists share the biases of their society and often perform research that supports the status quo.
5. Because science rests on observation rather than authority, it challenges political and religious orthodoxies and has a liberal influence on society.
6. Science has certain essential and practical limitations in achieving knowledge.
7. Essential limitations come from three considerations: Science must remain agnostic about questions that lie outside the realm of things on which every person can agree; science is culturally relative; science is necessarily incomplete and, therefore, always tentative.
8. Three considerations constitute practical limitations on science: Scientists often work on problems that seem capable of solution rather than the most important ones; some research is too expensive to conduct; some problems are too complex to study with present methods.

9. The responsibilities of the scientist include having as the goal of research that society will be benefited by the work. One problem is justifying pure research that has uncertain future payoff against applied research that may be of immediate significance. Another problem is the risk that new knowledge presents to society.
10. Science flourishes only in an atmosphere of free speech, including freedom of inquiry into unpopular ideas.
11. Scientists have a responsibility to educate the public about the nature and results of scientific research.

Suggestions for Further Reading

HOGAN, T. T., & EMLER, N. P. (1978). The biases in contemporary social psychology. *Social Research*, *45*, 478–534. This article suggests areas of social psychology in which biases have affected research.

VITZ, P. C. (1977). *Psychology as religion: The cult of self-worship*. Grand Rapids, MI: Eerdmans. Although this volume deals primarily with personality theorists, it shows clearly the biases that influence how researchers approach their subject areas.

Reading Between The Lines

Epilogue.1 The Liberated Female Rat

For many years researchers who studied sexual behavior in rats found that the male rat was the active partner, whereas the female was more passive. During these studies, the rats were housed in small arenas that kept the animals close to each other. Martha McClintock and Norman Adler (1978) studied the sexual behavior of rats in larger and more complex environments. They found that the female rat actually controlled the initiation and timing of sexual behavior by soliciting the male. What reasons can you think of for the failure of researchers to discover this fact for so many years?

Exercises

Epilogue.1 Science as Liberal

Describe several social issues on which the findings of scientists have had a liberal influence.

Epilogue.2 Science as Conservative

Describe several social issues on which the findings of scientists have been used to resist change. (You may be able to think of issues on which scientists have lined up on both sides.)

Epilogue.3 Limitations of Science

List several theoretical or social problems that science may never be able to solve, and give reasons.

Epilogue.4 Political Influences on Science

Look in the "News & Comment" section of the journal *Nature* for an example of the influence of the political process on the funding of scientific projects. What group or individual is attempting to influence the project? What is their special or vested interest in the matter?

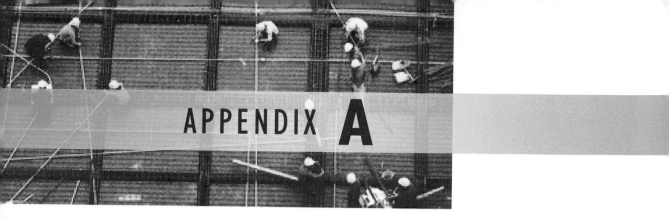

APPENDIX A

Random-Number Table

See page 232–234 for directions in the use of this table.

RANDOM-NUMBER TABLE

```
9 9 0 4 8 2 9 1 6 0 6 6 3 5 3 3 3 1 9 5 8 0 2 0 8 4
5 5 5 7 0 4 8 5 9 2 8 1 9 4 3 4 2 1 7 3 6 6 6 2 4 1
5 2 3 4 1 8 5 6 2 3 9 3 4 2 1 3 9 7 9 9 5 9 8 9 6 1
2 1 2 8 8 1 2 9 4 5 9 2 6 6 6 1 6 2 9 7 9 0 8 5 7 3
0 4 7 1 4 3 8 7 0 7 5 8 3 4 0 8 0 5 1 6 2 5 7 0 2 0
5 4 8 8 0 4 1 8 1 0 7 2 3 9 2 9 7 2 5 2 1 0 7 7 3 7
6 9 1 2 3 0 3 6 6 1 6 7 6 0 3 5 0 4 5 3 8 2 6 5 1 6
5 8 8 7 4 2 2 7 5 6 3 6 5 8 8 8 3 9 6 9 7 0 8 2 1 8
7 6 7 8 8 2 8 8 4 3 8 2 7 3 7 8 2 8 4 1 7 3 0 7 1 5
5 5 8 9 9 8 1 0 0 1 1 2 9 8 7 5 8 7 5 1 6 4 1 3 3 7
0 0 3 7 3 5 0 2 3 1 7 1 0 2 0 3 5 2 6 3 5 1 6 1 2 6
8 0 9 2 4 8 2 3 0 6 0 0 4 3 0 2 3 3 3 2 9 8 6 4 7 0
9 2 5 5 3 0 2 5 8 3 1 5 7 6 0 0 4 8 0 9 4 4 4 1 2 9
0 0 8 3 8 6 0 5 7 9 3 9 6 3 6 6 6 9 3 3 0 7 5 9 2 2
0 3 0 2 6 2 5 0 8 4 9 7 7 0 6 6 8 7 6 2 6 9 3 3 3 8
9 2 2 1 2 3 3 3 6 1 6 0 8 0 0 9 7 0 2 7 5 7 3 6 2 8
6 2 3 8 3 5 3 1 7 4 3 4 9 6 1 5 2 2 1 2 0 4 9 1 5 3
6 4 3 3 1 8 8 3 0 5 9 9 0 3 9 6 7 7 2 9 3 2 4 8 8 7
2 3 4 7 5 9 2 8 4 0 1 8 1 2 6 6 5 3 9 3 9 7 8 3 9 4
0 7 3 5 0 7 4 8 9 4 3 2 6 1 1 1 9 5 7 8 5 2 7 1 8 7
8 6 8 4 5 6 9 8 0 0 4 1 3 9 6 2 0 9 3 1 4 9 2 3 5 4
9 5 1 8 3 3 5 1 1 0 5 8 8 0 3 3 4 7 2 8 2 0 5 1 9 0
4 5 2 6 4 5 1 7 2 8 3 6 1 3 8 5 3 5 5 0 5 1 1 0 1 0
5 1 9 3 3 9 1 5 2 3 7 5 4 0 4 4 6 4 6 9 3 8 7 1 9 5
4 8 5 4 8 6 0 0 3 0 7 3 5 6 3 3 3 9 0 4 3 0 0 3 1 9
8 3 0 0 6 2 2 2 9 1 1 0 4 3 6 1 2 3 1 1 1 2 3 4 3 1
6 2 2 0 6 3 7 0 8 6 4 6 9 3 6 2 4 5 5 7 0 4 2 2 5 6
4 8 6 0 5 3 6 2 9 1 0 8 2 1 7 4 2 5 4 9 8 8 3 6 2 9
3 9 0 1 2 4 1 7 4 6 9 2 9 5 1 2 6 5 6 8 2 6 7 5 9 0
9 2 2 7 1 4 7 5 9 1 8 9 9 5 6 2 7 8 1 5 5 1 1 2 1 2
7 7 7 3 3 5 2 4 8 2 1 0 3 0 0 4 8 5 5 9 2 6 4 4 7 6
8 3 8 8 2 4 0 2 0 5 7 3 8 7 5 5 9 3 9 5 7 1 6 7 9 6
4 7 1 1 1 2 9 6 7 3 0 7 4 4 3 8 1 3 1 1 9 0 4 0 7 7
4 5 9 8 6 1 1 5 1 1 1 7 4 6 7 4 7 2 4 7 5 8 6 3 4 9
5 1 2 7 7 6 1 6 2 2 6 2 4 8 7 5 0 5 3 9 9 3 8 0 8 6
2 2 2 4 9 2 8 3 3 0 8 1 4 6 0 4 6 6 2 6 2 5 4 1 2 2
3 7 5 2 9 4 4 6 9 3 0 2 4 8 3 8 3 1 3 7 8 7 5 8 8 7
9 3 8 8 1 2 0 6 1 2 3 6 8 7 7 1 9 0 9 2 1 4 0 5 3 0
1 6 8 5 9 1 0 9 9 0 5 5 0 8 8 9 5 5 1 2 7 6 8 8 6 9
5 8 0 3 6 7 6 5 6 4 8 7 9 6 0 1 4 8 3 3 9 6 1 7 2 7
9 7 2 6 2 2 1 4 4 3 4 0 7 7 4 2 4 3 8 5 8 6 5 7 0 0
8 5 5 3 8 9 4 4 2 8 3 5 8 0 1 4 1 9 9 7 2 4 7 0 0 7
7 9 6 9 1 7 6 6 4 0 7 4 1 5 1 4 2 3 4 3 3 5 9 7 9 9
7 9 8 5 7 4 3 3 4 1 5 5 7 1 3 1 7 9 2 9 3 6 7 9 7 8
9 6 1 6 0 6 7 1 8 8 4 9 2 3 8 8 5 2 3 2 6 9 6 0 5 6
9 6 1 9 4 2 9 6 0 5 9 4 9 8 6 8 1 1 8 3 5 8 9 6 8 1
0 0 1 5 2 4 3 4 0 4 4 2 4 3 9 8 1 6 2 6 2 5 3 4 7 6
4 8 8 8 4 9 9 6 1 8 4 3 8 3 0 1 3 4 5 7 0 6 1 6 3 2
8 6 2 8 4 7 1 3 3 6 5 7 9 3 3 8 9 2 7 5 6 3 0 6 1 6
7 0 5 8 0 2 3 2 0 5 5 0 5 0 3 9 1 7 5 4 5 1 9 9 1 0
```

Note: The *Instructor's Manual* lists a computer program that will generate more tables of random numbers.

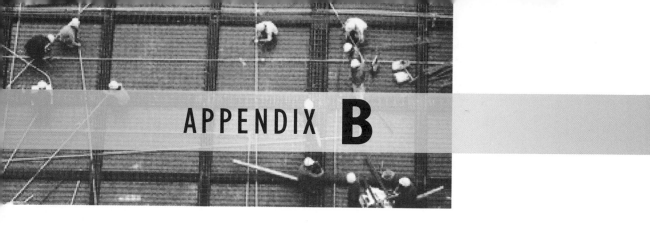

APPENDIX B

Population Data Set

This table represents a population of 64 individuals, identified in the column labeled *ID* by the numbers one through 64. Of these individuals, 29 are male and 35 are female, as indicated by M or F in the second column. Columns A through G give values of seven different variables for these individuals. The data approximate a normal distribution and have a known mean and standard deviation. Data in columns F and G are correlated. This data set is intended to be useful for exercises in random sampling, tabulating, and plotting results of hypothetical experiments, performing statistical analyses, and interpreting data. Several exercises in various chapters refer to these data. Other exercises could readily be developed. The means and standard deviations of the various columns and the correlation between columns F and G are given in the *Instructor's Manual*.

ID	Sex	A	B	C	D	E	F	G	ID	Sex	A	B	C	D	E	F	G
1	F	1	6	11	5	8	11	11	36	F	6	5	8	7	10	14	13
2	F	4	3	8	8	10	12	12	37	F	4	7	9	11	9	12	12
3	F	2	4	6	7	9	8	9	38	M	4	5	10	9	12	14	13
4	M	3	6	7	8	9	10	11	39	F	3	6	8	6	11	11	9
5	M	6	8	10	10	13	16	16	40	M	5	5	8	8	11	13	10
6	F	3	7	9	9	10	12	11	41	M	2	6	7	7	8	15	12
7	F	5	6	7	7	11	14	12	42	F	3	7	9	8	9	12	11
8	M	5	6	8	10	11	8	8	43	M	3	7	7	9	11	10	11
9	F	4	5	8	8	10	9	9	44	F	6	5	8	6	11	14	12
10	F	3	8	7	8	12	10	12	45	M	5	6	10	7	10	12	12
11	M	5	4	9	9	10	14	14	46	M	4	6	8	8	9	8	12
12	F	3	7	5	9	11	12	12	47	M	5	4	9	10	7	14	15
13	F	3	7	8	8	9	11	11	48	M	6	5	8	8	12	14	14
14	M	5	8	7	10	10	12	15	49	F	4	7	7	9	11	11	13
15	M	4	6	8	7	8	12	13	50	F	5	6	9	9	9	14	14
16	M	4	5	7	8	11	11	12	51	F	4	7	10	7	9	14	12
17	F	3	8	9	9	12	13	15	52	M	3	5	8	9	10	11	12
18	M	5	5	6	6	10	15	15	53	F	2	8	9	10	10	11	12
19	M	4	6	8	8	10	9	10	54	M	4	6	7	8	11	11	12
20	M	2	7	7	7	11	9	9	55	M	4	7	8	7	9	12	11
21	M	5	6	7	7	11	12	12	56	M	5	5	9	9	10	14	14
22	F	3	5	8	9	10	11	12	57	M	6	6	9	9	12	11	11
23	M	5	4	10	8	10	15	13	58	F	4	8	6	7	10	10	11
24	F	4	7	9	9	9	13	13	59	M	3	6	9	10	10	12	11
25	F	5	6	7	7	9	12	12	60	F	6	4	8	8	9	14	14
26	F	3	7	6	7	10	12	12	61	F	2	5	9	9	11	11	11
27	F	4	5	8	8	8	12	12	62	F	4	7	7	8	10	11	12
28	M	4	6	7	9	9	11	13	63	F	4	9	8	7	12	12	11
29	M	5	5	8	7	11	13	12	64	F	7	6	6	8	8	13	15
30	F	3	7	9	6	10	12	9									
31	M	2	6	6	6	9	13	15									
32	F	4	4	10	8	8	12	12									
33	F	5	7	7	6	10	12	11									
34	F	4	5	9	8	9	13	12									
35	F	3	6	8	8	11	12	6									

APPENDIX **C**

Suggested Answers to *Reading Between the Lines*

1.1 Guns Don't Kill People; People Kill People _____

The gun lobby assumes that people have free will and that they choose to kill. It follows from this that people who kill are different from ordinary people who would use a gun only in self-defense. The anti-gun lobby argues that the presence of a gun is a stimulus to use the gun. The two sides make different assumptions about the importance of determinism versus free will. One slogan might be *guns turn people into killers*. The gun control lobby's slogan *guns don't die; people do* is less to the point but may be a better slogan because of its emotional appeal.

1.2 Is Prayer Effective? _____

Sir Francis Galton assumed that these groups would have the same longevity except for the effect of prayer. It is likely that being royalty is more stressful than being a scientist or a member of the gentry. Other factors could be hereditary weaknesses caused by inbreeding or simply the fact that royalty tend to be related to one another and therefore are not a random sample of the population. Ways of knowing used by Galton include logic and the scientific method.

1.3 Imagine that Precognition Does Occur _____

ESP challenges several basic limiting assumptions of science: that effects cannot precede causes, that we know the world only through the senses, and that mere thought cannot influence the world except via our bodies. If ESP did exist, most of human society as we know it would be impossible! There would

429

be few secrets, and the daily lottery would be bankrupt. All banks would fail because their safes would be cracked by psychic means, and the stock market would cease to function. Most of these effects would occur even if only a few people had ESP and if it worked only part of the time. In addition, the various state lotteries that are conducted every day would not show the constant conformity to the laws of probability that they do. ESP violates the assumption of causality: If we can foretell the future, then effects (our knowledge) precede their cause (the events foretold). ESP also violates the scientific goal of looking for regularities and laws: Most ESP experiments are aimed at finding an irregularity—something that cannot be explained by science.

1.4 Reincarnation

The claim of reincarnation is virtually impossible to test, which seems to make it all the more appealing to some people. It is not hard to come up with alternative hypotheses, however. Hypnosis causes an increase in the ability to imagine scenes and events. Psychologists know that it is difficult to distinguish imagined events from real ones. The recall of past lives under hypnosis is just one example of the ability to imagine fictitious events. An interesting exercise is to relax and recall various scenes from your past, going back as far as you can. Then, imagine yourself 10 or 20 years from now.

Most people can imagine the future about as vividly as they can recall the past. If you have little difficulty imagining what has not yet happened, what does that say about the ability to *recall* a past life? Although people may claim to be able to recall historical facts or to speak foreign languages that they could not have known in their present lives, research shows that they are actually using bits of information they have learned by ordinary means in their present lives, which they remember by means of hypnosis.

3.1 The Causes of Child Abuse

Leroy Pelton suggests that the idea that child abuse is unrelated to social class is politically convenient, both to mental health professionals and to politicians. The mental health professionals would like to see the problem of child abuse as part of their turf so they could benefit from funding available for the study and cure of child abuse. If child abuse is caused by poverty instead, the mental health profession receives no benefit. Politicians, for their part, may prefer to see child abuse as psychologically caused because that view permits them to seek a technological solution instead of resolving the more difficult causes of poverty.

4.1 The Authoritarian Personality

Families with high levels of status concern and repressive disciplinary procedures tend to come from the lower social classes. They are less educated and more conservative. These values are passed along to their children through principles of social learning. Thus, the children learn to be prejudiced and discriminatory from their parents via such mechanisms as instrumental conditioning and modeling. This explanation is thought by many investigators to be more parsimonious than that of Adorno et al. (1950). Adorno et al. studied working-class people who generally have stricter child-rearing practices than do the middle-class researchers. Racism is also a common attitude among working-class people. Some researchers have suggested that the reason a correlation was found between authoritarianism and child-rearing practices was that the researchers had used a particular population in which these characteristics were common. According to this interpretation, authoritarianism is not a personality trait, but a cultural norm.

4.2 Life Events and Illness

The measurement of life events in retrospective research takes place, by definition, after the person has suffered the illness. Therefore, it is impossible to measure the number of life events before the illness strikes. Having the illness is likely to influence the recall and interpretation of life events (Brown & Harris, 2001). People who are sad are known to recall more sad events from the past than are people who are not sad. In addition, people seek to find consistency among the events that happen to them. They are likely to reinterpret past events to provide some explanation of their illness. For example, one study found that mothers of Down syndrome children recalled more emotional shocks during pregnancy than did mothers of normal children. The syndrome is caused by a chromosomal abnormality, however, so it is impossible for emotional stress during pregnancy to be the cause. The mothers must have searched their memories for stressful events that might explain the abnormal offspring.

5.1 Testing for Independence of Dimensions

Children with ADHD are characterized by an inability to maintain the optimal levels of activity and attention that are necessary for everyday tasks. In this study, medications and behavioral therapies were the independent variables. If participation in behavioral therapy required a certain amount of attention, then the benefits of the therapy might not be possible when the child was in the placebo condition. When the medication was presented at a higher rate, more attention may have been available to a child than when the medication was presented at a lower dose. Therefore, until an effective dosage of medication was reached, behavioral therapy would not be possible.

6.1 Do Younger Infants Prefer Simpler Patterns?

Because all the cards were the same size, the less complex cards had the largest squares. In other words, size of square was perfectly confounded with complexity.

Miranda and Fantz (1971, as cited by cited by Fantz, Fagan, & Miranda, 1975) repeated the study but varied the number of squares independently of the size of the squares. They presented infants with cards that had 2, 8, or 32 black squares. The size of the squares was varied such that three of the cards had the same total amount of black area. These three cards constituted the replication of the earlier study. In addition, other cards were made in which size and number varied independently. The patterns used are shown in Figure C.1.

Considering only the three cards that were similar to the previous study, Miranda and Fantz found the same results as Brennan and Moore: There was a tendency for infants to prefer the simpler patterns when the size of the square was confounded with number. However, there was also a strong tendency for the infants to prefer both larger squares, when number was held constant, and more numerous squares, when size was held constant. Therefore, if number is taken as a measure of complexity, even newborn infants prefer greater complexity to less. The previous experiments had pitted two strong tendencies against one another: preference for greater size and preference for greater complexity. In that situation, the preference for size had won out. In another study, Fantz et al. found that older babies tended to be less controlled by pattern size and more by complexity alone, which would explain the apparent developmental trend toward greater complexity found by the previous investigators.

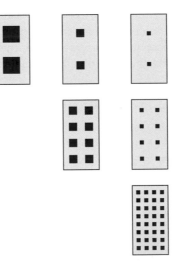

FIGURE **C.1** Stimulus patterns. Number of squares varies across rows, and size of squares varies across columns. The three cards along the diagonal have the same total black area.

("Early Visual Selectivity" by R. L. Fantz, et al, 1975, in *Infant Perception: From Sensation to Cognition: Vol. 1. Basic Visual Processes,* ed. by L. B. Cohen and P. Salapatek, © 1975 by Academic Press. Reprinted by permission of Elsevier.)

6.2 Is There a Bias Against Men? _____

The participants in this experiment were in a small-group situation and reported their responses orally. Even though the groups were constructed such that there were an equal number of men and women in each group, it is possible that group dynamics influenced the outcome of the study. Women are often more verbal than men, so it is possible that the results reflect bias that arises primarily from females, rather than a cultural bias per se.

7.1 Brain Damage Sometimes Produces Obesity in Rats _____

The successful investigators were using female rats, and the others were using males. Female rats consistently showed obesity after the lesions, whereas males showed it to a lesser degree (Valenstein, Cox, & Kakolewski, 1969).

7.2 Mozart Effect–Shmozart Effect _____

Because the Mozart music was upbeat, it likely increased both mood and arousal (Thompson, Husain, & Schellenberg, 2001). It is possible that either of these changes accounts for the increase in spatial reasoning observed by Rauscher, Shaw, and Ky (1993).

The results of this experiment have been hotly contested, with some successes and some failures to replicate the experiment. Steele, Bass, and Crook (1999) replicated the study but used different spatial reasoning questions. Otherwise, the experiment was similar to the original. We may consider this experiment to be a systematic, rather than an exact, replication. Nevertheless, there were so many experiments with findings on both sides of the debate that several meta-analyses have been conducted. The most recent of the meta-analyses (Pietschnig, Voracek, & Formann, 2010) concludes that although a small effect may exist, some experimenter bias may have inflated the results.

The dust probably will not settle for some time, but we can note how long it may take for an influential experiment to be replicated and how difficult it may be to decide when an experiment is similar enough to constitute a replication.

8.1 Aggression and XYY Males _____

Stephan Chorover (1979) points out several problems with the study. First, the mothers were not told that the chromosome test was part of an experiment or that it was funded by an agency concerned with crime and delinquency. The experimenters implied that the chromosome test was part of the hospital's routine practice and that it was a service to the family. Second, the parents were told of their child's condition, which probably would have an effect on how they treated the child. They might consider that he was a "bad seed" and was doomed to a life of crime, thus creating a self-fulfilling prophecy. Or they might have been overly concerned with controlling his aggressive tendencies. The study was actually one on the effects of having the XYY condition and having the parents know that the child had the condition. A more adequate design would have included a group that was told that their child had the condition when the child did not. That design, of course, would introduce new ethical problems.

9.1 Red Wine Reduces Heart Attacks

People who regularly drink red wine may be wealthier than people who do not regularly drink alcohol. If this is the case, then these people would also be able to afford to buy healthy, balanced foods, which also affect heart attack frequency. These factors would also predict a lower-than-average number of heart attacks.

10.1 Subliminal Seduction

A reader of that issue of *Playboy* would have seen many other pictures of naked women but few, if any, of other wreaths. Therefore, the wreath would be a more distinctive stimulus than would one more naked woman. Without clothes, there are not many features that would distinguish one *Playboy* model from another. Certainly a blonde would not be unusual. The explanation in terms of subliminal perception of the fancied appearance of the wreath seems gratuitous in view of this explanation. Significantly, no reference to a scientific journal is given in which one might examine the evidence more closely. This case is typical of the rest of the evidence for subliminal perception cited in the book.

11.1 Thirst in Brain-Damaged Rats

Christopher Coburn and Edward Stricker proposed that the brain-damaged rats failed to respond to the intraperitoneal injections because these injections caused more stress than the other means of changing salt balance. There is evidence that rats with damage to this area of the brain are unable to react well to stress. In other words, these animals may have been too sick to drink. The other means of inducing changes in salt balance were not as stressful, and therefore the brain-damaged rats were able to respond normally. Subsequent studies (Saad et al., 1996) have indicated that the lateral preoptic area contains fibers that are involved in both the inhibition and the facilitation of drinking in response to salt balance.

12.1 Electrical Inhibition of Aggression in a Charging Bull

Notice that the bull turned to one side when he stopped. The caudate nucleus is involved in the control of motor movements. The bull likely stopped because the involuntary movement to one side caused by the stimulation interfered with his charge. He may have been just as aggressively motivated as before but unable to carry out his intentions (Valenstein, 1977).

12.2 Clever Hans

Hans was picking up subtle cues from his questioners. Oskar Pfungst, a psychologist, found that Hans gave the correct answer only when the questioner knew the correct answer. Pfungst had one person think up a number and whisper it in Hans' ear. A second person did the same and asked Hans to add them up. Hans was at a complete loss in this situation. It was also necessary for Hans to be able to see the questioner. When blinders were placed on him, he struggled to view the questioner.

Pfungst knew by then that Hans relied on visual cues from the questioner, but what were they? Pfungst eventually noticed that all of the questioners made an extremely slight inclination of the head when a question was posed. This head movement caused Hans to start tapping. When Hans had made the correct number of taps, the questioner raised his head and Hans stopped tapping. Pfungst was able to cause Hans to start and stop tapping by merely moving his head without saying a word to Hans. So Hans was just an ordinary horse that had been well trained to respond to subtle visual cues.

Clever Hans was no isolated phenomenon. In addition to the potential for circus acts that such animals have, scientific interest has been created over whether chimpanzees are able to use sign language to communicate with people. Terrace (1979) concluded on the basis of his experiments that previous research that seemed to show that chimpanzees could communicate in this way was subject to the Clever Hans effect. Terrace's conclusions are controversial, but they show how difficult it may be to rule out such subtle biases in research.

13.1 Ulcers in Executive Monkeys

Because the animals were not randomly assigned to the executive position, it is possible that those that learned faster were predisposed to ulcers (Weiss, 1968, 1971). When Weiss replicated the study using the proper controls, he found that the executive animals developed fewer ulcers than the control animals. We should note that Weiss used rats instead of monkeys, so a possible species difference may exist. Nevertheless, many researchers believe the executive monkey study has joined the ranks of nonreplicable studies.

13.2 Memory for Words

It is not possible to assign words randomly to conditions in an experiment on memory. Some words are nouns, some are common, some are short, and so forth. Therefore, it is necessary to select words that meet particular criteria. Thus, experiments on verbal memory are quasi experiments, according to our terminology. In any quasi experiment, it is possible that another variable is confounded with the variable on which you are selecting. In this case, Michael McCloskey eventually realized that the highly related words tended to be more familiar to the subjects as well: Robins and oaks are more familiar than penguins and mahoganies. McCloskey (1980) repeated his earlier study, this time measuring the familiarity of the words. He found that familiarity caused a large part of the effect he had previously found and had attributed to similarity. He was able to show, however, that similarity also played a role in the results, when familiarity was controlled.

14.1 "You Can Prove Anything with Statistics"

The y-axis is not labeled! The origin of the graph is actually $2,150 and the top of the graph is $2,400. Draw a rough sketch of what the graph would look like with an origin of $0 to see a more accurate view of the difference between the two proposals.

15.1 How Much Significance Should Be Placed on Significance

It is always difficult to try to compare two things that were tested separately rather than directly compared, and the results can be misleading. In this instance, the apparent differences between the two drugs' rate of suicidal incidents were due to differences in the placebo groups. The comparison group for the first anti-depressant was abnormally low (even though they had been appropriately randomly selected), giving the appearance that the drug was strongly associated with suicidal incidents.

Epilogue.1 The Liberated Female Rat

Most of the researchers were males who let their biases toward human females determine how they looked at the behavior of rats. Notice that Martha McClintock is a woman. In the female rat, conception can occur only when the uterus is prepared by hormones that are triggered by sexual activity. Therefore, the sexual behavior must be properly timed before successful mating can occur. For this reason, the female rat logically should be in control of the timing of sexual activity.

APPENDIX D

Key for Identifying Appropriate Graphs and Statistics

The following key will help you to decide which graphical and statistical procedures are appropriate for various kinds of questions, types of data, and experimental designs. The way to use it is to ask a series of questions, starting at the top. Each question is numbered at the left. On the right side of each line, you will find either the appropriate procedure or a number. If a procedure is listed, you have your answer. If a number is listed, look for that number on the left side of the page, where there will be another question. This will lead either to a procedure or to another number, and so on. You may have used keys like this one to identify flowers, insects, and the like. A key table is logically identical to a tree diagram but permits many more branches without becoming impossible to represent on a single sheet of paper.

Key to Graphical and Statistical Procedures

1.0	Purpose of procedure is to		
	1.1	Describe data	**2.0**
	1.2	Make estimates about population means	**14.0**
	1.3	Draw inferences	**15.0**
2.0	Purpose of description is to		
	2.1	Summarize data	**3.0**
	2.2	Measure degree of a relationship	**13.0**

	2.3	Make a prediction based on correlation coefficient	linear regression
3.0	TYPE OF SUMMARY DESCRIPTION DESIRED IS		
	3.1	Graphical	4.0
	3.2	Numerical	9.0
4.0	PURPOSE OF GRAPHICAL DESCRIPTION IS TO DISPLAY		
	4.1	Categorical data	bar graph
	4.2	Frequencies or numbers of cases	5.0
	4.3	Quantitative data	6.0
5.0	PURPOSE IS TO SHOW FREQUENCIES OR NUMBER OF CASES		
	5.1	At particular values of a dependent variable	frequency distribution
	5.2	At or below particular values of a dependent variable	cumulative frequency distribution
6.0	PURPOSE IS GRAPHICAL DESCRIPTION OF QUANTITATIVE DATA FOR		
	6.1	Two variables	7.0
	6.2	Three variables	8.0
7.0	GRAPHICAL DESCRIPTION OF QUANTITATIVE DATA WITH TWO VARIABLES FOR		
	7.1	Individuals	scattergram
	7.2	Functional relationships between variables	graph of function
	7.3	Time as the independent variable	time series
8.0	GRAPHICAL DESCRIPTION OF QUANTITATIVE DATA WITH THREE VARIABLES WHEN THERE ARE		
	8.1	Two independent variables and one dependent variable	contour graph
	8.2	Locations in two-dimensional space that have some characteristic	data map
	8.3	Quantitative data that cannot easily be displayed numerically	data points are pictures
9.0	PURPOSE IS NUMERICAL DESCRIPTION OF		
	9.1	Typical case	10.0
	9.2	Variability of cases	12.0
10.0	NUMERICAL DESCRIPTION OF TYPICAL CASE WHEN		
	10.1	Data are categorical	mode
	10.2	Data are quantitative	11.0
11.0	DESCRIBE TYPICAL QUANTITATIVE DATA WHEN		
	11.1	Data are skewed, or you want the middle score	median
	11.2	You want an average based on all the scores, or you plan to do further calculations, or you want to relate average to normal curve	mean
	11.3	You want the most common score	mode

12.0 MEASURE OF VARIABILITY APPROPRIATE FOR THE

12.1	Mode	range
12.2	Median	interquartile range, semi-interquartile range
12.3	Mean	variance, standard deviation

13.0 PURPOSE IS TO MEASURE DEGREE OF A RELATIONSHIP WHEN DATA ARE

13.1	Ranks (ordinal)	Spearman correlation coefficient, ρ
13.2	Ordinal, interval, or ratio	Pearson r correlation coefficient

14.0 ESTIMATES ABOUT POPULATION MEAN FOR

14.1	One group of subjects tested once	confidence interval for the mean
14.2	Two matched groups, or one group tested twice	confidence interval for difference between means for correlated samples
14.3	Two independent groups	confidence interval for difference between means for independent groups

15.0 PURPOSE IS TO DRAW INFERENCES WHEN DATA ARE

15.1	Frequencies in categories	16.0
15.2	Scores, quantities, or amounts	17.0

16.0 INFERENTIAL STATISTIC FOR FREQUENCIES WHEN

16.1	Data are distributed over levels of one variable, and you want to compare obtained distribution with hypothesized distribution	Chi-Square test of goodness of fit
16.2	Data are arranged in a two-way contingency table	Chi-Square test of independence

17.0 INFERENTIAL STATISTIC FOR SCORES, QUANTITIES, OR AMOUNTS WHEN THERE ARE

17.1	One group of subjects	18.0
17.2	Two groups of subjects or two conditions	20.0
17.3	Three or more groups of subjects or conditions	21.0

18.0 INFERENTIAL STATISTIC ON QUANTITIES FOR ONE GROUP OF SUBJECTS

18.1	Hypothesis test for population mean	19.0
18.2	Hypothesis test for difference between means	t-test for correlated samples
18.3	Hypothesis test of strength of a linear relationship between two variables	significance of Pearson correlation coefficient

19.0 TEST HYPOTHESIS ABOUT POPULATION MEAN WHEN THE POPULATION STANDARD DEVIATION IS

19.1	Known	**normal curve test**
19.2	Not known	**t-test for population mean**

20.0 HYPOTHESIS TEST, QUANTITATIVE DATA, TWO GROUPS OF SUBJECTS OR TWO CONDITIONS, WITH

20.1	Matched groups or within-subjects design	**t-test for correlated samples**
20.2	Independent groups	**t-test for independent samples**

21.0 HYPOTHESIS TEST FOR SCORES, THREE OR MORE CONDITIONS OR GROUPS OF SUBJECTS, WITH

21.1	Three or more levels of one independent variable	**22.0**
21.2	Two independent variables	**23.0**

22.0 TEST HYPOTHESIS STATISTIC FOR THREE OR MORE LEVELS OF ONE INDEPENDENT VARIABLE IN A

22.1	Between-subjects design	**one-way ANOVA**
22.2	Within-subjects design	**one-way, repeated-measures ANOVA**

23.0 INFERENTIAL STATISTIC FOR TWO INDEPENDENT VARIABLES WHEN

23.1	Both independent variables tested between subjects	**two-way ANOVA**
23.2	Both independent variables tested within subjects	**two-way, repeated-measures ANOVA**
23.3	One independent variable tested between subjects and one tested within subjects	**two-way, mixed-design ANOVA**

REFERENCES

Adorno, T. W., Frenkel-Brunswik, E., Levinson, D. J., & Sanford, R. N. (1950). *The authoritarian personality.* New York: Harper & Row.

Alberto, P. A., & Troutman, A. C. (2006). *Applied behavior analysis for teachers* (7th ed.). Columbus, OH: Merrill.

American Association for Public Opinion Research. (2008). *Guidelines and considerations for survey researchers when planning and conducting RDD and other telephone surveys in the U.S. with respondents reached via cell phone numbers.* Retrieved October 29, 2008, from http://www.aapor.org/uploads/Final_AAPOR_Cell_Phone_TF_report_041208.pdf

American Psychological Association. (1995). Behavioral research under attack: APA picks up the gauntlet. *Psychological Science Agenda, 8*(4), 2.

American Psychological Association. (2010a). *Ethical principles of psychologists and code of conduct.* Retrieved from http://www.apa.org/ethics/code/index.aspx

American Psychological Association. (2010b). *Publication manual of the American Psychological Association* (6th ed.). Washington, DC: Author.

American Psychological Association Committee on Animal Research and Ethics (2010). *Guidelines for ethical conduct in the care and use of animals.* Retrieved from http://www.apa.org/science/anguide.html

Anastasi, A., & Urbina, S. (1997). *Psychological testing* (7th ed.). Upper Saddle River, NJ: Prentice Hall.

Angier, N. (1995, August 29). New view of family: Unstable but wealth helps. *The New York Times,* pp. B5, B7.

A political attack on peer review. (2005). *Nature Neuroscience, 8,* 1273.

Appelbaum, P. S., Roth, L. H., Lidz, C. W., Benson, P., & Winslade, W. (1987). False hopes and best data: Consent to research and the therapeutic misconception. *Hastings Center Report, 17*(2), 20–24.

Aronson, E., Wilson, T., & Brewer, M. (1998). Experimentation in social psychology. In D. Gilbert, S. Fiske, & G. Lindzey (Eds.), *Handbook of social psychology* (4th ed., Vol. 1, pp. 99–142). New York: Oxford University Press.

Arseneault, L., Milne, B. J., Tayler, A., Adams, F., Delgado, K., Caspi, A., & Moffitt, T. (2008). Being bullied as an environmentally mediated contributing factor to children's internalizing problems. *Archives of Pediatric and Adolescent Medicine, 162*(2), 145–150.

Association for the Advancement of Psychology. (1981, August). Administration intensifies attack on social science research. *Advance,* pp. 3–5.

Azar, B. (2000). A web of research. *Monitor on Psychology, 31,* 42–47.

Babich, F. R., Jacobson, A. L., Bubash, S., & Jacobson, A. (1965). Transfer of a response to naive rats by injection of ribonucleic acid extracted from trained rats. *Science, 149,* 656–657.

Barak, A., Hen, L., Boniel-Nissim, M., & Shapira, N. (2008). A comprehensive review and a meta-analysis of the effectiveness of internet-based psychotherapeutic interventions. *Journal of Technology in Human Services, 26*(2/4), 109–160. doi:10.1080/15228830802094429

Barber, T. X. (1976). *Pitfalls in human research: Ten pivotal points.* New York: Pergamon Press.

Barlow, D. H., & Hersen, M. (1984). *Single case experimental designs* (2nd ed.). New York: Pergamon Press.

Barlow, D. H., Nock, M. K. & Hersen, M. (2008). *Single case experimental designs* (3rd ed.). New York: Pergamon Press.

Barrass, R. (2003). *Scientists must write: A guide to better writing for scientists, engineers, and students* (2nd ed.). London: RoutledgeFalmer.

Bartlett, T. (2010a, August 19). Document sheds light on investigation at Harvard. *The Chronicle of Higher Education.* Retrieved from http://chronicle.com/article/Document-Sheds-Light-on/123988/

Bartlett, T. (2010b, October 26). Did Marc Hauser get a raw deal? *The Chronicle of Higher Education*. Retrieved from http://chronicle.com/blogs/percolator/did-marc-hauser-get-a-raw-deal/27446

Bartoshuk, L. M., Duffy, V. B., Chapo, A. K., Fast, K., Yiee, J. H., Hoffman, H. J., et al. (2004). From psychophysics to the clinic: Missteps and advances. *Food Quality and Preference, 15*, 617–632.

Bartoshuk, L. M., Duffy, V. B., Fast, K., Green, B. G., Prutkin, J. M., & Snyder, D. J. (2002). Labeled scales (e.g., category, Likert, VAS) and invalid across-group comparisons: What have we learned from genetic variation in taste? *Food Quality and Preference, 14*, 125–138.

Beck, A. T., Epstein, N., Brown, G., & Steer, R. A. (1988). An inventory for measuring clinical anxiety: Psychometric properties. *Journal of Consulting and Clinical Psychology, 56*, 893–897.

Bekelman, J. E., Li, Y., & Gross, C. P. (2003). Scope and impact of financial conflicts of interest in biomedical research: A systematic review. *Journal of the American Medical Association, 289*, 454–465.

Bennof, R. J. (2007). *President's FY budget requests 1% increase in R&D funding*. InfoBrief Science Resource Statistics. Retrieved November 30, 2008, from http://www.nsf.gov/statistics/infbrief/nsf07327/

Bernstein, I. (1978). Learned taste aversion in children receiving chemotherapy. *Science, 200*, 1302–1303.

Billingsley, R., Lang, F. F., Slopis, J. M., Schrimsher, G. W., Alter, J. L., & Moore, B. D. (2002). Visuo-spatial neglect in a child following subcortical tumor resection. *Developmental Medicine & Child Neurology, 44*, 191–200.

Blair, I. V., Judd, C. M., & Chapleau, K. M. (2004). The influence of afrocentric facial features in criminal sentencing. *Psychological Science, 15*, 674–679.

Blass, E. M., & Epstein, A. N. (1971). A lateral preoptic osmosensitive zone for thirst in the rat. *Journal of Comparative and Physiological Psychology, 76*, 378–394.

Blough, D. S. (1956). Dark adaptation in the pigeon. *Journal of Comparative and Physiological Psychology, 49*, 425–430.

Bohan, J. S. (1993). Regarding gender: Essentialism, constructionism, and feminist psychology. *Psychology of Women Quarterly, 17*, 5–21.

Boring, E. G. (1954). The nature and history of experimental control. *American Journal of Psychology, 67*, 573–589.

Boring, E. G. (1969). Perspective: Artifact and control. In R. Rosenthal & R. L. Rosnow (Eds.), *Artifact in behavioral research* (pp. 1–11). New York: Academic Press.

Bouchard, T. J. (1999). Genes, environment, and personality. In S. J. Ceci & W. M. Williams (Eds.), *The nature-nurture debate: The essential readings* (pp. 97–103). Malden, MA: Blackwell.

Boyack, K. W., Klavans, R., & Börner, K. (2005). Mapping the backbone of science. *Scientometrics, 64*, 351–374.

Brady, J. V., Porter, R. W., Conrad, D. G., & Mason, J. W. (1958). Avoidance behavior and the development of gastroduodenal ulcers. *Journal of Experimental Analysis of Behavior, 1*, 69–72.

Braun, K. A., Ellis, R., & Loftus, E. F. (2002). Make my memory: How advertising can change our memories of the past. *Psychology & Marketing, 19*, 1–23.

Brehm, J. W. (1966). *A theory of psychological reactance*. New York: Academic Press.

Breland, K., & Breland, M. (1961). The misbehavior of organisms. *American Psychologist, 16*, 681–684.

Brennan, W. M., Ames, E. W., & Moore, R. W. (1966). Age differences in infants' attention to patterns of different complexities. *Science, 151*, 354–356.

Brown, G. W., & Harris, T. (2001). *Social origins of depression*. New York: Free Press.

Burgess, J. W. (1984). Do humans show a "species typical" group size? Age, sex and environmental differences in the size and composition of naturally occurring casual groups. *Ethology and Sociobiology, 5*, 51–57.

Byrne, W. L. (Ed.). (1970). *Molecular approaches to learning and memory*. New York: Academic Press.

Byrne, W. L., Samuel, D., Bennett, E. L., Rosenzweig, M. R., & Wasserman, E. (1966). Memory transfer. *Science, 153*, 658–659.

Campbell, D. T. (1975). On the conflict between biological and social evolution and between psychology and moral tradition. *American Psychologist, 30*, 1103–1126.

Campbell, D. T. (1979). "Degrees of freedom" and the case study. In T. D. Cook & C. S. Reichardt (Eds.), *Qualitative and quantitative methods in evaluation research* (pp. 49–67). Beverly Hills, CA: Sage.

Chalmers, A. F. (1999). *What is this thing called science?* (3rd ed.). Indianapolis, IN: Hackett Press.

Chang, L. (2002). A comparison of samples and response quality obtained from RDD telephone survey methodology and internet survey methodology. *Dissertation Abstracts International: Section B: The Sciences & Engineering, 62* (8–B), 3845.

Chiu, A. Y., Perez, P. E., & Parker, R. N. (1997). Impact of banning alcohol on outpatient visits in Barrow, Alaska. *Journal of the American Medical Association, 278*(21), 1775–1777.

Chorover, S. L. (1979). *From genesis to genocide*. Cambridge, MA: MIT Press.

Coburn, P. C., & Stricker, E. M. (1978). Osmoregulatory thirst in rats after lateral preoptic lesions. *Journal of Comparative and Physiological Psychology, 92*, 350–361.

Collett, P., & Marsh, P. (1974). Patterns of public behavior: Collision avoidance on a pedestrian crossing. *Semiotica, 12*, 281–299.

Committee on the Use of Animals in Research. (1991). *Science, medicine and animals*. Washington, DC: National Academy Press.

Cook, T. D., & Campbell, D. T. (1979). *Quasi experimentation: Design and analysis issues for field settings*. Chicago: Rand McNally.

Cotman, C. W., & McGaugh, J. L. (1980). *Behavioral neuroscience*. New York: Academic Press.

Craik, F. I. M., & Tulving, E. (1975). Depth of processing and the retention of words in episodic memory. *Journal of Experimental Psychology: General, 104*, 268–294.

Cressey, D. R. (1971). *Other people's money: A study in the social psychology of embezzlement*. Belmont, CA: Wadsworth.

Crumbaugh, J. C. (1966). A scientific critique of parapsychology.

International Journal of Neuropsychiatry, 2, 523–531.

Danziger, K. (1979). The social origins of modern psychology. In A. R. Buss (Ed.), *Psychology in social context* (pp. 27–45). New York: Irvington.

Darley, J. M., & Latané, B. (1968). Bystander intervention in emergencies: Diffusion of responsibility. *Journal of Personality and Social Psychology, 8,* 377–383.

Davis, A. (n.d.). *The Georgie project.* Retrieved from http://grants.nih. gov/grants/policy/air/dog_days.htm

Deangelis, T. (2003). Does industry funding deserve a bad rap? *Monitor on Psychology, 34*(7), 28–31.

Debono, K. G., & Kline, C. (1993). Source expertise and persuasion: The moderating role of recipient dogmatism. *Personality and Social Psychology Bulletin, 19,* 167–173.

Delgado, J. M. R. (1969). *Physical control of the mind.* New York: Harper & Row.

DeWall, C. N., MacDonald, G., Webster, G. D., Masten, C. L., Baumeister, R. F., Powell, C., ... Eisenberger, N. I. (2010). Acetaminophen reduces social pain: Behavioral and neural evidence. *Psychological Science, 21*(7), 931–937.

Diener, E., Fraser, S. C., Beaman, A. L., & Kelem, R. T. (1976). Effects of deindividuation variables on stealing among Halloween trick-or-treaters. *Journal of Personality and Social Psychology, 33,* 178–183.

Domjan, M. (2008). Claiming credit in the interdisciplinary age. *APS Observer, 21*(4), 13–18.

Donders, F. C. (1969). Over de snelheid van psychische processen [On the speed of psychological processes]. (W. Koster, Trans.), In W. Koster, (Ed.), *Attention and performance II.* Amsterdam: North-Holland. (Original work published 1868.)

Doty, R. L. (1975). Influence of menstrual cycle on volunteering behavior. *Nature, 254,* 139–140.

Eggertson, L. (2010). Lancet retracts 12-year-old article linking autism to MMR vaccines. *CMAJ, 182*(4), E199–E200. doi:10.1503/cmaj.109-3179

Ekman, P., & Friesen, W. V. (1975). *Unmasking the face: A guide to recognizing emotions from facial clues.* Englewood Cliffs, NJ: Prentice-Hall.

Ekman, P., & Friesen, W. V. (1976). Measuring facial movement. *Environmental Psychology and Nonverbal Behavior, 1,* 56–75.

Ekman, P., & Friesen, W. V. (1978). *Facial action coding system.* Palo Alto, CA: Consulting Psychologists Press.

Ekman, P., Friesen, W. V., & O'Sullivan, M. (1988). Smiles when lying. *Journal of Personality and Social Psychology, 54,* 414–420.

Evans, C. (1973). Parapsychology— what the questionnaire revealed. *New Scientist, 57,* 209.

Ephron, D. (2008). *The biscuit breaker.* Retrieved November 30, 2008, from http://www.newsweek.com/id/164497

Fantz, R. L., Fagan, J. F., & Miranda, S. B. (1975). Early visual selectivity. In L. B. Cohen & P. Salapatek (Eds.), *Infant perception: From sensation to cognition: Vol. 1. Basic visual processes* (pp. 249–345). New York: Academic Press.

Faye, C., & Bazar, J. (2007). Exploring the pages of psychology's past: Archival research in the history of psychology. *APS Observer, 20*(9), 49–50.

Festinger, L. (1957). *A theory of cognitive dissonance.* Evanston, IL: Row, Peterson.

Festinger, L., Riecken, H. W., Jr., & Schachter, S. (1956). *When prophecy fails.* Minneapolis, MN: University of Minnesota Press.

Ficbert, M., & Meyer, M. (1997). Gender stereotypes: A bias against men. *The Journal of Psychology, 131,* 407–410.

Fink, A., & Kosekoff, J. (2005). *How to conduct surveys: A step-by-step guide* (3rd ed.). Beverly Hills, CA: Sage.

Fisher, W. A. (1990). Understanding and preventing teenage pregnancy and sexually transmitted disease/ AIDS. In J. Edwards, R. S. Tindale, L. Heath, & E. J. Posavac (Eds.), *Social influence processes and prevention* (pp. 71–101). New York: Plenum Press.

Forgas, J. P. (1987). The role of physical attractiveness in the interpretation of facial expression cues. *Personality and Social Psychology Bulletin, 13,* 478–489.

Friedman, M. I., & Stricker, E. M. (1976). The physiological psychology of hunger: A physiological perspective. *Psychological Review, 83,* 409–431.

Gaito, J. (1980). Measurement scales and statistics: Resurgence of an old misconception. *Psychological Bulletin, 87,* 564–567.

Gergen, K. J. (1994). Exploring the postmodern: Perils or potentials? *American Psychologist, 49,* 412–426.

Gergen, K. J. (2001). Psychological science in postmodern context. *American Psychologist, 56,* 803–813.

Gernsbacher, M. A. (2006). How to spot bias in research. *APS Observer, 19*(11), 5, 30.

Gilligan, C. (1993). *In a different voice: Psychological theory and women's development.* Cambridge, MA: Harvard University Press.

Goffman, E. (1971). *Relations in public.* New York: Basic Books.

Goldberg, A. M., Zurlo, J., & Rudacille, D. (1996). The three Rs and biomedical research. *Science, 272* (5267), 1403.

Golder, S. A., & Macy, M. W. (2011). Diurnal and seasonal mood vary with work, sleep, and daylength across diverse cultures. *Science, 333*(6051), 1878–1881. doi:10.1126/science.1202775

Gormally, J., Black, S., Daston, S., & Rardin, D. (1982). The assessment of binge eating severity among obese persons. *Addictive Behaviors, 7,* 47–55.

Gould, S. J. (1979, July). The father of Jensenism (review of Hearnshaw). *Psychology Today,* pp. 104–106.

Grattan, L. M., Roberts, S., Mahan, W. T., McLaughlin, P. K., Otwell, S., & Morris, J. G. (2011). The early psychological impacts of the deepwater horizon oil spill on Florida and Alabama communities. *Environmental Health Perspectives, 119*(6), 838–843. doi:10.1289/ehp.1002915

Greenberg, D. S. (2008). NIH Grants: Trust but don't verify. *APS Observer, 21*(8), 13.

Haig, B. D. (2002). Truth, method, and postmodern psychology. *American Psychologist, 57,* 457–458.

Harris, I., & Miniussi, C. (2003). Parietal lobe contribution to mental rotation demonstrated with rTMS. *Journal of Cognitive Neuroscience, 15*(3), 315–323.

Hawkes, N. (1979). Tracing Burt's descent into fraud. *Science, 205,* 673–675.

Hawkins, D. M. (1980). *Identification of outliers.* London: Chapman & Hall.

Hearnshaw, L. S. (1979). *Cyril Burt, psychologist.* Ithaca, NY: Cornell University Press.

Hetherington, M. M., & Rolls, B. J. (1987). Methods of investigating human eating behavior. In F. M. Toates & N. E. Rowland (Eds.), *Feeding and drinking* (pp. 77–109). New York: Elsevier.

Hoffman, R. E., Gueorguieva, R., Hawkins, K., Varanko, M., Boutros, N. N., Wu, Y., et al. (2005). Temporoparietal transcranial magnetic stimulation for auditory hallucinations: Safety, efficacy and moderators in a fifty patient sample. *Biological Psychiatry, 58*(2), 97–104.

Holden, C. (1979). Ethics in social science research (news and comment). *Science, 206*, 537–540.

Holland, A. L., McBurney, D. H., Moossy, J., & Reinmuth, O. M. (1985). The dissolution of language in Pick's disease with neurofibrillary tangles: A case study. *Brain and Language, 24*, 36–58.

Hoskins, C. N. (1988). *Partner relationship inventory.* Palo Alto, CA: Consulting Psychologists Press.

Hunt, N., & Silverstone, T. (1995). Does puerperal illness distinguish a subgroup of bipolar patients? *Journal of Affective Disorders, 34*(2), 101–107.

Institute of Laboratory Animal Resources Commission on Life Sciences National Research Council. (1996). *Guide for the care and use of laboratory animals* (rev., NIH 78–23). Washington, DC: National Academy Press. US Government Printing Office.

Jaffee, S. R., Caspi, A., Moffitt, T. E., Polo-Tomás, M., & Taylor, A. (2007). Individual, family, and neighborhood factors distinguish resilient from non-resilient maltreated children: A cumulative stressors model. *Child Abuse & Neglect, 31*(3), 231–253.

Jaschik, S. (2008). Fending off attacks on social science. *Inside Higher Ed.* Retrieved December 1, 2008, from http://insidehighered.com/news/2007/05/04/nsf

Jay, T. (2009). The utility and ubiquity of taboo words. *Psychological Science, 4*, 153–161.

Jenni, D. A., & Jenni, M. A. (1976). Carrying behavior in humans: Analysis of sex differences. *Science, 194*, 859–860.

Johnson, D. H. (2001). Three ways to use databases as tools for psychological research. *APS Observer, 14*, 7–8.

Johnson, D. H. (2002). The power of psychology's databases. *APS Observer, 15*, 7–10.

Jones, P. E. (1995). Contradictions and unanswered questions in the Genie case: A fresh look at the linguistic evidence. *Language & Communication, 15*(3), 261–280.

Jorgensen, D. L. (1989). *Participant observation: A methodology for human studies.* Newbury Park, CA: Sage.

Joynson, R. B. (1989). *The Burt affair.* London: Routledge.

Kandel, E. R. (2007). *In search of memory: Emergence of a scientific mind.* New York: W.W. Norton.

Karlsson, T., Börjesson, A., Adolfsson, R., & Nilsson, L.-G. (2002). Successive memory test performance and priming in Alzheimer's disease: Evidence from the word-fragment completion task. *Cortex, 38*(3), 341–355.

Keogh, E., & Witt, G. (2001). Hypoalgesic effect of caffeine in normotensive men and women. *Psychophysiology, 38*(6), 886–895.

Kernis, M. H., Zuckerman, M., & McVay, E. (1988). Motivational factors affecting performance: The importance of perceived locus of control. *Personality and Social Psychology Bulletin, 14*, 524–535.

Key, W. B. (1973). *Subliminal seduction.* Englewood Cliffs, NJ: Prentice-Hall.

Kirk, E. E. (1996). *Evaluating information on the internet* (Cited on Johns Hopkins University Library Web page). Retrieved from http://www.jessebethel.net/imc/kirk_evalinfo.html

Kirk, R. E. (1994). *Experimental design: Procedures for the behavioral sciences* (3rd ed.). Pacific Grove, CA: Wadsworth.

Kohlberg, L. (1981). *The philosophy of moral development* (Vol. 1). San Francisco, CA: Harper & Row.

Kolata, G. (1987). How to ask about sex and get honest answers. *Science, 236*, 82.

Koocher, G. P., & Keith-Spiegel, P. (1998). *Ethics in psychology: Professional standards and cases* (2nd ed.). New York: Random House.

Kornhauser, A., & Sheatsley, P. B. (1976). Questionnaire construction and interview procedure. In C. Selltiz, L. S. Wrightsman, & S. W. Cook (Eds.), *Research methods in social relations* (3rd ed., pp. 541–573). New York: Holt, Rinehart & Winston.

Kratochwill, T. R., & Levin, J. R. (Eds.). (1992). *Single-case research design and analysis: New directions for psychology and education.* Hillsdale, NJ: Erlbaum.

Krosnick, J. A. (1999). Survey research. *Annual Review of Psychology, 50*, 537–567.

Kuhn, T. S. (1996). *The structure of scientific revolutions* (3rd ed.). Chicago, IL: University of Chicago Press.

Kuriki, I., Ashida, H., Murakami, I., & Kitaoka, A. (2008). Functional brain imaging of the Rotating Snakes illusion by fMRI. *Journal of Vision, 8*(10), 1–10. doi:10.1167/8.10.16

Langston, W. (2010). *Research methods laboratory manual for psychology* (3rd ed.). Pacific Grove, CA: Wadsworth.

Lansford, J. E., Chang, L., Dodge, K. A., Malone, P. S., Oburu, P., Palmerus, K., et al. (2005). Physical discipline and children's adjustment: Cultural normativeness as a moderator. *Child Development, 76*, 1234–1246.

Lasswell, H. (1951). *The analysis of political behavior: An empirical approach.* London: Routledge.

Laudan, L. (1977). *Progress and its problems: Towards a theory of scientific growth.* Berkeley and Los Angeles, CA: University of California Press.

Laudan, L. (1996). *Beyond positivism and relativism: Theory, method, and evidence.* Boulder, CO: Westview Press.

Legrand, L. N., Iacono, W. G., & McGue, M. (2005). Prediction addition: Behavioral genetics uses twins and time to decipher the origins of addiction and learn who is most vulnerable. *American Scientist, 93*, 140–147.

Lettvin, S. Y., Maturana, H. R., McCulloch, W. S., & Pitts, W. H. (1959). What the frog's eye tells the frog's brain. *Proceedings of the Institute of Radio Engineers, 47*, 1940–1951.

Lewis, I. M., Watson, B. C., & White, K. M. (2009). Internet versus paper-and-pencil survey methods in psychological experiments: Equivalence testing of participant responses to health-related messages. *Australian Journal of Psychology, 61*(2), 107–116.

Lorenz, K. Z. (1958, June). The evolution of behavior. *Scientific American,* pp. 67–78.

Mackintosh, R. J. (Eds.). (1995). *Cyril Burt: Fraud or framed?* New York: Oxford University Press.

McBurney, D. H., & Gent, J. F. (1979). On the nature of taste qualities. *Psychological Bulletin, 86*, 151–167.

McBurney, D. H., Levine, J. M., & Cavanaugh, P. H. (1977). Psychophysical and social ratings of human body odor. *Personality and Social Psychology Bulletin, 3*, 135–138.

McCabe, S. E., Boyd, C. J., Cranford, J. A., & Teter, C. J. (2009). Motives for nonmedical use of prescription opioids among high school seniors in the United States: Self-treatment and beyond. *Archives of Pediatrics & Adolescent Medicine, 163*(8), 739–744. doi:10.1001/archpediatrics.2009.120

McClintock, M., & Adler, N. T. (1978). The role of the female during copulation in wild and domestic rats (*Rattus norvegicus*). *Behaviour, 68*, 67–96.

McCloskey, M. (1980). The stimulus familiarity problem in semantic memory research. *Journal of Verbal Learning and Verbal Memory, 19*, 485–502.

McCloskey, M., & Glucksberg, S. (1979). Decision processes in verifying category membership statements: Implications for models of semantic memory. *Cognitive Psychology, 11*, 1–37.

McConnell, J. V. (1962). Memory transfer through cannibalism in planarium. *Journal of Neuropsychiatry, 3*(Suppl. 1), 542–548.

McGinnies, E. (1949). Emotionality and perceptual defense. *Psychological Review, 56*(5), 244–251. doi:10.1037/h0056508

Mednick, M. T. (1989). On the politics of psychological constructs: Stop the bandwagon, I want to get off. *American Psychologist, 44*, 1118–1123.

Milgram, S. (1963). Behavioral study of obedience. *Journal of Abnormal and Social Psychology, 67*, 371–378.

Mill, J. S. (2006). *Collected works of John Stuart Mill system of logic. In Ratiocinative and inductive (vol. 7: Books I–III and vol. 8: Books IV–VI)*. Indianapolis, IN: Liberty Fund, Inc.

Miller, G. A. (1956). The magical number seven plus or minus two: Some limits on our capacity for processing information. *Psychological Review, 63*, 81–97.

Miller, N. E. (1984). Value and ethics of research on animals. *Laboratory Primate Newsletter, 23*(3), 1–10.

Miller, N. E. (1985). The value of behavioral research on animals. *American Psychologist, 40*, 423–440.

Miranda, S. B., & Fantz, R. L. (1971). Distribution of visual attention by newborn infants among patterns varying in size and number of details. *Proceedings of the 79th Annual Convention of the American Psychological Association, 6*, 181–182.

Moffat, A. S. (1991). Another sex survey bites the dust. *Science, 253*, 1483.

Mollenauer, S., Bryson, R., & Phillips, C. (1991). Voluntary exercise: Effects of ethanol-induced sleep in the C57BL/6J mouse. *Bulletin of the Psychonomic Society, 29*, 217–219.

Morgan, D. L., & Morgan, R. K. (2001). Single-participant research design. *American Psychologist, 56*(2), 119–127.

Moshagen, M., Musch, J., & Erdfelder, E. (2011). A stochastic lie detector. *Behavior Research Methods*. (Advance online publication). doi:10.3758/s13428-011-0144-2

Mozzoni, M. P., & Hartnedy, S. (2000). Escape and avoidance hypothesis testing using an alternative treatment design. *Behavioral Interventions, 15*, 269–277.

Murray-Harvey, R. (2010). Relationship influences on students' academic achievement, psychological health and well-being at school. *Educational and Child Psychology, 27*(1), 104–115.

National Institutes of Health. (1996). *Public health service policy on humane care and use of laboratory animals*. Bethesda, MD: Author.

National Science Board. (2010). *Science and engineering indicators 2010*. Retrieved January 10, 2012, from http://www.nsf.gov/statistics/seind10/c4/c4s1.htm

Neuman, W. L. (1999). *Social research methods: Qualitative and quantitative approaches* (6th ed.). Needham Heights, MA: Allyn & Bacon.

Newport, F. (2001). *What can we learn from Americans' views about the death penalty?* Retrieved from Gallup Poll website: http://www.gallup.com/poll/4666/what-can-learn-from-americans-views-about-death-penalty.aspx

Nicholl, C. S., & Russell, R. M. (1990). Analysis of animal rights literature reveals the underlying motives of the movement: Ammunition for counteroffensive by scientists. *Endocrinology, 127*, 985–989.

Niederkrotenthaler, T., & Sonneck, G. (2007). Assessing the impact of media guidelines for reporting on suicides in Austria: Interrupted time series analysis. *Australian and New Zealand Journal of Psychiatry, 41*, 419–428.

Nisbett, R. E. (1968). Determinants of food intake in human obesity. *Science, 159*, 1254–1255.

Nolen-Hoeksema, S., & Girgus, J. S. (1994). The emergence of gender differences in depression during adolescence. *Psychological Bulletin, 115*(3), 424–443.

Noll, J. G., Zeller, M. H., Trickett, P. K., & Putnam, F. W. (2007). Obesity risk for female victims of childhood sexual abuse: A prospective study. *Pediatrics, 120*(1), e61–e67. doi:10.1542/peds.2006-3058

Orne, M. T., & Evans, F. J. (1965). Social control in the psychological experiment: Antisocial behavior and hypnosis. *Journal of Personality and Social Psychology, 1*, 189–200.

Pachter, W. S., Fox, R. E., Zimbardo, P., & Antonuccio, D. O. (2007). Corporate funding and conflicts of interest: A primer for psychologists. *American Psychologist, 62*(9), 1005–1015. doi:10.1037/0003-066X.62.9.1005

Parker, E. S., Cahill, L., & McGaugh, J. L. (2006). A case of unusual autobiographical remembering. *Neurocase, 12*, 35–49.

Pelham, W. E., Burrows Maclean, L., Gnagy, E. M., Fabiano, G. A., Coles, E. K., Tresco, K. E., et al. (2005). Transdermal methylphenidate, behavioral, and combined treatment for children with ADHD. *Experimental and Clinical Psychopharmacology, 13*, 111–126.

Pelton, L. H. (1978). Child abuse and neglect: The myth of classlessness. *American Journal of Orthopsychiatry, 48*, 608–617.

Perez, J. C. (2007). Facebook's Beacon more intrusive than previously thought. *PC World*. Retrieved from http://www.pcworld.com/article/140182/facebooks_beacon_more_intrusive_than_previously_thought.html

Petticrew, M., Cummins, S., Ferrell, C., Findlay, A., Higgins, C., Hoyd, C., ... & Sparks, L. (2005). Natural experiments: An underused tool for public health? *Public Health, 119*(9), 751–757. doi:10.1016/j.puhe.2004.11.008

Phillips, D. P. (1974). The influence of suggestion on suicide: Substantive and theoretical implications of the Werther effect. *American Sociological Review, 39*, 340–354.

Pietschnig, J., Voraceka, M., & Formann, A. K. (2010). Mozart effect-Shmozart effect: A meta-analysis. *Intelligence, 38*(3), 314–323.

Pinel, J. P. J. (1969). A short gradient of ECS-produced amnesia in a one-trial appetitive learning situation. *Journal of Comparative and Physiological Psychology, 68,* 650–655.

Plato. (1995). *Phaedrus* (A. Nehamas & P. Woodruff, Trans.). Indianapolis, IN: Hackett Press.

Posavac, E. J., & Carey, R. G. (1997). *Program evaluation: Methods and case studies* (5th ed.). Englewood Cliffs, NJ: Prentice-Hall.

Price, J., & Davis, B. (2008). *The woman who can't forget. The extraordinary story of living with the most remarkable memory known to science. A memoir.* New York: Free Press.

Puglisi, T. (2001). IRB review: It helps to know the regulatory framework. *APS Observer, 14*(5), 1.

Rauscher, F. H., Shaw, G. L., & Ky, K. N. (1993). Music and spatial task performance. *Nature, 365*(6447), 611.

Regan, T. (1983). *The case for animal rights.* Berkeley, CA: University of California Press.

Regan, T. (2001). The case for animal rights. In C. Cohen & T. Regan (Eds.), *The animal rights debate* (pp. 127–222). Lanham, MD: Rowman & Littlefield.

Resnik, D. B. (2007). Conflicts of interest in scientific research related to regulation or litigation. *Journal of Philosophy, Science and Law, 7,* 1–12.

Robinson, J. P., Shaver, P. R., & Wrightsman, L. S. (Eds.). (1991). *Measures of personality and social psychology attitudes.* San Diego, CA: Academic Press.

Rosenthal, R. (1976). *Experimenter effects in behavioral research* (Enlarged ed.). New York: Irvington.

Rosenthal, R., & Fode, K. L. (1963). The effect of experimenter bias on the performance of the albino rat. *Behavioral Science, 8,* 183–189.

Rosnow, R. L., & Rosnow, M. (2006). *Writing papers in psychology* (7th ed.). Pacific Grove, CA: Brooks/Cole.

Ross, L., Lepper, M. R., & Hubbard, M. (1975). Perseverance in self-perception and social perception: Biased attributional processes in the debriefing paradigm. *Journal of Personality and Social Psychology, 32,* 880–892.

Rubin, L. B. (1979). *Women of a certain age: The mid-life search for self.* New York: Harper & Row.

Saad, W. A., Luiz, A. C., Camargo, L. A. D. A., Renzi, A., & Manani, J. V. (1996). The lateral preoptic area plays a dual role in the regulation of thirst in the rat. *Brain Research Bulletin, 39,* 171–176.

Sedikides, C., Devine, P. G., & Furman, R. W. (1991). Social perception in multitarget settings: Effects of motivated encoding strategies. *Personality and Social Psychology Bulletin, 17,* 625–632.

Shadish, W., Cook, T. D., & Campbell, D. T. (2002). *Experimental and quasi-experimental designs for generalized causal inference.* Boston, MA: Houghton Mifflin Company.

Sharpe, R. S., & Johnsgard, P. A. (1966). Inheritance of behavioural characters in F. Mallard × pintail (*Anas platyrynchos* L. × *Anas acuta* L.) hybrids. *Behaviour, 27,* 259–272.

Shaw, J. I. & Skolnick, P. (2005). Effects of psycholegal knowledge on decision-making by mock juries. *Applied Psychology in Criminal Justice, 1*(2), 90–109.

Shergill, S. S., Brammer, M. J., Fukuda, R., Williams, S. C. R., Murray, R. M., & McGuire, P. K. (2003). Engagement of brain areas implicated in processing inner speech in people with auditory hallucinations. *British Journal of Psychiatry, 182,* 525–531.

Shumway-Cook, A., Hutchison, S., Kartin, D., Price, R., & Woollacott, M. (2003). Effect of balance training on recovery of stability in children with cerebral palsy. *Developmental Medicine and Child Neurology, 45,* 591–602.

Shweder, R. A. (1982). Liberalism as destiny. *Contemporary Psychology, 27,* 421–424.

Shweder, R., Mahapatra, M., & Miller, J. G. (1987). Culture and moral development. In J. Kagan & S. Lamb (Eds.), *The emergence of morality in young children* (pp. 1–83). Chicago, IL: University of Chicago Press.

Sidman, M. (1988). *Tactics of scientific research: Evaluating experimental data in psychology.* Boston, MA: Authors Cooperative.

Siegfried, T. (2010a). Odds are, it's wrong. *Science News, 177*(7), 26–29.

Siegfried, T. (2010b). Staying on the lookout for rumors disguised as news. *Science News, 178*(7), 2.

Singh, D. (1993). Adaptive significance of female physical attractiveness: Role of waist-to-hip ratio. *Journal of Personality and Social Psychology, 65,* 293–307.

Singh, N. N., Dawson, M. J., & Gregory, P. R. (1980). Suppression of chronic hyperventilation using response-contingent aromatic ammonia. *Behavior Therapy, 11,* 561–566.

Skinner, B. F. (1950). Are theories of learning necessary? *Psychological Review, 57,* 193–216.

Skinner, B. F. (1956). A case history in scientific method. *American Psychologist, 11,* 221–233.

Skinner, C. H., Skinner, A. L., & Armstrong, K. J. (2000). Analysis of a client-staff-developed shaping program designed to enhance reading persistence in an adult diagnosed with schizophrenia. *Psychiatric Rehabilitation Journal, 24*(1), 52–57.

Skitka, L. J., & Sargis, E. G. (2006). The internet as psychological laboratory. *American Review of Psychology, 57,* 529–555.

Skoe, E. E. A., Hansen, K. L., Morch, W. T., Bakke, I., Hoffmann, T., Larsen, B., et al. (1999). Care-based moral reasoning in Norwegian and Canadian early adolescents: A cross-national comparison. *Journal of Early Adolescence, 19,* 280–291.

Smith, M. B. (1994). Selfhood at risk: Postmodern perils and the perils of postmodernism. *American Psychologist, 49,* 405–411.

Smith, P. M., & Torrey, B. B. (1996). The future of the behavioral and social sciences. *Science, 271,* 611–612.

Stafford, T. (1991). Animal lib. In J. Williams (Ed.), *Animal rights and welfare* (pp. 40–48). New York: Wilson. (Reprinted from *Christianity Today, 34*(9), 18–23.)

Steele, K. M., Bass, K. E., & Crook, M. D. (1999). The mystery of the Mozart effect: Failure to replicate. *Psychological Science, 10,* 366–369.

Steinar-Jonsson, S. M., & Fisher, K. (1996). Phantom pain—psychological conceptualization and treatment: A case report. *Behavioural & Cognitive Psychotherapy, 24*(3), 275–281.

Sternberg, R. J. (2003). *The psychologist's companion: A guide to scientific writing for students and researchers* (4th ed.). New York: Cambridge University Press.

Stevens, J. C., & Rubin, L. L. (1970). Psychophysical scales of apparent heaviness and the size-weight illusion. *Perception and Psychophysics, 8*, 225–230.

Stone, A. A., Broderick, J. E., Schwartz, J. E., & Schwarz, N. (2008). Context effects in survey ratings of health, symptoms, and satisfaction. *Medical Care, 46*, 662–667.

Strayer, D. L., Drews, F. A., & Johnston, W. A. (2003). Cell phone-induced failures of visual attention during simulated driving. *Journal of Experimental Psychology: Applied, 9*, 23–32. doi:10.1037/1076-898X.9.1.23

Strunk, W., Jr., & White, E. B. (2000). *The elements of style: With index* (4th ed.). Englewood Cliffs, New York: Longman.

Sullivan cancels teen sex survey. (1991, September/October). *Psychological Science Agenda*, p. 7.

Swerdlow, P. (2000). Use of humans in biomedical experimentation. In F. L. Macrina (Ed.), *Scientific integrity* (2nd ed., pp. 137–151). Washington, DC: ASM Press.

Tamashiro, D. J. (2003). How to get published. *APS Observer, 16*(8), 27–28.

Tanner, L. (2008). *Psychologists vote against role in Gitmo interrogations.* Retrieved September 18, 2008, from http://tinyurl.com/4cgbv7

Terrace, H. S. (1979, June). How Nim Chimpsky changed my mind. *Psychology Today*, pp. 65–76.

Thompson, A. (2007). *'Meteorite' crash breeds mass hysteria.* Retrieved October 15, 2008, from http://www.space.com/scienceastronomy/070926_meteorite_hysteria.html

Thompson, W. F., Husain, G., & Schellenberg, G. (2001). Arousal, mood, and the Mozart effect. *Psychological Science, 12*(3), 248–251.

Truman, J. L., & Rand, M. R. (2010). National crime victimization survey: Criminal victimization, 2009. *Bureau of Justice Statistics.* Retrieved from http://bjs.ojp.usdoj.gov/content/pub/pdf/cv09.pdf

Trumpy, F. D. (1983–1984). An investigation of the reported effect of transcendental meditation on the weather. *Skeptical Inquirer, 8*, 143–148.

Tucker, W. H. (1997). Re-reconsidering Burt: Beyond a reasonable doubt. *Journal of the History of the Behavioral Sciences, 33*, 145–162.

Tufte, E. R. (2001). *The visual display of quantitative information* (2nd ed.). Chesire, CT: Graphics Press.

Tukey, J. W. (1977). *Exploratory data analysis.* Reading, MA: Addison-Wesley.

Turner, E. H., Matthews, A. M., Linardatos, E., Tell, R. A., & Rosenthal, R. (2008). Selective publication of antidepressant trials and its influence on apparent efficacy. *The New England Journal of Medicine, 358*, 252–260.

Valenstein, E. S. (1977). *Brain control.* New York: Wiley.

Valenstein, E. S., Cox, V. C., & Kakolewski, J. W. (1969). Sex differences in hyperphasia and body weight following hypothalamic damage. *Annals of the New York Academy of Sciences, 157*, 1030–1046.

von Hippel, W. & Gonsalkorale, K. (2005). "That is bloody revolting!" Inhibitory control of thoughts better left unsaid. *Psychological Science, 16*(7), 497–500. doi:10.1111/j.0956-7976.2005.01563.x

Wade, N. (2010, August 20). Harvard finds scientist guilty of misconduct. *New York Times.* Retrieved from http://www.nytimes.com/2010/08/21/education/21harvard.html

Wagenaar, W. A. (1969). Note on the construction of diagram-balanced Latin squares. *Psychological Bulletin, 72*, 384–386.

Wakefield, A. J., Murch, S. H., Anthony, A., Linnell, J., Casson, D. M., Malik, M., ... Walker-Smith, J. A. (1998). Ileal-lymphoid-nodular hyperplasia, non-specific colitis, and pervasive developmental disorder in children. *Lancet, 351*(9103), 637–641.

Walker, L. R. (1982, September). Empirical tests of famous sayings. *USAir*, pp. 64–68.

Wallenstein, M. B., & Nock, M. K. (2007). Physical exercise for the treatment of non-suicidal self-injury: Evidence from a single-case study. *American Journal of Psychiatry, 164*, 350–351.

Wandell, B. A., & Pugh, E. N., Jr. (1980). A field-additive pathway detects brief-duration, long-wavelength incremental flashes. *Vision Research, 20*, 613–624.

Wansink, B., & Kim, J. (2005). Bad popcorn in big buckets: Portion size can influence intake as much as taste. *Journal of Nutrition Education and Behavior, 37*, 242–245.

Washington, K., Deitz, J. C., White, O. R., & Schwartz, I. S. (2002). The effects of a contoured foam seat on postural alignment and upper-extremity function in infants with neuromotor impairments. *Physical Therapy, 82*, 1064–1076.

Webb, E. J., Campbell, D. T., Schwartz, R. D., & Sechrest, L. (1999). *Unobtrusive measures.* Thousand Oaks, CA: Corwin Press.

Weisberg, H. F., & Bowen, B. D. (1977). *An introduction to survey research and data analysis.* San Francisco, CA: Freeman.

Weiss, J. M. (1968). Effects of coping responses on stress. *Journal of Comparative and Physiological Psychology, 65*, 251–260.

Weiss, J. M. (1971). Effects of coping behavior in different warning signal conditions on stress pathology in rats. *Journal of Comparative and Physiological Psychology, 77*, 1–13.

West, S. G. (2009). Alternatives to randomized experiments. *Current Directions in Psychological Science, 18*, 299–304.

Wilkinson, L. (1999). Statistical methods in psychology journals: Guidelines and explanations. *American Psychologist, 54*(8), 594–604.

Wittman, F. D. (1989). Planning and programming server intervention initiatives for fraternities and sororities: Experiences at a large university. *Journal of Primary Prevention, 9*, 247–269.

Yin, R. K. (2008). *Case study research: Design and methods* (4th ed.). Newbury Park, CA: Sage Publications.

Zimmerman, D. H., & West, C. (1975). Sex roles, interruptions and silences in conversation. In B. Thorne & N. Henley (Eds.), *Language and sex: Difference and dominance* (pp. 105–129). Rowley, MA: Newbury House.

NAME INDEX

SUBJECT INDEX

Note: Page numbers followed by "*f*" and "*t*" denote figures and tables, respectively.

Chapter 13

Conclusion

The first unit in the prophecy (chapters 1–8) is directed to the dispirited Jews who had returned from the Captivity to rebuild the community and reestablish true worship at Jerusalem. The visions and messages of those chapters were to reconfirm the fact of Jehovah's control of world events and to promise His protection of His people. Though much of the message is relevant to the people of that time, there are also predictions of God's coming blessing in the Millennium through His servant the Branch.

The second unit is quite different as a literary genre. It is what scholars refer to as apocalyptic, but this should not be understood to imply that the events will not happen. They will. The theme running through this section is the holy warfare between God and the forces of evil. This warfare will focus on God's people Israel, who will be attacked by the anti-God confederacy but defended by God himself. An ultimate victory will obviously ensue, and God will establish His long promised kingdom on earth.

In addition, the "Branch" of the first unit is called the "pierced one" and "the smitten one" in the second unit. This suffering servant (as Isaiah refers to Him) will be the one through whom God will effect redemption for His people Israel.

The Book of Zechariah is, therefore, an extremely important work in God's revelation. It is a comforting word because it shows God's intervention in and control of the affairs of men. It is disturbing for it predicts catastrophic events for Israel and the world. It is finally encouraging because it predicts the redemptive work of the Savior and the establishment of God's physical rule among men when there will truly be peace on earth and good will toward men.

For Further Study

1. Explain the purpose of the two major sections of the book.

2. Now that you have finished the book, go back to the first question and answer it again.